ARTFORMS

AN INTRODUCTION TO THE VISUAL ARTS

DUANE PREBLE
UNIVERSITY OF HAWAII, EMERITUS

SARAH PREBLE
HAWAII STATE LIBRARY

SEVENTH EDITION

REVISED BY
PATRICK FRANK
UNIVERSITY OF KANSAS

Prentice
Hall

Upper Saddle River, NJ 07458

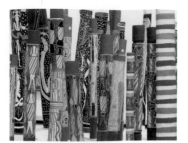

About the Cover

Paddy Dhathangu (b. 1915), David Malangi (b. 1927), George Malibirr (1934–1998), Jimmy Wululu (b. 1936) and other Ramingining Artists. "The Aboriginal Memorial" 1987–1988. Wood, ochres, installation of 200 hollow-log coffins, height from 40.0 to 327.0 cm. Purchased with the assistance of funds from Gallery admission charges and commissioned 1988. Collection: National Gallery of Australia, Canberra/ARS-NY.

Library of Congress Cataloging-in-Publication Data
Preble, Duane.
    Artforms : an introduction to the visual arts / Duane Preble, Sarah Preble,
Patrick Frank.—7th ed.
      p.   cm.
    Includes bibliographical references and index.
    ISBN 0-13-089979-8
    1. Composition (Art) 2. Visual perception. 3. Art—History.
I. Preble, Sarah. II. Frank, Patrick, 1953-III. Title.
N7430.P69   2002
700—dc21   00-052464
          CIP

Editorial Director: Charlyce Jones Owen
Publisher: Bud Therien
AVP, Director of Production and Manufacturing: Barbara Kittle
Senior Production Editor: Harriet Tellem
Prepress and Manufacturing Manager: Nick Sklitsis
Marketing Manager: Sheryl Adams
Creative Design Director: Leslie Osher
Interior and Cover Design: Anne DeMarinis

Line Art Supervisor: Guy Ruggiero
Electronic Art Coordinator: Joh Lisa
Copy Editor: Janet Masterson
Editorial Assistant: Wendy Yurash
Photo Research: Francelle Carapetyan
Photo Permission Manager: Kay Dellosa
Photo Permission Specialist: Carolyn Gauntt

This book was set in 11/14 Garamond by TSI Graphics and was printed
and bound by RR Donnelley, Willard, OH. The cover was printed by Phoenix Color Corporation.

© 2002 by Pearson Education
Upper Saddle River, NJ 07458

Printed in the United States of America

10 9 8 7 6 5 4 3

ISBN 0-13-089979-8

Prentice Hall International (UK) Limited, *London*
Prentice-Hall of Australia Pty. Limited, *Sydney*
Prentice-Hall Canada Inc., *Toronto*
Prentice-Hall Hispanoamericana, S.A., *Mexico*
Prentice-Hall of India Private Limited, *New Delhi*
Prentice-Hall of Japan, Inc., *Tokyo*
Pearson Education Pte. Ltd., *Singapore*
Editora Prentice-Hall do Brasil, Ltda., *Rio de Janeiro*

TO ALL WHO COME TO KNOW THE ARTIST WITHIN

CONTENTS

PREFACE

From the first edition in 1972, ARTFORMS has been as visually exciting as the individual works of art that are reproduced in it. ARTFORMS grew out of a desire to introduce art through an engaging visual experience. It is written and designed to help readers build an informed foundation for individual understanding and enjoyment of art. By introducing art theory, practice, and history in a single volume, this book aims to draw students into a new or expanded awareness of the visual arts. The goal is to engage readers in the process of realizing their own innate creativity.

In keeping with this philosophy, the seventh edition of ARTFORMS is a careful blending of the strengths of its earlier editions—clear organizational structure, straightforward writing, and high quality images—and a number of important changes. Twenty-eight new illustrations of contemporary art works have been added, including those of many new artists in a wide range of media, from graphic design and architecture to installation and ceramics. Contemporary artists represented in this book for the first time include Willie Cole, Rachel Whiteread, Mel Chin, Zaha Hadid, Sarah Charlesworth, Xu Bing, Tunga, Charles Ray, William Kentridge, Tibor Kalman, and others. Moreover, I have continued the effort begun in the last edition to reflect the ever-broadening canon of art history by making this edition the most inclusive yet. I have added works by Sonia Delaunay, Tarsila do Amaral, Norman Lewis, Carlos Frésquez,

and Alicia Candiani, among others, to make this book the best available survey of the world-wide range of art production.

In addition, I have done major updating in several sections to reflect recent developments in art issues and advances in scholarship. Essays on restoration of art works, censorship, and return of cultural property have been rewritten with new information. I included a photograph of the back view of the Venus of Lespugue to show recent groundbreaking research on textile arts from the Stone Age. The chapter on Islamic Arts has been expanded.

The most important change in this edition, however, is in the bridges it builds to the digital world. A new section of Chapter 10 describes art made on computers, with an historical overview and contemporary works. A new essay, "The Digital Revolution and the Arts," highlights how all areas of art creation, preservation, and study have been affected by the advent of digital technology. This book itself makes groundbreaking use of that technology, displaying interviews with contemporary artists on an interactive CD-ROM that is included with the book. A new feature in the text, Artists at Work, introduces six artists and cues the reader to the CD in which the artists themselves discuss their creations. Thus the page of text is linked to the digital image.

Part One: Art Is . . . (Chapters 1 and 2) introduces the nature of art, aesthetics, and creativity, and discusses the purposes of art and visual communication. Strongly believing that we are all artists at heart, we include an essay on children and their "Early Encounters with the Artist Within," and a section on the works of untrained artists.

Part Two: The Language of Visual Experience (Chapters 3–6) presents the language of vision: visual elements, principles of design, and style. Experience with the language of visual form introduced in Chapters 3 through 5 provides a foundation for developing critical thinking and for considering evaluation and art criticism, discussed in Chapter 6.

The visual and verbal vocabulary covered in Part Two prepares the reader to sample the broad range of art disciplines, media, and processes presented in Part Three: Two-Dimensional Arts (Chapters 7–11) and Part Four: Three-Dimensional Arts (Chapters 12–14). In these two parts we discuss the classical media used in drawing, painting, sculpture, and architecture and the latest developments in photography, video, film, computer imaging, craft, and environmental art.

Part Five: Art as Cultural Heritage (Chapters 15–20) and Part Six: The Modern World (Chapters 21–25) introduce historic world styles and related cultural values. Part Six devotes four comprehensive chapters to the many artistic developments of the modern Western world from the late eighteenth century to the present. That each new technique in the history of art relies heavily on its predecessors becomes obvious in these chapters. Chapter 25: Recent Diversity discusses art of the last two decades and the multifaceted and changing roles of artists today. It ends with a section on the Global Present, emphasizing the international aspects of the contemporary art world.

In addition to a revised Glossary, Pronunciation Guide, and Selected Readings, the back matter of ARTFORMS includes an annotated listing of Web sites related to art: images, artists, museums, art organizations, magazines, and other sources. The three-page Timeline is illustrated and includes additional information on both Western and non-Western art.

The seventh edition of ARTFORMS offers a variety of updated ancillaries, including a large collection of high-quality slides (available to qualified adopters), carefully selected to represent the diversity of artists shown in the book; and an ARTFORMS Web site with links to museums and other Web sites, videotapes of interviews with artists, an audio pronunciation guide, and chapter guides with summaries and learning objectives.

The title of this book has a dual meaning. It evolved from the original title, which was a condensation of the concluding sentences of the draft for the first edition: "Man creates art. Art creates man." Man Creates Art Creates Man was further condensed to contain the idea in one word, ARTFORMS: As we create forms, we are in turn formed by what we have created.

Beyond fostering appreciation of major works of art, this book's primary concern is to open eyes and minds to the richness of the visual arts as unique forms of human communication and to convey the idea that the arts enrich life best when we experience, understand, and enjoy them as integral parts of the process of living.

Although ARTFORMS is filled with pictures of art objects, the subject is not just human accomplishment; it is human potential. These works are shown for themselves and for what they indicate about the process that brought them into being. The arts enable us to experience the past, see the present, and anticipate the future. We hope that readers will share our conviction that the arts give voice to the heart of humanity.

Patrick Frank

ACKNOWLEDGMENTS

Research for seven editions of ARTFORMS has taken us around the world and into the studios of many fellow artists. We have found it highly rewarding to meet and talk with artists as well as collectors, gallery and museum staff members, photographers, and scholars who generously shared their works and expertise with us. We greatly appreciate the help and encouragement of the many people who have been directly involved in this team effort; we regret that space does not permit us to name them all. A few people deserve special mention for their major contributions.

Publisher Bud Therien's patience, down-to-earth manner, and wide experience were invaluable assets in this revision. Production Editor Harriet Tellem kept us all focused with her efficiency and eye for detail. These characteristics were fortunately not allowed to overshadow her sense of humor, a valuable asset in a project such as this. Francelle Carapetyan of Image Research was superb in tracking down artists, slides, prints, and permissions from around the globe. She consistently went above and beyond the call of duty as she cajoled and pleaded with people and institutions, sometimes at odd hours of the night and sometimes in languages other than English. Marketing Director Sheryl Adams gave valuable feedback on how to keep this book the bestseller that it is. Her staff oversees this book's journey into professors' offices at all kinds of educational institutions, and we are grateful for their dedication and effort over the life of this edition. Assistant Editor Kimberly Chastain supervised the production of the *Artforms* CD-ROM. She and her staff broke new ground in the search for ways to integrate digital technology with the printed page. Invaluable assistance was also provided by Natasha Morse. All of these persons made special contributions to this book, and their efforts and dedication mark its every page.

Most important of all has been the continuing guidance of original authors Duane and Sarah Preble. They have been always willing to help with information and advice from their wisdom of seven editions of experience. As this book continues to evolve to meet changing times, it will always remain faithful to the original vision that they had.

We express our appreciation to the following reviewers, who offered many helpful suggestions during the revision of the text:

Fred C. Albertson, The University of Memphis
Donald Alexander, Louisiana State University—Shreveport
Carol Ventura, Tennesee Technological University
Stephen Smithers, Indiana State University
Sarah E. McCormick, Kapiolani Community College
Elizabeth A. Winga, North Iowa Area Community College
Ted Kerzie, California State University Bakersfield
Herbert R. Hartel, Jr., John Jay College, Cuny
Pamela A. Lee, Washington State University
Gene Hood, University of Wisconsin Eau Claire

Crucial to this book are the artists, past and present, known and unknown, whose art is presented here and those people who have had the foresight to preserve meaningful products of human creativity. It has indeed been an awe-inspiring experience to be part of a cooperative venture as large and complex as the publication of ARTFORMS.

Patrick Frank

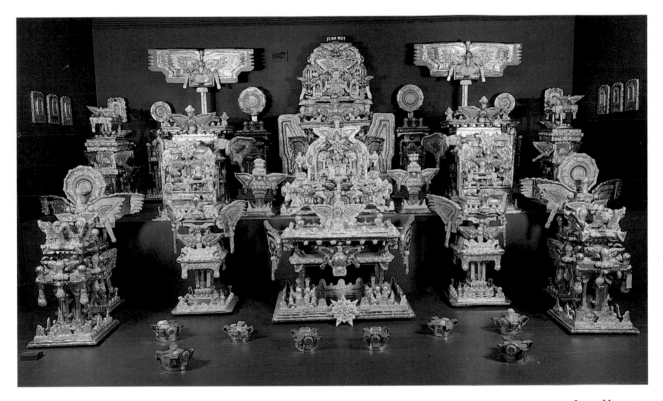

James Hampton.
THRONE OF THE THIRD HEAVEN OF THE NATION'S
MILLENIUM GENERAL ASSEMBLY. c. 1950–1964.
National Museum of American Art, Smithsonian Institution. Washington, D.C.
Photograph: Art Resource, NY.

PART ONE
Art Is . . .

CONSIDER . . .

Have you ever tried to explain something to someone—then used a pencil to show exactly what you meant?

Are any paintings, posters, or photographs displayed where you live or work? If so, how do you feel about them? Do they enhance your life?

Do you think artists are born with special gifts, or do you think they acquire skills through practice and effort?

Most of us were active artists as children, and then we stopped making art. Do you still draw or paint or take photographs? If not, why not?

Do you think that most societies use art in the same way? Is art a concept, a process, or is it objects? Can societies with no word for art still have art?

CHAPTER ONE

THE NATURE OF ART

Art is not something apart from us. It grows from common—as well as uncommon—human insights, feelings, and experiences. When we are so deeply moved by an experience that we want to share it with others, we are where art begins.

Art does not need to be "understood" to be enjoyed. Like life itself, it can simply be experienced. Yet the more we understand what art can offer, the richer our experience of it will be.

For example, Wassily Kandinsky's work COMPOSITION IV, while it may at first appear to be a strange jumble, comes from common feelings. Kandinsky, one of the great innovators of modern art, tried for years to create works that did not "copy" anything in the external world. Rather, he wanted the forms and colors on the canvas to communicate his inner state of mind without referring to anything seen. He would often merely improvise with paint, expressing himself spontaneously from moment to moment. This quest of his was an outgrowth of his spiritual yearnings: He thought that the world is too materialistic; and if art depends on reproducing the visual world, it also is too materialistic.

He later wrote about COMPOSITION IV, detailing how some of the elements of the painting correspond to inner states. The large blue patch at the center "gives the whole picture a cold tone."[1] This blue area contrasts with the lighter and sweeter colors elsewhere in the work. He noticed elements from landscape in the painting that he called figures, horses, and a castle. He gave them those names because he found that such shapes often bubbled up in his mind as he was working. Just as anyone's mood is usually a mixture of various feelings, this painting communicates a complex emotional moment that includes the sweetness and coldness of the colors with a sense of motion in the outlined forms. Through a work such as this, he wrote, "the artist purposely sets the soul vibrating."[2]

WHAT IS ART?

Art—like beauty, truth, and life itself—is larger than any single definition. One widely used dictionary defines art in this way:

art (art), *n. 1. the quality, production, or expression of what is beautiful, appealing, or of more than ordinary significance.*[3]

Within this book a *work of art* is the visual expression of an idea or experience formed with skill through the use of a medium. A *medium* is a particular material, along with its accompanying technique. (The plural is *media.*) Artists select media that best suit the ideas and feelings they wish to present. When a medium is used in such a way that the object or performance contributes to our un-

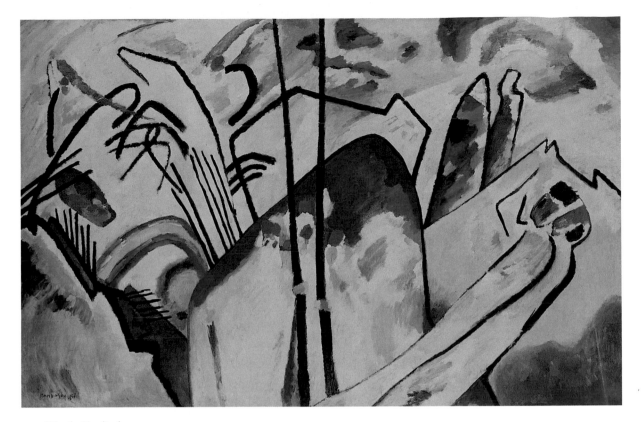

1   Wassily Kandinsky.
COMPOSITION IV. 1911.
Oil on canvas. 62¹³⁄₁₆" × 98⅝".
Kunstsammlung Nordrhein-Westfalen, Düsseldorf.
Photographer: Walter Klein,© 2002 Artists Rights Society
(ARS), NY/ADAGP, Paris.

derstanding or enjoyment of life, we experience the final product as art.

Media in use for many centuries include clay, fiber, stone, wood, and paint. By the mid-twentieth century, modern technology had added new media, including video and computers, to the nineteenth-century contributions of photography and motion pictures. Art made with a combination of different materials is referred to as *mixed media.*

When people speak of *the arts,* they are usually referring to music, dance, theater, literature, and the visual arts. Each art form is perceived in different ways by our senses, yet each grows from a common need to give expressive substance to feelings, ideas, insights, and experiences. Here, the focus is the visual arts, including drawing, painting, sculpture, film, and architecture.

Much of our communication is verbal, yet any single medium of expression has its limitations. Cer-tain ideas and feelings can be communicated only through visual forms, while other insights can be expressed only through music. American painter Georgia O'Keeffe said: "I found that I could say things with colors and shapes that I couldn't say in any other way—things I had no words for."[4] The arts provide ways to communicate meanings that go far beyond ordinary verbal exchange. The entire range of thought, feeling, and observation is the subject of art.

IS ART A NECESSITY?

Is it necessary for us to give physical form to things we feel, think, and imagine? Must we gesture, dance, draw, speak, sing, write, and build? To be fully human, it seems that we must. In fact, the ability to create is one of the special characteristics of being human. The urge to make and enjoy what we call art has been a driving force throughout human history.

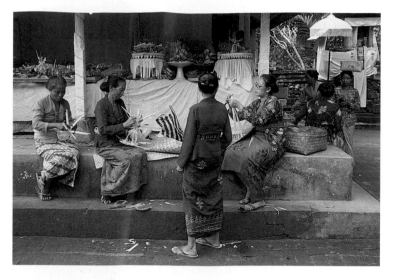

2   PREPARING FOR A FESTIVAL.
Bali. 1992.
Photograph: Hefner Visual Communications.

All societies have produced objects and rituals that extend communication and meet physical and spiritual needs. Some objects—from simple tools to vast temple complexes—have been designed to meet both physical and spiritual needs simultaneously.

There are societies whose languages have no word for art, yet people in these societies are abundantly creative and live artfully. The Balinese—shown here in the photograph PREPARING FOR A FESTIVAL—say "We have no art—we do everything as well as we can." At their best, the arts can express important values, take care of practical needs, and give form to the spiritual life of both individuals and communities. Because the arts express, enhance, and embody creative energy, they often act as ritual, magic, and practical technology all at once. Arts such as singing, dancing, carving, or painting bring participants into unity with nature's forces and thereby give access to the creative energy of the universe. In many traditional, nonindustrial societies the artistic expressions of spiritual life are not treasured as entertaining performances or decorative objects, but as harmonizing vehicles of power, as offerings of praise and gratitude. It is the

creative process and the power of the object that are of value, rather than the object itself.

Because our high-tech, multicultural society has few shared traditions, we have few traditional art forms. Most of us tend to think of "art" as something produced only by "artists"—uniquely gifted people. Because art is often separated from community life in contemporary society, many people believe they have no artistic talent. This belief makes them hesitate to create their own art or even to explore the art of others. Today, works we call art are often displayed in galleries and museums—far removed from the everyday life experiences of the people who created them or view them.

This situation is unfortunate; people living in highly technological societies need art as much as the members of culturally rich, traditional societies need art. Science and the arts serve humanity in complementary ways. Both involve creative thinking and problem solving. Science seeks answers to questions about the outer, physical world; these answers form the basis of our technology. The arts foster the development of our inner world—the intuitive, emotional, spiritual, and creative aspects of being human. Reality is explained through the sciences and revealed through the arts. People need both science and art if they are to balance function with meaning.

History provides the best evidence of our need for the arts. When a dictator or conquering group seeks domination over a people, and perhaps has already won a military victory, the next step is to find ways to destroy the culture—to eliminate the language, traditions, and the arts of the oppressed. Artists of all kinds are among the first to be controlled or silenced. Hitler's and Stalin's control of the arts, and the suppression of the languages and ritual arts of Native Americans, immediately come to mind.

As groups and individuals, we can survive incredible physical hardships far more easily than the loss of our personal creativity and cultural foundations. Our languages, our arts, our traditions, and beliefs are at the core of who we are.

PURPOSES AND FUNCTIONS OF ART

Art can inspire, beautify, inform, persuade, entertain, and transform. It can also deceive, humiliate, and anger. Art can arouse our emotions, spark our imaginations, delight our senses, lead us to think and see in new ways, and help each of us develop a personal sense of beauty and truth. A given work of art may serve several functions all at once.

When we look at art of the past—or even current art—we cannot always know exactly what its creators had in mind. To understand their purposes and functions, we find it is useful to place art and artifacts in contexts and categories.

Art for Communicating Information

Because art can make a strong statement, one clearly understood by a broad spectrum of people, it is often used to impart information in both literate and nonliterate societies. During the Middle Ages in Europe, stained-glass windows and church sculpture taught Bible stories to an illiterate population.

At Chartres Cathedral, near Paris, a stained glass window called THE TREE OF JESSE depicts the genealogy of Jesus Christ, beginning with the Jewish patriarch Jesse (at the bottom below the tree). The vertical sequence presenting the four kings culminates in depictions of Mary the mother of Jesus, and at the top, Christ himself. Many later artists in the European tradition, especially portrait painters, have had as their primary goal the mere recording of information for posterity.

Art continues to inform nonliterate as well as literate people around the world. Photography, film, and television have proven to be particularly useful for recording and communicating. Through artistic presentation, information often becomes more accessible and memorable than it would be through words alone.

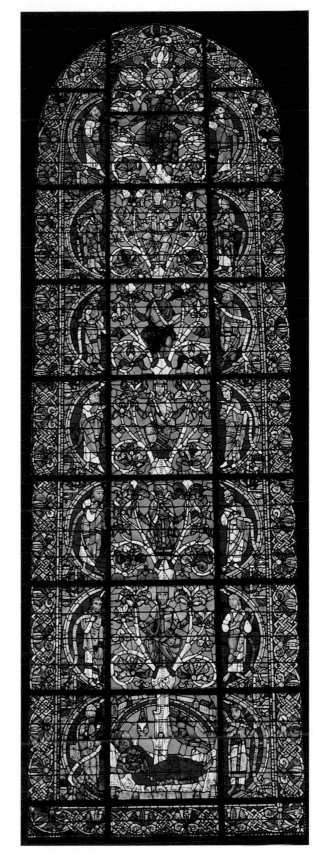

3   THE TREE OF JESSE.
West facade, Chartres Cathedral. c. 1150–1170.
Stained glass.
Photograph: Laura Lushington, Sonia Halliday Photographs.

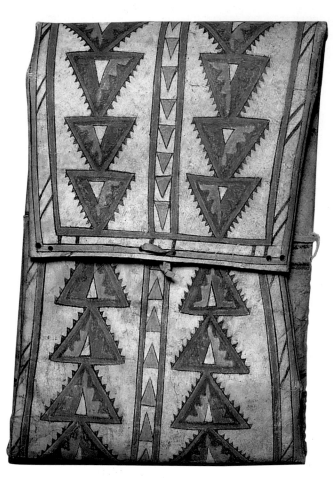

4   BLACKFEET PARFLECHE. 1885.
Rawhide, pigment. 21" × 14".
University of Pennsylvania Museum, Philadelphia.
(Neg. #T4–826c.2)

Art for Day-to-Day Living

Objects of all kinds, from ancient, carefully crafted flint knives to sleek sports cars, have been conceived to delight the eye as well as to serve more obviously useful functions. Well-designed utilitarian objects and spaces—from chairs to communities—bring pleasure and efficiency into our daily lives. For example, the BLACKFEET PARFLECHE is a rawhide envelope that was useful for carrying personal goods in that nomadic Native American society. However, it is also decorated with colorful symbolic forms that refer to the tribe's communal life and to the forces of nature. Women made these parfleches by stretching out pieces of rawhide in the sun to dry, then applying paints pigmented with earthen powders.

Many societies value the artistic embellishment of everyday things. This DISH from ancient Persia is simply decorated in a few colors. The circular patterns in the central motif echo the shape of the plate itself. Dancing around its border is a line of stylized Arabic writing from Muslim scripture which underlines the plate's function in hospitality: "Generosity is one of the qualities of the people of Paradise."

In a general sense, the visual arts include all human creations in which visual form has been a

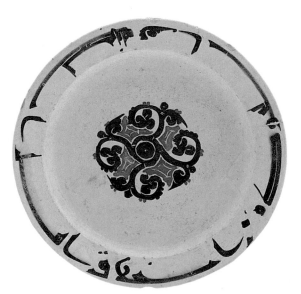

5   DISH.
10th Century. East Iran.
Lead-glazed earthenware with colored slips. Diameter 8¼".
Courtesy Freer Gallery of Art, Smithsonian Institution, Washington, D.C. (F1965.27)

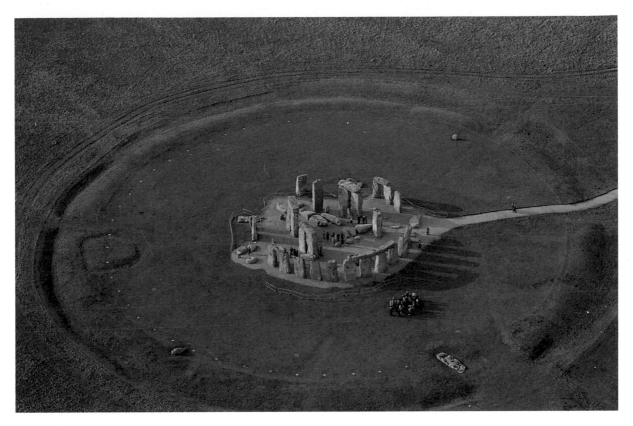

6 STONEHENGE. Wiltshire, England. c. 2000 B.C.E.
Photograph: Aerofilms.

major consideration during their design and production. Nearly all the objects and spaces we use in our private and public lives were designed by art and design professionals. The best of our buildings, towns, and cities have been designed with the quality of their visual form—as well as their other functions—in mind. Each of us is involved with art/design whenever we make decisions about how to style our hair, what clothes to wear, or how to furnish and arrange our living spaces. As we make such choices, we are engaged in universal art-related processes—making visual statements about who we are and the kind of world we like to see around us.

Art for Spiritual Sustenance

In many societies, all the arts have a spiritual component. Spiritual and/or magical purposes apparently motivated the making of the world's earliest carvings and cave paintings. Long before the developments of farming and writing, the arts helped sustain bands of hunter-gatherers. What motivated prehistoric peoples to carve, draw, and paint? Survival needs? The desire to record events? The need to magically control the animals they hunted for food? Or simply the urge to create?

Among the best-known ritual structures built by stone-age human beings is the complex of huge boulders at STONEHENGE, England. It was constructed at a time when religion and science were one unified quest for understanding. Four series of giant stones, surrounding an altar stone, stand within a circular trench 300 feet in diameter. Most archaeologists agree that STONEHENGE was built in several phases, around 2000 B.C.E., to serve some sort of religious or scientific function. Few scholars agree on the specific purpose of the stone monument, but some have concluded that STONEHENGE was used to calculate solar and lunar movements, including eclipses.

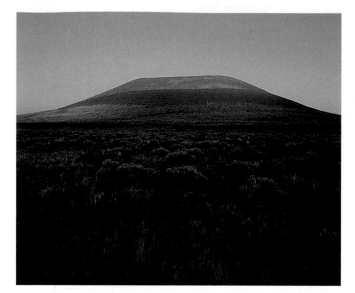

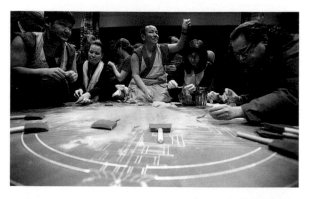

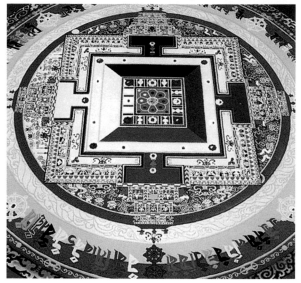

7   James Turrell. RODEN CRATER.
Work in progress. 1980 to the present.
Photograph: Barbara Gladstone Gallery.

8   WHEEL OF TIME.
Tibetan sand mandala.
a. Being created.
b. Completed.
Photographs: José R. Lopez, *New York Times* Pictures.

Sculptor James Turrell is currently working to provide a direct, intense experience of nature through his RODEN CRATER project near Flagstaff, Arizona. The extinct volcano will be used to focus attention on celestial phenomena.

Turrell's concept is to keep the site—a beautiful, quiet, natural environment—as unchanged as possible. He designed underground rooms from which to view the changing light of the sky, using orientations involving the equinoxes, solstices, and moon cycles. The perception of the viewer is the "art" in this work. Turrell poses questions, rather than giving answers. As the space, light, and darkness are seen and experienced from different elevations, enclosures, and open spaces along the rim, the viewer, with no distractions from civilization, has the opportunity to respond to the majesty of nature.

In the context of Tibetan Buddhism, art making is a meditative group process requiring concentration and focused attention. In 1997 three Tibetan monks from the American Nagyal Monastery spent three weeks at the Asia Society in New York City making a traditional *mandala* (a sacred circle). Working eighteen-hour days for three weeks, they produced a Tibetan mandala made of colored sand called WHEEL OF TIME. The monks followed ancient traditional practices as they created their contemporary symbol. After celebrating and sharing the work, they destroyed it to symbolize the impermanence of life.

All of the world's major religions have used art to inspire and instruct the faithful, even though some great spiritual leaders, including Moses and Mohammed, cautioned their followers against worshiping idols. Art continues to fulfill personal, spiritual needs for many people.

Art for Personal and Cultural Expression

Certain artists reveal themselves and their heritage so clearly that we feel we know them. Seventeenth-century Dutch artist Rembrandt van Rijn expressed his attitude toward life through well over one thousand paintings, drawings, and prints.

From the age of twenty until his death at sixty-three, Rembrandt drew and painted dozens of self-portraits. He was fascinated by the expressive possibilities of the human body and found himself to be the most readily available model. Like a good actor, he used his own face as a resource for studying life.

In most of his self-portraits, Rembrandt viewed himself straightforwardly and with the same interest that he brought to his other human subjects. Rembrandt's SELF-PORTRAIT of 1658 is brought to life by the eyes, which suggest a man of penetrating insight. By studying himself carefully, he went beyond himself; he created a visual statement about how it feels to be alive, to be human.

Korean-American artist Yong Soon Min projects an altogether more contemporary sense of the self in her mixed media piece DWELLING. Born in a small village in Korea just before the end of the Korean war, she and her mother joined her father in California when she was seven. Thus while she was raised mainly in the United States, it is not her native land; yet on trips back to Korea she feels distant from her country of origin as well.

DWELLING is an effort to express this divided cultural background. The artist inserted personal mementoes into a traditional Korean-style dress and hung it over a pile of books, maps, and photographs. Inside the dress, barely visible, is a script from a Korean poet which gives voice to the loss of identity. The hauntingly empty dress seems to

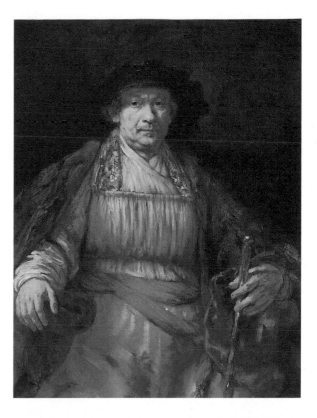

9   Rembrandt van Rijn.
SELF-PORTRAIT. 1658.
Oil on canvas. 33¼" × 26".
© The Frick Collection, New York.

10   Yong Soon Min.
DWELLING. 1994.
Mixed media. 72" × 42" × 28".
Photo by Erik Landsberg. Courtesy of the artist.

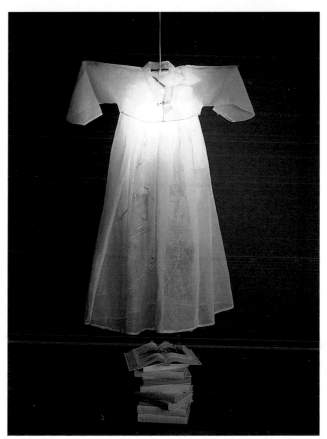

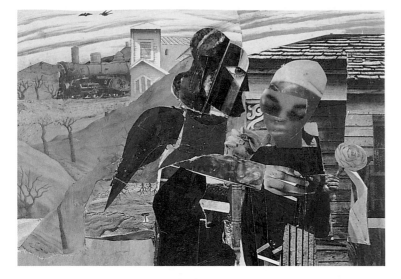

11 Romare Bearden.
PREVALENCE OF RITUAL: TIDINGS. 1967.
Photomontage. 36" × 48".
© Romare Bearden Foundation/Licensed by VAGA, New York, NY.

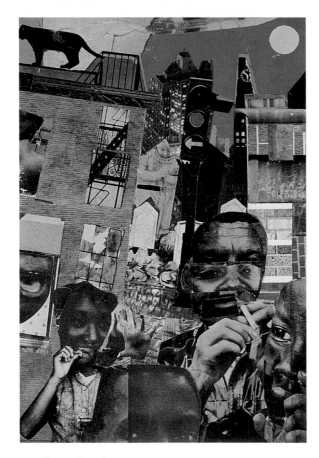

12 Romare Bearden.
ROCKET TO THE MOON. 1971.
Collage on board. 13" × 9 ¼".
© Romare Bearden Foundation/Licensed by VAGA, New York, NY.

await a Korean occupant who will never put it on. This sense of divided nationality is increasingly common among Americans, many of whom were born elsewhere.

Twentieth-century American artist Romare Bearden was fascinated by the pageant of daily life he witnessed in the rural South and in Harlem, New York. Bearden created memorable images of humanity by observing, distilling, then reconstructing the life he saw around him. In TIDINGS an angel seems to bring solace or release to an introspective young woman. Borrowed picture fragments with a few muted colors make up an otherwise gray world. There is a mood of melancholy and longing. Does the train suggest departure from this world or escape to the lure of a better life in the North?

In ROCKET TO THE MOON, collage fragments build a scene of quiet despair and stoic perseverance. A barely visible rocket heads for the moon, while urban life remains punctuated by two red stoplights. The artist makes an ironic visual statement: Bearden placed America's accomplishments in space next to our inner cities' stalled social and economic progress.

Rembrandt and Bearden were concerned with the effectiveness of their communication to others, but equally important was meeting their own inner needs for expression. Within the broad range of the visual arts, there is a considerable difference in the amount and type of personal expression. The designs of a coin or a telephone offer much less information about the personal concerns of the artist than do the designs of a painting or a piece of sculpture.

An element of self-expression exists in all art, even when the art is produced cooperatively by many individuals, as in filmmaking and architecture. In each case, the intended purpose for the art affects the nature and degree of the personal expression.

Romare Bearden paid tribute to the richness of his African-American experience through his art. He sought :

to paint the life of my people as I know it . . . because much of that life is gone and it had beauty.[5]

The child of educated, middle-class parents, Bearden spent his early childhood in rural North Carolina, then moved north with his family to Harlem, in New York City. He had a brief stint as a professional baseball player for the Boston club of the now-defunct Negro Leagues. He attended New York University, where he earned a degree in mathematics and drew cartoons for the *NYU Medley.* He went on to draw humorous and political cartoons for magazines and a newspaper. During the Depression he attended the Art Students League in New York, where he was encouraged to say more in his drawings than he said in his cartoons. He held his first exhibition in a private studio in 1940—about the same time that he became a social worker in New York, a job he held on and off until 1966.

After serving in the army during World War II,

Bearden used his G.I. Bill education grant to study at the Sorbonne in Paris. There he came to know a number of intellectuals and writers of African descent, including poet Leopold Senghor and novelist James Baldwin. Bearden was inspired to make the philosophical perspective of his ethnic heritage a cornerstone of his art. He said of his experience at the Sorbonne, "The biggest thing I learned was reaching into your consciousness of black experience and relating it to universals."[6]

Bearden was critical of programs that supported African-American artists by encouraging them to work in European academic traditions rather than those of their own lives. He believed that, just as African Americans had created their own musical forms such as jazz and blues, they should invent their own visual art. He urged fellow African-American artists to create art out of their own life experiences, as had jazz greats Ellington, Basie, Waller, and Hines, who were among Bearden's friends. Bearden himself was a musician and songwriter who said he

painted in the tradition of the blues.

He combined his stylistic search with institutional activism. In 1963, he founded the Spiral Group, an informal group of African-American artists that met in his studio. A year later, he became art director of the Harlem Cultural Council, a group devoted to recognizing and promoting the arts of Harlem residents.

His study of art history led Bearden to admire Cubist and Surrealist paintings and African sculpture, as well as work by earlier European masters. These works of art were among the many important influences on his creative development. Also important was the rapid-cut style of contemporary documentary film makers. Bearden worked in a variety of styles prior to the 1960s, when he arrived at the combined collage and painting style for which he is best known.

Although he learned from direct association with the previous generation of international artists, Bearden's focus remained the African-American experience. He kept a list of key events from his life on the wall of his studio. Often, Bearden drew upon memories of his

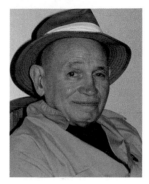

13   ROMARE BEARDEN.
Photograph: Bernard Brown.

childhood in rural North Carolina. The idea of homecoming fascinated him. He said, "You can come back to where you started from with added experience and you hope more understanding. You leave and then return to the homeland of your imagination."[7]

Despite his emphasis on his own experiences, Bearden cannot simply be labeled an African-American artist because his work has meaning both for and far beyond that community. He said, "What I try to do with art is amplify." If he had just painted a North Carolina farm woman, "it would have meaning to her and people there. But art amplifies itself to something universal."[8]

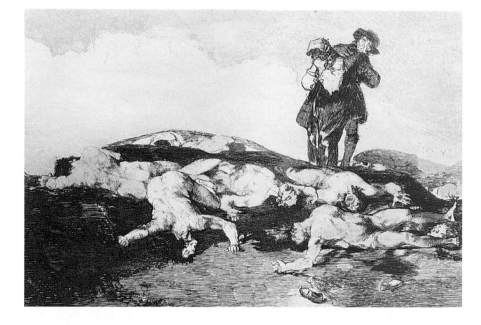

14 Francisco Goya.
THE DISASTERS OF WAR,
NO. 18: BURY THEM AND
SAY NOTHING. 1818.
Etching and aquatint.
5⅞" × 8⅜"
S.P. Avery Collection, Miriam &
Ira D. Wallach Division of Art,
Prints and Photographs.
The New York Public Library,
Astor, Lenox and Tilden
Foundations.

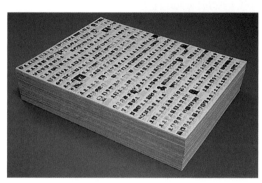

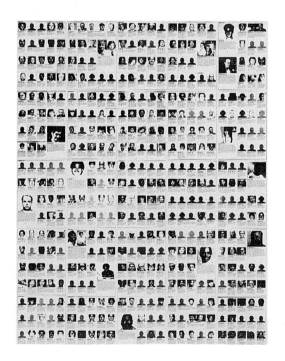

Art for Social and Political Purposes

Artists in many societies have sought to criticize or influence values and public opinion through their work. Often this attempt is clear and direct, as with Francisco Goya's expression of outrage at the Napoleonic wars in his country. THE DISASTERS OF WAR vividly documents atrocities committed by Napoleon's troops as they took over Spain in 1808. In a similar vein is the work of Cuban-American artist Félix González-Torres. In 1990, he printed large sheets with photographs and information on all of the victims of gunfire in the United States in a randomly selected week. UNTITLED (DEATH BY GUN) was reproduced in what the artist called "endless copies," which were then placed in a stack on the floor of the art gallery, free for the taking by viewers. González-Torres said of these pieces, "I need the public to complete the work. I ask the

15 Félix González-Torres.
UNTITLED (DEATH BY GUN). 1990.
Offset print on paper. 44½" × 32½".
a. Installation view.
b. Single sheet.
Museum of Modern Art, New York. Purchased in part with funds
from Arthur Fleisher, Jr. and Linda Barth Goldstein.
Photographs: © 2000 The Museum of Modern Art, NY.

public to help me, to take responsibility, to become a part of my work, to join in."[9]

Sometimes the artist's social comment is far less obvious, but still sincerely felt. The Chinese painter Bada Shanren of the seventeenth century was deeply dissatisfied with the foreign rulers of his country; as a political statement he frequently painted melons, a sign in China of new birth and new beginnings (see Chapter 18). The seeds inside the melons symbolize the previous Chinese royal line to which the artist was still faithful. Although it was not an outright protest, most educated persons understood the meaning.

Architecture, painting, and sculpture—and more recently film and television—have been used to project and glorify images of deities, political leaders, and now corporations. In seventeenth-century France, King Louis XIV built an enormous palace with a formal garden at Versailles. Its purpose was to symbolize the strength of the monarchy—to impress and intimidate the nobility with the Sun King's power (see Chapter 17).

Advertising designers often use the persuasive powers of art to present a version of the truth. We see their messages every day on television and in the print media. Not all persuasive art is commercial, however. Art can be an effective instrument for educating, directing popular values, molding public opinion, and gaining and holding political power. Art, like science, is not inherently good or evil. It is the way art is used that makes the difference.

Political and religious leaders wielded the power of art to help control the minds of the masses long before the advent of modern communications media. In the twentieth century, art's capacity to influence behavior has been greatly increased by photography, film, and television. Adolf Hitler's ability to inspire people to follow his mad dreams was greatly intensified and extended by the masterful filmmaking of Leni Riefenstahl. In her 1934 film TRIUMPH OF THE WILL, Riefenstahl created what Hitler ordered: a highly effective instrument for political propaganda. Writing about her experiences, she said her aim was to bring the word of the Führer to the German people and to the world.

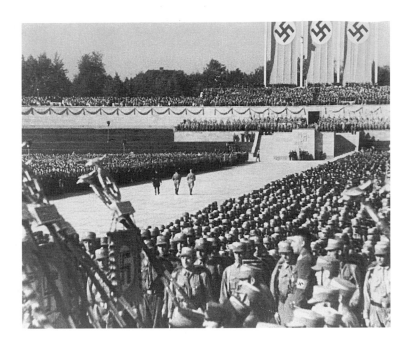

16   Leni Riefenstahl.
TRIUMPH OF THE WILL. 1934.
Film.
The Museum of Modern Art Film Stills Archive, New York.
Photograph: Leni Riefenstahl

The major question raised by Riefenstahl's work for Hitler goes far beyond the Nazi films she produced. What is an artist's moral responsibility? What is the impact of such powerful artistic achievement on the whole human race? In this case an artist of great talent applied her artistic ability to influence the hearts and minds of millions of people—with disastrous results.

Many artists, including political cartoonists and photographers, have used their art to protest injustice and to promote peace, environmental protection, and human rights. Margaret Bourke-White's photograph LOUISVILLE FLOOD VICTIMS on page 161 is a protest against racial and social inequality; Picasso's GUERNICA on page 119 is a strong antiwar statement.

The art of our culture reflects who we are and what our relationships are to our surroundings and to one another. Art can provide beauty and inspiration, but it may also uncover disturbing truths. In the powerful distortions in some works of art we may recognize destructive aspects of ourselves and of society. This very recognition can inspire inner development and an increased social and political

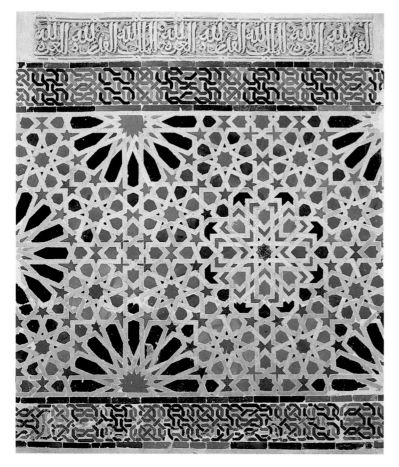

17 DECORATIVE PANEL FROM THE ALHAMBRA.
Granada. Nasrid Period, 14th Century. Glazed mosaic tile. 60" × 50⅝".
Museo de la Alhambra.
Photograph: Sheldan Collins.

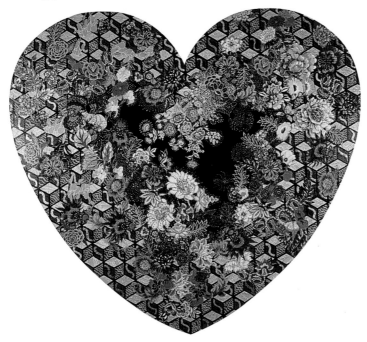

awareness. Today, when cross-cultural understanding, open-mindedness, and creative problem solving are urgently needed, art can elevate our consciousness and deepen our humanity.

Art for Visual Delight

Many of us probably think of visual delight as the first function of art. Indeed, art can provide pleasure, enjoyment, amusement, diversion, and embellishment in our world. Art that is visually attractive and well crafted can "lift us above the stream of life," as a noted aesthetician once put it.[10] In contemplating such works, we may be so absorbed that we forget where we are for a moment.

Islamic cultures have traditionally been among the world's best at producing objects of this sort. For example, the fourteenth-century DECORATIVE PANEL FROM THE ALHAMBRA is made of colored mosaic tile laid in dazzling patterns. Our eyes follow pathways that enclose geometric figures of many different shapes, sizes, and colors. These small polygons are included in a larger rhythm of black starbursts between rows of geometric interlace. The piece shown here is only a small fragment of the lower portion of a wall enclosing a room in the Alhambra, a palace that dates from the time of Islamic occupation of Spain (711–1492).

Some contemporary artists have achieved decorative effects with very different materials. Miriam Schapiro's HEARTLAND depends partly on sheer size for its impact, since it measures nearly seven by eight feet. Here, a rich texture of mixed media calls to mind traditional art forms of quilting and flower arranging which were once exclusively the province of women. The piece actually combines paint, fabric, and glitter in a collage format whose feminine elements led Schapiro to coin the term "femmages" to describe them. The lush colors, bold patterns, and symbolic meanings of the shape of the work combine to create a garden of visual delight.

18 Miriam Schapiro.
HEARTLAND. 1985.
Acrylic, fabric, and glitter on canvas. 85" × 94".
Collection of Orlando Museum of Art, Orlando, Florida.
Gift of the Women for Special Acquisitions and the Council 101.
Photograph: © Miriam Shapiro.

CHAPTER TWO

AWARENESS, CREATIVITY, AND COMMUNICATION

T here are as many ways to create as there are creative people. The creative process often begins when one is inspired by an idea or faced with a problem.

VISUAL THINKING

Much of our thinking is visual thinking. To visualize is to use imagination and visual memory to preview events or plans before they occur. Most of the things we make begin with a mental picture. This is true for a meal, a vacation, a painting, or a building. Visualization is used by all artists. Some plan their works by mentally picturing them as completed images; others visualize their pieces as they develop them, letting one idea lead to another.

Our experiences influence both inner visualization and outer seeing. For example, ten people painting the same subject—even working from the same vantage point—will make ten different images based on their experiences, values, and interests. An English botanist, a Peruvian developer, and a Japanese photographer each see the same landscape differently

We have a variety of responses to a given subject over time. When we look at a picture of a house, for example, we see an enclosed volume. On an intellectual level we may assume it contains rooms, while our emotions may lead us to make associations with "home." Creative visual thinking draws from varied levels of meaning and integrates the complementary modes of rational and intuitive intelligences associated with the right and left sides of the brain.

PERCEPTION AND AWARENESS

Of all our planet's resources, the most precious is human awareness.

Don Fabun[1]

Perception and awareness are closely related. To *be aware* means to be conscious, to know something. To *perceive* is to become aware through the senses, particularly through sight or hearing, and to understand through that awareness.

In the visual arts, we seek awareness through our sense of sight and through the development of visual thinking. Surprising as it may seem, much of our sensory awareness is learned. The eyes are blind to what the mind cannot see. The following story provides an unusually dramatic example.

Joey, a New York City boy with blind parents, was born with cerebral palsy. Because of his disabilities, as well as those of his parents, Joey was largely confined to his family's apartment. As he grew older, he learned to get around the apartment in a walker. His mother believed him to be of normal intelligence, yet clinical tests showed him to be blind and mentally retarded. At age five Joey was admitted to a school for children with a variety of disabilities, and for the first time he had daily contact with people who could see. Although he bumped into things in his walker and felt for almost everything, as a blind person does, it soon became apparent that Joey was not really blind. *He simply had never learned to use his eyes.* The combined disabilities of Joey and his parents had prevented him from developing normal visual awareness. After working with specialists and playing with sighted children for a year, his visual responses were normal. Those who worked with him concluded that Joey was a bright and alert child.

To varying degrees, we are all guided—or limited, as Joey was—in the growth of our awareness by parents, teachers, and others who influence us.

Even common words and concepts can sometimes limit our sensory impressions. When we look at an object only in terms of a label or a stereotype, we miss the thing itself; we tend to see a vague something called "tree" or "chair" rather than *this* tree, this *particular* chair, or this *unique* object or person. As artist Robert Irwin pointed out, "seeing is forgetting the name of the thing one sees."[2]

As we become more conscious of our own sensory experiences, we open up new levels of awareness. Ordinary things become extraordinary when seen without prejudgment. Is Edward Weston's photograph of a pepper meaningful to us because we like peppers so much? Probably not. To help us see anew, Weston created a memorable image on a flat surface with the help of a common pepper. A time exposure of over two hours gave PEPPER #30 a quality of glowing light—a living presence that resembles an embrace. Through his sensitivity to form, Weston revealed how this pepper appeared to him. Notes from his *Daybook* communicate his enthusiasm about this photograph:

August 8, 1930
I could wait no longer to print them—my new peppers, so I put aside several orders, and yesterday afternoon had an exciting time with seven new negatives.

First I printed my favorite, the one made last Saturday, August 2, just as the light was failing—quickly made, but with a week's previous effort back of my

immediate, unhesitating decision. A week?—Yes, on this certain pepper,—but twenty-eight years of effort, starting with a youth on a farm in Michigan, armed with a No. 2 Bull's Eye [Kodak] 3½ × 3½, have gone into the making of this pepper, which I consider a peak of achievement.

It is a classic, completely satisfying—a pepper— but more than a pepper: abstract, in that it is completely outside subject matter . . . this new pepper takes one beyond the world we know in the conscious mind.[3]

Weston's photograph of a seemingly common object is a good example of the creative process at work. The artist was uniquely aware of something in his surroundings. He applied a great deal of creative effort in achieving the image that he wanted. The photograph that resulted not only represents the object, but communicates a deep sense of wonder about the natural world and its processes. Thus the work combines awareness, creativity, and communication.

LOOKING AND SEEING

Degrees of visual awareness can be distinguished by the verbs "look" and "see." Looking implies taking in what is before us in a purely mechanical way; seeing is a more active extension of looking. If we care only about function, we simply need to look quickly at a doorknob in order to grasp and turn it. But when we get excited about the shape and finish of a doorknob, or the bright clear quality of a winter day, we go beyond simple functional looking to a higher level of perception called "seeing."

The twentieth-century French artist Henri Matisse wrote about the effort it takes to move beyond stereotypes and to see fully:

To see is itself a creative operation, requiring an effort. Everything that we see in our daily life is more or less distorted by acquired habits, and this is perhaps more

19 Edward Weston.
PEPPER #30. 1930.
Photograph.
© 1981, Center for Creative Photography,
Arizona Board of Regents.

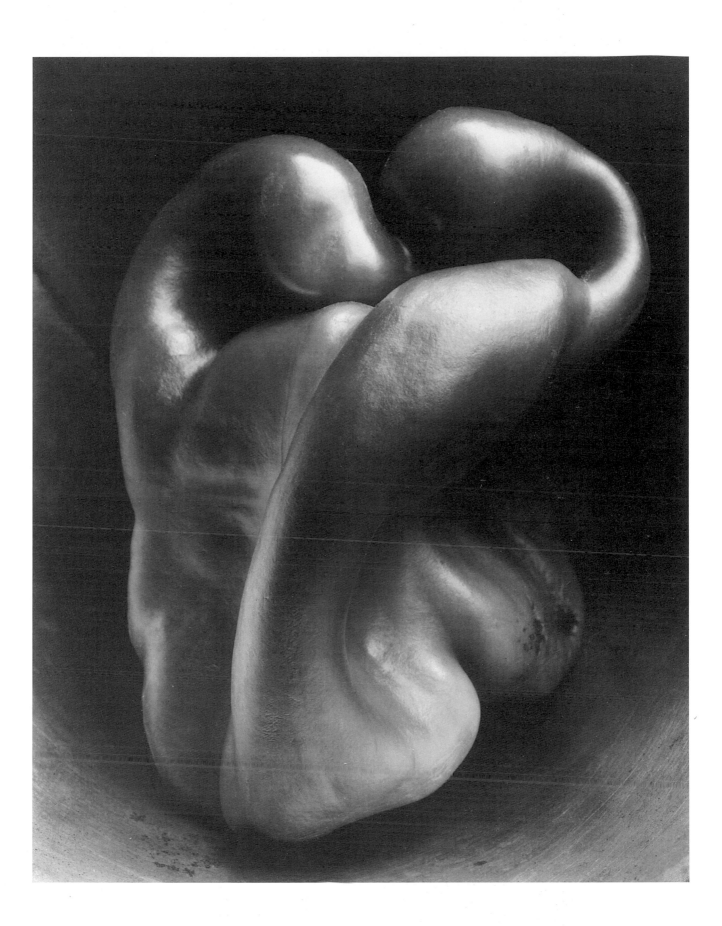

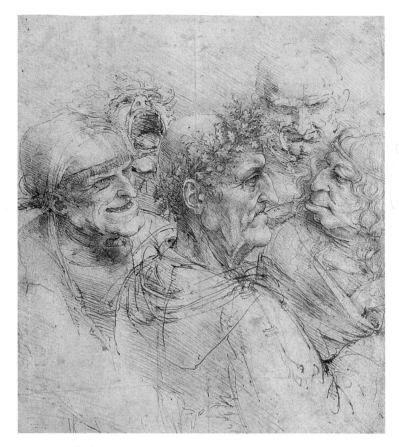

20 Leonardo da Vinci (1452–1519).
A GROUP OF FIVE GROTESQUE HEADS. c. 1490.
Pen and brown ink. 10¼" × 8½".
The Royal Collection Windsor Castle.
© 2002, Her Majesty Queen Elizabeth II.

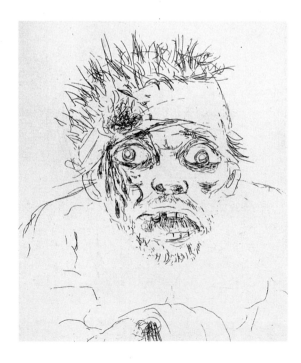

evident in an age like ours when cinema, posters, and magazines present us every day with a flood of ready-made images which are to the eye what prejudices are to the mind. The effort needed to see things without distortion takes something very like courage.[4]

AESTHETICS, ART, AND BEAUTY

Aesthetics refers to an awareness of beauty or to that quality in a work of art or other manmade or natural form which evokes a sense of elevated awareness in the viewer. Some people equate the word "aesthetic" with taste. Many artists and art critics oppose this view, maintaining that art has nothing to do with taste; they think that so-called good taste can actually limit an honest response. "Good taste" almost always refers to an already established way of seeing. Innovative artists, seeking new ways of seeing, often challenge the established conventions of taste.

In the West, contradictory views exist regarding "art" and "beauty." Beginning with the ancient Greeks, Westerners have been preoccupied with beauty. Criteria for beauty, as well as art, often are based on culturally accepted standards rather than individual responses or personal intuition.

Today we often use the word "beautiful" to refer to things that are simply pretty. "Pretty" means pleasant or attractive to the eye, whereas "beautiful" means having qualities of a high order, qualities that delight the eye, engage the intellectual or moral sense, or do all these things simultaneously. In the words of architect Louis Kahn, "Beautiful doesn't necessarily mean good-looking."[5]

It is important to consider possibilities beyond the conventional or established standards of beauty and ugliness. If art's only function were to please the senses, ugliness would have no place in art. But since we don't expect all works of drama or literature to be pretty or pleasant, why should we have different expectations of the visual arts? Leonardo da Vinci, Otto Dix, Vincent van Gogh, and Jean-Michel Basquiat—artists from different times and

21 Otto Dix. DER KRIEG (WOUNDED SOLDIER). 1924.
Etching. 7¾" × 5½".
Galerie der Stadt, Stuttgart.
© 2002 Artists Rights Society (ARS), NY/VG Bild-Kunst, Bonn.

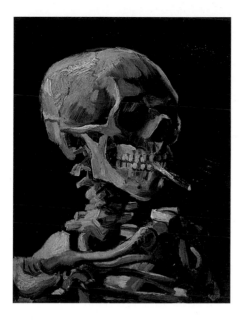

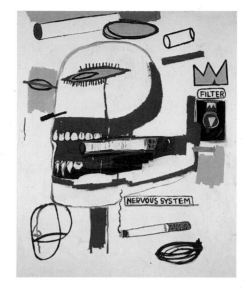

22 Vincent van Gogh.
SKULL WITH A BURNING CIGARETTE. 1885–1886.
Oil on canvas. 32" × 24½".
Van Gogh Museum (Vincent Van Gogh Foundation), Amsterdam.

23 Jean-Michel Basquiat.
TOBACCO. 1984.
Acrylic and oil crayon on canvas. 86" × 68".
Courtesy Galerie Bruno Bischofberger, Zurich.
© 2002 Artists Rights Society (ARS),
NY/ADAGP, Paris.

places—explored dimensions of "ugliness" in relation to their own concerns and personal modes of expression.

Street life fascinated Italian Renaissance artist Leonardo da Vinci. He was particularly interested in studying people of striking appearance, people either very beautiful or very ugly. Leonardo found ugliness to be as worthy of attention as beauty. In fact, he considered ugliness a variation of beauty, and this feeling can be seen in his FIVE GROTESQUE HEADS. In his *Treatise on Painting,* he advised others always to carry a pocket notebook in which to make quick drawings of what they observed. He also drew from memory, as described by sixteenth-century artist and biographer Giorgio Vasari:

Leonardo used to follow people whose extraordinary appearance took his fancy, sometimes throughout a whole day, until he could draw them as well by memory as though they stood before him.[6]

Unlike Leonardo's drawing, in which ugly people are gracefully drawn, every line in Otto Dix's etching carries the grotesque quality of the larger subject—the horror of war.

Dix, who served in the German army for four years during World War I, depicted the terrible anguish of war in his etching WOUNDED SOLDIER. In the economically and politically troubled 1920s, he criticized his society for its decadence. With unrelenting honesty, Dix documented the brutalities of gas and trench warfare. As his etching illustrates, even horrible events can provide the basis for constructive communication through art. Artists can help us to learn without our having to live through such horrors.

Vincent van Gogh's SKULL WITH A BURNING CIGARETTE presents another aspect of what we humans consider ugly: reminders of death, the skeleton. The skeleton seems eerily lit as it basks in an earthy brown glow before an overwhelmingly dark background.

In contrast to the careful brushwork of van Gogh is the intentionally blunt, bad-boy, street-painting style of Jean-Michel Basquiat. Basquiat's direct approach, as seen in TOBACCO, evolved from his early experience as a teenage graffiti artist.

The sociocultural context of his life was the foundation for Basquiat's art. He was born in Brooklyn to a Haitian father and Puerto Rican mother; his parents divorced and his mother ended up in a mental institution. After gaining attention for his graffiti-like street paintings, Basquiat was rather suddenly brought into the hyped environment of the New York gallery world. The pressure was enormous. TOBACCO is about death from addiction, a subject he knew all too well. Basquiat died from a heroin overdose at age twenty-seven.

ART AND EXPERIENCE

Art encourages us to experience our lives more vividly by causing us to reexamine our thoughts and renew our feelings. The essence of art is the spark of insight and the thrill of discovery—first experienced by the maker, then built into the work of art, and finally experienced by the viewer. Russian novelist and philosopher Leo Tolstoy described the process:

To evoke in oneself a feeling one has experienced, and having evoked it . . . , then by means of movement, line, color, sounds or forms expressed in words, so transmit that same feeling—this is the activity of art.[7]

As we live our lives, experiences flow past in a stream of what may seem like disconnected events and impressions. Art helps us to become aware of the significance of the moment and the interrelationships of events—and thereby to experience life fully.

While animals are keenly aware of their world through their senses, human beings have lost some of the ability to experience life intensely in the present moment. Caught up in thoughts and emotions, and often separated from direct experiences with nature, many of us adopt dulled, programmed responses to our environments.

The best art can cut through our tendency to experience life with prejudgment. Such art sharpens our perceptions of life by re-creating human experience in fresh forms, bringing a new sense of the significance and connectedness of life.

CREATIVITY

The source of all art, science, and technology—in fact, all of human civilizations—is creative imagi-

nation, or creative thinking. As scientist Albert Einstein declared, "Imagination is more important than knowledge."[8]

What do we mean by this ability we call creativity? Psychologist Erich Fromm wrote:

In talking about creativity, let us first consider its two possible meanings: creativity in the sense of creating something new, something which can be seen or heard by others, such as a painting, a sculpture, a symphony, a poem, a novel, etc., or creativity as an attitude, which is the condition of any creation in the former sense but which can exist even though nothing new is created in the world of things. . . .

What is creativity? The best general answer I can give is that creativity is the ability to see (or to be aware) and to respond.[9]

Creativity is as fundamental to experiencing and appreciating a work of art as it is to making one. Insightful seeing is itself a creative act; it requires open receptivity—putting aside habitual modes of thought.

Studies of creativity have described traits of people who have maintained or rediscovered the creative attitude. These include the abilities to:

- wonder and be curious
- be open to new experience
- see the familiar from an unfamiliar point of view
- take advantage of accidental events
- make one thing out of another by shifting its function
- generalize from particulars in order to see broad applications
- synthesize, integrate, find order in disorder
- be in touch with one's unconscious, yet be intensely conscious
- be able to analyze and evaluate
- know oneself, have the courage to be oneself in the face of opposition
- be willing to take risks
- be persistent: to work for long periods—perhaps years—in pursuit of a goal

I'd like to study the drawings of kids. That's where the truth is, without a doubt.
André Derain[10]

The arts come from innately human needs to create and to communicate. They come from the desire to explore, confirm, and share special observations and insights— a fact readily apparent in nine-year-old Kojyu's SEARCHING FOR BUGS IN THE PARK. The arts are one of the most constructive ways to say "I did it. I made it. This is what I see and feel. I count. My art is me." Unfortunately, the great value of this discover-and-share, art-making process is only rarely affirmed in today's busy homes and schools.

We include art by children as the best way—other than actual hands-on art-making processes—to help you reexamine your relationship to your own creative powers and perhaps even to guide you as you prepare to become a parent, a teacher, or a caregiver for children.

Children use a universal visual language. All over the world, drawings by children ages two to six show similar stages of mental growth, from exploring with mark-making to inventing shapes to symbolizing things seen and imagined. Until they are about six years old, children usually depict the world in symbolic rather than realistic ways. Their images are more mental constructions

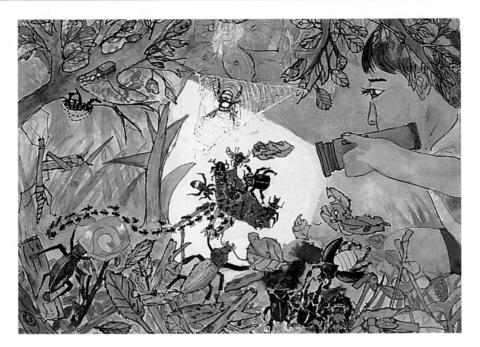

than records of visual observations.

During the second year of life, children enjoy making marks, leaving traces of their movements. Sensitive exploration is visible in FIRST LINES, by a one-and-a-half-year-old child. After marking and scribbling, making circles and other shapes fascinates young children. The HOUSE shape is by a two-year-old. HAND WITH LINE AND SPOTS is by a three-year-old, as is the smiling portrait of GRANDMA in which self-assured lines symbolize a happy face, shoulders, arms, body, belly button, and legs.

Being the son of a salt-water fish collector, and watching an octopus, gave almost four-year-old

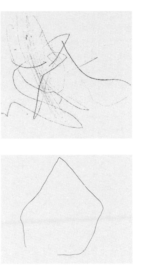

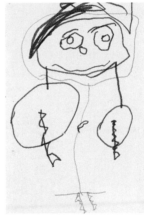

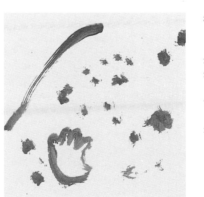

24 Kojyu, age 9.
SEARCHING FOR BUGS
IN THE PARK.
25 FIRST LINES.
26 Alana, age 2.
HOUSE.
27 Alana, age 3.
GRANDMA.
28 Jeff, age 3.
HAND WITH LINE
AND SPOTS.
Photographs: Duane Preble.

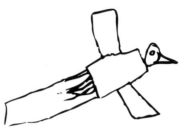

OCTOPUS

29 Jason, almost 4.
MOTHER
OCTOPUS WITH
BABIES.

30 Yuki, age 8.
I CAN RIDE,
I CAN RIDE MY
UNICYCLE.
Photographs: Duane
Preble.

31 Anonymous Child. BIRDS.
  a. This picture shows one child's drawing of a bird
     before exposure to coloring books.

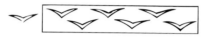

  b. Then the child colored a workbook illustration.

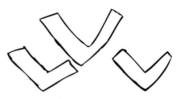

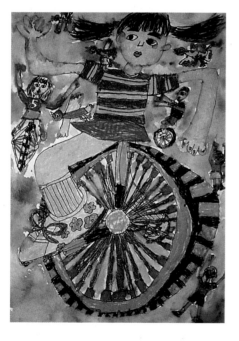

  c. After coloring the workbook birds, the child
     lost creative sensitivity and self-reliance.
     (a, b, and c) Creative Mental Growth
     by Victor Lowenfeld, MacMillan,1975, p23. Reproduced by
     permission of Pearson Education.

Jason the idea for his drawing of a smiling MOTHER OCTOPUS WITH BABIES. The excitement of joyful play with friends on unicycles inspired eight-year-old Yuki's I CAN RIDE, I CAN RIDE MY UNICYCLE. Notice how she emphasized her own image by greatly exaggerating her size relative to others and how she included important information, such as her right leg seen through the spokes of the wheel.

Young children often demonstrate an intuitive sense of composition. Unfortunately, we lose much of this intuitive sense of balanced design as we begin to look at the world from a conceptual, self-conscious point of view. Most children who have been given coloring books, workbooks, and pre-drawn printed single sheets become overly dependent on such impersonal, stereotyped props. In this way, children often lose the urge to invent unique images based on their own experiences. A child's two drawings of BIRDS show this process: The child first interprets the bird in a personal, fresh way, but later adopts the trite forms of a conventional workbook. Without ongoing opportunities for personal expression, children lose self-confidence in their original creative impulses.

Children begin life as eager learners. If they are loved and cared for, they soon express enthusiasm for perceiving and exploring the world around them. Research shows that parents' ability to show interest in and empathy for their child's discoveries and feelings is crucial to the child's brain development. Before the age of one, and well before they talk, babies point tiny fingers at wonderful things they see. Bodies move in rhythm to music. Ask a group of four-year-olds "Can you dance?" "Can you sing?" "Can you draw?" and they all say, "Yes! Yes!" Ask twelve-year-olds the same questions, and they will too often say "No, we can't." Such an unnecessary loss has ominous implications for the spiritual, economic, social, and political health of society.

Most abilities observed in creative people are also characteristic of children during interactions with the world around them. What becomes of this extraordinary capacity? According to John Holt, author of *How Children Fail,*

We destroy this capacity above all by making them afraid— afraid of not doing what other people want, of not pleasing, or of making mistakes, of failing, of being wrong. Thus we make them afraid to gamble, afraid to experiment, afraid to try the difficult and unknown.[11]

As Fromm said, creativity is an *attitude*. We all have the potential to be creative, yet most of us have not been encouraged to develop our creativity.

Though certain aspects of creativity seem very similar worldwide, each culture has specific ways of thinking about the subject. In Chinese painting, for example, the artist is not expected merely to copy the appearance of the subject of the work, but rather to *understand* it deeply and communicate that understanding. In that tradition, paintings of bamboo are fairly common; but an artist who masters the subject is one who can go beyond mere appearances and harmonize his or her spirit with that of the plant. The eleventh-century poet and painter Su Xi once described the creative process as an intuitive grasping of the subject, not a laborious copying of its every detail: "Painters of today draw joint after joint and pile up leaf on leaf. How can that become a bamboo? When you are going to paint a bamboo, you must first realize the thing completely in your mind."[12] He once praised the artist Yu Ko by saying that Yu was transformed into the bamboos that he painted.

Native American pottery painters of the Southwest offer another perspective on creativity. These artists decorate their earthenware vessels with symbolic forms that are meant to recall the natural surroundings. Each tribal group generally uses a basic set of commonly understood symbols, which the artists, who traditionally are women, may vary and combine at will. When an anthropologist interviewed several of these potters in the 1920s, most said that they first dreamed of the designs that they would paint on their pots. Each said that she fully conceived the design in her mind before painting it.

Creativity developed through art experiences enhances creative problem solving and communicating in other areas of life. Opportunities for creative expression are extremely important: They develop our abilities to integrate experiences of the outside world with those of our inner selves.

UNTRAINED AND FOLK ARTISTS

The urge to create is universal; it has little to do with art training. We satisfy our artistic sensibilities every day in a variety of ways. Those with little or no formal art education who make objects commonly recognized as art are identified as either *untrained artists* or *folk artists*.

Art by untrained artists, also called *naive* or *outsider artists*, is made by people who are largely unaware of art history or the art trends and fashions of their time. Unlike folk art, which is made by people working within a tradition, art by untrained artists is personal expression created apart from any conventional practice or style.

Many untrained artists seem to develop their art spontaneously, without regard to art of the past

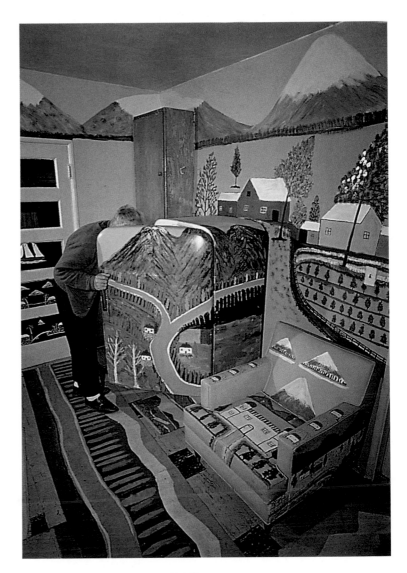

32   SANFORD DARLING IN HIS KITCHEN.
Photograph: Ralph Crane.
Life Magazine. © TimePix.

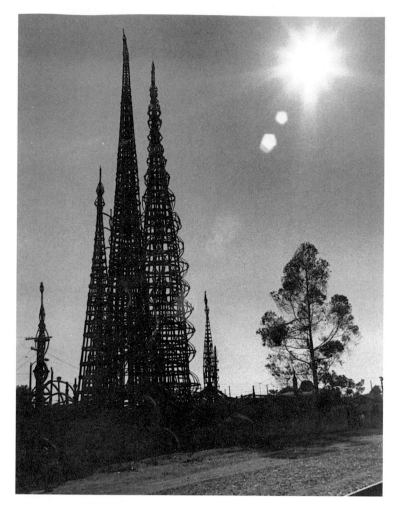

33 Sabatino "Simon" Rodia.

a. NUESTRO PUEBLO.
Watts, California. 1921–1954.
Mixed media. Height 100'.
Photographs: Duane Preble.

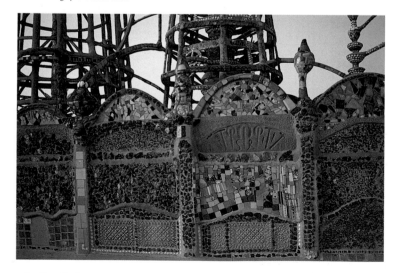

b. Detail of NUESTRO PUEBLO.
Enclosing wall with construction-tool impressions.

or present. Sanford Darling was sixty-three, retired, and recently widowed when he began to paint (previous page). Using a three-inch brush and green semigloss enamel, he painted his first picture—on a wall of his house in Santa Barbara, California. Over a period of years, he covered the rest of his house inside and out, with landscapes and other scenes from his memory. Among Darling's images were things he had seen during a six-month tour of the South Pacific and the Orient as well as scenes from his youth on a Wisconsin farm. He continued to paint pictures on his furniture and on the backs of small rugs. His kitchen was eventually dominated by landscapes, including a river that flowed across the refrigerator.

The sculptural spires in Watts, California, known commonly as "Watts Towers," were titled NUESTRO PUEBLO (OUR PEOPLE) by Sabatino Rodia, the Italian tile setter who built them. Rodia exemplifies the artist who visualizes new possibilities for ordinary materials. He worked on his cathedral-like towers for thirty-three years, making the fantastic structures from cast-off materials such as metal pipes and bed frames held together with steel reinforcing rods, mesh, and mortar. Incredibly, he built the towers without power tools, rivets, welds, or bolts.

As the towers rose in his tiny triangular backyard, he methodically covered their surfaces with bits and pieces of broken dishes, tile, melted bottle glass, shells, and other colorful "junk" from the vacant lots of his neighborhood. Rodia's towers and the ideas they represent are testimony to the artist's creativity and incredible perseverance.

Another striking work by an untrained artist in this century is the THRONE OF THE THIRD HEAVEN OF THE NATION'S MILLENNIUM GENERAL ASSEMBLY, which James Hampton built in his garage over a fourteen-year span. The artist brought home pieces of furniture and other found objects, which he laboriously covered with gold and silver foil and arranged symmetrically. Hampton, a Baptist minister and night janitor at government buildings in Washington, D.C., believed that Jesus was coming again soon. His reading of the last book of the New

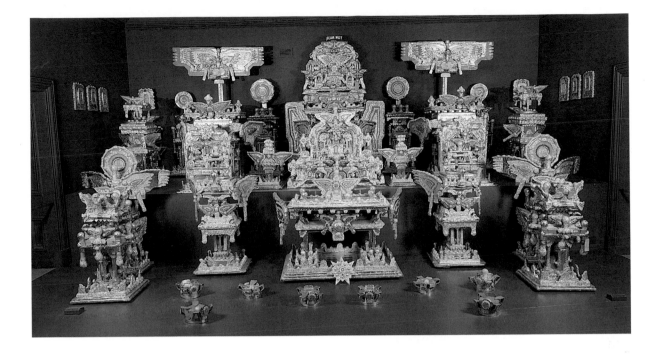

Testament, Revelation, convinced him that when Jesus returned, he would need a throne to sit on. Between about 1950 and 1964, he actually built one. No one knew of this project until Hampton died, and relatives going through his possessions found this amazing work. It now occupies an entire gallery in the Smithsonian Institution.

Folk art applies to art by artists who are part of established traditions of style, theme, and craftsmanship. In earlier times, particularly in rural areas, communication and influences from beyond one's immediate community were limited, and thus many folk art traditions remained relatively unchanged for long periods.

When the Southwest was a Spanish colony, a folk tradition of painting religious imagery evolved in the Roman Catholic churches. Small panels were made for private devotion in homes. Since the saints, or *santos,* were the most common subjects, the artists who painted or sculpted them were known as *santeros.* One of the best known of these traditional artists was José Rafael Aragón, who was active during the middle of the nineteenth century. His FLIGHT INTO EGYPT shows a crowned Mary carrying the infant Jesus, with Joseph behind and a dove representing the Holy

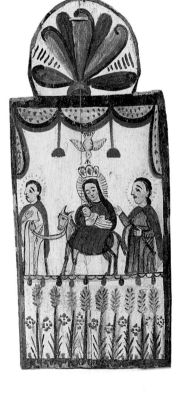

34 James Hampton.
THRONE OF THE THIRD HEAVEN OF THE NATION'S MILLENNIUM GENERAL ASSEMBLY. c. 1950–1964. Gold and silver aluminum foil, colored Kraft paper, plastic sheets over wood, paperboard and glass. 180 pieces. 10'6" × 27' × 14'6".
National Museum of American Art, Washington, D.C./Art Resource, NY.

35 José Rafael Aragón.
FLIGHT INTO EGYPT. c. 1850. Gesso and water-soluble paint on wood. 20½" × 8¾".
Museum of New Mexico collections. Museum of International Folk Art, Santa Fe. Photograph: Blair Clark.

Spirit above. They are led by an angel in white as they flee the persecution of King Herod that is related in the Bible. The simplicity of this work contributes to its mood of sweetness, communicated by subtle facial expressions and gestures. Aragón was among the busiest painters of his day, as he executed works in churches across the area that is now central New Mexico. His volume of work was so enormous that he had a workshop and assistants; as a result, it became difficult to tell which images were made by his own hand.

TRAINED ARTISTS

In the past, the world's trained artists generally learned by working as apprentices to accomplished masters. (With a few notable exceptions, women were excluded from such apprenticeships.) Through practical experience, they gained necessary skills and developed knowledge of their society's art traditions. Today most art-educated American artists are "trained" in art schools, or in college or university art departments. Learning in such settings develops sophisticated knowledge of alternative points of view, both contemporary and historical.

In contrast to untrained artists, who demonstrate unmannered originality, trained artists often show a self-conscious awareness of their relationship to art history. This can be either an asset or a burden. Knowledge of art history provides a wealth of material to draw from but can lead to an egocentric struggle to be profound and original.

Whether outsider, folk, or trained, artists must be independent thinkers and must have the courage to go beyond group mentality. In this way artists offer not what others have seen, but fresh insights that extend the experiences of those who see their art.

VISUAL COMMUNICATION

The language of vision determines, perhaps even more subtly and thoroughly than verbal language, the structure of our consciousness.

S. I. Hayakawa[13]

The most direct avenue to the mind is by way of the eyes. As S. I. Hayakawa pointed out, our visual experience of the world is so profoundly influential that it constitutes a nonverbal language all its own. This is the language that art uses to communicate.

In art, the visual experience is essential. Words used to describe that experience are simply a means of discussing our perceptions. Words can help us analyze—and therefore better understand—the infinite ways in which artists construct visual forms.

Since words and visual images are two different "languages," talking about visual arts with words is always an act of translation—and is one step removed from actually experiencing art. In fact, our eyes have their own connections to our minds and emotions. Only by cultivating these connections are we able to take full advantage of what art has to offer.

In the context of art, an artist's interpretation of a subject is more important than the actual subject being used. Subjects don't make art, artists do. How the image is composed, how materials and techniques are employed, what is emphasized, and what left out—all this becomes the basis for an in-depth experience of a work of art.

ART AND APPEARANCES

Art involves interpretation rather than replication. A real horse, a painting of a horse, and a sculpture of a horse each has its own reality—and each of these realities is substantially different from the others.

Artists may depict much of what they see in the physical world, they may alter appearances, or they may invent forms not seen in either the natural or human-made world. Regardless of their approaches, most artists invite viewers to see beyond mere appearances. The terms *representational, abstract,* and *nonrepresentational* (or *nonobjective*) are used to describe an artwork's relationship to the physical world.

Representational Art

Representational art (sometimes called *objective* or *figurative art*) depicts the appearance of things. It represents—presents again—objects we recognize from the everyday world. Objects that representational art depicts are called *subjects.*

Representational art includes a wide range of styles, from the fool-the-eye realism of William Harnett to personally expressive images such as those by Rembrandt (see page 9), to distortions such as those in Romare Bearden's art (page 10).

The most "real" looking paintings are in a style called *trompe l'oeil* (pronounced "tromp loy")—French for "fool the eye." Paintings in this illusionistic style impress us because they look so "real." In Harnett's painting A SMOKE BACKSTAGE, the assembled objects are close to life-size, which contributes to the illusion. We almost believe that we can reach out and touch an actual pipe.

Belgian painter René Magritte presents the viewer with a different pictorial and written statement about the nature of representational art. The subject of the painting appears to be a pipe, but written in French on the painting are the words, *"Ceci n'est pas une pipe."* ("This is not a pipe.") The viewer wonders, "If this is not a pipe, what is it?" The answer, of course, is that it is a painting! Magritte's title, THE TREASON OF IMAGES, suggests what the artist had in mind.

Matisse told of an incident that illustrated his views on the difference between art and nature. A woman visiting his studio pointed to one of his paintings and said, "But surely, the arm of this woman is much too long." Matisse replied, "Madame, you are mistaken. This is not a woman, this is a picture."[14]

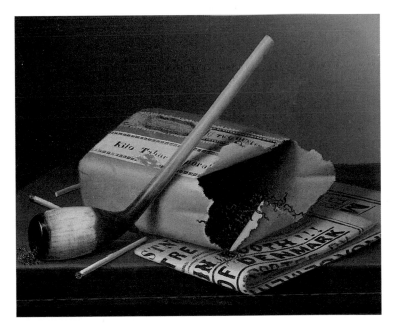

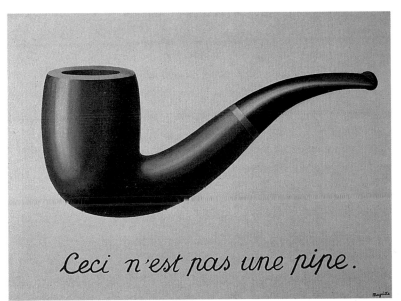

36   William Harnett. A SMOKE BACKSTAGE. 1877. Oil on canvas. 7" × 8½".
Honolulu Academy of Arts. Gift of John Wyatt Gregg Allerton, 1964.(3211.1).

37   René Magritte. LA TRAHISON DES IMAGES (CECI N' EST PAS UNE PIPE), 1929. Oil on canvas. 60 × 81 cm.
Los Angeles County Museum of Art, Los Angeles. Giraudon/Art Resource, NY. © 2002 C. Herscovici, Brussels/Artists Rights Society (ARS), New York.

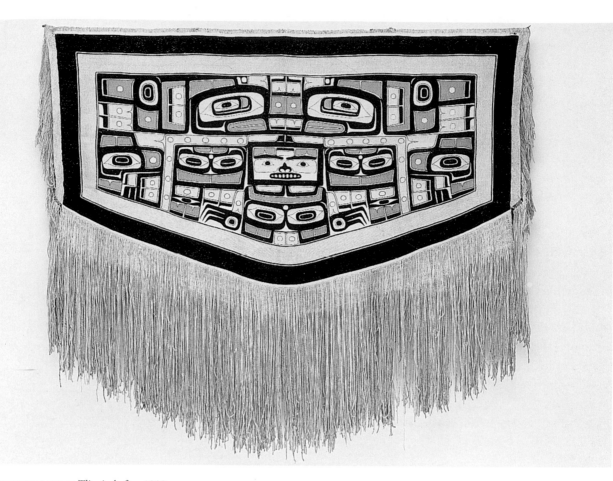

38 CHILKAT BLANKET. Tlingit, before 1928.
Mountain goat wool and shredded cedar bark. 4'7" × 5'4".
Neg./Transparency no. 3804.
Courtesy Department of Library Services,
American Museum of Natural History, New York.
Photograph: Steve Myers.

Abstract Art

"To abstract" means to extract the essence of an object or idea. In art, the word *abstract* can mean either (1) works of art that have no reference at all to natural objects, or (2) works that depict natural objects in simplified, distorted, or exaggerated ways. In this book, we use abstract in the second sense.

In abstract art the artist changes the object's natural appearance in order to emphasize or reveal certain qualities. Just as there are many approaches to representational art, there are many approaches to abstraction. We may be able to recognize the subject matter of an abstract work quite easily, or we may need the help of a clue (such as a title). The interaction between how an actual subject typically looks and how a particular artist presents it is part of the pleasure and challenge of abstract art. In a basic sense, all art is abstraction because it is not possible for an artist to reproduce exactly what is seen.

Abstraction in one form or another is a common art style in many cultures besides Western modern art. Native peoples of the Northwest coast decorate many objects with forms abstracted from the shapes of animals that populate their mythology. For example, the CHILKAT BLANKET woven by

Tlingit women contains in its center a face of such a composite figure. Below the face, along the bottom edge, claw feet point outward. Elsewhere in the design, shapes that symbolize eyes, fins, and wings of other animals fill the surface in a symmetrical arrangement. This blanket, once the prized possession of a high tribal official, was woven in a regional style. The weaver employed abstraction in the decorative use of meaningful symbols connecting seen and unseen spheres.

Varying degrees of abstraction are evident in Theo van Doesburg's series of drawings and paintings, ABSTRACTION OF A COW. The artist apparently wanted to see how far he could abstract the cow through simplification and still have his image symbolize the essence of the animal. Van Doesburg used the subject as a point of departure for a composition made up of colored rectangles. If we viewed only the final painting, and none of the earlier ones, we would see it as a nonrepresentational painting.

Nonrepresentational Art

A great deal of the world's art was not meant to be representational at all. Amish quilts, many Navajo textiles, and most Islamic wood carvings consist primarily of flat patterns that give pleasure through mere variety of line, shape, and color. *Nonrepresentational* art (sometimes called *nonobjective* or *nonfigurative* art) presents visual forms with no specific references to anything outside themselves. Just as we can respond to the pure sound forms of music, so we can respond to the pure visual forms of nonrepresentational art.

While nonrepresentational art may at first seem more difficult to grasp than representational or abstract art, it can offer fresh ways of seeing. Absence of subject matter actually clarifies the way all visual form affects us. Once we learn how to "read" the language of vision, we can respond to art and the world with greater understanding and enjoyment.

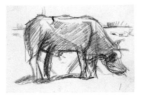

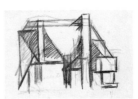

39 Theo van Doesburg (C.E.M. Kupper).
ABSTRACTION OF A COW.

Studies for composition
(THE COW). c. 1916.
Pencil on paper. Each 4⅝" × 6¼".
The Museum of Modern Art, New York. Purchase.
Photograph © 1999 The Museum of Modern Art, NY.
© 2002 Artists Rights Society (ARS), NY/Beeldrecht, Amsterdam.

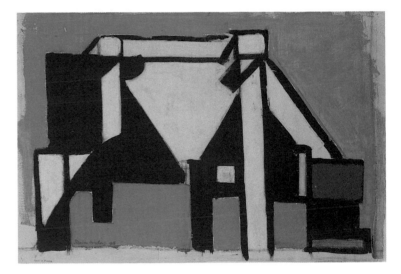

Theo van Doesburg (C.E.M. Kupper).
COMPOSITION (THE COW) c. 1917 (DATED 1916).
Tempera, oil and charcol on paper. 15⅝" × 22¾".
The Museum of Modern Art, New York. Purchase. Photograph © 2002 The Museum of Modern Art, NY. © 2002 the Arts Rights Society (ARS), NY/Beeldrecht, Amsterdam.

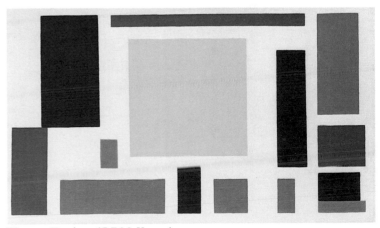

Theo van Doesburg (C.E.M. Kupper).
COMPOSITION (THE COW). c. 1917.
oil on canvas. 14¾" × 25".
The Museum of Modern Art, New York. Purchase.
Photograph © 2002 The Museum of Modern Art, NY.
© 2002 Artists Rights Society (ARS), NY/Beeldrecht, Amsterdam.

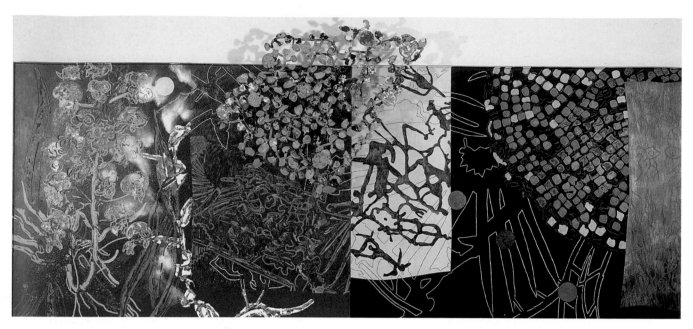

40 Nancy Graves.
FOOTSCRAY, from the AUSTRALIAN SERIES. 1985.
Oil, acrylic, and glitter on canvas with painted aluminum sculpture.
6'4½" × 14'5" × 12½" (diptych).
© Nancy Graves Foundation/Licensed by VAGA, NY.

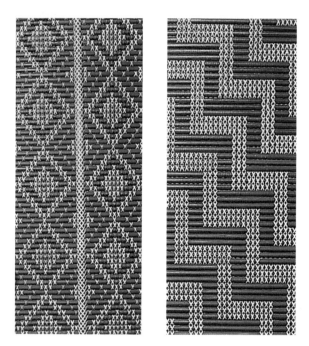

41 TUKUTUKU PANELS.
Maori peoples, New Zealand. 1930s.
Dyed plaited flax strips over wood laths.
Dimensions variable.
Collection of the Museum of New Zealand,
Te Papa Tongarewa, Wellington, New Zealand, F236, F238.

Two widely different types of nonrepresentational art are pictured here. In FOOTSCRAY, the work of the American painter-sculptor Nancy Graves, oil paint on canvas combines with brightly colored aluminum elements that hover above the surface of the work. The forms in the piece suggest organic, exuberant motion.

In New Zealand, Maori women working in pairs weave strips of dyed flax into geometric patterns called TUKUTUKU PANELS. These patterns are traditional in Maori societies and they have names such as "sand flounder," "human ribs," and "albatross tears." The panels are woven in specific sizes to fit between the wooden uprights of meeting houses where religious ceremonies are held. A given meeting house may contain *tukutuku* panels of many different designs, giving the room a rich and varied visual texture.

Whereas the makers of the TUKUTUKU PANELS used naturally dyed flax to create elegantly rhythmic, yet strictly geometric, traditional designs, Graves employed manmade materials, bright synthetic colors, and a dynamic, irregular composition to create FOOTSCRAY. These contrasting works show that even in nonrepresentational art, an extremely wide variety of forms, compositions, moods, and messages are possible.

FORM AND CONTENT

Form is what we see; content is what we interpret as the meaning of what we see. In this book *form* refers to the total effect of the combined visual qualities within a work, including such components as materials, color, shape, line, and design. *Content* refers to the message or meaning of the work of art—what the artist expresses or communicates to the viewer. Content determines form and is expressed through it; thus the two are inseparable. As form changes, content changes—and vice versa.

For example, the valentine ♥ heart—which is used to represent the human heart—is a symbol of love. If someone were to give you a huge, beautifully made red velvet valentine, so large it had to be pulled on a cart, you would probably be overwhelmed by the gesture. The content would be Love! But if you were to receive a faint photocopied outline of a heart on a cheap piece of paper, you might read the content as: *love*—sort of—a very impersonal kind. And if you were to receive a shriveled, greenish brown, slightly moldy image of a heart, you might read the content as *Ugh!*

One way to understand how art communicates experience is to examine works that have the same subject but vary greatly in form and content. THE KISS by Auguste Rodin and THE KISS by Constantin Brancusi show how two sculptors interpret an embrace. In Rodin's work, the life-size human figures represent Western ideals of the masculine and feminine: Rodin captured the sensual delight of that highly charged moment when lovers embrace. Our emotions are engaged as we overlook the hardness of the marble out of which the illusion was carved. The implied natural softness of flesh is accentuated by the rough texture of the unfinished marble supporting the figures.

In contrast to Rodin's sensuous approach, Brancusi used the solid quality of a block of stone to express lasting love. Through minimal cutting of the block, Brancusi symbolized—rather than illustrated—the concept of two becoming one. He chose geometric abstraction rather than representational naturalism to express love. Rodin's work expresses the *feelings* of love while Brancusi's expresses the *idea* of love.

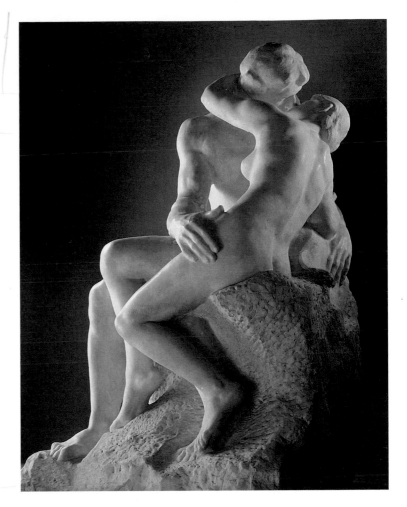

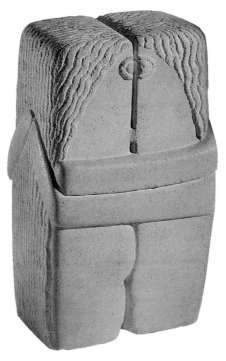

42 François Auguste René Rodin.
THE KISS. 1886.
Marble. Height 5'11¼".
Musée Rodin, Paris, France.
Photograph: Bruno Jarret.
© 2002 Artists Rights Society (ARS) NY/ADAPG,Paris.

43 Constantin Brancusi.
THE KISS. c. 1912.
Limestone.
23" × 13" × 10".
Philadelphia Museum of Art.
The Louise and Walter Arensberg Collection.
Photograph: Graydon Wood.
© 2002 Artists Rights Society (ARS) NY/ADAGP, Paris.

SEEING AND RESPONDING TO FORM

The creative act is not performed by the artist alone; the spectator brings the work in contact with the external world by deciphering and interpreting its inner qualifications and thus adds his contribution to the creative act.

Marcel Duchamp[15]

Obviously, effort is required to produce a work of art. Less obvious is the fact that responding to a work of art also requires effort. The artist is the source or sender; the work is the medium carrying the message. We, as viewers, must receive and experience the work if the communication is to be complete. In this way, we become active participants in the creative process.

Whether we realize it or not, learning to respond to form is part of learning to live in the world. We guide our actions by "reading" the forms of people, things, and events that make up our environment. Even as infants, we have an amazing ability to remember visual forms such as faces, and we interpret content based on our previous experiences with these forms. Each form is capable of evoking some kind of response from each of us.

Subject matter can interfere with our perception of form. One way to learn to see form without subject is to look at pictures upside down. Inversion of recognizable images frees the mind from the process of identifying and naming things. Familiar objects become unfamiliar, enabling the artist to concentrate on the design. Art teachers have found that having students copy a picture placed upside down can dramatically improve seeing, and thereby improve representational drawing skills, by encouraging concentration on spatial relationships rather than on preconceptions.

Another exercise in learning to see form is to search for images that are visually similar in form but dissimilar as nameable objects. For example, in VISUAL METAPHOR when we notice that the form of fingers supporting a head is similar to roots grasping a rock (in an inverted photograph), we are see-

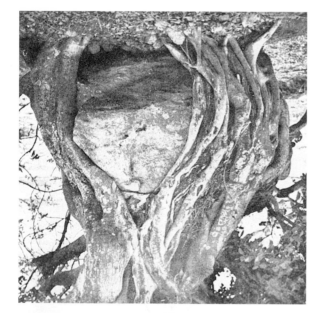

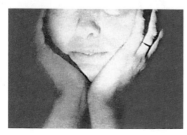

44　VISUAL METAPHOR. Student Project. Photographs: Duane Preble.

45　Elliott Erwitt. FLORIDA. 1968. Photograph. Photograph: Magnum Photos Inc.

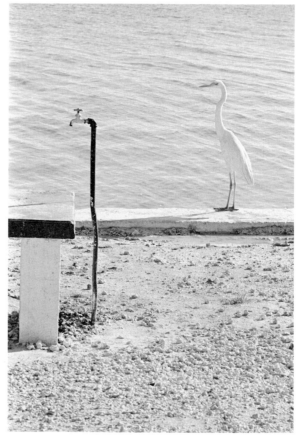

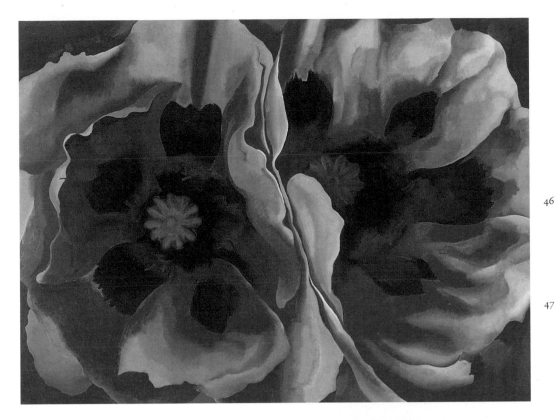

ing beyond names to pure form. Such similarities can become visual metaphors, as in Elliott Erwitt's photograph, FLORIDA.

Georgia O'Keeffe responded to nature's forms in her own way. In paintings such as ORIENTAL POP-PIES and JACK-IN-THE-PULPIT NO. V, she shared her awareness. She said of these paintings:

Everyone has many associations with a flower—the idea of flowers. Still—in a way—nobody sees a flower —really—it is so small—we haven't the time—and to see takes time, like to have a friend takes time. If I could paint the flower exactly as I see it no one would see what I see because I would paint it small like the flower is small.

So I said to myself—I'll paint what I see—what the flower is to me but I'll paint it big and they will be surprised into taking time to look at it.[16]

Those who have seen O'Keeffe's paintings of flow-ers and the American Southwest often go on to see actual flowers and desert landscapes in new ways.

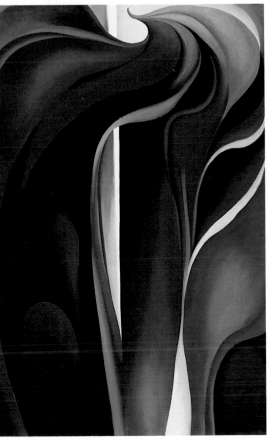

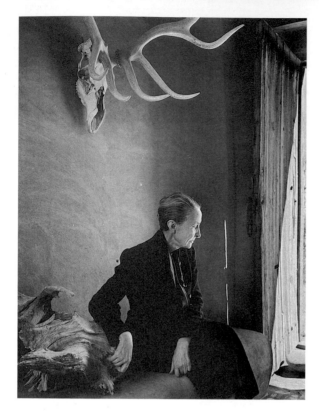

48   Yousuf Karsh.
GEORGIA O'KEEFFE.
1956.
Photograph.
Woodfin Camp & Associates.
Photograph: Yousuf Karsh.

During her long, productive life, Georgia O'Keeffe became nearly as well known as her distinctive paintings. She represented, to many people, the popular concept of the isolated, eccentric "artist." She lived a spare, often solitary life, and approached both her life and her art in her own unique way.

O'Keeffe was born in Sun Prairie, Wisconsin, and spent her childhood on her family's farm. While in high school, she had a memorable experience that gave her a new perspective on the art-making process. As she passed the door to the art room, O'Keeffe stopped to watch as a teacher held up a jack-in-the-pulpit plant so that the students could appreciate its unusual shapes and subtle colors. Although O'Keeffe had enjoyed flowers in the marshes and meadows of Wisconsin, she had done all of her drawing and painting from plaster casts or had copied them from photographs or reproductions. This was the first time she realized that one could draw and paint from real life. Twenty-five years later she produced a powerful series of paintings based on flowers.

O'Keeffe studied at the Art Institute of Chicago, the Art Students League in New York, and Columbia University Teachers College. From Arthur Wesley Dow of Columbia she learned to appreciate Japanese design, to fill space in a beautiful way, and to balance light and dark. As a student she was also influenced by the first wave of European abstract paintings reaching the United States from Europe.

From 1912 to 1918, she spent four winters teaching school in the Texas Panhandle. The Southwest landscape left a strong impression on her and influenced her later decision to move to New Mexico —where the desert became her favorite subject.

O'Keeffe's first mature artworks, produced in 1915, consisted of abstract charcoal drawings suggesting natural forms and vivid watercolor landscapes. A friend of O'Keeffe's showed those drawings to influential photographer and gallery owner Alfred Stieglitz, who exhibited them in his avant-garde Gallery 291 in New York. Thus began one of the best-known artistic and romantic liaisons of the twentieth century. O'Keeffe and Stieglitz were married in 1924, and O'Keeffe's work was exhibited annually in various galleries owned by Stieglitz until his death in 1946. They were strong supporters of one another's work.

Although associated with American modern artists, O'Keeffe developed her own style, which is both sensuous and austere. Her paintings of the 1920s include the series of greatly enlarged flowers, landscapes, and geometrically structured views of New York City. In her mature style, O'Keeffe rejected realism in favor of simplified flat patterns and color harmonies inspired by Japanese art.

From 1929 to 1949 O'Keeffe spent summers in Taos, New Mexico, surrounded by the desert she loved. After Stieglitz died she settled permanently on an isolated ranch near the village of Abiquiu, where she remained until her death in 1986 at age ninety-eight. In people's minds she lives on as a model of creative individuality and strength.

ICONOGRAPHY

As we have noted, form conveys content even when no nameable subject matter is represented. But when subject matter is present, meaning is often based on traditional interpretations.

Iconography is the symbolic meaning of signs and subjects. Not all works of art contain iconography. In those that do, it is often the symbolism (rather than the obvious subject matter) that carries the deepest levels of meaning. The identification and specific meanings of significant subjects, motifs, forms, colors, and positions are the central concern of iconographic interpretation.

Examples of iconography from different times and places reveal a wealth of cultural meanings. Today, the term iconography is usually associated with a religious or cultural area of study, such as Egyptian or Christian iconography.

The primary subject in Albrecht Dürer's THE KNIGHT, DEATH AND THE DEVIL is a man in armor on horseback; behind him are a corpselike figure and a horned monster. Meanings of the objects in the detailed scene would have been well known to Christians of Dürer's time because they were familiar with Christian iconography. The knight in armor, for instance, symbolized the good Christian who follows the right path despite the persistence of Death and the Devil.

The knight must ride through the darkness of the "valley of the shadow of death" to reach the City of God, seen in the background. An hourglass in the hand of Death symbolizes human mortality or the brevity of life. Serpents in Death's hair are ancient symbols of death and also Christian symbols of the Devil. The dog, a symbol of faithfulness in both religion and marriage, symbolizes the faith the knight must have if he is to reach his goal. A dragon-like lizard, representing evil, is going in an opposing direction. Dürer organized all these separate references in a way that leaves no doubt that the Christian knight will reach his goal. The idealized form and dominant central position of the knight and his powerful horse convey a sense of assurance.

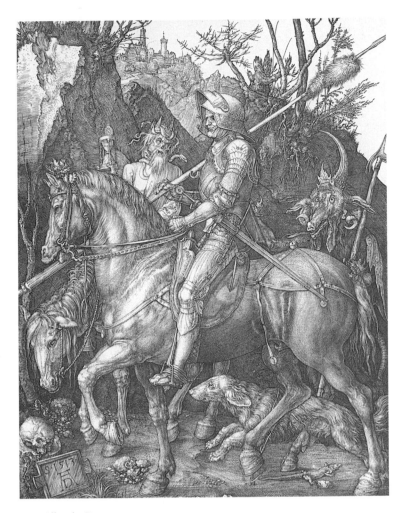

49   Albrecht Dürer.
THE KNIGHT, DEATH AND THE DEVIL. 1513.
Engraving. 9¹¹⁄₁₆" × 7⁹⁄₁₆".
The Brooklyn Museum of Art, New York.
Gift of Mrs. Horace O. Havemeyer. 54.35.6.

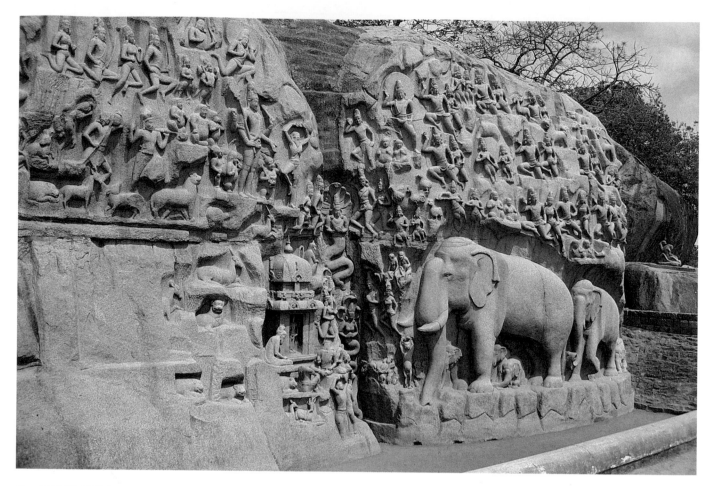

50   DESCENT OF THE GANGES.
   Māmallapuram, India. 7th Century. Granite. Height approximately 30'.
  a. Overview.
   Dr. Jerome Feldman, Hawaii Pacific University.

An excellent example of Hindu iconography called DESCENT OF THE GANGES was carved in a huge granite outcropping in the town of Māmallapuram, in southern India. Included in the large composition are over a hundred human figures, deities, flying pairs of angels without wings, lifesize elephants, and a variety of other animals, all converging at the Ganges River in an elaborate depiction of intertwining Hindu legends. As in Dürer's engraving, the composition is filled with symbolic subject matter.

The center of the carving symbolizes the descent of the sacred Ganges from heaven to earth, making the land fertile. The cobra-like figures of the King and Queen of the Nagas are serpent deities that portray the great river. While these figures dominate the center of the relief, other legends are incorporated into the composition.

In front of the largest elephant is a wonderful depiction of a cat and mice. According to an old folk tale, a cat pretending to be an ascetic stood beside the Ganges with upraised paws and gazed at the sun. The cat convinced the mice that it was holy and thus worthy of worship. As the mice closed their eyes in reverence, the cat snatched them for dinner.

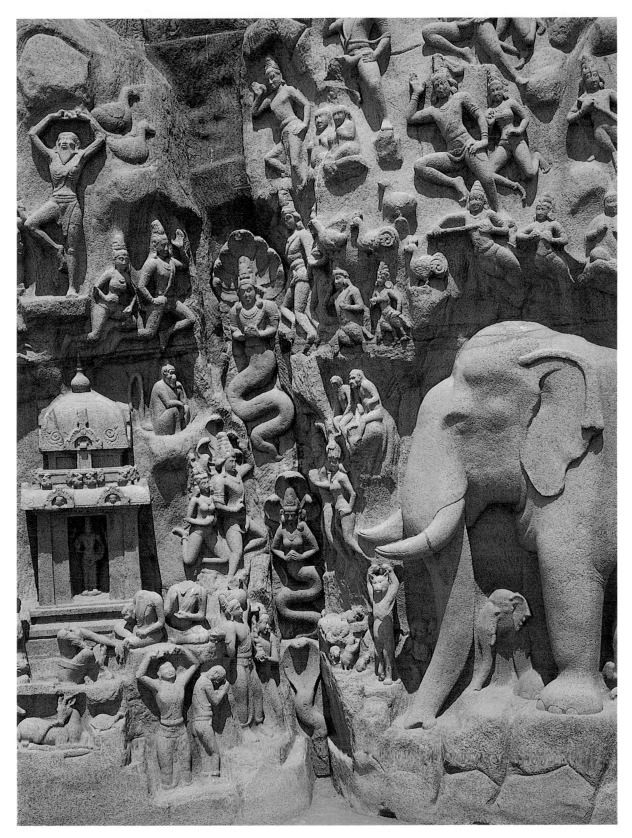

b. Detail.
Photograph: Duane Preble.

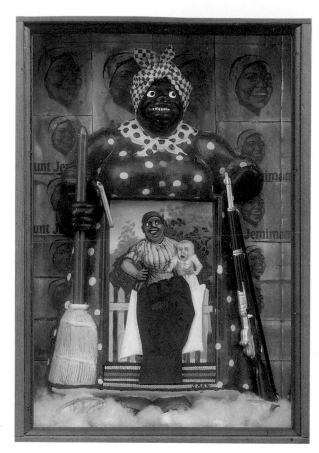

The whole sculpture relates to the annual miracle of the return of the life-giving waters of the river. Appropriately, the many figures appear to be emerging from the stone as if from flowing water.

In modern America the most pervasive art forms are mass-media advertising images, and they too have their iconography. Some artists have used such commercial images to comment on the cultural environment of their times. In 1972 Betye Saar created a mixed media assemblage titled THE LIBERATION OF AUNT JEMIMA. The work confronts viewers with a startling group of faces and figures designed to shake us out of complacency and complicity. Even now, decades after its creation, the figure of Aunt Jemima can dredge up painful feelings associated with racial stereotyping.

Contrasts between a broom and a rifle add to the message. The whole construction is punctuated with an icon of very different purpose: the defiant, upraised clenched fist, a salute and primary symbol of the Black Power movement. By making this hand large, and by placing it in the lower central position, in front of the woman holding the baby, Saar made her meaning abundantly clear: no more of this demeaning nonsense!

51 Betye Saar.
THE LIBERATION OF AUNT JEMIMA. 1972.
Mixed media. 11¾" × 8" × 2¾".
University of California, Berkeley Art Museum.
Purchased with the aid of funds from the National Endowment for the Arts.
Photograph: Benjamin Blackwell.

ARTISTS AT WORK

CARLOS FRÉSQUEZ

Contemporary Mexican-American artist Carlos Frésquez offers an even wider range of iconographic symbols in his oil painting YELLOW WALL. The imagery in this work refers to realities as diverse as pre-conquest Mexico, European modern art, television cartoons, and thrift shops. See him discuss how he uses these diverse sources in the video interview on the CD-ROM that accompanies this book.

Using the coded visual language of iconography, artists can add layers of meaning to their works. They always place such forms and symbols in compositions of formal visual elements—the subject of our next chapter.

Carlos Frésquez.   52
MI CASA ES SU CASA: YELLOW WALL (WEST). 1997.
Mixed media with objects on panel.
11 ft. × 8 ft.
Courtesy of the artist.

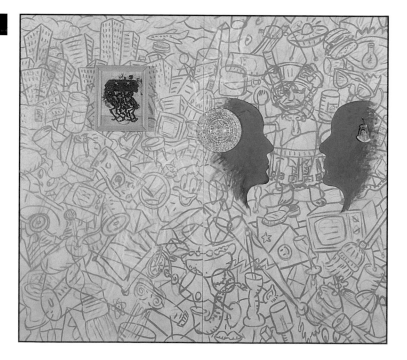

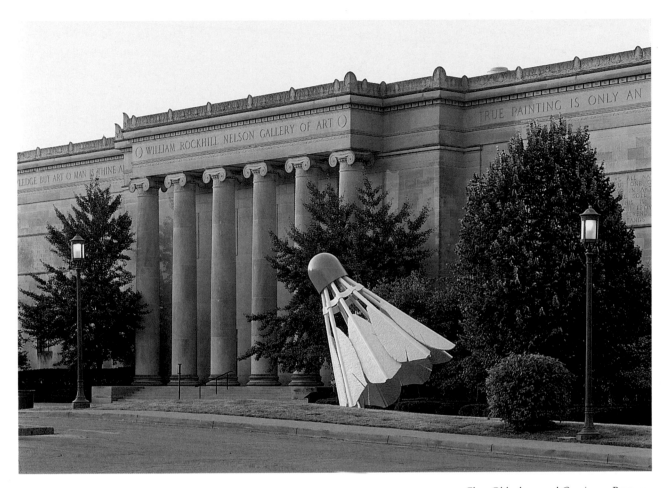

Claes Oldenburg and Coosje van Bruggen.
SHUTTLECOCKS. 1994.
Commissioned by Nelson-Atkins Museum of Art and the Morton I.
Sosland family, Kansas City, MO.

PART TWO
The Language of Visual Experience

CONSIDER . . .

Have you ever arranged a group of pictures on the wall of your home? How did you know when the arrangement looked "right"?

Have you ever been in a room where the space felt oppressive? What caused that feeling, and how would you change the space in order to alter the mood?

Why is handwriting sometimes accepted as legal evidence in court? What does that tell you about individual drawing styles?

How do cartoonists show the passage of time? How do they show movement? What other visual media can express time or movements?

Does color affect your emotions? What color would you choose to express sadness? Joy? Boredom? Anger? Do you avoid using certain colors in your clothing or in your art?

CHAPTER THREE

VISUAL ELEMENTS

Remember that a picture—before being a war horse, a nude woman, or some anecdote—is essentially a plane surface covered with colours assembled in a certain order.

Maurice Denis[1]

Painter Maurice Denis might have gone on to say that the *plane,* the two-dimensional picture surface, can also be covered with lines, shapes, textures, and other aspects of visual form (visual elements). Sculpture consists of these same elements organized and presented in three-dimensional space. Because of their overlapping qualities, it is impossible to draw rigid boundaries between the elements of visual form.

For example, a glance at Swiss artist Paul Klee's LANDSCAPE WITH YELLOW BIRDS reveals his playful interpretation of the subject. Fluid, curving *lines* define abstract *shapes.* Klee simplified and flattened the solid *masses* of natural plant and bird forms so that they read as flat shapes against a dark background *space.* Such abstraction emphasizes the fantastic, dreamlike quality of the subject. The whimsical positioning of the upside-down bird suggests a moment in *time* without *motion. Light* illuminates and enhances the yellow *color* of the birds and the unusual colors of the leaves. Surface *textures* provide further interest in each area of the painting.

This chapter introduces the visual elements identified in LANDSCAPE WITH YELLOW BIRDS: line, shape, mass, space, time, motion, light, color, and texture. Not all these elements are important, or even present, in every work of art; many works emphasize only a few elements. In order to understand their expressive possibilities, it is useful for us to examine—one at a time—some of the expressive qualities of each of the aspects of visual form.

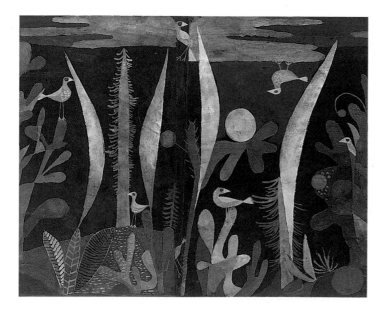

53   Paul Klee.
LANDSCAPE WITH YELLOW BIRDS. 1923.
Watercolor, newspaper, black base. 14" × 17⅜".
Photograph: Hans Hinz/Artothek.
© 2002 Artists Rights Society (ARS), NY/VG Bild-Kunst, Bonn.

LINE

We write, draw, plan, and play with lines. Our individualities and feelings are expressed as we write our one-of-a-kind signatures or make other unmechanical lines. Line is our basic means for recording and symbolizing ideas, observations, and feelings; it is a primary means of visual communication.

Our habit of making all kinds of lines obscures the fact that pure geometric line—line with only one dimension, length—is a mental concept. "Line" does not exist in the three-dimensional physical world. "Lines" are actually linear forms in which length dominates over width. Wires and branches are long cylinders, whereas cracks and grooves are long, narrow depressions. Wherever we see an edge, we can perceive the edge as a line—the place where one object or plane appears to end and another object or space begins. In a sense, we often "draw" with our eyes, converting edges to lines.

In art and in nature, we can consider *lines* as paths of action—records of the energy left by moving points. Many intersecting and contrasting linear paths form the composition in Ansel Adams' photograph RAILS AND JET TRAILS.

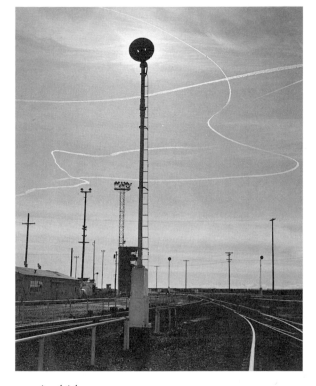

54 Ansel Adams.
RAILS AND JET TRAILS, ROSEVILLE, CALIFORNIA. 1953.
Photograph.

Characteristics of Line

Lines can be active or static, aggressive or passive, sensual or mechanical. Lines can indicate directions, define boundaries of shapes and spaces, imply volumes or solid masses, and suggest motion or emotion. Lines can also be grouped to depict qualities of light and shadow and to form patterns and textures. Note the line qualities in these LINE VARIATIONS.

55 LINE VARIATIONS.

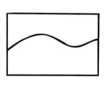

a. Actual line.

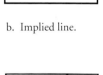

b. Implied line.

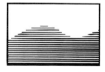

c. Actual straight lines and implied curved line.

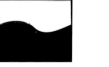

d. Line created by an edge.

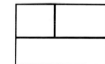

e. Vertical line (attitude of alert attention); horizontal line (attitude of rest).

f. Diagonal lines (slow action, fast action).

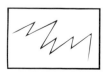

g. Sharp, jagged line.

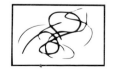

h. Dance of curving lines.

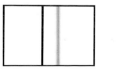

i. Hard line, soft line.

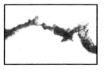

j. Ragged, irregular line.

56 Agnes Martin. MOUNTAIN. c. 1960.
Pen and ink and pencil. 9⅜" × 11⅞" (24 × 30.2 cm).
Museum of Modern Art, New York. Ruth Vollmer Bequest.
Photograph © 2002 The Museum of Modern Art, NY.

Consider the range of qualities expressed in Agnes Martin's simple and solid MOUNTAIN, in the vibrant energy of painted lines in Bridget Riley's CURRENT, and in the spontaneous dance of gestural line in Jackson Pollock's DRAWING. ACROBATS is one of many whimsical pieces of wire sculpture in which Alexander Calder took advantage of the descriptive and expressive potential of lines.

Recording the contours of three-dimensional objects as outlines (edges) of shapes on a two-dimensional surface is a fundamental process of drawing—and one of the most important functions of line in art. In the descriptive drawing BLUE GINGER, contour lines depict the edges of leaves. Notice the contrasting ways contour lines are used to express lyric sensuality and brusque aggressiveness in the Japanese woodcut prints by Kiyonobu (WOMAN DANCER WITH FAN AND WAND) and Kiyotada (ACTOR IN A DANCE MOVEMENT).

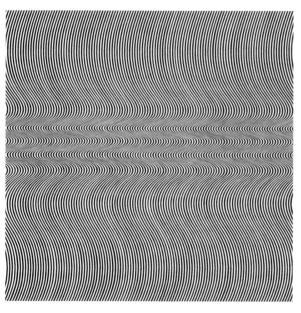

57 Bridget Riley.
CURRENT. 1964.
Synthetic polymer paint on composition board.
58⅜" × 58⅞" (148.1 × 149.3 cm).
The Museum of Modern Art, New York. Philip Johnson Fund. Photograph © 2001 The Museum of Modern Art, New York.

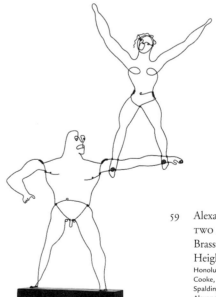

59 Alexander Calder (1898–1976).
TWO ACROBATS. 1928.
Brass wire.
Height with base 34".
Honolulu Academy of Arts, Gift of Mrs. T.A. Cooke, Mrs. W.F. Dillingham and Mrs. P.E. Spalding, 1937. #4595. © 2002 Estate of Alexander Calder/Artists Rights Society (ARS), NY.

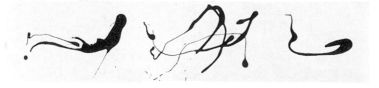

58 Jackson Pollock.
DRAWING. 1950.
Duco on paper. 56.6 × 152.2 cm.
Staatsgalerie, Stuttgart.
© 2002 The Pollock–Krasner Foundation/Artists Rights Society (ARS), New York.

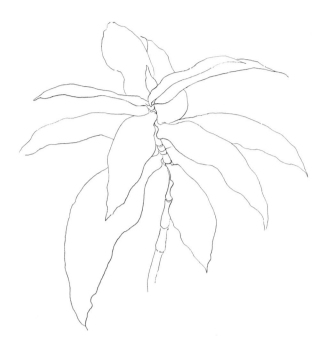

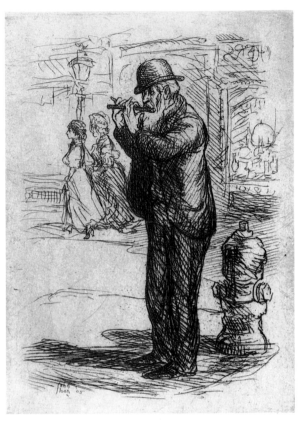

60 Duane Preble.
BLUE GINGER. 1993.
Pencil. 13¾" × 11".

63 John Sloan.
THE FLUTE PLAYER. 1905.
Etching. 3³⁄₁₆" × 2¾"; sheet 8 × 6".
Philadelphia Museum of Art: Purchased: Lessing J. Rosenwald gift and Farell Fund
Income. 1956-35-61. Photo by Lynn Rosenthal, 2000.

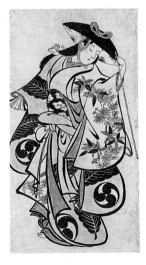 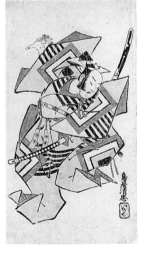

61 Attributed to
Torii Kiyonobu I.
WOMAN DANCER WITH
FAN AND WAND. c. 1708.
Hand-colored woodcut.
21¾" × 11½".
Metropolitan Museum of Art,
New York. Harris Brisbane Dick
Fund, 1949. Photo © 1979 The
Metropolitan Museum of Art.

62 Torii Kiyotada (Japanese),
c.1710–1740.
AN ACTOR OF THE
ICHIKAWA CLAN IN A
DANCE MOVEMENT. C.
1715. Hand-colored
woodcut. 11¼" × 6".
The Metropolitan Museum of Art,
New York. Harris Brisbane Dick
Fund, 1949.

Many kinds of prints are made up entirely of lines. Artists give these lines varying weights and functions, as we can see in the small etching THE FLUTE PLAYER. John Sloan used very light lines to suggest objects far away, as in the background at the upper where lines indicate the edges of the lamppost. The lines are thicker and heavier where they describe nearer objects, such as the fire hydrant. Heavy lines close together help to emphasize the central figure of the flute player. In addition, Sloan deftly suggested the roundness of the figure by shading it from light to dark with parallel crossed lines called *crosshatching*. The density of the lines changes with the degree of shading on the subject. In the brightest areas, such as the flat street, there are no lines at all. Even a small work such as this—which is reproduced here near full size—the artist makes sophisticated use of line.

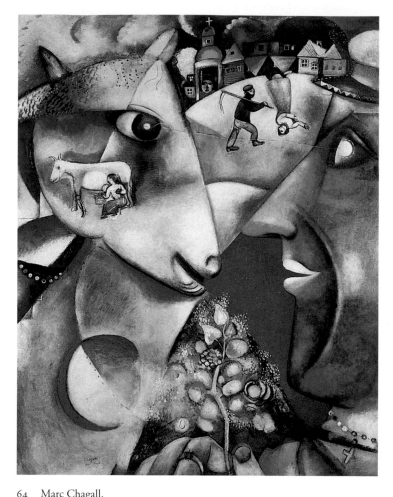

Implied Line

Implied lines suggest visual connections. Implied lines that form geometric shapes can serve as an underlying organizational structure. In I AND THE VILLAGE, Marc Chagall used implied lines to create a circle that brings together scenes of Russian Jewish village life. Notice that he also drew in the implied sightline between man and animal.

SHAPE

The words shape, mass, and form are sometimes used interchangeably. Here *shape* is used to refer to the expanse within the outline of a two-dimensional area or within the outer boundaries of a three-dimensional object. When we see an animal in daylight, we may respond to its mass. If it is silhouetted against a sunset, we may see it only as a flat shape. A shape becomes visible when a line or lines enclose an area or when an apparent change in value (lightness or darkness), color, or texture sets an area apart from its surroundings. In BLUE GINGER (preceding page), lines define variations in similar leaf shapes.

We can approach the infinite variety of shapes through two general categories: geometric and organic. *Geometric shapes*—such as circles, triangles, and squares—tend to be precise and regular. *Organic shapes* are irregular, often curving or rounded, and seem relaxed and more informal than geometric shapes. The most common shapes in the human-made world are geometric. Although some geometric shapes exist in nature—in such forms as crystals, honeycombs, and snowflakes—most shapes in nature are organic.

In I AND THE VILLAGE, Chagall used a geometric structure of circles and triangles to organize the organic shapes of people, animals, and plants. He softened the severity of geometric shapes to achieve a natural flow between the various parts of the painting. Natural subjects were abstracted toward geometric simplicity in order to strengthen visual impact and symbolic content.

64 Marc Chagall.
I AND THE VILLAGE. 1911.
Oil on canvas. 75⅝" × 59⅝".
The Museum of Modern Art, New York. Mrs. Simon Guggenheim Fund.
Photograph ©2002 The Museum of Modern Art, New York. © 2002 Artists Rights Society (ARS), NY/ADAGP, Paris.

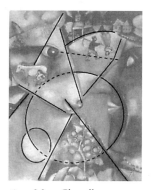

64B Marc Chagall.
I AND THE VILLAGE. 1911.
Oil on canvas. 75⅝" × 59⅝".
The Museum of Modern Art, New York. Mrs. Simon Guggenheim Fund.
Photograph ©2002 The Museum of Modern Art, New York. © 2002 Artists Rights Society (ARS), NY/ADAGP, Paris.

When a shape appears on a *picture plane* (the flat picture surface), it simultaneously creates a second shape out of the background area. The subject or dominant shapes are referred to as *positive* or *figure shapes;* background areas are *negative* or *ground shapes.* The figure-ground relationship is a fundamental aspect of perception; it allows us to sort out and interpret what we see. Because we are conditioned to see only objects, and not the spaces between and around them, it takes a shift in awareness to see the negative shapes in A SHAPE OF SPACE. An artist, however, must consider both positive and negative shapes simultaneously, and treat them as equally important to the total effectiveness of an image.

Interactions between figure shapes and ground shapes are heightened in some images. NIGHT LIFE can be seen as white shapes against black or as black shapes against white, or the figure-ground relationship can shift back and forth. In both this and M. C. Escher's woodcut SKY AND WATER, the shifting of figure and ground contributes to a similar content: the interrelatedness of all things.

In the upper half of Escher's print, we see dark geese on a white ground. As our eyes move down the page, the light upper background becomes fish against a black background. In the middle, however, fish and geese interlock so perfectly that we are not sure what is figure and what is ground. As our awareness shifts, fish shapes and bird shapes trade places, a phenomenon called *figure-ground reversal.*

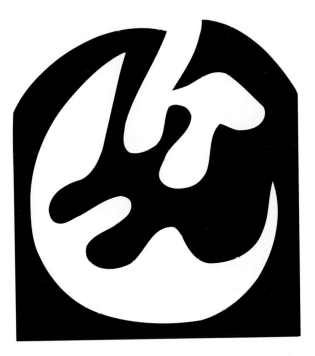

66   Duane Preble
NIGHT LIFE (figure-ground reversal).

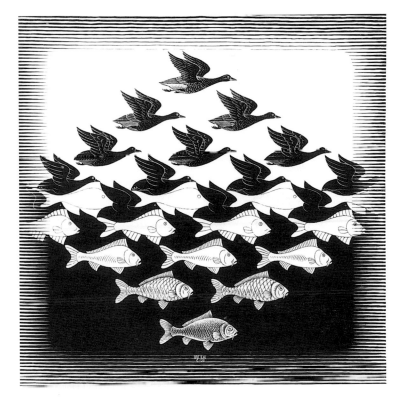

67   M. C. Escher.
SKY AND WATER I. 1938.
Woodcut. 17⅛" × 17¼".

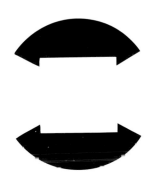

65   A SHAPE OF SPACE.
(implied shape).

MASS

Whereas a two-dimensional area is referred to as a shape, a three-dimensional area is called a *mass*—the physical bulk of a solid body of material. When mass encloses space, the space is called *volume*. The word *form* is sometimes used instead of mass to refer to physical bulk.

Mass in Three Dimensions

Mass is often a major element in sculpture and architecture. Unusually large, compact, or impressive mass was one of the dominant characteristics of ancient Egyptian architecture and sculpture. Egyptians sought this quality and perfected it because it expressed their desire to make art for eternity.

QENNEFER, STEWARD OF THE PALACE, was carved from hard black granite and retains the cubic, blocklike appearance of the quarried stone. None of the limbs projects outward into the surrounding space. The figure sits with knees drawn up and arms folded, the neck obscured by a ceremonial headdress. The body is abstracted and implied with minimal

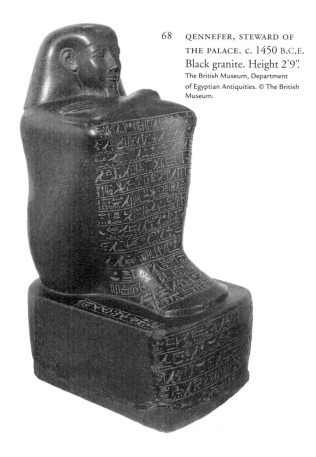

68 QENNEFER, STEWARD OF THE PALACE. c. 1450 B.C.E. Black granite. Height 2'9".
The British Museum, Department of Egyptian Antiquities. © The British Museum.

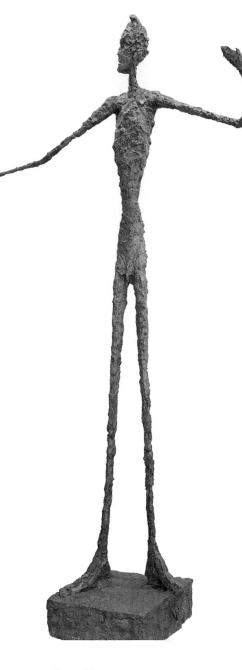

69 Alberto Giacometti.
MAN POINTING. 1947.
Bronze. 70½" × 40¾" × 16⅜".
The Museum of Modern Art, New York.
Gift of Mrs. John D. Rockefeller III.
Photograph © 2002 The Museum of Modern Art, NY.
© 2002 Artists Rights Society (ARS), NY/ADAGP, Paris.

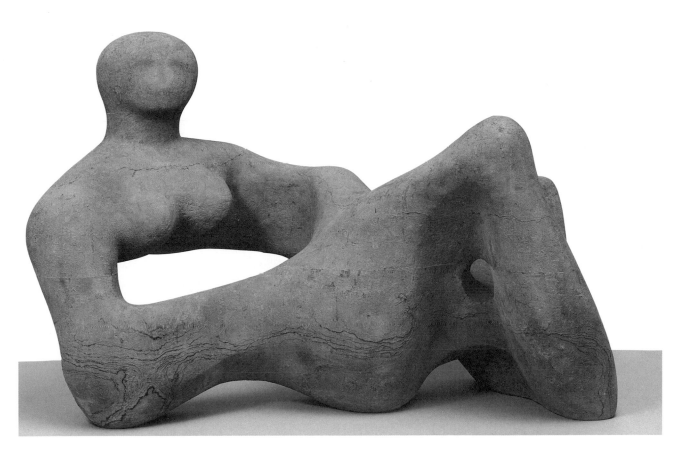

70   Henry Moore.
RECUMBENT FIGURE. 1938.
Green hornton stone. Length 54".
Tate Gallery, London/Art Resource, NY.

suggestion. This piece is a prime example of *closed form*—form that does not openly interact with the space around it. Here, compact mass symbolizes permanence. Egyptian portrait sculpture acted as a symbolic container for the soul of an important person in order to insure eternal afterlife.

In contrast to the compact mass of the Egyptian portrait, contemporary sculptor Alberto Giacometti's MAN POINTING conveys a sense of fleeting presence rather than permanence. The tall, thin figure appears eroded by time and barely existing. Because Giacometti used little solid material to construct the figure, we are more aware of a linear form in space than of mass. The figure reaches out; its *open form* interacts with the surrounding space, which seems to overwhelm it, suggesting the fragile, impermanent nature of human existence.

Giacometti's art reveals an obsession with mortality that began when he was twenty, following the death of an older companion. Later, the fleeting essence of human life became a major concern visible in his work. For Giacometti, both life and the making of art were continuous evolutions. He never felt that he succeeded in capturing the changing nature of what he saw, and therefore he considered all of his works unfinished.

In RECUMBENT FIGURE Moore related the rounded forms of a woman's body to the wind-worn stone and bone forms he had admired since childhood. Moore made his abstract figure relatively compact, but he put a large hole through the figure, allowing space to flow through as well as around the form. In this way he created a dynamic, interactive relationship between mass and space. Notice that in talking about mass, we have also had to talk about space. An object is perceived in relation to the space it occupies, and the character of that interaction carries some of the work's meaning.

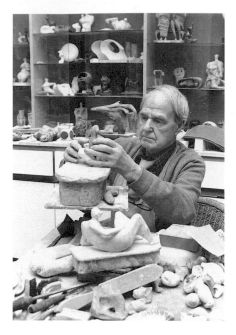

71   HENRY MOORE.
Photograph: © Gemma Levine.

When Henry Moore was eleven years old, he learned one day in Sunday school about a man named Michelangelo. Deeply impressed by stories of the artist's greatness, he decided to become a sculptor himself—a *great* sculptor. This was an unusual dream for someone of Moore's background, for he lived in a small town in the bleak north country of England, the ninth of ten children of a coal miner. But he never gave up on his dream and neither did his parents nor his teachers. After serving as a soldier in World War I, Moore was accepted at the Leeds School of Art, and from there he won a scholarship to the Royal College of Art in London.

Moore's training was conservative and academic. He insisted later that all art students should have a thorough grounding in drawing and anatomy to anchor their work. In his art, however, he rejected such classical ideals of beauty in favor of something he felt was ultimately more powerful and primal—a language of expressive form such as he found in the sculpture of various ancient cultures, in ancient stone monuments such as Stonehenge (page 7), and in the sea-worn boulders and cliff formations of the English coast ("nature sculptures," he called them).

In one important respect, though, Moore was deeply nourished by the Western tradition, for he believed that the human body was the basic subject for sculpture and through it one could say everything that needed to be said. He abstracted and opened the figure to bring human form into resonance with the natural forms he loved. "I am trying to add to people's understanding of life and nature," he said simply, "to help them open their eyes and to be sensitive."[2]

Mass in Two Dimensions

With two-dimensional media, such as painting and drawing, mass must be implied. In HEAD OF A YOUNG MAN, Picasso drew lines that seem to wrap around and define a head in space, implying a solid mass. The drawing gives the appearance of mass because the lines both follow the curvature of the head and build up dark areas to suggest mass revealed by light. Picasso's use of lines convinces us that we are seeing a fully rounded head. At the same time, the vigor of Picasso's lines calls our attention to the flat surface, reminding us that the image is a two-dimensional drawing.

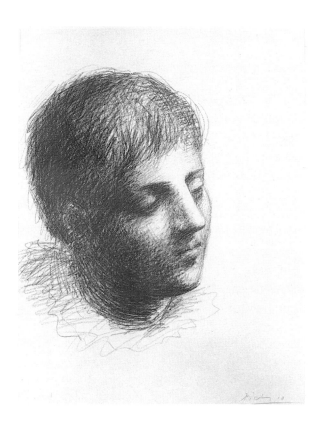

72   Pablo Picasso (Spanish, 1881–1973).
HEAD OF A YOUNG MAN. 1923.
Grease crayon on pink Michallet laid paper. 24½" × 18⅝".
Brooklyn Museum of Art, Carll H. de Silver Fund. 39.18/
© 2002 Estate of Pablo Picasso/Artisys Rights Society (ARS), New York.

SPACE

Space is the indefinable, general receptacle of all things—the seemingly empty space around us. It is continuous, infinite, and ever present. The visual arts are sometimes referred to as *spatial* arts because most of these art forms are organized in space. In contrast, music is a *temporal* art because musical elements are organized primarily in time. In film, video, and dance, form is organized in both time and space.

Space in Three Dimensions

Of all the visual elements, space is the most difficult to convey in words and pictures. To experience three-dimensional space, we must be in it. We experience space beginning with our own positions in relation to other people, objects, surfaces, and voids at various distances from ourselves. Each of us has a sense of personal space—the area surrounding our bodies —that we like to protect, and the extent of this invisible boundary varies from person to person and from culture to culture.

Architects are especially concerned with the qualities of space. Imagine how you would feel in a small room with a very low ceiling. What if you raised the ceiling to fifteen feet? What if you added skylights? What if you replaced the walls with glass? In each case you would have changed the character of the space and, by doing so, would have radically changed your experience.

Whereas we experience the outside of a building as mass in space, we experience the inside as volume and as a sequence of enclosed spaces. Cesar Pelli's design for the recently completed NORTH TERMINAL at Ronald Reagan Washington National airport takes the passenger's experience of space into account. There are many large windows that afford exterior views of the runways and also of the Potomac River and the nearby Washington Monument. The interior is divided into many small domed modules: "The module has an important psychological value in that each one is like a very large living room in size," the architect said.[3] "It's a space that we experience in our daily life. . . . The domes make spaces designed on the scale of people, not on the scale of big machines."

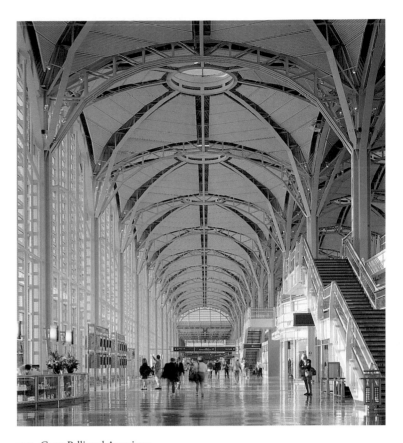

73 a. Cesar Pelli and Associates.
NORTH TERMINAL RONALD REAGAN WASHINGTON NATIONAL AIRPORT. 1997.
Photographer Jeff Goldberg/ Esto Photographics, Inc.

b. CLOSE-UP INTERIOR
Photographer Jeff Goldberg/ Esto Photographics, Inc.

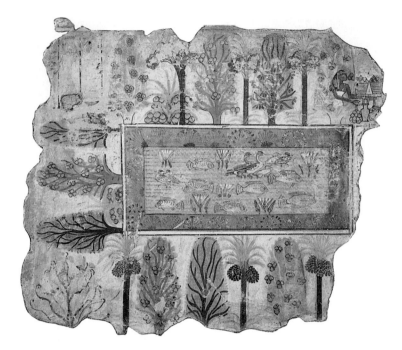

74 POND IN THE GARDEN.
WALL PAINTING FROM THE TOMB OF NEBAMUN.
Egypt. c. 1400 B.C.E.
Paint on dry plaster.
British Museum, London.
Photograph: © The British Museum.

75   CLUES TO SPATIAL DEPTH.

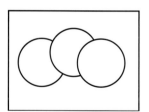

a. Overlap.

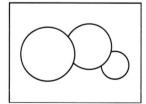

b. Overlap and diminishing size.

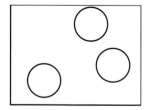

c. Vertical placement.

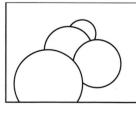

d. Overlap, vertical placement, and diminishing size.

Space in Two Dimensions

With three-dimensional objects and spaces, such as sculpture and architecture, we must move around to get the full experience. With two-dimensional works, such as drawing and painting, we see the space of the surface all at once. In drawings, prints, photographs, and paintings, the actual space of each picture's surface *(picture plane)* is defined by its edges—usually the two dimensions of height and width. Yet within these limited boundaries, an infinite number of spatial qualities can be implied.

Paintings from ancient Egypt show little or no depth. Early Egyptian painters made their images clear by portraying objects from their most easily identifiable angles and by avoiding the visual confusion caused by overlap and the appearance of diminishing size. POND IN A GARDEN demonstrates this technique. The pond is shown from above while the trees, fish, and birds are all pictured from the side. The Egyptian artist felt no need for a single point of view or vantage point.

Implied Depth

Almost any mark on a picture plane begins to give the illusion of a third dimension: depth. Clues to seeing spatial depth are learned in early childhood. A few of the major ways of indicating space on a picture plane are shown in the diagrams of CLUES TO SPATIAL DEPTH.

When shapes overlap, we immediately assume from experience that one is in front of the other (diagram a). Overlapping is the most basic way to achieve the effect of depth on a flat surface. The effect of overlap is strengthened by *diminishing size,* which gives a sense of increasing distance between each of the shapes (diagram b). Our perception of distance depends on the observation that distant objects appear smaller than near objects. A third method of achieving the illusion of depth is *vertical placement:* objects placed low on the picture plane (diagram c) appear to be closer to the viewer than objects placed high on the plane. This is the way we see most things in actual space. Creating illusions of depth on a flat surface usually involves one or more such devices (diagram d).

We may be conscious of both the flat surface and the illusion of depth when we examine a picture. Artists can emphasize either the reality or the illusion—or strike a balance between these extremes. For centuries, Asian painters have paid careful attention to the relationship between the reality of the flat picture plane as well as the implied depth they wish to create. Mu Qi's ink painting SIX PERSIMMONS has only a subtle suggestion of depth in the overlap of two of the persimmons. By placing the smallest persimmon lowest on the picture plane, Mu Qi further minimized the illusion of depth; since we interpret the lower part of the picture as being closer to us, we might expect the persimmon there to be larger.

The persimmons appear against a pale background that works as both flat surface and as infinite space. The shapes of the fruit punctuate the open space of the ground. Imagine what would happen to this painting if some of the space at the top were cut off. Space is far more than just what is left over after the important forms have been placed; it is an integral part of the total visual design.

Linear Perspective. In general usage, the word perspective refers to point of view. In the visual arts, *perspective* can refer to any means of representing three-dimensional objects in space on a two-dimensional surface. In this sense it is correct to speak of the perspective of Persian miniatures, Japanese prints, Chinese Song Dynasty paintings, or Egyptian paintings—although none of these styles uses a system that is in any way similar to the linear perspective system we use, which was developed during the Italian Renaissance. It is a difference in intention rather than in skill that results in various methods for depicting depth.

In the West, we have become accustomed to *linear perspective* (also called simply *perspective*), a system designed to depict the way objects in space appear to the eye. This system was developed by Italian architects and painters in the fifteenth century, at the beginning of the Renaissance.

Linear perspective is based on the way we see. We have already noted that objects appear smaller when seen at a distance than when viewed close up.

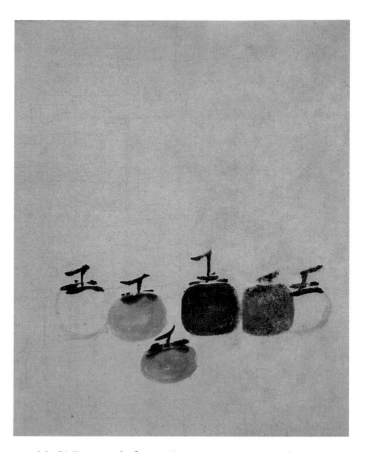

76   Mu Qi (Japanese, d. after 1279). SIX PERSIMMONS. c. 1269.
Pen and Ink on paper. width 36.2 cm.
Daitoku-ji Monastery, Kyoto, Japan. The Bridgeman Art Library International Ltd.

Because the spaces between objects also appear smaller when seen at a distance, parallel lines appear to converge as they recede into the distance, as shown in the first of the LINEAR PERSPECTIVE diagrams (following page). Intellectually, we know that the edge lines of the road must be parallel, yet they seem to converge, meeting at last at what is called a *vanishing point* on the horizon—the place where land and sky appear to meet. On a picture surface, the horizon (or *horizon line*) also represents your eye level as you look at a scene.

Eye level is an imaginary plane, the height of the artist's eyes, parallel with the ground plane and extending to the horizon, where the eye level and ground plane appear to converge. In a finished picture, the artist's eye level becomes the eye level of anyone looking at the picture. Although the horizon is frequently blocked from view, it is necessary for an artist to establish the combined eye-level/horizon line to construct images using linear perspective.

With the LINEAR PERSPECTIVE system, an entire picture can be constructed from a single, fixed position called a *vantage point,* or *viewpoint.* Diagram a. shows one-point (one vanishing point) perspective, in which the parallel sides of the road appear to converge and trees in a row appear smaller as their distances from the vantage point increases.

Diagram b. shows cubes drawn in one-point linear perspective. The cubes at the left are at eye level; we can see neither their top nor their bottom surfaces. We might imagine them as buildings.

The cubes in the center are below eye level: We can look down on their tops. These cubes are drawn from a high vantage point, a viewing position above the subject. The horizon line is above these cubes and their perspective lines go up to it. We may imagine these as boxes on the floor.

The cubes at the right are above our eye level; we can look up at their bottom sides. These cubes are drawn from a low vantage point. The horizon line is below these cubes and their perspective lines go down to it. Imagine that these boxes are sitting on a glass shelf high above our heads.

In *one-point perspective,* all the major receding "lines" of the subject are actually parallel, yet visually they appear to converge at a single vanishing point on the horizon line. In *two-point perspective,* two sets of parallel lines appear to converge at two points on the horizon line, as in diagram c.

When a cube or any other rectilinear object is positioned so that a corner, instead of a side, is closest to us, we need two vanishing points to draw it. The parallel lines of the right side converge to the right; the parallel lines of the left side converge to the left. There can be as many vanishing points as there are sets and directions of parallel lines.

Horizontal parallel lines moving away from the viewer above eye level appear to go down to the horizon line; those below eye level appear to go up to the horizon line. It is easy to find the eye level in diagram a. because the horizon line is visible; it is not so easy to find it in the painting THE SCHOOL OF ATHENS.

In THE SCHOOL OF ATHENS, Raphael invented a grand architectural setting in the Renaissance style to provide an appropriate space for his depiction of the Greek philosopher-teachers Plato and Aristotle and their students. The size of each figure is drawn to scale according to its distance from the viewer; thus the entire group seems natural. Lines superimposed over the painting reveal the basic one-point perspective system used by Raphael. However, the cube in the foreground is not parallel to the picture plane or to the painted architecture and is in two-point perspective.

Raphael used the visual dynamics of perspective for symbolic emphasis. We infer that Plato and Aristotle are the most important figures in this painting because of their placement at the center of receding archways in the zone of greatest implied depth.

If the figures are removed, as shown in the computer-modified image by Harry Clow, our attention is pulled right through the painted surface into implied infinite space. Looking at the figures without their architectural background defined by perspective, we are unable to recognize Plato and Aristotle, much less be aware of their importance.

77 LINEAR PERSPECTIVE.

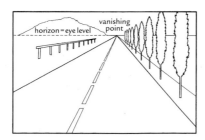

a. One-point linear perspective.

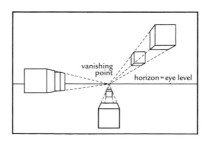

b. One-point linear perspective. Cubes above eye level, at eye level, and below eye level.

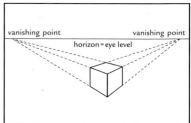

c. Two-point linear perspective.

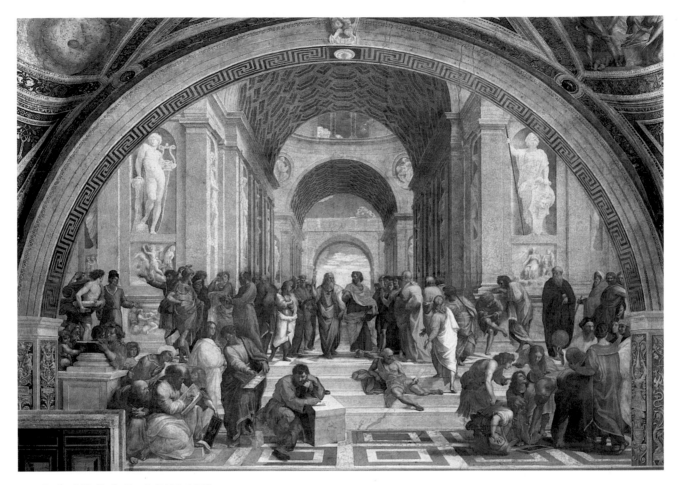

78   Raphael (Raffaello Santi) (1483–1520).
      THE SCHOOL OF ATHENS. 1508. Fresco. Approximately 18' × 26'.
      Erich Lessing/Art Resource, NY.

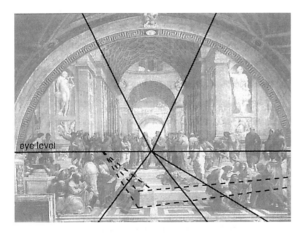

Perspective lines showing eye level, main vanishing point, and
left vanishing point for the stone block in the foreground.

78B   Raphael (Raffaello Santi) (1483–1520).
      THE SCHOOL OF ATHENS. 1508.
      Erich Lessing/Art Resource, NY.

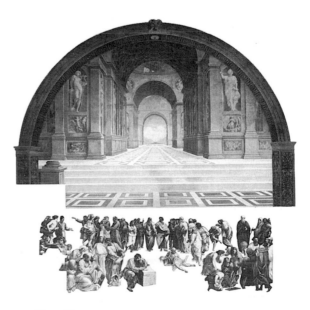

79   Harry Clow.
      Study of Raphael's THE SCHOOL OF ATHENS.
      Mitchell Beazley International Ltd.

Atmospheric Perspective. *Atmospheric* or *aerial perspective* is a nonlinear means for giving an illusion of depth. The illusion of depth is created by changing color, value, and detail. In visual experience of the real world, as the distance increases between the viewer and faraway objects such as mountains, the increased quantity of air, moisture, and dust causes the distant objects to appear increasingly bluer and less distinct. Color intensity is diminished, and contrast between light and dark is reduced.

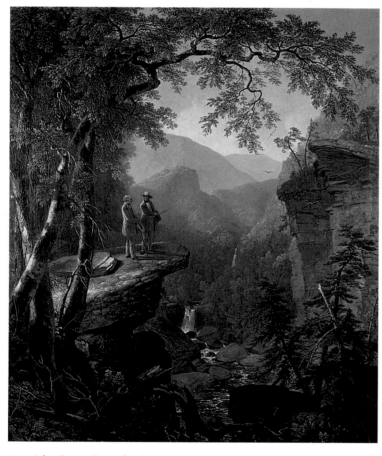

80   Asher Brown Durand.
KINDRED SPIRITS. 1849.
Oil on canvas. 44" × 36".
Collection of the New York Public Library,
Astor, Lenox and Tilden Foundations.

Asher Brown Durand used atmospheric perspective in his painting KINDRED SPIRITS to provide a sense of the vast distances in the North American wilderness. The illusion of infinite space is balanced by dramatically illuminated foreground details, by the figures of the men, and by Durand's lively portrayal of trees, rocks, and waterfalls. We identify with the figures of painter Thomas Cole and poet William Cullen Bryant as they enjoy the spectacular landscape. As in THE SCHOOL OF ATHENS, the implied deep space appears as an extension of the space we occupy.

Traditional Chinese landscape painters have differed from their European counterparts in their use of atmospheric perspective. In Shen Zhou's painting POET ON A MOUNTAIN TOP, near and distant mountains are suggested by washes of ink and color on white paper. The light gray of the farthest mountain implies space and atmosphere. Traditional Chinese landscape paintings present poetic symbols of landforms rather than realistic representations. Whereas KINDRED SPIRITS draws the viewer's eye into and through the suggested deep space, POET ON A MOUNTAIN TOP leads the eye across (rather than into) space.

A third system for suggesting depth is isometric perspective, which is employed by engineers and is often used by traditional Asian artists. In isometric perspective, parallel lines remain parallel; they do not converge as they recede. Instead, rectangular planes that turn away from the viewer are drawn as parallelograms. The illustration ISOMETRIC PERSPECTIVE shows a cube drawn in isometric perspective. Industrial designers and architects also find isometric perspective useful because it enables them to maintain accurate measurements in working drawings. The detail from the Chinese hanging scroll EIGHTEEN SCHOLARS shows furniture and another hanging scroll in isometric perspective.

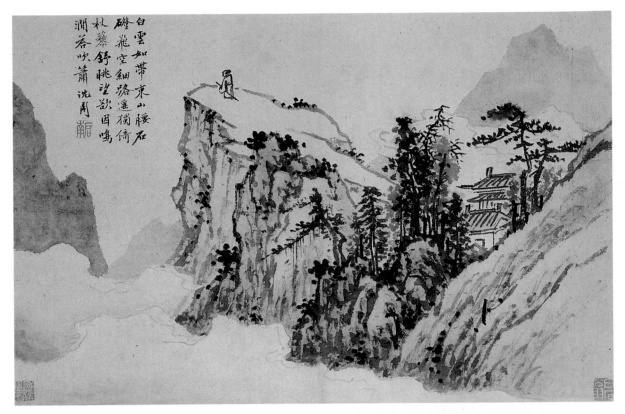

81   Shen Zhou, Chinese (1427–1509).
POET ON A MOUNTAIN TOP (CHANGI–LI YUAN–T'IAO).
Series: LANDSCAPE ALBUM: FIVE LEAVES by Shen Zhou, ONE
LEAF by Wen Cheng–Ming (Shen Shih–t'ien Wen Cheng-
ming shan-shui-ho-chuan). Ming Dynasty, (1368–1644).
Album leaf mounted as a handscroll. Ink on paper.
17¼" × 504¾". Overall (43.8 × 1282.1 cm).
The Nelson-Atkins Museum of Art, Kansas City, Missouri.
(Purchase: Nelson Trust) 46–5½.

82   ISOMETRIC PERSPECTIVE.

83   Anonymous.
Detail of EIGHTEEN SCHOLARS.
Song Dynasty (960–1279).
Hanging scroll. Ink and color on silk.
67⅞" × 40¼".
National Palace Museum, Taipei, Taiwan.

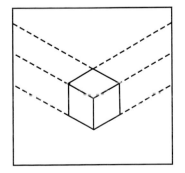

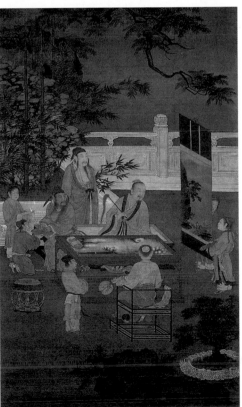

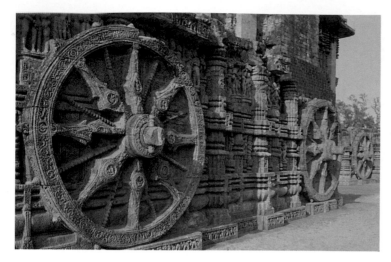

84 WHEELS OF THE SUN CHARIOT.
Surya Deul Temple, Konarak, India. c. 1240.
Photograph: Prithwish Neogy.

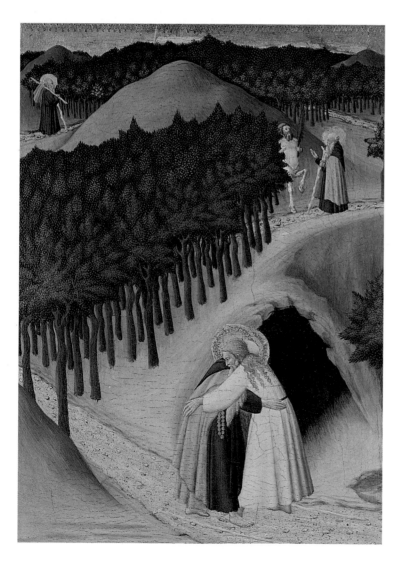

TIME AND MOTION

Time is a nonspatial continuum—the fourth dimension—in which events occur in succession. Because we live in a combined environment of space and time, our experience of time often depends on our movement in space and vice versa. Although time itself is invisible, it can be made perceptible in art. Time and motion become major elements in visual media such as film, video, and kinetic (moving) sculpture.

Many traditional Asian philosophies and religions teach that time is cyclic. The Wheel of the Law in Buddhism, which originated in ancient Hindu symbolism, stands for time seen in the cycle of the seasons; in the cycle of birth, death, and rebirth; and in longer cycles of celestial creation, preservation, dissolution, and re-creation. This view of time is one of the symbolic references expressed in WHEELS OF THE SUN CHARIOT of Surya Deul Temple at Konarak, India.

The Judeo-Christian tradition of Western culture teaches that time is linear—continually moving forward. Sassetta implied the passage of linear time in his painted narration of THE MEETING OF SAINT ANTHONY AND SAINT PAUL. The painting depicts key moments during Saint Anthony's progression through time and space, including the start of his journey in the city, which is barely visible behind the trees. He first comes into view as he approaches the wilderness; we next see him encountering the centaur; finally, he emerges into the clearing in the foreground, where he meets Saint Paul. The road on which he travels implies continuous forward movement in time.

85   Sassetta and Workshop of Sassetta.
THE MEETING OF SAINT ANTHONY AND SAINT PAUL. c. 1440.
Tempera on panel, .475 × .345 (18¾" × 13⅝"); framed:
.616 × 1.254 × .076 (24¼ × 49⅜ ×3).
© 2001 Board of Trustees, The National Gallery of Art, Washington, D.C.
Samuel H. Kress Collection. 1939.1.239.(404)/PA

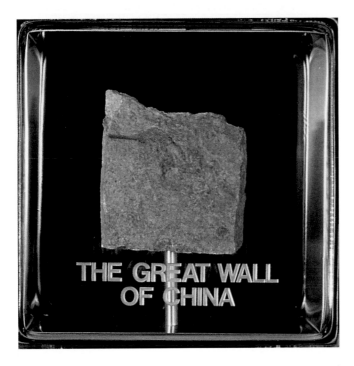

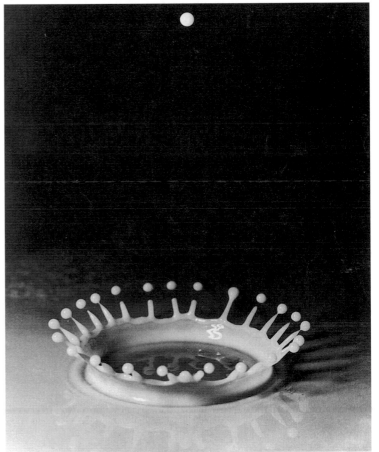

KRISTIN JONES AND ANDREW GINZEL

Contemporary artists have found new ways to include time in their works. Kristin Jones and Andrew Ginzel suggest the passage of time in an understated way in their work called MNEMONICS, which was created for Stuyvesant High School in New York City. They embedded objects from remote times and places in over 400 glass bricks distributed around the school in no apparent order. Each graduating class contributes its own brick as well, so that the building itself mirrors the passage of time.

86   Kristin Jones and Andrew Ginzel.
MNEMONICS.
Detail of Installation at Stuyvesant High School, NYC.
Photograph courtesy of the artists.

Stopped Time

The desire to record events in time goes back to before written history. More recently, this urge helped to inspire the development of photography. Initially, only static, inanimate objects could be photographed, but improvements in the process made it possible to photograph people standing or sitting very still; and, by the end of the nineteenth century, even a galloping horse could be photographed.

In the early twentieth century, electronics engineer Harold Edgerton explored the unseen world of things in high-speed motion. He invented the strobe light and pioneered its use in photography. In stroboscopic photography light pulses flash on a moving subject at regular intervals in order to "stop" the action and record it (without blurring) on film. Such means have greatly increased our understanding of the changes in objects as they move. Edgerton's high-speed photograph of a MILK SPLASH (revealed by a flash of light no more than 1/100,000 of a second) shows the beauty of the "crown" of a milk drop, which is not visible to the unaided human eye.

87   Harold Edgerton.
MILK SPLASH RESULTING FROM DROPPING A BALL. 1936.
Photograph.
© Harold and Esther Edgerton Foundation, 1999. Courtesy of Palm Press, Inc.

Manipulated Time

The word *movies* underscores the central feature of the filmmaker's art: the appearance of motion. In films, still pictures are shown at the rate of twenty-four images per second, creating the illusion of actual motion. Past, present, and future time can be implied and intermixed, and events that occur too quickly or too slowly to be perceived can be made visible by slowing them down or speeding them up. In both film and television, the impression of time can be compressed, expanded, run backward, and rerun. Contemporary music videos often present widely disparate moments of time in quick succession, as if time moves in a series of sudden jumps of unpredictable length. This creates a feeling of disjunction from the passage of clock time.

Implied Motion

To give lifelike feeling, artists often search for ways to create a sense of movement. Sometimes movement itself is the subject or a central quality of the subject. One of the world's most appealing depictions of movement is that of the DANCING KRISHNA, portraying a moment in India's ancient legend of the god Krishna when Krishna, as a playful child, has just stolen his mother's butter supply and now dances with glee. Bronze provides the necessary strength to hold the dynamic pose as the energy-radiating figure stands on one foot, counterbalancing arms, legs, and torso.

A sense of motion can be created by actual or implied changes in position. In 1884, American painter and pioneer photographer Thomas Eakins used a single camera and a movable photographic plate to capture sequential images that show the movements of a MAN POLE VAULTING. Eakins also designed a camera with revolving discs to produce stop-action stills, anticipating the principle of the motion picture camera.

Early multiple-exposure photographs of figures in motion influenced Italian Futurist painter Giacomo Balla. In DYNAMISM OF A DOG ON A LEASH, Balla suggests movement through rhythmic repetition. His painting depicts the concept presented in the *Futurist Painting Technical Manifesto* of 1910:

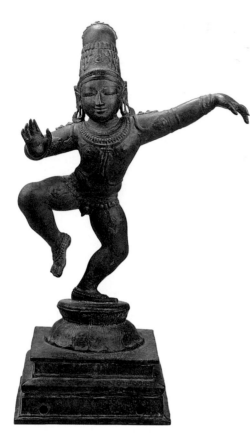

88   DANCING KRISHNA.
     Tanjor, Tamil Nadu. South India. Chola Dynasty.
     c. 1300. Bronze, 23⅝".
     Honolulu Academy of Arts. Partial gift of Mr. & Mrs. Christian H. Aall,
     partial purchase, The Jhamandas Watumull Family Fund, 1997.(8640.1).
     Photograph: Shuzo Uemoto.

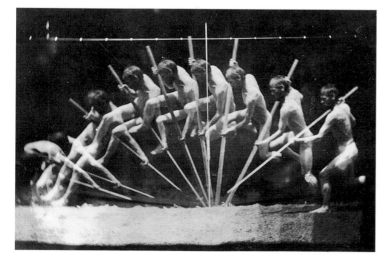

89   Thomas Eakins.
     MAN POLE VAULTING. 1884.
     Multiple-exposure photograph of George Reynolds. 3¾" × 4¾".
     The Metropolitan Museum of Art, New York. Gift of Charles Bregler, 1941 (41.142.11).

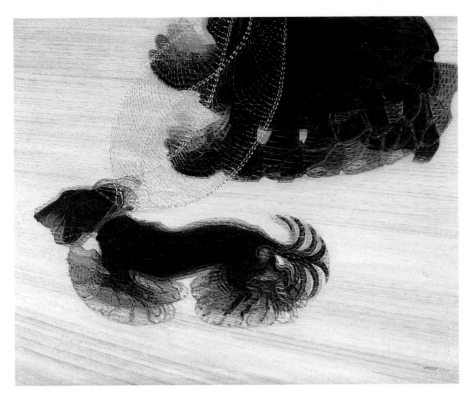

In fact, all things move and run, all things change rapidly. The profile before our eyes is never static but constantly appears and disappears. Given the persistence of the image in the retina, moving objects are multiplied, changing their shapes as they pursue one another like lively vibrations across space.[4]

Actual Motion

Before the advent of electric motors, artists created moving sculpture by harnessing the forces of wind and water. Fountains, kites, banners, and flags have been popular since ancient times.

Alexander Calder's mobiles, such as BIG RED, rely on air movement to perform their subtle dances. Calder, a leading inventor of kinetic sculpture, was one of the first twentieth-century artists who made movement a major feature of their art.

LIGHT

Our eyes are light-sensing instruments. Everything we see is made visible by the radiant energy we call light. Sunlight, or natural light, although perceived as white, actually contains all the colors of light that make up the visible part of the electromagnetic

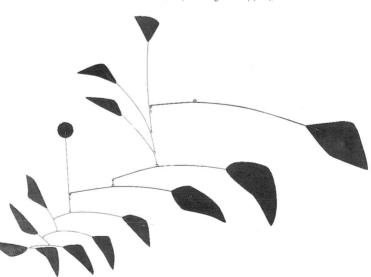

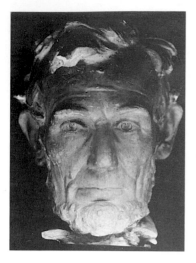

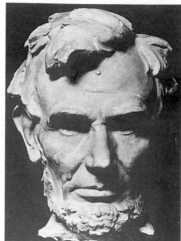

92   Daniel Chester French (1850–1931).
      ABRAHAM LINCOLN, detail of seated figure,
      1922. Professional historical composite
      photograph of full–size plaster head, 6 ¾" × 9⅜"
   a. As originally lit by daylight.
   b. With the addition of artificial light.
      Chesterwood, A National Trust Historic Site, Stockbridge, MA.
      Photograph: De Witt Ward.

spectrum. Light can be directed, reflected, re-fracted, diffracted, or diffused. The various types of artificial light include incandescent, fluorescent, neon, and laser. The source, color, intensity, and direction of light greatly affect the way things appear; as light changes, surfaces illuminated by it also appear to change.

Seeing Light

A simple shift in the direction of light dramatically changes the way we perceive the sculpture of ABRA-HAM LINCOLN by Daniel Chester French. When the monumental figure was first installed in the Lincoln

Memorial in Washington, D.C., the sculptor was disturbed by the lighting: The character of the Lin-coln figure was radically altered by sunlight reflected from the floor of the entrance to the building. Light alone had changed the content of French's portrait from wise leader to frightened novice. The problem was corrected by placing spotlights in the ceiling above the statue. Because the spotlights are stronger than the natural light reflected from the white mar-ble floor, they illuminate the figure with the kind of overhead light we are accustomed to seeing.

Light coming from a source directly in front of or behind objects seems to flatten three-dimensional form and emphasize shape. Light from above or from the side, and slightly in front, most clearly reveals the form of objects in space.

In art terminology, *value* (sometimes called *tone*) refers to the relative lightness and darkness of surfaces. Value ranges from white through various grays to black. Value can be considered a property of color or an element independent of color. Subtle relationships between light and dark areas deter-mine how things look. To suggest the way light re-veals form, artists use changes in value. A gradual shift from lighter to darker tones can give the illu-sion of a curving surface, while an abrupt value change usually indicates an abrupt change in sur-face direction.

Implied Light

The diagram DARK/LIGHT RELATIONSHIPS shows that we perceive relationships rather than isolated forms: the gray bar has the same gray value over its entire length, yet it appears to change from one end

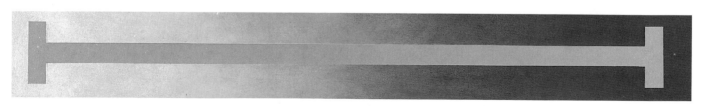

93   DARK/LIGHT RELATIONSHIPS.
      Value scale compared to uniform middle gray.

to the other as the value of the background changes.

The DRAWING OF LIGHT ON A SPHERE illustrates *chiaroscuro*—the use of gradations of light and shade, in which forms are revealed by the subtle shifting from light to dark areas, without sharp outlines. This technique, developed in the Renaissance, makes it possible to create the illusion that figures and objects depicted on a flat surface appear as they do in natural light conditions. Chiaroscuro, originally an Italian word, is now used in English to describe the interaction of light and shade in two-dimensional art. The word's origins suggest its meaning: *chiaro* means light or clear, and *oscuro* means dark or obscure.

Using charcoal and white chalk on middle-value paper, Annibale Carracci used chiaroscuro to create the illusion of roundness in his drawing HEAD OF A YOUTH. The face on its brighter side is close to the shade of the paper. At times the distinction between subject and background is difficult to see, as in the clothing. On the areas where light strikes the subject most directly, the artist used white chalk, as on the forehead and nose, making these areas brighter than the background. Areas around the mouth and chin are delicately shaded, showing that the artist is sensitive to the subtlest curves of the face. The shadowy areas stand in contrast both to the white highlights and to the color of the paper; the darkest area, at the left, forms a silhouette against the background.

The choice of colored paper is in some ways advantageous because we tend to perceive white areas as flooded with light. Middle-value paper tends to heighten the contrasts of light and dark within the subject itself.

The preoccupation with mass or solid form as revealed by light is a Western tradition which began in the Renaissance. Most of the world's pictoral art before the twentieth century did not show shadows. When the Japanese first saw Western portraits, they wanted to know why one side of the face was dirty!

Color, direction, quantity, and intensity of light strongly affect our moods, mental abilities,

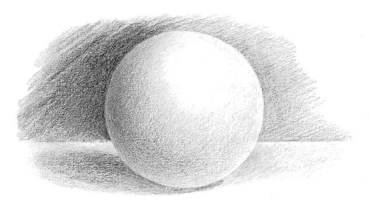

94 DRAWING OF LIGHT ON A SPHERE.
Value gradations suggest light on a curving surface.

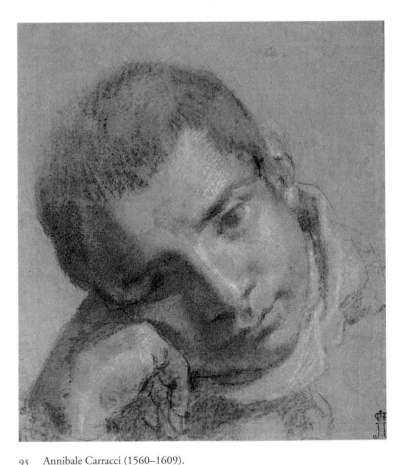

95 Annibale Carracci (1560–1609).
HEAD OF A YOUTH.
Charcoal and white chalk on green/grey paper. 27.1 × 24 cm.
Hermitage, St. Petersburg, Russia. The Bridgeman Art Library International Ltd.

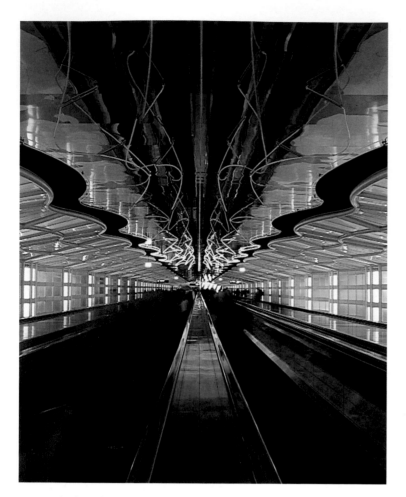

96   Michael Hayden. SKY'S THE LIMIT. 1987.
United Airlines Terminals, O'Hare International Airport, Chicago.
Neon tubes, mirrors, controlled by computers with synchronized sounds.
Length 744'.
Churchill & Klehr Photography.

and general well-being. California architect Vincent Palmer has experimented with the color and intensity of interior light, and he has found that he can modify the behavior of his guests by changing the color of the light around them. Light quality affects people's emotions and physical comfort, thereby changing the volume and intensity of their conversations and even the lengths of their visits.

As light technology has developed, and people have increased their awareness of the important functions of light, lighting design has become more important. Qualities of light must be carefully considered in most of the visual arts, but especially in photography, cinematography, television, stage design, architecture, and interior design.

Light as a Medium

Some contemporary artists use artificial light as their medium. Michael Hayden employs neon light with spectacular effect in his installation SKY'S THE LIMIT. The sculpture runs the entire length of the ceiling of an underground pedestrian walkway in the United Airlines Terminal at Chicago's O'Hare Airport. The work modifies space in a cycle of changing, moving light patterns, as neon tubes of colored light turn on and off in computer-timed sequences with musical accompaniment.

Light used in combination with visual media and sound has become of increasing interest to contemporary artists. Lighting has also become important in performances of all kinds, including rock concerts and videos.

COLOR

Color, a component of light, affects us directly by modifying our thoughts, moods, actions, and even our health. Psychologists, as well as designers of schools, offices, hospitals, and prisons, have acknowledged that colors can affect work habits and mental conditions. People surrounded by expanses of solid orange or red for long periods often experience nervousness and increased blood pressure. In contrast, some blues have a calming effect, causing blood pressure, pulse, and activity rates to drop to below normal levels.

Dressing according to our color preferences is one way we express ourselves. Leading designers of everything from clothing and cars to housewares and interiors recognize the importance of individual color preferences, and they spend considerable time and expense determining the colors of their products.

Most cultures use color symbolically, according to established customs. Leonardo da Vinci was influenced by earlier European traditions when he wrote, "We shall set down for white the representative of light, without which no color can be seen; yellow for earth; green for water; blue for air; red for fire; and black for total darkness."[5] In traditional painting in North India, flat areas of color are used to suggest certain moods, such as red for anger and blue for sexual passion. The artist may paint the sky or the ground with a bright shade that relates not to the appearance of the area, but to the feeling appropriate to the work. In spoken Austrian German, yellow describes a state of envy or jealousy, while blue means intoxicated.

In China and Japan, traditional painters have often limited themselves to black ink on white. Before the mid-nineteenth century, color was used in limited, traditional ways in Western art. In the 1860s and 1870s, influenced by the new science of color, the French Impressionist painters revolutionized the way color was seen and used.

The Physics of Color

What we call "color" is the effect on our eyes of light waves of differing wavelengths or frequencies. When combined, these light waves make white light—the visible part of the electromagnetic spectrum. Individual colors are components of white light.

The phenomenon of color is a paradox: color exists only in light, but light itself seems colorless to the human eye. All objects that appear to have color are merely reflectors or transmitters of the colors that must be present in the light that illuminates them. In 1666, British scientist Sir Isaac Newton discovered that white light is composed of all the colors of the spectrum. He found that when the white light of the sun passes through a glass prism, it is separated into the bands of color that make up the *visible spectrum,* as shown in the diagram WHITE LIGHT REFRACTED BY A PRISM.

Because each color has a different wavelength, each travels through the glass of the prism at a different speed. Red, which has the longest wavelength, travels more rapidly through the glass than blue, which has a shorter wavelength. A rainbow results when sunlight is refracted and dispersed by the spherical forms of raindrops, producing a combined effect like that of the glass prism. In both cases, the sequence of spectral colors is: red, orange, yellow, green, blue, and violet.

Pigments and Light

Our common experience with color is provided by light reflected from pigmented surfaces. Therefore the emphasis in the following discussion is on pigment color rather than on color coming from light alone.

When light illuminates an object, some of the light is absorbed by the surface of the object and some is reflected. The color that appears to our eyes as that of the object (called *local color* or *object color*) is determined by the wavelengths of light being reflected. Thus a red surface illuminated by white light (full-spectrum light) appears red, because it reflects mostly red light and absorbs the rest of the spectrum. A green surface absorbs most of the spectrum except green, which it reflects; and so on with all the hues.

When all the wavelengths of light are absorbed by a surface, the object appears black; when all the wavelengths are reflected, the surface appears white. Black and white are not true colors: white, black, and their combination, gray, are *achromatic* (without the property of hue) and are often referred to as *neutrals.*

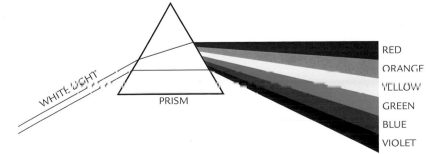

RED
ORANGE
YELLOW
GREEN
BLUE
VIOLET

WHITE LIGHT

PRISM

97   WHITE LIGHT REFRACTED
BY A PRISM.

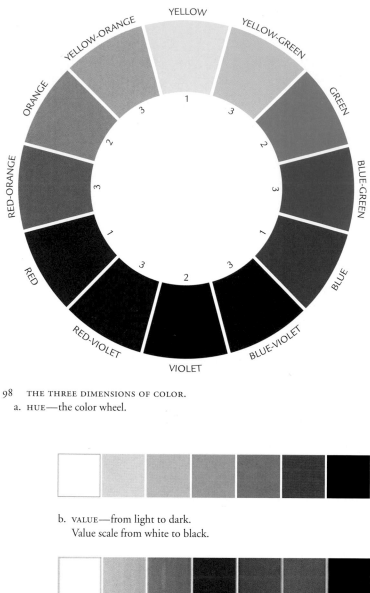

98 THE THREE DIMENSIONS OF COLOR.
   a. HUE—the color wheel.

b. VALUE—from light to dark.
   Value scale from white to black.

+ WHITE   PURE HUE   + BLACK

Value variation in red.

PURE HUE   DULLED   PURE HUE

c. INTENSITY—from bright to dull.

Each of the millions of colors human beings can distinguish is identifiable in terms of just three variables: hue, value, and intensity.

- *Hue* refers to a particular wavelength of spectral color to which we give a name. Colors of the spectrum—such as yellow and green—are called hues.

- *Value* refers to relative lightness or darkness from white through grays to black. Pure hues vary in value. On THE THREE DIMENSIONS OF COLOR chart, hues in their purest state are at their usual values. Pure yellow is the lightest of hues; violet is the darkest. Red and green are middle-value hues. Black and white pigments can be important ingredients in changing color values. Black added to a hue produces a *shade* of that hue. For example, when black is added to orange, the result is a brown; when black is mixed with red, the result is maroon. White added to a hue produces a *tint.* Lavender is a tint of violet; pink is a tint of red.

- *Intensity,* also called *saturation,* refers to the purity of a hue or color. A pure hue is the most intense form of a given color; it is the hue at its highest saturation, in its brightest form. With pigment, if white, black, gray, or another hue is added to a pure hue, its intensity diminishes and the color is thereby dulled.

When the pigments of different hues are mixed together, the mixture appears duller and darker because pigments absorb more and more light as their absorptive qualities combine. For this reason, pigment mixtures are called *subtractive color mixtures.* Mixing red, blue, and yellow will produce a dark gray, almost black, depending on the proportions and the type of pigment used.

Most people are familiar with the three PIGMENT PRIMARIES: red, yellow, and blue. Printers use *magenta* (a bluish red), *yellow,* and *cyan* (a greenish blue) because magenta and cyan provide the specific purplish red and greenish blue that work best for four-color printing.

A lesser-known triad is the three LIGHT PRI-MARIES: red-orange, green, and blue-violet—actual electric light colors that produce white light when combined. Such mixtures are called *additive color mixtures*. Combinations of the light primaries produce lighter colors: red and green light, when mixed, produce yellow light. Color television employs additive color mixture.

Color Wheel

The color wheel is a twentieth-century version of the circle concept first developed in the seventeenth century by Sir Isaac Newton. After Newton discovered the spectrum, he found that both ends could be combined into the hue red-violet, making the color wheel concept possible. Numerous color systems have followed since that time, each with its own basic hues. The color wheel shown here is based on twelve pure hues and can be divided into the following groups:

- *Primary hues* (see 1 on the color wheel): red, yellow, and blue. These pigment hues cannot be produced by an intermixing of other hues. They are also referred to as primary colors.
- *Secondary hues* (see 2 on the color wheel): orange, green, and violet. The mixture of two primaries produces a secondary hue. Secondaries are placed on the color wheel between the two primaries of which they are composed.
- *Intermediate hues* (see 3 on the color wheel): red-orange, yellow-orange, yellow-green, blue-green, blue-violet, and red-violet. Each intermediate is located between the primary and the secondary of which it is composed.

The blue-green side of the wheel is *cool* in psychological temperature, and the red-orange side is *warm*. Yellow-green and red-violet are the poles dividing the color wheel into warm and cool hues. The difference between warm and cool colors may come chiefly from association. Relative warm and cool differences can be seen in any combination of hues. Color affects our feelings about size and distance as well as temperature. Cool colors appear to contract and recede; warm colors appear to expand and advance, as in the WARM/COOL COLORS diagram.

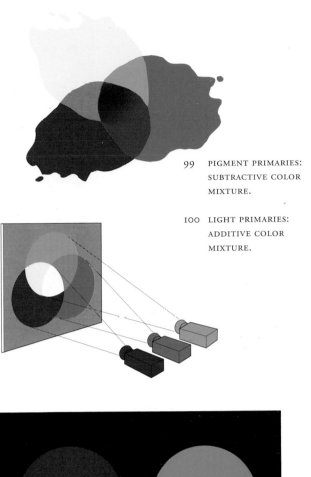

99   PIGMENT PRIMARIES: SUBTRACTIVE COLOR MIXTURE.

100   LIGHT PRIMARIES: ADDITIVE COLOR MIXTURE.

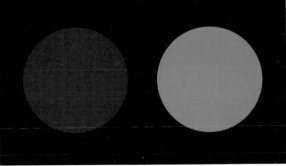

101   WARM/COOL COLORS.

Color sensations more vibrant than those achieved with actual pigment mixture can be obtained when dots of pure color are placed together so that they blend in the eye and mind, to create the appearance of other hues. This is called *optical color mixture*. For example, we see rich greens when many tiny dots or strokes of yellow-green and blue-green are placed close together.

a. Yellow.

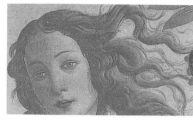

b. Magenta.

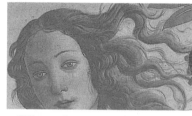

c. Yellow and magenta.

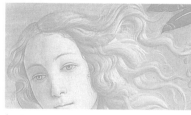

d. Cyan.

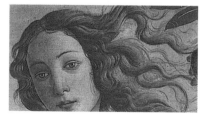

e. Yellow, magenta, and cyan.

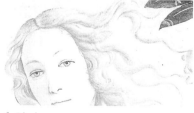

f. Black.

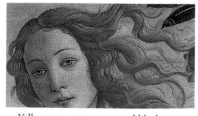

g. Yellow, magenta, cyan, and black.

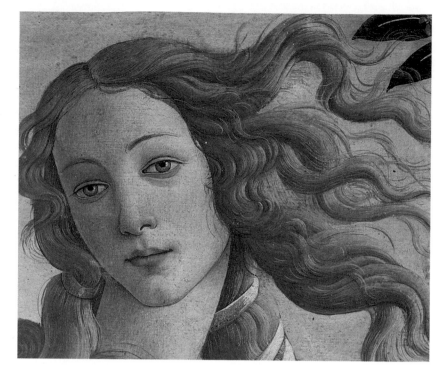

103   COLOR PRINTING

h. Color printing detail of Sandro Botticelli's BIRTH OF VENUS, 1486. Detail.
Tempera on canvas, 175 × 134 cm. Uffizi, Florence, Italy.

Erich Lessing/Art Resource, NY.

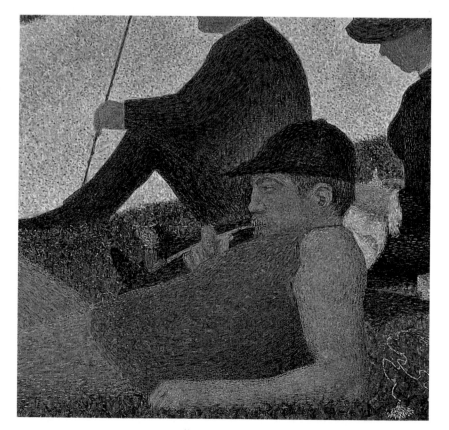

102   OPTICAL COLOR MIXTURE. Detail of Georges Seurat's (French, 1859–1891),
A SUNDAY ON LA GRANDE JATTE–1884, 1884–86.
Oil on canvas, 207.6 × 308 cm.

Helen Birch Bartlett Memorial Collection, 1926.224.

Photograph: © 2001 The Art Institute of Chicago. All Rights Reserved.

Painter Georges Seurat developed this concept in the 1880s as a result of his studies of Impressionist paintings and recent scientific discoveries of light and color. He wanted his paintings to capture the brilliance and purity of natural light. Seurat called his method divisionism; it is now usually called *pointillism*. The result is similar to modern four-color printing, in which tiny dots of ink in the printer's three primary colors—magenta (a bluish red), yellow, and cyan (a greenish blue)—are printed together in various amounts with black ink on white paper to achieve the effect of full color. Seurat, however, used no black. Compare the detail of Seurat's A SUNDAY ON LA GRANDE JATTE with the color separations and the enlarged detail of the reproduction of Botticelli's BIRTH OF VENUS. (The complete paintings appear in chapters 21 and 17.) The eye perceives subtle blends as it optically mixes tiny dots of intense color both in Seurat's painting and in four-color printing.

Color Schemes

Color groupings that provide distinct color harmonies are called *color schemes*.

Monochromatic color schemes are based on variations in the value and intensity of a single hue. In a monochromatic scheme, a pure hue is used alone with black and/or white, or mixed with black and/or white. Artists may choose a monochromatic color scheme because they feel that a certain color represents a mood. Pablo Picasso, for example, made many blue paintings in the early years of the twentieth century, at a time in his life when he was very poor. Other artists adopt the monochromatic color scheme as a kind of personal discipline, in order to experiment with the various shades and gradations of a relatively narrow band of the spectrum. James McNeill Whistler did just that in the 1870s when he embarked on a series of works called NOCTURNES. The series began when he noticed that after sunset the world becomes in effect more monochromatic as the brightest hues disappear. The challenge, which he met in NOCTURNE: BLUE AND GOLD—OLD BATTERSEA BRIDGE, is to create a visually rich surface with limited tonal means. The gold flecks are the only counterfoil to the monochromatic blue-green scheme.

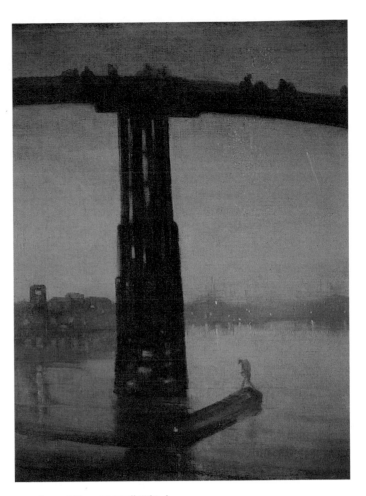

104 James Abbott McNeill Whistler.
NOCTURNE: BLUE AND GOLD—OLD BATTERSEA BRIDGE.
1872–1875.
Tate Gallery, London, Great Britain. Erich Lessing/Art Resource, NY.

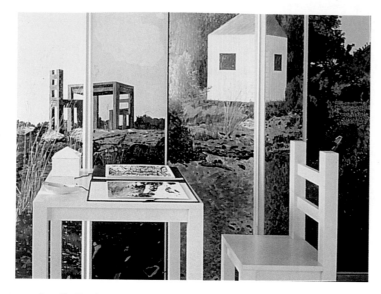

105 Jennifer Bartlett.
VOLVO COMMISSION. 1984.
Relaxation room, detail: table, painted wood, 29" × 35" × 35";
chair, painted wood, 35" × 18" × 18"; portfolio of twenty-four
drawings, pen, brush, and ink on paper, 20" × 16"; house cigarette
box, painted wood, 5" × 5"; boat ashtray, silver, 5" × 2"; screen,
enamel on six wood panels, 6' × 10'3".
Volvo Corporate Headquarters, Sweden.
Courtesy of the artist.

Analogous color schemes are based on colors adjacent to one another on the color wheel, each containing the same pure hue, such as a color scheme of yellow-green, green, and blue-green. Tints and shades of each analogous hue may be used to add variations to such color schemes.

Jennifer Bartlett's three-dimensional installation VOLVO COMMISSION uses the analogous colors yellow-orange, yellow, and yellow-green, which are adjacent to one another in the spectrum and on the color wheel. The analogous color scheme supports the mood of quiet relaxation appropriate to the pleasant rural subject.

Complementary color schemes emphasize two hues directly opposite each other on the color wheel, such as red and green. When actually mixed together as pigments in almost equal amounts, complementary hues form neutral grays; but when placed side by side as pure hues, they contrast strongly and intensify each other. Complementary hues red-orange and blue-green tend to "vibrate" more when placed next to each other than do other complements because they are close in value and produce a strong warm/cool contrast. The complements yellow and violet provide the strongest value contrast possible with pure hues. The complement of a primary is the opposite secondary, which is obtained by mixing the other two primaries. For example, the complement of yellow is violet.

Keith Haring's untitled shows the effect of complementary colors. The bright red and green are near-opposites on the color wheel. When seen together they vibrate. This "loud" color scheme supports the simple execution and brash subject matter of the painting in providing an almost comically crude effect. The artist used Dayglo paints, which are known for their gaudy brightness.

These examples provide only a basic foundation in color theory. In fact, most artists work intuitively with color harmonies more complex than the schemes described above.

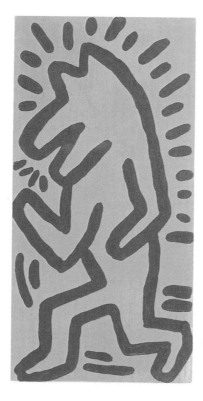

106 Keith Haring.
UNTITLED. 1982.
Dayglo paint on wood.
8⅝" × 4⅜".
Courtesy, Tony Shafrazi Gallery, New York.

TEXTURE

In the visual arts, *texture* refers to the tactile qualities of surfaces or to the visual representation of those qualities. As children, we explored our surroundings by touching everything within reach, and we learned to equate the feel with the look of surfaces. As adults we know how most things feel, yet we still enjoy the pleasures that touching gives; we delight in running our hands over the fur of a pet or the smooth surface of polished wood.

All surfaces have textures that can be experienced by touching or through visual suggestion. Textures are categorized as either actual or simulated. *Actual* textures are those we can feel by touching, such as polished marble, wood, sand, or swirls of thick paint. *Simulated* (or implied) textures are those created to look like something other than paint on a flat surface. A painter can simulate textures that look like real fur or wood but to the touch would feel like smooth paint. Artists can also invent actual or simulated textures. We can appreciate most textures even when we are not permitted to touch them, because we know, from experience, how they would feel.

Meret Oppenheim's fur-covered teacup, titled OBJECT, is a rude tactile experience. She presented an intentionally contradictory object designed to evoke strong responses ranging from revulsion to amusement. The actual texture of fur is pleasant, as is the smooth texture of a teacup, but the idea of touching one's tongue to fur rather than porcelain is startling. Abundant social and psychological implications are intended.

Sculptors and architects make use of the actual textures of their materials and the relationships between them. They can also create new textures in the finishing of surfaces. Compare the eroding surfaces of Giacometti's figure on page 46 with the youthful, skinlike textures of the figures in Rodin's THE KISS on page 31, which in itself has strong textural contrast. Each artist used texture to heighten emotional impact.

Texture is also extremely important for an appreciation of much of the world's ceramic art. For

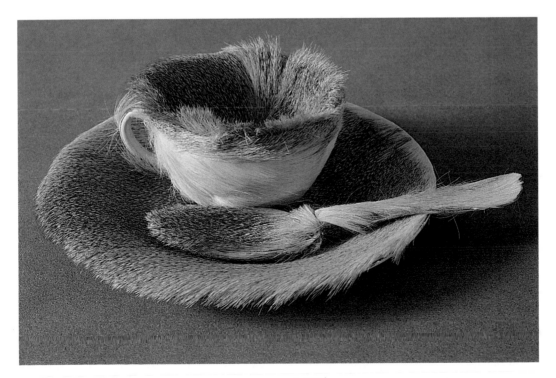

107   Meret Oppenheim. OBJECT (LE DEJEUNER EN FOURRURE). 1936.
Fur covered cup 4⅜" (10.9 cm.) diameter; saucer 9⅜" (23.7 cm) diameter; spoon 8" (20.2 cm) long; overall height 2⅞" (7.3 cm).
The Museum of Modern Art, New York. Purchase.
Photograph: © 2002 The Museum of Modern Art, NY. © 2002 Artists Rights Society (ARS), NY/ProLitteris, Zurich.

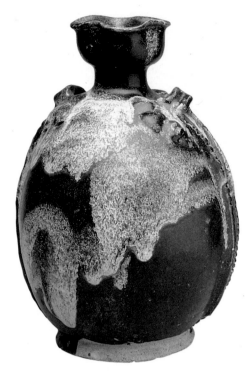

108 FLASK.
China, Tang Dynasty, 9th century.
Stoneware with suffused glaze. Height 11½".
Metropolitan Museum of Art. Gift of Mr. and Mrs. John R. Renke, 1972.
Photograph: Schecter Lee.

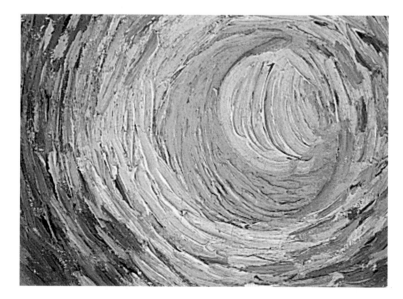

109 Vincent van Gogh.
Detail of STARRY NIGHT. 1889.
Oil on canvas. 29" × 36¼" (73.7 × 92.1 cm).
The Museum of Modern Art, New York. Acquired through the Lillie P. Bliss Bequest.
Photograph: © 2002 The Museum of Modern Art, New York.

example, handling the FLASK from Tang Dynasty China is likely to be even more interesting than looking at it. The potter achieved the complex texture of the surface by splashing a lighter glaze of a different chemical composition over the original dark glaze. Incomplete mixing of the two left a mottled surface. Elsewhere in the body of the piece, the clay has loops and ridges that disclose the origin of the shape to be the leather flasks carried by horsemen. These varied textures make our experience of this object multi-sensory.

A painter may develop a rich tactile surface as well as an implied or simulated texture. We can see actual texture on a two-dimensional surface in the detail of van Gogh's STARRY NIGHT (the entire painting appears in chapter 21). With brush strokes of thick paint, called *impasto,* van Gogh invented textural rhythms that convey his intense feelings.

Five centuries earlier painter Jan van Eyck used tiny brush strokes to show, in minute detail, the incredible richness of various materials. In his painting of GIOVANNI ARNOLFINI AND HIS BRIDE, van Eyck simulated a wide range of textural qualities. In the section of the painting reproduced here (close to actual size) we see the smooth textures of the mirror, amber beads, metal chandelier, a corner of a whisk broom, and the fur of the man's coat. Many other textures can be seen in the entire painting reproduced in chapter 17.

We have explored some of the expressive powers of the visual elements. The ways in which the elements work together according to the principles of design are the focus of the next chapter.

110 Jan van Eyck. Detail of GIOVANNI ARNOLFINI AND HIS BRIDE. 1434.
(See page 298.)
National Gallery, London.
Bridgeman Art Library, NY.

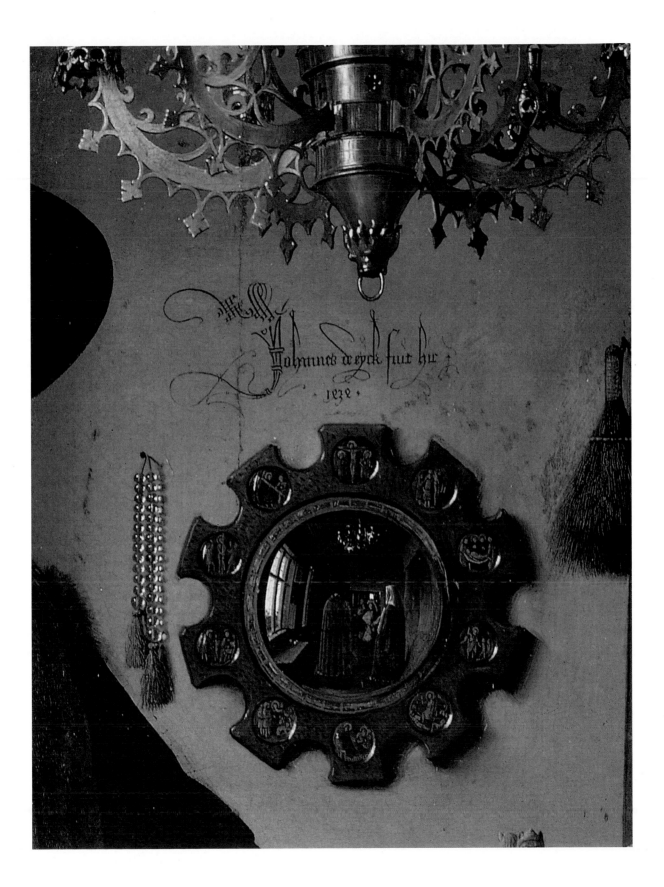

CHAPTER FOUR

PRINCIPLES OF DESIGN

Organized perception is what art is all about.

Roy Lichtenstein[1]

We are continually affecting and being affected by design—our own designs and the designs of others. Whenever we select clothing, place items on a plate, arrange furniture, or hang pictures, we are designing. The process of selecting and ordering the objects and events in our daily lives is related to the design process in art. Like all of us, artists and designers organize visual elements in order to create meaningful and interesting form. In two-dimensional arts, such as painting and photography, this organization is usually called *composition,* but a broader term that applies to the entire range of visual arts is *design.* The word *design* indicates both the process of organizing visual elements and the product of that process.

Design is a result of our basic need for meaningful order. Our desire to unify our experiences of forms is at the root of our appreciation for design. Some designs are so well integrated that they have qualities beyond a mere sum of their parts. Such designs are said to be beautiful, interesting, absorbing, or surprising.

There are no absolute rules for good design. There are only principles or general guidelines for effective visual communication. We study them for the same reason artists do: to develop our innate design sense, to give ourselves a vocabulary for talking to one other about what we see, and to become more sensitive to the expressive and relational qualities of form. In this chapter we look at seven key terms (or pairs of terms) used to identify major principles of design:

> unity and variety
> balance
> emphasis and subordination
> directional forces
> contrast
> repetition and rhythm
> scale and proportion

Together, such terms provide an understanding not only of how artists work but also of how design affects us. The process at its best is a lively, open dialogue between the intention and intuition of the designer and the character of the materials he or she has used.

UNITY AND VARIETY

Unity and variety are complementary concerns. *Unity* is the appearance or condition of oneness; *variety* provides diversity. In design, unity is used to describe the feeling that all the elements in a work belong together and make up a coherent and harmonious whole. When a work of art has unity, both the artist and the viewer feel that any change would damage overall quality.

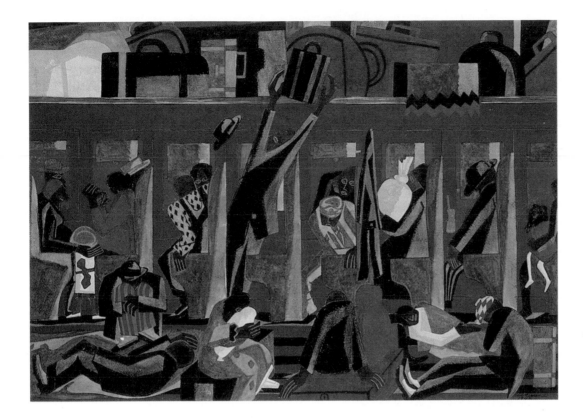

III Jacob Lawrence.
GOING HOME. 1946.
Gouache.
21½" × 29½".
Private collection, courtesy of DC Moore Gallery, NY. Artwork copyright Gwendolyn Knight Lawrence, courtesy of the Jacob and Gwendolyn Lawrence Foundation. Photograph: Joe Painter.

Variety acts as a counterbalance to extreme unity. The balance between the boredom of too much sameness and the chaos of uncontrolled variety creates continuity, vitality, and interest in both art and life.

Artists select certain aspects of visual form in order to clarify and intensify the expressive character of their subjects or themes. In his painting GOING HOME, Jacob Lawrence abstracted the elements of his subject, people traveling on a train. He established visual themes with the lines, shapes, and colors of the train seats, figures, and luggage, and then he repeated and varied those themes. Notice the varied repetition in the green chair seats and window shades. As a unifying element, the same red is used in a variety of shapes. The many figures and objects in the complex composition form a unified design through the artist's skillful use of abstraction, theme, and variation.

Lawrence is known for the lively harmony of his distinctive compositions. Although he has made

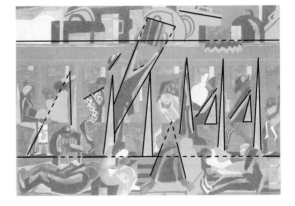

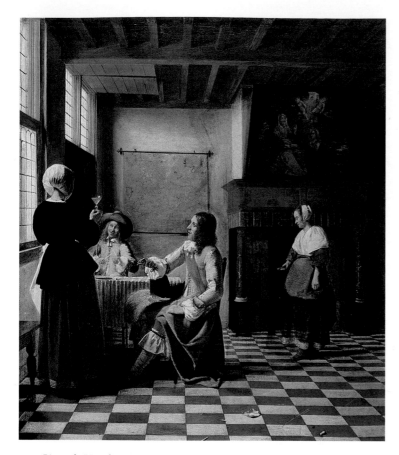

112 Pieter de Hooch.
INTERIOR OF A DUTCH HOUSE. 1658.
Oil on canvas. 29" × 35".
© National Gallery, London.

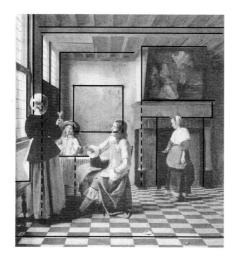

a conscious decision to work in an unsophisticated manner, he is keenly aware of the importance of design. Lawrence studies other artists' work, and he has been influenced by a number of nineteenth- and twentieth-century painters whose works he finds particularly forceful. He said "I like to study the design to see how the artist solves his problems and brings his subjects to the public."[2]

The flat quality of GOING HOME contrasts with the illusion of depth in Pieter de Hooch's INTERIOR OF A DUTCH HOUSE. Each artist depicted a scene from daily life in a style relevant to the century in which he painted. In each case, the painter's use of space helped unify the composition. By setting the scene indoors, de Hooch "borrowed" the unity that architecture imposes on actual space in order to unify pictorial space and provide a cohesive setting for the interaction of figures.

Pattern refers to a repetitive ordering of design elements. In de Hooch's painting, the pattern of floor tiles and windows plays off against the larger rectangles of map, painting, fireplace, and ceiling. These rectangular shapes provide a unifying structure. De Hooch repeated the horizontal and vertical proportions that begin with the format (nearly square) of the picture plane. He then created a whole family of varied rectangles, as indicated in the accompanying diagram. The shapes and colors in the figures around the table relate to the shapes and colors of the figures in the painting above the fireplace—another use of theme and variation.

Alberto Giacometti's sculpture CHARIOT brings together diverse subjects—a standing female figure and two wheels. Unity is achieved through the use of thin lines and rough texture in the figure, wheels, and axle, as well as through the use of bronze for the entire piece. The unity provided by the consistent handling of these elements leads us to see all aspects of the sculpture as a single mysterious entity. Our interest is held by the varied components and by the tension of the figure poised precariously atop a two-legged table on wheels. And these bring us to the principle called balance.

BALANCE

For sculptors such as Giacometti, balance is both a visual issue and a structural necessity. The dynamic interplay between opposing forces is one of the basic conditions of life. The dynamic process of seeking balance is equally basic.

Balance is the achievement of equilibrium, the condition in which acting influences are held in check by opposing forces. We often crave balance in life and in art, and we may be disturbed when we feel its absence. In art, our instinct for physical balance finds its parallel in a desire for visual balance. A painting can depict an act of violence or imbalance—a frenzied battle or a fall from a tightrope; however, unless the painting itself is balanced, it will lack the expressive power necessary to convince us that the battle was terrible, the fall disastrous. Instead, it will merely convince us that it is not a very good painting. For examples of well-balanced paintings of chaotic events, see Delacroix's DEATH OF SARDANAPALUS in chapter 21 and Picasso's GUERNICA in chapter 23.

The two general types of balance are symmetrical (formal) and asymmetrical (informal).

Symmetrical Balance

Symmetrical balance is the near or exact matching of left and right sides of a three-dimensional form or a two-dimensional composition.

Architects often employ symmetrical balance to give unity and formal grandeur to a building's facade or front side. For example, in 1792 James Hoban won a competition for his DESIGN FOR THE PRESIDENT'S HOUSE, a drawing of a symmetrical, Georgian-style mansion. Today, two centuries and several additions later, we know it as the WHITE HOUSE.

In architecture, as in other visual arts, symmetrical design is useful because it is easier to comprehend than asymmetry. Symmetry is also useful because it creates a powerful unity—even in large, complex buildings—setting them apart from nearby structures. Symmetry tends to be visually inactive. We certainly want our symbolically

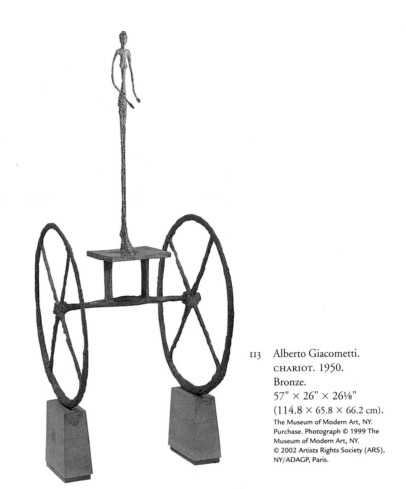

113   Alberto Giacometti.
CHARIOT. 1950.
Bronze.
57" × 26" × 26⅛"
(114.8 × 65.8 × 66.2 cm).
The Museum of Modern Art, NY.
Purchase. Photograph © 1999 The
Museum of Modern Art, NY.
© 2002 Artists Rights Society (ARS),
NY/ADAGP, Paris.

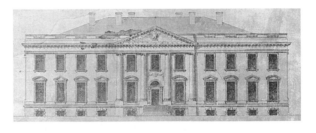

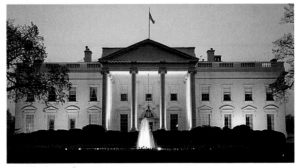

114   James Hoban.
A DESIGN FOR THE PRESIDENT'S HOUSE. 1792.
a.   Elevation.
Maryland Historical Society, Baltimore.
b.   WHITE HOUSE.
Front view. 1997.
The Image Bank.
Photograph: Antonio M. Rosario.

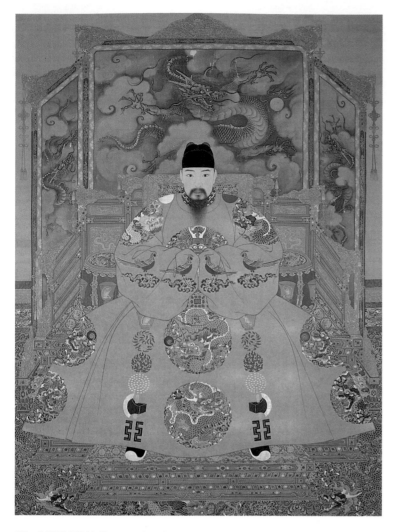

115　PORTRAIT OF THE HUNG-CHIH EMPEROR.
Ming Dynasty, 15th Century.
Hanging Scroll. Ink and color on silk. 82" × 61".
National Palace Museum, Taipei, Taiwan, Republic of China.

important buildings to seem motionless and stable. All the qualities that make symmetry desirable in architecture make it generally less desirable in sculpture and two-dimensional art. Too much symmetry can be boring. Although artists admire symmetry for its formal qualities, they rarely employ it rigidly. Artists usually do not want their work to seem static.

Probably one of the most symmetrical paintings ever made is the PORTRAIT OF THE HUNG-CHIH EMPEROR, executed by an anonymous court artist in fifteenth-century China. The ruler sits stiffly facing us, hands concealed by his rich garments. Only a few asymmetrical dragons on the screen behind him and in the medallions on his cloak relieve the overall rigidity of the composition. Color in the painting is symmetrically placed, yet its richness also serves to lighten the air of formality and reserve that the symmetrical composition creates. The emperor wanted to convey a sense of dignity, permanence, and majesty to all who came into his presence, and this artist's use of symmetry contributes strongly to that impression.

Asymmetrical Balance

With *asymmetrical balance,* the two sides are not the same. Instead, various visual phenomena are balanced—according to their visual and referential weights—around a felt or implied center of gravity. For example, in THE EVENING GLOW OF THE ANDO, the composition as a whole seems balanced, but only because dramatic imbalances are held in check. The strong diagonal of the wall and floor is accented by the heads of the two subjects, one of whom is reading a poem. This diagonal provides the focus of the composition. The curves of the water in the upper left have no counterpart except for the curves of the figures at the center. The lightness of the water and the tree branches is balanced by the solidly anchored candle lamp that the other figure is adjusting. The horizontal lines of the ground and the floorboards give a vertical rhythm to the composition, but these are often broken or missing. The artist has engaged and balanced complex energies in a knowing and tasteful way typical of the best Japanese prints. Asymmetrical balance is far more difficult to achieve than symmetrical balance, but it is more flexible, subtle, and dynamic.

What exactly are the visual properties or weights of colors and forms, and how does an artist go about balancing them? As with design itself, there are no rules, only principles. Here are a few about visual balance:

- A large form is heavier, more attractive, or more attention-getting than a small form. Thus, two or more small forms can balance one large form.
- A form gathers visual weight as it nears the edge of a picture. In this way, a small form near an edge can balance a larger form near the center.
- A complex form is heavier than a simple form. Thus, a small complex form can balance a large simple form.

The introduction of color complicates these principles. Here are three color principles that overturn the three principles of form just given:

- Warm colors are heavier than cool colors. A single small yellow form can therefore balance a large dark blue form.
- Intense colors are heavier than weak or pale colors (tints and shades). Hence, a single small bright blue form near the center can balance a large pale blue form near an edge.
- The intensity, and therefore the weight, of any color increases as the background color approaches its complementary hue. Thus, on a green background, a small simple red form can balance a large complex blue form.

Although guidelines such as these are interesting to study and can be valuable to an artist if she or he gets "stuck," they are really "laboratory" examples. The truth is that most artists rely on a highly developed sensitivity to what "looks right" in order to arrive at a dynamic balance. Simply put, a picture is balanced when it feels balanced.

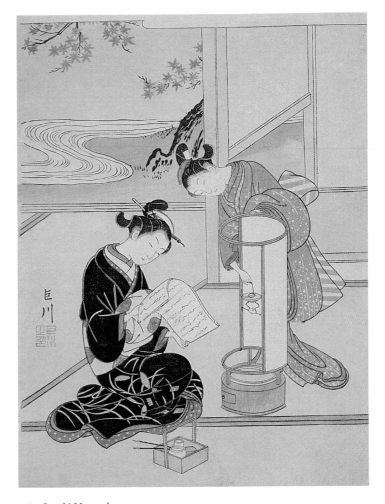

116   Suzuki Haranobu.
THE EVENING GLOW OF THE ANDO, from the series
EIGHT PARLOR VIEWS. Edo period. 1766.
Color woodblock print. 11¼" × 8½".
The Art Institute of Chicago. Clarence Buckingham Collection, 1928.900.
Photograph: © 1997, The Art Institute of Chicago. All rights reserved.

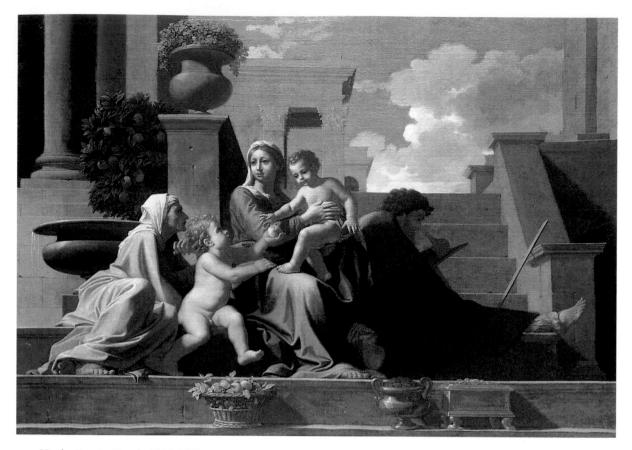

117 Nicolas Poussin, French, 1594–1665.
THE HOLY FAMILY ON THE STEPS. 1648.
Oil on canvas. 72.4 × 111.7 cm.
© The Cleveland Museum of Art. 2001, Leonard C. Hanna Jr. Fund, 1981.18.

A classic example of balance in Western art is Nicolas Poussin's HOLY FAMILY ON THE STEPS. Poussin combined both asymmetrical and symmetrical elements in this complex composition. He grouped the figures in a stable, symmetrical pyramidal shape. The most important figure, the infant Jesus, is at the center of the picture, the strongest position. In case we don't see that right away, Poussin guided our attention by making the traditional red and blue of Mary's robes both light and bright, and by placing Jesus's head within a halolike architectural space.

But then Poussin offset the potential boredom of this symmetry with an ingenious asymmetrical color balance. He placed Joseph, the figure at the right, in deep shadow, undermining the clarity of the stable pyramid. He created a major center of interest at the far left of the picture by giving St.

Elizabeth a bright yellow robe. The interest created by the blue sky and clouds at the upper right counterbalances the figures of St. Elizabeth and the infant John the Baptist. But the final master stroke that brings complete balance is Joseph's foot, which Poussin bathed in light. The brightness of this small, isolated shape with the diagonal staff above it is enough to catch our eye and balance the color weights of the left half of the painting.

While the overall composition of HOLY FAMILY ON THE STEPS is balanced asymmetrically, the painting's center of gravity is still the central vertical axis. In JOCKEYS BEFORE THE RACE on the other hand, Edgar Degas located the center of gravity on the right. To reinforce it, he drew it in as a pole. At first glance, all our attention is drawn to our extreme right, to the nearest and largest horse. But the solitary circle of the sun in the upper left exerts a strong fascination. The red cap, the pale pink jacket of the distant jockey, the subtle warm/cool color intersection at the horizon, and the recession of the horses all help to move our eyes over to the left portion of the picture, where a barely discernible but very important vertical line directs our attention upward.

In JOCKEYS BEFORE THE RACE, a trail of visual cues moves our attention from right to left. If we are sensitive to them, we will perform the act of balancing the painting. If we are not, the painting will seem forever unbalanced. Degas, who was known for his adventurous compositions, relied on the fact that seeing is an active, creative process and not a passive one.

Notice that both Poussin and Degas used strong diagonals in their designs. In the Poussin, Elizabeth's robe at the lower left begins an implied diagonal line that continues up through the cloud at the upper right. In the Degas, the large horse in the lower right, our first center of attention, is counterbalanced by the sun in the upper left. Diagonal opposition is common in asymmetrical compositions, and looking for it can often help you find the key to the balance.

A good way to explore a picture's balance is to imagine it painted differently. Block out Joseph's light-bathed foot in the Poussin, then see how the lack of balance affects the picture. Cover the jockey's red cap in the Degas and you'll see a spark of life go out of the painting.

Asymmetrical balance in architecture is difficult to show in photographs. In Frank Lloyd Wright's FALLING WATER (chapter 14), we can sense that the asymmetrically placed horizontal forms are firmly held, visually, by the implied gravity of the vertical tower. But what we cannot see is how the play of forms would shift constantly if we were to walk around the house, how the forms maintain a balance that we could see from every angle.

Besides the visual balance we seek in all art, works of sculpture and architecture need structural balance or they will not stand up. Feelings about visual balance are intimately connected to our experience with actual physical balance. It appears

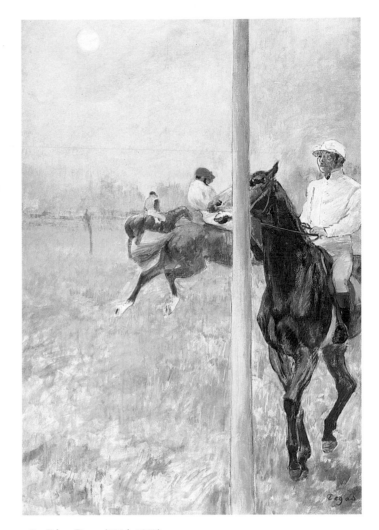

118 Edgar Degas (1834–1917).
JOCKEYS BEFORE THE RACE. C. 1878–1879.
Oil essence, gouache and pastel. 42½" × 29".
The Barber Institute of Fine Arts, The University of Birmingham/Bridgeman Art Library.

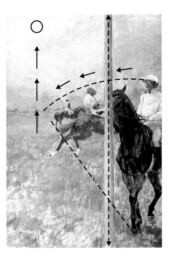

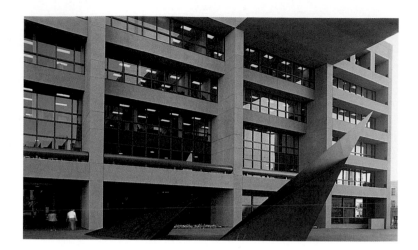

119   Beverly Pepper.
EXCALIBUR. San Diego
Federal Courthouse. 1975–1976.
Steel painted black. 32' × 40' × 60'.
Photograph: Courtesy of the Artist

that Beverly Pepper designed her large sculpture EXCALIBUR to look somewhat unbalanced as a way of giving an intriguing tension to her soaring diagonal structures. We know the triangular forms are securely attached to the ground, yet they look precarious. If we view the work from this and other angles, the smaller piece seems to provide an anchor—a visual pull that acts as a counterweight to the larger form.

EMPHASIS AND SUBORDINATION

Emphasis is used to draw our attention to an area or areas. If that area is a specific spot or figure, it is called a *focal point*. Position, contrast, color intensity, and size can all be used to create emphasis.

Through *subordination,* an artist creates neutral areas of lesser interest that keep us from being distracted from the areas of emphasis.

Emphasis, subordination, and directional forces are ways in which an artist balances and controls the sequence of our seeing and the amount of attention we pay to the various parts of any work of art. We have seen them at work in the two paintings we have just examined.

In HOLY FAMILY ON THE STEPS, Poussin placed the most important figure in the center, the strongest location in any visual field. In JOCKEYS BEFORE THE RACE, Degas took a different approach, using size, shape, placement, and color to create areas of emphasis *away* from the center. The sun is a separate focal point created through con-

trast (it is lighter than the surrounding sky area and the only circle in the painting) and through placement (it is the only shape in that part of the painting). Sky and grass areas, however, were painted in muted color with almost no detail so that they would be subordinate to, and thus support, the areas of emphasis.

DIRECTIONAL FORCES

Directional forces are "paths" for the eye to follow provided by actual or implied lines. Implied directional lines may be suggested by a form's axis, by the imagined connection between similar or adjacent forms, or by the implied continuation of actual lines. Studying directional lines and forces often reveals a work of art's underlying energy and basic visual structure.

Looking at JOCKEYS BEFORE THE RACE, we find that our attention is pulled to a series of focal points: the horse and jockey at the extreme right, the vertical pole, the red cap, the pink jacket, and the blue-green at the horizon. The dominant directional forces in JOCKEYS are diagonal. The focal points mentioned above create an implied directional line. The face of the first jockey is included in this line.

The implied diagonal line created by the bodies of the three receding horses acts as a related directional force. As our eyes follow the recession, encouraged by the attraction of the focal points, we perform the act of balancing the composition by correcting our original attraction to the extreme right.

Just as our physical and visual feelings for balance correspond, so do our physical and visual feelings about directional lines and forces. The direction of lines produces sensations similar to standing still (|), being at rest (—), or being in motion (/). Therefore, a combination of vertical and horizontal lines provides stability. For example, columns and walls and horizontal steps provide a stable visual foundation for HOLY FAMILY ON THE STEPS. The vertical pole and horizon provide stability in Degas's JOCKEYS.

Francisco Goya's print BULLFIGHT provides a fascinating example of effective design based on a dramatic use of directional forces. To emphasize the drama of man and bull, Goya isolated them in the foreground as large, dark shapes against a light background. He created suspense by crowding the spectators into the upper left corner.

Goya evoked a sense of motion by placing the bullfighter exactly on the diagonal axis that runs from lower left to upper right (diagram a). He reinforced the feeling by placing the bull's hind legs along the same line.

Goya further emphasized two main features of the drama by placing the man's hands at the intersection of the image's most important horizontal and vertical lines. He also directed powerful diagonals from the bull's head and front legs to the pole's balancing point on the ground (a). The resulting sense of motion to the right is so powerful that everything in the rest of the etching is needed to balance it.

By placing the light source to the left, Goya extended the bull's shadow to the right, in order to create a relatively stable horizontal line. The man looks down at the shadow, creating a directional force that causes us also to look. When we do, we realize that the implied lines reveal the underlying structure to be a stable triangle (diagram b). Formally, the triangle serves as a balancing force; psychologically, its missing side serves to heighten the tension of the situation.

The dynamism of the man's diagonal axis is so strong that the composition needed additional balancing elements; thus Goya used light to create two

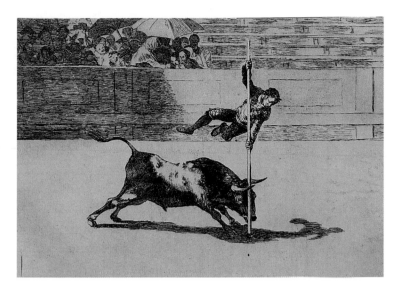

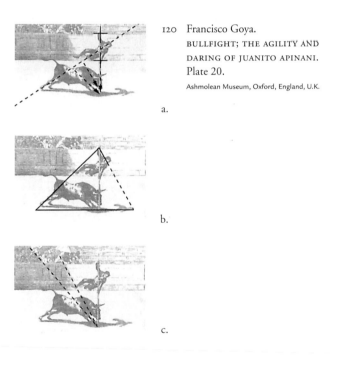

120 Francisco Goya.
BULLFIGHT; THE AGILITY AND DARING OF JUANITO APINANI. Plate 20.

Ashmolean Museum, Oxford, England, U.K.

a.

b.

c.

more diagonals in the opposite direction (diagram c). The area of shadow in the background completes the balance by adding visual weight and stability to the left.

It has taken many words and several diagrams to describe the visual dynamics that make the design of Goya's etching so effective. However, our eyes take it in instantly. Good design is efficient; it communicates its power immediately.

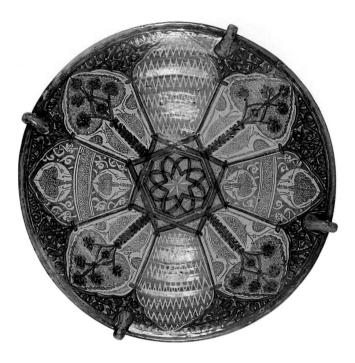

121   LUSTER-PAINTED BOWL.
Hispano-Moresque, Manises. Spain. c. 1400.
Tin-glazed earthenware painted in cobalt blue and luster.
Height 5½", diameter 17⅘" (E643).
Courtesy of the Hispanic Society of America, NY.

CONTRAST

Contrast is the juxtaposition of strongly dissimilar elements. Dramatic effects can be produced when dark is set against light, large against small, bright colors against dull. Without contrast, visual experience would be monotonous.

Contrast can be seen in the thick and thin areas of a single brush stroke. It can also be seen in the juxtaposition of regular geometric and irregular organic shapes, or in hard (sharp) and soft (blurred) edges. Contrast can provide visual interest, emphasize a point, and express content.

In the LUSTER-PAINTED BOWL, for example, the gold luster contrasts strongly with the blue accents. There is also a great deal of contrast among the eight petal-shaped segments that radiate from the central starburst. These segments are divided and decorated quite differently, creating a richly varied surface. Four of the petals have a blue tree shape, which in Muslim mythology refers to the Tree of Life described in the Quran, the Muslim holy book. They provide the major rhythm of the com-position, while the other four petals alternate between a simple zigzag and a doubled tree separated by a band. After a moment's look, we realize that the vivid and rich contrasts of this piece are subjected to a rigorous balancing scheme based on the repetition of radiating shapes. This discovery soon gives way to admiration for the designer's ability to harmonize such disparate elements.

REPETITION AND RHYTHM

The repetition of visual elements give a composition unity, continuity, flow, and emphasis. As we saw earlier, de Hooch's INTERIOR OF A DUTCH HOUSE (page 74) is organized around the repetition of rectangular shapes.

In Raphael's MADONNA OF THE CHAIR, curved shapes echo the circular format of the painting. The curve of the edge of the painting is repeated in the curve of Mary's head, neck, and arm, and in the interlocking curve of the infant Jesus. The repeated curves provide flow and continuity, while the vertical axis of the chair post stabilizes the curving directional forces that dominate the composition.

In the visual arts, *rhythm* is created through the regular recurrence of elements with related variations. Rhythm refers to any kind of movement or structure of dominant and subordinate elements in sequence. We generally associate rhythm with temporal arts such as music, dance, and poetry. Visual artists also use rhythm, as an organizational and expressive device.

Repetition and rhythm are effectively employed in one of history's most carefully observed and elegantly painted depictions of flying birds: THE HUNDRED GEESE. (Only a small section of the handscroll is shown here.) There is some controversy over who painted it and when, but no one can question the painter's incredible awareness of birds in flight and at rest and the skillful use of ink gradations. It is likely that the artist's intention for this section of the scroll was to show the same bird in various stages of flight, emerging from the distance and coming into sharper focus. The artist succeeded in creating the illusion of space and continuous motion long before the inventions of film and television.

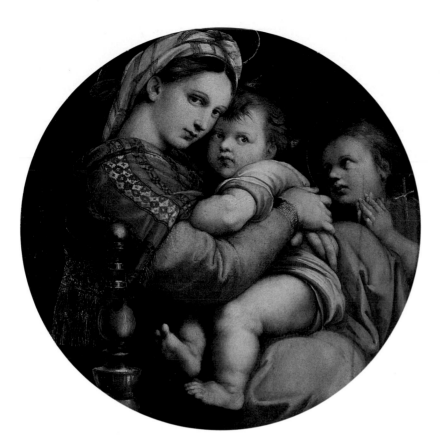

122 Raphael Sanzio.
MADONNA OF THE CHAIR. c. 1514.
Oil on wood. Diameter 2'4".
Pitti Gallery, Florence.
Photograph: Scala/Art Resource, NY.

123 Detail of THE HUNDRED GEESE.
c. 1270–1300. Ink on paper,
handscroll. 14⅜" × 29'8½".
Traditionally attributed to Ma Fen,
but probably an anonymous artist of
the early Yuan dynasty, China.
Honolulu Academy of Arts.
Gift of Mrs. Charles M. Coke, 1927. (2121).

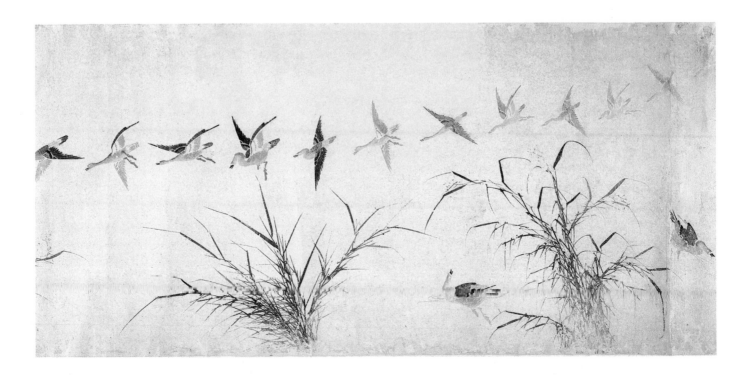

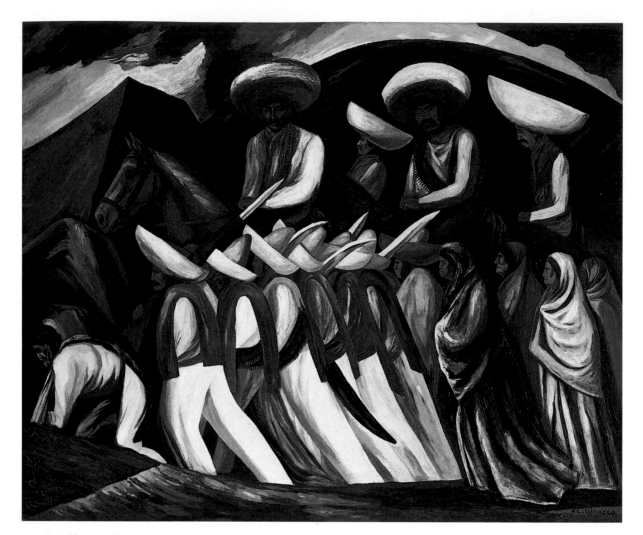

124 José Clemente Orozco.
ZAPATISTAS. 1931.
Oil on canvas. 45" × 55"(114.3 × 139.7 cm)
The Museum of Modern Art, New York. Anonymous gift.
Photograph © 2002 The Museum of Modern Art, New York. © Orozco Valladares
Family. Reproduction authorized by the Instituto Nacional de Bellas Artes.

A strong rhythm dominates José Clemente Orozco's ZAPATISTAS. The line of similar, diagonally placed figures grouped in a rhythmic sequence expresses the determination of oppressed people in revolt. The rhythmic diagonals of their hat brims, bayonets, and swords all contribute to a feeling of action. In fact, diagonal lines dominate the entire composition.

Rhythm plays a different role in the Chola Dynasty sculpture DANCING KRISHNA (page 58). The extended, bent, or curving limbs abolish the symmetry of the human body and suggest rather the vigorous rhythms of a joyous dance.

SCALE AND PROPORTION

Scale is the size relation of one thing to another. *Proportion* is the size relationship of parts to a whole.

Scale is one of the first decisions an artist makes when planning a work of art. How big will it be? We experience scale in relation to our own size, and this experience constitutes an important part of our response to works of art.

We see many relationships in terms of scale. You have probably noticed that when a short person stands next to a tall person, the short one seems shorter and the tall one taller. Their relationship exaggerates the relative difference in their heights. In the diagram SCALE RELATIONSHIPS, the inner circles at the center in both groups are the same size, but they appear to be quite different.

Claes Oldenburg and Coosje van Bruggen's SHUTTLECOCKS is a contemporary example of distortion of scale. The artists arrayed four huge metal shuttlecocks on the lawns ouside the north and south façades of the Nelson-Atkins Museum of Art in Kansas City, Missouri. Each is an outlandish seventeen feet high and weighs over 5,000 pounds. Since badminton is played on grass, it appears that the shuttlecocks fell during a game among giants who used the museum as a net. SHUTTLECOCKS thus uses distortion of scale to poke gentle fun at the museum, mocking its rather prim look with a playfully irreverent attitude.

When the size of any work is modified for reproduction in a book, its character changes. The sizes of almost all the art objects in this book have been changed to fit the photographic reproductions of them on the pages. One of the few exceptions is Rembrandt's SELF-PORTRAIT IN A CAP. This tiny etching, which the artist did when he was twenty-four years old, is reproduced here the actual size of the original print. It captures a fleeting expression of intense surprise. At this scale, it reads as an intimate notation of human emotion. On the other

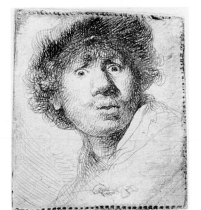

127 Rembrandt van Rijn.
SELF-PORTRAIT IN A CAP, OPEN MOUTHED AND STARING. 1630. Etching. 2" × 1⅞".
Copyright British Museum.

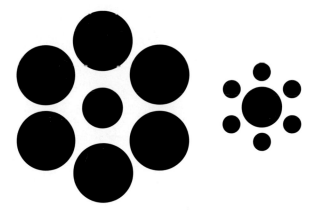

126 SCALE RELATIONSHIPS.

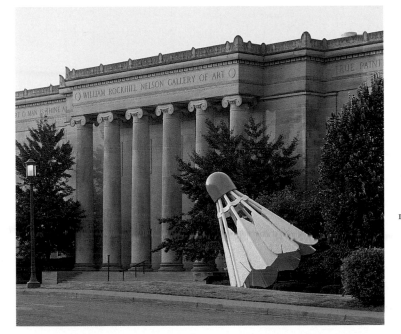

125 Claes Oldenburg (b. Sweden, 1929) and Coosje van Bruggen (b. Netherlands 1942). SHUTTLECOCKS. 1994. One of four. Aluminum, fiberglass-reinforced plastic, and paint, 215¾" × 209" × 191 ¾" (548 × 530.9 × 487 cm).
The Nelson-Atkins Museum of Art, Kansas City, MO. Purchase: acquired through the generosity of the Sosland Family. Photograph: E.G. Schempf. © 1994 The Nelson Gallery Foundation. All Production Rights Reserved.

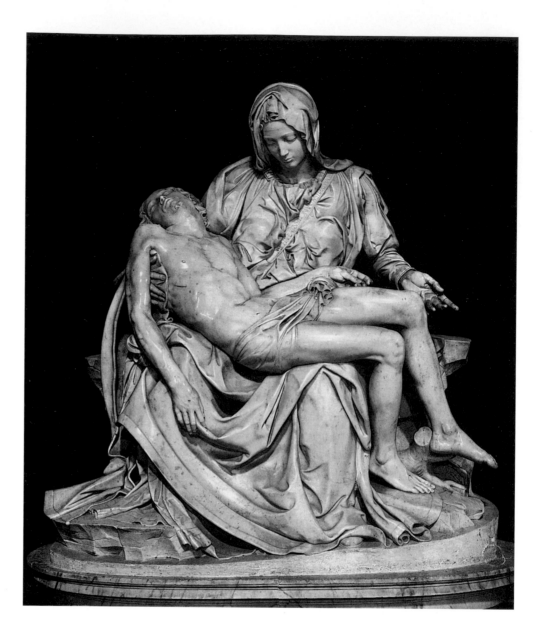

128　Michelangelo Buonarroti.
PIETÀ. 1501.
Marble. Height 6'8½".
St. Peter's Basilica, Rome.
Photograph: Alinari/Art Resource, NY.

hand, many large-sized works have been reduced in this book to tiny fractions of their actual sizes, thereby greatly changing the impact of each. Because works of art are distorted in a variety of ways when they are reproduced, it is important to experience original art whenever possible.

The term *format* refers to the size and shape—and thus to the scale and proportion—of a two-dimensional picture plane, such as a piece of paper, a canvas, a book page, or a video screen. For example, the format of this book is a vertical 8½ by 11-inch rectangle, the same format used for computer paper and most notebooks. Three common formats favored by traditional painters in China and Japan have been the long horizontal hand-scroll, the tall, vertical hanging scroll, and the fan. The circular or "tondo" format was used during the Renaissance by Raphael (see page 83) and others. Some recent artists have used huge formats.

The format an artist chooses affects the total composition (design) of a particular work. Matisse made this clear in his *Notes of a Painter:*

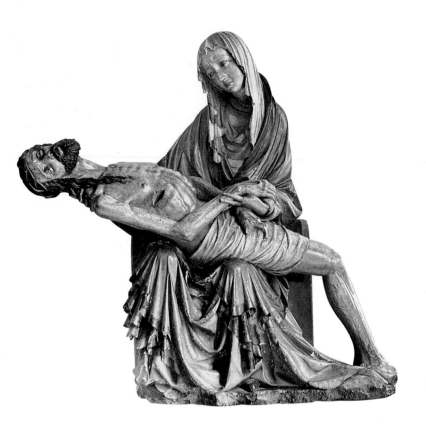

129 Master of the Beautiful Madonna.
PIETÀ. c. 1415.
Polychromed stone.
St. Mary's Church, Gdansk, Poland.
Photograph: Ryzard Petrajtis.

Composition, the aim of which should be expression, is modified according to the surface to be covered. If I take a sheet of paper of a given size, my drawing will have a necessary relationship to its format. I would not repeat this drawing on another sheet of different proportions, for example, rectangular instead of square.[3]

Size relationships within a work of art often express symbolic meaning. The use of unnatural proportions to show the relative importance of figures is called *hierarchical scale*. In Egyptian art, the relative importance of figures in a composition often dictates their size, so that rulers appear much larger than servants or captives.

Change in proportion can make a major difference in how we experience a given subject. This becomes apparent when we compare two *pietà*s (*pietà,* Italian for "pity," refers to a depiction of Mary holding and mourning over the body of Jesus).

Creating a composition with an infant on its mother's lap is much easier than showing a fully grown man in such a position. In his most famous PIETÀ, the young Michelangelo solved the problem by dramatically altering the human proportions of Mary's figure. Michelangelo made the heads of the two figures the same size but greatly enlarged Mary's body in relation to that of Christ, disguising her immensity with folds of drapery. Her seated figure spreads out to accommodate the almost hor-

izontal curve of Christ's limp body. Imagine how the figure of Mary would appear if she were standing. Michelangelo made Mary's body into that of a giant; if she were a living human being rather than a work of art, she would stand at least eight feet tall!

Because the proportions of the figure of Christ are anatomically correct and there are abundant naturalistic details, we overlook the proportions of Mary's figure; yet the distortion is essential to the way we experience the content of the work.

Compare Michelangelo's work with another PIETÀ, created almost a century earlier by an unknown sculptor. In the earlier work, the proportions are true to life, yet at first they seem unnatural. Christ's body appears to stick out awkwardly, without support. The sense of discomfort caused by the more normal proportions emphasizes the grief and tension appropriate to the subject. Such emphasis on suffering contrasts with the emphasis on serenity in Michelangelo's design.

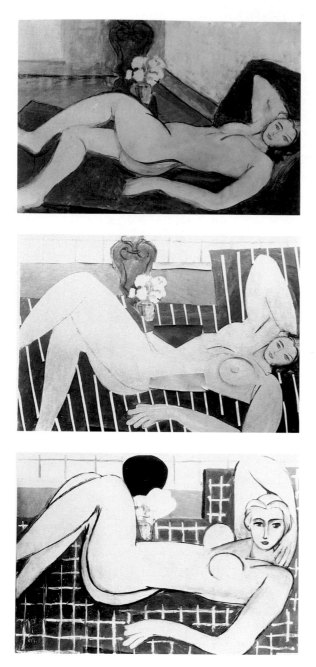

130　Henri Matisse.
Photographs of three states of LARGE RECLINING NUDE.
a. State I, May 3, 1935.
b. State IX, May 29, 1935.
c. State XII, September 4, 1935.
The Baltimore Museum of Art. The Cone Collection.
© 2002 Succession H. Matisse, Paris/Artists Rights Society (ARS), NY.

DESIGN SUMMARY

A finished artwork affects us because its design seems inevitable. However, design is not inevitable at all. Faced with a blank piece of paper, an empty canvas, a lump of clay, or a block of marble, an artist begins a process involving many decisions, false starts, and changes in order to arrive at an integrated whole. This chapter has presented some of the principles of design that guide the art-making process.

By photographing the progress of his painting LARGE RECLINING NUDE, Henri Matisse left us a rare record of the process of designing. He took twenty-four photographs over a period of four months; three of them are reproduced here.

The first version (State 1) is by far the most conventional: The proportions of the model's body on the couch and the three-dimensional space of the room seem ordinary. This stage of the work shows that the artist understood the traditional rules of picture construction, but this is only the start of a fascinating journey.

By State 9, Matisse had introduced a number of bold changes. Because the model's head and crooked right arm did not give the proper accent to that side of the composition, he greatly enlarged the arm. He added more curves to the torso, and he put the legs together to provide a balancing accent on the left side. The space of the room now has a new look because he removed the diagonal; this change flattened the composition, highlighting its two-dimensional design. The model's left arm is now closer to a ninety-degree angle, which makes it seem to support more weight; this is a stronger effect than that of the rubbery arm in the first photo. The boldest change regards the couch. Now it is far larger, with vertical white stripes in a rhythmic pattern. Since the stripes are parallel, they do not function as perspective lines; rather, the couch appears to be tipped toward us. Matisse kept the potted flowers and the chair, but he simplified the chair and placed the flowers on the couch.

By the time the artist took our third photograph (State 13), he had introduced even more changes, to compensate for some of the bold effects

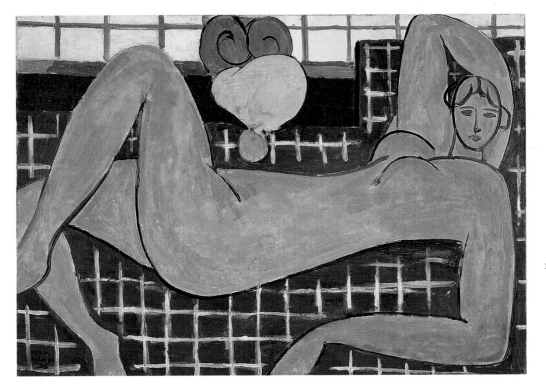

131 Henri Matisse (French, 1869–1954).
LARGE RECLINING NUDE.
Oil on canvas. 26" × 36½"
(66 x 92.7 cm).
The Baltimore Museum of Art: The Cone Collection,
formed by Dr. Claribel Cone and Miss Etta Cone of
Baltimore, Maryland. BMA 1950.258.
© 2002 Succession H. Matisse, Paris/Artists Rights
Society (ARS), NY.

he had introduced earlier. The model's head is larger and placed upright, so that it fits better into the shape of the raised arm. He simplified the curves of the torso and created a new position for the left arm, a compromise between its position in the first photo and the second one. The legs are now almost a unit, their bulky mass balancing the verticals and diagonals on the right. He added horizontal lines to the couch, making a pattern of squares that parallel the framing edges of the painting. This net-like motif is repeated in the larger squares on the back wall of the room. The composition is already interesting, but Matisse did not stop here.

The final version shows further refinements and a few discoveries. Because the model's left arm probably still seemed weak, Matisse finally fixed it in the corner of the work at a strong angle aligned with the picture frame. The head is smaller, because the new position of the arms provides enough visual weight on that side of the work. He intensified the pattern on the back wall, so that it

now serves as a variation of the motif on the couch. He gave new functions to the shapes and lines of the chair back and flowers by emphasizing their curves. They now echo the shapes of the body and balance the rigidity of the squares in the couch and wall. The position of the legs is the biggest change. By moving one of them down, he created a "pinwheel" effect that the arms carry through, adding a new circular element to the design of the whole. Finally, he repositioned the model's entire body at a slight angle from the horizontal.

Matisse's keen sense of design and restless experimentation produced a work in which powerful forces in the composition are balanced with seemingly simple means. He wrote that the expressiveness of a work does not rest merely on facial expressions or gestures of figures:

The entire arrangement of my picture is expressive: the place occupied by the figures, the empty spaces around them, the proportions, everything has its share.[4]

When French artist Henri Matisse was eighteen years old, his father sent him to Paris to study law. A year later he passed his examinations and took a dull job as a clerk in a lawyer's office. Then an attack of appendicitis changed the direction of his life. During the long convalescence at his parents' home, his mother tried to amuse him with a gift of a box of paints, brushes, and a do-it-yourself book on painting. The result was extraordinary. By the age of twenty-one, Matisse knew he wanted to be a painter. He returned to Paris and became a full-time art student. In the methodical manner of a lawyer, he began his artistic career by becoming thoroughly proficient in the traditional techniques of French art. Throughout his life he worked at adding to both his knowledge and his skills, while being careful to preserve his original freshness of vision.

For Matisse, a painting was a combination of lines, shapes, and colors before it was a depiction of nameable objects. His personal style was based on intuition; yet he acknowledged the importance of his years of study. He carefully assimilated influences from the arts of the Near East and Africa and from other painters.

Matisse's primary interest was to express his passionate feeling for life

through the free use of visual form, with the human figure his main subject.

What interests me most is neither still life nor landscape but the human figure. It is through it that I best succeed in expressing the nearly religious feeling that I have towards life.[5]

His search for expressive means caused him to question or abandon many of the "rules" of art as it was then understood. For example, he often used colors that did not correspond to what the eye sees, but rather to what he felt inside. He also simplified and flattened his compositions, because he felt that adding too much detail to a work took away feeling. For these and other innovations in painting style, he was once called a "wild beast"—*fauve* in French. The name stuck, and Fauvism took its place among the most important modern art movements.

Matisse sought to hide his own artistic struggles so that his work would appear effortless and light. He was concerned, however, that young people would think he had created his paintings casually —even carelessly—and would mistakenly conclude that years of disciplined work and study were unnecessary.

We find evidence of Matisse's sense of delight throughout most of his work—even his self-portrait has an expressive, playful quality.

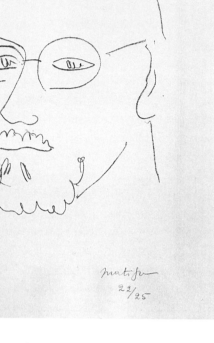

The dominant qualities in Matisse's art are lyric color and vitality. Behind the playful appearance lie radiant big-heartedness, grace, and wisdom. Although he lived through both world wars and was aware of acute suffering, Matisse chose to express joy and tranquility in his art.

What I dream of is an art of balance, of purity and serenity, devoid of troubling or depressing subject matter, an art which might be for every mental worker . . . businessman or writer, like an appeasing influence, like a mental soother, something like a good armchair in which to rest from physical fatigue.[6]

132   Henri Matisse.
SELF-PORTRAIT, THREE-QUARTER VIEW. 1948.
Lithograph printed in black composition.
9 1/16" × 7 3/16"
(23 × 18.3 cm).

CHAPTER FIVE

STYLE

The word "style" is common in everyday speech. Designers try to influence our purchases with frequent changes of clothing and car styles. We wear our hair in particular styles. We recognize the distinctive styles of our favorite musicians. We even speak of the style of an era, such as 1980s-style music. Style is a consistent, recognizable, and noteworthy manner of expression or way of behaving.

In art, *style* refers to a consistent and characteristic handling of media, elements of form, and principles of design that make a work of art identifiable as the product of a particular culture, period, region, group, or person. Some art styles are more distinct and easily identifiable than others. Individual and shared values, experiences, and techniques are among the major sources of artistic styles. During the course of a lifetime, an artist may change his or her style; likewise, culture or period styles change across time and space.

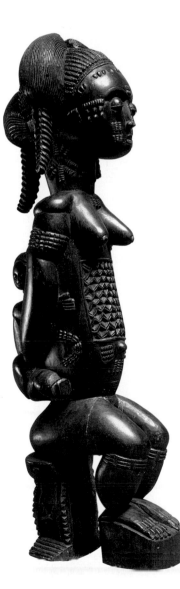

133 SPIRIT SPOUSE.
Côte D'Ivoire. Baule Culture, early 20th Century. Wood. Height 17".
University of Pennsylvania Museum, Philadelphia, T4.827c.2.

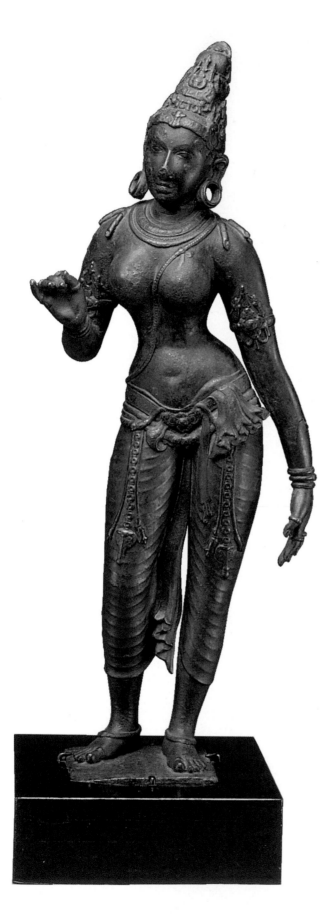

CULTURAL STYLE

Just as a society develops its own language and customs, so it develops its own beliefs (religion) and style of material forms (clothing, buildings, art of all kinds). Taken together, these social and physical forms comprise "culture." Each society finds ways to represent what it values or feels is important.

Style is an important part of every culture's identity. It comes from the culture and expresses its values. Just as an artist is the product of a culture, so too he or she is the product of the experience of a particular era. Within any culture, styles undergo changes over time while still expressing the broad cultural viewpoint.

Two examples of female spirit figures illustrate some of the differences found in cultural styles. Both the SPIRIT SPOUSE from Africa (preceding page) and the PARVATI from India represent an ideal woman as each culture perceives her. The African piece, from the Baule Culture of Côte D'Ivoire, shows the typical hairstyle and body markings of that society. In addition, we see the typically abstract sculptural style of the Baule: an elongated torso with vigorously modeled flesh curves in the hips, breasts, and arms.

The PARVATI differs from the Baule figure in many respects. The straight-backed and solemn mood of the African work gives way in the PARVATI to curving sensuousness highlighted by the narrow waist and full breasts. The weight rests mostly on one leg, providing a foundation for the contours of the spine as it seems to shift at hips, waist, and neck. The PARVATI's gestures are relaxed and elegant, and her clothing is typical of the Chola Dynasty from which she came.

Some of the differences are due to the use of different media—one figure is wood and the other is bronze—but cultural differences in the way a human body is visualized account for most of the variation in style between these two works. And each, of course, differs from the same subject rendered in the Classical Greek way (see VENUS DE MEDICI in chapter 16).

134   STANDING PARVATI.
Chola Dynasty, c. 900. Bronze. Height 27⅜".
The Metropolitan Museum of Art.
Photograph: Schecter Lee.
© 1986 The Metropolitan Museum of Art, 57.51.3.

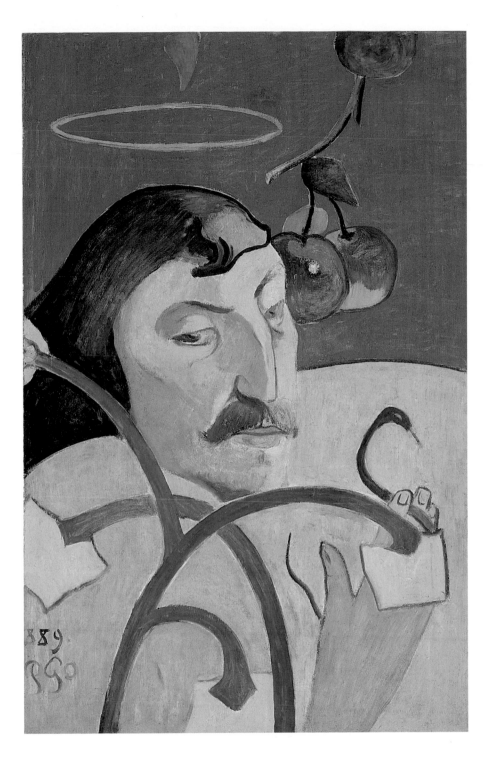

PERIOD STYLE

As noted above, styles often change over time. Popular concerns may shift, based on economic and political changes, new technology, or religious insights. Sometimes a mere thirst for something new takes over. Most cultures of the world have gone through various periods, and frequently these result in new art styles.

One such period style in Europe, *Art Nouveau* (French for "new art"), was an international decorative style of the late nineteenth and early twentieth centuries. The style is characterized by sinuous lines or contours, sometimes called "whiplash" lines to describe their serpentine curves and how they reverse themselves in unexpected ways. Art Nouveau appeared in nearly all art forms, from furniture and housewares to posters, typography, jewelry, glass, painting, sculpture, and architecture. Its sources include an antimechanical, return-to-crafts movement in England, the flat, curving shapes and patterns of Japanese woodcut prints (see page 45), decorative linear plant forms, and the art of Symbolist painters such as Paul Gauguin. Notice, for example, the line quality of the vinelike snake in Gauguin's SYMBOLIST SELF-PORTRAIT WITH HALO.

Although they drew from many sources, the artists who worked in the Art Nouveau style were antihistorical. They tried to free themselves from what they saw as superficial realism and the revivals of earlier historical styles. Art Nouveau reached its peak around 1900 and dominated the arts of Europe and the United States until World War I. The elegant linear embellishment in Victor Horta's STAIRCASE, TASSEL HOUSE, Henry van de Velde's twisting, turning, plantlike CANDELABRUM, and the flamboyant curves in Alphonse Mucha's poster advertising the bicycle company CYCLES PERFECTA are typical of Art Nouveau.

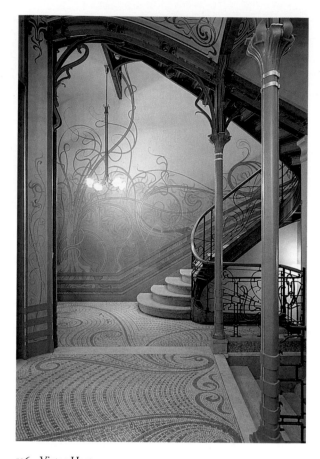

136 Victor Horta.
    STAIRCASE, TASSEL HOUSE, BRUSSELS. 1892–1893.
    © 2002 Artists Rights Society (ARS), NY/SOFAM, Brussels.

137 Henry van de Velde.
    CANDELABRUM. c. 1902.
    Silver-plated bronze.
    Industrial Arts Museum, Trondheim, Norway.

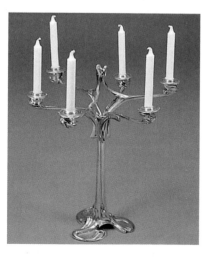

138 Alphonse Mucha.
    CYCLES PERFECTA. Poster. c. 1900.
    Poster Photo Archives, Posters Please, New York.
    © 2002 Artists Rights Society (ARS), NY/ADAGP, Paris.

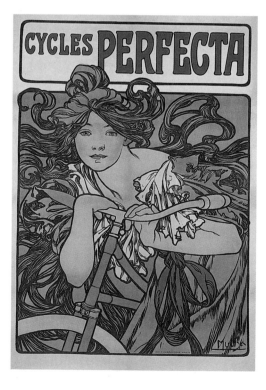

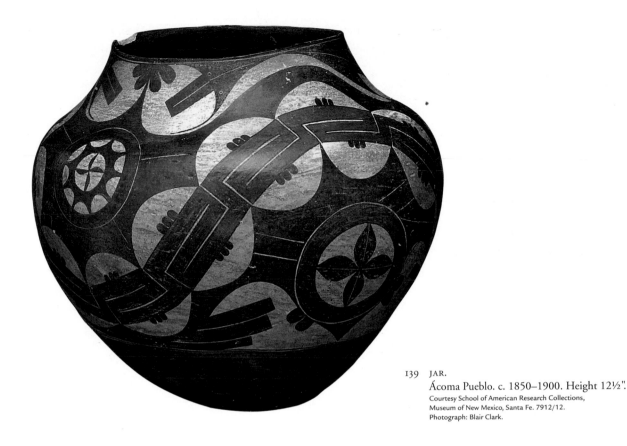

139 JAR.
Ácoma Pueblo. c. 1850–1900. Height 12½".
Courtesy School of American Research Collections,
Museum of New Mexico, Santa Fe. 7912/12.
Photograph: Blair Clark.

REGIONAL STYLE

Just as a cultural style may vary over time and give rise to different period styles, so it may vary across geographical space, leading to diverse regional styles. This variation typically occurs with language and speech patterns in different regions of a country, but it can also happen with art. Such regional variation may be due to a conscious decision, or it may be caused by a mere lack of communication over distance. For example, many art historians believe that a distinct regional variation was visible in abstract paintings produced in California compared with those made in New York in the 1940s and 1950s. Hindu sculpture of North India differs markedly from the same subjects sculpted in South India. There are several regional versions of Maya architecture, depending on whether a building is located in the Yucatan peninsula, the Guatemalan highlands, or the jungles of Chiapas. Traditional

Maori wood carving was done so differently in various regions of New Zealand that even inexperienced viewers can tell them apart. Renaissance painting in Venice is noticeably different from Renaissance painting in Florence or Rome.

Three ceramic jars made in different Pueblo villages in the late nineteenth and early twentieth centuries illustrate similarities and variations within the regional pottery style of the Pueblo peoples of New Mexico. The jars are similar in size and shape, but are different in surface decoration, with each bearing a design that is typical of the pottery produced by the artists of its Pueblo.

The JAR from Ácoma Pueblo is decorated in large swaths—the brick-red elements seem to wander over the entire surface, draping over the shoulders of the jar like a garland. This undulating form divides the pot into irregularly shaped large areas.

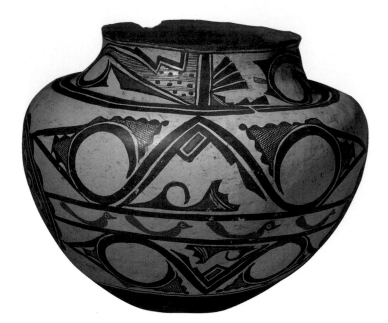

On the Zuni WATER JAR the design is divided by vertical lines into sections in which other lines define circular and triangular areas.

In San Ildefonso Pueblo, María Martínez and her husband developed another distinctive style, seen in our third example. The San Ildefonso BLACK ON BLACK STORAGE JAR has contrasting curvilinear and rectilinear shapes. This jar also features the subtle contrast of matte black and shiny black areas.

All three Pueblo styles exhibit related approaches to interacting figure and ground shapes. In Pueblo pottery generally, the painters (who are mostly women) employ abstract signs that symbolize natural forces, but in these three jars both the symbols and the organization of the painted designs are distinctly different from one another.

140 WATER JAR.
Zuni Pueblo. c. 1882.
National Museum of Natural History, Smithsonian Institution, Neg. #83–9425. Artifact #66395.
© Smithsonian Institution

141 María and Julian Martínez.
BLACK ON BLACK STORAGE JAR. c. 1942.
San Ildefonso Pueblo.
Matte black on polished black earthenware.
Height: 18¾"
#31959/12.
School of American Research Collections in the Museum of New Mexico.
Photograph: Doug Kahn.

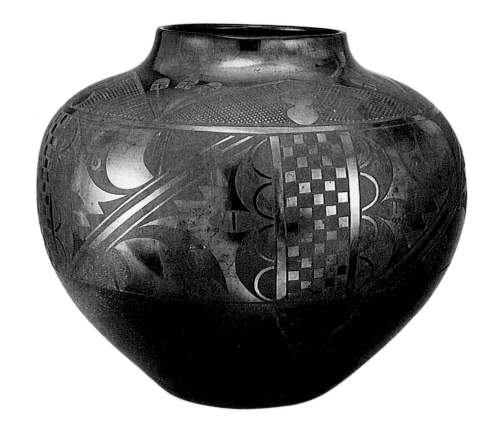

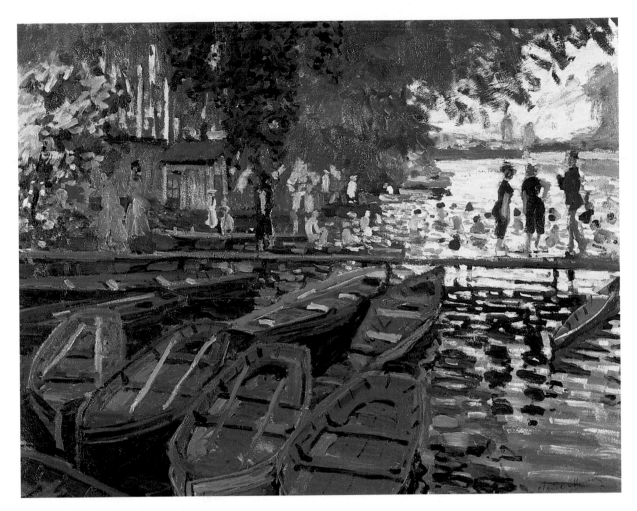

142 Claude Monet (1840–1926).
BATHERS AT LA GRENOUILLÈRE. 1859.
Oil on canvas. 28½" × 35⅞".
National Gallery, London. Art Resource, NY.

GROUP STYLE

Sometimes artists form alliances, exhibit together, and publicize their aims as a group as they develop and promote a distinctive style. This phenomenon is most common in modern European art, in which many such movements followed each other in quick succession. One of the best-known group styles is Impressionism, a late nineteenth-century French style of painting. Impressionists depicted scenes of contemporary life and landscape in a freely painted, light, colorful manner that was quite unlike the tightly polished, dark-toned canvases of the popular style of the academies of the time. Claude Monet and Pierre-Auguste Renoir, early advocates of this new approach, were part of a loosely knit group that included Edgar Degas, Edouard Manet, and Mary Cassatt, an American living in Paris.

Rather than depict myths or scenes from ancient Rome, members of the group painted their fleeting impressions of the leisure activities, urban scenes, and rural landscapes of their day. The Impressionists were among the first artists to paint outdoors, directly from their subjects. Until then, the standard practice was to sketch the subject, then complete the painting in the studio.

Another revolutionary feature of the style was the unfinished quality of the completed paintings.

In contrast to most other European painters of the time, Impressionists did not hide their brush strokes. Monet and Renoir developed the rapid painting techniques the Impressionists used for representing transitory effects of light. Monet's BATHING AT GRENOUILLÈRE and Renoir's BALL AT THE MOULIN DE LA GALETTE reveal the artists' interest in the ways light activates color to create the mood of a particular moment and place.

The Impressionists' subject matter included indoor as well as outdoor subjects and was largely urban and middle-class in outlook. Even when an Impressionist artist looked at a country landscape, it was often from a city dweller's point of view.

Although Impressionism is now the best-known and best-appreciated group style in Western art, it was not always so. From its inception, the approach was highly controversial, and this controversy led the artists to form a group and exhibit together in the 1870s and 1880s. The Impressionists' way of seeing and painting laid the groundwork for many of the revolutionary movements and styles of the twentieth century. (More discussion of Impressionism is found in chapter 21.)

143   Pierre-Auguste Renoir.
LE MOULIN DE LA GALETTE, MONTMARTE. 1876.
Oil on canvas. 51½" × 69".
Musée d'Orsay, Paris.
Giraudon/Art Resource, NY.

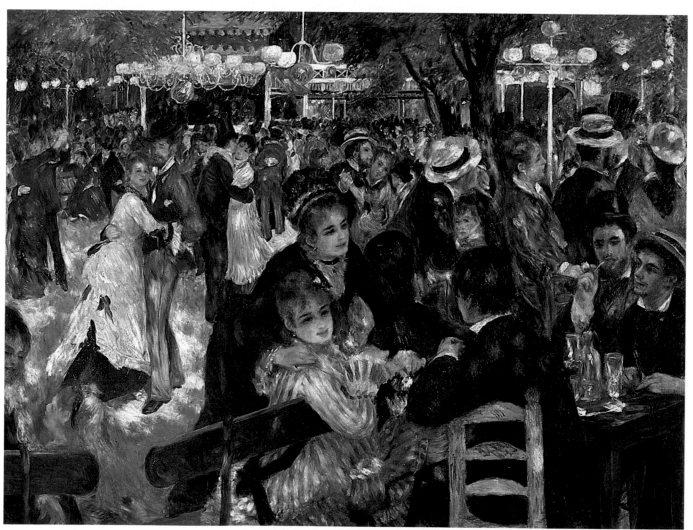

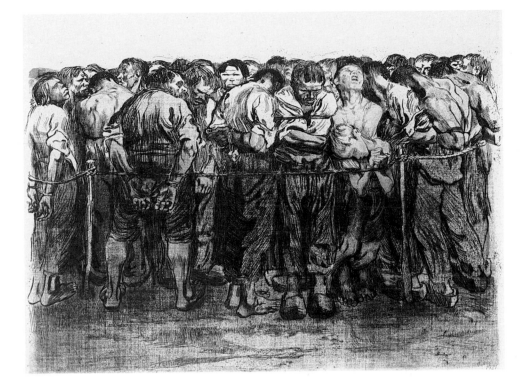

144 Käthe Kollwitz.
THE PRISONERS. 1908.
Etching and soft-ground.
12⅞" × 16⅝".
Library of Congress, Washington, D.C.
© 2002 Artists Rights Society (ARS),
New York/VG Bild–Kundt, Bonn.

PERSONAL STYLE

Just as each of us has a recognizable style of writing that is part of our expressive identity, individual artists often have characteristic modes of personal expression. The idea that a personal style is important or worth cultivating seems particularly characteristic of European art since the Renaissance. Most Westerners want to know who made a certain work, and they admire an artist who can develop and express a unique way of seeing. Personal styles evolve naturally as artists assimilate influences and evolve. An artist's early works are often linked with the art of their culture, period, peers, and teachers. As the artist's ideas evolve, wide variations in style can occur. Even when an artist's basic attitude remains the same, experiences, influences, and affiliations with other artists and art movements can generate major changes in style.

A majority of the world's cultures have held personal style to be a low priority. Some examples are Ancient Egyptian, Islamic, Medieval European, and (until recently) Native American. In all of these societies, signed works are uncommon, and a work is considered a success if its maker expresses the values of the culture by showing an understanding of its traditional art style.

The works of the two artists we consider next demonstrate individual, consistent points of view and therefore show fairly consistent personal styles, with some important variations over time. Each of these artists shows a unity of vision or purpose that differs markedly from her contemporaries. Although their lives overlapped in time, they came from different countries and held very different attitudes. Käthe Kollwitz was primarily interested in depicting people; Louise Nevelson preferred to work with nonrepresentational forms.

The personal style of Käthe Kollwitz is based on strong social conscience and a desire to use art as a tool against injustice. Although the three prints reproduced here were made over a period of twenty-six years, they are remarkably consistent in style and mood. THE PRISONERS, done in 1908, was one of a series of prints inspired by Kollwitz's interest in a peasant revolution that occurred in Germany in

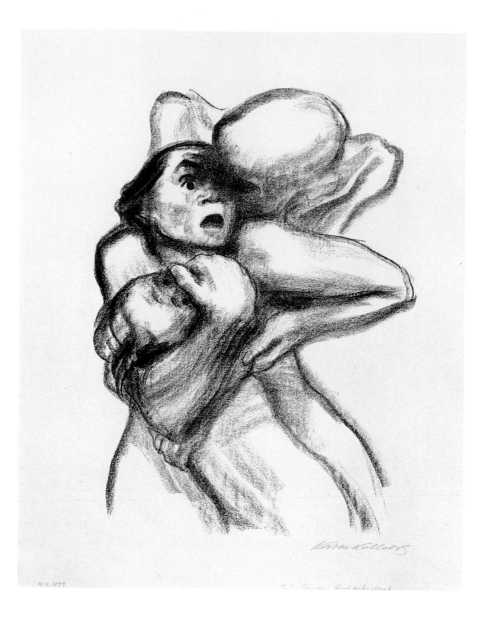

145   Käthe Kollwitz.
DEATH SEIZING A WOMAN. 1934.
Plate IV from the series DEATH
(1934–1936).
Lithograph, printed in black.
20" × 14⁷/₁₆".
The Museum of Modern Art, New York. Purchase.
© 2002 Artists Rights Society (ARS), NY/VG
Bild–Kundt, Bonn.

1525. She felt sympathy for the rebels, who wanted a reduction in their rents, liberty to move from one farm to another, and freer rights to hunt and fish. Their uprising was not successful, but Kollwitz saw it as foreshadowing many modern concerns about human rights. These prisoners could be from almost any period.

DEATH SEIZING A WOMAN was one of eight prints in Kollwitz's last major print series. She reduced the idea to its essentials to increase the print's dramatic impact. The mother clutches her child in a protective grasp and stares ahead in terror, as a symbolic figure of death presses down on her. Bold, converging lines focus attention on the mother's expression of fear. The strong sculptural quality in Kollwitz's drawings and prints developed from her study of Rembrandt, as well as from her own experience making sculpture.

Her SELF-PORTRAIT (see next page) depicts a person of insight, strength, and humility. Kollwitz's powerful graphic images are pleas for compassion. In the face of war, death, and human cruelty, they encourage empathy, charity, and conscience.

It is not surprising that Käthe Kollwitz became an artist of fiercely independent views. She was born in Königsberg, East Prussia, to parents who had strong moral and social convictions. The values of her father (a social-democrat) and her maternal grandfather (a rebel Lutheran pastor) were early influences on the direction of her life and art.

By the time Kollwitz was five, she was drawing extensively; by the time she was twelve, her father, who had already recognized her artistic potential, made sure she received the best art training available. At sixteen, Kollwitz made her first narrative drawings of workers. Although few academies or colleges accepted women, she continued her advanced studies with the help of several older artists and was finally able to attend the Women's Art School in Munich.

When she was nineteen, she realized that her ideas would be most powerfully expressed if she limited herself to black and white. From then on her work took the form of drawings, prints, and sculpture. In her diary she wrote:

In my own work I find that I must keep everything to a more and more abbreviated form . . . so that all the essentials are strongly stressed and the inessentials almost omitted.[1]

At twenty-three she married Karl Kollwitz, a doctor who had decided to practice medicine in one of Berlin's poorest districts. The couple acted as social workers, often welcoming troubled people into their home.

Kollwitz worked as a graphic artist and sculptor through her years of motherhood and right up to her death at seventy-seven. Her haunting images express strength, compassion, and self-discipline. A strong identification with the suffering of others is seen in her prints and drawings, many of which appear to be self-portraits. Although she lost a son in World War I and a grandson in World War II, her personal grief was secondary to her abiding concern for humanity. Kollwitz dreamed of a united world—one that would elevate human life above the misery she expressed in much of her art.

The tragic situation in post–World War I Germany led her to use art as a tool for social change. Believing that art should be for everyone, she chose not to make expensive paintings. Instead, she made inexpensive prints (posters, lithographs, and woodcuts) that ordinary people could afford. The seriousness of her art is balanced by her technical mastery and her ability to construct formal beauty.

In 1919, Kollwitz was elected the first woman member of the Prussian Academy of Arts in Berlin, a position that included full professor status. But her anti-Nazi sympathies caused her expulsion from that teaching position in 1933. The Nazis considered her degenerate and forbade exhibition of her work.

She died in 1945, just days before World War II ended, outlawed in her own country but recognized internationally as one of the world's outstanding artists. Prior to the middle of the twentieth century, Kollwitz was one of the few women artists whose greatness was publicly recognized.

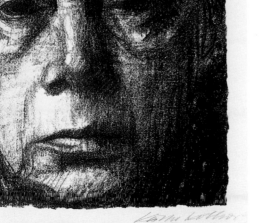

146   Käthe Kollwitz (German, 1867–1945).
SELF-PORTRAIT. 1934.
Lithograph. 8 1/16" × 7 3/16".

Louise Nevelson was born more than forty years after Kollwitz, yet both lived through the first forty-five years of this century. Whereas Kollwitz was interested in figurative art, Nevelson's work is nonrepresentational.

Nevelson began making sculpture out of scrap wood in the 1950s. She was an early exponent and leading practitioner of sculpture as environment. Some of her relief walls extend around entire rooms. In the work pictured behind her on the following page, she carefully combined pieces of wood with bits of old furniture and architectural trim. Each compartment is both a composition in itself and part of a complex total form. Nevelson painted such stacked-box constructions a single unifying color, usually black, white, or gold—colors she considered aristocratic.

In the late 1960s and 1970s, Nevelson turned from wood to plastic and aluminum, then to steel—a material suitable for large outdoor works. SHADOWS AND FLAGS, a group of seven pieces, stands in what is now Louise Nevelson Plaza in New York City.

Calling herself an "architect of shadows," Nevelson was concerned with space and shadow in all her assemblages. She described her sculpture in various media as variations on a theme, revealing a unity of approach to form. She stated:

Different people have different memories. Some have memories for words, some for action—mine happens to be for form.[2]

Our discussion of the purposes and language of art has laid the groundwork for us to consider in the next chapter how individual works are evaluated.

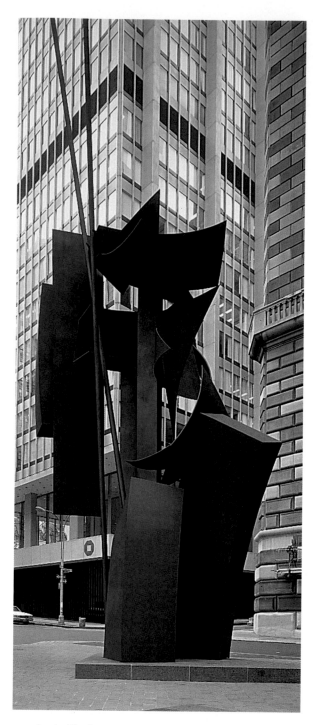

147 Louise Nevelson.
Detail of SHADOWS AND FLAGS.
Louise Nevelson Plaza, New York. 1977–1978.
Painted cor-ten steel. Height 72'.
One of seven sculptures.
Photograph: © 1978 Tom Crane, Photography Inc.
© 2002 Estate of Louise Nevelson/Artists Rights Society (ARS), NY.

It wasn't until she was in her fifties that Louise Nevelson was considered a leading American sculptor.

Born Louise Berliawsky in Russia, she was brought to the United States by her parents when she was five. Her family settled in Rockland, Maine, where they lived near a few other Jewish families, isolated from the life of the town.

In school, problems with the new language caused her to discover that she could better express herself through art. Her success in drawing gave her the sense of self-worth she needed and led her to dream of becoming an artist. Of the visual arts, she later said: "It's the quickest way of communicating, and I think it's the most joyous."[3]

After graduating from high school she married businessman Charles Nevelson, partly as a way to escape the limits of her small town. The couple moved to New York City when she was twenty. There—following the birth of her son—she pursued her interest in the arts by studying music, drama, poetry, and dance, as well as the visual arts.

Focusing her career, Nevelson—now thirty— began to study art seriously at the Art Students League. Then, in 1931, in a gesture of indepen-

dence, she sailed alone to Europe to study with Hans Hofmann, the foremost teacher of the new abstract art.

In her search for self-fulfillment, she divorced her husband and for more than twenty years struggled to survive as an artist. Despite many years of rejection and neglect, Nevelson managed to develop a highly original body of work.

Early in her career, Nevelson worked in a variety of styles and media, making drawings, prints, and paintings, as well as sculpture in stone, bronze, clay, and wood. It was not until the 1950s that she developed her mature style based on solid geometric forms. Nevelson's best-known works are large assemblages made up of numerous boxes filled with "found" wood fragments she picked up on the streets of New York City and in vacant lots and lumber yards.

She had this to say about the origin and evolution of her constructive style:

I never wanted to make sculpture. I didn't want to make anything like that. I felt my great search was for myself, the inner being of myself, and that was the best way I knew to project how I was feeling about everything in the world. Consequently, it wasn't that I made anything for anybody. Now, we call it "work" and I don't like to call it work at all. It really is a projection of an awareness. People don't un-

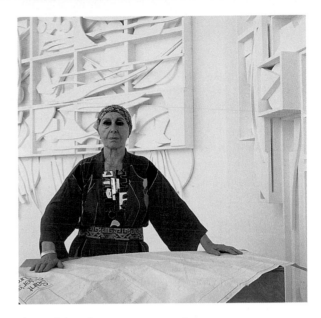

148   **LOUISE NEVELSON.** Photograph: © 1984 Hans Namuth.

derstand that when you project from yourself you are really at the height of your awareness, and that means you are at your best.[4]

Nevelson's sculpture demonstrates her belief that, in art as well as in life, it is not what you start with that counts; it is what you make of it. From scrap, she created regal structures with an air of timelessness. They are at once old and new. They have lived, and they are alive. Nevelson captured the essence of the art process:

The joy, if you want to call it that, of creation, is that it opens life to you. . . . It opens and you become more aware and more aware and that is the wonder of it.[5]

CHAPTER SIX

EVALUATION AND CRITICISM

Before exploring further the many ways of making art, it is important that we consider two interrelated issues: art evaluation (is the art worthwhile?) and art criticism (who decides whether it is worthwhile?).

EVALUATION

Have you ever heard someone say, "I don't know anything about art, but I know what I like"? Each of us decides what she or he likes or doesn't like many times a day. When we select one thing over another, or appreciate the special value of something, we are evaluating.

Creative experience is also a process of selecting and evaluating. For the artist, the creative process involves selecting and evaluating each component before deciding to include it in the final form. After the work is completed, the viewer's enjoyment comes from sensing the quality that has been achieved. How do artists and viewers evaluate art to determine whether it has quality?

Quality is relative. How a work of art is evaluated varies from person to person, from culture to culture, and from age to age. In Mexico before the Spanish Conquest, the Aztecs judged art to be good if it continued the style of the Toltecs, an ancient neighboring people that the Aztecs admired. In traditional Chinese art criticism, painters were urged to go beyond mere representation of the outward appearance of their subject matter. Good art was a matter of successfully understanding and communicating the inner spirit or "life breath" of the subject. If an artist failed to attain this goal, the term used to describe such modest achievement was "skillful."

In the European tradition, few famous artists or styles have had unchanging reputations. The Impressionist painters of the late nineteenth century were ridiculed by critics, museum curators, and the public. Their style differed too radically from those of their predecessors for easy acceptance in their own time. Today, Impressionist paintings have an honored place in museums and are eagerly sought by the public.

Value judgments in art necessarily involve subjectivity. It is not possible to measure artistic quality objectively in the same way that we measure the wingspan of an airplane or the capacity of a computer. In this regard it is useful for us to compare SHY GLANCE, a work generally regarded as "bad," with almost any of the other portraits illustrated in this book. The painter of SHY GLANCE lacks skill in color shading (the cheek is blotchy), anatomy (the eyebrow is too narrow and the forehead bulges), composition (it is difficult to tell positive from negative space), and brushwork (the hair and eyelashes!).

The feeling it communicates is almost embarrassingly sweet. Nevertheless, the work has an obvious sincerity and enthusiasm that may lead some viewers to enjoy it even if they regard it as a failure.

Those who seek a yardstick for measuring artistic quality often apply some of the principles the ancient Greeks believed art must contain: truth, beauty, order, harmony, and moral goodness. These qualities also inspire the best art of the Renaissance (see chapter 17), which many believe to have been among the greatest art periods in European history. In the late twentieth century, however, there is much less agreement on the meaning of these concepts than there was in either of those earlier periods. This divergence of opinion on artistic quality generally has two causes: the rapid changes taking place in modern society, and the increased drawing together and interchange among world cultures.

Prior to the nineteenth and twentieth centuries, cultural changes occurred slowly. People within each society had generally agreed-upon values and standards in nearly all areas, including the arts. During our century of rapid change, many artists have intentionally sought to go beyond or to deny long-established traditions. Related shifts in thinking have occurred in science and philosophy.

Strangely, it is easier for many people to accept the work of pioneering scientists than that of pioneering artists. If we close our eyes and minds to new work that is hard to understand, we will miss the opportunity to learn from fresh insights. Our concept of what is "good art" changes as we mature and develop our aesthetic awareness and critical thinking skills.

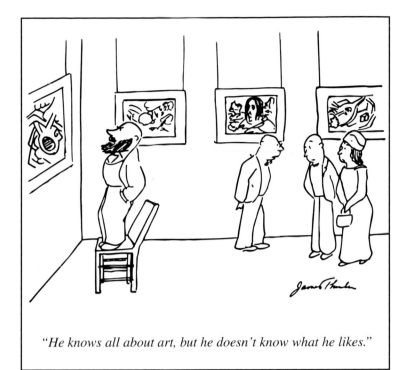

"He knows all about art, but he doesn't know what he likes."

149   James Thurber.
Men, Women and Dogs. Copyright © 1943 by James Thurber.
Copyright renewed 1971 by Helen Thurber and Rosemary A. Thurber.
Reprinted by arrangement with Rosemary A. Thurber and the Barbara
Hogenson Agency.

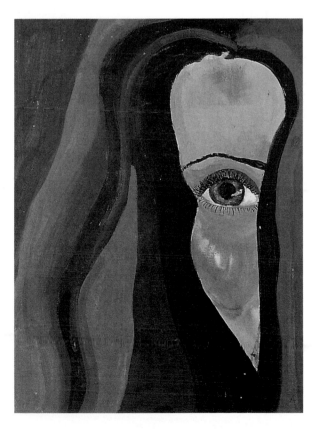

150   Dawn Marie Jingagian.
SHY GLANCE. 1976.
Acrylic on canvas. 18" × 24".
Museum of Bad Art, Dedham, MA.

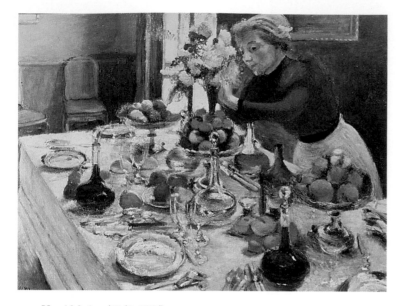

151   Henri Matisse (1869–1954).
LA DESSERTE. 1897.
Oil on canvas. 39½" × 51½".
Private collection/Bridgeman Art Library International Ltd., London/New York. PHD30074.
© 2002 Succession H. Matisse, Paris/Artists Rights Society (ARS), NY.

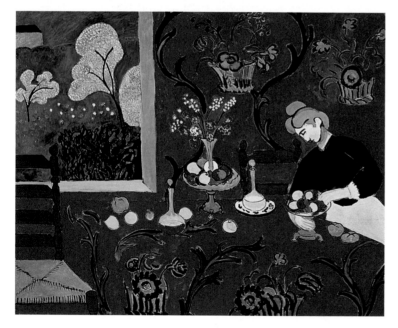

152   Henri Matisse (1869–1954).
HARMONY IN RED. 1908–1909.
Oil on canvas. 72" × 97".
State Hermitage Museum, St. Petersburg, Russia. Scala/Art Resource, NY.
© 2002 Succession H. Matisse, Paris/Artists Rights Society (ARS), NY.

An artist's own process of evaluation can cause a major shift in the evolution of his or her own work. Within little more than a decade, 1897–1909, the young Henri Matisse made a radical change in style. The depiction of light in Matisse's painting LA DESSERTE shows the influence of Impressionism. If this were as far as he progressed, Matisse would not be considered one of the twentieth century's leading artists. Building on all he had learned from both traditional and innovative artists, he began searching for his own path. Between 1908 and 1917, and after revolutionizing his use of color, Matisse made trips to Algeria and Morocco, where Islamic arts inspired him to use bold shapes in rhythmic patterns.

Matisse's painting HARMONY IN RED shows his break-through change. The subject matter is almost identical to that in LA DESSERTE, yet the overall effect could hardly be more different. The dominant warm red, set off by blues and greens, brings the tablecloth and wall together. Although the subjects—table, room, and window-framed landscape—immediately suggest depth, Matisse translated the third dimension of the real world into a lively flat surface. The tabletop has become an ambiguous plane of color upon which bright shapes rest weightlessly. Every area of the painting is charged with vitality. It was these qualities in Matisse's work that greatly influenced generations that followed.

Many people may find themselves baffled by works of art whose cultural roots are foreign to them. For example, Michelangelo's PIETÀ (see page 86) would be strange, if not repugnant, to a person from a traditional Islamic culture, where representation of the human form in art is considered blasphemous. Likewise, the hastily brushed landscape painting by Shen Zhou (see page 55) may mystify Western viewers who are unfamiliar with the Zen Buddhist philosophies that helped to give it birth.

When we look at a work of art and find that we are pleased (or displeased), it is useful for us to know why. We tend to like what is familiar and easy to comprehend. In order to increase our enjoyment of art, it is necessary to increase our visual awareness and knowledge. Teachers, authors, and art critics can offer their insights and add new dimensions to our understanding. With effort, we can learn to recognize aesthetic quality even in works we would not want to live with.

Whether you are approaching art for your own enjoyment or for a class assignment, it is most rewarding to begin with an open, receptive mind—to go beyond prejudgments. Give yourself time to get acquainted and to respond.

In addition to making drawings or composition studies of significant works, one of the best ways to experience a work of art is to write about it. When the writing describes a visual form, the process of interpretive translation from visual to verbal can greatly heighten your personal experience not only of the particular work being written about, but also of all subsequent encounters with art and art-making. Levels of awareness in other areas also may be enhanced.

Writing even a paragraph or brief essay causes you to take time to engage in seeing and responding to a work of art, to become conscious of the reasons for your initial gut-level reaction. Senses, emotions, and memories come together with knowledge as you think about how to communicate through words what you see and feel.

You might start by considering what you see. Describe its physical qualities. What is it made of? How big is it? Go into detail about what you see. As you are writing, describe the work as if you were helping a blind person "see" it. What colors and shapes are used? What subjects (if any) are represented?

What you have just done is the beginning of formal analysis—a discussion of the way various visual elements and design principles affect viewers' thoughts and feelings. Terms introduced in chapters 2 through 5 will be helpful; use them to describe the use of elements such as line, shape, color, and space. How was the work designed? Is it balanced? What is emphasized? Rhythm? Proportion? Contrast? Does it have unity as well as variety?

Follow the analysis of form with a subjective interpretation of the meaning or symbolism of the work. How does the work make you feel? How or why does it evoke these feelings? Think again about your first description. At this point, go well beyond "I like it" or "I don't like it." Then inform yourself about the cultural background of the object and the artist, keeping in mind that the functions of art vary widely across the globe. If it came from a culture remote from your own, assess how well it meets or expresses the values of that culture.

Can you tell what the artist had in mind? If so, was that intention realized? Was it worth the effort? Is it valuable from your point of view?

The process just described is a simplified version of the one used by an art critic.

ART CRITICISM

The term *art criticism* refers to making discriminating judgments, both favorable and unfavorable. Art criticism may include the above process (description, formal analysis, interpretation, and value judgment) and also biographical and historical information.

Biographical or historical information often provides clues to a work's context and therefore to its intended meaning. Criteria on which many art professionals agree include degree of originality, sensitivity to the appropriate choice and use of materials, and consistency of concept, design, and execution.

Art critics evaluate art exhibitions and events and publish their views in newspapers, magazines, exhibition catalogues, and books. While critics or teachers may express personal judgment on a work, one of their primary functions is to help others look closely at the art and make their own evaluations. By opening the dialogue for others to discuss the issues, critics help viewers clarify their own positions regarding meaning and quality.

Ideally, each person who views a work of art will make his or her own evaluations of its quality, but preconceptions often cloud the process. Many of us read the artists' names and titles of works in museums before we allow ourselves to respond. For example, we have heard that Leonardo da Vinci's MONA LISA (chapter 17) is a great work of art. If this assertion is foremost in our minds when we see

MONA LISA, our direct experience of the painting is affected by our preconception—by the idea that it is great art hanging in the Louvre Museum in Paris. This preconception is increased by the fact that it is largely obscured by the crowds of people who flock to see it. The painting's fame not only prevents many people from making their own judgments; it also causes the gallery to be so crowded that we can barely see it at all.

The art market can also cloud the problem of evaluating art. The artistic fashions of the moment, and the accompanying high prices, may be the result of market "hype" rather than the presence of new art of high quality or the rediscovery of earlier art of long-standing value. When a work sells at an auction for thousands, even millions, of dollars, does its high price make it an exceptionally good work of art?

The two principal functions of art criticism can best be summarized as education (helping the public understand art) and evaluation (making judgments about it based on values or beliefs). Although both functions are important, most critics practicing today probably see themselves more as teachers than as judges.

An example of the educational function of art criticism occurs in the work of American Willard Huntington Wright, who was active in the early twentieth century. At that time, modern art was highly controversial; many thought it represented insanity, anarchism, or even the decline of civilization. Wright took it upon himself to explain modern art in numerous magazine articles and in a book he authored in 1915. Modern art, he said, was not revolutionary, but evolutionary. It was a logical outgrowth of tendencies occurring in art for at least the previous fifty years. Writing of a 1917 exhibition of American modern art, he said, "Not one man represented in this exhibition is either a charlatan or a maniac; and there is not a picture here which, in the light of the ideal, is not intelligi-

ble and logically constructed in accordance with the subtler and more complex creative spirit which is now animating the world of art."[1] He attempted to show that just as science progresses, art continues to evolve toward new forms.

An example of evaluative art criticism exists in the work of the most famous art critic in the history of China, Dong Qichang, who lived in the sixteenth and early seventeenth centuries. He divided Chinese painting into two schools, Northern and Southern, and said that the Southern School was the source of most of the innovations in art of his country. Southern painting was free, spontaneously composed, more loosely brushed, and done primarily by artists who worked in isolation. For these reasons it was more creative than Northern School art, which was tightly brushed, carefully composed, and usually done by artists who worked for royal courts and academies. Works by "Northern" artist Tang Yin and "Southern" artist Yu-Jian are pictured in chapter 18.

Even though some "Northern" artists lived in the South of China, and vice versa, Dong Qichang's division was not merely his personal taste; the distinction between the schools paralleled the differences in the two leading schools of Buddhism at the time that he was writing. The fact that he could support his quality judgments by recourse to philosophy and religion gave his pronouncements about art great weight with his contemporaries and succeeding generations.

Whatever his or her point of view, the task of a critic is to make well-supported judgments, not comments based only on personal taste. He or she must establish criteria broad enough to encompass a wide range of aesthetic styles and intentions.

Although we can describe, analyze, interpret, and appraise art, there is no absolutely correct way to evaluate art. The process of evaluation is rewarding in itself because it draws the viewer into the creative process.

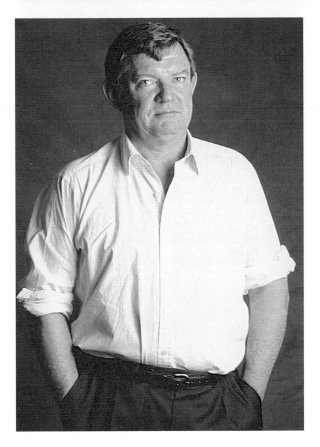

153   ROBERT HUGHES.
Photograph: Joyce Ravid/Outline.

As his 1991 book title suggests, Robert Hughes is *Nothing If Not Critical*. The outspoken art critic became known to millions for his art reviews in *Time* magazine and for his 1980 television series on modern art and the accompanying book, both titled *The Shock of the New.*

Born in Australia, Hughes dropped out of the Sydney University School of Architecture in his senior year to write his first book, *The Art of Australia.* He was working as a cartoonist for a small magazine in Sydney in 1958 when the art critic was fired. Hughes remembers the editor rushing into his office shouting, "I've just fired the art critic . . . you must know something about art. You are now the art critic."[2]

Hughes emigrated to England in 1964 and "lucked into" freelance critic jobs with London newspapers in 1966, but he says he didn't really get in gear until he got to America in 1970. He has been the art critic for *Time* since 1970, sending in twenty-four art reviews a year from his home on Shelter Island, at the tip of Long Island, New York.

Whether he is writing about a contemporary artist or one who lived hundreds of years ago, Hughes' personal convictions are passionately stated. He is at his most witty and provocative when he writes about contemporary art, and he can be as eloquent when he contemptuously dismisses works as when he raves about particular pieces and artists.

Drawing . . . is not what [this artist] does. . . . He never learned to do it, and probably never will. . . . The line has all the verve of chewed string. It starts here and finishes there, but that's all you can say for it: nothing happens along the way.[3]

Hughes prefers to write about art he likes—and there is a great deal that he does. Hughes admires artists who, like himself, are forthright, brave, and without pretense. He wrote a rave review of an exhibit of the works of nineteenth-century painter Georges Seurat:

One of the miracles of his art is his ability to analyze light, not through the simple juxtaposition of dabs of color but by a layering of tiny brush marks built up from the underpainted ground, so that the eventual surface becomes a fine-grained pelt, seamless and yet infinitely nuanced, from which captured light slowly radiates.[4]

Although his writings are widely read, Hughes is not among the handful of twentieth-century critics who have had a strong influence on the directions and fortunes of art. Often at odds with art galleries and museums, Hughes is a critic not only of art and artists, but of the cultural context in which art is created, exhibited, and sold. He is recognized as a "quixotic upholder of a cultural and intellectual standard he alternately mourns, celebrates, and nurtures."[5]

In 1997, Hughes produced a major book and an accompanying eight-hour television series titled *American Visions: The Epic History of American Art.* One reviewer called it a "triumph of popular criticism." It is a refreshingly idiosyncratic survey of art in America rather than a party-line history of American art. It is not art as isolated elite decoration, but art within the richly varied, always changing contexts and places of American life, shaped by and at times shaping "the deep currents moving in the society around it."

Hughes' critical approach is a valuable one. He believes that the work of a critic is to open up the discussion, to challenge us to make up our own minds after we have read his opinion. "Criticism isn't about saying 'I think this, therefore you should think this.' It's about getting people to look and to think, and to do it on their own," Hughes states firmly.[6]

. . . or, *How to Enjoy Looking at Art Without Being Overwhelmed by Museum Fatigue*

Art museums can be mind-expanding or sleep-inducing, depending on how you approach them. It is a mistake to enter a museum with the belief that you should like everything you see—or even that you should see everything that is there. Without selective viewing, the visitor to a large museum is likely to come down with a severe case of museum exhaustion.

The English word *museum* comes from the Greek *mouseion,* "place of the muses." "Muse" indicates the spirit or power believed to be capable of inspiring and watching over poets, musicians, and other artists—or any source of inspiration. A museum is for musing, a place devoted to collecting, caring for, studying, and displaying objects of lasting value and interest.

Unfortunately, museum visitors are often overwhelmed by the many rooms full of art and background information. Some may feel that they should have an extensive knowledge of art history before they even enter a museum. Even the entrance to a museum can be a bit intimidating ("Step this way. Serious art. No smiling.") or it can be inviting and welcoming ("Come on in. Relax. Make yourself comfortable.").

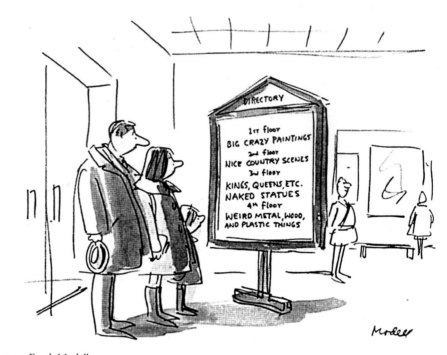

154   Frank Modell.
© The New Yorker Collection, 1983
Courtesy of the Cartoonbank.com. All Rights Reserved.

There is a way to enjoy an art museum without experiencing overload. If you were to go to a fine restaurant and try to sample everything on the menu, you would probably get sick. In both restaurants and museums, selection is the key to a positive experience.

It makes sense to approach an art museum the way a seasoned traveler approaches a city for a first visit: Find out what there is to see. In the museum, inquire about the schedule of special shows, then see those exhibitions and outstanding works that interest you. Museums are in the process of rethinking their buildings and collections in order to meet the needs of changing populations and changing values. It is not unusual to find video exhibits, performances of all kinds, and film showings as part of regular museum programming.

If you are visiting without a specific exhibition in mind, follow your interests and instincts. Browsing can be highly rewarding. Zero in on what you feel are the highlights, savoring favorite works and unexpected discoveries.

If you are traveling abroad, you will find *Mona Winks* to be a useful guide to many of Europe's top museums. This light-hearted book includes a collection of self-guided tours covering the highlights of some twenty European museums and cultural centers.[7]

Don't stay too long in a museum. Take breaks. Perhaps there is a garden or cafe in which you can pause for a rest. The quality of your experience is not measured by the amount of time you spend in the galleries or how many works you see. The most rewarding experiences can come from finding something that "speaks" to you, then sitting and enjoying it in leisurely contemplation.

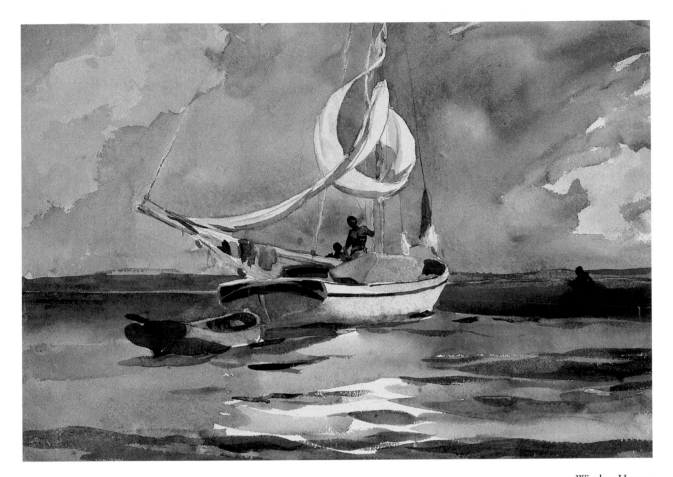

PART THREE
Two-Dimensional Arts

CONSIDER . . .

Have you ever said, I can't draw? Does not being able to draw mean you can't write your name or draw a map? What do people really mean when they say they can't draw?

Imagine an art gallery containing two framed artworks. One is a large, colorful painting and the other is a small black-and-white print. Would you approach each of them in the same way? How might your experience of them be different?

Can exposure to television, with its immediacy and vivid action, dull one's response to painting?

A primary function of the camera is that it "stops" time. We use photography to keep exact records of visual events. Does the camera ever lie?

Are new communications media such as the Internet, fax machines, and cable television bringing the world closer together? Are they building understanding between people of different cultures?

CHAPTER SEVEN

DRAWING

The desire to draw is as natural as the desire to talk. As children, we draw long before we learn to read and write. In fact, making letter forms is a kind of drawing—especially when we first learn to "write." Some of us continue to enjoy drawing; others return to drawing as adults. Those who no longer draw probably came to believe they did not draw well enough to suit themselves or others. Yet drawing is a learned process. It is a way of seeing and communicating, a way of paying attention.

In the most basic sense, to draw means to pull, push, or drag a marking tool across a surface to leave a line or mark. Most people working in the visual arts utilize drawing as a major tool for visual thinking—for recording and developing ideas.

Because drawing is less abstract than writing, developing drawing skills may be easier than learning to write. Drawing is the most immediate and accessible way to communicate through imagery. Through drawing we can share ideas, feelings, experiences, and imaginings. Sometimes a drawing does several of these things simultaneously.

The lines in Pamela Davis's drawing of CAROL are lively and inventive, describing the way the subject appeared to Davis as she drew. She shaded the central area by smearing the felt-tip pen lines with wet fingers.

Many people find it valuable to keep a sketchbook handy to serve as a visual diary, a place to de-

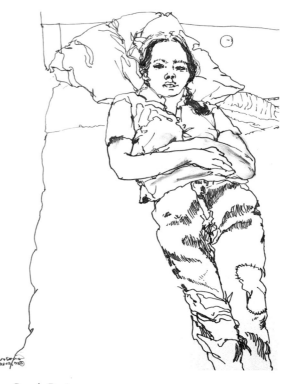

155   Pamela Davis.
CAROL. 1973.
Felt-tip pen. 19⅓" × 17".
Courtesy of the artist.

velop and maintain drawing skills and to note whatever catches the eye or imagination. From sketchbook drawings, some ideas may develop and reach maturity as finished drawings or complete works in other media. Leonardo da Vinci kept many of his exploratory drawings and writings in notebooks. He drew this study of THREE SEATED FIGURES next to idea sketches for some mechanical devices. Another study, DESIGNS FOR INVENTIONS, is the work of Iris, age eight. These two sets of drawings made to aid visual thinking—one by a world-renowned artist, scientist, and engineer and one by an untrained child—underscore the essence of the thinking and drawing process.

Drawing from direct observation is neither more nor less important than drawing from imagination or memory. However, the process of drawing from observation helps people learn to see more attentively and develops the ability to draw from either memory or imagination. In *The Zen of Seeing* (from which the PENCIL DRAWING is taken), medical doctor Frederick Franck describes drawing as a means to heighten visual awareness:

I have learned that what I have not drawn, I have never really seen, and that when I start drawing an ordinary thing I realize how extraordinary it is, sheer miracle: the branching of a tree, the structure of a dandelion's seed puff.[1]

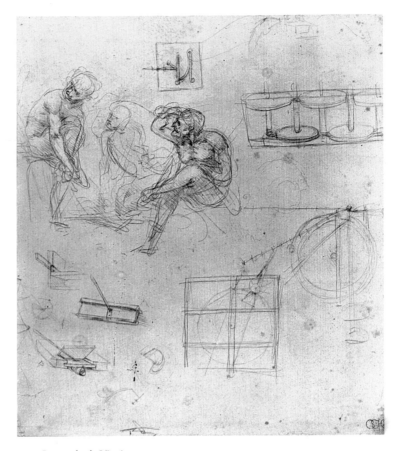

156 Leonardo da Vinci.
THREE SEATED FIGURES AND STUDIES OF MACHINERY. c. 1490.
Silver-point on very pale pink, prepared surface.
Ashmolean Museum, Oxford.

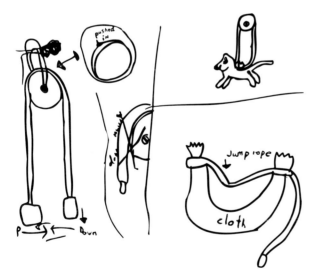

157 Iris Chamberlain, age 8.
DESIGNS FOR INVENTIONS. 1992.
Felt-tip pen. 8⅓" × 11".

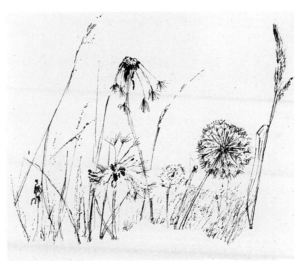

158 Frederick Franck.
PENCIL DRAWING from his book *The Zen of Seeing*.
© 1973, reprinted with permission of Alfred A. Knopf, Inc.

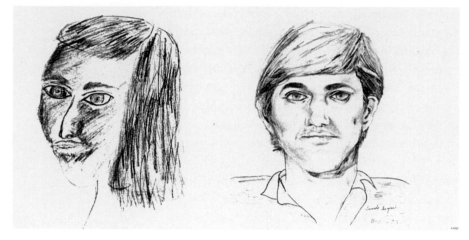

159   Gerardo Campos,
      September 2, 1973 (left).
      Gerardo Campos,
      November 10, 1973 (right).
      From Betty Edwards,
      Drawing on the Right Side
      of the Brain.

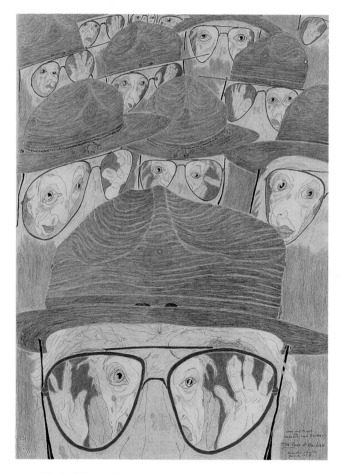

160   Elizabeth Layton (1909–1993).
      THE EYES OF THE LAW. 1985. Crayon, colored
      pencil on paper.
      Spencer Museum of Art: Gift of Don Lambert and the Artist.

Through her classes and her book *Drawing on the Right Side of the Brain,* Betty Edwards has created effective sequences of mind-releasing exercises that enable people to draw what they see. When her students make a shift from verbally dominated preconceptions to pure visual awareness, they really begin to see what they are looking at. Before-and-after student drawings, such as those shown above, show the typical change in the ability to see—and thus to draw in a representational style—achieved in just a few weeks.

Learning to draw to your own satisfaction can transform your outlook on life. Elizabeth Layton was in her late sixties and had been suffering from depression for many years when she took a drawing course that "turned her around." She learned to create representational images with blind (or pure) contour drawing. This drawing method emphasizes the edge lines of a subject. After learning contour drawing, Layton drew with enthusiasm and gained wide recognition for the quality of her drawings.

Her most common subject was herself and her experiences, which she learned to depict with a keen and sometimes ironic visual sense. Her 1985 drawing THE EYES OF THE LAW is a humorous collection of the reflections in a crowd of policemen's mirrored sunglasses. In each lens we see a different view of her aged face.

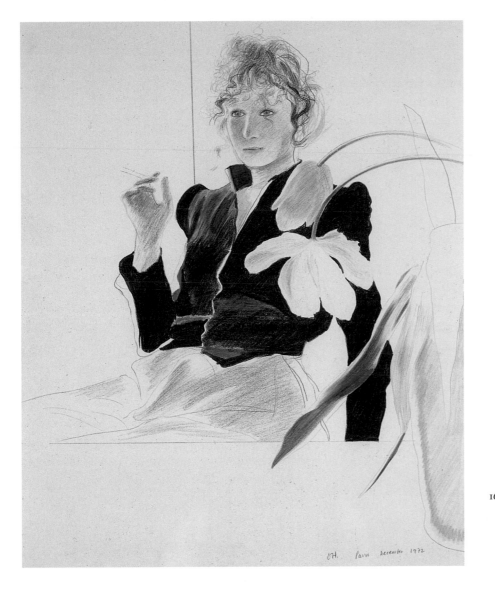

161 David Hockney.
CELIA IN A BLACK
DRESS WITH WHITE
FLOWERS. 1972.
Crayon. 17" × 14".
© David Hockney 1972.

In drawing, as in every human activity, it seems that some people have more natural aptitude than others. David Hockney feels his great interest in drawing spurred him to draw frequently, and this constant practice developed whatever ability he had. And it seemed he was drawing all the time—twelve hours a day when he was in art school. Hockney's intriguing crayon drawing CELIA IN A BLACK DRESS WITH WHITE FLOWERS exemplifies the level of expertise he developed. Hockney wrote:

Obviously I had some facility, more than other people, but sometimes facility comes because one is more interested in looking at things, examining them, and making a representation of them, more interested in the visual world, than other people are.[2]

Some artists, like Picasso, demonstrated exceptional drawing ability as young children. Others, such as Paul Cézanne and Vincent van Gogh, did not show obvious drawing ability when they committed themselves to art. Their skills developed through diligent effort. In spite of early difficulties, they succeeded in teaching themselves to draw. Seeing and drawing are learned processes, not just inborn gifts.

Van Gogh learned a great deal about both seeing and painting through his practice of drawing. He was just beginning his short career as an artist when he made the drawing of a CARPENTER shown below. Although stiff, and clumsy in proportion, the drawing reveals van Gogh's careful observation and attention to detail. OLD MAN WITH HIS HEAD IN HIS HANDS, made two years after his CARPENTER, shows that van Gogh had learned a great deal about seeing and drawing in those two years. By this time, van Gogh was able to portray the old man's grief as well as the solidity of the figure and to give a suggestion of his surroundings. The groups of parallel lines appear to have been drawn quickly, with sensitivity and self-assurance.

Good drawing may appear deceptively simple, yet it can take years of patient work to be able to draw easily and effectively. According to one account, a person viewing a portrait drawn by Matisse with only a few lines asked the artist with some disgust, "How long did it take you to do this?" "Forty years," replied Matisse (see his SELF-PORTRAIT on page 90).

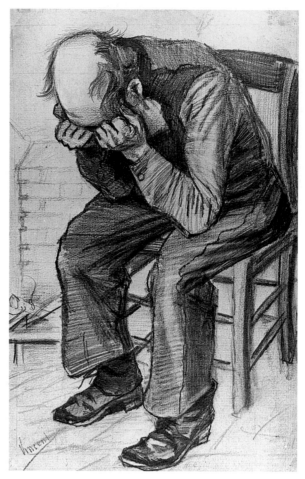

163   Vincent van Gogh.
OLD MAN WITH HIS HEAD IN HIS HANDS. 1882.
Pencil on paper. 19¹¹⁄₁₆" × 12³⁄₁₆".
Vincent van Gogh Foundation/Van Gogh Museum, Amsterdam.

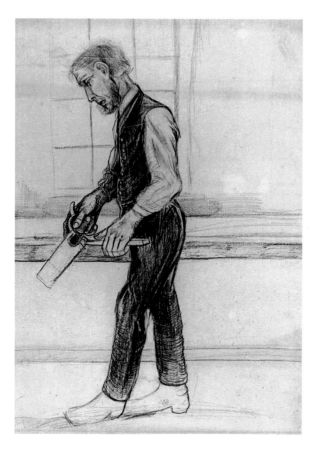

162   Vincent van Gogh.
CARPENTER. C. 1880.
Black crayon. 22" × 15".
Rijksmuseum Kröller-Müller, Otterlo, Netherlands.

Today the art of Vincent van Gogh is internationally known and admired. It is hard to believe that van Gogh worked as an artist for only ten years and that during his lifetime his art was known only to a few. In fact, he sold only one painting.

Van Gogh was born in the Netherlands. His father was a minister, his grandfather a famous preacher; three uncles, and later his brother, were art dealers—a background that paved the way for Vincent's lifelong concern with both art and religion.

From age sixteen, he worked for a firm of art dealers, first in The Hague and later in London and Paris. During this period he began what was to become his famous correspondence with his brother Theo. It is primarily through these extraordinary letters (published in the book *Dear Theo*) that we have come to know van Gogh's short, intense, yet highly creative life.

After six years working for art dealers, he returned to the Netherlands to study theology. In 1878, at age twenty-five, he became a lay preacher among impoverished miners in Belgium. Although not successful at preaching, van Gogh was effective at nursing victims of mining disasters and disease. When his compassion spurred him to give most of his own clothes and other possessions to the poor, the missionary society that had hired him dismissed him for his literal interpretation of Christ's teachings.

Van Gogh remained in Belgium, living in acute poverty and spiritual turmoil until he decided to apply himself to becoming an artist. He made his commitment to art not because he possessed any obvious talent, but because he saw art as the means through which he could communicate with others. Although determined to be a painter, van Gogh believed that he had to master drawing before he allowed himself to use color. Miners and farm laborers were his first models. As he worked on developing his skill, Vincent—the name he used to sign his finished works—was supported by his brother Theo, who regularly sent money and provided encouragement through his letters.

Van Gogh studied briefly at the art academy in Antwerp, Belgium, but he was largely self-taught. In 1886 he joined his brother in Paris, where he met the leading French Impressionist and Post-Impressionist painters. Under their influence van Gogh's paintings, which had been limited to the somber tones of traditional Dutch painting, became much lighter and brighter in color (see his SELF-PORTRAIT WITH GRAY HAT).

In 1888 he moved to southern France, where—in less than two years—he produced most of the paintings for which he is known. There, armed with the Impressionists' bright, free color, and inspired by the intense semitropical light, van Gogh took color even further. He developed a revolutionary approach to color based on the way colors and color combinations symbolize ideas and emotional content. His new understanding of expressive color led him to write that "the painter of the future will be a colorist such as has never existed."[3]

Van Gogh's use of pure colors and his bold strokes of thick paint created images of emotional intensity that had a great impact on artists—especially Expressionist painters—of the twentieth century. Before van Gogh, most Western painters used color to describe the appearance of their subjects. After van Gogh, painters began to realize that color could make visible feelings and states of mind.

From his teenage years, van Gogh's intense personality caused him to be rejected by the women with whom he fell in love, and later it drove away potential friends, such as Paul Gauguin. Such rejection contributed to several emotional breakdowns. Spells of fervent painting were interrupted by periods of illness and depression. Increasing illness led him voluntarily to enter a mental hospital for several months. After leaving the hospital he returned to Paris, then settled in a nearby town under the watchful eye of a doctor

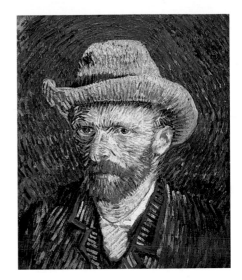

164   Vincent van Gogh.
SELF PORTRAIT WITH GRAY HAT. 1887.
Oil on canvas. 17¼" × 14¾".
Vincent van Gogh Foundation/Van Gogh Museum, Amsterdam.

known to be a friend of artists. There, in a frenzy of creative productivity, he completed about seventy paintings in sixty-five days—the last two months of his life. Van Gogh's loneliness and despair drove him to suicide at age thirty-seven.

An emphasis on the tragic aspects of van Gogh's now legendary life has produced a popular view of the man that tends to obscure his great contribution to art. In spite of his difficulties, van Gogh produced almost two thousand works of art within a mere ten years. Although most of his contemporaries could not see the value of his art, his paintings and drawings are displayed today in major museums worldwide, and exhibitions of his works attract record crowds.

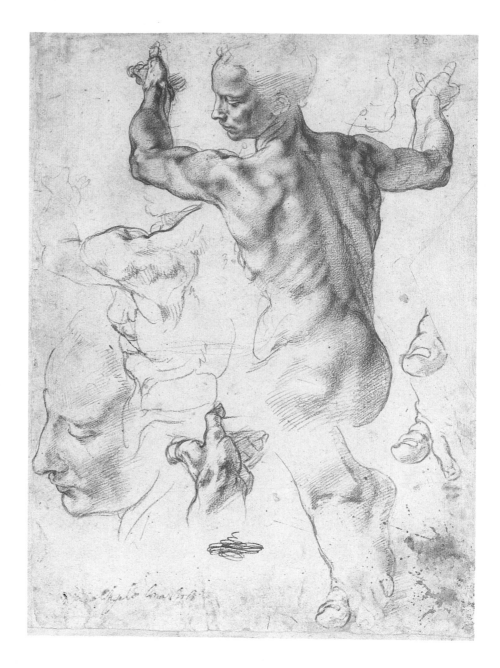

165 Michelangelo Buonarotti.
Studies for the LIBYAN SIBYL on the
Sistine Chapel ceiling. c. 1508.
Red chalk. 11⅜" × 8⅜".

PURPOSES OF DRAWING

A drawing can function in one or more of three ways:

- as a personal notation, sketch, or record of something seen, remembered, or imagined
- as a study for another, usually larger and more complex work such as a sculpture, a building, a film, a painting—or another drawing
- as an end in itself, a complete work of art

When Michelangelo made his detailed studies for the LIBYAN SIBYL, he had no idea that reproductions of his sheet of working drawings would be ad-mired almost as much as his finished painting of the figure on the ceiling of the Sistine Chapel.

This magnificent drawing of a mythical female figure was drawn from a male model. The studies are a record of search and discovery as Michelangelo carefully drew what he observed. His under-standing of anatomy helped him to define each muscle. The flow between the head, shoulders, and arms of the figure is based on Michelangelo's feel-ing for visual continuity as well as his attention to detail. The parts of the figure that he felt needed further study he drew repeatedly. To achieve the dark reds, Michelangelo evidently licked the point of the chalk.

A simple, tiny sketch, quickly done, can be the starting point for a far larger and more complex work. In such drawings an artist can work out problems of overall design or concentrate on small details. Picasso did many studies in preparation for a major painting, GUERNICA—a huge work measuring more than 11 feet high by 25 feet long (a larger reproduction appears in chapter 23). Forty-five of Picasso's studies are preserved; nearly all are dated.

The first drawing for GUERNICA shows what can be identified in later stages as a woman with a lamp, apparently an important symbol to Picasso. The woman leans out of a house in the upper right. On the left appears a bull with a bird on its back. Both the bull and the woman with the lamp are major elements in the final painting. The first drawing was probably completed in a few seconds, yet its quick gestural lines contain the essence of the large, complex painting.

Although artists do not generally consider their preliminary sketches as finished pieces, studies by leading artists are often treasured both for their intrinsic beauty and for what they reveal about the creative process. Picasso recognized the importance of documenting the creative process from initial idea to finished painting:

It would be very interesting to preserve photographically, not the stages, but the metamorphoses of a picture. Possibly one might then discover the path followed by the brain in materializing a dream. But there is one very odd thing to notice, that basically a picture doesn't change, that the first "vision" remains almost intact, in spite of appearances.[4]

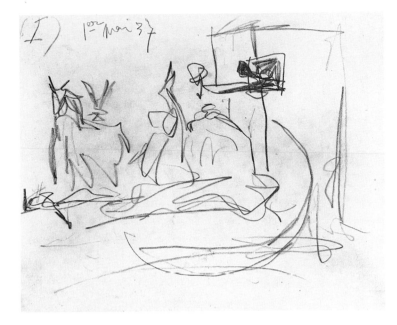

167   Pablo Picasso.
FIRST COMPOSITION STUDY FOR GUERNICA. May 1, 1937.
Pencil on blue paper. 8¼" × 10⅝".
Museo Nacional Centro de Arte Reina Sofia.
© 2002 Estate of Pablo Picasso/Artists Rights Society (ARS), NY.

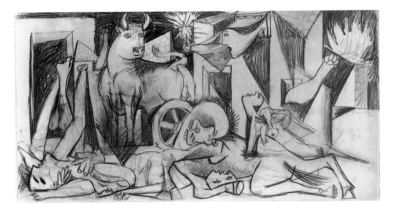

168   Pablo Picasso.
COMPOSITION STUDY FOR GUERNICA. May 9, 1937.
Pencil on white paper. 9½" × 17⅞".
Museo Nacional Centro de Arte Reina Sofia.
© 2002 Estate of Pablo Picasso/Artists Rights Society (ARS), NY.

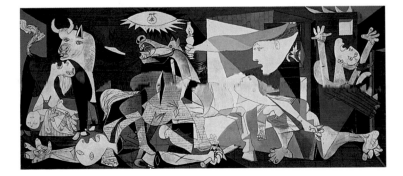

166   Pablo Picasso (1881–1973).
GUERNICA. 1937.
Oil on canvas. 11'5½" × 25'5¼".
Museo National Centro de Arte Reina Sofia, Madrid. John Bigelow Taylor/Art Resource NY.
© 2002 Estate of Pablo Picasso/Artists Rights Society (ARS), NY.

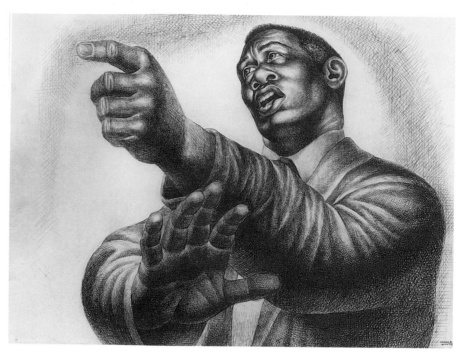

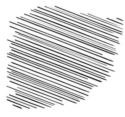

169   TYPES OF HATCHING.
a. Hatching.

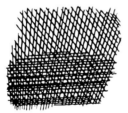

b. Cross-hatching.

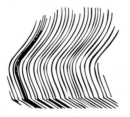

c. Contour hatching.

Another type of preparatory drawing is the cartoon. The original meaning of cartoon, still used by art professionals, is a full-sized drawing made as a guide for a large work in another medium, particularly a fresco painting, mosaic, or tapestry.

In today's common usage, the word *cartoon* refers to a narrative drawing emphasizing humorous or satirical content. Cartoons and comics are among the most widely enjoyed drawings. Young people fond of drawing cartoons often go on to develop their drawing skills in other ways.

Each drawing tool and each type of paper has its own characteristics. The interaction between these materials and the technique of the artist determines the nature of the resulting drawing. The illustration DRAWING TOOLS shows the different qualities of marks made by common drawing tools.

TYPES OF HATCHING shows how values can be built up with parallel lines, called *hatching,* or with *cross-hatching* of various types. Charles White used cross-hatched ink lines in PREACHER to build up the figure's mass and gesture in a forceful manner. Through the use of *contour hatching,* White gave the figure a feeling of sculptural mass. The strongly foreshortened right hand and forearm add to the drawing's dramatic impact.

DRY MEDIA

Dry drawing media include pencil, charcoal, conté crayon, and pastel. Drawing pencils include those made of graphite varying from soft (dark) to hard (light) and high-quality colored pencils in a wide range of colors.

Darkness and line quality are determined both by the degree of hardness of the pencil and by the texture of the surface to which it is applied. Paper with some *tooth* or surface grain receives pencil marks more readily than paper that is smooth. Pencil lines can vary in width or length, can be made by using the side of the pencil point in broad strokes, and can be repeated as hatching. A considerable range of values can be produced by varying the pressure on a medium-soft drawing pencil.

A rich variety of values and inventive shapes made with light and dark grades of drawing pencils fills Judith Murray's drawing OBSIDIAN. Flying shapes in rhythmic patterns play off against each other in a lively improvisation. The central black curving shape rises, helped by the energy of the shapes below and around it. Diagonally positioned, crystal-like triangular structures soar and return in dynamic interplay.

The sticks of charcoal used today are similar to those used by prehistoric peoples to draw on cave walls. With charcoal, dark passages can be drawn quickly. The various hard-to-soft grades now available provide a flexible medium for both beginning and advanced artists. Because not all charcoal particles bind to the surface of the paper, charcoal is

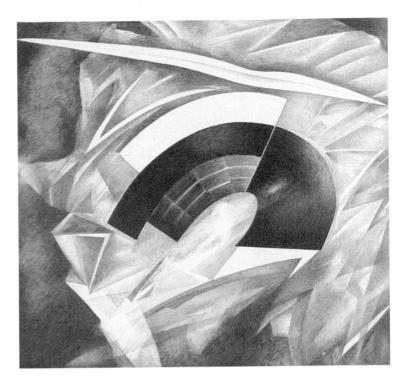

172   Judith Murray.
OBSIDIAN. 1988.
Pencil on arches paper. 17½" × 19¼".
Courtesy of the artist.
Collection of Howard and Terry S. Walters, Summit, NJ.

easy to smudge, blur, or erase. This quality is both an advantage and a drawback: it enables one to make changes readily, but finished works can easily smear. A completed charcoal drawing may be set or "fixed" with a thin varnish called *fixative,* which is sprayed over it to help bind the charcoal to the paper. Charcoal produces a wide range of light to dark values from soft grays to deep velvety blacks.

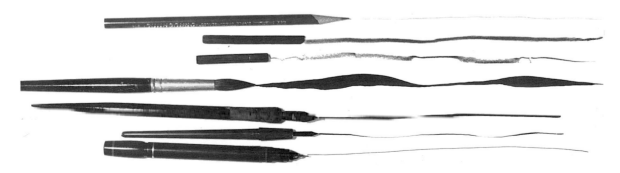

171   DRAWING TOOLS AND THEIR CHARACTERISTIC LINES.

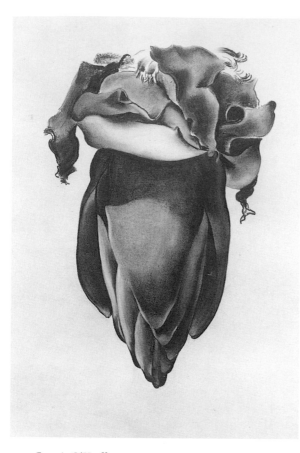

173   Georgia O'Keeffe.
BANANA FLOWER. 1933.
Charcoal and black chalk on paper. 21¾" × 14¾".
The Museum of Modern Art, New York.
Given anonymously (by exchange). Photograph: © 2002 Museum
of Modern Art, NY. © 2002 The Georgia O'Keeffe Foundation/Artists
Rights Society (ARS), NY.

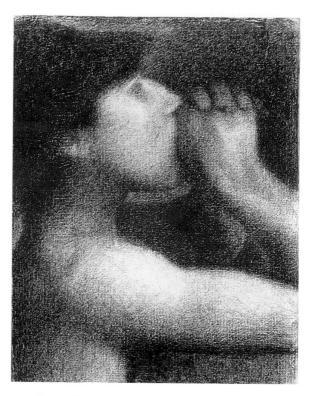

174   Georges Pierre Seurat (French, 1859–1891).
L'ECHO, STUDY FOR UNE BAIGNADE, ASNIERES. 1882–1891.
Black conté crayon. 12¹⁵⁄₁₆" × 9⁷⁄₁₆".
Yale University Art Gallery, New Haven. Bequest of Edith Malvina K. Wetmore.
1966.80.11

Georgia O'Keeffe took full advantage of charcoal in her drawing of a BANANA FLOWER. Charcoal provided her with the means to draw with powerful precision. Here she dramatized the monumental sculptural mass and unique structure of her subject. Although O'Keeffe is best known for her colorful paintings of enlarged close-up views of flowers (see page 33), in this drawing she has achieved a comparable impact with just black and white.

Conté crayon is a semi-hard chalk with enough oil in the binder to cause it to adhere to smooth paper. It can produce varied lines or broad strokes that are relatively resistant to smudging. Wax-based crayons, such as those given to children, are avoided by serious artists; they lack flexibility, and most fade over time. Because the strokes do not blend easily, it is difficult to obtain bright color

mixtures with wax crayons. Many professional artists now use oil crayons.

Georges Seurat used conté crayon to build up the illusion of three-dimensional form through value gradations (*chiaroscuro*) in his drawing L'ECHO. Seurat actually drew a multitude of lines; yet in the final drawing the individual lines are obscured by the total effect of finely textured light and dark areas. He selected conté crayon on rough paper as a means of concentrating on basic forms and on the interplay of light and shadow.

Natural chalks of red, white, and black have been used for drawing since ancient times. Pastels, produced since the seventeenth century, have characteristics similar to those of natural chalk. They have a freshness and purity of color because they are comprised mostly of pigment, with very little binding material. Because no drying is needed, there is no change in color, as occurs in some paints when they dry. Soft pastels do not allow for much detail—they force the user to work boldly. Blending of strokes with fingers or a paper stump made for the purpose produces a soft blur that lightly mixes the colors. Pastels yield the most exciting results when not overworked.

Venetian portraitist Rosalba Carriera made dozens of works with pastels in the early eighteenth century. Her ALLEGORY OF PAINTING depicts one of her favorite students at work. The hard, fine-grained pastels in common use at that time give the finished work a smooth surface that makes possible fine color shadings. Because of the artist's light, deft touch with short strokes of the pastel, the work resembles an oil painting in its appearance, an effect promoted by the very smooth paper. Carriera was in demand to make pastel portraits throughout Germany, France, and North Italy until poor eyesight forced her retirement in 1746.

French artist Edgar Degas shifted from oil painting to pastels in his later years, and occasion-ally he combined the two. He took advantage of the rich strokes of color and subtle blends possible with pastel. Although carefully constructed, his compositions look like casual, fleeting glimpses of everyday life. In BREAKFAST AFTER THE BATH, bold contours give a sense of movement to the whole design.

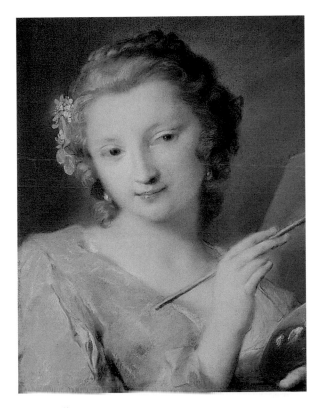

175 Rosalba Carriera.
ALLEGORY OF PAINTING. C. 1720.
Pastel on paper. 17¾" × 13¾".
Samuel H. Kress Collection. Photograph © 2001 Board of Trustees, National Gallery of Art, Washington, D.C. 1939.1.136.(247)/DR

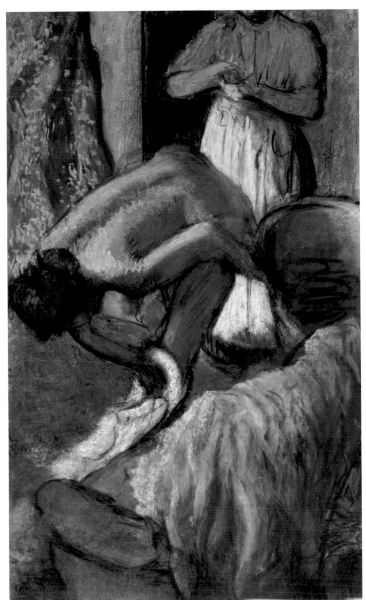

176 Edgar Degas (1834–1917).
LE PETIT DEJEUNER APRES LE BAIN (JEUNE FEMMME S'ESSUYANT).
c. 1894. Pastel on paper. 99.7 × 59.7 cm.
© 2002 Christie's Images Limited.

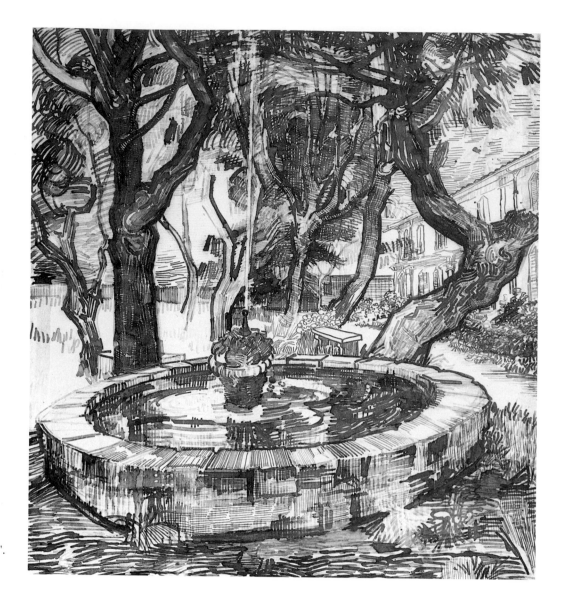

177 Vincent van Gogh.
THE FOUNTAIN IN THE
HOSPITAL GARDEN. 1889.
Pen and ink. 18⅞" × 17¾".
Vincent van Gogh Foundation/
Van Gogh Museum, Amsterdam.

LIQUID MEDIA

Black or colored inks are the most common draw-ing liquids. Some brush drawings are made with *washes* of ink thinned with water. Such ink draw-ings are similar to watercolor paintings. Felt- and fiber-tipped pens are widely used recent additions to the traditional pen-and-ink media.

In THE FOUNTAIN IN THE HOSPITAL GARDEN, van Gogh used a Japanese bamboo pen and ink for his vigorous lines, varying the darkness of lines by using both full strength and diluted ink. Rhythmic line groups suggest the play of light and shadow on the various surfaces.

Nineteenth-century Japanese artist Hokusai, a skilled and prolific draftsman, is said to have cre-ated about 13,000 prints and drawings during his lifetime. He experienced the feelings of self-doubt known to many, yet he prevailed with courage and humor. His statement about the development of his artistic ability should encourage any young per-son to persevere:

I have been in love with painting ever since I became conscious of it at the age of six. I drew some pictures which I thought fairly good when I was fifty, but really nothing I did before the age of seventy was of any value at all. At seventy-three I have at last caught every aspect of nature—birds, fish, animals, insects, trees, grasses, all. When I am eighty I shall have developed still further and will really master the secrets of art at ninety. When I reach one hundred my art will be truly sublime, and my final goal will be attained around the age of one hundred and ten, when every line and dot I draw will be imbued with life.

(signed) Hokusai
The art-crazy old man[5]

In TUNING THE SAMISEN, the expressive elegance of Hokusai's lines was made possible by his control of the responsive brush. In Asia, traditional writing and drawing are done with the same brushes. These brushes are ideal for making calligraphic lines because they hold a substantial amount of ink and readily produce both thick and thin lines. Hokusai played the uniformly thin lines of head, hands, and instrument against the bold spontaneous strokes indicating the folds of the kimono. As the woman tuned the strings of her samisen, he captured a moment of concentration with humor and insight.

Rembrandt also used brush and ink, plus wash, for the drawing of his wife, SASKIA ASLEEP. The result is at once bold and subtle, representational and abstract, finished and unfinished. Rembrandt's spontaneous line technique bears comparison to the Oriental brush-painting tradition seen in the works of Hokusai. While Rembrandt used shading to give the illusion of three-dimensional form, Hokusai suggested the mass of the figure with line alone.

In many societies, drawing is a stepping-stone to other art forms. Works perfected in other media often begin as drawings. In this sense, drawing is the foundation for the media we consider next.

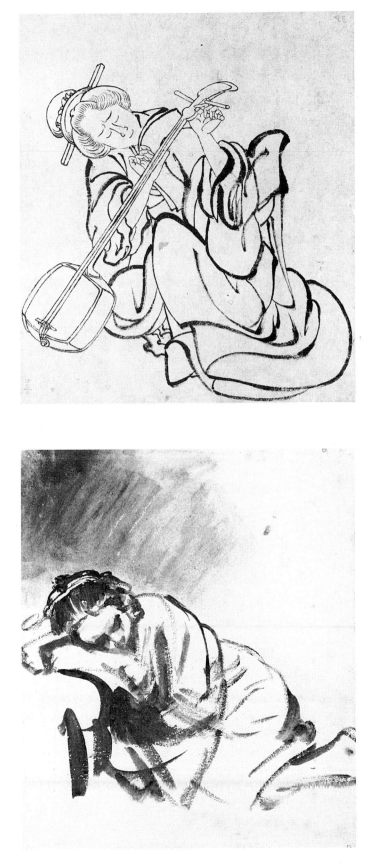

178   Hokusai.
TUNING THE SAMISEN.
c. 1820–1825.
Brush drawing. 9¾" × 8¼".
Courtesy of Freer Gallery of Art, Smithsonian
Institution, Washington, D.C. (F1904.241).

179   Rembrandt van Rijn.
SASKIA ASLEEP. c. 1642.
Brush and wash. 9½" × 8".
Copyright The British Museum.

CHAPTER EIGHT

PAINTING

To many people in the Western world, the word art means painting. The long, rich history of painting, the strong appeal of color, and the endless image-making possibilities explain painting's popularity.

Drawing and painting are closely related, somewhat overlapping processes. In fact, many paintings, such as Winslow Homer's SLOOP, NASSAU (overleaf), are essentially brush drawings over light pencil sketches. Paintings tend to be larger, more formal, more colorful, and they are often completed more slowly than drawings—but there are many exceptions. There is no distinct separation between painting and drawing.

Painting is often drawing with paint. In Gerhard Richter's UNTITLED, the medium, paint, and the process of its application are a major part of the message. Richter's invented landscape suggests rugged forms in the foreground and an open, distant sky. Large brush strokes of thickly applied oil paint contrast with the smooth gradations of paint in the sky area.

The people who made the earliest cave paintings used natural pigments obtained from plants and nearby deposits of minerals and clays. Pigments used in cave paintings at Pont d'Arc, France—including blacks from charred woods and earth colors—have lasted more than 30,000 years.

In Rembrandt's time, the seventeenth century, painters or their assistants mixed finely ground pigments with oil by hand until the paint reached a desirable fineness and consistency. Today high-quality paints are packaged in convenient tubes or jars, ready for immediate use.

Paints consist of three components: pigment, binder (or medium), and vehicle. The *pigment* provides color; the *binder* mixes with the pigment to hold the pigment particles together without dissolving them and to attach the pigment to the surface; and the *vehicle* spreads the pigment. With oil paints, turpentine, or its substitute, is the vehicle and linseed oil is the binder. With traditional tempera, water is the vehicle and egg yolk is the binder.

Pigments are powdered coloring agents that have long been derived from plant, animal, and mineral sources. In the nineteenth and twentieth centuries, major advances in the chemical industry made it possible to produce synthetic pigments that extend the available range of colors. The durability of both natural and synthetic pigments has also been improved. Most of the same pigments are used in manufacturing both the various paint media and the dry drawing media, such as colored pencils and pastels.

In the broad context of the whole field of visual arts, *medium* means a material and its accompanying technique. In the context of painting, *medium* can also refer to the binder, or mixture of binder and vehicle, added to paint to facilitate its application without diluting color intensity.

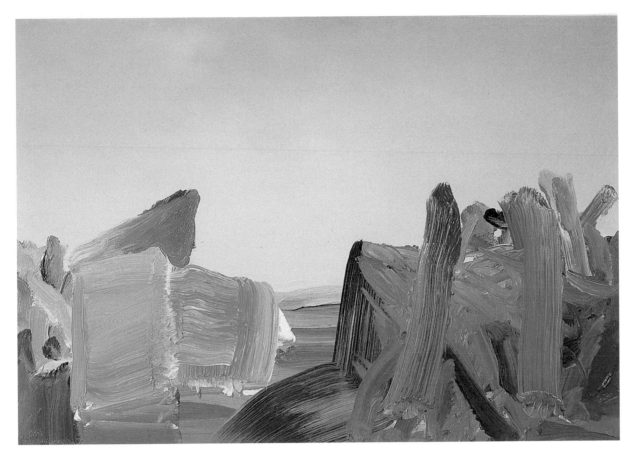

180 Gerhard Richter.
ABSTRACT PAINTING (551-4). 1984.
Oil on canvas. 17" × 23⅝".
© Gerhard Richter.

Paints are usually applied to a flat *support*, such as stretched canvas for oils or paper for watercolors. To achieve a *ground* (the prepared surface to which the paint is applied), the surface of the support (usually canvas) is prepared by sizing or priming, or both. Because supports are often too absorbent to permit controlled application of paint, a *size*, or sealer, is usually applied to lessen absorbency and fill in the pores of the material. For oil painting in particular, size is needed on canvas and paper to protect them from disintegrating from the drying action of linseed oil in oil paint. To complete the surface preparation for painting, an opaque *primer*, or *ground*, usually white, is often applied after or instead of sizing. Sizing and priming are unnecessary for watercolors; a paper surface provides both the support and the ground.

A student or beginning artist will want to experiment with the various types of paint available, learning firsthand the possibilities of each paint medium. Watercolor, tempera, oils, and synthetic or acrylic paints are among today's choices, but for the last five hundred years, oil paint has been the favorite medium of most Western painters. In recent years artists have begun to use synthetic (usually acrylic) paints for spraying, pouring, dripping, and other innovative methods of application. Each type of paint has its own unique advantages and disadvantages.

WATERCOLOR
Watercolor paintings are made by applying pigments suspended in a solution of water and gum arabic (a resin from the acacia tree) to white paper.

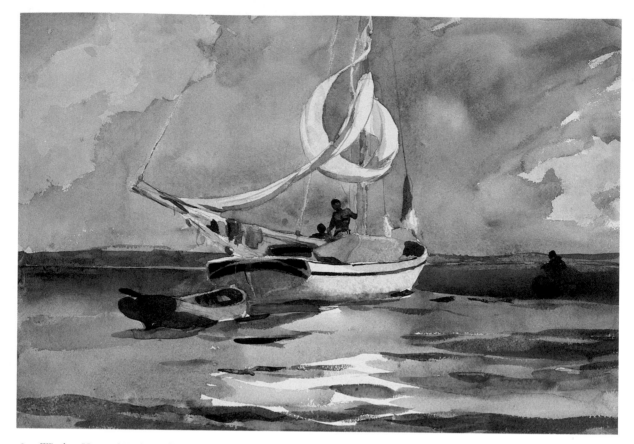

181 Winslow Homer (1836–1910).
SLOOP, NASSAU. 1899.
Watercolor and graphite on off-white wove paper. 14⅞" × 21⁷⁄₁₆".
The Metropolitan Museum of Art. Amelia B. Lazarus Fund, 1910 (10.228.3).
Photograph: © 1989 The Metropolitan Museum of Art.

Rag paper is the preferred support because of its superior absorbency and unchanging whiteness. Blocks of paint available in metal or plastic boxes are modern versions of the dried blocks of watercolor used for thousands of years. Professional artists use high-quality pigments sold in tubes.

Watercolor is basically a staining technique. The paint is applied in thin, translucent washes that allow light to pass through the layers of color and to reflect back from the white paper. Highlights are obtained by leaving areas of white paper unpainted. Opaque (nontranslucent) watercolor is sometimes added for detail. Watercolors are well suited to spontaneous as well as carefully planned applications. Despite the simple materials involved, watercolor is a demanding medium because it does not permit easy changes or corrections. If you overwork a watercolor, you lose its characteristic freshness.

Watercolor's fluid spontaneity makes it a favorite medium for painters who want to catch quick impressions outdoors. The translucent quality of watercolor washes particularly suits depictions of water, atmosphere, light, and weather.

American artist and illustrator Winslow Homer was one of the best watercolorists. In SLOOP, NASSAU, Homer used the bright whiteness of the bare paper to form the highlights of ocean waves, boat, and sails. From light pencil lines to finished painting, his whole process is visible. Homer captured the mood of weather—in this case, the particular qualities of light and color in the calm just before a storm. For Homer, a keen observer of nature, a quick impression made with watercolor was visually stronger than a painting filled with carefully rendered details.

Homer's watercolors are distinguished by their strong design. In SLOOP, NASSAU, he created rhythms with the loops of the sails, the repeated lines of the boats, the softly undulating waves, and the storm clouds. With a couple of short, deft strokes, he painted a third figure to the right—an essential element in the balance of the composition.

Opaque watercolor (sometimes called *gouache*) has been widely used for centuries. It was common in book illustration during the European Middle Ages, and also in traditional Persian art (see chapter 19 for an example). Gouache is like watercolor except that the medium includes small amounts of chalk powder. It is popular in our times with designers and illustrators because of its ease of use and low cost. Jacob Lawrence used gouache to good advantage in his work GOING HOME (see page 73). Here we see the typical opaque appearance of the colors. The speed of application of gouache also helps to suggest the rapid movements of the figures in the work.

In traditional Chinese watercolor technique, the artist employs black ink as well as color and often uses the water-based ink without color. The Chinese regard painting as descended from the art of calligraphy, which is also done in black ink. Thus a skillfully made black ink painting is a fully developed artwork, accorded at least as much honor as a painting with color.

One of the best examples of the use of ink is DWELLING IN THE FUCHUN MOUNTAINS, a work painted in 1350 by Huang Gongwang, one of China's most highly regarded artists. In this segment of a much larger work, we see many different types of brush strokes, from dark flecks in the tree leaves in the foreground, to pale dry strokes in the background, to thin washes in the far distance. Despite the painting's casual quality, the brushwork is in some places highly detailed. The work is over twenty feet long, and took the artist more than three years to complete. It demonstrates mastery of a variety of brushstrokes and control of ink in a wide range of tones, qualities admired in traditional Chinese painting.

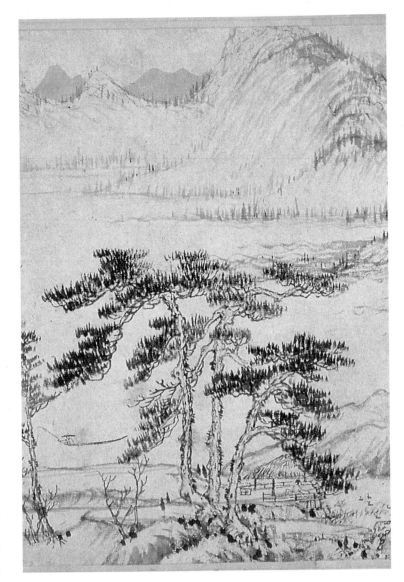

182 Huang Gongwang.
DWELLING IN THE FUCHUN MOUNTAINS.
Section of a handscroll.
Yuan Dynasty. 1350.
Ink on paper. 12½" high.
National Palace Museum, Taipei, Taiwan, Republic of China.

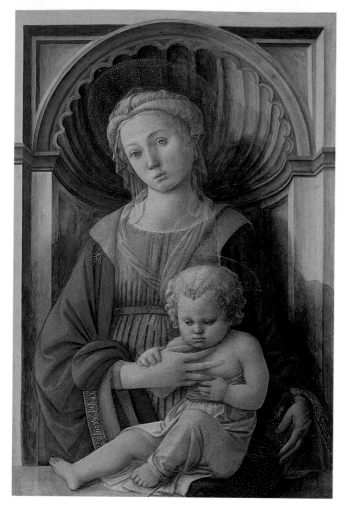

183 Fra Filippo Lippi.
MADONNA AND CHILD. C. 1440–1445.
Tempera on wood. 31⅜" × 20⅛"; framed 46⅛ × 33⅝ × 3¾
Samuel H. Kress Collection.
Photograph © 2001 Board of Trustees, National Gallery of Art, Washington.
1939.1.290.(401)/PA.

TEMPERA

Tempera was used by the ancient Egyptians, Greeks, and Romans. It was highly developed during the Middle Ages, when it was used for small paintings made on wood panels. Since ancient times the principal tempera medium has been egg tempera, in which egg yolk, or occasionally egg white, is the binder. (The binding qualities of egg yolk are well known to anyone who has washed breakfast dishes.) Today the word *tempera* is sometimes used to include water-soluble paints with binders of glue, casein, egg,

or egg and oil emulsion. All tempera paints are water-thinned.

Egg tempera has a luminous, slightly *matte* (not shiny) surface when dry. Its clear, brilliant quality results from painting on a ground of very white gesso. *Gesso,* a preparation of chalk or plaster of Paris and glue, is applied to a support as a ground for tempera and oil paintings.

Egg tempera is good for achieving sharp lines and precise details, and it does not darken with age. However, its colors change during drying, and blending and reworking are difficult because tempera dries rapidly. Traditional tempera painting requires complete preliminary drawing and pale underpainting because of its translucency and the difficulty in making changes. Overpainting consists of applying layers of translucent paint in small, careful strokes. Because tempera lacks flexibility, movement of the support may cause the gesso and pigment to crack. A rigid support, such as a wood panel, is required.

Fra Filippo Lippi was one of the finest colorists of his day. In MADONNA AND CHILD, he methodically built up thin layers of color, creating a smooth, almost luminous surface. Tempera is well suited for depicting translucencies such as those created by Lippi in the halo and the sheer neck scarf. His naturalistic yet poetic portrayal brought a worldly dimension to religious subject matter.

OIL

In the Western world, oil paint has been a favorite medium for five centuries. Pigments mixed with various vegetable oils, such as linseed, walnut, and poppyseed, were used in the Middle Ages for decorative purposes, but not until the fifteenth century did Flemish painters fully develop the use of paint made with linseed oil pressed from the seeds of the flax plant. In this early period, artists applied oil paint to wood panels covered with smooth layers of gesso, as in the older tradition of tempera painting.

The van Eyck brothers, Hubert and Jan, are credited with developing oil painting techniques and bringing them to their first perfection. They achieved glowing, jewel-like surfaces that remain

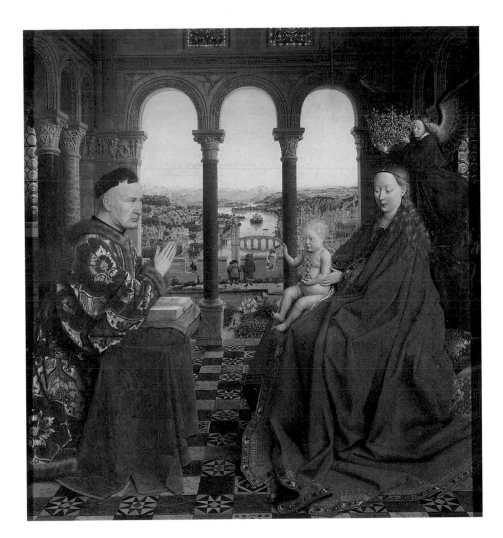

184 Jan van Eyck.
MADONNA AND CHILD WITH THE
CHANCELLOR ROLIN. c. 1433–1434.
Oil and tempera on panel. 26" × 24⅜".
Musée du Louvre, Paris.
Photograph: Erich Lessing/Art Resource, NY.

amazingly fresh to the present day. Jan van Eyck's MADONNA AND CHILD WITH THE CHANCELLOR ROLIN is an example of his early mastery of the oil technique.

MADONNA AND CHILD WITH THE CHANCELLOR ROLIN was painted on a small gesso-covered wood panel. After beginning with a brush drawing in tempera, van Eyck proceeded with thin layers of oil paint, moving from light to dark and from opaque to translucent colors. The luminous quality of the surface is the result of successive oil glazes. A *glaze* is a very thin, transparent film of color applied over a previously painted surface. To produce glazes, oil colors selected for their transparency are diluted with glazing medium—usually a mixture of oil, thinner, and varnish. Glazes give depth to painted surfaces by allowing light to pass through and reflect from lower paint layers.

Here the sparkling jewels, the textiles, and the furs are each given their own refined textures. Within the context of the religious subject, van Eyck demonstrated his enthusiasm for the delights of the visible world. Veils of glazes in the sky area provide atmospheric perspective and thus contribute to the illusion of deep space in the enticing view beyond the open window. The evolution in the new oil painting technique made such realism possible.

Oil has many advantages not found in other traditional media. Compared to tempera, oil paint can provide both increased opacity—which yields better covering power—and, when thinned, greater transparency. Its slow drying time, first considered a drawback, soon proved to be a distinct advantage, permitting strokes of color to be blended and repeated changes to be made during the painting

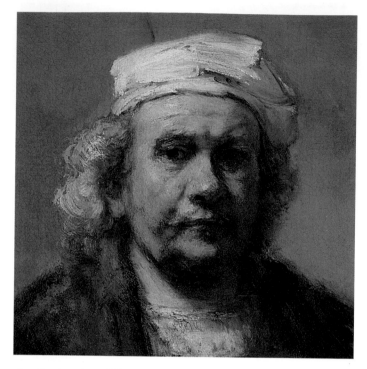

185   Rembrandt van Rijn.
       Detail of SELF-PORTRAIT. 1663.
       Oil on canvas. Full painting 45" × 38".
       Kenwood House/English Heritage Photo Library.

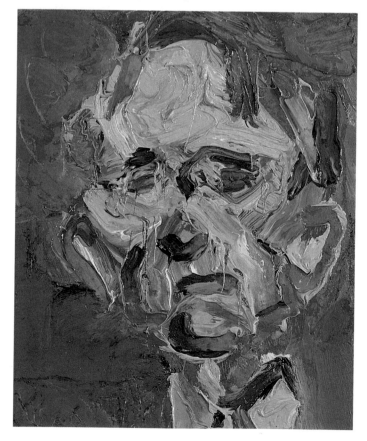

process. Unlike pigment in tempera, gouache, and acrylics, pigment colors in oil change little when drying; however, oil medium (primarily linseed oil) has a tendency to darken and yellow slightly with age. Because of the flexibility of dried oil film, sixteenth-century Venetian painters who wished to paint large pictures could replace heavy wood panels with canvas stretched on wood frames. A painted canvas not only is light in weight, but also can be unstretched and rolled (if the paint layer is not too thick) for transporting. Canvas continues to be the preferred support for oil paintings.

Oil can be applied thickly or thinly, wet into wet or wet onto dry. When applied thickly, it is called *impasto*. When a work is painted wet into wet and completed at one sitting, the process is called the *direct painting* method.

Rembrandt used this method in his SELF-PORTRAIT. The detail here shows how the impasto of light and dark paint both defines a solid-looking head and presents the incredible richness of Rembrandt's brushwork.

In Rembrandt's SELF-PORTRAIT and in Frank Auerbach's HEAD OF MICHAEL PODRO, the artists' responsiveness to both the reality of their subjects and the physical nature of paint and painting is clearly visible. Because the thick, paste-like quality of oil paint is celebrated rather than hidden, viewers participate in the process of conjuring up images when viewing Rembrandt's rough strokes and Auerbach's smears and globs of paint. Both artists created paintings that project strong images when seen at a distance and present amazingly rich tactile surfaces when viewed close up.

The wide range of approaches possible with oil paint becomes apparent when we compare van Eyck's subtly glazed colors with the impasto surfaces of Rembrandt and Auerbach.

In one sense, the story of painting is about the visual magic that people around the world have

186   Frank Auerbach.
       HEAD OF MICHAEL PODRO. 1981.
       Oil on board. 13" × 11".
       Photograph: Marlborough Fine Art Ltd., London.

been able to conjure up with various paint media. Within a single painting, a unique world is created; but that world is often influenced by, if not inspired by, the artist's own daily life. Such is the case with Grace Hartigan's CITY LIFE. A street vendor's fruit stand is the jumping-off point for an exuberant feast of dancing lines and colorful shapes piled one on top of another. Hartigan's sensitivity to sumptuous color and her skill with bold brush work heightened her expressive response to the lively, moving complexity of her urban environment.

Joan Mitchell used oil paint to spontaneously re-create emotional states in abstract visual form. BORDER is painted very loosely in a complex mix of rich, sensuous colors. The composition is subtly symmetrical (note the light vertical green stripe near the top center), and colors are applied with a combination of care and abandon. To arrive at the bright and lush yellows, blues, greens, and reds, the artist avoided overmixing her colors. She also allowed the texture of the paint to play a major role in the work by varying its thickness over a wide range. She made the yellow strokes with a dry brush; she allowed some of the blues to run; reds give accents at carefully selected points. We can actually follow the creation of this work, layer by layer and color by color, as we look at this embodiment of a warm—even exciting—mood.

ACRYLIC

Foremost among the synthetic painting media currently in wide use are *acrylics.* Pigments are suspended in acrylic polymer medium, which provides a fast-drying, flexible film. These relatively permanent paints can be applied to a wider variety of surfaces than traditional painting media. Most acrylics are water-thinned and water-resistant when dry. Because acrylic resin medium is highly transparent, colors can maintain a high degree of intensity; but unlike oils, acrylics rarely darken or yellow with age. Their rapid drying time restricts blending and reworking possibilities, but it greatly reduces the time involved in layering processes such as glazing.

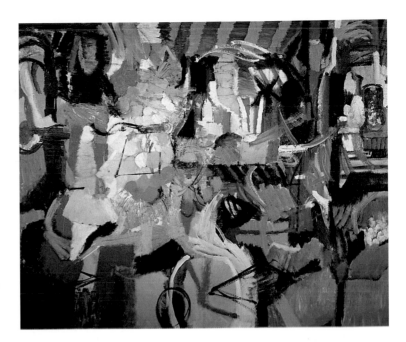

187 Grace Hartigan.
CITY LIFE. 1956.
Oil on canvas. 81" × 98½".
Collection of the National Trust for Historic Preservation, Pocantico Historical Area.

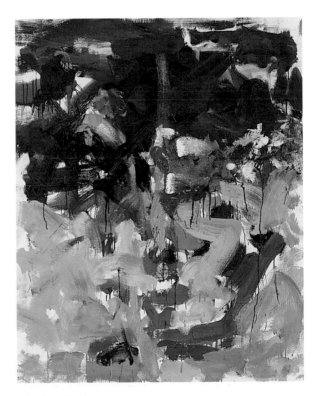

188 Joan Mitchell.
BORDER. 1989.
Oil on canvas. 45½" × 35".
Courtesy Robert Miller Gallery.
© The Estate of Joan Mitchell.

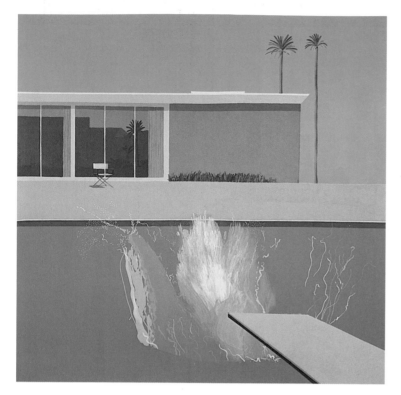

189 David Hockney.
A BIGGER SPLASH. 1967.
Acrylic on canvas. 96" × 96".
The Tate Gallery, London.

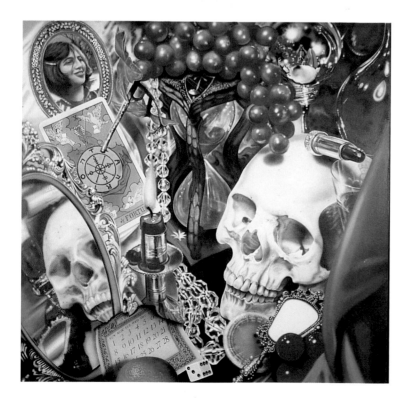

Acrylics work well when paint is applied quickly with little blending—witness the splash in David Hockney's A BIGGER SPLASH—or when it is brushed on in flat areas as in the rest of the painting. The strong contrast between the dramatic freedom of the paint application of the splash and the thinly painted, geometric shapes of house, chair, pool rim, and diving board gives lively energy to the suburban scene.

In recent years many painters have used airbrushes to apply acrylics and other types of paint. An *airbrush* is a small-scale paint sprayer capable of projecting a fine, controlled mist of paint. It provides an even paint application without the personal touch of individual brush strokes, and it is therefore well suited to the subtle gradations of color values found in many paintings of the 1960s and 1970s, such as Audrey Flack's WHEEL OF FORTUNE.

ENCAUSTIC

In the ancient medium of *encaustic,* pigments are suspended in hot beeswax, resulting in lustrous surfaces that bring out the full richness of colors. The Egyptian city of Fayum, when that area was a Roman province, became a center of encaustic painting during the second century. Fayum portraits, such as the PORTRAIT OF A BOY, were memorials to the deceased, painted directly on their wooden coffins. In these portraits lifelike vigor and the sense of individuality remain strong, and colors have retained their intensity after almost two thousand years.

Early practitioners found it difficult to keep the wax binder of encaustic at the right temperature for proper handling; with modern electrical heating devices, it is easier to maintain workable temperatures. Nevertheless, encaustic is used by only a few painters today. One of the best-known proponents of encaustic painting is Jasper Johns, whose TARGET WITH FOUR FACES is pictured in chapter 24.

190 Audrey Flack.
WHEEL OF FORTUNE. 1977–1978.
Oil over acrylic on canvas. 96" × 96".
Photograph courtesy of Louis K. Meisel Gallery, New York.

The painter works quickly in a rapid staining process similar to watercolor. Lime, in contact with air, forms transparent calcium crystals that chemically bind the pigment to the moist lime-plaster wall. The lime in the plaster thus becomes the binder, creating a smooth, extremely durable surface. Once the surface has dried, the painting is part of the wall. Notice the texture of the plaster in the detail from Diego Rivera's SUGAR CANE. Completion of the chemical reaction occurs slowly, deepening and enriching the colors as the fresco ages. Colors reach their greatest intensity fifty to one hundred years after a fresco is painted, yet the hues always have a muted quality.

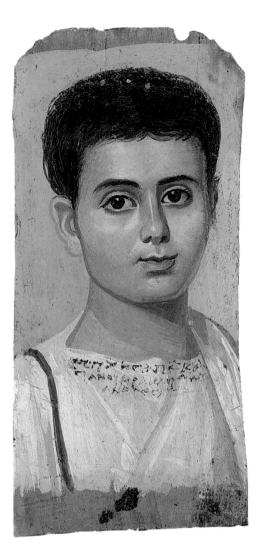

191 PORTRAIT OF A BOY.
From Fayum, Lower Egypt. ca. 50–100 C.E.
Encaustic on limewood. 15⅜" × 7½".
Metropolitan Museum of Art, New York.
Gift of Edward S. Harkness, 1918. (18.9.2)
Photograph: © 1998 The Metropolitan Museum of Art.

FRESCO

True fresco, or *buon fresco,* is an ancient wall-painting technique in which very finely ground pigments suspended in water are applied to a damp lime-plaster surface. Generally, a full-size drawing called a *cartoon* is completed first, then transferred to the freshly laid plaster wall before painting. Because the plaster dries quickly, only the portion of the wall that can be painted in one day is prepared; joints are usually arranged along the edges of major shapes in the composition.

192 Diego Rivera.
Detail from SUGAR CANE. 1931.
Fresco on plaster, 58" × 95".
Philadelphia Museum of Art: Gift of Mr. and Mrs. Herbert Cameron Morris.
1943–46–2. © 2002 Banco de Mexico Diego Rivera & Frida Kahlo Museums Trust. Av. Cinco de Mayo No. 2, Col. Centro, Del. Cuauhtemoc 06059, Mexico, D.F. Reproduction authorized by the Instituto National de Bellas Artes and Literature.

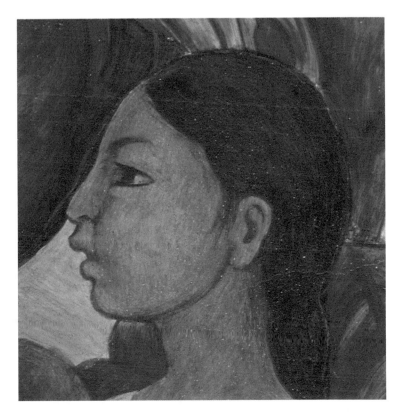

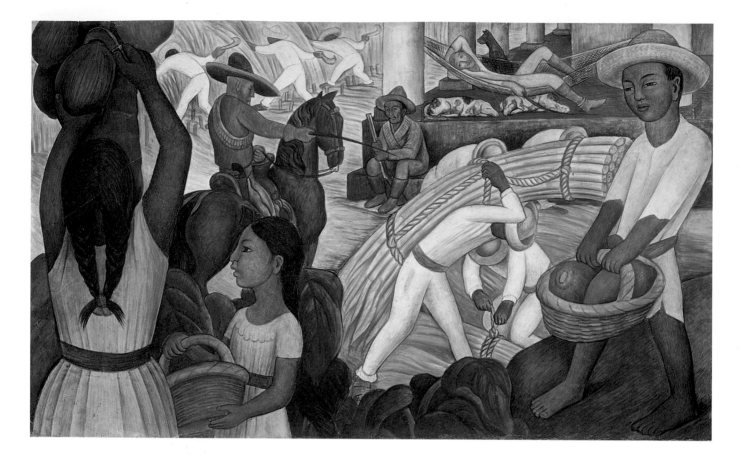

The artist must have the design completely worked out before painting, because no changes can be made after the paint is applied to the fresh plaster. It may take twelve to fourteen straight hours of work just to complete two square yards of a fresco painting. Fresco technique does not permit the delicate manipulation of transitional tones; but the luminous color, fine surface, and permanent color make it an ideal medium for large murals.

Secco fresco (dry fresco), another ancient wall-painting method, is done on finished, dried lime-plaster walls. With this technique, tempera paint is applied to a clean, dry surface or over an already dried *buon fresco* to achieve greater color intensity than is possible with *buon fresco* alone.

Fresco has been used in Asian and Western cultures for at least four thousand years. In Renaissance Italy it was the favored medium for painting on church walls. Probably the best known fresco paintings are those by Michelangelo on the Sistine Chapel ceiling in the Vatican in Rome, Italy. After

193　Diego Rivera.
SUGAR CANE. 1931.
Fresco on plaster. 58" × 95".

the Renaissance and Baroque periods, fresco became less popular, eclipsed by the more flexible oil medium. However, a revival of the fresco technique began in Mexico in the 1920s, encouraged by the new revolutionary government's support for public murals.

By leading the revival in fresco mural painting for public buildings, Diego Rivera was able to break away from the limited studio and gallery audience and make art a part of the life of the people. His style blends European and native art traditions with contemporary subject matter. SUGAR CANE is one of eight portable frescoes that Rivera made for his 1931–1932 exhibition at the Museum of Modern Art in New York.

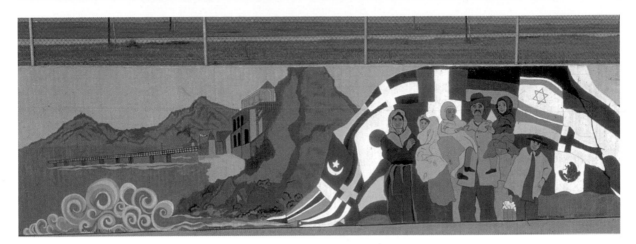

The world's largest painting is fourteen feet high and stretches for a half mile along the side wall of a drainage ditch in the San Fernando Valley. Not able to take it in all at once, viewers must contemplate it from a bike path or through the windows of their passing cars. This colossal project is the brainchild of Judy Baca, who for twenty years has combined art with community activism.

She was inspired by the mural paintings of Mexican artists of the 1920s and 1930s, who decorated public buildings with scenes of their country's history and life. They showed through their work how art could become, rather than a luxurious private possession, a vehicle of community awareness and empowerment. Baca studied mural painting at the Siqueiros workshop in Cuernavaca, Mexico. Returning home, she took the muralist message into diverse neighborhoods, recruiting over four hundred teenagers and young adults to help make THE GREAT WALL OF LOS

ANGELES over a period of several summers beginning in 1976.

The U.S. Army Corps of Engineers gave permission for the Mural Makers (as they called themselves) to decorate a long swath of cement that bordered one side of the Tujunga Wash Flood Control Channel in the Los Angeles suburb of Van Nuys. Baca recalled how the idea was born:

When I first saw the wall, I envisioned a long narrative of another history of California: one which included ethnic peoples, women, and minorities who were so invisible in conventional textbook accounts. The discovery of California's multicultured peoples was a revelation to me.[1]

THE GREAT WALL presents a sweeping panorama of the history of California. Beginning with the Native American cultures of the area, it continues with the Roman Catholic missions, and moves on to the Anglicization of the state when it became part of the United States with the Treaty of Guadalupe

Hidalgo in 1848. The twentieth-century section includes the Dust Bowl migrants of the 1930s, the dawn of the movie and aviation industries, and the impact of World War II.

Many parts of the mural highlight histories that are often left untold. One panel tells graphically how the building of Dodger Stadium in 1962 dislodged a Mexican-American neighborhood. Another depicts the forced incarceration of Japanese Americans in "relocation" camps after the Pearl Harbor attack that started World War II in the Pacific. A third deals with the blacklisting of dozens of Hollywood writers for suspected Communist affiliations during the height of the Cold War. THE GREAT WALL's size parallels its expansive, inclusive vision of the history of California.

Getting it done was a monumental task. Baca paid all of the workers, to help both the pocketbooks and the pride of the young people she recruited. Many of the Mural Makers were former gang mem-

194 Judy Baca, director; Isabel Castro, designer. GREAT WALL OF LOS ANGELES, IMMIGRANT CALIFORNIA, 1976–1983, Tujunga Wash, Studio City, CA.
Photograph: Social and Public Art Resource Center (SPARC), Venice, CA.

a. 1900 IMMIGRANT CALIFORNIA.

bers, juvenile delinquents, or ex-offenders on parole; painting the mural was their first job. She organized the workers into crews, taking care that each unit was multiethnic. They worked from Monday through Thursday during the summer; on Fridays they heard lectures about the history they were depicting. Most decisions were made by consensus, and everyone who helped to paint the mural had a chance to help design its contents. Funding sources included federal youth job programs, foundation grants, donations of supplies, and private contributions.

The mural's impact on the lives of those who painted it is well documented. Many disadvantaged youths got needed job skills. Social service referrals to counseling or drug treatment were readily

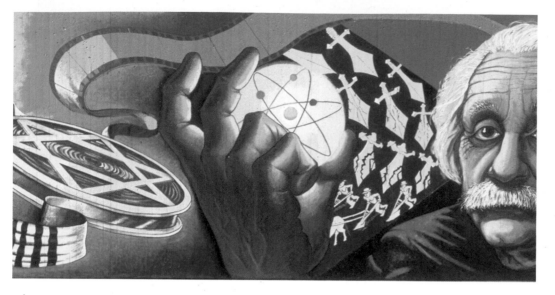

b. JEWISH ARTS AND SCIENCE.

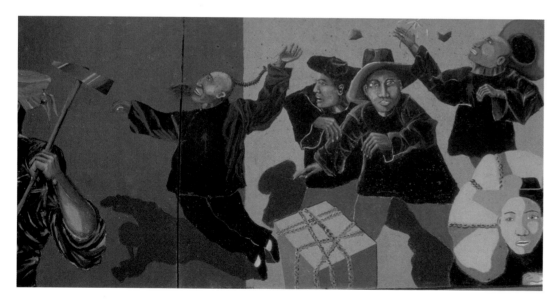

c. CHINESE IMMIGRANTS AND THEIR ROLE IN BUILDING THE RAILROADS.

available. For the first time, hundreds learned of their history and how it related to the state as a whole. One participant recalled, "After my first year on the mural, I left with a sense of who I was and what I could do that was unlike anything I'd ever felt before."[2]

Government funding cutbacks and skyrocketing liability insurance premiums forced work to a halt in 1983, but Baca insists that THE GREAT WALL is not complete yet. She went on to found SPARC, the Social and Public Art Resource Center, a group that has sponsored more than seventy smaller murals all over greater Los Angeles. SPARC recruits youth, gang members, middle-class parents, and even the elderly to work on murals in their own communities. SPARC has convinced dozens of illegal graffiti artists to work on the right side of the law.

But her biggest project has remained THE GREAT WALL OF LOS ANGELES. Always visible along Coldwater Canyon Avenue, it draws tourists, artists, and high school history classes, among its many viewers. As one teenager who worked on THE GREAT WALL said, "I hope when the public comes to admire our mural they'll share the magic and emotion that our crew shared with one another."[3]

CHAPTER NINE

PRINTMAKING

The term *printmaking* describes a variety of media developed to create multiple images. So much in our society is printed—newspapers, books, posters, magazines, greeting cards, billboards—that it is hard to imagine a time in which all human-made images were produced by hand, one at a time. Before 1415, every book and manuscript in Europe was hand-lettered and hand-illustrated. In contrast, multiple copies of *Artforms* are printed quickly by a mechanical printing method called *offset lithography.*

The technologies for both printing and paper-making came to Europe from China. By the ninth century, the Chinese were printing pictures; by the eleventh century, they had invented (but seldom used) movable type. Printmaking was developed in Europe by the fifteenth century—first to meet the demand for inexpensive religious icons and playing cards, then to illustrate books printed with the new European movable type. Since the fifteenth century, the art of printmaking has been closely associated with the illustration of books.

Before the twentieth century, most printing was for the purpose of commercial reproduction rather than making original art. As recently as the late nineteenth century, printmakers were still needed to copy drawings, paintings, and even early photographs by making plates to be used, along with movable type, for illustrating newspapers and books.

As photomechanical methods of reproduction were developed, handwork played a decreasing role in the printing process. Artists, however, have continued to use the old handcrafted printmaking processes to take advantage of their uniquely expressive properties. By designing and printing multiple originals, today's printmakers can sell their works for much less than one-of-a-kind paintings. Such works, conceived as *original prints,* are not to be confused with reproductions (see the discussion at the end of this chapter).

Nearly all original prints are numbered to indicate the total number of prints *pulled,* or printed, in the edition, and to give the number of each print in the sequence. The figure 6/50 on a print, for example, would indicate that the edition totaled fifty prints and that this was the sixth print pulled.

As part of the printmaking process, artists make prints called progressive proofs at various stages to see how the image on the block, plate, stone, or screen is developing. When a satisfactory stage is reached, the artist makes a few prints for his or her record and personal use. These are marked AP, meaning *artist's proof.*

Printmaking methods range from simple to complex. Traditionally, these methods are divided into four basic categories: relief, intaglio, planographic (lithography), and stencil (screen-printing).

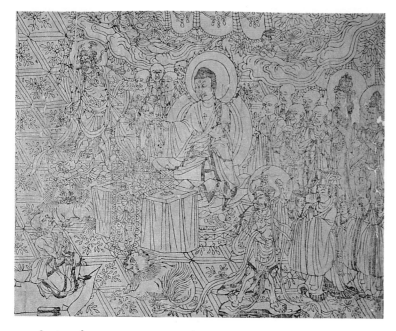

195 Section of THE DIAMOND SUTRA.
Chinese Buddhist text 868.
Scroll, woodblock print on paper.
Length of entire scroll 18'.
By permission of The British Library. OR.8210f2.

RELIEF

In a *relief* process, the printmaker cuts away all parts of the printing surface not meant to carry the ink, leaving the design to be printed "in relief" at the level of the original surface. The surface is then inked, and the ink is transferred to paper with pressure. Relief processes include *woodcuts, wood engravings,* and *linoleum cuts* (or *linocuts*). Marks made by rubber stamps and wet tires are examples of relief-printed marks in the everyday world.

The traditional woodcut process lends itself to designs with bold black-and-white contrast. The image-bearing block of wood, usually a soft wood, is a plank cut along the grain. Color can be printed with single or multiple blocks. As with most printmaking techniques, when more than one color is used, individually inked blocks—one for each color—are carefully *registered* (lined up) to ensure that colors will be exactly placed in the final print.

Block printing from woodcuts originated in China, where the desire to spread the Buddhist religion greatly influenced the type of prints produced. THE DIAMOND SUTRA is one of the world's oldest surviving books. It opens with a woodblock print of the Buddha, surrounded by attendants and guardians, preaching to an old man seen in the lower left. (The swastika on the Buddha's chest is an ancient symbol of his enlightenment.) An inscription states that it was made in 868 for free distribution, an apparent act of religious goodwill. The hard wood of this early print makes possible the many fine lines in the design, which is similar in style to stone carvings from the same time period. It is in excellent condition despite its age, because the work was hidden in a cave for many centuries.

Woodblock printing became a highly developed art in Japan in the seventeenth through the nineteenth centuries. Japanese woodblock prints were made through a complex process that used multiple blocks to achieve subtle and highly integrated color effects. Since they were much cheaper than paintings, these prints were the preferred art form for middle-class people who lived in the capital city of Edo (now known as Tokyo). Their subject matter included famous theater actors, night life, landscapes, and even erotic pictures. Japanese prints were among the first objects of Asian art to be appreciated by European artists, and many Impressionist and Post-Impressionist painters were strongly influenced by them.

Japanese artist Hokusai's color woodcut prints have become well known around the world. Hokusai worked in close collaboration with highly skilled craftsmen to realize the final prints. For each of his woodcuts, specialists transferred Hokusai's watercolor brush painting to as many as twenty blocks, then cut the blocks. In Hokusai's famous print WAVE AT KANAGAWA, a clawing mountain of water dwarfs tiny fishermen in their boats, climaxing the rhythmic curves of the churning ocean. The only stable element is the distant peak of Mt. Fuji. A more realistic rendering would not

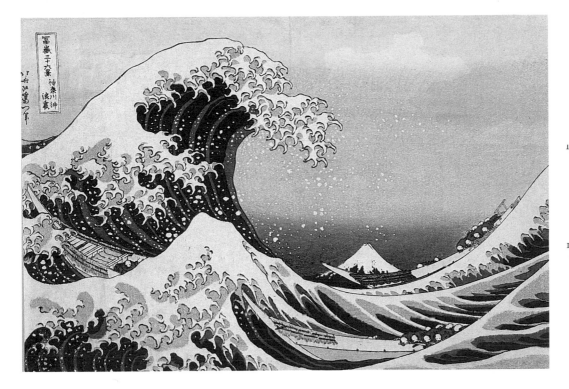

196 Katsushika Hokusai
(1760–1849).
THE WAVE. c 1830.
Color woodblock print.
10¼" × 15⅛

Private Collection. Art Resource , New York.

197 Emil Nolde (German,
1867–1956).
PROPHET. 1912.
Woodcut. (Schiefler/Mosel
1966 [W] 110. only);
Image 12½" × 8¹³⁄₁₆";
Sheet. 15¾" × 13¹⁵⁄₁₆".

Photograph © Board of Trustees, National
Gallery of Art, Washington, D.C. Rosenwald
Collection. 1943.36698. (B–9059)/PR.

have been as effective in capturing the awesome power of the sea. This print is one of Hokusai's thirty-six famous views of Mount Fuji seen from various locations.

The stylized detail in Hokusai's print is quite different from the intentional roughness of the woodcut PROPHET by German artist Emil Nolde. Each cut in the block contributes to the expressive image of an old man's face and reveals the character of the wood and the wood-cutting process. The light-and-dark pattern created through simplification of the features gives emotional intensity to the image. Nolde's direct approach is a recent development in the long tradition of German printmaking that included the work of Albrecht Dürer.

The linoleum cut is a modern development in relief printing. The artist starts with the rubbery, synthetic surface of linoleum and gouges out white areas not intended to take ink. The material is softer than wood and has no grain, characteristics that allow rounder and more numerous gouges.

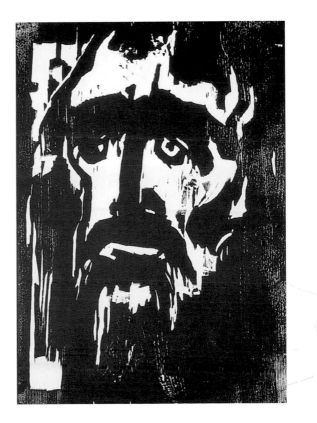

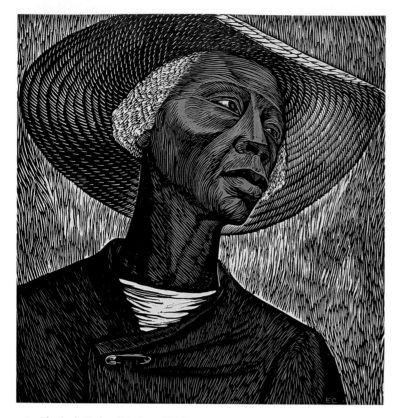

198 Elizabeth Catlett (Mexican, 1919).
SHARECROPPER. 1970.
Color linocut on cream Japanese paper. 15⅓" × 10⅛".
Restricted gift of Mr. and Mrs. Robert S. Hartman. 1992.182.
Photograph: © 2002 The Art Institute of Chicago. All rights reserved.
© Elizabeth Catlett/Licensed by VAGA, NY.

An example of a linoleum cut (or linocut) is SHARECROPPER by Elizabeth Catlett, in which the even white gouges betray the soft material. This work also typifies Catlett's lifelong devotion to creating dignified images of African Americans in art.

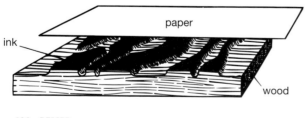

199 RELIEF.

INTAGLIO

Intaglio printing is the opposite of relief: areas below the surface hold the ink. *Intaglio* comes from the Italian *intagliare,* "to cut into." The image to be printed is either cut or scratched into a metal surface by steel- or diamond-tip tools, or etched into the surface by acid. To make a print, the printmaker first daubs the plate with viscous printer's ink, then wipes the surface clean, leaving ink only in the etched or grooved portions. Damp paper is then placed on the inked plate, and a print is made when the dampened paper picks up the ink in the grooves as it passes beneath the press roller. The pressure of the roller creates a characteristic plate mark around the edges of the print. Intaglio printing was traditionally done from polished copper plates, but now zinc, steel, aluminum, and even plastic are often used. Engraving, drypoint, and etching are intaglio processes.

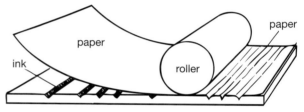

200 INTAGLIO.

Engraving

In *engravings,* lines are cut into the polished surface of the plate with a *burin,* or engraving tool. This exacting process takes strength and control. Lines are made by pushing the burin through the metal to carve a groove, removing a narrow strip of metal in the process. A clean line is desired; thus, any rough edges of the groove must be smoothed down with a scraper. Engraved lines cannot be as freely drawn as etched lines because of the pressure needed to cut the grooves. The precise, smooth curves and parallel lines typical of engravings are obvious in the engraved portraits that appear on the paper currency we use.

We can see the complex richness of engraved lines in Albrecht Dürer's magnificent engraving THE KNIGHT, DEATH AND THE DEVIL, reproduced here close to its actual size. Thousands of fine lines define the shapes, masses, spaces, values, and textures

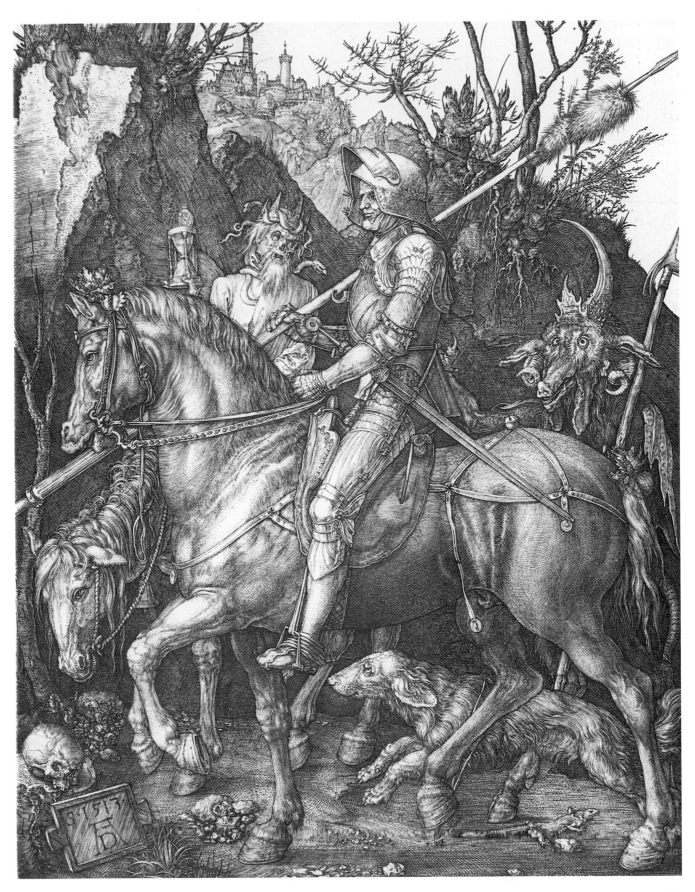

201   Albrecht Dürer (1471–1528). THE KNIGHT, DEATH AND THE DEVIL. 1513.
Engraving Page: 10 × 7⅞", Plate: 9⅝ × 7½.
Brooklyn Museum of Art, New York. Gift of Mrs. Horace O. Havemeyer. 54.35.6.

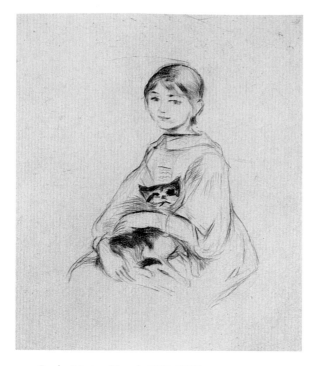

202 Berthe Morisot (French, 1841–1985).
LITTLE GIRL WITH CAT. 1888–90.
Drypoint. 1953.697.(B–21058)/PR.
Photograph by Ricardo Blanc © 2002 Board of Trustees, National Gallery of Art,
Washington, D.C. Rosenwald Collection.

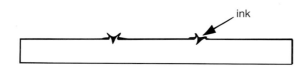

203 DRYPOINT PLATE.

of the depicted objects. The precision of Dürer's lines seems appropriate to the subject—an image of the noble Christian knight moving with resolute commitment, unswayed by the forces of chaos, evil, and death that surround him (a discussion of the print's iconography appears on page 35).

Drypoint

Drypoint is similar to line engraving. Using a thin, pencil-like, pointed tool with a steel or diamond tip, the artist digs lines into a soft copper or zinc plate. The displaced metal leaves a *burr*, or rough edge, similar to the row of earth left by a plow. The burr catches the ink and, when printed, leaves a slightly blurred line. Because the burr is fragile and deteriorates rapidly from the pressure of the printing press rollers as prints are made, drypoint editions are by necessity small. Skillful draftsmanship is required, for drypoint lines are difficult to execute and almost impossible to correct. The soft, somewhat sketchy line quality in Berthe Morisot's gentle depiction of LITTLE GIRL WITH CAT is characteristic of drypoint prints.

Etching

The process of making an *etching* begins with the preparation of a metal plate with a *ground*—a protective coating of acid-resistant material that covers the copper or zinc. The printmaker then draws easily through the ground with a pointed tool, exposing the metal. Finally, the plate is immersed in acid. Acid "bites" into the plate where the drawing has exposed the metal, making a groove that varies in depth according to the strength of the acid and the length of time the plate is in the acid bath.

Because they are more easily produced, etched lines are generally more relaxed or irregular than engraved lines. We can see the difference in line quality between an etching and an engraving—the freedom versus the precision—by comparing the lines in Rembrandt's etching CHRIST PREACHING with the lines in Dürer's engraving THE KNIGHT, DEATH AND THE DEVIL.

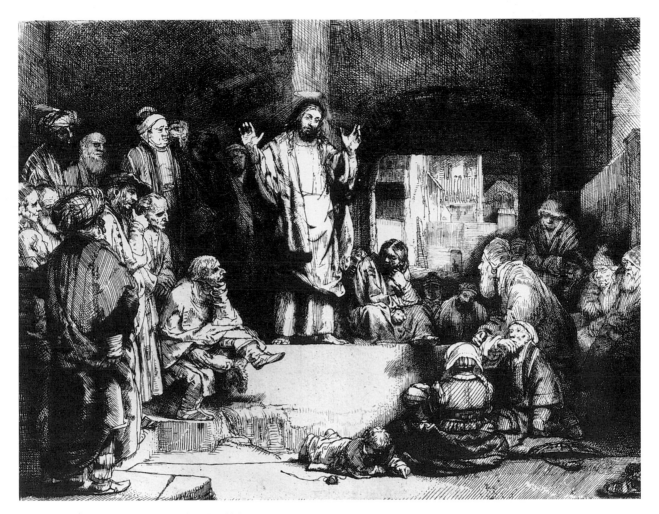

204 Rembrandt Harmensz van Rijn (1606–1669).
CHRIST PREACHING. c. 1652.
Etching. 61⅟₁₆" × 8⅛".
The Metropolitan Museum of Art.
Bequest of Mrs. H.O. Havemeyer Collection, 1929. (29.107.18).

In CHRIST PREACHING, Rembrandt's personal understanding of Christ's gentle compassion is in harmony with the decisive yet relaxed quality of the artist's etched lines. This etching shows Rembrandt's typical use of a wide range of values, achieved with drypoint as well as etching. Skillful use of light and shadow draws attention to the figure of Christ and gives clarity and interest to the whole image. In a composition in which each figure is similar in size, Rembrandt identifies Jesus as the key figure by setting him off with a light area below, a light vertical band above, and implied lines of attention leading to him from the faces of his listeners.

Aquatint is an etching process used to obtain shaded areas in black-and-white or color prints. Contemporary aquatints are prepared with acid-resistant spray paints. When the plate is placed in acid, the exposed areas between the paint particles are eaten away to produce a rough surface capable of holding ink. Values thus produced can vary from light to dark, depending on how long the plate is in the acid. Because aquatint is not suited to making thin lines, it is usually combined with a linear print process such as engraving, drypoint, or line etching.

American artist Mary Cassatt's prints and paintings show the influence of the strong flat shapes and elegant lines of Japanese woodblock prints. She was

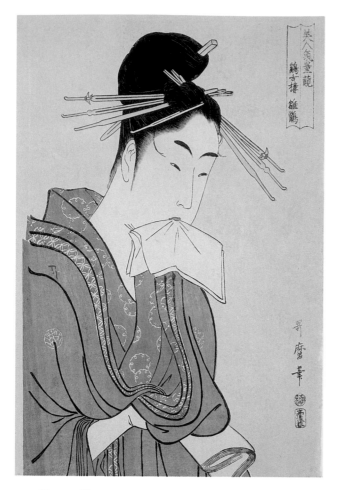

205 Kitagawa Utamaro.
A COMPETITIVE SHOWING OF BEAUTIES:
HINZAURU OF THE HEIZETSURO.
c. 1796.
Woodblock print. 15⅓" × 10⅛".
Clarence Buckingham Collection, 1925.3047.
Photograph courtesy of the Art Institute of Chicago.

206 Mary Cassatt. THE LETTER. 1891.
Drypoint, soft ground etching, and aquatint.
13⅝" × 8¹⁵⁄₁₆".
The Metropolitan Museum of Art. Gift of Paul J. Sachs, 1916.
Photograph: © 1991 The Metropolitan Museum of Art, NY.

especially drawn to the work of Kitagawa Utamaro, who frequently made prints depicting fashionable ladies. Cassatt owned many prints by Utamaro, including A COMPETITIVE SHOWING OF BEAUTIES: HINZAURU OF THE HEIZETSURO in which a woman holds a scarf in her lips while dressing. Cassatt borrowed the composition of this work for her own print THE LETTER. She made the fine lines in the dress using drypoint, and the flat color areas with aquatint.

LITHOGRAPHY

Etching and engraving date to the fifteenth and sixteenth centuries respectively, but lithography was not developed until early in the nineteenth century.

Lithography is a surface or planographic printing process based on the mutual antipathy of oil and water. It lends itself well to a direct manner of working because the artist draws an image on the surface of the stone or plate, without any cutting. Its directness makes lithography faster and somewhat more flexible than other methods. A lithograph is often difficult to distinguish from a drawing.

Using litho crayons, litho pencils, or a greasy liquid called *tusche,* the artist draws the image on flat, fine-grained Bavarian limestone (or on a metal surface that duplicates the character of such stone). After the image is complete, it is chemically treated with gum arabic and a small amount of acid to "fix" it on the upper layer of the stone. The surface is then dampened with water and is inked. The oil-

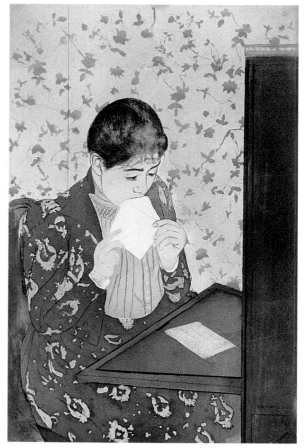

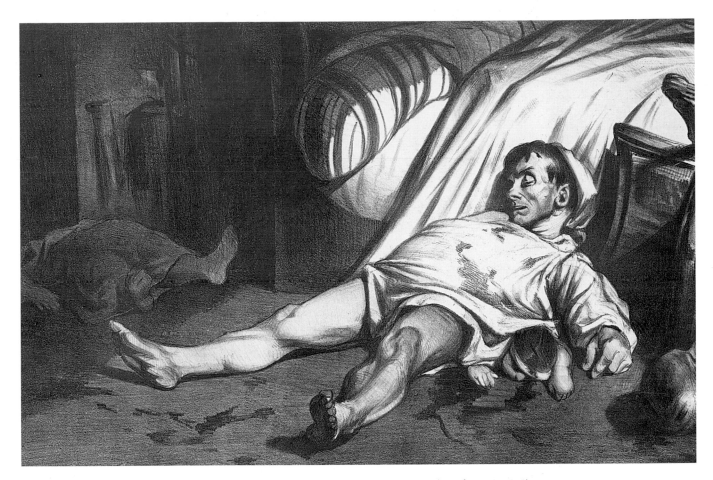

based ink is repelled by the water in the blank areas, but it adheres to the greasy area of the image. As in other print processes, when the surface is covered with paper and run through a press, the image is transferred to the paper.

Although lithography was a new medium in the early 1800s, it had a major impact on society because prints could be produced quickly and easily. Before the development of modern printing presses, it provided the illustrations for newspapers, posters, and handbills. Honoré Daumier, one of the first great lithographic artists, made his living drawing satirical and documentary lithographs for French newspapers. His personal style was well suited to the direct quality of the lithographic process.

In RUE TRANSNONAIN, Daumier carefully reconstructed an event that occurred during a period of civil unrest in Paris in 1834. The militia claimed that a shot was fired from a building on Transnonain Street. Soldiers responded by entering the apartment

207 Honoré Daumier (French, 1808–1879). RUE TRANSNONAIN, April 15, 1834. Lithograph. 11¼" × 17⅜".
© The Cleveland Museum of Art, 2001. Gift of Ralph King. (1924.809).

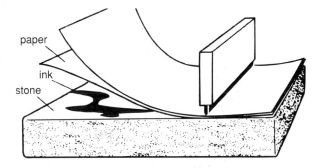

208 LITHOGRAPHY.

and killing all the occupants including many innocent people. Daumier's lithograph of the event was published the following day. The lithograph clearly reflects the artist's feelings, but it also conveys information in the way news photographs and television do today. Rembrandt's influence is evident in the composition of strong light and dark areas that increase the dramatic impact of Daumier's image.

The freedom and directness of lithography made the technique ideal for the spontaneous, witty approach of Henri de Toulouse-Lautrec. In the space of about ten years, this prolific artist created over three hundred lithographs. Many of them were designed as posters advertising everything from popular nightclub entertainers to bicycles. His posters of cabaret singer and dancer Jane Avril made her a star and simultaneously gave Parisians of the 1890s a firsthand look at "modern art" by a leading artist. Toulouse-Lautrec's innovations in lithography, including spatter techniques, large format, and use of vivid color, greatly influenced both lithography and graphic design in the twentieth century.

The popular lithographic poster JANE AVRIL appears to have begun with an awkward photograph and come to life in a dynamic oil sketch. The sketch was then incorporated as the key element in a strong lithograph, drawn with brush and liquid tusche on the litho stone. Compare the angles of the feet and legs in the photograph with those in the sketch. Toulouse-Lautrec used diagonal lines and curves to introduce a sense of motion missing in the photograph. In the print he placed Jane Avril in a nightclub setting and balanced her figure with the silhouetted shape of a bass player. A dark line emerging from the bass frames the dancer. Toulouse-Lautrec's strong use of shapes and fluid brush lines retains much of the vigor of the sketch and reflects his admiration for Japanese prints.

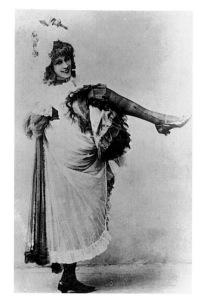

209 Henri de Toulouse-Lautrec.
JANE AVRIL. c. 1893.
Photograph.
Edita S.A., Lausanne, Switzerland.

210 Henri de Toulouse-Lautrec.
JANE AVRIL DANSANT. c. 1893.
Oil study on cardboard.
38" × 27".
A.C. Cooper (Colour) Ltd. Private collection.

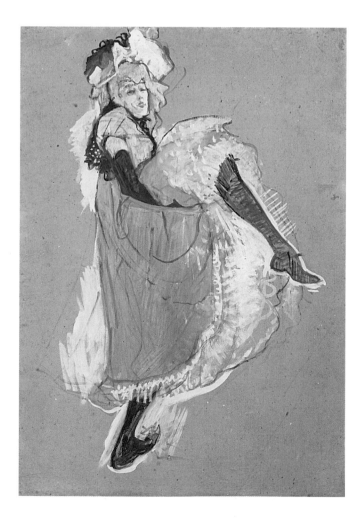

211 Henri de Toulouse-Lautrec.
JANE AVRIL. JARDIN DE PARIS. c. 1893.
Color lithograph. 50⅝" × 37".
The Metropolitan Museum of Art. Harris Brisbane Dick Fund, 1932.

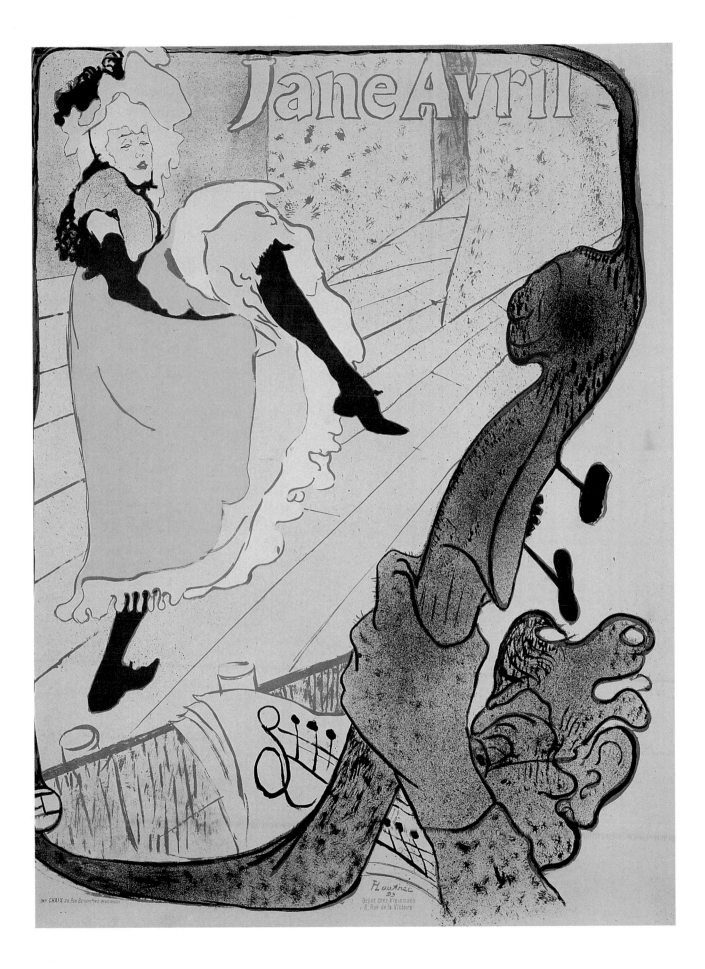

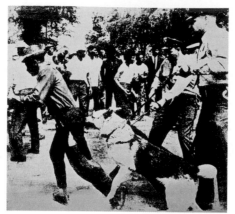

212 Andy Warhol (1928–1987).
LITTLE RACE RIOT. 1964.
Synthetic polymer paint
and silkscreen ink on
canvas. 30" × 33".
Art Resource, NY. ©2002 Andy Warhol
Foundation for the Visual Arts/Artists
Rights Society (ARS), New York.

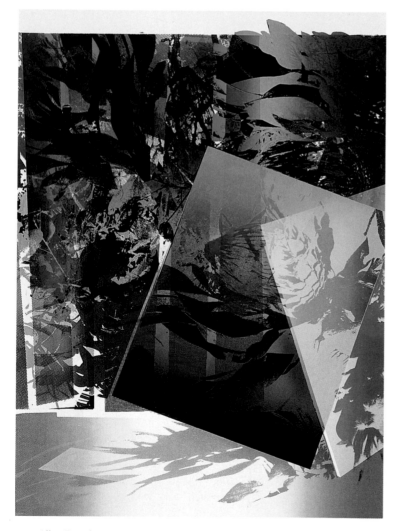

213 Allyn Bromley.
GREENHOUSE SERIES: PROTEA.
1987. Screenprint. 30" × 22".
Courtesy of the artist.

SCREENPRINTING

Modern *screenprinting* is a refinement of the ancient and relatively simple technique of stencil printing. Early in this century, stencil technique was improved by adhering the stencil to a screen made of silk fabric stretched across a frame (synthetic fabric is used today). With a rubber-edged tool (called a *squeegee*), ink is then pushed through the fabric in the open areas of the stencil to make an image of the stencil on the material being printed. Because silk was the traditional material used for the screen, the process is also known as *silkscreen* or *serigraphy* (*seri* is Latin for silk).

Screenprinting is well suited to the production of images with areas of uniform color. Each separate color requires a different screen, but registering and printing are relatively simple. There is no reversal of the image in screenprinting—in contrast to relief, intaglio, and lithographic processes in which the image on the plate is "flopped" in the printing process. The medium also allows the production of large, nearly mass-produced editions without loss of quality.

The latest development in screenprinting is the photographic stencil, or *photo screen,* achieved by attaching light-sensitive gelatin to the screen fabric.

Capitalizing on the impersonal, mass-media look provided by this technique, Andy Warhol popularized photo-screenprinting. LITTLE RACE RIOT is a work derived from a news photograph of a 1964 civil rights demonstration. Warhol expanded the photograph and transferred it to a silkscreen, thus magnifying its flat, impersonal character.

In contrast to Warhol's opaque, flat areas of color, Allyn Bromley's prints are comprised of overlapping translucent layers of color. She has brought a painterly quality to the previously flat, posterlike look of screenprinting. In PROTEA, Bromley combined photographic as well as hand-drawn images.

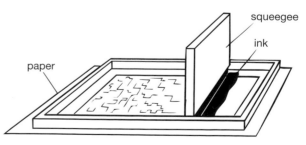

214 SCREENPRINTING.

215 Willie Cole.
STOWAGE. 1997.
Woodcut, printed in black,
composition: 49⁹⁄₁₆" × 95⁹⁄₁₆".
The Museum of Modern Art, New York.
Jacqueline Brody Fund and The Friends of
Education Fund. Photograph © 2002 The
Museum of Modern Art, New York.

CURRENT DIRECTIONS

Experimental printmaking in recent years has taken two general directions: use of experimental printing matrices, and use of digital technology. Each has altered the boundaries of the medium.

Willie Cole's mother and grandmother supplemented the family income by doing laundry, including ironing. The artist commonly repaired their broken irons, keeping them if they were beyond repair. To create his large 1997 woodcut STOWAGE, he cut round holes in a wood plank and imprinted the scorch that twelve different irons made. The shape in the center of the print was transferred from an ironing board.

The work is about more than ironing, though. Cole noticed how the shape of the board resembled the shape of slave ships that brought his ancestors from Africa. The twelve scorches represent African tribes that made up the cargo. Suddenly we see a visual parallel between ancient and modern "slavery."

Digital technology has altered printmaking at a more basic level by eliminating the tangible plate. The matrix can be made not by hand but with a keyboard and mouse. Some artists make digital prints using painting and photograph programs, and then erase the matrix files when the "edition" is complete. This technology allows for the creation of prints that are not original in the traditional sense, because they are infinitely reproducible.

Argentine artist Alicia Candiani combines digital and traditional technologies in prints that question stereotypical representations of women. Beginning with antique photographs, she alters and crops them with a scanner and photo manipulation program. She then superimposes other types of imagery, as we see in her 1999 work NO TE SALVES AHORA (DO NOT SAVE YOURSELF NOW). A female figure is posed to resemble a national symbol, as she wears a toga and a starred laurel wreath. She holds in her hand a staff with the cap and wreath that also appear on the Argentine flag. The star from her hair is echoed in the field at the left. Across most of the surface the artist has spread a dense array of lines that come from dressmaking patterns. This complex layering of personal and national symbols describes some of the ways in which the female identity is constructed in society. The work questions whether women can ever save themselves from stereotypes and become fully human.

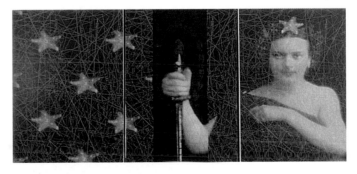

216 Alicia Candiani.
NO TE SALVES AHORA (DO NOT SAVE YOURSELF NOW).
1998.
Digital print on paper, tryptich 40" × 84".
Courtesy the artist.

The concept of original "fine" prints may seem out of place at a time when good reproductions are readily available. Although reproductions are merely mechanically made copies, without the exact color or texture of the original, they do make the art of the world available to all of us as never before.

Original prints, regardless of type, are those printed by the artist or under the artist's supervision from matrices made by, or in collaboration with, the artist. The term *reproduction* signifies a photomechanical copy of an original work of art. Any print that is made from a preexisting work of art, whether through photographic techniques or by skilled copyists, is a reproductive print or reproduction. Any work that is made by photographic reproduction is not an original print.

The terms original print and fine print signify the artist's intent: to create multiple originals, rather than copies of a single, preexisting original, such as a painting. The printmaker works directly to create the printing surface on stone, wood, metal, plastic, or any material that may be used to transfer images or make impressions. This can include digital files created and printed by an artist.

Buying original prints by artists, especially young or emerging artists, is an excellent way to acquire and enjoy original works of art at modest expense. However, the buyer should beware. The recent practice of selling photomechanical reproductions at high prices, under the guise of "limited edition prints," has confused many people who are unaware of the difference between reproductions and original prints. The advertising of art as a commodity for investment has led unscrupulous dealers to intentionally obscure the distinction between original prints and reproductions. It is important for buyers to recognize the difference between inexpensively produced reproductions, which should sell for a few dollars, and original prints that should be priced as works of art.

Some artists use photomechanical means to reproduce their own pieces; these reproductions are then sold as "signed prints" or posters, sometimes called "art prints." The marketing of signed reproductions is based on the artist's feeling that it is most important to get one's work seen and be able to make a living from selling it. This practice raises ethical and practical questions about the value and quality of an original, the value of a signature on a reproduction, and the extent to which art should be shaped and motivated by profit.

How can you tell a reproduction from an original print? If close scrutiny with a magnifying glass reveals a rigid pattern of small dots of the type shown at the top of page 66, then the work is a reproduction, not a handmade original print. But there are exceptions; some highly sophisticated printing systems, including laser scanners, produce reproductions that do not have dot patterns. Original serigraphs (screenprints) have layers of ink that look like paint on top of, rather than absorbed by, the paper. Original etchings and engravings are produced with a printing press, which causes the edge of the plate to leave an indentation in the paper called a *plate mark.*

Most original prints are signed and numbered by the artist in the lower margin to indicate personal involvement and approval. Original prints are usually produced in quantities called limited editions. All the prints in an edition are nearly identical, and each is called an original work. The artist generally destroys the plate, block, or screen after the edition has been printed in order to ensure the integrity of his or her work. In many states laws now require artists to provide cancellation proofs when they sell limited editions of their prints. A cancellation proof shows that the original printing surface has indeed been permanently altered (frequently with a big X across the image), and that no further prints of the original image can be made. Such regulation by law is designed to protect both artists and buyers against abuses of the traditional printmaking edition system.

The hands-on involvement of the originating artist is the crucial factor determining the value of a fine print: Original prints are always printed by the artist or by a printer working directly under the artist's supervision. Any work produced through photomechanical processes or without the artist's personal involvement from start to finish is a reproduction.

Before purchasing an original print, buyers should request complete disclosure information, including the name of the artist who created the matrix used to make the print; the method used for printing; the type of paper used; the name of the printer, if different from the artist; the number of impressions in existence; the manner in which the prints in the edition are numbered and identified; the number of artist's proofs; and the current status of the original matrix. With protection of the integrity of original prints, it is possible for people to purchase high-quality art at affordable prices.

CHAPTER TEN

CAMERA ARTS AND COMPUTER IMAGING

When we are captivated by the compelling realism of photography, film, or television, we can easily forget that the camera arts are recent extensions of a long pictorial tradition based on the desire to make lifelike images of our significant experiences. Each new technique in the history of art relies heavily on its predecessors.

Photography has been influenced by Western painting, and in turn it has influenced painting. Cinematography grew from and continues to rely on the basic principles of still photography. And television is influenced by painting, photography, and cinematography. When we are impressed by the beauty of a particular shot in a film or video, we often say it looks like a painting. In turn, television and other photographic imagery influence the more traditional visual and performing arts. Apart from all these mutual influences, cameras and computers provide means through which both past and present art can be reproduced and enjoyed by people in all parts of the world.

PHOTOGRAPHY

Photography literally means "light-writing," although a more accurate description would be "light-drawing." Like drawing, photography can be either an art form or a practical tool. Beyond its many uses in journalism, science, advertising, pub-

lic relations, and other fields—as well as for recording family history—photography offers the artist a powerful means of expression.

Many nineteenth-century inventions changed the way we live; but of all of them, photography had the greatest impact on the way we see. As an art form, photography reveals the photographer's personal way of seeing and responding. Given the same subject, ten photographers will make ten different photographs, because each photographer conveys what he or she feels is most significant about the subject. Individual styles would not be evident in photographs if photography were not a means of personal expression and communication.

Although ads for some cameras would have us believe that a particular brand will almost automatically produce "great pictures," it is the photographer, not the equipment, that makes the difference between an ordinary snapshot and a work of art. Beyond selecting camera, lens, and film, a skilled photographer makes many choices about light, angle, focus, distance, and composition. The best photographers have learned to visualize their photographs before releasing the shutter. Depending on how it is used, the camera can either enhance or dull our visual awareness. American photographer Ansel Adams spoke of the need to give considerable time and effort to the making of a photograph for the result to be worthwhile.

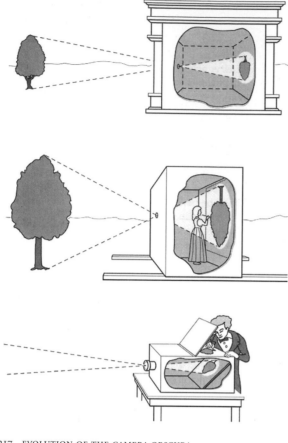

217 EVOLUTION OF THE CAMERA OBSCURA,
PREDECESSOR OF THE MODERN CAMERA.
a. Sixteenth-century camera obscura.
b. Seventeenth-century portable camera obscura.
c. Seventeenth–nineteenth-century table model camera obscura.

I have often thought that if photography were difficult in the true sense of the term—meaning that the creation of a simple photograph would entail as much time and effort as the production of a good watercolor or etching—there would be a vast improvement in total output. The sheer ease with which we can produce a superficial image often leads to creative disaster. We must remember that a photograph can hold just as much as we put into it, and no one has ever approached the full possibilities of the medium.[1]

Edwin Land, who developed the Polaroid instant camera, also emphasized the process of making a photograph when he described how even automatic, "instant" cameras can help us learn to see:

At its best, photography can be an extra sense, or a reservoir for the senses. Even when you don't press the trigger, the exercise of focusing through a camera can make you better remember thereafter a person or a moment. When we had flowers in this office recently to use as test objects, it was a great experience to take pictures of them. I learned to know each rose. I now know more about roses and leaves, and that enriched my life. Photography can teach people to look, to feel, to remember in a way that they didn't know they could.[2]

The Evolution of Photography

The basic concept of the camera preceded actual photography by more than three hundred years. The desire of Renaissance artists to make accurate depictions of nature was the impetus behind the eventual invention of photography as we know it.

The forerunner of the modern camera was the *camera obscura,* literally "dark room." The concept of photography grew out of the observation that reflected sunlight passing through a small hole in the wall of a darkened room projects onto the opposite wall an inverted image of whatever lies outside. In the fifteenth century, Leonardo da Vinci described the device as an aid to observation and picture making.

As a fixed room, or even as a portable room, the camera obscura was too large and cumbersome to be widely used. In the seventeenth century, when it was realized that the person tracing the image did not have to be inside, the CAMERA OBSCURA evolved into a portable dark box. During the course of this pre-camera evolution, a lens was placed in the small hole to improve image clarity. Later an angled mirror was added to right the inverted image, enabling anyone, skilled or unskilled, to trace the projected pictures with pen or pencil (see the table model CAMERA OBSCURA).

It was not until about 1826 that the first vague photographic image was made by Joseph Nicéphore Niépce. He recorded and fixed on a sheet of pewter an image made by exposing the sensitized metal plate to light for eight hours. During the next

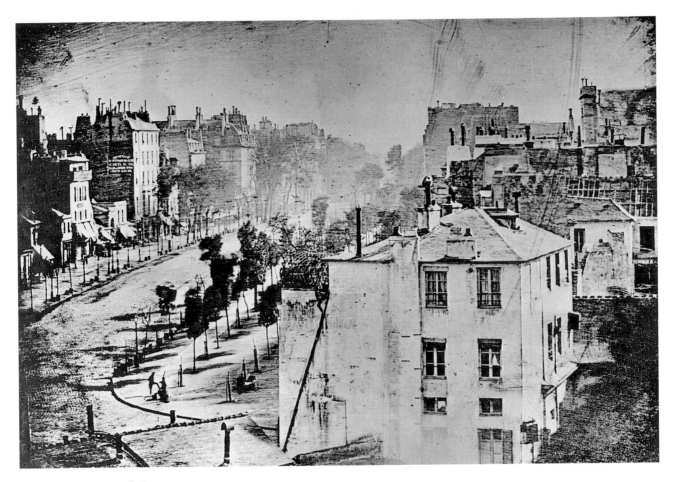

218 Louis Jacques Mandé Daguerre.
LE BOULEVARD DU TEMPLE. 1839.
Daguerreotype.
Bayerisches National Museum, Munich (R6312).

decade, the painter Louis Daguerre further perfected Niépce's process and produced some of the first satisfactory photographs, known as *daguerreotypes.*

At first, because the necessary exposure times were so long, photography could record only stationary objects. In Daguerre's photograph of LE BOULEVARD DU TEMPLE, taken in Paris in 1839 (the year his process was made public), the streets appear deserted because moving figures made no lasting light impressions on the plate. However, one man, having his shoes shined, stayed still long enough to become part of the image. He is visible on the corner in the lower left, the first person to appear in a photograph. It was a significant moment in history: At last images of people and things could be made without the hand of a

trained artist. Although some painters at the time felt the new medium was unfair competition and spelled the end of their art, the invention of photography actually marked the beginning of a period when art would be more accessible to all through photographic reproductions; it also marked not the end but the beginning of new approaches to painting, complemented by the new art of photography.

Before the development of the camera, it was usually only royalty and the wealthy who could afford to have their portraits painted. By the mid-nineteenth century, people of average means were going in great numbers to photography studios to sit unblinking for several minutes in bright sunlight to have their portraits made with the camera.

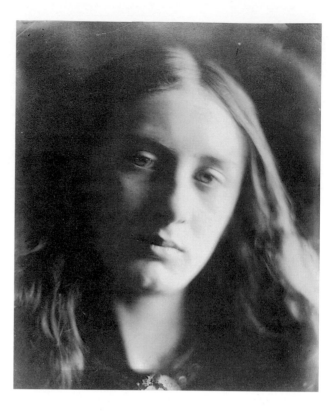

219   Julia Margaret Cameron.
JULIA JACKSON. March 1866.
Albumen silver print from wet-collodion
glass negative. 33.8 × 28 cm.
Gernsheim Collection, Harry Ransom Humanities Research
Center, The University of Texas at Austin.

From the beginning, portrait photography was heavily influenced by the traditions of portrait painting. The art of portrait photography was raised to a high level by English artist Julia Margaret Cameron. By 1864, she had become an avid photographer and had begun to create some of the most expressive portraits ever made with a camera. Cameron pioneered the use of close-ups and carefully controlled lighting to enhance the images of her subjects, who were often family members and famous friends. Her portrait of JULIA JACKSON is an excellent example. Cameron's use of raking light and a soft focus combine with Jackson's intense gaze and slight tilt of the head to suggest thoughtful energy.

Many nineteenth-century photographers looked for ways to duplicate what painters had already done—and thereby failed to find their medium's unique strengths. Painters, meanwhile—partially freed by photography from their ancient role as recorders of events, places, and people—looked for other avenues to explore. Yet some leading painters were greatly influenced by photography.

The Technology of Photography

Although the technology of modern cameras can be complex, the basic unit is still simply a lightproof box with an opening, or *aperture,* set behind a *lens* designed to focus, or order, the light rays passing through it. It also has a *shutter* to control the length of time the light is allowed to strike the light-sensitive film or plate held within the body of the camera.

HUMAN EYE AND CAMERA enables us to compare the camera to a simplified drawing of the human eye. The major differences are that the eye receives a continuous flow of changing images that are interpreted by the brain, whereas the still camera depends on light-sensitive film or a digital scanner to record an image and can only pick up a single image at a time. Also, with a pair of eyes, we see in stereoscopic vision, while a camera's vision is monoscopic. Monoscopic vision tends to flatten the visual field; with stereoscopic vision we see slightly more of an object from two different angles, thereby heightening our perception of depth.

The adjustable aperture in the lens of a sophisticated camera is similar to the changing pupil of the human eye, as seen in PUPIL OF EYE AND CAMERA LENS APERTURE. By changing the aperture, a photographer adjusts the amount of light entering the camera and simultaneously determines the depth of the area in sharp focus—called the *depth of field*—in the photograph. A large aperture gives a relatively shallow depth of field. By closing down the size of the opening, the photographer increases the area in focus, as seen in DEPTH OF FIELD WITH APERTURE ADJUSTMENTS.

To understand the relationship between depth of field and aperture, hold your thumb about a foot in front of your face and focus your eyes on it. Notice how objects behind it are out of focus. Now curl the fingers of your other hand to make a very small tunnel and hold it up to one eye. The light reflected off your thumb will pass through the tunnel to your eye. As you look at your thumb through the small opening or aperture, you will notice that both your thumb and what is just behind it come into sharper focus.

The various types of *film* are essentially transparent plastic strips or single sheets coated with light-sensitive emulsion. Exposed and developed print film is called a *negative* because the light and dark areas of the original subjects are reversed. Color positive film, such as slide film, produces a positive image that can be projected or printed.

Digital cameras have evolved very rapidly, so that now their picture quality rivals that of conventional negative film. These cameras direct focused light onto a scanner instead of film. Images are stored in digital files for easy downloading to a computer, where they can be manipulated in many ways and then printed.

In cameras of all types, the quality of the lens is most important. Lenses are designed to gather and concentrate a maximum amount of available light in order to transmit a sharply focused image quickly. The most versatile cameras allow for interchangeable lenses capable of various angles of view. The ANGLE OF VIEW diagram (following page) shows approximate angles of view with normal, telephoto, and wide-angle lenses. A zoom lens permits the focal length of the lens to be adjusted to various distances from close to far.

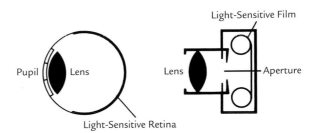

220 HUMAN EYE AND CAMERA.

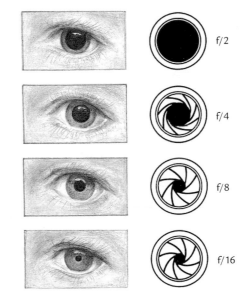

221 PUPIL OF EYE AND CAMERA LENS APERTURE.

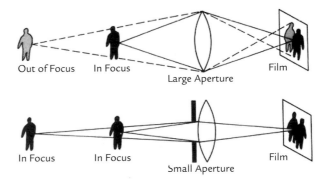

222 DEPTH OF FIELD WITH APERTURE ADJUSTMENTS.

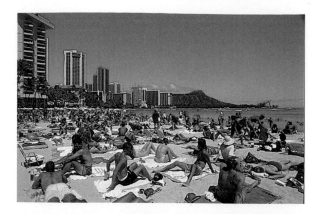

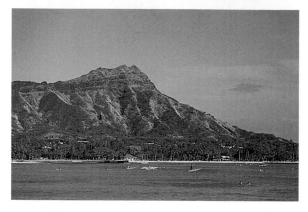

224 PHOTOGRAPHS OF WAIKIKI AND DIAMOND HEAD.
  a. With a wide-angle (24 mm) lens.
  b. With a telephoto (135 mm) lens.
    Photographs: Duane Preble

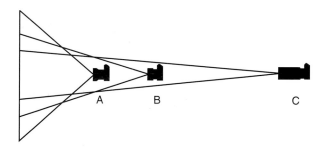

223 ANGLE OF VIEW.
  a. Wide-angle lens.
  b. Normal lens.
  c. Telephoto lens.

The PHOTOGRAPHS OF WAIKIKI AND DIAMOND HEAD were taken from the same position, on the same beach, on the same day, using different lenses. The shot taken with a wide-angle lens takes in the crowded beach and massive high-rise hotels of the new Waikiki, while the telephoto shot edits out the congested resort area to show only a few surfers enjoying the waves—to imply an unspoiled island paradise. As this example shows, photography is not always objective, as many would believe. It can stretch the truth, and it can mislead.

Photography as an Art Form

In the beginning, much of the public was reluctant to put photography on the same plane as other art forms because of its reliance on a mechanical device. Today, however, most people agree that the camera can be a vehicle for personal expression, symbolic communication, and eye-catching compositions. An early crusader in the art photography movement was American Alfred Stieglitz, who opened a photography gallery in New York City in 1905. The gallery, which was called 291 after its address on Fifth Avenue, showed only photography until 1908, when Stieglitz began to exhibit painting and sculpture as well. He also founded an influential magazine, *Camera Work,* which published photography along with essays about modern art and culture.

Stieglitz's own photography was almost always "straight"—that is, produced with no technical manipulation of the negative. In his 1903 photograph THE FLATIRON BUILDING, Stieglitz arranged visual fields so that they echo each other. The basic shape of the foreground tree is answered in the stand of trees in the middle ground, but the fork of its branches also suggests the angle of the building (the "Flatiron" of the title). Like the foreground tree, this building seems to emerge from the ground, an impression supported by the row of seats in the snowy park. The recession of the ground from front to back of the picture is contradicted above the horizon, where the Flatiron and the black tree branches seem to touch. In his early photographs, Stieglitz showed the poetry he saw in urban reality. His imagery of this period reflects the influence of French Impressionist painting.

One of photography's special strengths is its ability to capture a moment in time. French photographer Henri Cartier-Bresson captured a subtle moment of urban drama in BEHIND THE GARE ST. LAZARE, PARIS. Here he released the shutter at exactly the right moment to capture a man leaping over a puddle. The man's shape is echoed in both his own shadow and that of the dancer in the poster behind, just as semicircular ripples find a parallel in the round shapes close by in the water. For Cartier-Bresson, good photography is a matter of capturing the decisive moment:

To me, photography is the simultaneous recognition, in a fraction of a second, of the significance of an event as well as of a precise organization of forms which give that event its proper expression.[3]

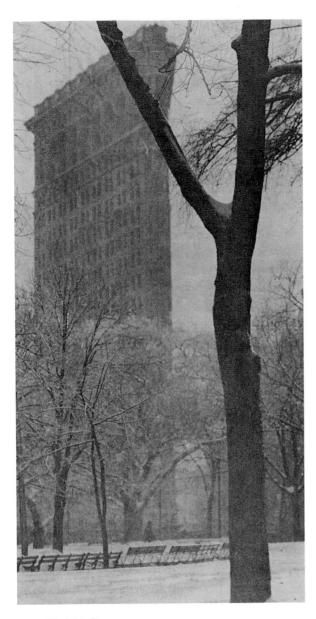

225   Alfred Stieglitz.
THE FLATIRON BUILDING. 1903.
Photograph from *Camera Work* (Vol. IV, 1903).
6⅝" × 3¼".
The Metropolitan Museum of Art. The Alfred Stieglitz Collection 1933.

226   Henri Cartier-Bresson.
BEHIND THE GARE ST. LAZARE, PARIS. 1932.
Photograph.
© Henri Cartier-Bresson/ Magnum Photos.

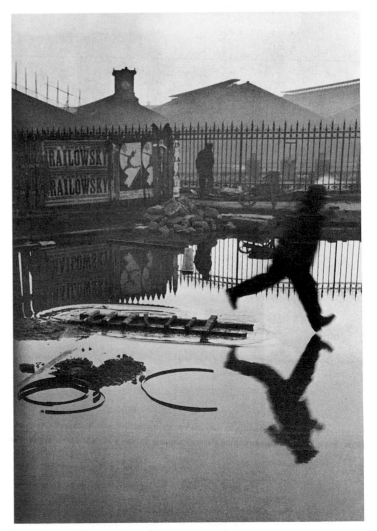

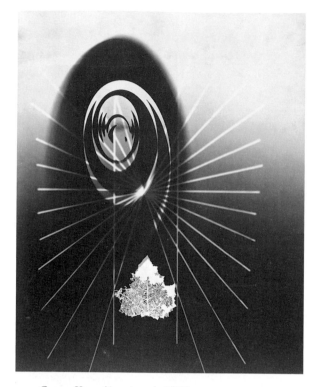

227 Gyorgy Kepes (American, b. 1906).
PHOTOGRAM. 1939.
Photogram on silver gelatin paper, n.d.
15¾" × 19⅔".
Gift of Katherine Kuh, 1954.1340.
Photograph: © 1998 The Art Institute of Chicago.

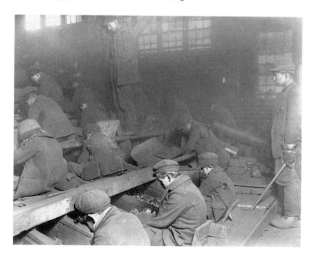

228 Lewis Hine.
COAL BREAKERS, PENNSYLVANIA. 1910.
Photograph.
International Museum of Photography at George Eastman House,
Rochester, New York.

Other photographers went beyond the camera itself to achieve more inventive effects. Hungarian-born Gyorgy Kepes made his PHOTOGRAM by placing objects on light-sensitive paper, exposing the paper to sunlight, and then developing the print with standard methods. The 1939 work shown here combines manufactured and organic forms in a composition that evokes mystery. Kepes' sensitive control of black-to-white values and visual relationships makes this an intriguing image.

Photography and Social Change

Each generation now produces its own set of memorable photographs. Such photographs move us not only because of the way their subjects are presented, but because we know the photographer was there. We join the photographer as witnesses. The significance of such images lies not simply in their ability to inform us, but in their power to stir our emotions.

Only a few decades after the invention of the medium, photographers began to bring public attention to human suffering caused by war, poverty, hunger, and neglect. The new tool made visual statements believable in ways that no other media could. Of all the arts, photography is uniquely suited not only to documenting historic events and social problems, but to bringing about the kind of empathetic awareness that can lead to social reform.

Early in this century, long before television, American sociologist Lewis Hine used his skill as a photographer to communicate his concern for the plight of working children. COAL BREAKERS, PENNSYLVANIA is one of a series of photographs that show young children working long hours in coal yards, cotton mills, and food-processing factories. These photographs brought such abuses to the attention of the public and played a significant role in the creation of child labor laws.

During the Great Depression of the 1930s, a number of photographers sparked public concern for those less fortunate than themselves. Margaret Bourke-White's LOUISVILLE FLOOD VICTIMS confronts us with the brutal difference between the glamorous life promised in advertising and the real-

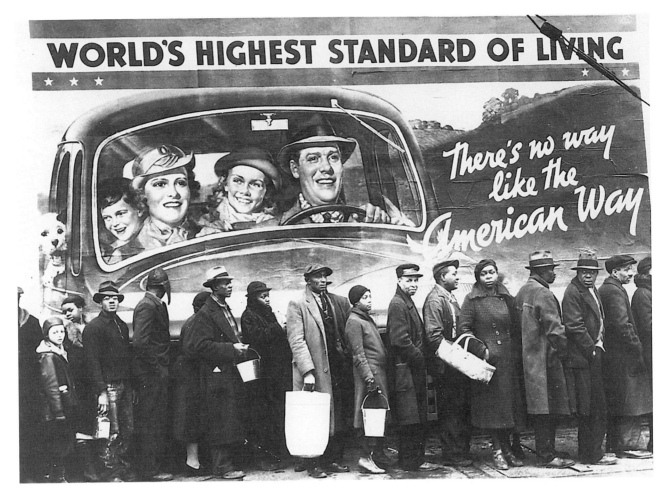

229 Margaret Bourke-White.
LOUISVILLE FLOOD VICTIMS. 1937.
Photograph.
LIFE Magazine ©TimePix.

ity that many face every day. If it were not for the dated styles of the car and clothing, this photograph could be about today's homeless.

In the same decade, Bourke-White introduced the concept of the photographic essay—an approach that was soon adopted by other photographers. A *photo essay* is a collection of photographs on a single subject, arranged to tell a story or convey a mood in a way not possible with a single photograph. Photo essays are now an important part of international journalism.

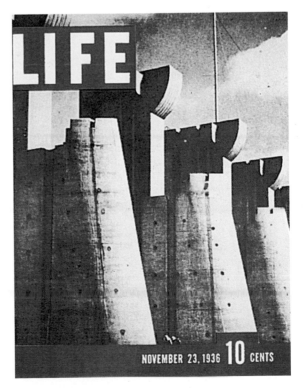

230 Margaret Bourke-White. FORT PECK DAM.
First *Life* Magazine cover, November 23, 1936.
Time Life Syndication.
LIFE Magazine © TimePix.

Few photographers have had a greater impact on the American public than Margaret Bourke-White. A pioneer in photojournalism, she made memorable images of most of the world's major events for nearly thirty years.

Her early family environment encouraged her to expand the boundaries of a woman's traditional role: "Learning to do things fearlessly was considered important by both my parents," she said.[4] She began to use a camera seriously when she took a group of landscape photographs in upstate New York that she sold to help pay her tuition at Cornell University. By 1927, she had her own studio in Cleveland, where she specialized in photographing industrial buildings such as steel mills.

Her life changed radically in the spring of 1929, when she got a call from Henry Luce, the publisher of *Time* magazine. He was founding a new magazine of American business, to be called *Fortune,* and he wanted to pioneer a new visual approach. Bourke-White recalled Luce's concept: "Pictures and words would be conscious partners . . . The camera would act as interpreter, recording what modern industrial civilization is, how it looks, how it meshes.

"This was the very role I believed photography should play . . . I could see that this whole concept would give photography greater opportunities than it had ever had before."[5]

Thus began one of the most important partnerships in American journalism. She photographed American businesses from all angles, capturing everything "from the steam shovel to the board of directors." She climbed on buildings, stood in swamps, and suspended herself in midair, as we can see in MARGARET BOURKE-WHITE ATOP THE CHRYSLER BUILDING. Luce sent her to Russia to record the process of industrialization under Stalin's five-year plan.

When the Depression took hold in the United States, Bourke-White collaborated on a book documenting its effects. With writer Erskine Caldwell, she made *You Have Seen Their Faces,* a record of individual suffering and endurance in the face of the economic crisis. In 1936, when Henry Luce founded *Life,* Bourke-White became its lead photographer. Her photograph of the FORT PECK DAM in Montana was used as the cover for the first issue.

Her work with *Life* anchored the rest of her career. She recalled, "I loved the swift pace of *Life* assignments, the exhilaration of stepping over the threshold into a new land. Everything could be conquered. Nothing was too difficult. And if you had a stiff deadline to meet, all the better. You said yes to the challenge."[6] The Air Force sent her as a war correspondent to most of the battle fronts of Europe in

World War II, and she was among the photographers allowed to record the liberation of the Buchenwald concentration camp in 1945.

Her pace hardly slackened when the war ended. Besides regular assignments within the U.S. borders, she witnessed and photographed for the rest of the world the decolonization of India, the Korean war, and struggles of South African gold miners. She was negotiating to be the first photographer sent to the moon when Parkinson's disease forced her retirement.

She said that she never recalled consciously choosing between marriage and a career, but as she grew older she realized that hers was "a life into which marriage doesn't fit very well. If I had had children, I would have charted a widely different life. . . . Perhaps I would have worked on children's books instead of going to wars. . . . One life is not better than the other; it is just a different life."[7] What settled the matter for her was probably this feeling: "There is nothing else like the exhilaration of a new story boiling up. To me this was food and drink."[8]

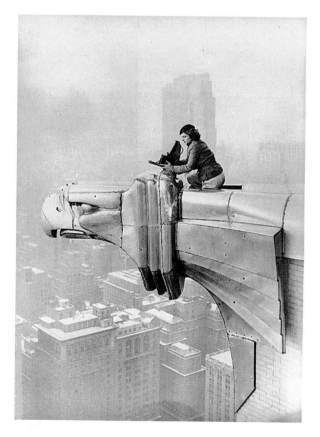

231   MARGARET BOURKE-WHITE ATOP THE CHRYSLER BUILDING. 1934.
LIFE Magazine © Time Inc.
Photograph: Oscar Grauber.
Courtesy of Margaret Bourk-White Estate.

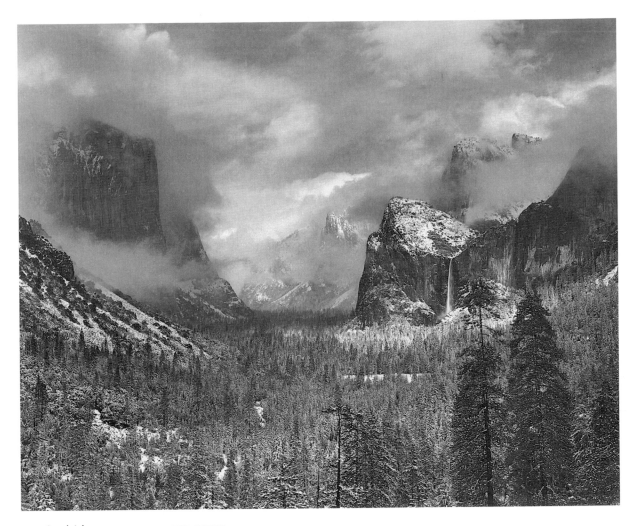

232　Ansel Adams. CLEARING WINTER STORM,
YOSEMITE NATIONAL PARK, CALIFORNIA. 1944.
Photograph.

In addition to focusing on social problems, photography has aided environmentalists. Ansel Adams used the power of his photographs and his reputation as an artist to increase public awareness of the beauty of nature and to draw attention to the great need for conservation of the natural environment. The symphonic grandeur of CLEARING WINTER STORM, YOSEMITE NATIONAL PARK reflects his vision of the eloquence of nature's design. His dramatic orchestration of a range of white to black values creates a brilliant image of the cathedral-like grandeur of Yosemite Valley. The stark beauty of the massive rock peaks contrasts with the soft intermingling of clouds.

Adams viewed aspects of nature as the symbols of spiritual life, capable of transcending the often conflicting prescriptions of society. In his majestic black-and-white photographs, which reflect a life-long passion for art and nature, nature becomes a timeless metaphor for spiritual harmony.

Recent photographers who are concerned about the environment are more likely to record the damage that we have done to nature, rather than its splendor, which they regard as endangered. Many photographers today present disturbing images of nuclear test sites, suburban sprawl, landfills, and other "open sores" in an attempt to warn us about our destructive exploitation of the Earth.

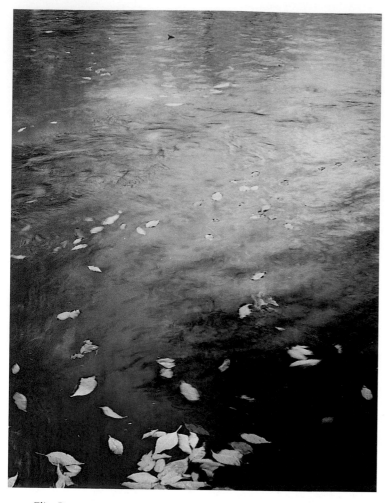

233 Eliot Porter.
POOL IN A BROOK, POND BROOK, NEW HAMPSHIRE, 1953.
Dye transfer print, 10¹¹⁄₁₆ × 8⁵⁄₁₆. (P1989.19.23)
© 1990 Amon Carter Museum,
Fort Worth, Texas. Bequest of Eliot Porter.

Color Photography

Photography began as a black-and-white (sometimes brown-and-white) process. For the first one hundred years, black and white was the only practical option for photographers. Through much of the twentieth century, technical problems with color persisted: film and printing papers were expensive, and, over time, color prints frequently faded. Even when fairly accurate color became available, many photographers felt that color tended to dilute the abstract power of the black-and-white image.

The development of color photography took a step forward in 1907 with the invention of positive color transparencies. In 1932, the Eastman Kodak Company began making color film. Then, in 1936, the invention of Kodachrome provided an even simpler technique that substantially improved the versatility and accuracy of color film. Further progress in the relative permanence of color prints has led to several decades of creative activity in color photography.

For those who accept its potential and its complexity, color expands expressive possibilities because it is the most evocative element in visual language.

By the time Eliot Porter took up color photography, he was already well known as a black-and-white photographer with an eye for subtle detail. He printed his own negatives with meticulous care. Rather than travel the world looking for sensational vistas, Porter took the time to notice the beauty in nature close at hand. A tireless, patient photographer, he was known to wait for hours or days for the right light and weather conditions before making a photograph such as POOL IN A BROOK.

Pushing the Limits

Artists have explored a variety of techniques to go beyond photography's assumed limits. The term *photomontage* describes the technique in which parts of photographs are cut out and reassembled to form new, often thought-provoking combinations.

The manipulated images of Jerry Uelsmann have added new dimensions to the art of photography and encouraged younger photographers to go beyond straightforward photography. In the darkroom—which he called "a visual research lab"—Uelsmann combined parts of images from several negatives to make one print. By manipulating the print, he achieved a mysterious quality that creates an other-wordly and dreamlike mood. In the UNTITLED print seen on the next page, trees float above the reflected image of a giant seed pod, invoking a mood of timeless generative forces. Uelsmann explained his intentions:

I am involved with a kind of reality that transcends surface reality. More than physical reality, it is emotional, irrational, intellectual, and psychological. It is because of the fact that these other forms of reality don't exist as specific, tangible objects that I can honestly say that subject matter is only a minor consideration which proceeds after the fact and not before.[9]

Sonia Landy Sheridan has pioneered the use of color photocopy machines and computers as artists' tools. These tools support her research in the creative use of imaging technology, which she calls "generative systems." In FLOWERS, the translucent colors that fill the background were produced by shining fluorescent and tungsten lights into the copy machine. Trained as a traditional artist, Sheridan began to shift in the late 1960s to creative uses of technological processes. Rather than wait for technology to catch up to her ideas, she worked with the 3M Company to develop tools to generate some of the images she envisioned.

The advent of digital photography, coupled with the expanding capabilities of photo-editing computer programs, is now radically altering the art of photography. Images that were once "handcrafted" in the darkroom can now be adjusted using a keyboard and mouse. Editing software allows many types of alterations, from resizing to color alterations to layering of images.

The invention of photography and the increasing availability of photographs and cameras have changed art more than any other invention to date, liberating it from its former narrative and documentary roles. Artists were empowered to explore more freely their own personal thoughts and meanings.

FILM: THE MOVING IMAGE

For thousands of years, artists have attempted to depict motion and how events occur over time. Prehistoric people portrayed animals in cave paintings

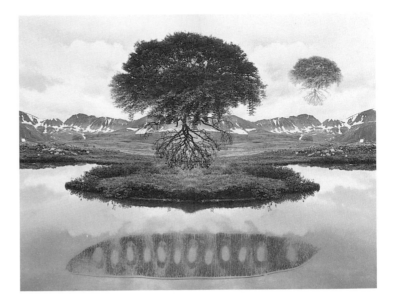

234   Jerry Uelsmann.
UNTITLED. 1969. Photograph.
Courtesy of the artist.

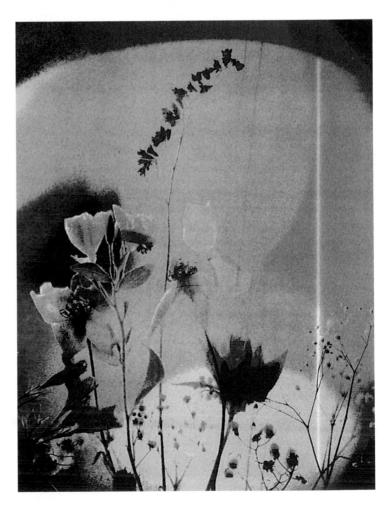

235   Sonia Landy Sheridan.
FLOWERS. 1976.
3M color-in-color print. 8½" × 11".
Courtesy of the artist.

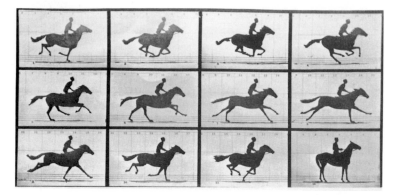

237 Eadweard Muybridge.
GALLOPING HORSE.
1878. Photographs.
Library of Congress.

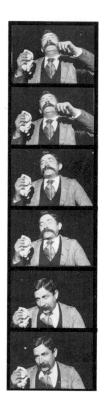

236 Thomas Edison and
W. K. Dickson.
FRED OTT'S SNEEZE.
1889. Film.
Library of Congress.

ings gave the illusion of motion. By spinning draw-ings of various stages of a movement in a *magic lantern,* or flipping them in a *flip book,* viewers experienced a flickering appearance of movement. The magic lantern/flip book phenomena led the way to the invention of cinematography. When camera lenses and film evolved to the point where they could capture clear photographs of each stage of an object in motion, technology made motion pictures possible.

Leland Stanford (the founder of Stanford University) made a bet in 1870 that all four of a horse's hooves came off the ground when it ran. To settle the bet, Eadweard Muybridge lined up a series of still cameras close together along the side of a race track; each camera was fixed with a string to be tripped by the horse's front legs as it ran by. When the resulting pictures of a GALLOPING HORSE were reviewed, it was evident that all four hooves left the ground. When Muybridge projected his still photographs in rapid succession, he discovered that the horse appeared to gallop. Others soon began experimenting with sequences of projected photographs, and cinematography was born, changing forever the way we see movement.

By 1889, Thomas Edison and his assistant, William Dickson, had developed a motion picture camera that used rolls of coated celluloid film to capture fourteen to twenty-four still pictures per second. Anything that moved, traffic in the street, a kiss—even FRED OTT'S SNEEZE—offered a way to demonstrate the new, highly entertaining technology.

The illusion of motion is made possible by the *persistence of vision,* the brief retention of an image by the retina of our eyes after a stimulus is removed; and the process of *perception,* by which the mind attempts to make sense of incomplete information.

Film and Visual Expression

First and foremost, a movie is a visual experience. Film's rhythmic, time-based structure makes motion picture photography a very different sort of visual art from painting or even from still photography. Whereas a painter or photographer designs a single moment, a filmmaker must design sequences that work together in time as well as space.

and carvings in ways that suggested action. Assyrians, Egyptians, and Romans presented time progressions in low-relief sculpture; French artists of the Middle Ages painted frescoes in strips to show episodes from biblical stories; and Chinese and Japanese artists painted scrolls that told stories in visual segments as their paintings were unrolled a section at a time. But only with the development of movies in the late nineteenth century did motion and time find full, lifelike expression.

Before movies, it was discovered that looking at rapidly changing short sequences of still draw-

Each piece of film photographed in a continuous running of the camera is called a *shot*. Film makes possible a dynamic relationship among three kinds of movement: the moving objects within a shot, the movement of the camera toward and away from the action, and the movement created by the sequence of shots.

Much of the power of film comes from its ability to reconstruct time. Film is not inhibited by the constraints of clock time; it can convincingly present the past, the present, and the future, or it can mix all three in any manner. Film time can affect us more deeply than clock time, because film sequences can be constructed to approximate the way we feel about time. In addition to editing, filmmakers can manipulate time by slowing or accelerating motion. The filmmaker's control over time, sequence, light, camera angle, and distance can create a feeling of total, enveloping experience so believable that it becomes a new kind of reality.

Making a film is a collaborative effort, coordinated and given a coherent form by the director. Leading directors have created their own styles and are known for certain kinds of content.

Technical Developments:
Creating a New Language of Vision

The recognition of film as a significant art form came slowly. At first, film was nothing more than a novelty. In order to gain public acceptance, early filmmakers tried to make their movies look like filmed theatrical performances. Actors made entrances and exits in front of a fixed camera as though it too were a member of the audience at a stage play. Early films not only were limited to a fixed view, but also were silent because the technology for recording sound on film was not perfected until more than thirty years after the invention of motion picture photography. Total reliance on the visual image forced pioneer filmmakers to develop the visual language of film that continues to be basic to the art.

Between 1907 and 1916, American director D. W. Griffith helped bring the motion picture from its infancy as an amusement to full stature as a means of artistic expression. Griffith introduced the moving camera by releasing it from its fixed, stagebound position in order to better express narrative content. The camera was placed where it would best reveal the dramatic meaning of each scene. A scene thus came to be composed of several shots taken from different angles, thereby greatly increasing the viewer's feeling of involvement.

Assembling a scene from several shots involves *film editing,* a process in which the editor selects the best shots from raw footage, then reassembles them into meaningful sequences and finally into a total, unified progression.

Narrative editing was introduced by Edwin S. Porter in his 1903 film THE GREAT TRAIN ROBBERY, the first film to use a nonlinear time line. Porter set

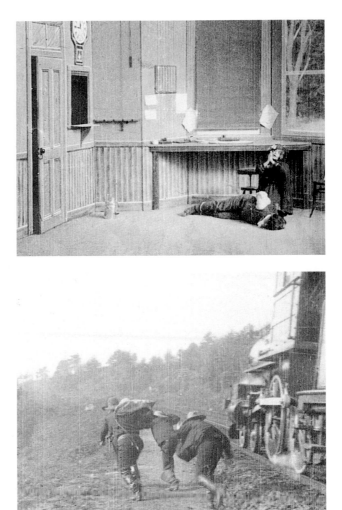

238 Edwin S. Porter.
THE GREAT TRAIN ROBBERY. 1903.
Film. 12 minutes.
The Museum of Modern Art Film Stills Archive, New York.

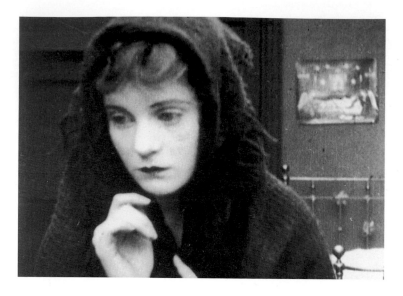

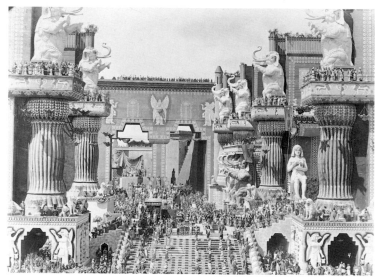

239 D. W. Griffith.
INTOLERANCE. 1916.
Film.
a. Close-up ("Little Dear One").
b. Longshot (Belshazzar's Feast).
The Museum of Modern Art Film Stills Archive, New York.

up his camera in several locations to shoot the various parts of the story; then he glued all the shots together and projected them in a logical sequence designed to tell a story. The nearly twelve-minute film was taken in fourteen scenes, each one a single shot. Action cuts back and forth between a telegraph operator and the bandits who force him to help them rob a train. Later, Griffith used parallel editing to compare events occurring at the same time in different places (person in danger and approach of would-be rescuer) or in different times, as in his film INTOLERANCE, in which he cut back and forth among four stories set in four periods of history.

To underscore the importance of editing, we have only to consider the *cutting ratio.* The cutting ratio tells how much film footage was discarded, compared to what was finally used. In the traditional Hollywood movie, the ratio is at least ten to one, or ten feet thrown away for every foot used. To fine-tune a motion picture, the editor will sometimes add or remove just a few inches of film—equal to less than one second of viewing time.

One of film's most characteristic techniques was discovered when Griffith's camera operator accidentally let the shutter of his camera close slowly, causing the light to gradually darken. Griffith decided that this might be a good way to begin and end love scenes. *Fading in* or *fading out* remains a common transition between scenes.

Griffith was the first to use the close-up and the longshot while most movies were still stagebound. A *close-up* shows only the actor's face. Today the close-up is one of the most widely used shots; but when Griffith first wanted to try a close shot, his cameraman balked at the idea of a head without a body! In a *longshot* the camera photographs from a distance to emphasize large groups of people or a panoramic setting.

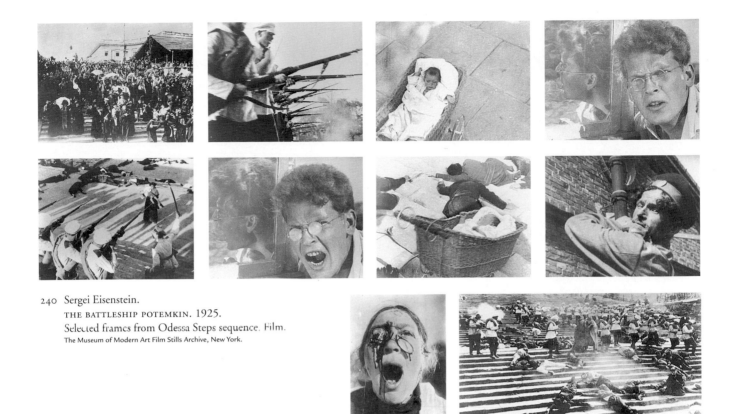

240 Sergei Eisenstein.
THE BATTLESHIP POTEMKIN. 1925.
Selected frames from Odessa Steps sequence. Film.
The Museum of Modern Art Film Stills Archive, New York.

An International Language

When films were silent, movies could be produced in many countries for an international audience, without concern for language barriers. Following the Russian Revolution in 1917, Sergei Eisenstein emerged as a major film artist, honored as much in the West as in the Soviet Union. Eisenstein greatly admired Griffith's film techniques; after careful study, he developed them further, becoming one of the first filmmakers to produce epic films of high quality.

One of Eisenstein's major contributions was his skilled use of montage to heighten dramatic intensity. *Montage,* introduced by Griffith in 1916, is the editing technique of combining a number of very brief shots, representing distinct but related subject matter, in order to create new relationships, build strong emotion, or indicate the passage of time. With the use of montage, a great deal seems to happen simultaneously, in a short time.

In his film THE BATTLESHIP POTEMKIN, Eisenstein created one of the most powerful sequences in film history: the terrible climax of a failed revolt. The montage of brief shots, edited into a sequence of no more than a few minutes, effectively portrays the tragedy of the historic event. Rather than shoot the entire scene with a wide-angle lens from a spectator's perspective, Eisenstein took many close-ups to give viewers the sensation of being caught as participants in the middle of the violence. He intermixed hundreds of shots to create relationships among such elements as a crowd on the steps, a rolling baby carriage, a horror-stricken student, and a Cossack about to strike. Eisenstein personalized the story by alternating close-up shots of individuals with sweeping scenes of chaos. The juxtaposition of movement and motionlessness, close-ups and longshots, gives audiences a powerful sense of the fear and tragedy that took place.

Charlie Chaplin came to prominence about 1915, when pressure from audiences and industry competition caused "stars" to be created and publicized. After starting his career as a member of a pantomime troupe, he became not only the leading comedian of his time, but also a director, producer, writer, and even composer. He built a team consisting of cameraman, leading lady, and comic actors,

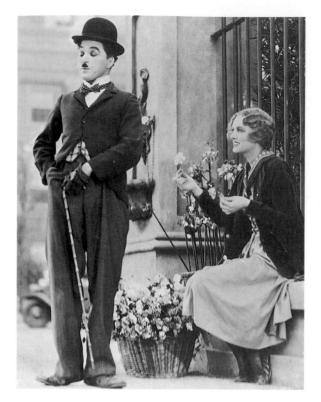

241　Charlie Chaplin.
CITY LIGHTS. 1931.
Film.
The Museum of Modern Art Film Stills Archive,
New York.

who worked with him for many years. A perfectionist, he reshot particular scenes dozens, even hundreds of times. In 1931, four years after the introduction of sound in film, Chaplin chose to stay with the silent tradition in CITY LIGHTS (except for music and sound effects), even though "talkies" were then being made by all other Hollywood filmmakers.

The arrival of sound in 1927 added a new dimension to film, but it did not change the medium's fundamental visual grammar. Color was introduced in the 1930s; the wide screen and three-dimensional images in the 1950s; 360-degree projection was first seen by the public in the 1960s. Most of these techniques, however, had been conceived of and researched by 1910.

After World War I, Hollywood became the film capital of the world, a position it still holds. In the 1930s, most Hollywood films simply repeated plot formulas already proven successful at the box office. Then, in 1941, at age twenty-five, Orson Welles made his film debut with CITIZEN KANE, an international landmark in filmmaking. Welles coauthored the script, directed, and played the leading role in the thinly disguised account of the life of newspaper tycoon William Randolph Hearst. Because of its outstanding aesthetic quality and meaningful social message, CITIZEN KANE immediately set new standards for filmmaking. Welles and his cinematographer, Gregg Toland, pioneered the use of extreme camera angles. The low angle camera presents Kane (Welles) as a towering presence; another such angle is the tilt, shown here, which emphasizes Kane's crooked politics.

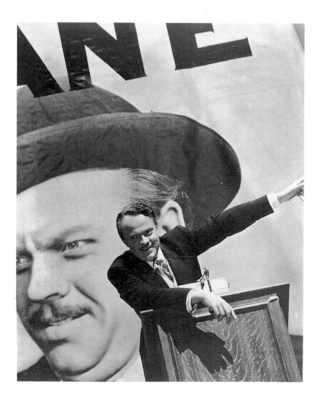

242　Orson Welles.
CITIZEN KANE. 1941.
Film.
The Museum of Modern Art Film Stills Archive,
New York.

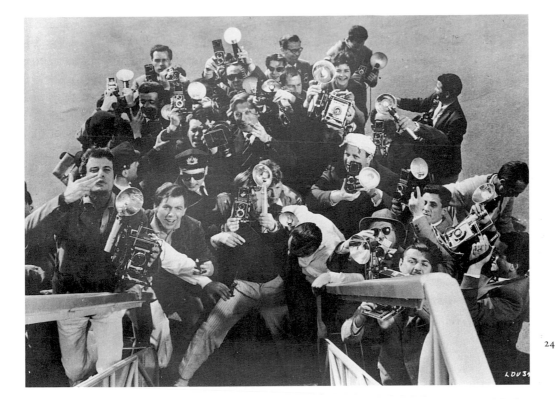

243 Federico Fellini.
LA DOLCE VITA. 1961.
Film.
Everett Collection, Inc.

Italian director Federico Fellini's 1961 film LA DOLCE VITA (The Sweet Life) foreshadows in memorable visual style many of today's critiques of the mass media. Marcello Mastroianni played the lead character, a tabloid journalist also named Marcello who makes his career reporting on sensations, scandals, and celebrities.

The protagonist follows the lifestyles of the rich and famous, dutifully attending spectacles of all kinds, from the exploits of American movie stars to decadent parties to religious visions. He frolics in a fountain at 4 A.M. with Anita Ekberg. He joins the media circus as thousands throng to a small town where two children say they saw the Virgin Mary. One of these fellow travelers is a photographer friend of Marcello's named Paparazzo, and ever since this film's release intrusive photographers throughout the world have been called *paparazzi*.

Questioned about his seeming tendency to exaggerate all he reports on, Marcello replies defensively, "The public demands exaggeration; but reasonably, when permitted, I can report events without exaggeration." At a party where the discussion has turned to art, Marcello announces that the art that he prefers is "a living art; a clear, honest style, without rhetoric and without subterfuge." The fact that he devotes his life to rhetoric and subterfuge is never more obvious, and he later tells a friend, "I am just wasting my days, uselessly."

The film might best be termed a tragicomedy, as it charmingly mocks the "Sweet Life" of its title. Shooting black-and-white scenes with a painter's eye toward tonal balance, Fellini humorously lampoons what he sees as the shallow lives of celebrities and the rich. The film uses many visual clues to help set up this complex mood. The first scene is one of the most striking: a helicopter with Marcello aboard carrying a large statue of Jesus over an ancient Roman aqueduct toward the Vatican. In the end, Marcello proves unable to resist the temptations of the "Sweet Life," as he plunges headlong into the world he reported on.

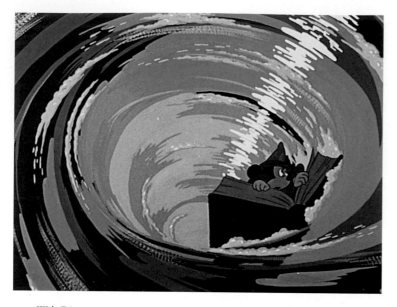

244 Walt Disney.
FANTASIA. 1940. Photograph: Photofest
Film.
The Sorcerer's Apprentice.
Photograph: © The Walt Disney Studios/Photofest.

Animation and Special Effects

Beginning with the development of FANTASIA in the late 1930s, Disney animators have meticulously explored the possibilities of animation. With FANTASIA, released in 1940, Disney created a new form of film that integrated classical music, painting, dance, and drama with a mix of human and cartoon characters as the stars.

The group effort began with a story conference in which artists and musicians brainstormed ways to realize Walt Disney's initial concept. Ideas were portrayed on storyboards outlining the story from which the director choreographed the action. A *storyboard,* a series of drawings or paintings arranged in a sequence like a comic strip, was used to visualize the major shots in the film. Layout artists made the story come alive as the spatial relationships were worked out. Animators dramatized individual characters in each action sequence. Disney's goal was always to create characters who gave the illusion—at twenty-four frames per second—that they

were not just moving, but thinking and feeling. Inkers traced the drawings onto cels (clear plastic sheets) for each frame and painters painted the reverse side. Each cel was then photographed, often using Disney's innovative multiplane camera for heightening the illusion of depth.

Russian animator Victor Petrov brought the old techniques of animation up to date in his 1999 feature film THE OLD MAN AND THE SEA, based on the novel by Ernest Hemingway. Working from a storyboard, the artist made a total of 29,000 paintings on glass panes, each illustrating a fraction of a second of the story. As the paintings were completed, his producers photographed them with a high-resolution digital camera. The entire process took several years. They then transferred the images to a type of 70mm film that requires special projectors. The movie can be seen only at large-format theaters, but because of its quality it can be projected onto screens up to eight stories high.

In recent years, some of the biggest box office successes have employed special effects made possible by a merging of old techniques and new technology. Teams of artists and technicians work with producer-directors such as George Lucas, creator of the *Star Wars* trilogy, to provide working sketches, models, animation, and sets that are fantastic yet believable.

Industrial Light and Magic (ILM), the special effects division of George Lucas's company, Lucasfilm Ltd., was the leading special effects studio of the late 1970s and 1980s. The ILM team took ideas from script to storyboard to models to film. ILM spent at least a week on a sequence that lasts less than two seconds in the finished film. Only with computers can the complex alignment of all the elements of camera, light, model, and background be achieved.

Lucas was also responsible for the increased use of computers to edit film. With Edit Droid, a device he developed, a film editor can rearrange film footage almost as easily as a text editor can move words or sections of copy on a word processor.

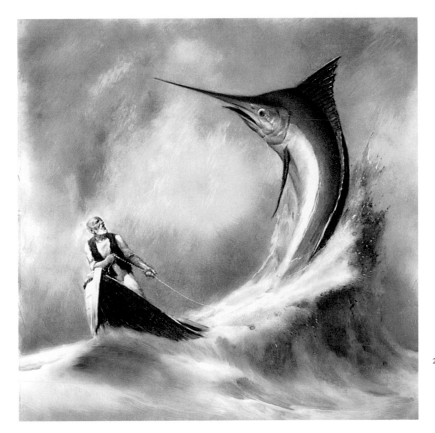

245 Victor Petrov.
THE OLD MAN AND THE SEA. 1940.
a.   Still from the film.
b.   The artist and the storyboard.
© 1999 Productions Pascal Blais, Inc. Imagica Corp.
Panorama Film Studio of Yaroslav.

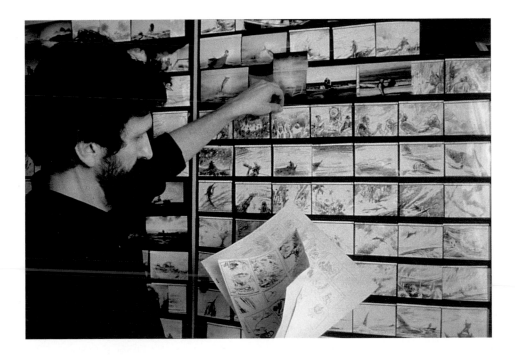

Many contemporary ideas about film design came together in BLADE RUNNER, Ridley Scott's 1982 science fiction classic. Set in Los Angeles in 2019, the movie presents the future city as a hi-tech metropolis that is also bleak, smog-ridden, and overcrowded with people from clashing cultures and nationalities. Scott believed that the visual impact of a film is as important as its actors. Thus he employed a large crew of well-known special effects artists, including Syd Mead and Douglas Trumbull, for computer animation and the creation of futuristic sets and props. The movie starred Harrison Ford in the role of a detective who must find and kill rebellious androids (mechanical humans), but most critics agreed that the performances by the actors playing the machines were the most compelling in the film. Ten years after its premiere, the director—taking advantage of the large home video rental market—re-edited BLADE RUNNER and released his own version of it on videocassette.

Digital animation now makes possible many kinds of highly sophisticated visual effects, such as the ability to present a digital storm at sea with waves sixty feet high, or, as in the well-known blockbuster *Titanic*, to drop real and virtual people at the same time from the upended stern of the fated ship. The 2000 Walt Disney Pictures feature film DINOSAUR contained not a single living actor or animal. All of the characters were created by computers, and in the film they bask in close-ups, cast shadows, and even splash through ponds. The directors endowed their digital creations with

246 Ridley Scott.
BLADE RUNNER. 1982/1993.
Film.
Photograph: Corbis/Sygma.

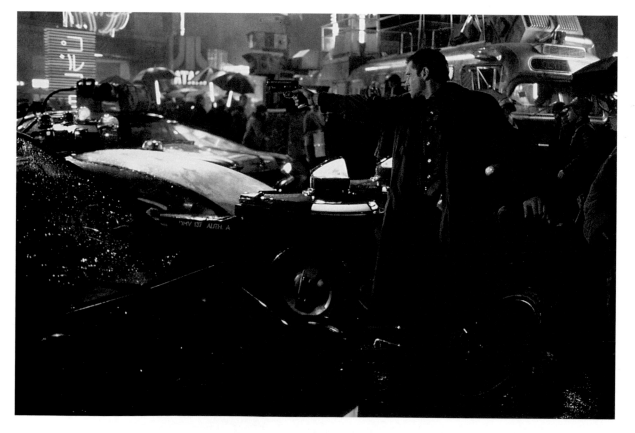

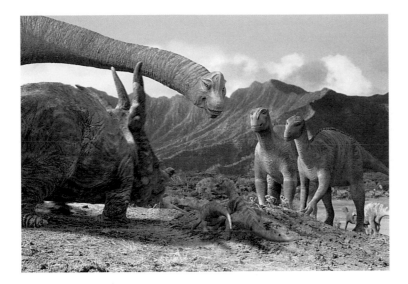

247 Still from DINOSAUR.
Walt Disney Co./Everett Collection.

human voices and placed them in real landscapes filmed in Hawaii, Venezuela, and Australia. The movie's special-effects climax came when the earth was struck by a giant asteroid, bringing about tremendous destruction, huge firestorms, and a mushroom cloud.

Today, most major Hollywood film studios are owned by large international corporations, and they have discovered that they can draw audience interest around the world with movies that employ luxurious special effects with a fast story line. To aid international receipts, these "blockbusters" generally do not rely on character development or social comment for their success, and they are promoted together with merchandise such as clothing or toys derived from the film, to aid their appeal to younger audiences. In this way a movie such as DINOSAUR can break box-office records in the United States, and then go on to attract large crowds in places as diverse as Moscow, Hong Kong, and Rio de Janeiro. Such international success is often required if the producer is to recoup the original expense of production and promotion, which can exceed $100 million.

Today, film is an international, intercultural language—the most persuasive of the arts. When the believable realism of photography was combined with the equally convincing appearance of motion, film became the supreme illusion of real-

ity. When visual motion was synchronized with sound, two major facets of total sensory experience were joined. Film can make us feel we are actually participating in events as they occur. No other medium is capable of engaging us so completely.

TELEVISION AND VIDEO

Television, literally "vision from afar," is the electronic transmission of still or moving images and sound by means of cable or wireless broadcast. In countries where commercial television dominates, it is primarily a distribution system for advertising, news, and entertainment.

Video Art

The Sony corporation set the stage for the beginning of video art in 1965 when it introduced the first portable video recording camera, the Portapak. Though it was cumbersome, some artists were drawn to the new medium because of its unique characteristics: The instant feedback of video does away with development times necessary for film. Video works can be stored on inexpensive cassettes that can be erased and re-recorded. In addition, because a video signal can be sent to more than one monitor, there is flexibility of presentation.

Early videos by artists were relatively simple, consisting mainly of recordings of the artists

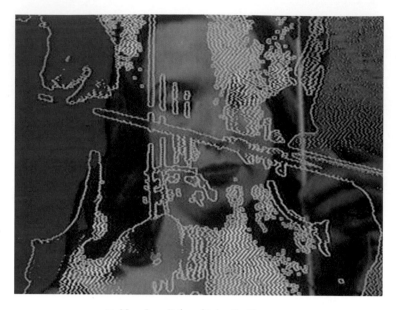

248 Nam June Paik and John Godfrey.
GLOBAL GROOVE.
Video.
Photograph: Michael Danowski. Courtesy of Electronic Arts Intermix, New York.

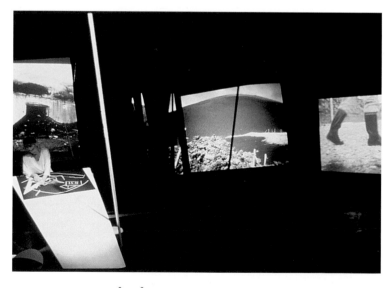

249 Joan Jonas.
VOLCANO SAGA. 1987.
Performance Still. Performing Garage, NY.
Pat Hearn Gallery, NYC.

themselves performing, or of dramatic scenes staged with only a few actors or props. Since no editing was possible, and the black-and-white image was incompatible with the color resolution of television broadcasts of the time, the medium was most suited to private screenings for small groups. In 1972, the compatibility issue was resolved with the introduction of standardized ¾-inch tape; this allowed artists to work with television production equipment, and even to broadcast the results of their labors. The 1980s brought vast improvements in video technology in the form of lighter cameras, color, and computerized editing.

In the short history of video art, some artists have consistently tried to expand the limits of the medium's technical capacities. A leader in this movement is the Korean-born artist Nam June Paik. With the help of foundation grants, he worked in partnership with public television labs in Boston to develop the first video synthesizer. This machine generated brilliant color patterns that could be programmed to develop from black-and-white input. Using it, he created GLOBAL GROOVE, a program that was broadcast over a public station in New York City.

Other video artists have used the medium to create and tell stories using themselves as actors. In her 1989 VOLCANO SAGA, Joan Jonas tells a story of a memorable trip to Iceland. Caught in a fierce windstorm, she was blown off the road and lost consciousness. Awakened by a local woman who offers help, the artist is magically transported back to ancient times in the company of Gundrun, a woman from Icelandic mythology who tells her dreams. The artist sympathizes with Gundrun's struggles in her ancient society, and returns to her New York home feeling a stronger kinship with women of the past. In the video, images move back and forth between past and present with the aid of overlays and an evocative musical score.

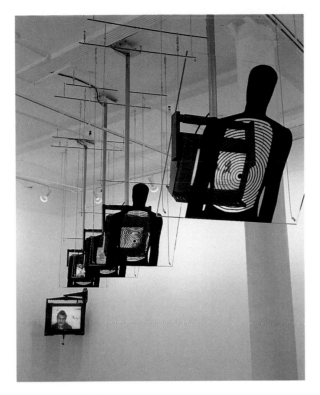

250 Dara Birnbaum. HOSTAGE. 1994.
6-channel video and interactive laser installation with
Peerless ceiling & wall mounts, and designed ceiling mounts
and plexiglass shields. Channels 1–5 videotape, color cycle
lengths vary from 01:43 to 02:35:29. Channel 6 on
videodisk with cycle length 11:06; all channels continuous
loop. Dimensions site specific.
Photograph: Geoffrey Clements, Installation: Paula Cooper Gallery, NY. Courtesy of
Paula Cooper Gallery.

Today's video artists often use the medium as
an element in three-dimensional installations. Dara
Birnbaum's HOSTAGE uses five monitors arranged
in an ascending arc together with target figures.
On the screens are borrowed images from a 1977
television news broadcast of a German hostage
explaining his captors' demands. These are interrupted with cuts to American news reports of
various other hostage-takings. The gallery environment is activated with sensors, so that viewers, by
moving about, cause the cuts from one scene to another, and are thus held "hostage" themselves by
being implicated in how the story unfolds on the
screens.

The onset of music video has blurred the line
between commercial television and video work by
artists. Here, many techniques that artists developed are used in sophisticated combinations as a
way to supplement the statements of popular
music performers.

DIGITAL ART FORMS

Computer screens are cathode ray tubes (CRTs)
just like TV screens. The artmaking capacity of
computer-linked equipment ranges from producing finished art, such as color prints, film, and
videos, to generating ideas for works that are ultimately made in another medium. Computers are
also used to solve design problems by facilitating
the visualization of alternative solutions. The
computer's capacity to store images-in-progress
enables the user to save unfinished images while
exploring ways of solving problems in the original. Thus sculptors, photographers, filmmakers,
designers, and architects can take advantage of the
tools created by programmers of computer software.

The multipurpose characteristics of the computer have accelerated the breakdown of boundaries between media specializations. A traditional
painter working with a computer can easily employ photo imaging or even add movement and
sound to a work. A photographer can retouch,
montage, change values, "paint over," or color
black-and-white images. Computers facilitate the
writing, design, and printing of books such as
Artforms.

Early computer art looks dull by today's standards. The first exhibition of computer-generated
digital imagery took place in a private art gallery in
1965; few claimed that it was art. Most of the earliest digital artists used computers to make drawings with a plotter, a small ink-bearing, wheeled
device that moves over a piece of paper drawing a
line in one color according to programmed in-
structions. With the help of technicians, Vera
Molnar made some of the most visually interesting

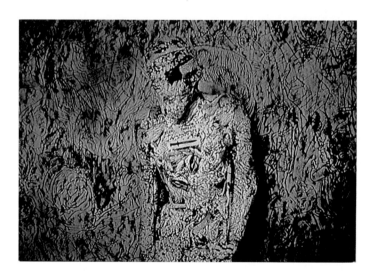

251　Vera Molnar.
PARCOURS: (MAQUETTE FOR AN ARCHITECTURAL ENVIRONMENT).
1976. Computer drawing.
Courtesy the artist.

252　Joseph Nechtaval. THE INFORMED MAN.
1986. Computer/robotic.
Acrylic on canvas. 82" × 116".
Collection Dannheisser Foundation, courtesy of the artist.

of these early efforts, such as her 1976 PARCOURS: (MAQUETTE FOR AN ARCHITECTURAL ENVIRONMENT). The computer was programmed to make subtle variations on a basic set of plotter movements, yielding a work that resembles a drawing quickly done by hand. In many of these early types of computer art, the plotter's motions were not entirely predictable, a fact that added to the attractiveness of the images. The expense and complexity of computer technology in those years, however, kept all but a few pioneer artists away from the medium.

The advent of faster computers, color printers, and interactive graphics changed the scenario in the middle 1980s; as the computer's abilities grew, more artists began to take interest. Joseph Nechtaval was close to the "cutting edge" at that time with his work THE INFORMED MAN. To make this work—he calls it a Scanamural—he first created an original image on a small transparency by chaotically combining a myriad of illegible information patterns in a photo editing program. He then scanned and enlarged the transparency to mural size by using computer-guided airbrushes. The re-

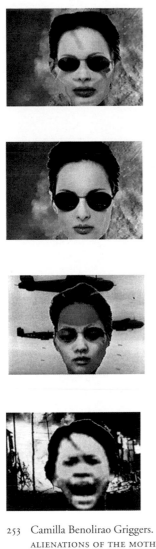

253 Camilla Benolirao Griggers.
ALIENATIONS OF THE MOTHER TONGUE. 1996.
Video with digital graphics and animation. 5 minutes.
Photo courtesy of the artist.

sulting large work resembles a very expressive painting with a human figure at its center.

Camilla Benolirao Griggers used video editing in her work ALIENATIONS OF THE MOTHER TONGUE. She began with a fashion photograph and introduced incremental changes in the subject's face, bit by bit, until by the last frame we have a horrifying image of destruction. She combined all the stages of the frame's evolution into a five-minute video that evolves from something glamorous and desirable into a cry of pain.

Both of these works show how the new digital technology has undercut the traditional truth value of photography. If images are so easy to manipulate, then the camera, if it is digital, can indeed be

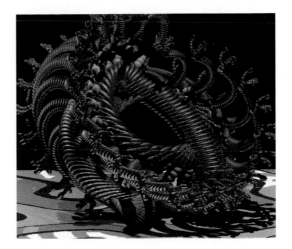

254 William Latham.
CR3Z/2. Photographic print. 1992. 5' × 5'.
© 2000 William Latham.

made to lie. Seeing is no longer believing, in the traditional sense of the term.

Digital artist William Latham moves even farther from reality in his digital works. With the aid of a mathematician, he writes programs that generate eerie digital beings. Latham said that his CR3Z72 grew and evolved in his computer, a digital plant grown in fertile binary soil under the care of the artist-gardener.

The digital artists considered so far use the computer to create art for the wall or the video screen; in that sense they are more traditional than the ones we consider next. This is because the digital revolution, besides generating new ways of making art, has also given rise to new ways of presenting it.

Some artists now create digital works for distribution on CD-ROMs, compact disks capable of storing and retrieving hundreds of megabytes of data. Artists' CD-ROM works usually include images, text, and video clips; since the amount of information is so voluminous, viewers at their terminals are usually free to exercise certain choices about how they navigate through the contents. This makes the presentation of the work interactive, that is, not entirely under the artist's control in the way that a movie or video is. Indeed the same viewer examining the same CD on different days may get an entirely different order of output. So far, artists who create for CD-ROMs tend to make works of two general types: either they tell a story that the viewer can unfold in different ways by

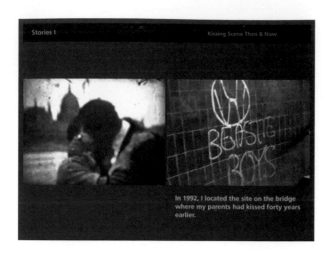

their interactive choices, or they archive works and information related to a theme that viewers can click through according to their interest.

A highly regarded example of the latter approach is Hungarian George Legrady's 1994 work AN ANECDOTED ARCHIVE FROM THE COLD WAR. This CD presents a wealth of mostly autobiographical information about the artist's experience growing up and living in a Communist country that threw off that system in 1991. The CD is organized into rooms patterned after a Communist workers' museum which has since closed. Included are home movies, interviews, family documents, photographs of old and new Hungary, news clippings in various media, and digital videos shot by the artist. Viewers navigate through this storehouse as if they are walking through a museum.

Along the way there are many visual surprises in store. To give just one example, in the room called "Stories I" we find a grainy home movie of the artist's parents kissing on a famous bridge over-looking the city of Budapest in 1952. Next to it is a video that the artist shot of a return visit to the same bridge 40 years later, when it was covered with graffiti. Legrady calls himself "an individual whose history and identity were shaped by the political events of the Cold War," and through his CD we get a poignant and fascinating view of his country's tumultuous evolution.

The newest digital medium is the World Wide Web, and many artists are beginning to take advantage of its free universal distribution to create works expressly for viewing there. Some create works for posting to their own web pages; in addition there are several sites that specialize in exhibiting web works and thus function like interactive galleries. A few museums have added collections of web works to their sites as well. Like other branches of digital art, web works have evolved rapidly since the first examples came out in the middle 1990s, in accordance with the increasing capabilities of web browsers and plug-in programs.

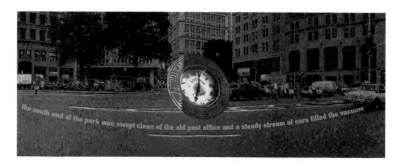

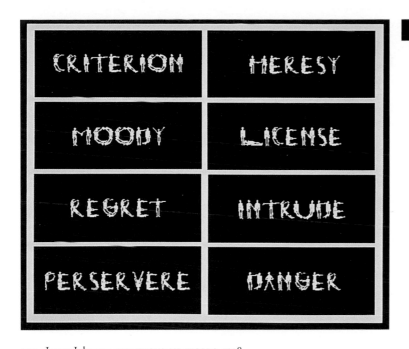

257 James Johnson. ONE THOUSAND WORDS. 1998.
Interactive www work. Screen shot from
IKWORDS, 1998. Net work, 7½" × 9".
© James Johnson.

JAMES JOHNSON

James Johnson, who began his digital art career working with a plotter, makes web works whose complexity is not apparent to the casual user. His interactive work ONE THOUSAND WORDS presents the viewer with an array. Clicking on any word will change it to another by selecting randomly from a large store. In this way, meanings and their combinations shift at random at a speed that the user determines. The work generates a welter of meanings, all presented in a unique type font that the artist himself invented.

One of the many ways in which web works differ from other kinds is that copyright protection is severely weakened, because viewers can download and print in unlimited quantities any phase of a web work. This does not worry Johnson, who says that art should be a gift. He discusses this and many other aspects of digital art creation, on the CD-ROM that accompanies this book.

The degree of sophistication of a web-based work is no indicator of its quality, however. As in other media, artists who are best at organizing meaningful visual information create the best web works.

Near the edge of the envelope in web works is Annette Weintraub, whose 1999 web work SAMPLING BROADWAY requires the most advanced plug-ins currently available. The work is an interactive journey up and down New York City's famous street, with sound effects, painterly washes of color, overlaid images, scrolling lines of poetry, and even Virtual Reality. Viewers can find and click on various "hot spots" in any screen for further images or sounds. As is evident from the screen shot pictured here, the work is not a mere movie, but an artist's imaginative transformation of a highly symbolic place.

In short, digital art is evolving as fast as computers themselves are. Its position now is similar to that of photography in its early years; that is, significant parts of the art world hang back from accepting it on an equal basis with other art forms, and a few even question whether digital art is indeed art. But the quality of works now being made is bringing the kind of attention that will eventually lead to changed attitudes. The art world has been very quick to adopt other aspects of digital technology; some of these are discussed in the essay that follows.

The impact of the new digital technology on the creation of art works has been important, but in other areas connected to art the impact has been greater. Computers are now integrally connected to the analysis, preservation, and sale of art works. Indeed the new technology has taken root in these areas sooner than it has in artists' studios.

There are several on-line art magazines, where internet surfers can go to find out where art shows are held and read reviews of current exhibitions in many parts of the world. Critical issues surrounding art are discussed, and scholars present new findings. Because the quality of images visible on a computer screen is still significantly below that of a printed page, digital magazines are far from replacing hard copy; for now they function as a supplement to paper-based art criticism and analysis.

Museum websites become more sophisticated with each passing year. Most museums have them, and usually they contain information about current special exhibitions, as well as on-line viewing of art works from their collections. Some museums create education modules on their sites so that the inter-

net public can learn in depth about the art on display. The most advanced museum websites have pioneered new methods of digital browsing of art works, placing more and more of the collection on-line and allowing for close-up, high-resolution views of selected parts of works. In this way they have narrowed the quality gap between screen images and printed photographs.

Likewise, the new technology has had an important impact on conservation of art works. From small pottery fragments dug up at an archaeological site, for example, computer programs can digitally reconstruct an entire piece. New three-dimensional laser scanners can track every square millimeter of sculptural works from several angles at once, making exact recordings of every surface possible. Painting conservators use computer-assisted mass spectrometers to analyze the chemical content of paint surfaces in order to aid in their cleaning and restoration.

On a more mundane level, there are several websites that track and post information on stolen art works. Dealers and auction houses make frequent recourse to such sites, to check on the legal status of works that they may buy or sell.

Increasingly, the internet is an important venue for the sale of art works as well. Many galleries and dealers have websites that post works for sale, saving art collectors a great deal of browsing time. On-line auctions are another fast-growing trend. At present, on-line auction sites have the status of a fad, as new ones spring up every month. Only a small portion of these will last, partly because it is difficult to assess the quality and much less the authenticity of a work posted on line. In addition, deceptive practices such as price collusion and false bids are easy to bring about and difficult to trace. For these reasons, most of the high-value works will continue to sell at live auctions and in dealers' galleries. But there is little doubt that on-line auctions of art works are here to stay because of the ease with which they bring in a wider public. On-line auctions are a highly visible phenomenon, widely reported in the media. But they represent only one facet of the continuing impact that computer technology is having on the art world.

There is one area that is still relatively untouched by digital technology: the study of art works. Only a tiny fraction of documents relating to the history of art have been placed on line. Thus, most art research still requires much more time in the library than at the computer screen. More important, no digital experience can quite take the place of standing before an actual work, or of meeting the person who created it face to face.

CHAPTER ELEVEN

GRAPHIC DESIGN AND ILLUSTRATION

Every manufactured object, printed image, and constructed space has been designed by someone. From clothing to airplanes, from homes to public buildings and community spaces, design is a basic necessity, not a cosmetic afterthought.

DESIGN DISCIPLINES

A professional designer's role is to enhance living by applying a developed sense of aesthetics and utility to the design of the human-made world. Design both shapes and expresses our cultural values. Some designers see themselves as artists, while others prefer to think of themselves as creative problem solvers. The design concepts introduced in chapter 4 provide a basis for understanding how designers apply their skills to design issues as they work to enhance the visual, informational, and mechanical qualities of our material environment.

As consumers, we are aware that some things are well designed and some are not. When the form and function of an object or image do not complement each other, the object or image is poorly designed. Good design solves problems; bad design creates problems.

Design disciplines include, but are not limited to, graphic design, industrial design, textile design, clothing design, interior design, architecture, and environmental design. In this chapter, the focus is on graphic design and illustration.

Of all the arts, graphic design comes closest to meeting us in our contemporary daily life. We interact with graphic design on an almost constant basis, and most designers have chosen it as their profession because they relish that close interaction with people in all situations. Many of our encounters with graphic design are even unintentional; we do not often seek out graphic design the way we might seek to view other art forms in a gallery or museum. This fact gives designers an unequalled opportunity to inform, persuade, delight, bore, offend, or repel us.

Text dominates Russian designer Alexander Rodchenko's sketch for a 1923 sign. GIVE ME SUN AT NIGHT! exclaims the text in the upper left. "Where do we find this?" reads the inscription just

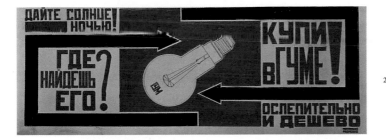

258 Aleksandr Rodchenko and Vladimir Maiakovskii. GIVE ME SUN AT NIGHT. Design for Poster, 1923. Gouache, ink, pencil, gelatin silver print. 4⅜" × 18".
Merrill C. Berman Collection. Photograph by Jim Frank. © Estate of Aleksandr Rodchenko/Licensed by VAGA, New York, NY.

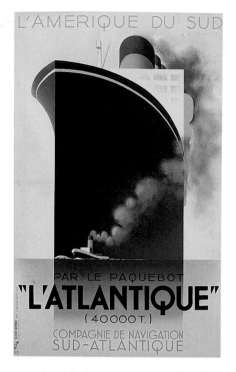

259 Cassandre (Adolpe Jean-Marie Moreall).
L'ATLANTIQUE, 1932.
Lithograph, 39½" × 24½".
Merrill C. Berman Collection. Photograph by Jim Frank.
©2002 Artists Rights Society (ARS), NY.

below. "Buy it at GUM," is the answer, referring to Moscow's largest department store. In the lower right, a slogan hammers the point home: "Blinding and cheap." In the center, surrounded by arrows, is the light bulb that will illuminate everyone at night. The designers had the formidable task of encouraging people to buy a product that was still not widely used at the time, so the tone is emphatic.

A great deal of graphic design has the goal of getting us to do something. The French designer Cassandre designed the poster L'ATLANTIQUE in 1932 in order to promote travel by ship. The text of the poster merely informs viewers that the ship weighs forty thousand tons, and frequently goes to South America under the auspices of the Sud-Atlantique steamship company. The designer made the image do most of the persuasion in this poster, as it dominates the composition. The angle of view is from below, as if we were bobbing on the ocean surface as the ship looms majestically above. The

implication is that if we travel by ship, we participate in something larger than life.

By far the most profound current influence on design in all areas—from print media to car design and architecture—is the digital revolution, comparable in its impact on human life to the Industrial Revolution. The internet and computer-generated imagery are changing not only design processes, but also the character of three-dimensional form and two-dimensional imagery.

Today's designers for the internet use photo editing programs, browser plug-ins and animation to create the next wave in graphic design. Eric Rodenbeck's THE EMPTY CITY is a slowly shifting array of words and phrases, most of them clickable links.

GRAPHIC DESIGN

The term *graphic design* refers to the process of working with words and pictures to create solutions to problems of visual communication. Much of graphic design involves designing materials to be printed, including books, magazines, brochures, packages, posters, and imagery for electronic media. Such design ranges in scale and complexity from postage stamps and trademarks to billboards, film, video, and web pages.

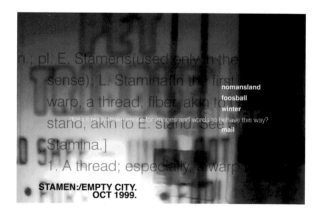

260 Eric Rodenbeck. THE EMPTY CITY. 1999.
Self-promotion piece for Stamen.com.
Screen shot from website.
Courtesy of the artist.

Graphic design is a creative process employing art and technology to communicate ideas. With control of symbols, type, color, and illustration, the graphic designer produces visual compositions meant to attract, inform, and persuade a given audience. Under the skilled guidance of a graphic designer, a message becomes visual, transcending words alone.

Signs and Symbols

Often the name, product, or purpose of a company or organization is given a distinctive and memorable appearance by a graphic designer. An identifying mark, or trademark, based on letter forms is known as a *logo* (short for *logotype*). An identifying mark based on pictorial (rather than typographic) sources is called a *symbol*.

Symbols that instantly communicate important information without words help meet the needs of travelers in foreign countries. When such symbols are not easily understood, they cause more problems than they solve. Designer Henry Dreyfuss recognizing the need for an international symbol system, pioneered the development of universally recognized SYMBOLS. His 1972 *Symbol Sourcebook* combined his own ideas with the work of other designers.

International symbols designed for the Olympic Games go beyond the limitations of verbal languages to guide people to game events. By comparing selected OLYMPIC PICTOGRAMS from 1976 to 1998, we can see how five different designers played with the same subject. The poster designed for the 1996 SUMMER GAMES includes

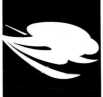

a. hotel   b. stop   c. drinking fountain

d. restaurant

261   Henry Dreyfuss. SYMBOLS. 1972.

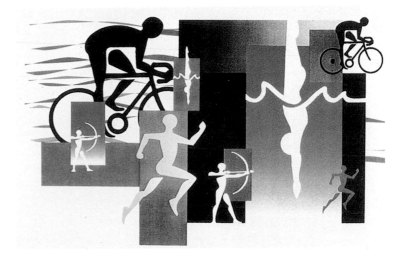

263   1996 SUMMER GAMES.
Museum and Olympics Studies Centre.
IOC/Olympic Museum Collection.

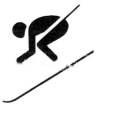
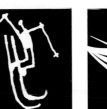

a. 1976.   b. 1988.   c. 1992.   d. 1994.   e. 1998.

262   OLYMPIC PICTOGRAMS—DOWNHILL SKIING.
Museum and Olympics Studies Centre.
IOC/Olympic Museum Collection.

pictograms inspired by the grace and strength of active human figures appearing on early Greek ceramic vessels.

For the design of a SYMBOL FOR A COFFEE HOUSE, designer Bruce Wynne-Jones created a one-line abstraction of a coffee cup with steam rising from the top. The curving thick and thin line suggests both depth and lyrical movement.

An organization's logo may change over time, reflecting a different cultural climate, a different set of goals, or new management. When the National Aeronautics and Space Administration (NASA) was founded in the late 1950s, the first of the NASA

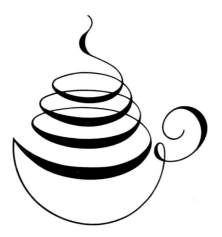

264 SYMBOL FOR A COFFEE HOUSE.
Esienberg and Associates, Dallas, Texas.
Arthur Eisenberg, creative director;
Bruce Wynne-Jones, art director/
designer/illustrator.

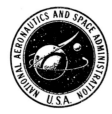 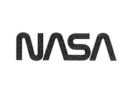

a. 1959.
Logo designer. c. 1959
James Modarelli (US).
10½" × 8". 1996–36–1

b. 1974.
Designers Danne &
Blackburn, NYC. 1973
10½" × 8". 1996–36–3

c. 1992.
Logo designer
James Modarelli (US).
11" × 8½". 1996–36–5

265 NASA LETTERHEAD STATIONERY.
Cooper-Hewitt, National Design Museum. Smithsonian Institution/Art Resource,
NY. Gift of NASA.

LOGOS used a celestial globe with the Earth, the Moon, and a stylized arrow symbolizing space flight (a). In 1974, with space travel more commonplace, the logo was changed to the stylized initials in red (b). The letters "A" symbolize rocket nose cones in this second NASA logo.

In the early 1990s, in the aftermath of federal budget cuts and with a demoralized atmosphere caused by the explosion of the space shuttle *Challenger*, the logo was redesigned. NASA decided to return to a version of its previous logo, which administrators thought better exemplified an optimistic and exploratory mood (c). This time they used the color blue to symbolize the heavens.

Typography
Letter forms are art forms. *Typography* is the art and technique of composing printed material from letter forms (*typefaces* or *fonts*). Designers, hired to meet clients' communication needs, frequently create designs that relate nonverbal images and printed words in complementary ways.

Just a few decades ago, when people committed words to paper, their efforts were handwritten or typewritten—and nearly all typewriters had the same typeface, the name of which was unknown to most users. Now anyone who uses a computer can select fonts and can create documents that look typeset, producing desktop publications such as newsletters and brochures. But computer programs, like pencils, paintbrushes, and cameras, are simply tools: They can facilitate artistic aims if their operator has artistic sensibilities.

Since the Chinese invention of printing in the eleventh century, thousands of typefaces have been created—helped recently by computer technology. For the text of *Artforms*, Adobe Garamond was selected for its grace and readability.

Many European-style type faces are based on the capital letters carved in stone by early Romans. **Roman** letters are made with thick and thin strokes, ending in *serifs*—short lines with pointed ends, at an angle to the main strokes. In typesetting, the term "roman" is used to mean "not italic." Sans serif (without serifs) typefaces have a modern

MOTHER ⊗ CHILD

266 Herb Lubalin, assisted by Alan Peckolick and Tom Carnase.
MOTHER & CHILD, logo for a magazine (never produced). 1965.
By permission of Herb Lubalin, Lubalin Peckolick Associates.

look due to their association with modernist designs. They are actually ancient in origin. **Black letter** typefaces are based on Northern medieval manuscripts and are rarely used today.

Graphic designer Herb Lubalin first gained an international reputation for his elegant typographic designs. In his most innovative work, form and content are inseparably united, as in his logo design intended for a magazine devoted to parenting, to be called MOTHER & CHILD. The magazine was never produced, but the logo—an apt symbol of the mother-and-child-relationship—is now well known to designers and students of design.

Today, many type designers are redesigning and updating old fonts, keeping in mind readability and contemporary preferences. Tobias Frere-Jones reworked the NOBEL font, updating a style invented in 1929 in Holland. He developed the font ARMADA to refer to the arches of nineteenth-century urban warehouses; his GARAGE GOTHIC is meant to recall the printing on parking garage tickets.

THREE INVENTED TYPEFACES are a playful departure from traditional type. House Industries created these three fonts based on crude handwriting, spoiled type, and doodling.

Posters, Advertisements, and Other Graphics

A poster is a concise visual announcement that provides information through the integrated design of typographic and pictorial imagery. In a flash, an effective poster attracts attention and conveys its message. The creativity of a poster designer is directed toward a specific purpose, which may be to advertise or to persuade.

The concept of the modern poster is more than a hundred years old, but it wasn't until the 1920s and 1930s that advances in printing methods made possible high-quality mass production. Since the 1950s, other means of advertising have overshadowed posters. While they now play a lesser role than they once did, well-designed posters still provide powerful means of instant communication. Posters of all sorts have become so popular as

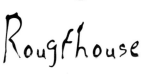

Nobel
Armada
Garage Gothic
Roughouse
Crackhouse
Housemaid

267 Tobias Frere-Jones.
THREE TYPEFACES: NOBEL™,
ARMADA™, GARAGE GOTHIC™.
1992–1994.
The Font Bureau, Boston.

268 THREE INVENTED TYPEFACES.
ROUGHHOUSE, CRACKHOUSE,
HOUSEMAID.
Designers (from top): Andy
Cruz, Jeremy Dean, Kristen
Faulker. 1992–1994.
House Industries, Wilmington, Delaware.

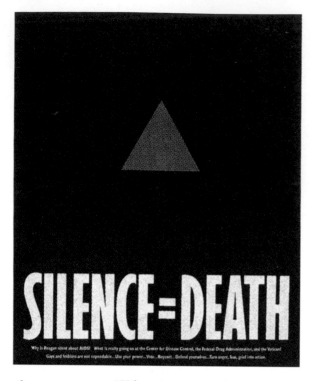

269 SILENCE=DEATH. 1986.
Poster. Offset lithograph.
Designed and published by the
Silence=Death Project, New York.
©Avram Finkelstein, Brian Howard, Oliver Johnston,
Charles Kreloff, Christopher Lione, Jorge Soccoras.

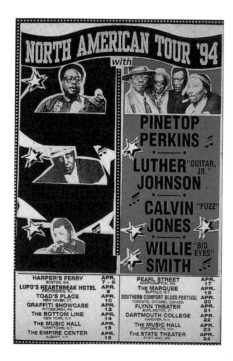

270 NORTH AMERICAN
TOUR '94. Poster. 1994.
Globe Poster Printing
Corporation, Francis.
Cicero. Silkscreen and
offset lithography.
33¾" × 22¹⁄₁₆".
Cooper-Hewitt National Design
Museum. Smithsonian Institution Art
Resource, NY. Gift of Globe Poster Print-
ing Corp., 1997-54-2.

inexpensive images to be framed and hung on walls that printing and selling posters have become big business. Poster design has influenced and been influenced by contemporary fine art.

The AIDS crisis presented a new set of social issues and problems in many American cities, and much graphic art was produced as advocacy for one point of view or another. The SILENCE=DEATH motif is still used on posters, T-shirts, bumper stickers, billboards, and handbills. It was developed by a group of six gay men who founded the Silence=Death Project in 1986. The composition as a whole is meant to resemble a corporate logo. The purple triangle is an inverted version of the insignia homosexuals were forced to wear in Nazi concentration camps. The slogan refers to the fact that the causes, treatment, and prevention of AIDS need to be openly discussed. It is not until the viewer comes close enough to read the inscription at the bottom of the poster that the epidemic is mentioned at all. This emblem became the most common graphic of the movement known as ACT UP (AIDS Coalition to Unleash Power), and one of the members of the Silence=Death Project went on to found Gran Fury, the graphic arts division of the movement.

Subcultures often have their own unique design styles. For example, when the Globe Poster company promoted NORTH AMERICAN TOUR '94, it used a brightly colored and highly readable style that its designers had pioneered a generation before. Globe set the standard for promotional design on behalf of soul, gospel, and blues performers, and the "Globe Style" is still the norm in many areas of the United States for such functions, giving almost instant recognizability.

A poster design for the fourth WORLD CONFERENCE ON WOMEN, held in Bejing in 1996, was created as a student project by Jialang Yin, in Germany. Leonardo's MONA LISA was used as a point of departure for an image that suggests the shared views and concerns of women throughout the world. Yin combined the two sets of words in the subtitle as an attention-getting, low-key surprise emphasizing important meanings.

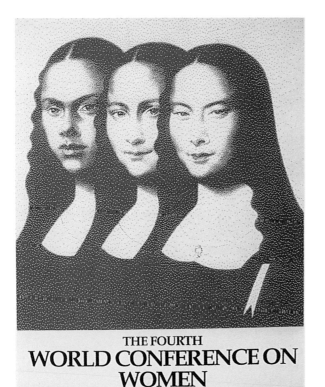

THE FOURTH
WORLD CONFERENCE ON WOMEN

ACTION FOR EQUALITYDEVELOPMENT ANDPEACE

1995 BEIJING

271   Jialang Yin.
WORLD CONFERENCE ON WOMEN.
Poster. 1996.

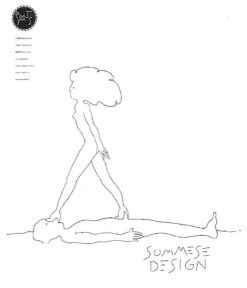

272   Kristin and Lanny Sommese.
SELF-PROMOTION POSTER.
Sommese Design.

Humor has great appeal. With a simple line drawing and a minimum of type, Kristin and Lanny Sommese created a playful SELF-PROMOTION POSTER for their design firm, SOMMESE DESIGN. The designers used humor to counter a longstanding gender imbalance. Designers at BBDO Canada won an award for their NEWSPAPER ADVERTISEMENT, a cheeky appropriation of text found on boxes.

Designers in recent years often use an offhand, low-key approach that does not seem very "designed" at all. Tibor Kalman created the album cover for LOST IN THE STARS (on the following page) by merely overlaying album information and small symbols over a photograph of the composer's face. This approach has proved very influential on designers today, many of whom are wary of too-elaborate design ideas. Kalman was himself something of a

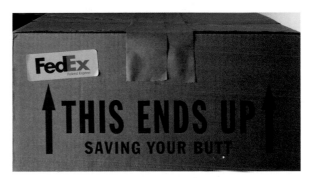

273   NEWSPAPER ADVERTISEMENT.
Creative Direction: Larry Tolpin, Stephen Creet,
Michael McLaughlin. BBDO Canada. 1998.

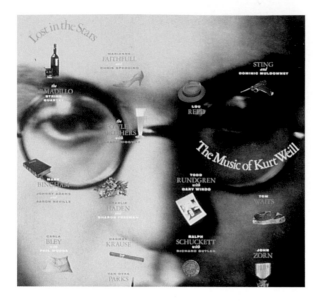

274 LOST IN THE STARS: THE MUSIC OF KURT WEILL. 1985.
Album cover. Art director: Tibor Kalman. Firm: M&Co.
Publisher: A&M Records, Hollywood. M&Co.
Collection Cooper–Hewitt, National Design Museum, Smithsonian Institution.
Art Resource, NY, NY/Art Resource, NY.

275 David Carson.
PAGES FROM RAY GUN MAGAZINE. 1993.
Offset lithograph. Ray Gun Publishing, Santa Monica, CA.
Ray Gun Magazine.

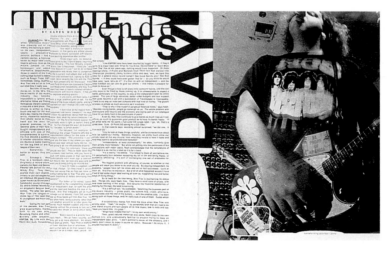

rebel in the design world. When accused of trying to make things look wrong, he said, "I am interested in quirkiness, insanity, unpredictablility."[1]

David Carson came from the world of punk, hardcore, and grunge music. His rough and expressive designs have enlivened compact disk cases, T-shirts, concert promotions, and independent magazines, or "zines." The PAGES FROM RAY GUN MAGAZINE is an example of his work at its most raw, where legibility is nearly sacrificed for expressiveness. The magazine completely avoids the slick look of most publications. This layout is the visual equivalent of the music it extols. Columns of text are unequal in size and look slapped on. Different fonts are combined in the heading, with the last word crossing a page break. The accompanying photograph is purposely out of focus and off-center.

In advertising, the arts frequently work together. Television advertising is a kind of operatic art form that calls on writers, musicians, and actors as well as directors, camera operators, and graphic designers. In printed advertising, a writer, a designer, and often an illustrator or photographer work as a team.

ILLUSTRATION

An *illustration* is a picture or decoration created to enhance the appearance of written material or to clarify its meaning. Illustrators create images for books, magazines, reports, CD cases, greeting cards, and advertisements.

Some of the most elaborate and sumptuous illustrations ever made were hand painted, however, modern illustration has evolved in conjunction with the development of printing processes. Nineteenth-century illustration usually required the insertion of a plate into the blocks of raised type (letters) that served as text. The plate, prepared by lithography, engraving, or etching, was inked and printed. The resulting page was then bound with the other pages of the text. Honoré Daumier was among the first to use lithography for illustration.

One of the great illustrators of all time was José Guadalupe Posada, a printmaker who worked in Mexico City in the years surrounding 1900. His illustrations were metal plates that his publisher mounted on a wood frame together with raised type to make flyers, single sheets that sold for one centavo. These sheets told stories of disasters, robberies, murders, and miracles: whatever would be of interest to the working classes of that time. LAS BRAVÍSIMAS CALAVERAS GUATEMALTECAS deals with the case

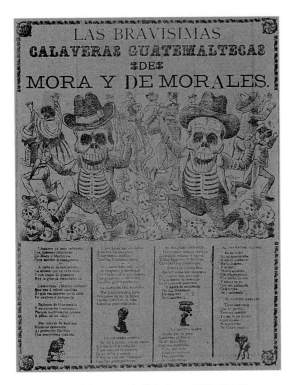

of two Guatemalans who were executed for carrying out a political assassination in 1907. As we see in the sheet, Posada's style was full of humor and energy. The criminals dance through a field of skulls as the general public flees in alarm. The skeleton has ancient roots in Mexico as a symbol of the dead, but here death is mocked in a high-spirited fashion.

Recent photomechanical reproduction processes have enabled illustrators to employ drawing, painting, and photographic techniques—with computers further extending the capabilities of illustrators. Although most illustration is now done with photography, some areas—notably children's books, fashion illustration, and greeting cards—continue to rely on drawn or painted images.

The distinction between illustrations and art displayed in galleries and museums has to do with the purpose the work is intended to serve, rather than the medium in which the work is made, since both illustrations and gallery art can be drawings, paintings, or photographs.

American illustrator Norman Rockwell was best known for the many *Saturday Evening Post* magazine covers he created between 1916 and 1963. He specialized in warm, humorous, often sentimental scenes of everyday small-town life, drawn with a wealth of meaningful detail. His 1946 illustration PORTRAIT is a quaintly humorous picture with several interesting details. On a basic level, it is rather charming that the museum worker carrying a frame has become a momentary work of art himself. Yet Rockwell set the scene in a portrait gallery, and all three figures in the paintings the custodian passes seem to look in his direction, as if surprised to see him join their number. The implied lines of their glances help to focus the composition. The worker's

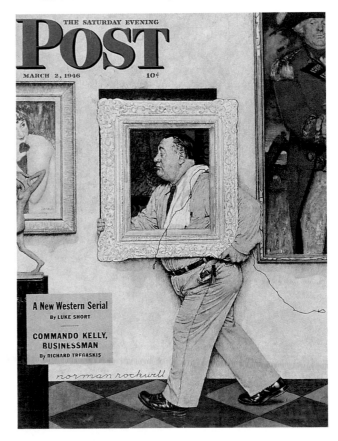

legs are echoed in the small piece of sculpture at the left. The wire dangling at the center suggests wayward but graceful right-to-left motion. After these close observations, it is not really surprising that a worker can be a work of art; surely this was part of Rockwells' egalitarian message.

Maurice Sendak's name has become synonymous with children's book illustration. Though he has illustrated many books by other authors, he is best known for those he wrote himself. His style varies from quite simple line drawings, with little or no indication of background, to elaborate cross-hatched and textured drawings in which every inch of the composition is filled.

Sendak's make-believe creatures delight adults as well as children. His READING IS FUN poster uses animals from his book *Where the Wild Things Are.* Sendak rejects the notion that illustrations for children's books must be devoid of anything frightening; his playfully menacing creatures provide children with a healthy way to confront some of their fears of the unknown. Sendak's work has had a strong influence on other illustrators.

Surprisingly, given his fame as an illustrator, Sendak believes that illustrations should be secondary to the text. When illustration is at its finest, however, pictures and text become inseparable.

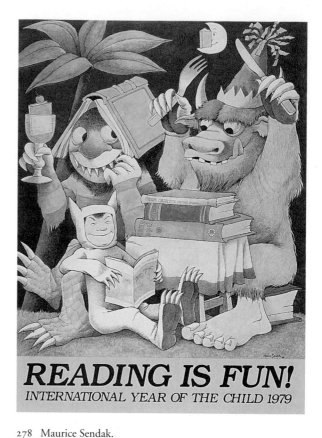

278 Maurice Sendak.
READING IS FUN. Poster.
©1979 by Reading Is Fundamental, Inc. Reprinted with permission.

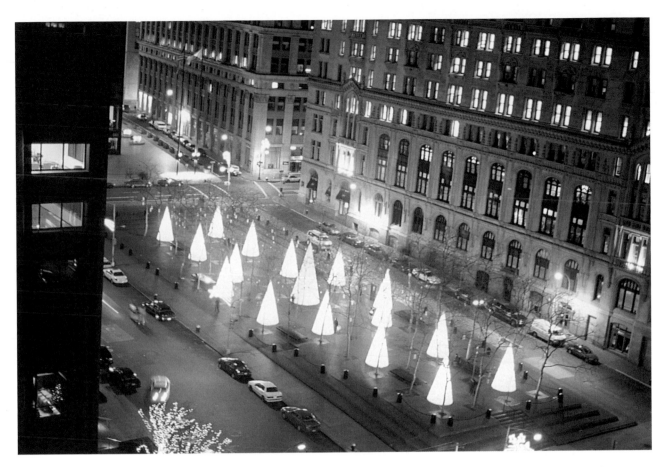

Ken Smith and Jim Conti.
GLOWING TOPIARY GARDEN. Liberty Plaza, New York City 1997–1998.
Height of cones, 16' to 24'.
Courtesy Ken Smith.

PART FOUR

Three-Dimensional Arts

CONSIDER . . .

In what ways does a sculpture of a human being differ from a painting of one?

The process of creating sculpture provides a kind of kinesthetic satisfaction that differs from the satisfaction derived from the production of two-dimensional art forms. Do you think some people prefer to make tactile sculptural art for this reason?

How does our experience of a sculpture or building or a garden differ from our experience of a drawing or a painting?

If something carefully handmade is utilitarian, can it still be art? Or should we call it a craft?

Is there a difference between art and craft?

CHAPTER TWELVE

SCULPTURE

S culpture exists in space, as we do. The total experience of a sculpture is the sum of its surfaces and profiles. Even when touching is not permitted, the perceived tactile quality is an important part of the way we experience sculpture.

FREESTANDING AND RELIEF SCULPTURE

Sculpture meant to be seen from all sides is called *in-the-round* or *freestanding.* As we move around it, our experience of a sculpture is the sum of its surfaces and profiles. No one had to suggest moving around Calder's OBUS to the little girl in our photograph. A single photograph shows only one view of a sculpture under one kind of light; thus unless we

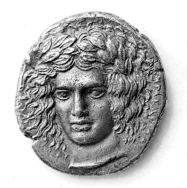

280 APOLLO. C. 415 B.C.E. Greek silver coin. Diameter 1⅛".
Photograph: Hirmer Fotoarchiv, Munich Germany.

can see many photographs or, better yet, a video, or best of all, view the piece firsthand, we receive only a limited impression of the sculpture.

A sculpture that is not freestanding but projects from a background surface is in relief. In *low-relief* (or *bas-relief*) sculpture, the projection from the surrounding surface is slight. As a result, shadows are minimal. Most coins, for example, are works of low-relief sculpture. A high point in the art of coin design was reached on the island of Sicily during the classical period of ancient Greece. The APOLLO coin, shown here slightly larger than actual size, has a strong presence in spite of being in low relief and very small.

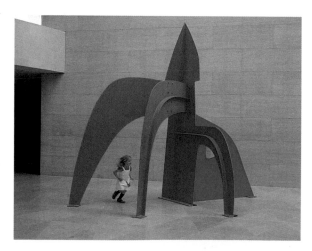

279 Alexander Calder.
OBUS. 1972.
Painted sheet metal. 142½" × 152" × 89⅝".
Mr. & Mrs. Paul Mellon Collection. Photograph © 2001 Board of Trustees, National Gallery of Art, Washington, D.C. 1983.1.49.(A–1859)/SC. © 2002 Estate of Alexander Calder/Artists Rights Society (ARS), NY. Photograph: Duane Preble.

Some of the world's best and most varied low-relief sculptures are found at the temple of Angkor Wat in Cambodia. This vast temple complex was the center of the Khmer empire in the twelfth century. It was here that Khmer kings sponsored an extensive program of sculpture and architecture. Within the chambers of the complex, carvings are in such delicate low relief that they are more like paintings than sculpture. One scene depicting an ARMY ON THE MARCH is a king's army commanded by a prince. The rhythmic pattern of the spear-carrying soldiers contrasts with the curving decorative patterns of the jungle foliage depicted in the background. The soldiers and background provide a base and setting for the prince, who stands with bow and arrow poised in his carriage on the elephant's back. Intricate detail covers entire surfaces of the stone walls. It seems as though the Khmer sculptor enjoyed contrasting the excellent formal discipline of the Khmer troops on the left with the chaotic disarray of the Thai troops on the right.

In *high-relief* sculpture, more than half of the natural circumference of the modeled form projects from the surrounding surface, and figures are often substantially undercut.

This is the case with Robert Longo's CORPORATE WARS: WALL OF INFLUENCE, where male and female figures convulse in painful conflict. In much of the composition there is extensive use of high-relief; in a few areas limbs and garments are barely raised from the background surface. Longo's use of dynamic gestures and diagonal placement of torsos and limbs make the sculpture feel very active. The charged emotional energy of the piece carries Longo's view of the horrors of corporate dog-eat-dog competition.

Longo works in a variety of media, including drawing, painting, sculpture, and film. He also is an actor, musician, and graphic designer. The focus of much of his work has been on expressing his horror at the prevalence of physical and psychological violence found in war, in mass media, and in life.

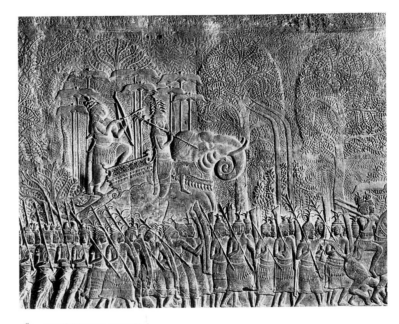

281 ARMY ON THE MARCH.
Angkor Wat, The Great Temple of the Khmers, Cambodia.
Sandstone.
Eliot Elisofon, LIFE Magizine © TimePix

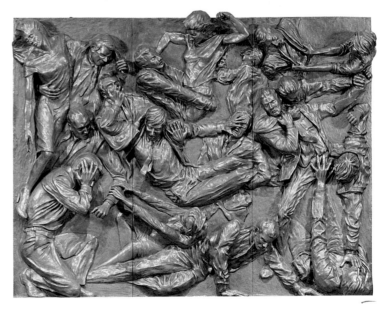

282 Robert Longo.
Middle portion, CORPORATE WARS: WALL OF INFLUENCE. 1982.
Cast aluminum. 7' × 9'.
Photograph: Courtesy of Metro Pictures.

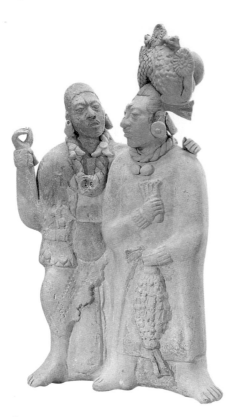

283 DOUBLE FIGURE, MAN AND FEMALE.
Mexican. c. 700 A.D.
Terracotta and paint.
10½" × 5¾" × 3⅜".
Honolulu Academy of Arts. Purchase 1973 (4184.1).

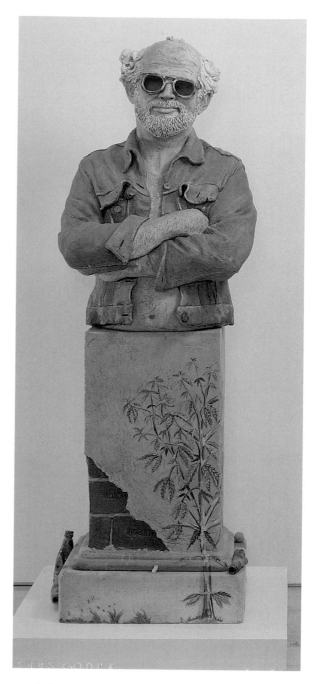

284 Robert Arneson.
CALIFORNIA ARTIST. 1982.
Stoneware with glazes. 68¼" × 27 ½" × 20¼".
San Francisco Museum of Modern Art. Gift of the Art Council.
© Estate of Robert Arneson/Licensed by VAGA, NY.

METHODS AND MATERIALS

Traditionally, sculpture has been made by modeling, casting, carving, constructing, and assembling, or a combination of these processes.

Modeling

Modeling is a *manipulative* and often *additive* process. Pliable material such as clay, wax, or plaster is built up, removed, and pushed into a final form.

Tool marks and fingerprint impressions are visible on the surface as evidence of the modeling technique employed to make MAYA MAN AND WOMAN. Body volume, natural gesture, and costume detail are clearly defined. The ancient Maya, who lived in what are now parts of Mexico, Guatemala, and Honduras, used clay to create fine ceramic vessels and lively naturalistic sculpture.

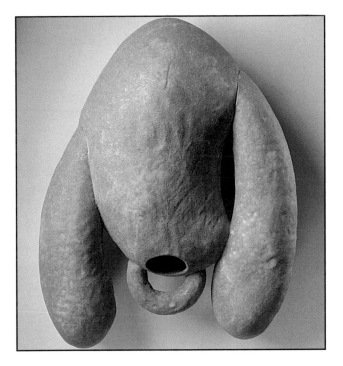

SCOTT CHAMBERLIN

Scott Chamberlin's AHYRE is a piece of terra cotta modeled into an abstract shape. He discusses his working methods and intended meanings for this work on the CD-ROM that accompanies this book.

285 Scott Chamberlin.
AHYRE. 1998.
Terra Cotta. 24" high.
Photograph by John Bobath. Courtesy the artist.

In their working consistencies, materials such as wax, clay, and plaster are soft. To prevent sagging, sculptors usually start all but very small pieces with a rigid inner support called an *armature*. When clay is modeled to form large sculptures, the total piece can be built in relatively small, separately fired, structurally self-sufficient sections, thereby eliminating the need for an armature.

This was the case when Robert Arneson employed the modeling process for building his self-portrait CALIFORNIA ARTIST. Arneson considered all art self-portraiture. He made this piece in response to an attack on his work by a New York critic, who said that, because of California's spiritual and cultural impoverishment, Arneson's work could have no serious depth or meaning.

Arneson created a life-sized ceramic figure with empty holes in place of eyes, revealing an empty head, depicted himself as a combination biker and aging hippie—complete with the appropriate visual clichés on and around the base. Those who think that clay is only for making bricks and dinnerware were acknowledged by Arneson, who put his name on the bricks, as any other brickmaker would. The artist stated his point of view:

I like art that has humor, with irony and playfulness. I want to make "high" art that is outrageous, while revealing the human condition which is not always high.[1]

Casting

Casting processes make it possible to execute a work in an easily handled medium (such as clay) and then to preserve the results in a more permanent material (such as bronze). Because most *casting* involves the substitution of one material for another, casting is also called the *substitution* or *replacement* process. The process of bronze casting was highly developed in ancient China, Greece, Rome, and parts of Africa. It has been used extensively in the West from the Renaissance to modern times.

Casting involves three broad steps. First, a *mold* is taken from the original work (also called the *pattern*). The process of making the mold varies, depending on the material of the original and the material used in the casting. Materials that can be poured and will harden can be used to cast: clay diluted with water, molten metal, concrete, or liquid plastic. Second, the original sculpture is removed from the mold and the casting liquid is poured into the resulting hollow cavity. Finally, when the casting liquid has hardened, the mold is removed.

casting. Most of our monuments in public parks were cast in bronze from artists' clay or wax models.

In recent years, many sculptors have turned to modern synthetic media such as plastics, which can be cast and painted to look like a variety of other materials. Cast polyvinyl resin can be made to resemble human flesh, and some artists have exploited this property to create sculptures of unbelievable realism by adding clothing. Viewers might be forgiven for approaching and conversing with Duane Hanson's GUARD, for example. It is difficult to tell whether it is a work of art or is protecting other works. Its presence in the gallery probably does help protect other works. Charles Ray's SELF-PORTRAIT is a little more witty, if that is possible. He made the statue taller than he actually

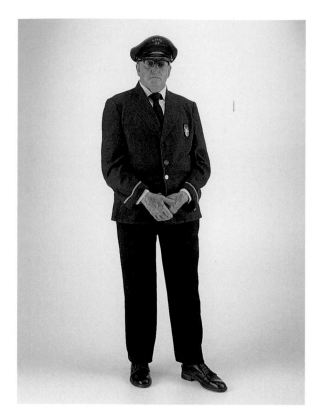

286 Duane Hanson (American, 1925–1996).
MUSEUM GUARD. 1975.
Polyester, fiberglass, oil and vinyl. 69" × 21" × 13".
Nelson-Atkins Museum of Art, Kansas City, MO. Gift of the Friends of Art.
Photograph by Robert Newcombe © 1995 The Nelson Gallery Foundation.
All Reproduction Rights Reserved. © Estate of Duane Hanson/Licensed by
VAGA, New York, NY.

Some casting processes employ molds or flexible materials that allow many casts to be made from the same mold; with other processes, such as the *lost wax process,* the mold is destroyed to remove the hardened cast, thus permitting only a single cast to be made.

Castings can be solid or hollow, depending on the casting method. The cost and the weight of the material often help determine which casting method will be used for a specific work.

The process of casting a large object like Giacometti's MAN POINTING (page 46) is extremely complicated. Except for small pieces that can be cast solid, most artists turn their originals over to foundry experts, who make the molds and do the

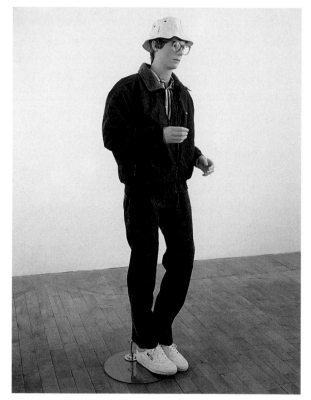

287 Charles Ray. SELF-PORTRAIT. 1990.
Mixed media. 75" × 26" × 20".
Collection of the Orange County Museum of Art, Museum purchase.

is—wouldn't we all like to be taller—and put a mannequin stand at the bottom. Both works play an elaborate game between human-made image and reality, but Ray's work adds a third possibility: Is it real, is it art, or something in between, such as a dummy? Is it dummy art?

Sculptors who attempt to fool our eyes with statues that resemble real people are working in an ancient Western tradition that values realism as evidence of artistic skill. According to myth, the Classical Greek artist Zeuxis once painted a man holding a bowl of grapes so realistically that a bird flew down and tried to eat the fruit. Zeuxis was unsatisfied with the work, however, because, he reasoned, if he had painted the man with equal skill, the bird would have been frightened off by the painted figure. Unfortunately, none of his works survive. The belief that the greatest artists are the best at capturing a likeness still holds much sway in our society, and artists such as Hanson and Ray make charming allusion to it in their works.

Sculpture made with materials such as polyvinyl or epoxy resin is often formed in separate pieces in plaster molds, then assembled and unified with the addition of more layers of plastic. Although molds are used, the initial pouring process differs from conventional casting because forms are built up in layers inside mold sections rather than being made out of material poured into a single mold all at once.

English artist Rachel Whiteread has used these new materials in fascinating cast pieces that turn empty spaces into solid volumes. She made her 1998 work WATER TOWER by pouring 9,000 pounds of clear urethane into a mold made from an actual tower. The piece looks as though the wooden container vanished, leaving only the water.

Carving

Carving away unwanted material to form a sculpture is a *subtractive* process. Michelangelo preferred this method. Close observation of his chisel marks

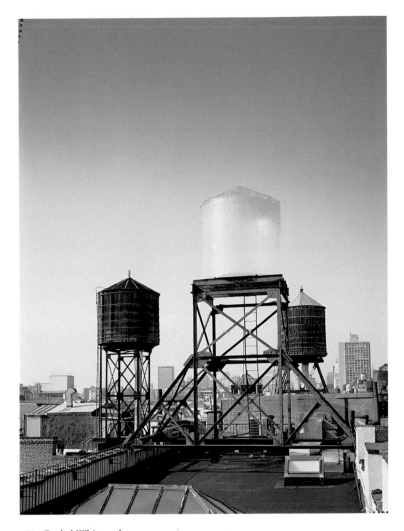

288　Rachel Whiteread.
PUBLIC ART FUND WATERTOWER PROJECT. 1997.
12' high, 9' diameter.
Courtesy of the artist and Luhring Augustine.

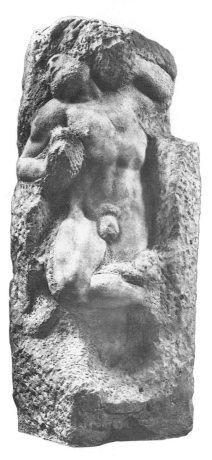

289 Michelangelo Buonarroti.
AWAKENING SLAVE.
1530–1534.
Marble. Height 9'.
Academy Gallery, Florence.
Alinari/Art Resource, NY.

290 MASSIVE STONE HEAD.
Possibly representing a
planetary deity.
12th–10th centuries B.C.E.
Olmec. Basalt. Height 65".
Anthropology Museum, Veracruz, Mexico.
Werner Forman/Art Resource, NY.

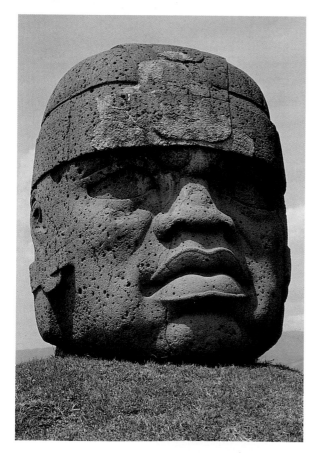

on the surfaces of the unfinished AWAKENING SLAVE reveals the steps he took toward increasingly refined cutting—even before he had roughed out the proportions of the figure from all sides. Because Michelangelo left this piece in an unfinished state, it seems as though we are looking over his shoulder midway through the carving process. For him, the act of making sculpture was a process of releasing the form he had seen in his mind's eye from within the block of stone. This is one of four unfinished figures, later called "Slaves," that Michelangelo abandoned in various stages.

Carving is the most difficult of the three basic sculptural methods because it is a one-way technique that provides little or no opportunity to correct errors. Before beginning to cut, the sculptor must visualize all angles of the finished form within the original block of material. Another example of Michelangelo's finished carving is his PIETÀ on page 86.

The various types of stone with their different characteristics greatly influence the type of carving that can be done with them. The marble that many sculptors in the European tradition prefer is typically soft and workable enough that it can be cut with a chisel. Final polishing with a light abrasive yields a smooth and creamy surface not unlike human skin. Jade, on the other hand, is so hard and brittle that it can be filed down only with friction. ARMY ON THE MARCH (page 195) was done in sandstone, a relatively soft and fine-grained stone that makes high detail possible using a combination of cutting and filing. The Olmecs of ancient Mexico used basalt, common in their area of the Gulf Coast. We can see its coarse-grained character in the MASSIVE STONE HEAD. Even though the sculptor achieved an intense facial expression, there is little detail. The relative hardness of the stone and the simple nature of the tools available meant that most of the original boulder-like shape of the stone had to be kept. The coarseness of basalt is even more obvious when we consider that this piece is nearly five and half feet tall and weighs several tons.

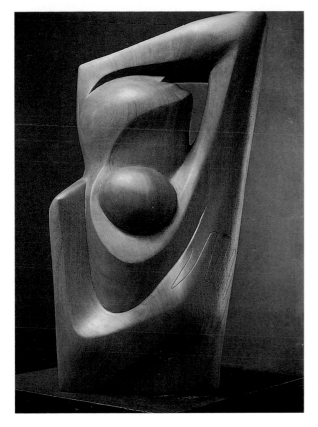

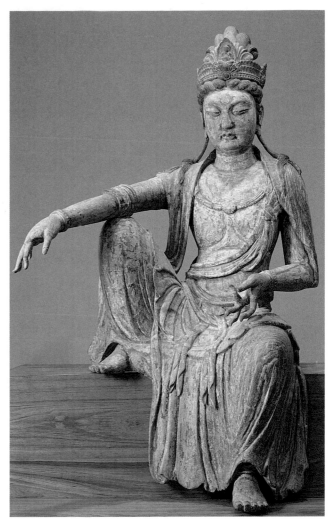

291 Elizabeth Catlett. MOTHER AND CHILD #2. 1971.
Walnut. Height 38".
Photograph by Samella Lewis.
© 2002 Elizabeth Catlett/Licensed by VAGA, NY.

292 KWAN YIN. BODHISATTVA. China, 13th–14th century
Northern Song Dynasty, *1027*
Wood. Height 67".
Honolulu Academy of Arts Purchase 1927. (2400)

In wood carving, walnut and cypress are preferred because of their strength and ease of working. The gesture of the mother in Elizabeth Catlett's carved MOTHER AND CHILD suggests anguish, perhaps over the struggles all mothers know each child will face. Both figures have been abstracted to their essence in a composition of bold sweeping curves and simplified shapes. Solidity of the mass is relieved by the open space between the uplifted chin and raised elbow and by the convex and concave surfaces. A subtle carved line indicating the mother's right hand accents the surface of the abstract form. The highly polished smooth wood invites the viewer to touch.

Carving from a single block of wood is risky because the outside of a piece of wood reacts to external moisture conditions much more readily than the inside, and the resulting expansion and contraction can lead to splits and cracks. The Chinese, who have traditionally excelled at wood carving, solved this problem many centuries ago by developing the technique called joined-block construction. Here, different parts of a sculpture are carved separately and fitted together; then the whole piece is hollowed out from behind. If the work is done well, as it is in KWAN YIN BODHISATTVA, the joints between the four pieces of wood are not noticeable except to experts. This work was originally painted, but in the intervening centuries the color has mostly worn away, leaving the grain of the cypress wood visible.

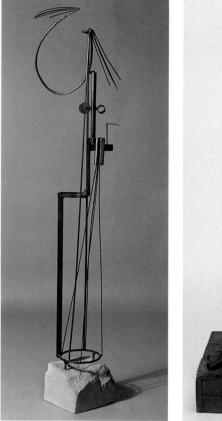

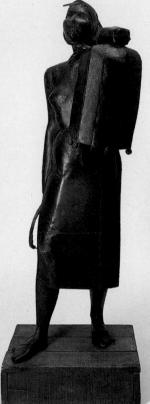

293 Julio González.
     MATERNITY. 1934.
     Welded iron. Height 49⅞".
     Tate Gallery, London/Art Resource, NY.
     ©2002 Artists Rights Society (ARS), New York.

294 Julio González.
     THE MONTSERRAT. 1936–1937.
     Sheet iron. Height 5'5".
     Stedelijk Museum, Amsterdam. ©2002 Artists Rights Society (ARS), New York.

Constructing and Assembling

For most of recorded history, the major sculpturing techniques in the Western world were modeling, carving, and casting. Early in the twentieth century, *assembling* methods became popular. Such works are called *constructions*.

In the late 1920s, Spaniard Julio González pioneered the use of the welding torch for cutting and welding metal sculpture. The invention of oxyacetylene welding in 1895 had provided the necessary tool for welded metal sculpture, but it took three decades for artists to realize the new tool's potential. González had learned welding while working briefly in an automobile factory. After several decades—and limited success—as a painter, González began assisting Picasso with the construction of metal sculpture. Subsequently González committed himself to sculpture and began to create his strongest, most original work. In 1932 he wrote:

The Age of Iron began many centuries ago by producing very beautiful objects, unfortunately mostly weapons. Today it makes possible bridges and railroads as well. It is time that this material cease to be a murderer and the simple instrument of an overly mechanical science. The door is wide open, at last! for this material to be forged and hammered by the peaceful hands of artists.[2]

González welded iron rods to construct his linear abstraction MATERNITY. It is airy and playful. In contrast, the MONTSERRAT, created a few years later, is a much more representational figure. The title, after Catalonia's holy mountain, suggests that the figure is a symbol of Spanish will and resistance to Nazi aggression.

The direct metalworking technique was quickly adapted by other leading sculptors, including Alexander Calder. He made several large-scale constructions out of steel which now decorate public spaces.

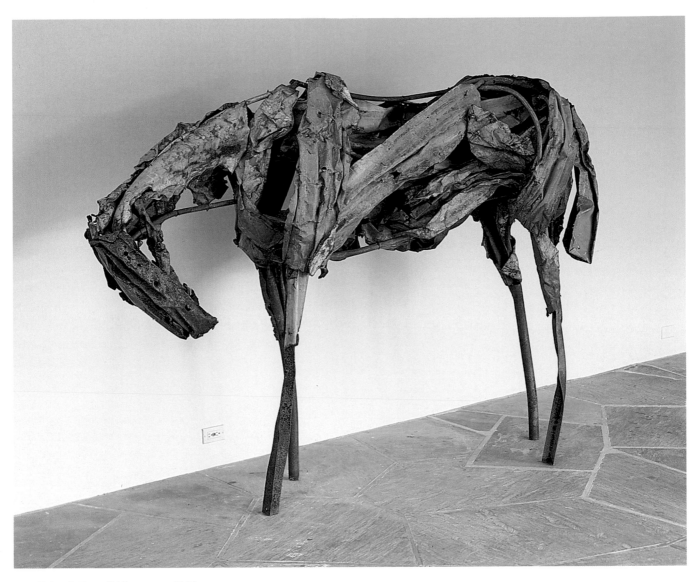

295 Deborah Butterfield. NAHELE. 1986.
Scrap metal. 72" × 102" × 39".
Courtesy The Contemporary Museum, Honolulu.
Gift of the Honolulu Advertiser Collection at Persis Corporation.

Since the 1970s, Deborah Butterfield has created figures of horses from found materials such as sticks and scrap metal. Much of Butterfield's time is spent on ranches in Montana and Hawaii where she trains and rides horses and makes sculpture. Painted, crumpled, rusted pieces of metal certainly seem an unlikely choice for expressing a light-footed animal, yet Butterfield's NAHELE and other abstract horses have a surprisingly lifelike presence. The artist intends her sculpture to *feel* like horses rather than simply look like them. The old car bodies she has used for many of her welded and wired metal horses add a note of irony: the scrapped autos take on a new life as a horse.

Some sculptors assemble found objects in ways that radically change the way we see familiar objects, yet the artists maintain enough of the objects' original characteristics and identities to invite us to participate in their transformation. Such work requires metaphorical visual thinking by both artists and viewers. This subcategory of constructed sculpture is called *assemblage*.

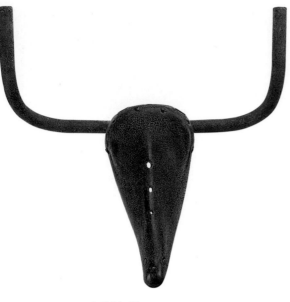

From salvaged fragments of daily life Picasso found a wealth of ready-made ingredients. For his assemblage BULL'S HEAD he cut the creative process to a single leap of awareness. Describing how it happened, Picasso said:

One day I found in a pile of jumble an old bicycle saddle next to some rusted handle bars . . . In a flash they were associated in my mind . . . The idea of this BULL'S HEAD *came without my thinking of it . . . I had only to solder them together . . .*[3]

Is Picasso's witty cast assemblage BABOON AND YOUNG a statement on evolution? First we notice the bulky mother ape with baby; on closer inspection we recognize some of the original ingredients of this assemblage: a large rubber ball for the torso; a strip of metal for the tail; ceramic handles for

296 Pablo Picasso.
BULL'S HEAD. 1943.
Bronze. Height 16⅛".
Seat and handles of a bicycle.
Reunion des Musees Nationaux/Art Resource, NY. © 2002 Estate of Pablo Picasso/Artists Rights Society (ARS), NY.

297 Pablo Picasso.
BABOON AND YOUNG. 1951.
Bronze (cast 1955), after found objects.
21" × 13¼" × 20¾".
The Museum of Modern Art, NY, Mrs. Simon Guggenheim Fund. Photograph © 2002 The Museum of Modern Art , NY © 2002 Estate of Pablo Picasso/Artists Rights Society (ARS), NY.

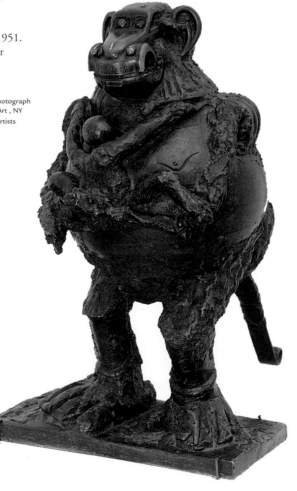

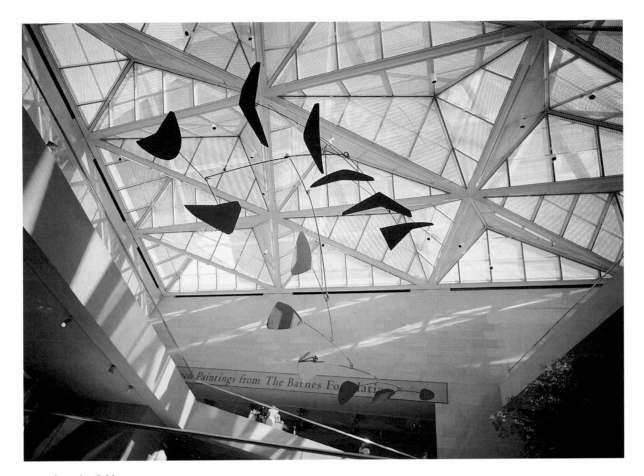

298 Alexander Calder.
UNTITLED. 1976.
Painted aluminum and tempered steel.
29'10½" × 76'.

ears; an upside-down toy car for the lower jaw; and for eyes, the heads of two people riding in another car. After sticking these found objects together with plaster, Picasso had the entire work cast in bronze.

Regarding unity and ambiguity in such constructions the artist said:

The thing that's marvelous about bronze is that it can give the most diverse objects such unity that sometimes it's difficult to identify the elements that make up the whole. But that's also a danger: [speaking of his BULL'S HEAD] *if you no longer see anything but the head of a bull, and not the bicycle seat and handlebar that formed it, the sculpture would lose its interest.*"[4]

KINETIC SCULPTURE

Alexander Calder was among the first to explore the possibilities of *kinetic sculpture*, or sculpture that moves. Marcel Duchamp christened Calder's kinetic sculptures *mobiles*—a word Duchamp had coined for his own work in 1914. Sculptors' traditional emphasis on mass is replaced in Calder's work by a focus on shape, space, and movement. By 1932, he was designing inventive wire and sheet-metal constructions. Calder's huge UNTITLED mobile is the centerpiece of the contemporary wing of the National Gallery of Art in Washington; its slow, graceful movement is caused by natural air currents within the building.

As a child, Alexander Calder made toys for his little sister and friends out of bits of wire, wood, and other odds and ends. This playful inventiveness never left him, and it leads viewers to see his mature sculptures as visual toys for adults. No other description quite explains the sense of well-being his sculptures can produce.

Alexander (Sandy) Calder was born in Lawton, Pennsylvania. His father and grandfather were both sculptors—you can see their work outdoors in many American cities. His mother was a painter. As artists, they encouraged creativity in their children, and young Sandy had his own workshop at home.

Despite his upbringing among artists, Calder decided on a career as an engineer, earning a degree from Stevens Institute of Technology in New Jersey. But after he had been out of school for a few years, he felt the urge to start drawing again. After studying at the Art Students League in New York, in 1925 he went to Paris, the center of new energy for art at the time.

Calder first enchanted European viewers with his delightful wire sculptures—whimsical three-dimensional drawings of animals and entertainers (see page 42). Perhaps his best-loved wire work is a grand troupe of circus performers and animals.

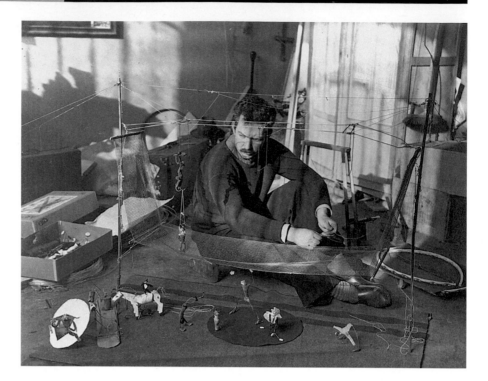

Today CIRCUS is in a museum, in a glass case where it can't be touched. But the artist used to treat his friends to gala performances, complete with music and lights, announcing each act like a ringmaster and putting his wire performers through their paces. Life, play, and art all merged in Calder's world.

A 1930 visit with Piet Mondrian opened Calder's eyes to the possibilities of abstraction. "I liked his paintings well enough," the sculptor later recalled. "But those little black or colored rectangles—I should have liked to see them move."[5] From this insight he developed his famous *mobiles*—delicately balanced constellations of metal discs on wires that move in the breeze or at a touch.

Calder became one of the most popular artists of his day. He married happily and had two daughters, one of whom carries on the family artistic tradition as a children's book illustrator. His time was divided between a farmhouse in France and one in Connecticut, and from his huge barnlike studios there emerged a long and joyous series of mobiles, stabiles (stationary constructions), paintings, jewelry, stage sets, and designs for tapestries and rugs.

Today Calder's large sculptures can be seen in many city squares and modern buildings. They have become a part of our daily lives, just as he wanted.

299   ALEXANDER CALDER WITH HIS CIRCUS. 1929.
Photograph: Andre Kertész. © Estate of Andre Kertész. Andre and Elizabeth Kertész Foundation.

"A sculpture must be as useful as signaling poles placed in sea-lanes and waterways, with their red discs, yellow squares, and black triangles," he said. "It must be designed as a real urban signal [as] well as a sculpture."[6] Calder's sculptures beam a strong signal of freedom and delight into modern life.

MIXED MEDIA

Today's artists frequently use a variety of media in a single work. Rather than being presented as a long list of materials, such combinations are sometimes identified as *mixed media*. The media may be all two-dimensional, all three-dimensional, or a mixture of the two. Often, the use of media responds to some cultural symbolism.

Cai Guo Qiang retold an ancient Chinese war story in his large work BORROWING YOUR ENEMY'S ARROWS: A crafty general dared the enemy to shoot at his boats as he floated by; the enemy obliged with such enthusiasm that the arrows helped the general's laden boats float higher.

Bessie Harvey follows ancient African tradition by picking up wood roots and working them into sculptures with the addition of other media. SNAKE THROUGH EYE is an assemblage of such wood pieces.

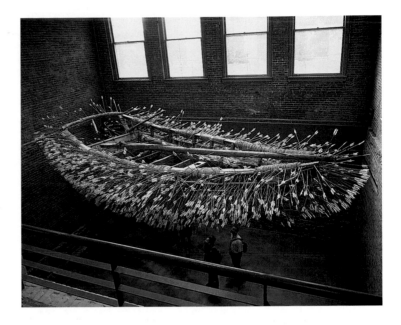

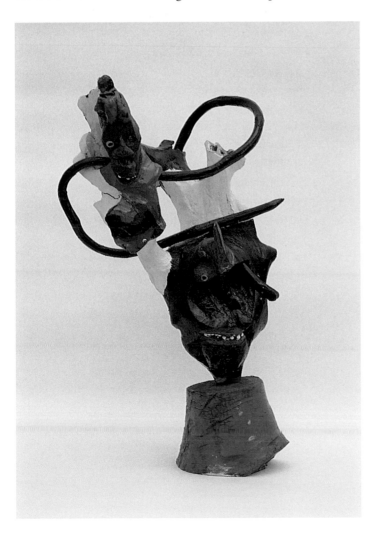

300 Cai Guo Qiang.
BORROWING YOUR ENEMY'S ARROWS. 1998.
Inside Out: New Chineese Art. P.S.1, New York.
Photo: Hiro Ihara. Courtesy of the artist.

301 Bessie Harvey.
SNAKE THROUGH EYE. 1989.
Painted wood. 24".
Photograph: Courtesy Cavin-Morris Gallery.

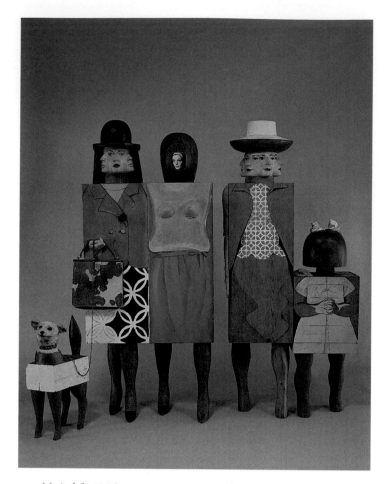

302 Marisol (b. 1930). WOMEN AND DOG. 1964.
Wood, plaster, synthetic polymer, taxidermed
dog head, and mixed media.
Whitney Museum of American Art, New York. Purchase, with funds
from the Friends of the Whitney Museum of American Art. 64.17a–g.
Photograph by Robert E. Mates © 1999: Whitney Museum of American Art, NY. Mairsol/Licensed by VAGA, New York, NY.

She described her working method, which involves seeing the finished piece in the raw found object: "You go to the wood pile and all at once you see a face, in any piece of wood, and it looks like it's just asking for help, for help to come out."[7]

Marisol, a Venezuelan who uses only one name, makes assembled wood sculpture in a more geometric style than Bessie Harvey. Typical of her work, WOMEN AND DOG incorporates both drawing and painting on the life-sized, boxy figures. Her work usually has a satirical edge to it, as the rigidity and multiple blank faces of the figures show. She most often lampoons political leaders and upper-class persons, a rather ironic fact since the artist herself comes from these social levels.

For almost four decades, Korean-born Nam June Paik has been the artist most identified with the fusion of art and technology. In chapter 10, Paik was introduced as the first to use video as an art medium. Here, we consider him as a major mixed-media artist.

From the beginning of his career, Paik has refused to conform to the demands of only one creative medium. He began by studying musical composition before moving on to visual art. In the 1960s he achieved art-world notoriety for creating a cello made from television monitors. He composed several works for his "TV cello." For a 1978 installation, he recorded videotapes of green landscapes, and played them on monitors placed in a bed of live plants. A recent installation made use of video monitors, sounds, projected imagery, and brightly colored laser beams.

In 1974 Paik, in harmony with computer development, envisioned a totally new kind of super highway made up of interactive technologies that would enable a new level of communication around the world. His 1997–1998 traveling installation exhibit, the *Electronic Super Highway*, filled with his recent video assemblages, incorporates over 650 working television monitors. He calls it "Cybertown." What could be more "mixed" than the ingredients of Paik's humorous INTERNET DWELLER: WOL.FIVE.YDPB listed in the caption of the piece shown here?

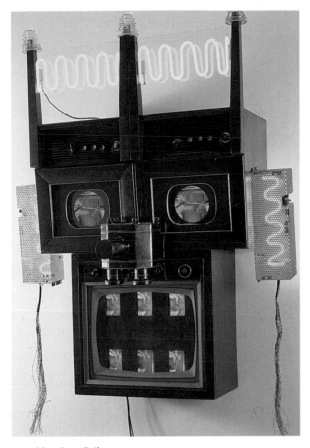

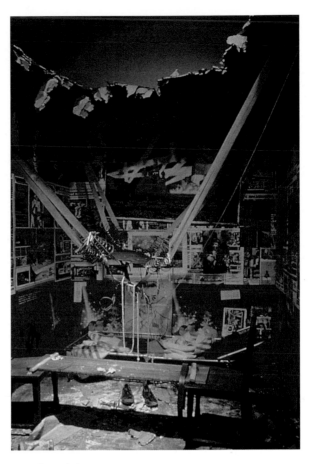

303   Nam June Paik.
INTERNET DWELLER: WOL.FIVE.YDPB. 1994.
Two Panasonic 10" televisions, six KTV 5" televisions, six
vintage television cabinets, projector, lantern, glass
insulators, neon, one laser disc player, one original Paik
laser disc.
Solway Gallery, Cincinnati, Ohio.
Photographers: Chris Gomien and Tom Allison.

304   Ilya Kabakov.
THE MAN WHO FLEW INTO SPACE FROM HIS APARTMENT.
From TEN CHARACTERS. 1981–1988.
Mixed media installation.
© Ilya Kabakov. Courtesy Barbara Gladstone. © 2002 Artists Rights Society (ARS),
New York.

INSTALLATIONS
AND SITE-SPECIFIC SCULPTURE

Recently, many artists have begun to use the three-dimensional medium of *installation* in an effort to tell a story visually. An installation artist transforms a space by bringing into it items of symbolic significance. This medium is most similar to constructed sculpture, but the artist constructs an entire environment within the gallery. A leader in this trend has been the Russian émigré artist Ilya Kabakov, whose work THE MAN WHO FLEW INTO SPACE FROM HIS APARTMENT was first exhibited in 1989, a year after he left the Soviet Union. It represents a cramped tenement apartment of the sort typical of the Russian middle classes, except that

the walls are covered with Communist posters and drawings by the room's imagined inhabitant. Looking at the piece, viewers can guess at the story line: The hero, feeling dejected and oppressed by life as he found it, literally blasted himself out of his cubicle, leaving behind a gaping hole in the ceiling directly above his abandoned shoes. Kabakov is committed to the installation style, because, he says, "it may unite—on equal terms, without recognition of supremacy—anything at all . . . Here, politics may be combined with the kitchen, objects of everyday use with scientific objects, garbage with sentimental effusions."[8]

A very different installation from Kabakov's was created by James Turrell within P.S.1, an old

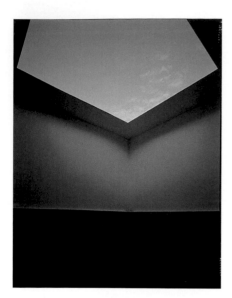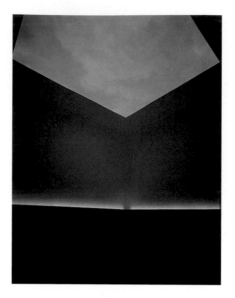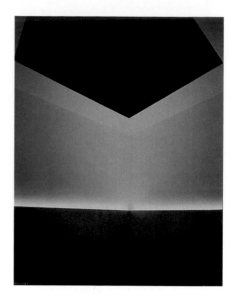

305 a-b-c.
James Turrell. MEETING. 1980–1986.
Installation at P.S.1, Long Island City, N.Y.
Courtesy Barbara Gladstone Gallery and P.S. 1.
Museum of Contemporary Art, NY.

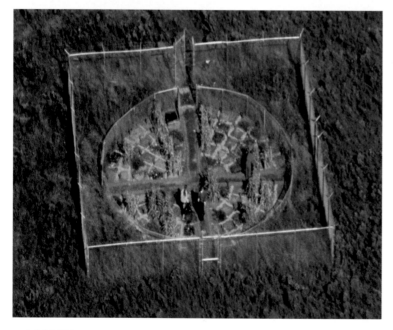

306 Mel Chin.
REVIVAL FIELD.
Pig's Eye Landfill, St. Paul, Minnesota. 1993.
Photo: David Schneider. Courtesy the artist.

work is one of a series of installations Turrell calls Skyspaces. The space is visited by appointment only, in dry weather, in late afternoon to early evening hours. It consists of a white room without windows or furniture except for a high-backed continuous bench built into the base of the four walls. Visitors slowly realize that most of the ceiling is not ceiling, but open sky. As evening comes, the natural light defining the space gradually fades to reveal a previously unseen warm light gently emerging from behind the high-backed seating. For many visitors, MEETING is a wonderful visual experience, a meditative spiritual renewal. It is a place where nature and human ingenuity conspire to transform one's sense of self and place.

Sculpture designed for a particular place—called *site-specific*—has become a major type of contemporary art. Many artists have sought to move beyond the limitations of sculpture as portable, collectible commodities and sculpture on pedestals, such as statues of historic figures. In addition, commissions for art in public places usually involve designing permanent works for specific locations. The best of site-specific sculpture interacts with its location in such a complete and complementary way that the surroundings become part of the piece and the sculpture helps define the character of the place.

public school in Long Island City that had been renovated to provide studio and exhibition spaces. MEETING, a site-specific permanent installation, is in a small square room on an upper floor. This

Mel Chin's REVIVAL FIELD is a site-specific work made for a landfill; over time, this work will reclaim a field polluted for years with toxic dumping of heavy metals. Working with scientists, the artist laid out a patch of land and planted it with crops that thrive on the very pollutants that caused the closure of the site in the first place. Chin believes that artists can help to solve social problems by conceiving of creative approaches. Since this is an art project, the bureaucratic holdups were minimal.

The piece, which must be seen from the air, took the form of a circle inscribed in a square. This is a highly meaningful symbol in both Asia and Europe, but it also has a practical purpose: The circle and the untreated surrounding area are exactly the same size, allowing for precise measurement of the work's progress in ridding the land of waste.

Although of great interest to today's artists, the idea of site-specific sculptural forms is not entirely new. One of the world's most impressive site-specific installations is the prehistoric monument at STONEHENGE (see page 7). Another site-specific work is the VIETNAM WAR MEMORIAL shown in chapter 25.

CHAPTER THIRTEEN

CLAY, GLASS, METAL, WOOD, FIBER

Traditionally in Western society, we have tended to separate the "crafts" from the "arts." Crafts are made with different media (clay, glass, wood, fiber) from those of art (paint, marble, bronze). Craft objects tend to be decorative, while art gener-

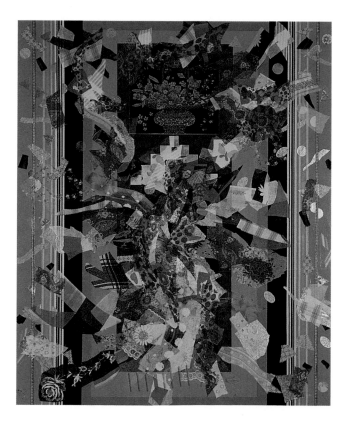

307 Miriam Schapiro.
PERSONAL APPEARANCE #3. 1973.
Acrylic and fabric on canvas. 60" × 50".
Collection Marilyn Stokstad, Lawrence, Kansas. Courtesy Bernice Stein-baum Gallery, Maimi, FL. Photo: Robert Hickerson

ally makes a personal statement. In addition, we have generally considered craft objects to be useful things, such as dishes, blankets, or jewelry, while art is meant to be only looked at and thought about, in a gallery or on a wall in someone's home.

All of that changed radically in the 1970s. Many artists began making unique objects for gallery exhibition out of craft media. Moreover, viewers at that time began to appreciate more and more the high level of skill, taste, and labor that go into the best craft work such as quilts, dishes, and stained glass. Industry and mass production reduced the demand for handmade things for daily use. Craft and art thus began to draw together, and the barrier between them began to break down.

This change in attitude brought Western thought in line with that of other cultures around the world and throughout history, who have not separated art and craft. Most of the world's cultures have regarded an excellent piece of pottery as highly as a painting, and a book illustration as equal in merit to a piece of sculpture; Western society is approaching this view as well.

The Canadian-born American artist Miriam Schapiro was a key figure in this transition. After spending many years making abstract paintings, in the early 1970s she began borrowing techniques from quilting in large works such as PERSONAL APPEARANCE #3. She selected and cut out pieces of fabric and actually glued them to the surface of the canvas, where they joined forces with acrylic paint in colorful, exuberant compositions.

She commented many times on her reasons for making this jump. Decoration, she said, is universal. The urge to embellish is both a worldwide phenomenon and a characteristic that art and craft share: "Decoration pulls us all together and is non-elitist, non-sexist, and non-racist." Hence the sumptuous richness of most of her work.

Along with many other artists who pierced the boundary between art and craft, Schapiro had a partially feminist intent as well. Traditional craft media such as ceramics and textiles have for centuries been a woman's province. Schapiro and many others feel that relegating craft to separate status demeans the achievements of women throughout history. Regarding her effort to heal the breach, to elevate craft, and join it with art. Shapiro said, "I dovetail my feminism with decoration."[1]

Industrial production coupled with feminism has thus made it possible for craft artists to produce purely expressive rather than only functional objects. Today, much work in traditional craft media functions as art does, to give pleasure and provoke thought. This chapter will explore many such works.

CLAY

Bits of broken clay pots found in archaeological sites provide valuable clues to thousands of years of human civilization. In addition to being one of the world's art media, clay has long been a valuable raw material. It offers flexibility of form, and also relative permanence due to its capacity to harden when exposed to heat, a process called *firing*.

The art and science of making objects from clay is called *ceramics*. A person who works with clay is called a *potter* or a *ceramist*. A wide range of objects, including tableware, dishes, sculpture, bricks, and many kinds of tiles, are made of clay. Most of the basic ceramic materials were discovered, and processes developed, thousands of years ago.

Clays are generally categorized in one of three broad types. *Earthenware* is typically fired at a relatively low temperature (approximately 1,100° C to 1,150° C), and is porous after firing. It may vary in color from red to brown to tan. Earthenware is the most common of the three types, and a great many of the world's pots have been made from it. *Stoneware* is fired at a higher temperature (1,200° C to 1,300° C) and is not porous. Its color is usually grayish or brown. Combining strength with easy workability, stoneware is the preferred medium of most of today's art potters. *Porcelain* is the rarest and most expensive of the three types. Made from deposits of decomposed granite, it becomes white and translucent after firing at a typically high temperature (1,350° C to 1,500° C). Also nonporous, it rings when struck. Porcelain was first developed in China, and even today in England and America the finest white dishes are called "China," no matter where they are made.

The ceramic process is relatively simple. Potters create functional pots or purely sculptural forms from soft, damp clay using hand-building methods such as slab, coil, or modeling, or by *throwing*—that is, by shaping clay on a rapidly revolving wheel. Invented in Mesopotamia about six thousand years ago, the potter's wheel allows potters to produce circular forms with great speed and uniformity. In the hands of a skilled worker, the process looks effortless—almost magical—but it takes time and practice to perfect one's technique.

After shaping, a piece is thoroughly dried. Next it is fired in a *kiln* (a kind of oven) where heat chemically transforms the clay into a hard, stone-like substance.

Two kinds of liquids are commonly used to decorate ceramics, though rarely on the same piece. A *slip* is a mixture of clay and water about the consistency of cream, sometimes colored with earthen powders. With this relatively simple technique, only a limited

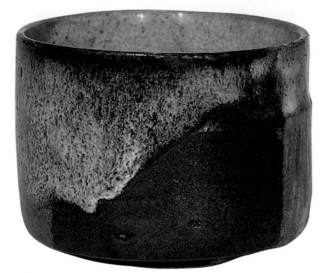

308 TEA BOWL.
Satsuma ware. 17th century.
Diameter of mouth 4⅕".
Courtesy of the Freer Gallery of Art, Smithsonian Institution, Washington D.C.
F1899.83.

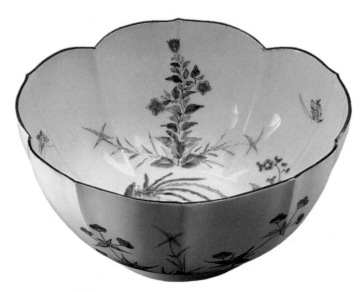

309 Kakiemon V.
BELL-FLOWER-SHAPED BOWL. 17th century.
Porcelain with overglaze enamels. Height 3".
Iris and B. Gerald Cantor Center for Visual Arts at Stanford University Museum
of Art (61.20). Gift of friends of Mrs. Phillip N. Lilienthal, Jr.
in honor of her 70th birthday, 1961.20.
Photograph: Frank Wing Photography.

range of colors is possible, but many ancient cultures made a specialty of this type of pottery decoration.

A *glaze* is a specially formulated liquid "clay paint" with a silica base. During firing, the glaze vitrifies (turns to a glass-like substance) and fuses with the clay body, creating a nonporous surface. Glazes can be colored or clear, translucent or opaque, glossy or dull, depending on their chemical composition. Firing changes the color of most glazes so radically that the liquid that the potter applies to the vessel comes out of the kiln an entirely different color.

Two seventeenth-century Japanese bowls—a TEA BOWL and a BELL-FLOWER-SHAPED BOWL—illustrate the extreme contrast in style that can occur when widely differing values, technique, and materials are applied to the making of objects with similar functions. The TEA BOWL, inspired by the Japanese tea ceremony, is of stoneware. Stoneware clays may contain impurities (including some that impart color) that make them appropriate for making unrefined wares. Earthy spontaneity, including graceful, unanticipated glaze drips, is highly valued by tea masters. In contrast, the porcelain BELL-FLOWER-SHAPED BOWL, delicate and fragile looking, was probably fired a total of three times: once with the raw white clay, once with a transparent glaze, and finally, at a lower temperature, to set the colored glazes. Porcelain is made with a fine-grained, translucent clay body. Both pieces are outstanding traditional examples, yet express greatly contrasting approaches within the same society.

Some present-day potters use ancient methods, firing their pots in open fires that reach only low and generally varied temperatures. A pioneer in the rediscovery of past techniques was the Hopi potter Nampeyo. Working in the 1890s in collaboration with anthropologists and archaeologists who were digging ancient ruins near her village, she learned the long-forgotten symbolic vocabulary of ancient wares, and in the process revitalized her own work and that of many other potters.

Traditional Native American ceramic arts had fallen into decline when Nampeyo first learned the trade from her grandmother. Most Indians in the Hopi region of Arizona, and even the Pueblo peoples of New Mexico, made very little pottery. The encroachment of mass produced goods, coupled with the severe poverty of both regions, led most Native families in the late nineteenth century to buy low-priced dishes and cooking utensils from white traders rather than pursue the ancient and time-consuming art of ceramics. Nampeyo's fusion of artistic talent and interest in the past sparked a pottery revival that spread throughout the Southwest and continues to this day.

The date of her birth is uncertain, since no one kept close records of such things in the village of Hano, on land that the Hopis called First Mesa. She was born into the Snake Clan, and was given the name Nampeyo, which means "Snake That Does Not Bite." There were no paved roads leading to the village, and the nearest city—Winslow, Arizona—was three days' journey away. In that isolated environment Nampeyo grew up. Her family responded to her early artistic interests by sending her to a neighboring village to learn pottery making from her grandmother, one of the few who still made pots. Her grandmother's large water jars were rather simply decorated, with only one or two designs on the face of each one.

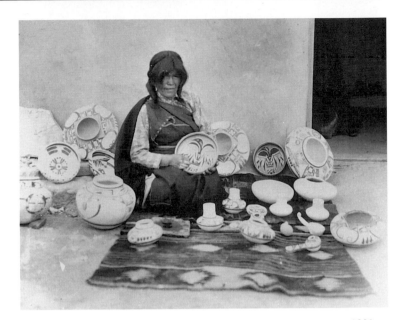

Sometime in the middle 1890s, Nampeyo began picking up broken shards of pottery from the nearby site of an ancient Hopi village called Sikyatki. This village had been abandoned well before the Spanish Conquest. The ancient pottery fragments were more ornate and abstract than the basic symbols that Nampeyo had been painting; she was fascinated by the ancient designs and began to incorporate them into her own pots.

In 1895, the anthropologist Jesse Walter Fewkes arrived to dig and study the ruins of Sikyatki, and his presence transformed Nampeyo's work. Her husband was one of several assistants to Fewkes; he helped with the digging and told the anthropologists what he knew about

310   NAMPEYO DECORATING POTTERY. 1901. Displaying pottery: ollas, dippers, bowls, vases, Hopi Tewa.
Courtesy of the Southwest Museum, Los Angeles.
Photograph: Adam Clark Vroman. N42363

the ancestral customs of the Hopi peoples. Fewkes and his assistants and students unearthed hundreds of burials, finding many more examples of ancient Hopi pottery in excellent condition. It was traditional to bury the dead with a seed jar, a low container with a narrow opening at the top, as a symbol of spiritual rebirth. These jars had abstract designs in brown or black over a rich yellow body. Her husband brought pieces home for Nampeyo, and soon she met Fewkes and accompanied him on digs.

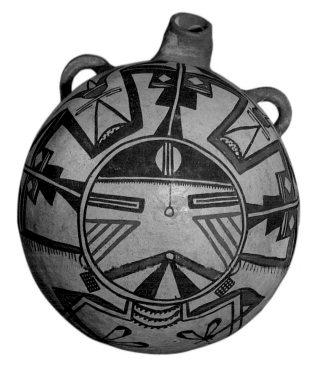

311   Nampeyo.
CANTEEN. C. 1880.
Polacca Polychrome Style C.
Arizona State Museum, University of Arizona, Tucson.
Miller Collection. ASM Cat. # 4099
Photograph: Helga Teiwes.

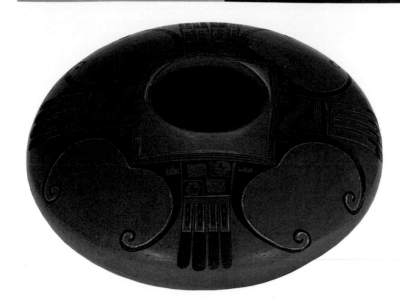

312 Nampeyo.
SEED JAR. c. 1915–1916.
Hopi.
Museum of Indian Arts & Culture/
Laboratory of Anthropolgy Collections, Museum of New Mexico Santa Fe.
Photograph: Doug Kahn.

Nampeyo invigorated her pottery by her sustained exposure to the work of her ancestors. She copied, studied, and practiced the ancient symbols. She mastered the shape of the traditional SEED JAR. Because the clay in the ancient pots was of finer quality than she was used to making, she sought new places to dig better clay from the earth. Fewkes, keenly interested in this revival of ancient techniques, took

Nampeyo to Chicago so that she could demonstrate her knowledge to the curators of the Field Museum of Natural History. She also demonstrated her skills to tourists and archaeologists at the Grand Canyon.

Once she learned the vocabulary of symbols, she found that she could freely adapt and combine them, rather than merely copy ancient models. She told an anthropologist, "When I first began to paint, I used to go to the ancient village and pick up pieces of pottery and copy the designs. That is how I learned to paint. But now I just close my eyes and see designs and I paint them."[2] Fewkes referred to her as "a thorough artist."

Probably Nampeyo's biggest surprise was that non-Native Americans were interested in buying her pots. She discovered that there was a ready market for pottery with the ancient designs. In this effort she was a pioneer. The relatively rare ancient pottery had always found buyers among a few select collectors; however, when Nampeyo began making pots in that style, to her delight she found that she could easily sell her entire production. She used the new income to support her entire extended family, and alleviate some of the poverty on First Mesa.

Nampeyo's success became a pattern that other Indian artists would follow. In the Pueblo of San Ildefonso, María Martínez and her husband, in collaboration with anthropologist Edgar Hewitt, soon reintroduced ancient black pottery from that Pueblo (see page 96). Lucy Lewis of Acoma was similarly inspired by ancient designs. The revival of Pueblo and Hopi pottery contributed to the creation, in 1932, of the Native American Arts and Crafts Board, the first government attempt to encourage Native creators to practice their traditional art forms.

Nampeyo continued to produce work herself until she began to lose her eyesight in the 1920s. Her husband painted some of her designs until his death in 1932. Today, her great-granddaughters continue the tradition.

In the mid-1950s, Peter Voulkos brought ceramic tradition together with modern art expression, and thus extended the horizons for both art and craft. He and a group of his students led the California sculpture movement that broke through preconceptions about limits of clay as a medium for sculpture. With his rebellious spirit, Voulkos revitalized ceramic art and helped touch off new directions in other craft media. His monumental GALLAS ROCK brings the emotional energy of Abstract Expressionist painting (see chapter 25) to three-dimensional form. He said that the basis of this work is "the core cylinder inside, with other cylinders going in different directions to take the weight of the slabs . . . . Outside and inside grew together." While working on it, he had to "relate everything at the same time and still keep the spontaneity."[3]

Both Peter Voulkos and Toshiko Takaezu were influenced by the earthiness and spontaneity of some traditional Japanese ceramics, such as the TEA BOWL as well as by expressionist painting, yet they have taken very different directions. Voulkos's pieces are rough and aggressively dynamic, while Takaezu's CERAMIC FORMS offer subtle, restrained strength. By

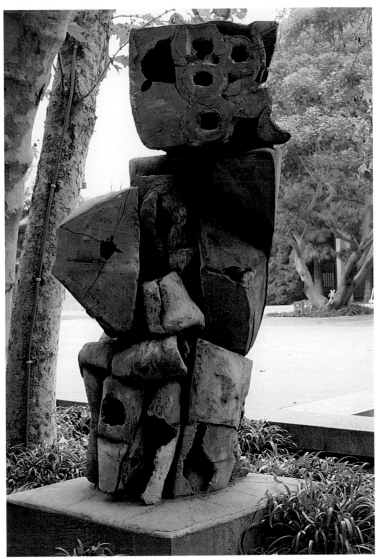

313 Peter Voulkos.
GALLAS ROCK. 1960.
Glazed ceramic. Height 6'.
University of California at Los Angeles.
Photograph: Duane Preble.

314 Toshiko Takaezu.
CERAMIC FORMS. 1986.
Stoneware.
Photograph: Macario, Kaneohe, Hawaii.
Courtesy of the artist.

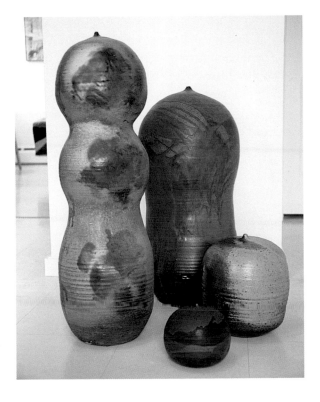

closing the top of container forms, Takaezu shifted attention to sculptural form, and thus provided surfaces for rich paintings of glaze and oxide. She reflects on her love of the clay medium:

When working with clay I take pleasure from the process as well as from the finished piece. Every once in a while I am in tune with the clay, and I hear music, and it's like poetry. Those are the moments that make pottery truly beautiful for me. [4]

Until the twentieth century, ceramic processes evolved very slowly. In recent years, new formulations and even synthetic clays have become available. Other changes have included more accurate methods of firing and improved techniques and equipment. The most significant change of all has come in the use of clay as a conceptual and sculptural art form.

GLASS

Glass has been used for at least four thousand years as a material for practical containers of all shapes and sizes. During the Middle Ages, stained glass was used extensively in Gothic churches and cathedrals (see page 5). Elaborate, blown-glass pieces have been made in Venice since the Renaissance. Glass is also a fine medium for decorative inlays in a variety of objects—including jewelry.

Glass is an exotic and enticing art medium. One art critc wrote, "Among sculptural materials, nothing equals the sheer eloquence of glass. It can assume any form, take many textures, dance with color, bask in clear crystallinity, make lyrics of light."[5]

Chemically, glass is closely related to ceramic glaze. As a medium, however, it offers a wide range of unique possibilities. Hot or molten glass is a sensitive, amorphous material that is shaped by blowing, casting, or pressing into molds. As it cools, glass solidifies from its molten state without crystallizing. After it is blown or cast, glass may be cut, etched, fused, laminated, layered, leaded, painted, polished, sandblasted, or slumped (softened for a controlled sag). The fluid nature of glass produces qualities of mass flowing into line as well as translucent volumes of airy thinness.

Although it is said that the character of any material determines the character of the expression, this statement is particularly true of glass. Molten glass requires considerable speed and skill in handling. The glassblower combines the centering skills of a potter, the agility and stamina of an athlete, and the grace of a dancer to bring qualities of breath and movement into crystalline form.

The person most responsible for making glass into an art form was Harvey Littleton. Formerly a ceramic artist, he started a glassblowing studio on the grounds of the Toledo Museum of Art in Ohio in 1962 and began experimenting with artistic glassmaking. With help from industrial technicians, he soon settled at the University of Wisconsin where he began the first instructional studio. A generation of glass workers studied with him, and they fanned out to start over 50 other university glass studios within ten years.

Kreg Kallenberger used carving and polishing to create FULL MOON IN CURTAIN CANYON from a solid piece of lead crystal. The carving marks on the sides duplicate the look of rocky canyon slopes, as the clear glass suggests crisp mountain air on a bright moonlit night.

The fluid and translucent qualities of glass are used to the fullest in Dale Chihuly's SEAFORM SERIES. Chihuly, a Littleton student, produces such pieces with a team of glass artists working under his direction. In this series, he arranges groups of pieces and carefully directs the lighting to create suggestions of delicate undersea environments.

METAL

Metal's primary characteristics are strength and formability. The various types of metal most often used for crafts and sculpture can be hammered, cut, drawn out, welded, joined with rivets, or cast. Early metalsmiths created tools, vessels, armor, and weapons.

A high point of metalwork production was reached in the Islamic cultures of the Middle East

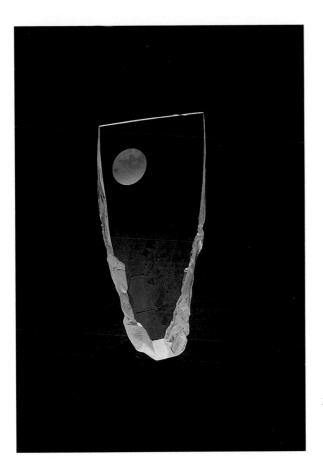

315 Kreg Kallenberger.
FULL MOON IN CURTIN CANYON. 1997.
Cut and polished lead crystal.
17 ½" × 9 ½" × 4".
Courtesy of Leo Kaplan Modern, New York.
Photo: Don Wheeler, Inc.

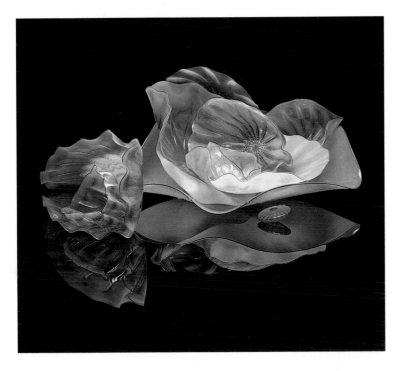

316 Dale Chihuly.
MAUVE SEAFORM SET WITH BLACK LIP WRAPS
from the "SEAFORMS" SERIES. 1985.
Blown glass.
Courtesy of Dale Chihuly.
Photograph: Dick Busher.

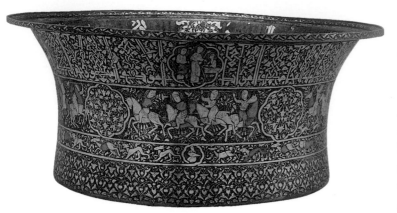

317 D'ARENBERG BASIN. Syria. 13th century.
Brass with silver inlay. 9" × 20".
Freer Gallery of Art, Smithsonian Institution, Washington, D. C. F1955.10.

318 Mark Pierce. EARRINGS. 1982.
Polished brass and luminar. 2¼" × 1⅜" × ½".
Courtesy of the artist.

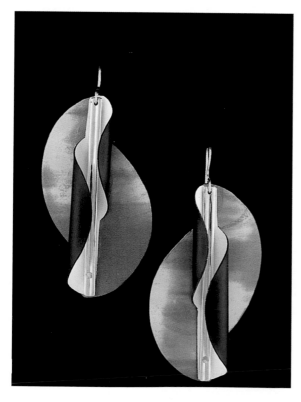

in the thirteenth and fourteenth centuries, where techniques of shaping and inlaying were practiced with unparalleled sophistication. The D'ARENBERG BASIN, named after a French collector who owned it for many years, was made for the last ruler of the Ayyubid Dynasty in Syria in the mid-thirteenth century. The body of the basin was first cast in brass; its extremely intricate design included lowered areas into which precisely cut pieces of silver were placed. Although most of the silver pieces are only a fraction of an inch in size, they enliven a carefully patterned design that occupies several finely proportioned horizontal layers. The lowest layer is a decorative pattern based on repeated plant shapes. Above is a row of animals that decorates a relatively narrow band. Some of these animals actually existed; some are imaginary. The next layer depicts a scene of princely pleasure, as well-attired people play a game similar to polo. The top layer contains more plant shapes between the uprights of highly stylized Arabic script that expresses good wishes to the owner of the piece. A central panel in this upper row depicts a scene from the life of Christ, who is regarded as an important figure in the Muslim religion.

Perhaps the largest number of craft artists using metal today are those who make jewelry. Contemporary jewelry often includes unusual materials, as well as the more traditional metals and precious stones. The best examples can be appreciated as miniature sculpture that involves the crafts of metalworking, enameling, and precise stone-cutting (lapidary).

Mark Pierce is one of the many craft artists who have recently explored new materials and techniques. Pierce invents jewelry forms by merging his experience as a painter with his work as a jewelry designer. Through research, Pierce developed the polymer-aluminum process he uses for creating EARRINGS and other jewelry.

Albert Paley's large, heavy, hand-wrought and forged GATE appears delicate when seen in a small reproduction. Paley began his metalworking career making jewelry and gradually shifted to creating larger pieces such as the GATE, commissioned for the entrance of the Renwick Gallery museum

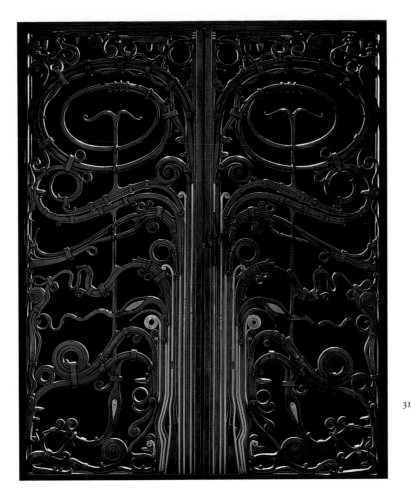

319 Albert Raymond Paley (b. 1944).
PORTAL GATES. 1974.
Forged steel, brass, copper, and bronze.
90¾" × 72" × 4".
National Museum of American Art, Smithsonian,
Washington, D. C./Art Resource, NY. Commissioned for
the Renwick Gallery (1975.117.1).

shop. Few artists today possess the technical skill required to forge red-hot iron. Paley enjoys handling a material that physically resists him. Whether he is working on small pieces or large ones, Paley employs a variety of metals, woven together in harmonious interplay. A lively relationship between lines and spaces creates the high energy of his ornamental gates. The curves—revealing Art Nouveau influence (see page 94)—have the sensual fluidity of hot pliable metal, while the center verticals recall the rigid strength of iron and steel. Bundles of straight lines unify and solidify the composition. The twelve-hundred-pound Renwick GATE took Paley and his assistant seven months to complete.

WOOD

The living spirit of wood is given a second life in handmade objects. Growth characteristics of individual trees remain visible in the grain of wood long after trees are cut, giving wood a vitality not found in other materials. Its abundance, versatility, and warm tactile qualities have made wood a favored material for human use and for art pieces.

Virginia Dotson makes elegant works that straddle the boundary between useful things and objects

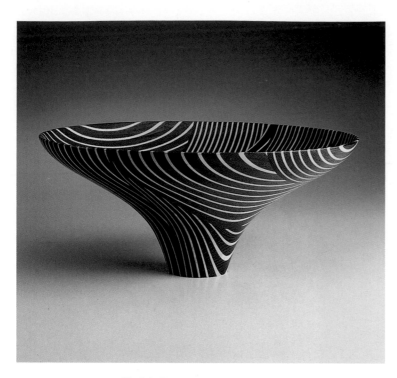

320 Virginia Dotson.
CROSS WINDS. 1989.
Wenge and maple, laminated and turned. 5¾" × 13⅛" × 13⅛".
Ronald C. Wornick Collection.

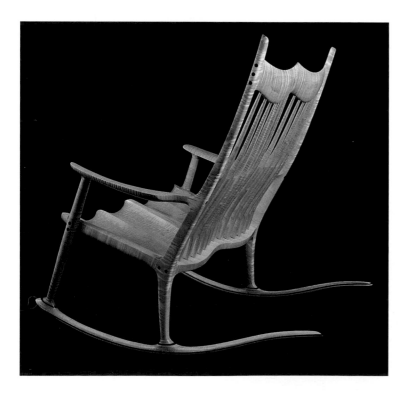

321 Sam Maloof.
DOUBLE ROCKING CHAIR. 1992.
Fiddleback maple and ebony.
42⅝" × 42" × 44½".
Courtesy of the artist.

just for contemplation. Her bowl CROSS WINDS includes two kinds of wood, inlaid, laminated, and turned on a lathe. While devoted to wood as a medium, she favors interaction with other types of artists. She said, "I love to look at work in other media and talk about common concerns with weavers, quilters, metal, and glass artists. This type of interaction has provided many insights for the personal involvement I have with my work."[6]

Most furniture purchased today is produced by industrial mass-production methods. However, those with the skill to make their own—or enough money to buy custom pieces—can enjoy living with handcrafted furniture.

Sam Maloof makes unique pieces of furniture and also repeats some designs he finds particularly satisfying. His DOUBLE ROCKING CHAIR and other designs show his thorough understanding of wood and of the hand processes he uses to shape wood into furniture. Flowing curves result from his sensitive melding of form and function. Although he employs assistants who help him duplicate his best designs, he limits quantity. Because he enjoys knowing that each piece is cut, assembled, and finished according to his own high standards, Maloof has rejected offers from manufacturers who want to mass-produce his designs. He prefers to retain quality control and the special characteristics that are inevitably lost when even the best designs are factory-produced rather than handmade. Many pieces of furniture are pleasing to look at, and many are comfortable to use, but relatively few fulfill both functions so successfully.

FIBER

Fiber art includes such processes as weaving (both loom and nonloom techniques), stitching, basketmaking, surface design (dyed and printed textiles), wearable art, and handmade paper-making. These fiber processes use natural and synthetic fibers in both traditional and innovative ways. Artists working with fiber (as with artists working in any medium) draw on the heritage of traditional practices and also explore new avenues of expression.

All weaving is based on the interlacing of lengthwise fibers, *warp*, and cross fibers, *weft* (also called *woof*). Weavers create patterns by changing the numbers and placements of interwoven threads, and they can choose from a variety of looms and techniques. Simple hand looms can produce very sophisticated, complex weaves. A large tapestry loom, capable of weaving hundreds of colors into intricate forms, may require several days of preparation before work begins.

Some of the world's most spectacular carpets came from Islamic Persia during the period of the Safavid Dynasty in the sixteenth century. Here, weavers employed by royal workshops knotted carefully dyed wool over a network of silk warps and wefts. THE ARDABIL CARPET, long recognized as one of the greatest Persian carpets, contains about three hundred such knots, over fine silk threads, per inch. Thus this carpet required approximately 25 million knots!

The design of the carpet is centered on a sunburst surrounded by sixteen oval shapes. Two mosque lamps of unequal size share space with an intricate pattern of flowers. At the corners of the main field, quarters of the central design are repeated. The work has a signature and date embedded in it, but the artist named must have been the designer, since no one person could tie so many knots in a lifetime. Another inscription expresses a prayer for safety, referring to the mosque as the house of God: "I have no refuge in this world other than thy threshold." This combination of luxurious workmanship and religious piety is common in Islamic arts.

Prolific, highly influential contemporary artist Diane Itter created a major body of work consisting of off-loom, small-scale knotted structures

322 THE ARDABIL CARPET. Tabriz. 1540.
Wool pile on silk warps and wefts. 34' × 17'6".
V & A Picture Library.

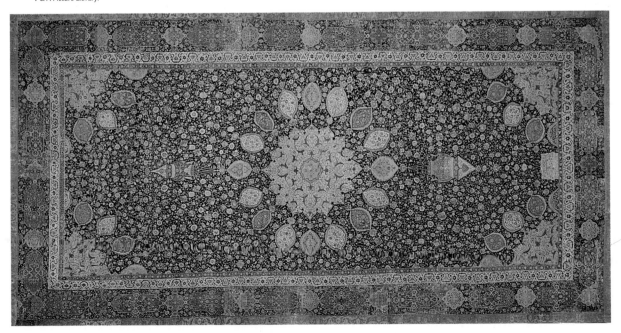

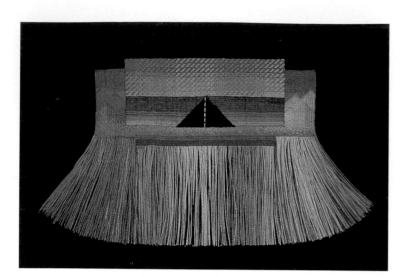

323 Diane Itter.
PATTERN SCAPE. 1985.
Linen, knotted. 10"× 11".
Photo courtesy of the American Craft Museum, New York, from the exhibition
"Craft, Today: Poetry of the Physical," 1986.

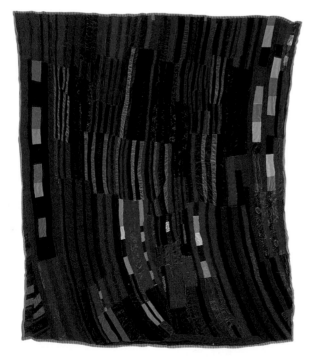

324 Pieced by Rosie Lee Tompkins; restructured and quilted
by Willia Ette Graham.
STRING. 1985.
Mixed fabrics. 100"× 85½".
Photograph courtesy of the
San Francisco Craft and Folk Art Museum.

made of linen threads. PATTERN SCAPE is one of Itter's many pieces made with a technique she developed. Working from the center out, through patterned repetition, she constructed complex color-rich forms thread by thread. Of her work she said:

I have come to realize what it is about the textile arts that fascinates me. Among other things . . . it is the capacity to be both painter and sculptor at the same time. That is, the visual image is created by the integration of color and structure—one cannot exist without the other. In addition, the textile arts allow me a way of working which is both personal and intimate yet potentially monumental in concept and universal in nature. By limiting both my technique (knotting) and my materials (linen) I am able to concentrate all my energies on full exploration of the visual image. After many years of working, I am still fascinated by the infinite variety of images I can create within the set limits. [7]

Many modern African-American quilt designs are inspired by traditional African textiles, while others are related to European-American quilt traditions.

STRING, a collaborative work, was pieced by Rosie Lee Tomkins and restructured and quilted by Willia Ette Graham. Its contrasting strips of light/dark, hot/cool colors flow in an inventive rhythmic pattern. The pieces are velvet, which gives the quilt an exceptionally rich surface that cannot be seen as well in a photograph as in the quilt itself. This quilt exhibits a strong African-American aesthetic of improvisation that contrasts with the regularity and frequent symmetry of European-American quilt styles. In its spontaneous energy and impact, STRING is related to the vital spirit of jazz.

Polly Apfelbaum dyes fabrics to create installations that show the influence of both modern abstract art and feminism. She said that she wanted to do a contemporary version of the traditional crazy quilt, in which random fragments of leftover cloth are stitched together in dazzling patterns. In this way she claims descent from the women who have traditionally woven and sewn most textiles. In

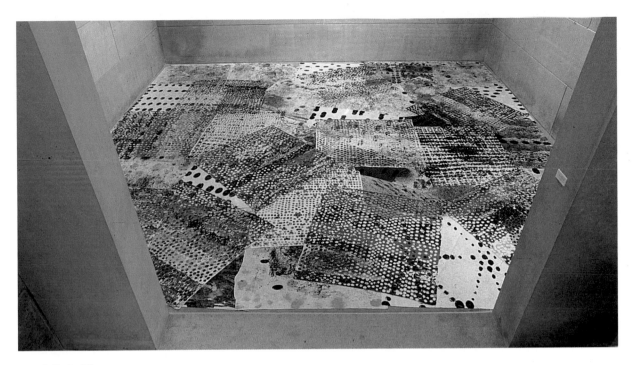

325 Polly Apfelbaum.
L'AVVENTURA. 1994.
Velvet and dye. Approx. 20' × 20'.
Courtesy D'Amelio/Terras.

326 Olga de Amaral.
GOLD MOUNTAIN. 1992.
Fiber, parchment, and gold leaf. 61" × 61".
Private Collection. Courtesy of Bellas Artes, Santa Fe, New Mexico.

L'AVVENTURA, she used bright colors to stain pieces of velvet. She cut regular holes in some of her dyed pieces to heighten the resemblance to quilts, and then installed them on the floor of a gallery, where they took up an entire room. The floor space was transformed into a jagged and overlapping composition that resembles that of Cubist paintings and collages.

Colombian artist Olga de Amaral draws on traditional sources closer to her own ethnic roots: goldsmithing and textiles of the native peoples of Andean South America. To make GOLD MOUNTAIN, she began with a loose network of fibers. Into this array she wove pieces of parchment covered with gold leaf. Because of their size (five to six feet on a side), she calls her works from this period "woven walls." The visual effect of GOLD MOUNTAIN is like a plush tapestry of shimmering texture.

Faith Ringgold's paintings, quilts, and soft sculptures speak eloquently of her life and ideas. Happy memories of her childhood in Harlem in the 1930s provide much of her subject matter.

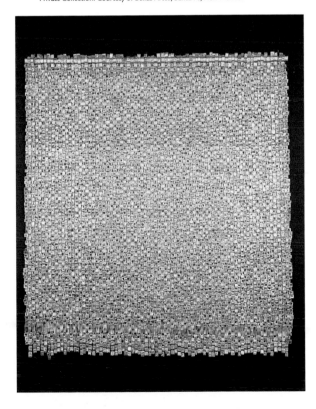

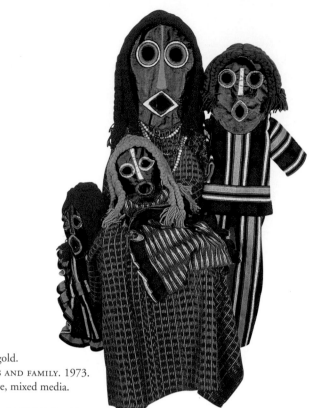

MRS. JONES AND FAMILY represents Ringgold's own family. Commitments to women, the family, and cross-cultural consciousness are at the heart of Ringgold's work. With playful exuberance and insight, she draws on history, recent events, and her own experiences for her depictions and narratives of class, power, race, and gender. Her highly sophisticated use of naiveté gives her work the appeal of the best folk art.

Innovations in off-loom fiber work have taken the fiber arts into the realm of sculpture in a variety of ways. Magdalena Abakanowicz has been at the leading edge of nontraditional uses of fiber since the 1960s. Her powerful series called BACKS has an unforgettable quality—at once personal and universal. The earthy color and textures of the formed burlap suggest the capacity to endure dire hardships and to survive with strength. Her forms have what she feels all art must have: mysterious, bewitching power. The artist speaks of her motives:

I want the viewer to penetrate the inside of my forms. For I want him to have the most intimate contact with them, the same contact one can have with clothes, animal skins, or grass.[8]

327 Faith Ringgold.
MRS. JONES AND FAMILY. 1973.
Soft sculture, mixed media.
74" × 69".
Artist's collection. © 1973 Faith Ringgold.

328 Magdalena Abakanowicz.
BACKS (IN LANDSCAPE). 1976–1982.
80 pieces, burlap and glue.
Photograph: © 1982 Dirk Bakker. Magdalena Abakonowicz.
Licensed by VAGA, NY. Marlborough Gallery, NY.

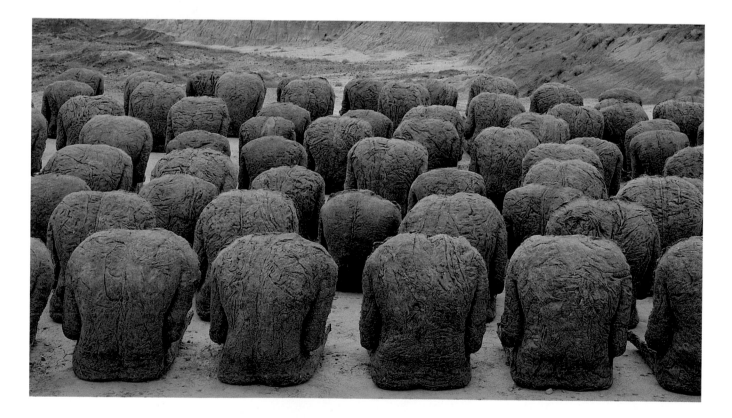

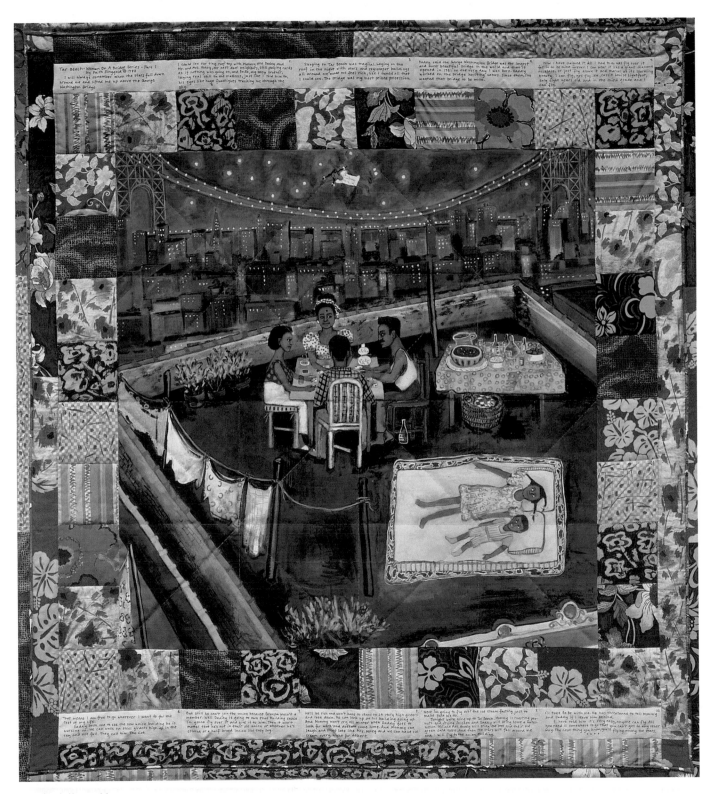

329 Faith Ringgold.
TAR BEACH. 1988.
Acrylic pieced and printed fabric. 74" × 69".
In the Collection of Solomon R. Guggenheim Museum, New York.
©Faith Ringgold Inc.

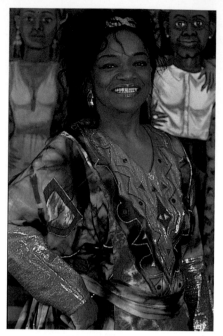

330   FAITH RINGGOLD.
With detail of
The Purple Quilt. 1986.
© Faith Ringgold, Inc.
Photographer: C'Love.

A prolific creator of many art forms, from paintings to quilts to children's books, Faith Ringgold has taken the reality of racial discrimination and made from it uplifting stories about finding sustenance and overcoming adversity.

Born in Harlem to working-class parents, she was encouraged as a child to succeed by their example. Acknowledging the double disadvantage of being an African-American woman, her parents taught her that "you have to be twice as good to go half as far."[9] Her mother was a seamstress and fashion designer, her father a sanitation truck driver. After receiving bachelor's and master's degrees in art from City College of New York, she taught in New

York City public schools from 1955 to 1972. She later recalled that the experience of teaching children encouraged her own creativity: "They showed me what it is to be free, to be able to express yourself directly."[10]

During the early years of her teaching career, she painted landscapes. But the civil rights movement of the 1960s encouraged her to address directly in her art the issues of inequality that seemed then to be present everywhere. She sought advice from the elder African-American artist Romare Bearden (see page 11), who included her work in a group show in Harlem in 1966. She also took part in several protest actions at New York museums, urging greater inclusion of African-

American artists and more outreach to ethnic minority neighborhoods.

Leaving her teaching position in 1972, she began to devote full time to art. She also began a ten-year collaboration with her mother in the creation of works on cloth. Quilt making had been a family tradition as far back as her great-great-grandmother, who had made them as a slave in Florida. Now the mother-daughter team collaborated on a new type of textile art that included images and stories on the sewn fragments. In addition to continuing ancient African textile art traditions, these cloth works were also portable.

Her themes are highly varied. Some are personal and autobiographical, such as *Change: Faith Ringgold's Over 100 Pound Weight Loss Performance Story Quilt.* Others expose injustice, such as *The Slave Rape Series,* which dealt with the mistreatment of African women in the slave trade. Some are about important African-American cultural figures, such as *Sonny's Quilt,* which depicts the jazz saxophonist Sonny Rollins, performing as he soars over the Brooklyn Bridge.

Typical of the artist's "Story Quilts" is TAR BEACH (on the preceding page), which tells the story of the fictional Cassie, an eight-year-old character who is based on Ringgold's own childhood memories. She would go up to the as-

phalt roof of her apartment building ("Tar Beach") with her family on hot nights, since there was no air conditioning in the home. Cassie describes Tar Beach as a magical place, with a 360-degree view of tall buildings and the George Washington Bridge in the distance. She dreams that she can fly, that she can do anything she imagines, as she lies on a blanket with her little brother. She dreams that she can give her father the union card that he has been denied because of his race. She dreams that she can let her mother sleep late, and eat ice cream every day for dessert. She even dreams that she can buy the building her father works in, and that her mother won't cry when her father can't find work. The quilt depicts the two children on the blanket, and her parents playing cards with the neighbors next to a table set with snacks and drinks. TAR BEACH was later made into a children's book, one of four that Ringgold has written.

The combination of fantasy and hard reality in this work, with imagination the key to overcoming obstacles, is typical of Ringgold's work as well as her life. Near the end of her memoir, she said, "I don't want the story of my life to be about racism, though that has played a major role. I want my story to be about attainment, love of family, art, helping others, courage, values, dreams coming true."[11]

CHAPTER FOURTEEN

ARCHITECTURE AND ENVIRONMENTAL DESIGN

Architecture and environmental design are arts with great potential for enhancing our lives. Every day we live, work, and move about in indoor and outdoor spaces that have been designed by individuals or teams. No matter how simple or complex, how rich or how poor our life situations, we can find comfort in making our surroundings beautiful. Margaret Courtney-Clarke's photograph of a woman painting an image of a chicken on the mud wall of her house embodies this idea. The title, BEAUTIFYING THE SPACE IN WHICH WE LIVE MAKES LIFE MORE BEARABLE, says it all.

In our modern and more specialized society, creative architects and environmental designers make their designs after hearing the needs and concerns of clients and those who will live with their designs. The work of professionals is in turn maintained, enhanced, or degraded by those who use the spaces.

ARCHITECTURE

Architecture is frequently overlooked and misunderstood as an art form—first, because of its constant presence; and second, because it is generally considered a necessity rather than an expressive statement. It is both. As the art form that often surrounds us in our daily lives, architecture has long made human survival both possible and enjoyable.

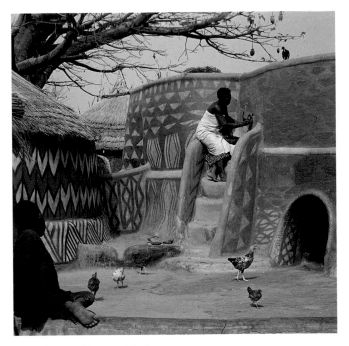

331 Margaret Courtney-Clarke.
BEAUTIFYING THE SPACE IN WHICH WE LIVE MAKES LIFE MORE BEARABLE.
From *African Canvas,* Namibia, Africa. 1990.
Photograph.
© Margaret Courtney-Clarke.

Architecture is the art and science of designing and constructing buildings for practical, aesthetic, and symbolic purposes. Since it grows out of basic human needs and aspirations, architecture offers one of the clearest records of a society's values. For at least five thousand years, people around the world have developed impressive techniques for building structures that go far beyond providing mere shelter.

Throughout most of recorded history, people built their own homes. The essential skills were passed on from generation to generation, from master to apprentice. Among the world's oldest surviving structures is the DOLMEN located in northwestern France. Its builders simply massed huge boulders to create a workable sheltered space.

Yet even before industrialization and the rapid growth of cities, much of the knowledge of the building crafts was lost to all but a few. In order to provide livable housing for the world's growing population, educated people need knowledge of architectural possibilities. One way to begin to find out what it takes to design buildings is to get directly involved with creating and building one. When architect Frank Lloyd Wright started an architecture school in Arizona, for example, he demanded that his students make their own dwellings from simple materials. No matter what sort of structure they are

332 DOLMEN.
Crocuno, north of Carnac, France.
Photographer: James Lynch. Ancient Art and Architecture Collection, Ltd.

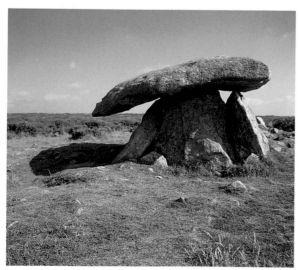

building, architects address and integrate three key issues: function (how a building is used); form (how it looks); and structure (how it stands up).

We come to understand a building through a succession of experiences in time and space. We cannot see or experience a building all at once as we do a painting; to enjoy the pleasures architecture offers, often we must explore buildings inside and out.

Walk around your house or apartment. How do you respond to the entrance? The height of the ceilings? Wall and floor colors, textures, materials? Window sizes and placements? The stairs, if any? Have you ever noticed how your response changes as you move from a dark, low-ceilinged entranceway to a bright, high-ceilinged room?

An Art and a Science

As an art, architecture is concerned with the design of the space-defining expressive form throughout a total structure.

As a science, architecture is a physics problem: How does a structure hold up its own weight and the loads placed on it? Architecture must be designed to withstand the forces of compression, or pushing ($\rightarrow\leftarrow$); tension, or pulling ($\leftarrow\rightarrow$); bending, or curving ($\mathcal{S}\ \mathcal{S}$); and any combination of these physical forces.

Contemporary architecture has three essential components, which might be compared to elements of the human body. These are a supporting skeleton or frame; an outer skin; and operating equipment, similar to the body's vital organs and systems. The equipment includes plumbing; electrical wiring; appliances; and systems for cooling, heating, and circulating air as needed. In earlier centuries, structures of wood, earth, brick, or stone had no such equipment, and the skeleton and skin were often one.

Styles, Materials, and Methods

The evolution of architectural techniques and styles has been determined by the materials available and by the changing needs and values of society. In ancient times, when nomadic hunter-gatherers became farmers and village dwellers, housing evolved from caves, huts, and tents to substantial structures. During the Middle Ages, the tallest buildings were stone churches; during our own age of commerce, the tallest buildings are office towers.

Because early building designers (as well as those in nonindustrialized countries today) could design structures only out of materials at hand, regional styles developed that blended well with their sites and climates. Modern transportation and the spread of advanced technologies have now made it possible to build almost anything anywhere. The consequence is a loss of a sense of place. Urban architecture in many parts of the world now looks very much alike.

Wood, Stone, and Brick Since the beginning of history, most structures have been made of wood, stone, earth, or brick. Each of these natural materials has its own strengths and weaknesses. For example, wood, which is light, can be used for roof beams; whereas stone, which is heavy and generally good for vertical supports, can be used for load-bearing walls but is not effective as a beam. Much of the world's major architecture has been constructed of stone because of its permanence, availability, and beauty. In the past, entire cities were built very slowly by cutting and placing stone upon stone.

Dry Masonry Probably the simplest building technique is to pile stones atop one another. The process has been used to make such rudimentary structures as markers, piles, and cairns throughout the world. When such massing is done with a con-

sistent pattern, the result is called masonry. In dry masonry, where no mortar is used, the weight of the stones themselves holds the structure up. If the stones are cut or shaped before use, they are *dressed*.

The GREAT ZIMBABWE ("Great Stone House") in East Africa is an elliptical structure that gave its name to the country in which it is located. Built sometime in the twelfth century, it was abandoned about three hundred years later. GREAT ZIMBABWE is nearly round, with several conical structures inside whose original function is still unknown. Its walls, made of dressed local stone, are approximately thirty feet high. For added stability, the walls were built up to fifteen feet thick at the base, tapering slightly toward the top. Roofing was probably grass or thatch held together with sticks. The structure is by far the largest part of a group of ancient stone dwellings, forming a trading city that may have held as many as twenty thousand people at its height. Though the outer walls of GREAT ZIMBABWE have openings in selected locations for entry and exit, there are no windows; because these tend to weaken

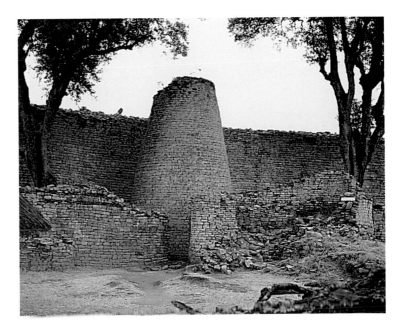

333   GREAT ZIMBABWE.
      Zimbabwe. Before 1450.
      Height of wall 30'.

   a. Plan.
   b. Interior.
   Casement Creative Services, Inc., ARPS/The Casement Collection.

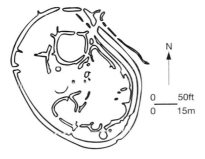

masonry walls, only structures that are considerably smaller can use them without external support.

GREAT ZIMBABWE is the largest ancient stone structure in Africa south of the great pyramids of Egypt, which are also built of dry masonry. Other notable examples of such buildings are Machu Picchu in Peru and the ancient pueblos of the American Southwest, such as Mesa Verde.

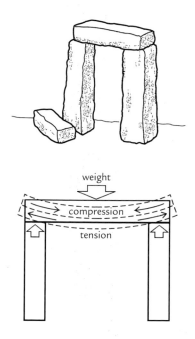

334 POST-AND-BEAM CONSTRUCTION.

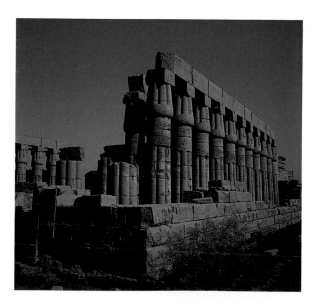

Post and Beam Prior to the twentieth century, two dominant structural types were in common use: post-and-beam (also called post-and-lintel) and arch systems, including vaulting. (The term *lintel,* preferred by art historians, is usually associated with stone; *beam,* preferred by today's architects and builders, is usually associated with wood, steel, and steel-reinforced concrete.) Most of the world's architecture, including modern steel structures, has been built with POST-AND-BEAM CONSTRUCTION. Vertical posts or columns support horizontal beams and carry the weight of the entire structure to the ground.

The form of post-and-beam buildings is determined by the strengths and weaknesses of the materials used. Stone beam lengths must be short and columns (posts) relatively thick to accommodate stone's brittleness. Wood beams may be longer, and posts thinner, because wood is lighter and more flexible. The strength-to-weight ratio of modern steel makes it possible to build with far longer beams and thus to create much larger interior spaces.

The monumental stone post-and-lintel structures of the Egyptian temples at Luxor appear to have been derived from earlier constructions in which supporting posts (columns) were made of bundles of reeds. A row of columns spanned or connected by beams is called a *colonnade,* as seen in the COLONNADE AND COURT OF AMENHOTEP III.

Following the lead of the Egyptians, the Greeks further refined stone post-and-beam construction. For more than two thousand years, the magnificence of the Parthenon and other classical Greek architecture has influenced the designers of a great many later buildings.

335 COLONNADE, COURT OF
AMENHOTEP III.
Temple of Amun-Mut-Khonsu.
View of the great court with
double row of papyrus-clustered
columns. 18th dynasty.
Luxor, Thebes, Egypt.
c. 1390 B.C.E.
© SEF/Art Resource, NY.

Round Arch, Vault, and Dome Both Egyptian and Greek builders had to place their columns relatively close together because stone is weak under the load-bearing stresses inherent in a beam. A structural invention had to be made before this physical limitation of short spans could be overcome and new architectural forms created. That invention was the semicircular or ROUND ARCH, which when extended in depth creates a tunnel-like structure called a BARREL VAULT. Roman builders perfected the round arch and developed the GROIN VAULT, formed by the intersection of two barrel vaults.

A *vault* is a curving ceiling or roof structure, traditionally made of bricks or blocks of stone tightly fitted to form a unified shell. In recent times, vaults have been constructed of materials such as cast reinforced concrete.

Early civilizations of western Asia and the Mediterranean area built arches and vaults of brick, chiefly for underground drains and tomb chambers. But it was the Romans who first used the arch extensively in above-ground structures. They learned the technique of stone arch and vault construction from the Etruscans, who occupied central Italy between 750 and 200 B.C.E.

A round stone arch can span a longer distance and support a heavier load than a stone beam because much lower levels of stress develop. The Roman arch is a semicircle made from wedge-shaped stones fitted together with joints at right angles to the curve. During construction, temporary wooden supports carry the weight of the stones. The final stone that is set in place at the top is called the *keystone*. When the keystone is placed, a continuous arch with loadbearing capacity is created. A series of such arches supported by columns forms an ARCADE.

As master builders, the Romans created cities, roads, and aqueducts throughout their vast empire in most of Europe, the Near East, and North Africa. The aqueduct called PONT DU GARD, near Nimes, France, is one of the finest remaining examples of the functional beauty of Roman engineering. The combined height of the three levels of arches is 161 feet. Dry masonry blocks, weighing

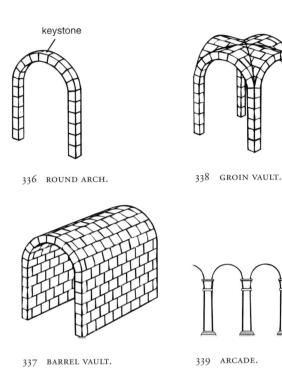

336 ROUND ARCH.

338 GROIN VAULT.

337 BARREL VAULT.

339 ARCADE.

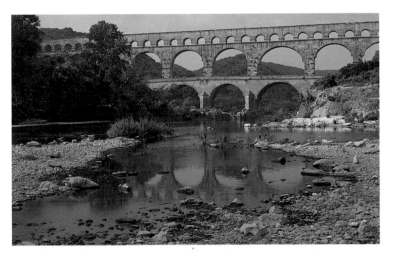

340 PONT DU GARD.
Nimes, France. 15 C.E.
Limestone. Height 161', length 902'.
Photograph: Duane Preble.

up to two tons each, make up the large arches of the two lower tiers. Water was once carried in a conduit at the top, with the first level serving as a bridge for traffic. That the aqueduct is still standing after two thousand years attests to the excellence of its design and construction.

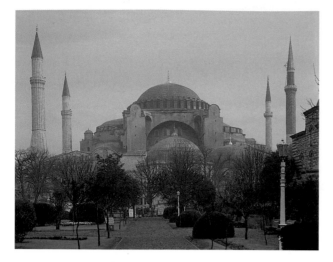

342 HAGIA SOPHIA. 532–535.
  a. Exterior.

Roman architects borrowed Greek column design and combined it with the arch, enabling them to greatly increase the variety and size of their architectural spaces. The Romans also introduced concrete as a material for architecture. Cheap, stonelike, versatile, and strong, concrete allowed the Romans to cut costs, speed construction, and build on a grand scale.

An arch rotated 180 degrees on its vertical axis creates a DOME. Domes may be hemispherical, semihemispherical, or pointed. In general usage the word *dome* refers to a hemispherical vault built up from a circular or polygonal base. The weight of a dome pushes downward and outward all around its circumference. Therefore, the simplest support is a cylinder with walls thick enough to resist the downward and outward thrust.

One of the most magnificent domes in the world was designed for the Byzantine cathedral of HAGIA SOPHIA (Holy Wisdom) in Istanbul, Turkey. It was built in the sixth century as the central sanctuary of the Eastern Orthodox Christian Church. After the Islamic conquest of 1453, *minarets* (towers) were added and it was used as a mosque. It is

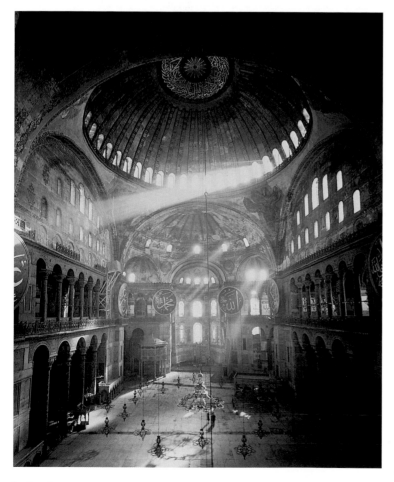

b. Interior.
  Photograph: Erich Lessing/Art Resource, NY.

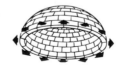

341 DOME.
  a. Dome
  (arch rotated 180°).

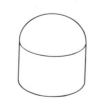

b. Dome on a cylinder.

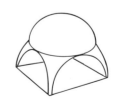

c. Dome on pendentives.

now a museum. In contrast to the PANTHEON'S dome on a cylinder, the dome of HAGIA SOPHIA rests on a square base.

HAGIA SOPHIA's distinctive dome appears to float on a halo of light—an effect produced by the row of windows encircling its base. The huge dome is supported on what appears to be a larger dome with its top and sides removed. Curving triangular sections called *pendentives* carry the enormous weight from the circular base of the upper dome downward to a square formed by supporting walls.

Pointed Arch and Vault After the rounded or semicircular arch and its offspring, the dome, the pointed *gothic arch* was the next great structural advance in the Western world. This new shape seems a small change, but its effect on the building of cathedrals was spectacular. Vaults based on the pointed arch made it possible to build wider naves. It was not merely the geometry of the pointed arch, but also the exterior buttresses and the trusses supporting the roof that allowed builders to go higher and to make thinner walls with larger window areas as we see in NOTRE DAME DE CHARTRES.

Although a pointed arch is steeper and therefore sends its weight more directly downward, a substantial sideways thrust must still be countered. Gothic builders accomplished this by constructing elaborate supports called *buttresses* at right angles to the outer walls. In the most developed Gothic cathedrals, the outward force of the arched vault is carried to large buttresses by stone half-arches called *flying buttresses.*

By placing part of the structural skeleton on the outside, Gothic builders were able to make their cathedrals higher and lighter in appearance. Since the added external support of the buttresses relieved the cathedral walls of much of their structural function, large parts of the wall could be replaced by enormous stained-glass windows, allowing more light (a symbol of God's grace and love) to enter the sanctuary. From the floor of the

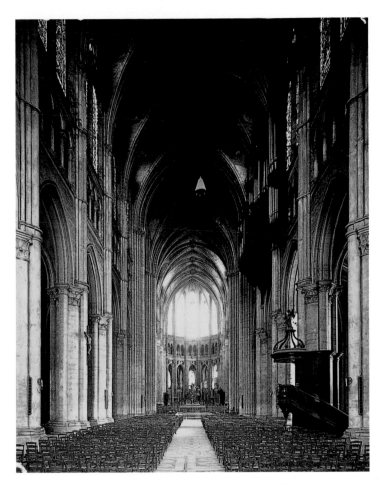

343 NOTRE DAME DE CHARTRES.
Chartres, France. 1145–1513.
Interior, nave. Height 122', width 53', length 130'.
Scala/Art Resource, New York.

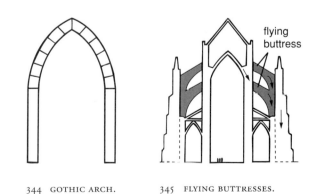

344 GOTHIC ARCH.   345 FLYING BUTTRESSES.

sanctuary to the highest part of the interior above the main altar, the windows increase in size. Stones carved and assembled to form thin ribs and pillars make up the elongated columns along the nave walls, which emphasize verticality and give the cathedral its active sense of upward thrust. (We discuss the stylistic features of Gothic architecture in more detail in chapter 16.)

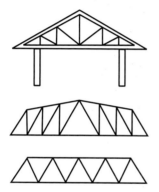

346 TRUSSES.

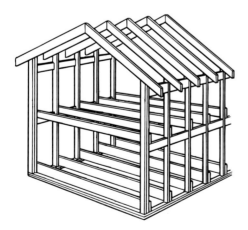

347 BALLOON FRAME.

After the Gothic pointed arch and vault, no basic structural technique was added to the Western architectural vocabulary until the nineteenth century. Instead, architects designed a variety of structures—at times highly innovative—in which combinations of borrowed elements played important new roles. Forms and ornamentation from the Greek and Roman periods were revived again and again and given new life in different contexts.

In the nineteenth century, eclectic and revival architecture consisted primarily of elements applied to exteriors, while interior spaces were designed in more contemporary ways, often taking advantage of new technical resources. By the mid-nineteenth century, the world was being transformed by science and industry. Major changes in materials and techniques have continued at an accelerating pace until the present. New inventions of the industrial age led to a revolution in architecture. First cast iron, then steel, then steel-reinforced concrete, electricity, and the invention of the high-speed elevator gave architects a set of materials and technologies that changed the design of buildings.

Truss and Balloon Frame Construction It is possible to build strong structures with relatively thin wooden boards. One method is to use TRUSSES, such as those used for structural support in Gothic cathedral roofs. A *truss* is a triangular framework used to span, reinforce, or support. Another method is balloon framing, in which heavy timbers are replaced with thin studs held together only with nails. In the nineteenth century, the availability of cheap wood in the United States led to the BALLOON FRAME innovation in wood construction for houses and other small structures. Old-timers, who were unwilling to use the new method, called it balloon framing because they thought it was as fragile as a balloon. The method—widely used since its 1833 introduction—helped to make possible the rapid settlement of America's Western frontier.

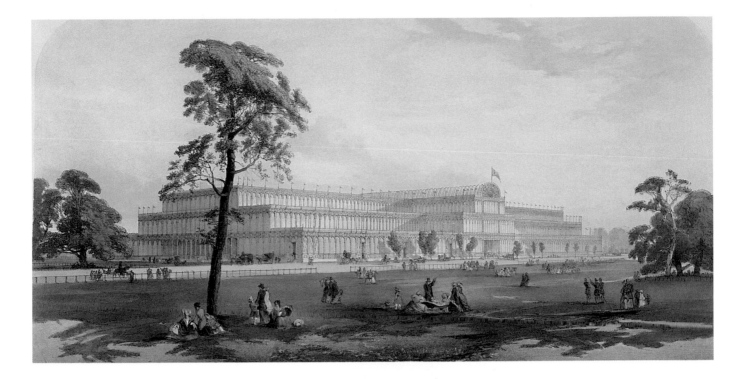

Cast Iron Cast iron became technically useful during the Industrial Revolution, and it led to new types of structures in which heavy, load-bearing walls were no longer needed. Iron has much greater strength than most stone and can span much larger distances. The engineering of structures with iron was a prelude to the development of steel toward the end of the nineteenth century and steel-reinforced concrete in the twentieth.

After the iron industry was established, cast and wrought iron became important building materials. Stronger and more fire-resistant than wood, iron led to lighter exterior walls and more flexible uses of interior space. Factories, bridges, and railway stations were among the new types of buildings for which cast iron was used.

The CRYSTAL PALACE, designed by Joseph Paxton, was a spectacular demonstration of what cast iron could do. It was built for the Great Exhibition of the Works of Industry of All Nations, the first international exposition, held in London in 1851. The building was designed to show off the latest mechanical inventions. It was built (from prepared materials) in six months and enclosed

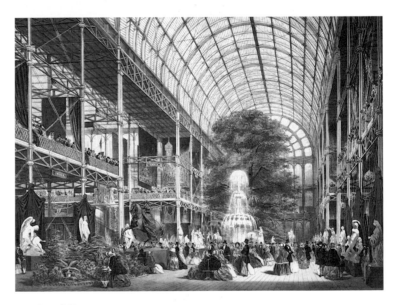

348   Joseph Paxton.
CRYSTAL PALACE. London. 1850–1851.
(damaged by fire in 1935).
Cast iron and glass.

a. Exterior.
Victoria and Albert Museum, London.
Crown Copyright.
Photograph: Stock Montage, Inc. © The Newberry Library.
b. Interior.
Etching by Lothar Buchar.
Victoria and Albert Museum, London.
Crown Copyright.

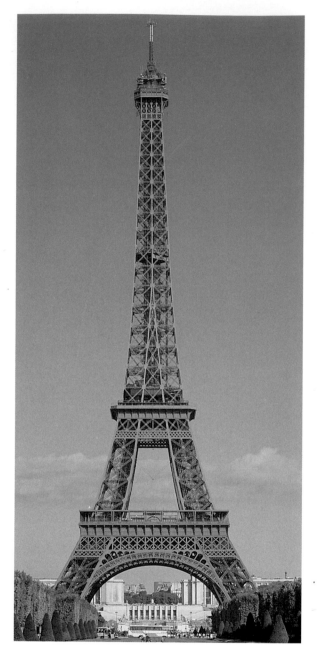

349 Gustave Eiffel.
EIFFEL TOWER. Paris. 1889.
Iron frame. Height: 984'.
Giraudon/Art Resource, New York.

twenty-one acres of park land! This was the first time new industrial methods and materials were eloquently presented in architecture. In its day, the CRYSTAL PALACE was recognized as a highly original expression of the spirit of the new age.

In this building there was no borrowing of earlier styles. Paxton used relatively lightweight, factory-made *modules* (standard-size structural units) of cast iron and glass. By freeing himself from past styles and masonry construction, Paxton created a whole new architectural vocabulary. The light, decorative quality of the glass and cast-iron units was created not by applied ornamentation, but by the structure itself. Paxton, inspired by leaf structures, said, "Nature gave me the idea." The modular units provided enough flexibility for the entire structure to be assembled on the site, right over existing trees, and later disassembled and moved across town.

Paxton's successful innovation was a new application of the concept "form follows function," expressed earlier by Renaissance architect Leon Battista Alberti and later made famous by American architect Louis Sullivan.

In Paris, the 984-foot EIFFEL TOWER, designed and built by civil and aeronautic engineer Gustave Eiffel in 1889, epitomizes the inventive spirit of the new cast-iron structures of the mid- to late-nineteenth century. At the time of its design and construction, the tower was highly controversial because of its disruption of the low skyline of Paris. (All cities were low-rise then.) When it was built, it was the world's tallest freestanding structure. Even now, as the city's most visible symbol, it dominates the Paris skyline.

Steel and Reinforced Concrete The next breakthrough in construction methods for large structures came between 1890 and 1910 with the development of high-strength structural steel, used by itself and as the reinforcing material in reinforced concrete. The extensive use of cast-iron skeletons in the mid-nineteenth century had prepared the way for multistory steel-frame construction in the 1890s.

New building techniques and materials, as well as new functional needs, demanded a fresh approach to structure and form. The movement began to take shape in commercial architecture, became symbolized by early skyscrapers, and found one of its first opportunities in Chicago, where the big fire of 1871 had cleared the way for a building boom.

Leading the Chicago school was Louis Sullivan, regarded as the first great modern architect. Sullivan, like Paxton, rejected eclectic practices and sought to meet the needs of his time by using building methods and materials made available by the new technology. Sullivan had a major influence on the early development of what became America's and the twentieth century's most original contribution to architecture: the "skyscraper."

The first skyscraper, Sullivan's WAINWRIGHT BUILDING in St. Louis, Missouri, was made possible by the invention of the elevator and by the development of steel used for the structural skeleton. The building breaks with nineteenth-century tradition in a bold way. Its exterior design reflects the internal steel frame and emphasizes the height of the structure by underplaying horizontal elements in the central window area. Sullivan demonstrated his sensitivity and adherence to the harmony of traditional architecture by dividing the building's facade into three distinct zones, reminiscent of the base, shaft, and capital of Greek columns. These areas also reveal the various functions of the building, with shops at the base, offices in the central section, and utility rooms at the top. The heavily ornamented band at the top (cornice) stops the vertical thrust of the piers located between the office windows.

The interdependence of form and function is found throughout nature. Sullivan's observation that "form ever follows function" eventually helped architects to break with their reliance on past styles and to rethink architecture from the inside out.[1]

In this spirit a new architecture arose in Europe between 1910 and 1930. It rejected decorative ornamentation and eclecticism, as well as traditional stone and wood construction, and it broke away from the earlier idea of a building as a mass.

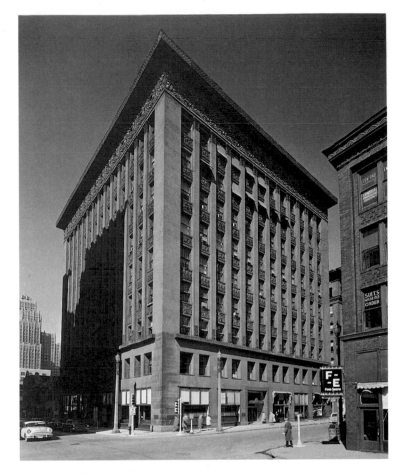

350 Louis Sullivan.
WAINWRIGHT BUILDING.
St. Louis, Missouri. 1890–1891.
Photograph: Hedrich Blessing, LTD.

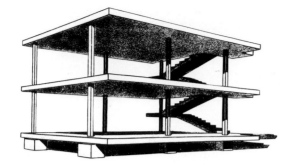

351 Le Corbusier.
DOMINO CONSTRUCTION SYSTEM. 1914–1915.

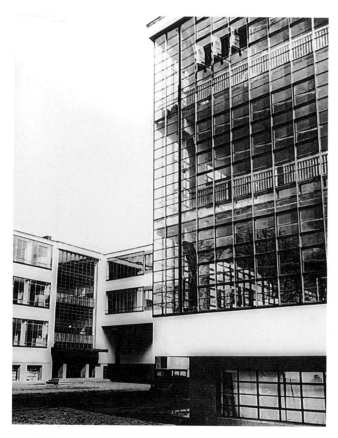

352 Walter Gropius.
BAUHAUS. Dessau, Germany. 1925–1926.
Bauhaus–Archiv Berlin. Photograph: Lucia Moholy
© VG Bild Kunst, Berlin, Germany 2001.

The resulting International Style (also called International Modern) expressed the function of each building, its underlying structure, and a logical (often asymmetrical) plan.

With a simple drawing of the DOMINO CONSTRUCTION SYSTEM, Le Corbusier—French architect, painter, and city planner—demonstrated the basic components of steel-column and reinforced-concrete-slab construction. This concept was used extensively later in the century as architects adopted the look, and sometimes the principles, of the International Style. Le Corbusier's idea of supporting floors and roof on interior load-bearing columns instead of load-bearing walls made it possible to vary the placement of interior walls and the nature of exterior coverings. His sense of style was inspired by the efficiency of machines and an awareness of the importance of natural light.

Walter Gropius carried out the principles of the International Style in his new building for the BAUHAUS when the school moved to Dessau, Germany. The workshop wing, built between 1925 and 1926, follows the basic concept illustrated in Le Corbusier's drawing. Because the reinforced-concrete floors and roof were supported by steel columns set back from the outer edge of the building, exterior walls did not have to carry any weight: they could be *curtain walls* made of glass. Even interior walls were non-load-bearing and could be placed anywhere they were needed for nonstructural purposes.

In the United States, the development of the high-rise building reached a climax in New York. On the city's small, heavily populated Manhattan Island, tall buildings provided a way to supply ever more residential and commercial space. By 1915, New York was suffering from poor air circulation and reduction of sunlight because so many skyscrapers were built straight up from the sidewalk. By the 1920s, a new *set-back* law required architects

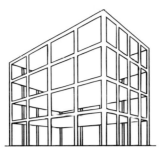

353 STEEL-FRAME CONSTRUCTION.

to terrace their structures back from the street to allow sunlight to enter what were becoming dark canyons.

Le Corbusier's idea for alleviating urban crowding by using tall, narrow buildings surrounded by open space, and Sullivan's concept for high-rise buildings that express the grid of their supporting STEEL-FRAME CONSTRUCTION came together in the SEAGRAM BUILDING, designed by Mies van der Rohe and Philip Johnson. Non-load-bearing glass walls had been a major feature of van der Rohe's plans for skyscrapers conceived as early as 1919, but it was not until the 1950s that he had the chance to build such structures. In the SEAGRAM BUILDING, interior floor space gained by the height of the building allowed the architects to leave a large, open public area at the base. The vertical lines emphasize the height and provide a strong pattern that is capped by a top section designed to give a sense of completion. The austere design embodies Mies van der Rohe's famous statement "Less is more."

Mies van der Rohe was a leading proponent of the International Style, which had an enormous, if sometimes negative, influence on world architecture. It has often replaced unique, place-defining regional styles. By mid-century, modern (now called modernist) architecture had become synonymous with the International Style. The uniformity of glass-covered rectilinear grid structures was considered the appropriate formal dressing for the bland anonymity of the modern corporation.

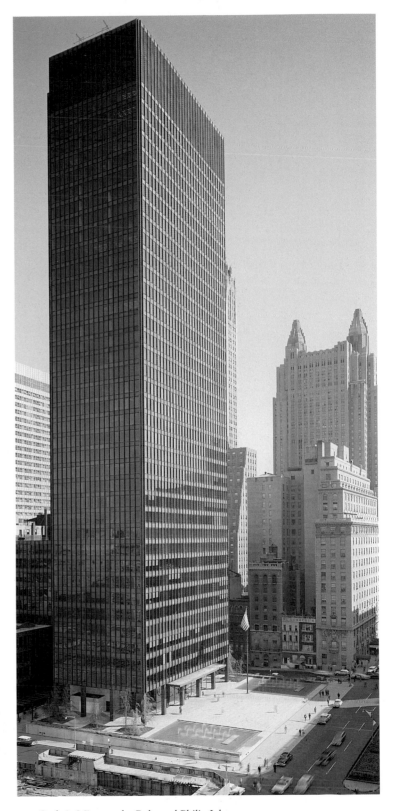

354 Ludwig Mies van der Rohe and Philip Johnson. SEAGRAM BUILDING. New York. 1956–1958. Photograph: Ezra Stoller © Esto.

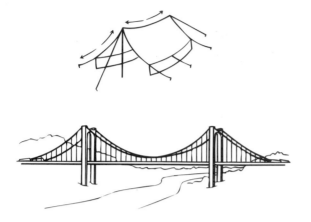

355 SUSPENSION STRUCTURES.

Other Innovations By the second half of the twentieth century, improved construction techniques and materials, new theories regarding structural physics, and computer analyses of the strengths and weaknesses in complex structures led to the further development of fresh architectural forms including hanging roofs and such innovations as the SHELL STRUCTURE, the FOLDED PLATE ROOF, and the PNEUMATIC or air-inflated structure.

Reinforced concrete and steel have provided the raw materials for a variety of new structural forms. The giant roofs of Kenzo Tange's indoor stadiums, built in Tokyo for the 1964 Olympics, are supported by a suspension structure of the type employed previously for bridge construction. Tange's tentlike OLYMPIC STADIUMS integrate spatial, structural, and functional requirements.

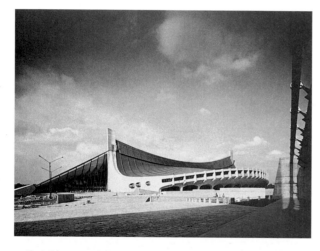

a. Exterior, natatorium.

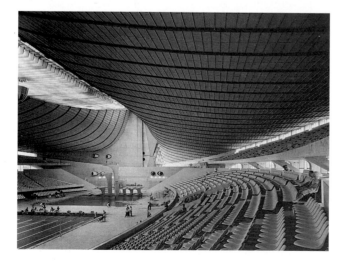

b. Interior, natatorium.
Photograph: Duane Preble.

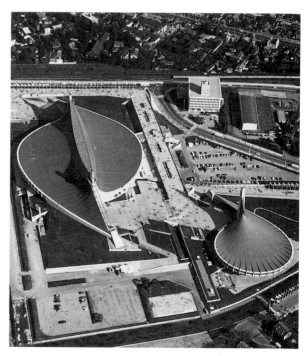

c. Aerial view.

356 Kenzo Tange.
OLYMPIC STADIUMS (YOYOGI SPORTS CENTER).
Tokyo, Japan. 1964.
Photographs a, c: Osamur Murai, Tokyo.

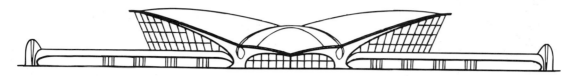

In the main building, which houses the swimming pools, Tange and structural engineer Yoshikatsu Tsuboi designed an interior space with seating for fifteen thousand. The vast open area under the roof was made possible by suspending the roof from steel cables strung from huge concrete abutments at either end of the building (rather than supporting the roof with interior columns). In spite of the structure's large size, the entire building complements rather than dwarfs human scale. Diving platforms, seats, and air-conditioning vent pipes on the end wall are part of the unified sculptural design.

An aerial view shows how the sweeping curves of the buildings unite the two structures and energize the spaces between and around them. The proportions of the many curves, both inside and out, give the complex a sense of graceful motion and balance.

The most recent use of the suspension technology was in the JEPPESEN TERMINAL BUILDING at Denver International Airport. Its roof is a giant tent composed of fifteen acres of woven fiberglass, making it the largest suspension building on earth. This white roofing material lets in large amounts of natural light without conducting heat, and it is coated with Teflon for water resistance and easy cleaning. Its exterior design was inspired by the snow-capped Rocky Mountains, which are visible from inside.

357 Eero Soarinen.
SHELL STRUCTURE (TWA TERMINAL).
Kennedy Airport, N.Y. 1956–1962.

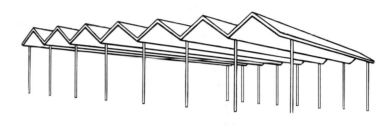

358 FOLDED PLATE ROOF.

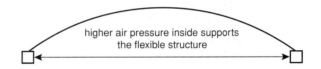

higher air pressure inside supports the flexible structure

359 PNEUMATIC STRUCTURE.

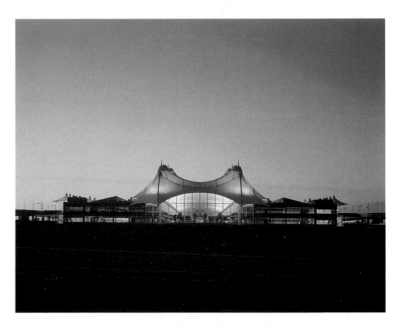

360 JEPPESEN TERMINAL BUILDING.
Denver International Airport.
1994. Fentress-Bradburn Architects.
Timothy Hursley Photography/Fentress Bradburn Architects Ltd.

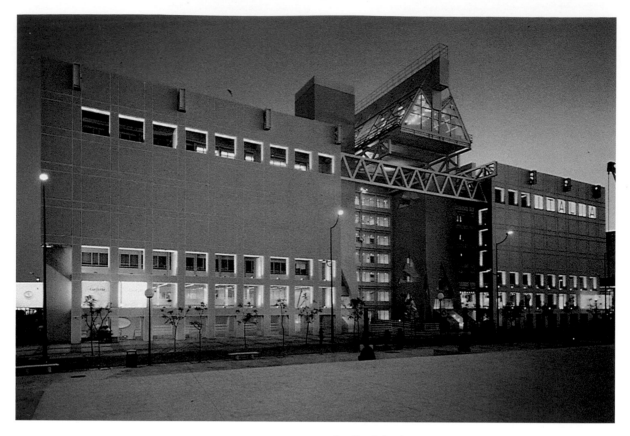

Many architects use world's fairs and expositions as opportunities to design innovative, experimental structures. The exterior of Gae Aulenti's ITALIAN PAVILION for Expo '92 in Seville is a shell with exhibition spaces recessed behind it. Ample windows on the lower stories make the building seem light and airy, its walls paper-thin. Triangular motifs mark the entrance. Once inside, visitors pass through an atrium that runs the length of the building. Waterfalls at each end fill shallow pools that reflect light from inside and out. Elegant proportions and tasteful use of asymmetrical details make this building a standout.

Aulenti is perhaps best known for her conversion of the 1906 Orsay Railroad Station into the MUSÉE D'ORSAY, the French national museum of nineteenth-century art. Working with a team of interior designers, she transformed the huge space into interconnected galleries that viewers can navigate easily, with sculpture displayed on levels exposed beneath the building's huge skylight.

361 Gae Aulenti.
ITALIAN PAVILION. Expo '92, Seville, Spain.
Index Ricerca Iconografica. I Guzzini, Centro Studie Ricerca.

362 Gae Aulenti.
MUSÉE D'ORSAY. Paris, France. 1986.
Index Ricerca Iconographica, Baldi.

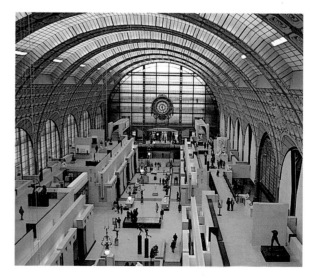

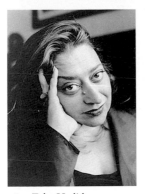

363   Zaha Hadid.
Photograph: Michael Wilson,
1998. Courtsey The Contempory
Arts Center, Cincinnati, Ohio.

One of the most creative and controversial architects now at work is Zaha Hadid. Indeed, many of her buildings have remained in the planning stages because they are too radical to be built. But her realized projects are adventurous designs that radically alter the viewer's experience of space.

Born in Baghdad, Iraq, as a young girl she worked weaving carpets. She has said that their intricate and dazzling designs later influenced her design ideas. She studied architecture at London's Architectural Association, where she was constantly challenged to reinvent modern architecture. This private academy was an incubator of new ideas where the teachers often threw practicality to the winds. Hadid's graduation project was to redesign a busy bridge over the Thames River so that people could live on it. The fact that few would want to live on a heavily trafficked bridge bothered neither her nor her teachers, who pronounced it excellent.

We see a basic example of Hadid's unique approach to design in the 1985 project MELBURY COURT APARTMENT, where the clients asked her to remodel the interior of their skylit 1940s flat. She began by removing most of the interior walls and replacing them with sweeping curves of glass. This gives the apartment curved hallways with mostly transparent walls which separate but also visually include other spaces. The idea, she said, was "to explode the rigid box of rooms . . . to create a generously fluid space around the central light well."[2] The furniture was installed on tracks and pivots to give added flexibility.

Most people's experience of built space comes from rectangular, orderly, self-contained, often symmetrical rooms. Her plan gives such a break from these kinds of spaces that she was soon termed a Deconstructive architect. That is, she makes buildings in such a way that they look flexed, twisted, crushed, or shattered: constructed and not constructed at the same time. She uses digital animation programs to help her visualize and develop her ideas.

Hadid is concerned about modern urban life, which is getting more closed-in and crowded in many parts of the world. Referring to Tokyo, she said, "In such a dense city, light and air are valuable commodities. We must release these spaces from their constricted sites and breathe light and air into the urban condition."[3] She sees her loose and open spaces helping to contribute to the liberation of people from surroundings that are at times oppressive.

When she designs, she refuses to be guided by previous examples. Compare, for example, the VITRA FIRE STATION with just about any other one on earth. Her angular arrangement of jagged masses is meant to suggest tensed energy, just as any fire station is poised and ready to dispense noisy trucks at any moment. The VITRA FIRE STATION looks unusual, but it does not sacrifice practicality. The garages in the rear have wide openings that point directly at the rest of the complex.

Hadid's practice has ranged widely. She has made an archaeological museum in Vienna, a music video pavilion in Holland. a sports complex in Abu Dhabi, the Irish Prime Minister's residence, and the new Contemporary Arts Museum in Cincinnati. The latter is her first building in the United States, and it is pictured at the end of chapter 25.

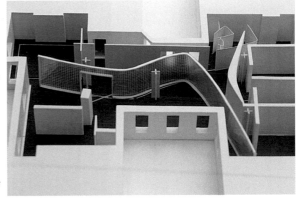

364   Zaha Hadid.
MELBURY
COURT
APARTMENT.
London.
1985.
Interior
remodeling.
Courtesy Office of
Zaha Hadid Ltd.

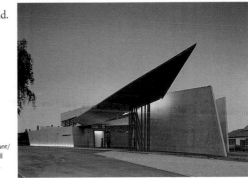

365   Zaha Hadid.
VITRA FIRE
STATION.
Vitra
Furniture
Company,
Weil-am-
Rhein,
Germany.
1993.
© Richard Bryant/
Esto/Arcaid. All
rights reserved.

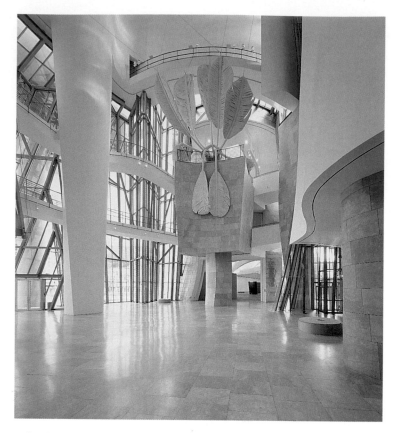

In recent years architect Frank O. Gehry has been selected to design several major show places for the performing and visual arts. The GUGGEN-HEIM MUSEUM BILBAO (GMB), completed at the harbor's edge in Bilbao, Spain, in the fall of 1997, is a spectacular example of Gehry's concept of architecture as functional sculpture. The design—he calls it a "metallic flower"—is a dramatic limestone-and-titanium surfaced cluster of soaring, all-but-dancing volumes climaxing in a gigantic, glass-enclosed atrium. Museum director Thomas Krens envisioned a museum that would celebrate the ever-evolving, at times large-scale inventions of leading contemporary artists while also featuring the art of the architecture—a great world-class museum for world-class art.

There is a feeling of active interplay among the geometrically loose, almost organic masses of the building's main components. With its suggestive boat-like forms and spaces, the museum is a major event in a bold urban-renewal plan aimed at cleaning up and revitalizing the deteriorated port area in

a. Interior.

366 Frank O. Gehry.
GUGGENHEIM MUSEUM BILBAO.
Bilbao, Spain. 1997.

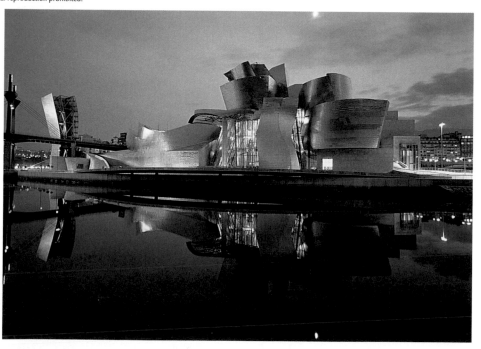

b. Exterior.

which it is built. In its sculptural break from traditional rectangular structures, the Bilbao museum relates to the ground-breaking main Guggenheim Museum in New York, designed in the 1950s by Frank Lloyd Wright. The GMB presents today's art objects in a space that offers an awesome experience in itself.

At Harare, Zimbabwe, a new office complex deals with a totally different set of purposes and challenges. THE EASTGATE COMPLEX is the first building in the world based on the heating and cooling principles of Africa's temperature-efficient termite mounds. Architect Mick Pearce succeeded in meeting the challenge to design an office block that would have a comfortable year-around indoor climate with no air-conditioning and almost no heating in a place where outside temperatures range from 35 degrees F at night to 104 degrees F during the day. Amazingly, the building uses less than ten percent of the energy consumed by conventional buildings of its size and density. Instead of an energy-gobbling glass skin, Pearce took what he calls a Gothic approach, inspired in part by the headdresses of the local Shona tribe and perhaps by the earthy textures of termite mounds.

Large public structures such as temples, churches, exposition halls, and stadiums have historically been at the forefront of architectural innovation, for into them an entire society puts its energy and resources. But one fundamental purpose of architecture is to provide us with a place to live, and our most intimate contact with architectural design is in our own homes.

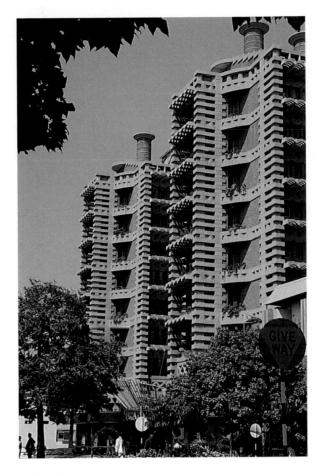

a. Exterior.

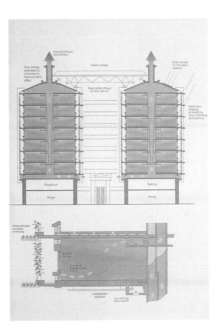

367 Mick Pearce.
THE EASTGATE COMPLEX.
Harare, Zimbabwe. 1996.
Wide Angle (PVT) Ltd.

b. Energy use.
Courtesy Pearce Partnership Architects, Harare.

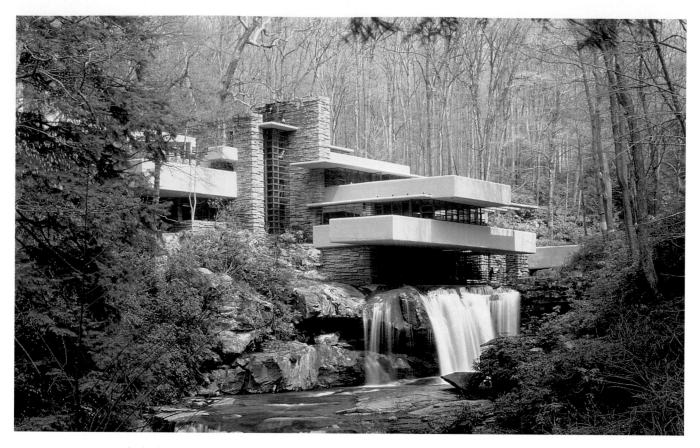

368 Frank Lloyd Wright.
FALLING WATER (EDGAR KAUFMANN RESIDENCE).
Bear Run, Pennsylvania. 1936.
Esto Photographics, Inc.

Designing with Nature

Major influences on mid-century American domestic architecture came from Japan through Frank Lloyd Wright. Wright was among the first to use open planning in houses. In a break with the tradition of closed, boxlike houses, Wright eliminated walls between rooms, enlarged windows, and discovered that one of the best ways to open a closed-in room was to place windows in corners. With these devices, he created flowing spaces that opened to the outdoors, welcomed natural light, and related houses to their sites and climates. Sliding glass doors were influenced by the sliding paper-covered *shoji* doors in traditional Japanese architecture.

Wright also made extensive use of the cantilever. When a beam or slab is extended a substantial distance beyond a supporting column or wall, the overhanging portion is called a *cantilever*. Before the use of steel and reinforced concrete, cantilevers were not used to a significant degree because the available materials could not extend far enough to make the concept viable.

One of the boldest and most elegant uses of the principle occurs in Wright's KAUFMANN RESIDENCE (also known as FALLING WATER) at Bear Run, Pennsylvania. Horizontal masses cantilevered from supporting piers echo the rock ledges on the site and seem almost to float above the waterfall. Vertical accents were influenced by surrounding tall, straight trees. The intrusion of a building on such a beautiful location seems justified by the harmony Wright achieved between the natural site and his equally inspiring architecture.

Frank Lloyd Wright, the most influential twentieth-century American architect, was born in Wisconsin, the son of a Baptist minister.

At age sixteen, Wright took a job with a local builder while studying civil engineering part-time at the University of Wisconsin. A year later, in 1887, he went to Chicago, where he worked as an apprentice in the newly formed architectural firm of Adler & Sullivan. When Louis Sullivan was designing the Wainwright Building (page 239), Wright was his chief draftsman. Eager to do his own work, Wright began designing houses on his own at night. Sullivan took offense at this practice, and Wright left the firm. Wright, however, was strongly influenced by Sullivan and continued throughout his life to refer to him as *Lieber Meister* (beloved master).

By 1893, Wright had opened his own office in the rapidly growing community of Oak Park, Illinois, where he designed a series of houses with low horizontal lines that echoed the flat prairie landscape. This distinctive approach became known as his Prairie Style.

That same year, at the Columbian Exposition in Chicago, Wright saw a Japanese tea house. The encounter led to a deep interest in Japanese architecture and long stays in Japan. He found the asymmetrical balance, large extended eaves, and flexible open plan (with sliding doors and walls) of traditional Japanese houses more sensitive to nature and to human life than the often static symmetry of traditional American homes.

Wright sought to bring his own poetic sense of nature into harmony with the new materials and the engineering technology of the machine age. In terms of both structure and aesthetics, Wright was a radical innovator. He used poured reinforced concrete and steel cantilevers in houses at a time when such construction was usually confined to commercial structures. His KAUFMANN RESIDENCE is dramatically cantilevered over a waterfall, and two of his major buildings were designed with flowing interior spaces and spiral ramps. Among his many notable buildings was the structurally innovative Imperial Hotel in Tokyo, built between 1916 and 1922. His use of the cantilever in this hotel was criticized as a violation of sound construction—until after the devastating quake of 1923, when it remained one of the few undamaged buildings in the city.

In his later years, Wright continued his large practice and devoted considerable time to writing and to teaching apprentices in his workshop-homes. Throughout his career Wright was guided by his awareness that buildings have a profound, life-shaping influence on the people who inhabit them.

Among Wright's many unrealized projects was a plan for a mile-high skyscraper. His last major work was the controversial Solomon R. Guggenheim Museum, built in the late 1950s. Its immense spiraling ramp enables viewers to see exhibitions in a clearly defined continuous path, but the sloping, eye-filling space tends to overpower the presentation of other works of art.

Wright's guiding philosophy is most apparent in his houses, where his concern for simplicity and his sensitivity to the character of space and materials express what he defined as an organic ideal for architecture. According to Wright, the word *organic* goes beyond its strictly biological meaning to refer to the integration of all aspects of a form, the part to the whole and the whole to the part. Thus, in architecture, one should determine the form of a building by designing in terms of the

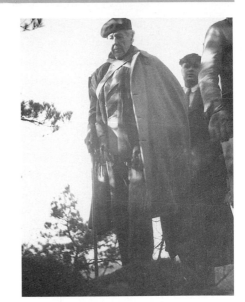

369   FRANK LLOYD WRIGHT. 1936.
Photograph: Edmund Teske. Courtesy The Frank Lloyd Wright Archives, Scottsdale, AZ.

unique qualities of the site, proceeding from the ground up, and honoring the character of the natural conditions as well as the materials and purposes of the structure. Wright spoke of organic architecture as having a meaning beyond any preconceived style:

exalting the simple laws of common sense—or of supersense if you prefer—determining form by way of the nature of materials, the nature of purpose so well understood that a bank will not look like a Greek Temple, a university will not look like a cathedral, nor a fire-engine house resemble a French château. . . . Form follows function? Yes, but more important now [with organic architecture] form and function are one.[4]

ENVIRONMENTAL DESIGN

Architecture and environmental design are about as far as we can get from art objects in museums. They are also among the most important of the arts in their impact on our daily lives.

Environmental design involves the design of communities and regions, from small gardens to large parks, from small neighborhoods to large urban areas. Professional fields of environmental design include architecture, landscape architecture, and transportation design. Overseeing all of these is the discipline of planning. Environmental designers help establish and work within zoning laws that determine land use and population density through open-space requirements. Such restrictions set height limits on buildings and establish setback laws that regulate building height and density and the dis-

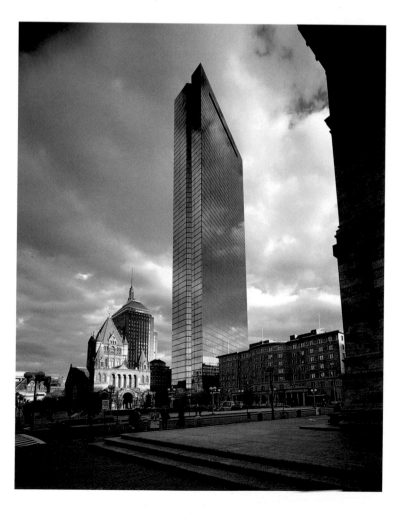

tance buildings must be from property lines. Visual contact with natural and manufactured landmarks is preserved or created through view corridors and view planes that prevent new construction from blocking visual contact with the beauty of such place-defining amenities.

Prior to the twentieth century, planned and unplanned urban centers grew slowly to meet the needs for protection, commerce, and communication. Traditions, relatively unchanging lifestyles, slow population growth, and the absence of powerful technologies limited the speed of change and the impact of humans on the rest of nature. As Earth's population rapidly increases, environmental planning and design, or their absence, will make an enormous difference in the quality of life.

On a small scale, the accidental city has intriguing variety and complexity; but in a large and rapidly expanding urban area, haphazard growth can be dehumanizing and dangerous. Master planner James Rouse pointed out that far too often:

. . . our cities grow by sheer chance, by accident, by the whim of the private developer and public agencies. A farm is sold and the land begins to sprout houses instead of potatoes. Forests are cut. Valleys are filled. Streams are turned into storm sewers. An expressway is hacked through the landscape. Then a cloverleaf, then a regional shopping center, then office buildings, then high-rise apartments. In this way, the bits and pieces of a city are splattered across the landscape. By this irrational process, non-communities are born, formless places without order, beauty or reason, with no visible respect for either people or the land.[5]

370 Henry Hobson Richardson.
TRINITY CHURCH. 1877.

I. M. Pei and Partners.
JOHN HANCOCK TOWER. 1974.
Copley Square, Boston.
Photograph: © Steve Rosenthal.

Changes within cities are being made all the time, with some sensitive blending of old and new. Sometimes incredible confrontations occur between the old and the new, as when the size of a new building causes it to dwarf older, smaller structures. The building of JOHN HANCOCK TOWER on Copley Square in Boston was widely publicized. Many people find it offensive because of its dominating size and incompatibility with the styles of nearby older buildings. Others enjoy its monumental height and the dramatic contrast of its sheer crystalline form with Henry Richardson's nineteenth-century TRINITY CHURCH.

Landscape architecture deals with the interrelationships among land forms and the plants and constructed elements on them. It is the art of working with both natural and human-made elements to provide visual enjoyment and refreshing places for relaxation and recreation. Landscape architects are trained in both the natural sciences and art. The essence of their work is designing with nature. Approaches range from formal, geometrically organized forms to informal, natural-looking compositions. Landscape architects frequently work with planners and architects to enhance the surroundings of buildings and to help buildings relate visually to their sites and to one another.

On another Manhattan site, landscape architect Ken Smith and lighting designer Jim Conti combined nature and culture in a subtle and witty manner with their GLOWING TOPIARY GARDEN. They remodeled the space of Liberty Plaza in the financial district for two months in midwinter of 1997-1998. A symmetrical array of cones made from white awning material were lit from within by pale neon tubes so that each cone glowed with soft pastel shades. The artists installed 200 wind chimes throughout the space, and added music clips of bell sounds. As passers-by traversed the site, the shifting colors of the cones coupled with the chimes and soft bells created a meditative environment that the artists said was influenced by Japanese Zen gardens. The shape of the cones also suggested Christmas trees, an appropriate seasonal hint.

The art-making processes found in other disciplines apply to solving environmental design issues. Whether we are creating something new or changing or preserving something that already exists, we face the challenge of being aware of the character of an existing place and all the factors that influence its form. Nowhere is the creative process more complex or needed than in the work of honoring and renewing the spirit of a place.

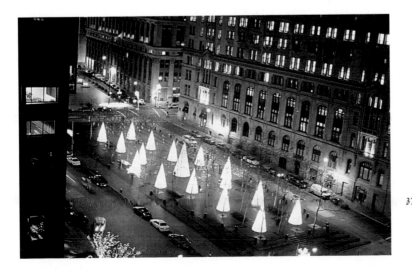

371 Ken Smith and Jim Conti.
GLOWING TOPIARY GARDEN.
Liberty Plaza, New York. 1997–1998.
Height of cones, 16' to 24'.
Courtesy Ken Smith.

By imagination and reason, we turn experience into foresight. We become the creators of our future, and cease to be slaves of our past.

Will Durant[6]

The evolutionary jump that lies ahead is . . . a tall one, for it means no more or less than changing ourselves by changing our surroundings, and learning to do this by choice and not by chance.

Humphry Osmond[7]

Moment-to-moment, day-to-day, we influence our surroundings and, in turn, are influenced by them. The original title of this book was *Man Creates Art Creates Man,* referring to the fact that "art" is not just pictures on the wall, or special performances, but the whole world of creative awareness and actions available to all. What human beings have invented and are inventing has an enormous impact on who we are and how we live. The process of caring for the spaces we live in is essential. Our sense of ourselves and our attitudes about life determine the way we live. Art is one name for how we manifest our being in the world—from the clothing we choose to wear to the spaces we select and shape for living.

What qualities in our surroundings make life both sustainable and worthwhile? What is behind the making of sense-pleasing, soul-satisfying places? How can neighbors work together to create and sustain rewarding communities? How can we work with nature to sustain and create viable and beautiful living environments for all? Such questions are behind the art of environmental design.

The more aware we are of what is possible, the more we can make a positive difference in our own lives and in the lives of others. Art cannot be forced or dictated; sources of aesthetic pleasure vary from person to person. Yet, when enough members of a community are aware of aesthetic values and realize that they affect results, whether they are consciously involved in the decision making or not, the rewarding art of place-making can begin.

Environmental issues are best addressed from the perspectives of many disciplines, including the sciences and the arts.

Some issues should be obvious: One doesn't build for a desert what would be best in a rain forest; one makes optimal use of natural light in indoor spaces to save energy costs. The visual arts heighten awareness (design/aesthetic sensitivity) and help develop visual thinking, making it possible to visualize options. The principles of effective visual design—such as harmony, proportion, balance, unity, and variety, introduced in chapter 4—apply as much to environmental design as to any of the other visual arts.

Many of us spend much of our time "capsulized." In a given work day, we might go from a home capsule to a car capsule to an elevator capsule to an office capsule, with only a distant through-windows contact with the larger environment. In this context, we are capsulized both physically and mentally; one state contributes to the other. How can we influence environmental decision making if we are not really in touch with our physical surroundings? The capsule is a metaphor for a mental box—a mind set that limits understanding of what is possible.

Feng shui, the ancient Chinese art of placement, teaches that everything has a life force *(ch'i).* If the environment is not harmonious, people will become ill, unhappy, and unproductive. Mystical meaning, practicality, and aesthetic sensibility are combined in this art that may deal with ecology, architecture, and the arrangement of furniture. In practice, Feng shui functions as both an art and a science.

When our senses are insulted by visual pollution and chaos, life is "diseased." While good design is not a cure-all, indoor and outdoor living spaces that are life supporting, rather than degrading, will reward our senses and greatly enhance our well-being. The goal is to see, to be aware of the art of living, and to enjoy the results of our own creative contributions.

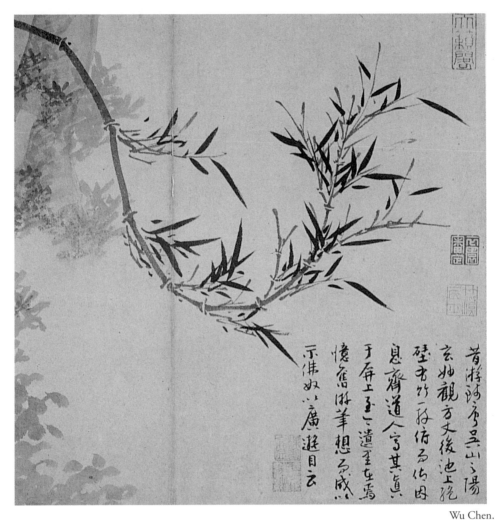

Wu Chen.
ALBUM LEAF from MANUAL OF INK BAMBOO.
1350. Ink on paper. 16⅞" × 20½".
National Palace Museum, Taipei.

PART FIVE
Art as Cultural Heritage

CONSIDER . . .

Picasso once said, "If a work of art cannot live always in the present it must not be considered at all." What do you think he meant?

Glance through chapters 18 to 20 without reading the text. How much can you learn about each civilization by looking at its art and architecture? For example, compare the Indian temple with the Japanese palace. What differences are apparent in each culture's view of beauty?

When you think of historic culture, what comes to your mind: dates, images, or political events?

Notice the change in the subject matter as you glance through chapter 21. How would you characterize the artistic interests of the eighteenth and nineteenth centuries, when compared with those of the Renaissance in chapter 17?

CHAPTER FIFTEEN

PREHISTORIC TO EARLY CIVILIZATION

Art history makes history visible and accessible. It is a record of how the people of the past—our ancestors—lived, felt, and acted in widely separated parts of the world at different periods of time.

Art history differs from other kinds of history because works of art from the past are with us in the present. One-to-one communication occurs even when artist and viewer are separated by thousands or even tens of thousands of years. This communicative power of art makes it possible for us to glimpse some of the experiences of those whose lives preceded ours, to better understand societies other than our own, and to see beyond our own cultural boundaries. Although interesting, old science is no longer of practical use; but old art can be as life-enriching as new art.

Our knowledge of art history is constantly growing. Excavations and restorations continue to bring ancient works to light. In rare cases such as the excavations of Pompeii in Italy, an entire city is being revealed.

Modern techniques of photo reproduction, printing, and electronic transmission have helped to make the art of the whole world available to us. Through reproductions, we can now see more fine works of ancient Egyptian and Chinese art, for example, than the people of those cultures were themselves able to see.

As numbers of years can be confusing when we study art history, let's consider numbers in terms of generations. Since the beginning of human life on Earth, the average time interval between the birth of parents and the birth of their offspring has varied from about eighteen to thirty-three years. When we figure that roughly twenty-five years is the average generation, we can come closer to the people of the past by realizing that most of us have three generations within our own families, and many have four. The United States became a country only nine generations ago; the Italian Renaissance occurred just twenty generations ago; Jesus Christ lived eighty generations ago; the Buddha (Siddhartha Gautama) lived about one hundred generations ago. In fact, the end of the prehistoric period occurred less than three hundred generations ago.

There is no "better" or "best" when we compare the art of different societies, or even the art of different times within the same society. Rather, differences in art reflect differences in points of view. Pablo Picasso put the subject of art history in perspective in this way:

To me there is no past or future in art. If a work of art cannot live always in the present it must not be considered at all. The art of the Greeks, the Egyptians, the great painters who lived in other times, is not an art of the past; perhaps it is more alive today than it ever was. Art does not evolve by itself, the ideas of people evolve and with them their mode of expression.[1]

THE PALEOLITHIC PERIOD

Roughly two million years ago, in east central Africa, early hominids made crude stone cutting tools. The making of these tools enabled our predecessors to extend their skills and thereby gain a measure of control over their surroundings. From such beginnings, human beings developed the abilities to reason and to visualize: to remember the past, to relate it to the present, and to imagine possible futures. As we became form-creating creatures, our ability to conceive mental images—and the development of hands capable of making those images—set us apart from other animals. Imagination is our special advantage.

About one million years ago in Africa, and more recently in Asia and Europe, people made more refined tools by chipping flakes from opposite sides of stones to create sharp cutting edges. It took another 250,000 years or so for human beings to develop choppers and hand axes that were symmetrical and refined in shape. An awareness of the relationship of form to function, and of form as enjoyable in itself, was the first step in the history of art.

Sprinkled powders and beads accompany many widely dispersed gravesites from about 100,000 years ago. These finds suggest to archaeologists that humans at that time practiced ritual burial, though the meaning of these decorative additions is unknown. Some very ancient rock carvings recently discovered in Australia await further testing, but are said to date back 75,000 years.

The most sophisticated examples of what we call prehistoric art were discovered during the last hundred years at many locations around the world. Current scientific dating places the earliest of these findings at about 40,000 years ago, toward the end of the last Ice Age. As the southern edge of the European ice sheet slowly retreated northward, hunter-gatherers followed the animals on which they depended for food. They carved and painted images of these animals on cave walls deep in the earth. The level of expertise demonstrated in these works suggests that they were preceded by generations of slow artistic development. However, researchers have not yet found any evidence of a long evolution of these art forms.

Hand-size carvings of female figures have been found in the areas now called Eastern and Western Europe. Shown here are two of the best known: the so-called VENUS OF WILLENDORF and VENUS OF LESPUGUE. In each of these figures, the exaggerated emphasis on hips and breasts implies a specific purpose that we can only guess. We might assume that prehistoric people gave primary credit to women for the most evident creative act: the birth of a new person. These figures may be the earliest known works of religious art, depicting the Paleolithic image of the Creator—the Great Mother Goddess. We refer to the Paleolithic period as the Stone Age, but that is mainly because only stone artifacts have survived. Some details on these figures suggest that their makers also practiced the arts of twining and braiding. For example, recent researchers believe that the VENUS OF LESPUGUE wears a skirt made from braided cords, and the VENUS OF WILLENDORF may sport a cap.

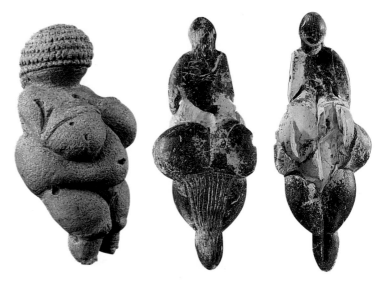

372 VENUS OF WILLENDORF. c. 25,000–20,000 B.C.E.
Limestone. Height 4½".
Naturhistorisches Museum, Vienna.
Photograph: Erich Lessing/Art Resource, NY.

373 VENUS DE LESPUGUE.
Mammoth ivory. Height 7¹³⁄₁₆".
Musée de l'Homme, Paris.
Scala/Art Resource/New York.
a. back view
b. front view

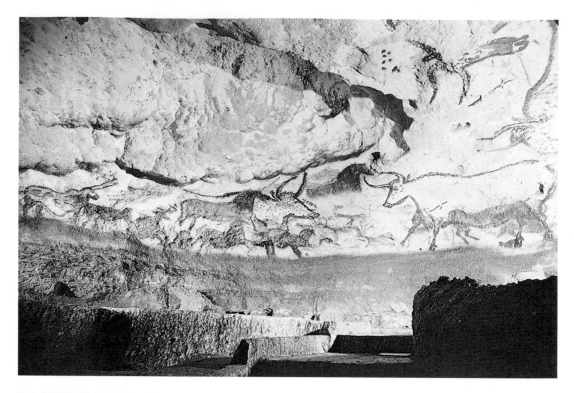

374   GREAT HALL OF BULLS, LEFT-HAND WALL.
      Lascaux Cave, Dordogne, France. c. 15,000–10,000 B.C.E.
      Polychrome rock painting.
      Photograph: Hans Hinz/Colorfoto Hinz, Basel, Switzerland.

375   WALL PAINTING OF ANIMALS.
      Chauvet Cave, Pont d'Arc, France. c. 28,000 B.C.E. Corbis/Sygma.

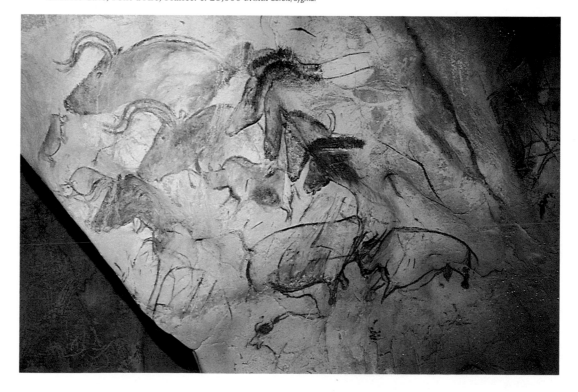

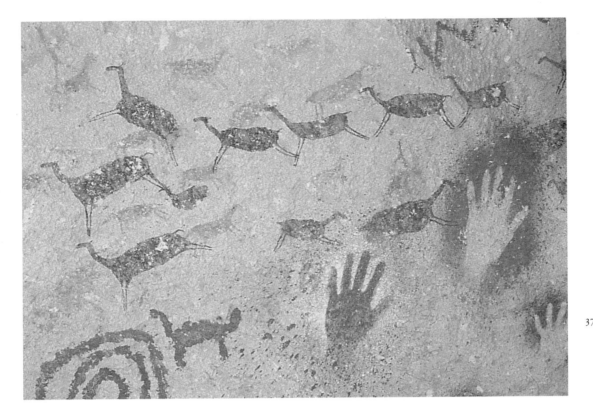

376 DEER AND HANDS.
Las Manos Cave,
Argentina.
c. 15,000 B.C.E.
Bruce Coleman Inc.
Photograph: Des and
Jen Barlett

Human figures rarely appear in Paleolithic paintings; those that do tend to be more simplified and abstract than the images of animals. Animals portrayed in sculpture and paintings of this period have an expressive naturalism. The oldest known paintings were found in 1994 in the Chauvet Cave in South Central France. The WALL PAINTING OF ANIMALS is among dozens of 30,000-year-old images painted with charcoal and earthen pigments on the cave walls. The unknown artists depicted in a lifelike fashion horses, rhinoceroses, tigers, and other large animals, many of them now extinct. Explorers found nearby a bear's skull placed in the middle of a flat stone slab in what may have been an altar.

Lascaux Cave in southern France contain examples of the magnificent art of the late Paleolithic period. On walls of the inner chambers, large and small animals were portrayed in as many as thirteen different styles, from small and delicate to very large and bold. The largest bull at Lascaux (at lower right of the GREAT HALL OF BULLS) is eighteen feet in length. Successive images were painted over earlier ones. Each of the vigorous, naturalistic styles was made in a different time period. Depictions are obviously based on careful observation gained through considerable direct contact with the animals that roamed the land at that time. The paintings were made by the light of oil-bearing stone lamps. At Lascaux, and at many other Paleolithic sites, geometric signs or symbols often appear along with the animal and occasional human figures.

Scholars long believed that the purpose of naturalistic Paleolithic art was to bring the spirits of animals into rituals related to the hunt. Many authors stress this theory. However, careful study of footprints and other archaeological remains has recently led some experts to theorize that Lascaux and similar sites were used as sanctuaries where youth were initiated in ceremonies based on symbolic and metaphysical associations with the portrayed animals.

Prehistoric Ice Age people, in what is now Southern Argentina, made paintings of their hands, probably by blowing earth colors as they placed their hands against the cave wall. DEER AND HANDS is similar to hand impressions and paintings of animals found on many continents.

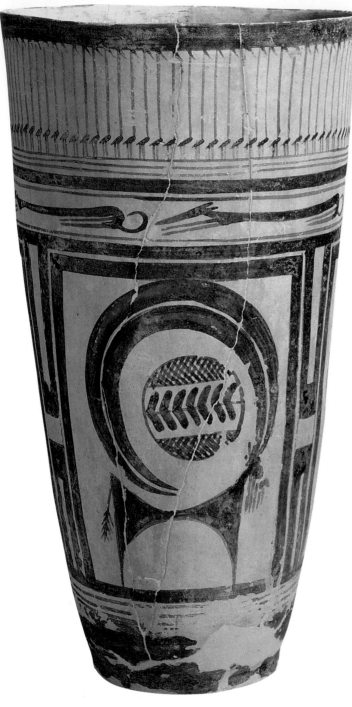

377 EARTHENWARE BEAKER. Susa, Iran. c. 4000 B.C.E.
Painted terra cotta. Height 11¼".
Musée du Louvre, Paris.
Reunion de Musée Nationaux/Art Resource/NY.

THE NEOLITHIC PERIOD

The transition from Old Stone Age, or Paleolithic, to New Stone Age, or Neolithic, cultures marked a major turning point in human history. Although there are comparable sites around the world, the New Stone Age seems to have occurred first in the Middle East, between 9000 and 6000 B.C.E., when people made the gradual transition from the precarious existence of nomadic hunters and food gatherers to the relatively stable life of village farmers and herders. The agricultural revolution—this major shift from nomadic groups to small agricultural communities—stabilized human life and produced early architecture and other technological developments. Out of necessity, people learned new techniques for working with seasonal rhythms. Because food and seeds had to be stored, it is not surprising that clay storage pots are among the most significant artifacts of the period.

Neolithic art reflects the great shift in living patterns. The vigorous, naturalistic art of Paleolithic hunters was largely replaced by the geometrically abstract art of Neolithic farmers. From about 10,000 to 3000 B.C.E., emphasis was placed on abstract designs used to enhance articles of daily use. The motifs, or dominant themes, used on clay pots were often derived from plant and animal forms.

The painted EARTHENWARE BEAKER is from Susa, the first developed city on the Iranian plateau. Solid bands define areas of compact decoration. The upper zone consists of a row of highly abstract long-necked birds, below which appears to be a band of dogs running in the opposite direction. The dominant image is an ibex or goat abstracted into triangular and circular shapes. The significant difference between the naturalism of Paleolithic animal art and the abstraction of Neolithic art becomes clear when we compare this goat with the naturalistic bulls of Lascaux.

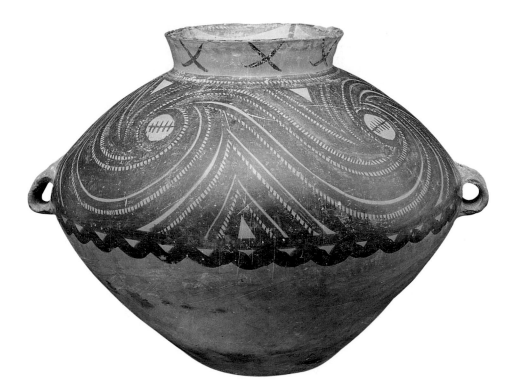

378 BURIAL URN.
Kansu type. Chinese, Neolithic period.
c. 2200 B.C.E.
Pottery with painted decoration.
Height 14⅛".
The Seattle Art Museum.
Eugene Fuller Memorial Collection (51.194).
Photo: Paul Macapia.

We can see how Neolithic abstract designs were derived from representational images in AN EVOLUTION OF ABSTRACTION, the series of drawings copied from pieces of pottery found in Shensi Province in China. As the decorative designs evolved over generations, the clearly recognizable bird image became more and more abstract, and eventually it formed the basis for the nonrepresentational band around the pot shown in the drawing. Such playing with figure-ground reversal is also found in modern painting and design.

Some of the finest Neolithic pottery was made in China. The well-preserved BURIAL URN from Kansu Province is decorated with a bold interlocking design, which may have been abstracted from spirals observed in nature. The design in the center of the spirals is probably derived from the bottoms of cowrie shells.

It is quite possible that nonrepresentational signs often found in Paleolithic caves along with

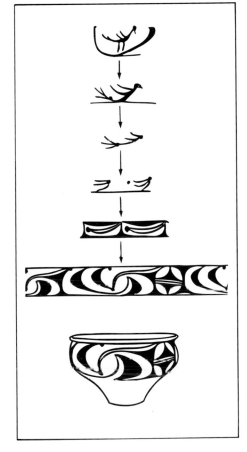

379 AN EVOLUTION OF ABSTRACTION.
From Neolithic pottery,
Shensi Province, China.
Courtesy of Charles Weber.

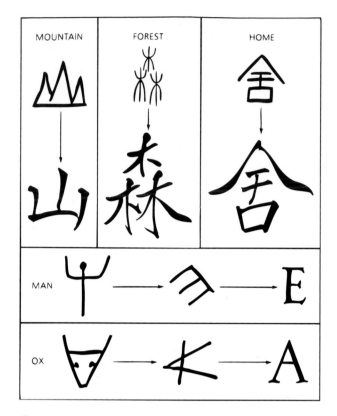

MOUNTAIN	FOREST	HOME
山	森	舍

MAN	Ψ → ∃ → E
OX	∀ → K → A

380 PICTOGRAPHS TO WRITING EAST AND WEST.

naturalistic images of animals were meant to communicate specific information. Many of the world's writing systems grew out of a search for visual equivalents for speech and were preceded by various types of pictography, or "picture writing." The pictographic origin of some characters in modern Chinese writing is well known. Less well known is that some letters of the Roman alphabet used in English came from pictographs that stood for objects or ideas.

THE BEGINNINGS OF CIVILIZATION

Artifacts indicate that early civilizations emerged independently, at different times, in many parts of the world. We use the term *civilization* to distinguish cultures, or composites of cultures, that have fairly complex social orders and relatively high degrees of technical development. Key elements are food production through agriculture and animal husbandry, metallurgy, occupational specialization, and writing. All of these developments were made possible by the move to cooperative living in urban as well as agricultural communities.

Among the earliest major civilizations were those in four fertile river valleys: the Tigris and Euphrates Rivers in Iraq, the Nile River in Egypt, the Indus River in west Pakistan and India, and the Yellow River in northern China.

381 EARLIEST CENTERS OF CIVILIZATION, 3500–1500 B.C.E.

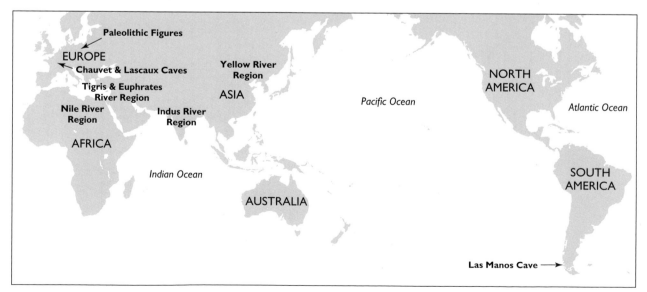

CHAPTER SIXTEEN

ANCIENT THROUGH MEDIEVAL IN THE MIDDLE EAST AND EUROPE

The ancient civilizations of Mesopotamia and Egypt were almost parallel in time, arising in the fourth millennium B.C.E. and lasting some three thousand years. Yet they were quite different from each other. Urban civilization developed earlier in Mesopotamia than it did in Egypt. The Nile Valley of Egypt was protected by formidable deserts, making it possible for the Egyptians to enjoy thousands of years of relatively unbroken self-rule. The Tigris–Euphrates Valley of Mesopotamia, however, was vulnerable to repeated invasion; the area was ruled by a succession of different peoples. Each civilization therefore developed its own distinctive art forms.

382 ZIGGURAT OF UR-NAMMU. Iraq. c. 2100 B.C.E.
 a. Reconstruction drawing.
   University of Pennsylvania Museum, Philadelphia #S8–55876.
 b. Incomplete restoration.
   Photograph: Superstock.

MESOPOTAMIA

It was the Greeks who named the broad plain between the Tigris and Euphrates Rivers Mesopotamia, "the land between the rivers." Today, this plain is part of Iraq. The first Mesopotamian civilization arose in the southernmost part of the plain in an area called Sumer. The Sumerian people developed the world's first writing, the wheel, and the plow.

In the city-states of Sumer, religion and government were one; authority rested with priests who claimed divine sanction. The Sumerians worshiped a hierarchy of nature gods in temples set on huge platforms called *ziggurats,* which stood at the center of each city-state. Ruins of many early Mesopotamian cities are still dominated by eroding ziggurats, such as the ZIGGURAT OF UR-NAMMU. The biblical Tower of Babel was probably a ziggurat.

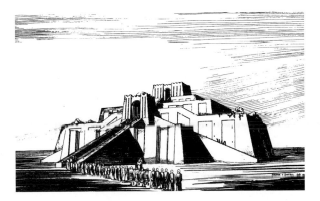

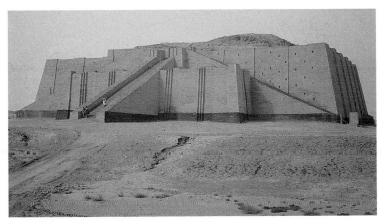

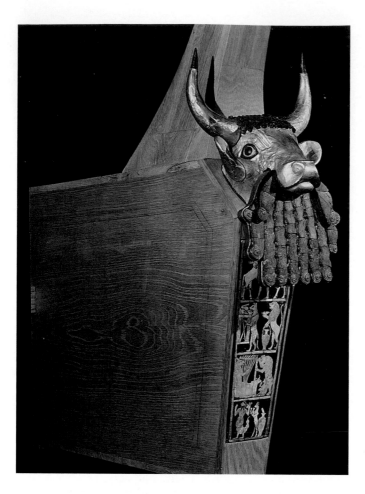

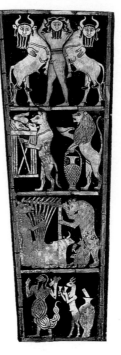

383 Reconstructed LYRE.
From "The King's
Grave" tomb RT 789,
Ur. c. 2650–2550
B.C.E. Reconstructed.
Wood with gold, lapis
lazuli, shell, and silver.
University of Pennsylvania
Museum, Philadelphia
(B 17694T4-29C), (#T4–109C3).

a. Soundbox.
b. Front plaque.

Ziggurats symbolized the concept of the "sacred mountain" that links heaven and earth. They were filled with sun-baked bricks and faced with fired bricks often glazed in different colors. Two or more successively smaller platforms stood on the solid base, with a shrine on the uppermost platform. On these heights, close to heaven, the city's deities might dwell, and there the ruling priests and priestesses had their sanctuaries. A lack of stone led to the use of brick and wood for building, and consequently very little Mesopotamian architecture remains.

We can imagine the splendor of Sumerian court life by studying the reconstruction of the elegant royal LYRE found in the king's tomb in the ancient city of Ur. The narrative panel on the front and the bull's head are original. The bearded bull's head is a symbol of royalty often seen in Mesopotamian art. In contrast, the bulls and other imaginative animals inlaid on the harp's soundbox are depicted in a simplified narrative style. They take on human roles, as do the animals in the later Greek fables of Aesop. The upper panel, which shows a man embracing two bearded bulls, is a type of heraldic design developed by the Sumerians that was to influence the art of many later cultures. Both the upper panel and the panel at the

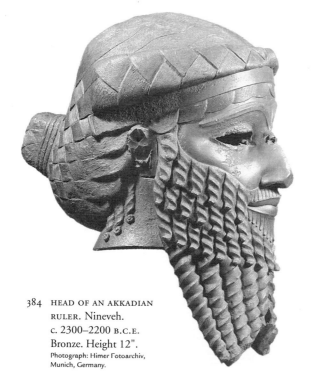

384 HEAD OF AN AKKADIAN
RULER. Nineveh.
c. 2300–2200 B.C.E.
Bronze. Height 12".
Photograph: Himer Fotoarchiv,
Munich, Germany.

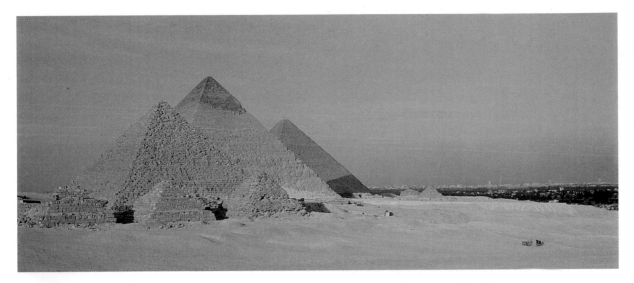

bottom—a goat attending a scorpion-man—are believed to be scenes from the great classic of Sumerian literature, the *Epic of Gilgamesh.*

The region of Mesopotamia north of Sumer was called Akkadia. By about 2300 B.C.E., the scattered city-states of Sumer had come under the authority of a single Akkadian king. The magnificent HEAD OF AN AKKADIAN RULER portrays such an absolute monarch. Clearly, this highly sophisticated work evolved from a long tradition. The elaborate hairstyle and rhythmic patterning show the influence of Sumerian stylization. The handsome face expresses calm inner strength. Such superb blending of formal design with carefully observed naturalism is a characteristic of both later Mesopotamian and Egyptian art.

Mesopotamia was an area of continual local rivalries, foreign invasions, and the rise and fall of military powers, yet this disorder did not prevent the development and continuity of cultural traditions.

EGYPT

Deserts on both sides of the Nile diminished outside influences and enabled Egypt to develop distinctive styles of architecture, painting, and sculpture that remained relatively unchanged for 2500 years—longer than the time from the birth of Christ to today. In our age of rapid cultural and technological change, it is difficult to imagine such artistic stability.

Among the most impressive and memorable works of Egyptian civilization are THE GREAT PYRAMIDS, gigantic mountain-like structures built as

385 THE GREAT PYRAMIDS. Giza, Egypt.
Pyramid of Mycerinus, c. 2500 B.C.E.; Pyramid of Chefren, 2650 B.C.E.; Pyramid of Cheops, c. 2570 B.C.E.

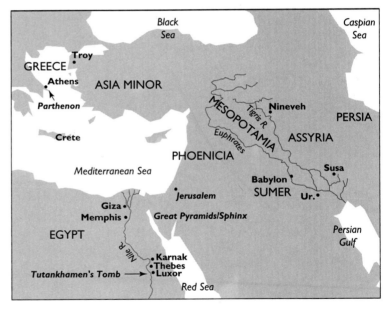

386 THE ANCIENT MIDDLE EAST.

burial vaults for pharaohs—rulers who were considered god-kings. Legions of workers cut huge stone blocks, moved them to the site, and stacked them, without mortar, to form the final pyramidal structure. The interiors are mostly solid, with narrow passageways leading to small burial chambers.

Egyptian religious belief was distinguished by its emphasis on life after death. Preservation of the body and care for the dead were considered essential

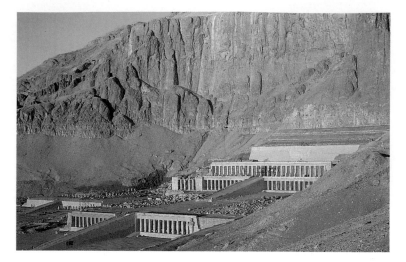

387 FUNERARY TEMPLE OF QUEEN HATSHEPSUT.
Deir el-Bahari. c. 1490–1460 B.C.E.
Tom Till Photography. © Tom Till.

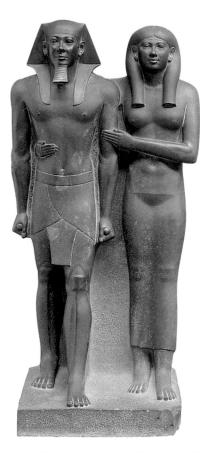

388 KING MYCERINUS AND A QUEEN. KHAMERERNEBTY.
Egypt, Giza, Old Kingdon, Dyanasty 4, reign of Mycerinus,
2532–2510 B.C.E. Schist. 54¹¹⁄₁₆" x 22⅜" x 21 ⁵⁄₁₆".

for extending life beyond the grave. Upon death, bodies of royalty and nobility were embalmed; together with accompanying artifacts, tools, and furniture, they were then buried in pyramids or in hidden underground tombs. Architects put great effort into preventing access to these funerary structures. As a result, most of what we know about ancient Egypt comes from such tombs.

Names of many Egyptian architects are known in association with their buildings. One of the finest and best-preserved examples of environmentally sensitive design is the FUNERARY TEMPLE OF QUEEN HATSHEPSUT, designed by Senmut, the queen's chancellor and architect. Here ramps and colonnades provide an elegant setting for ritual pageantry and complement the majestic cliffs of the site.

Egyptian sculpture is characterized by compact, solidly structured figures that embody qualities of strength and geometric clarity found in Egyptian architecture. The final form of a piece of sculpture was determined by an underlying geometric plan that was first sketched on the surface of the stone block. The sculptor of KING MYCERINUS AND QUEEN KHAMERERNEBTY paid considerable attention to human anatomy yet stayed within the traditionally prescribed geometric scheme. The strength, clarity, and lasting stability expressed by the figures result from this union of naturalism and abstraction. With formal austerity, the couple stands in the frontal pose (straight forward, not turning) that had been established for royal portraits. Even so, the figures express warmth and vitality; the queen touches Mycerinus in a sympathetic, loving way. Typical of sculpture of this era are the formal pose with left foot forward, the false ceremonial beard, and figures that remain attached to the block of stone from which they were carved.

Tutankhamen ("King Tut"), who died at age eighteen, is the best-known Egyptian pharaoh because his was the only Egyptian royal tomb discovered in modern times with most of its contents intact. The volume and value of the objects in the small tomb make it clear why grave robbers have been active in Egypt since the days of the first pharaohs. Tutankhamen's inlaid gold MASK FROM MUMMY CASE is but one of hundreds of extraordinary artifacts from the tomb. Its formal blend of naturalism and abstract idealism is distinctly Egyptian.

A feature of Egyptian painting, relief carving, and even sculpture in the round is the presentation of the human figure either in a completely frontal position or in profile. Egyptian artists portrayed each object and each part of the human body from what they identified as its most characteristic angle, thus avoiding the ambiguity caused by random or chance angles of view (see also page 50).

In the WALL PAINTING FROM THE TOMB OF NEBAMUN, the painter of the hunting scene presents a wealth of specific information without making the painting confusing. Flat shapes portray basic elements of each subject in the clearest, most identifiable way. The head, hips, legs, and feet of the nobleman who dominates this painting are shown from the side, while his eye and shoulders are shown from the front. Sizes of human figures are determined by social rank, a system known as *hierarchic scale;* the nobleman is the largest figure, his wife is smaller, his daughter smaller still.

The family stands on a boat made of papyrus reeds; plants grow on the left at the shore. The entire painting is teeming with life, and the artist has

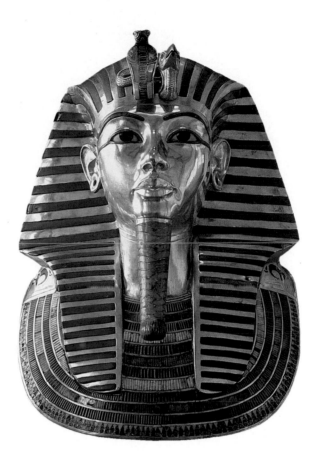

389 MASK FROM MUMMY CASE.
Tutankhamen. c. 1340 B.C.E.
Gold inlaid with enamel
and semiprecious stones.
Height 21¼".
Egyptian Museum, Cairo.
Photograph: Superstock, Inc.

390 WALL PAINTING FROM THE
TOMB OF NEBAMUN.
Thebes, Egypt. c. 1450 B.C.E.
Paint on dry plaster.
© British Museum, London.

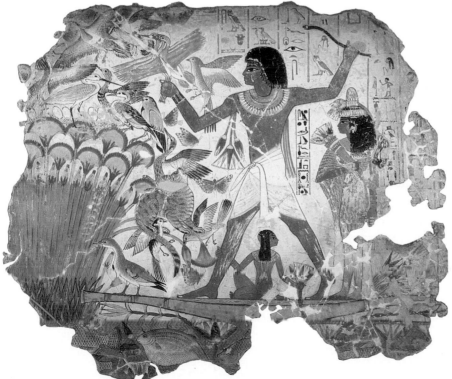

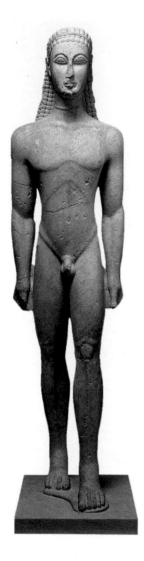

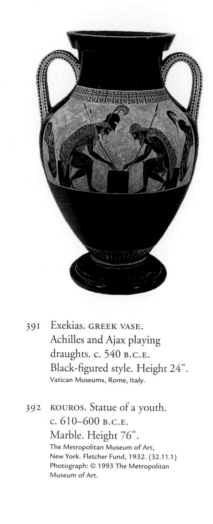

391 Exekias. GREEK VASE.
Achilles and Ajax playing
draughts. c. 540 B.C.E.
Black-figured style. Height 24".
Vatican Museums, Rome, Italy.

392 KOUROS. Statue of a youth.
c. 610–600 B.C.E.
Marble. Height 76".
The Metropolitan Museum of Art,
New York. Fletcher Fund, 1932. (32.11.1)
Photograph: © 1993 The Metropolitan
Museum of Art.

even taken great care to show life below the water's surface. Attention to accurate detail lets us identify species of insects, birds, and fish. The hieroglyphics—the picture writing of ancient Egyptian priesthood—can be seen behind the figures.

GREECE

The Greeks distinguished themselves from other peoples of Europe and Asia by their attitude toward being human. They came to regard humankind as the highest creation of nature—the closest thing to perfection in physical form, coupled with the power to reason. Greek deities had human weaknesses, and Greek mortals had godlike strengths.

With this attitude came a new concept of the importance of the individual. The Greek focus on

human potential and achievement led to the development of democracy and to the perfection of naturalistic images of the human figure in art. The philosopher Plato taught that behind the imperfections of transitory reality was the permanent, ideal form. Thus to create the ideal individual (the supreme work of nature) became the goal of Greek artists.

Greek civilization passed through three broad stages: the Archaic period, the Classical period, and the Hellenistic period. In the art of the Archaic period (from the late seventh to the early fifth centuries B.C.E.), the Greeks assimilated influences from Egypt and the Near East. Greek writers of the time tell us that Greek painters were often better known than Greek sculptors. Yet what we now see of Greek painting appears only on pottery because very few wall paintings survive. The elegant GREEK VASE shown here suggests the level of achievement of Greek potters as well as painters. It is in the Archaic, "black-figured" style and shows Achilles and Ajax, two heroes from Homer's epic poetry, playing draughts, what we now call checkers. Although their eyes are still shown from the front in the Egyptian manner, there is a new liveliness in the bodies.

Numerous life-size nude male and clothed female figures were carved in stone or cast in bronze during this era. The Archaic-style KOUROS, carved at about the same time the vase was painted, has a rigid frontal position that is an adaptation from Egyptian sculpture. (*Kouros* is Greek for male youth; *kore* is the word for female youth.) The Egyptian figure of MYCERINUS (page 264) and the KOUROS both stand with arms held straight at the sides, fingers drawn up, and left leg forward with the weight evenly distributed on both feet.

In spite of the similarity of stance, however, the character of Greek sculpture is already quite different from that of Egyptian. The KOUROS is freestanding, and it honors an individual who was not a supernatural ruler.

Within one hundred years after the making of the KOUROS figure, Greek civilization entered its Classical phase (480–323 B.C.E.). Greek aesthetic principles from this period provide the basis for the concept of classicism. *Classical* art emphasizes rational simplicity, order, and restrained emotion. The rigid poses of Egyptian and early Greek figures gave way to a greater interest in anatomy and more relaxed poses. Sculpture became increasingly naturalistic as well as idealized and began to show the body as alive and capable of movement.

The WARRIOR, one of two bronze sculptures found in 1972 in the Mediterranean off the coast of Italy, is a fine example of Greek Classicism. The figure stands with its weight resting on one foot. As a result, the hip and shoulder lines are no longer in a frontal, parallel position; instead, they counterbalance one another. This form of balance is known as *contrapposto,* meaning counterposed. The Greeks and then the Romans used it to give a lifelike quality to figures at rest. Centuries later, their sculpture would inspire Renaissance artists to use the same technique.

Classical Greek sculpture was much more than the accurate representation of live models. Greek sculptors infused life into bronze or marble, guided by the ideal proportions they established for the depiction of human figures. The WARRIOR shows a balance between the ideal male figure and a convincing image of a man in the prime of life. Details include eyes of bone and glass-paste, bronze eyelashes, nipples of copper, and silver-plated teeth.

The city-state of Athens was the artistic and philosophical center of Classical Greek civilization. Above the city, on a large rock outcropping called the Acropolis, the Athenians constructed one of the world's most admired structures, the PARTHENON. Today, even in its ruined state, the PARTHENON continues to express the ideals of the people who created it.

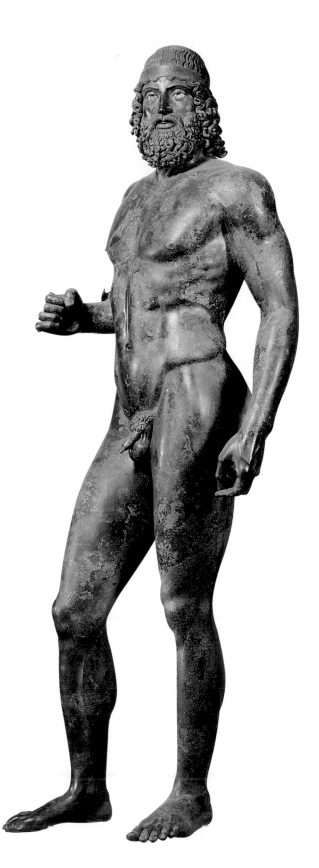

393 WARRIOR. 5th century B.C.E.
Riace bronze A, ¾ view. Height 78⅔".
Musea, Archeologica Naz. Reggia Calabria, Italy.
Scala/Art Resource, NY.

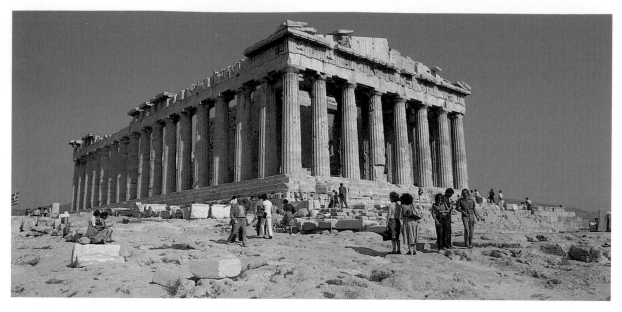

394   Ictinus and Callicrates. PARTHENON. Acropolis, Athens. 448–432 B.C.E.
   a. View from the northwest.

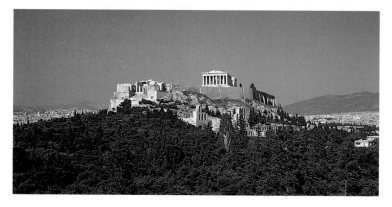

b. View from the southwest.
   Photographs: Duane Preble.

The largest of several sacred buildings on the Acropolis, the PARTHENON was designed and built as a gift to Athena Parthenos, goddess of wisdom, arts, industries, and prudent warfare, and protector of the Athenian navy.

When Ictinus and Callicrates designed the PARTHENON, they were following Egyptian tradition in temple design based on the post-and-beam system of construction (see page 232). In the PARTHENON, the Greek temple concept reached its highest form of development. The structure was located so that it could be seen against the sky, the mountains, or the sea from vantage points around the city, and it was the focal point for processions and large outdoor religious ceremonies. Rites were performed on altars placed in front of the eastern entrance. The interior space was designed to house a forty-foot statue of Athena. The axis of the building was carefully calculated so that on Athena's birthday the rising sun coming through the huge east doorway would fully illuminate the towering gold-covered statue.

In its original form, the PARTHENON exhibited the refined clarity, harmony, and vigor that are the basis of the Greek tradition. The proportions of the PARTHENON are based on harmonious ratios. The ratio of the height to the widths of the east and west ends is approximately 4 to 9. The ratio of the width to the length of the building is also 4 to 9. The diameter of the columns relates to the space between the columns at a ratio of 4 to 9, and so on.

None of the major lines of the building is perfectly straight. Many experts believe that the subtle deviations were designed to correct optical illusions. The columns have an almost imperceptible bulge (called *entasis*) above the center, which causes them to appear straighter than if they were in fact straight-sided, and this gives the entire structure a tangible grace. Even the steps and tops of doorways

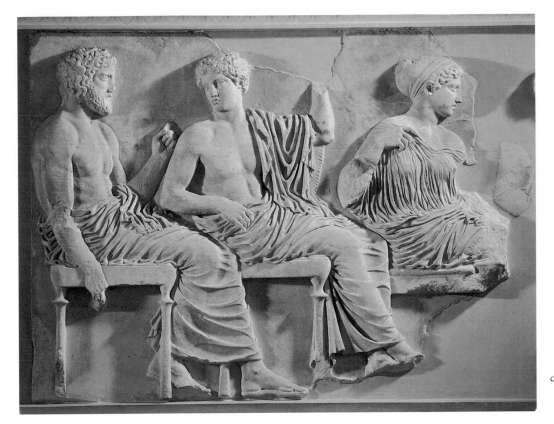

C. PARTHENON FRIEZE.
Poseidon, Apollo, and Artemis.
Photograph: Erich Lessing/Art Resource, NY.

rise slightly in perfect curves. Corner columns, seen against the light, are somewhat larger in diameter to counteract the diminishing effect of strong light in the background. The axis lines of the columns lean in a little at the top. If extended into space, these lines would converge 5856 feet above the building. These unexpected variations are not consciously seen, but they are felt, and they help make the building visually appealing.

The Greeks developed three ARCHITECTURAL ORDERS: Doric, Ionic, and Corinthian. Each order comprises a set of architectural elements and proportions. The most telling details for identification of the orders are the three types of *capitals* used at the tops of columns. Doric, which came first, is simple, geometric, and sturdy; Ionic is taller and more dynamic than Doric; Corinthian is complex and organic.

Although today we see Greek temples as white stone structures, some of the upper portions of exterior surfaces were once brightly painted. Parts of sculpture were also painted.

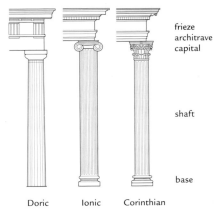

frieze
architrave
capital

shaft

base

Doric   Ionic   Corinthian

395   ARCHITECTURAL ORDERS.

Some of the finest Greek sculpture was made for the upper areas of the PARTHENON. Running along the exterior wall of the inner temple was a 524-foot-long relief sculpture of a procession in honor of Athena. As with the other figures on the frieze, the gods Poseidon, Apollo, and Artemis are depicted in ideal human form—noble and perfect.

396 VENUS DE MEDICI.
3rd century B.C.E.
Marble. Height 5'.
Uffizi Gallery, Florence.
Photograph: Scala/Art
Resource, NY.

VENUS DE MEDICI is a third-century B.C.E. Roman copy of a fourth-century B.C.E. Greek original. (Aphrodite, the Greek goddess of love and beauty, was known to the Romans as Venus.) The original sculpture was inspired by an Aphrodite by Praxitiles, one of the most famous sculptors of the Classical period. Because it was made to symbolize a goddess rather than to portray a real woman, the figure is more ideal than natural. Its refined profile is one of the most obvious features of the Greek idealization of human figures. But we can sense the emerging Hellenistic sensibility in the figure's sensuality—a mortal element foreign to Classical ideals.

After the decline of the Greek city-states at the end of the fourth century B.C.E., the art of the Mediterranean changed. Though it continued to be strongly influenced by earlier Greek art, and was often executed by Greek artists, it was produced for, and according to the preferences of, non-Greek patrons. Mediterranean art during this era is called *Hellenistic,* meaning Greek-like. The transition from Classical to Hellenistic coincided with the decline of Athens as a city-state after it fought a useless war with the neighboring city of Sparta, and with the rise of an absolute monarchy in Macedonia which soon took over the entire peninsula. Artists turned from the glorified idealizations of the Classical period to the subjective and imperfect aspects of life and humanity.

In the Hellenistic period, Greek art became more dynamic and less idealized. Everyday activities, historical subjects, myths, and portraiture were more common subjects for art than in the Classical period. Late, or Hellenistic, Greek art contrasts with Classical Greek art in that it is more expressive and frequently shows exaggerated movement.

THE LAOCOÖN GROUP is a Roman copy of a late Hellenistic work. In Greek mythology, Laocoön was the Trojan priest who warned against bringing the wooden horse into Troy during the Trojan War. Subsequently, he and his sons were attacked by serpents, an act the Trojans interpreted as a sign of the gods' disapproval of Laocoön's prophecy. Laocoön is shown in hierarchic proportion to his grown sons.

The rationalism, clarity, and restrained gestures of Classical sculpture have given way to writhing movement, tortured facial expressions, and strained muscles expressing emotional and physical anguish. When this sculpture was unearthed in Italy in 1506, it had an immediate influence on the young Michelangelo.

ROME

The Hellenistic era saw the rise of Rome, a formidable new force in the Mediterranean. By the second century B.C.E., Rome had become the major power in the Western world. At its height, the Roman Empire would include western Europe, North Africa, and the Near East as well as the shores of the Mediterranean (overleaf). The governance of a multitude of unique peoples and cultures was a prime example of the Roman genius for order and practical politics. Roman culture has affected our lives in many areas: our systems of law and government, our calendar, festivals, religions, and languages. We also inherited from the Romans the concept that art is worthy of historical study and critical appreciation.

The Romans were a practical, materialistic people, and their art reflects these characteristics. They made few changes in the general style of Greek art, which they admired, collected, and copied. But not all Roman art was imitative. Roman portraiture of the Republican period, such as the FEMALE PORTRAIT, achieved a high degree of individuality rarely found in Greek sculpture. The representationally accurate style probably grew out of the Roman custom of making wax death masks of ancestors for the family shrine or altar. Later, these images were recreated in marble to make them more durable. Roman sculptors observed and carefully recorded those physical details and imperfections that give character to each person's face.

The Romans' greatest artistic achievements were in civil engineering, town planning, and architecture. They created utilitarian and religious structures of impressive beauty and grandeur that were to have a major influence on subsequent Western architecture. As we saw in chapter 14, the

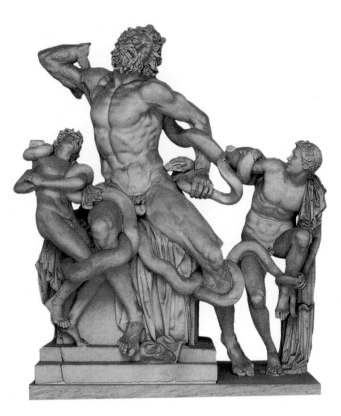

397   THE LAOCOÖN GROUP.
Roman copy of a 1st- or 2nd-century B.C.E. Greek original, perhaps after Agesander, Athenodorus, and Polydorus of Rhodes. c. 1st century C.E. Marble. Height 95¼".
Vatican Museum, Rome.
Photograph: Giraudon/Art Resource, NY.

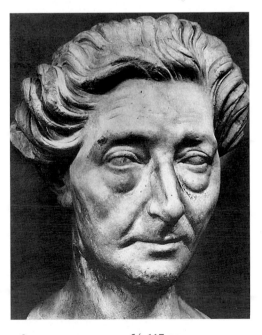

398   FEMALE PORTRAIT. c. 54–117 C.E.
Marble. Life-size.
Museo Profano Lateranese, Rome.
Photograph: Phaidon Press Limited, London.

399 PANTHEON. Rome. 118–125 C.E.
  a. View of the entrance.
    Photograph: Duane Preble.

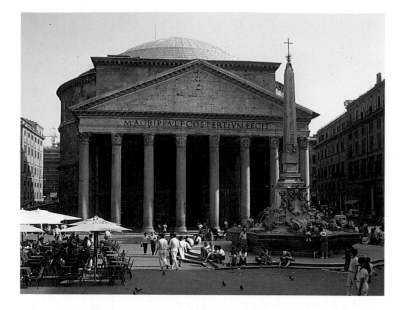

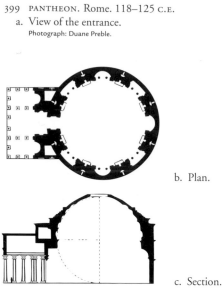

b. Plan.

c. Section.

outstanding feature of Roman architecture was the semicircular arch, which the Romans utilized and refined in the construction of arcades, barrel vaults, and domes (see the diagrams on pages 233–234).

By developing the structural use of concrete combined with semicircular arch and vault construction, the Romans were able to enclose large indoor spaces. Although a type of concrete was commonly used in Roman construction, the quality of cement (the chemically active ingredient in concrete) declined during the Middle Ages, and concrete was not widely used again until it was redeveloped in the nineteenth century.

In the PANTHEON, a major temple dedicated to all the gods, Roman builders created a domed interior space of immense scale. The building is essentially a cylinder, capped by a hemispherical dome, with a single entrance framed by a Greek porch, or *portico.*

Whereas Greek temples such as the PARTHENON were designed both as inner sanctuaries for priests and as focal points for outdoor religious cere-

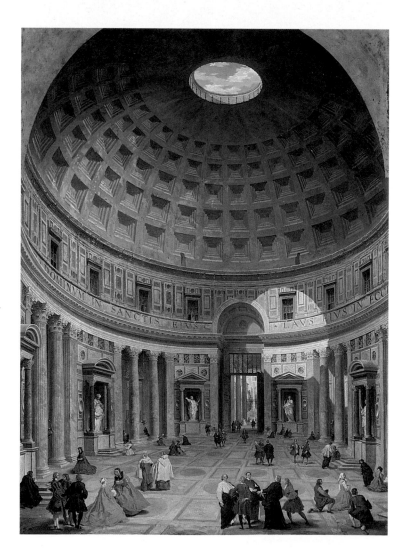

400 Giovanni Paolo Panini (Roman, 1691–1765).
    THE INTERIOR OF THE PANTHEON, ROME. c. 1734.
    Oil on canvas. 50½" × 39"; framed 56¾" × 45"
    Samuel H. Kress Collection.
    Photograph: Richard Carafelli.
    © 2001 Board of Trustees, National Gallery of Art, Washington, D.C.
    1939.1.24.(135)/PA.

monies, the PANTHEON was built as a magnificent, awe-inspiring interior space that complemented its once opulent exterior. To meet their preference for spacious interiors, the Romans developed many other great domed and vaulted buildings.

The PANTHEON's circular walls, which support the huge dome, are stone and concrete masonry, twenty feet thick and faced with brick. The dome diminishes in thickness toward the crown, and it is patterned on the interior surface with recessed squares called *coffers,* which both lighten and strengthen the structure. Originally covered with gold, the coffered ceiling symbolizes the dome of heaven. It was designed so that the distance from the summit to the floor is equal to the 143-foot diameter—making it a virtual globe of space. At the dome's crown, an opening called an *oculus,* or eye, thirty feet in diameter, provides daylight and ventilation to the interior. Neither verbal description nor views of the exterior and interior can evoke the awe one experiences upon entering the PANTHEON.

Wall paintings are among the most interesting art produced during the period of the Roman Empire. The majority known to us come from Pompeii, Herculaneum, or other towns buried—and thus preserved—by the eruption of Mt. Vesuvius in 79 C.E. In the first century, Roman artists continued the late Greek tradition of portraying depth in paintings of landscapes and urban views. The ROMAN PAINTING from a villa near Naples presents a complex urban scene painted with an unsystematic form of perspective. As is typical of Roman painting, the receding lines are not systematically related to one another to create a sense of common space, nor is there controlled use of the effect of diminishing size relative to distance. Compare this painting with Raphael's SCHOOL OF ATHENS on page 53. Perhaps the artist intended viewers simply to enjoy the pleasing interwoven shapes, patterns, colors, and varied scale rather than to "enter" the illusory space. After the collapse of the Roman Empire, even such suggestions of space were no longer applied, and the knowledge was forgotten until it was rediscovered and developed as a scientific system during the Renaissance, more than one thousand years later.

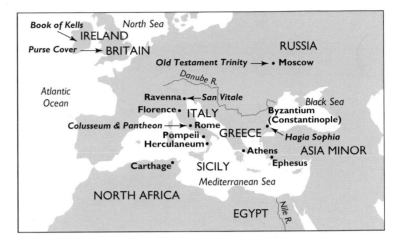

401   EUROPE FROM 117 TO 1400.

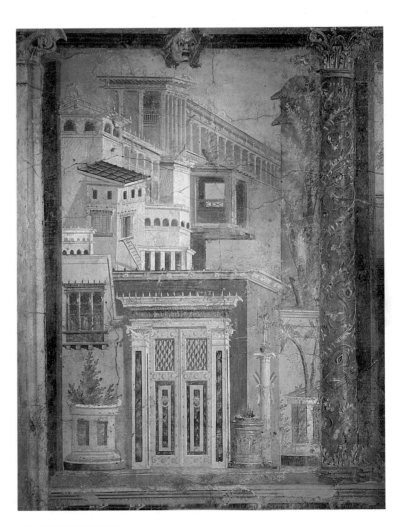

402   ROMAN PAINTING.
Detail of west wall in a villa at Boscoreale. 1st century B.C.E.
Fresco on lime plaster. Height: 8'.
The Metropolitan Museum of Art, New York. Rogers Fund, 1903. (03.14.13)
Photograph: © 1986 The Metropolitan Museum of Art.

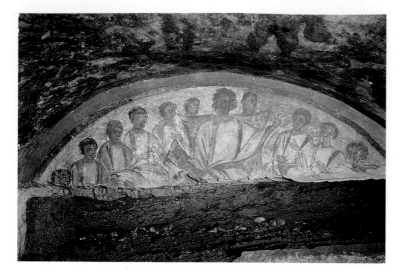

403 CHRIST TEACHING HIS DISCIPLES.
Catacomb of Domitilla, Rome. Mid-4th century C.E.
Photograph: Scala/Art Resource, NY.

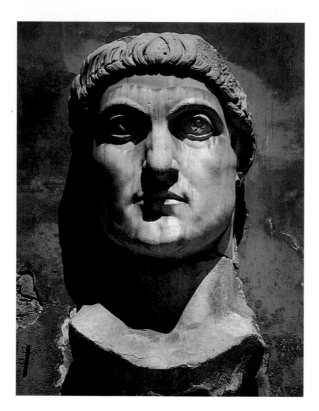

404 HEAD OF CONSTANTINE.
c. 312 C.E.
Marble. Height 8'.
Museo dei Conservatori, Rome.
Photograph: Duane Preble.

EARLY CHRISTIAN AND BYZANTINE ART

The Romans first regarded Christianity as a strange cult and suppressed it through law. Since it was illegal to be Christian, the followers of Christ were forced to worship and hide their art in underground burial chambers called *catacombs*. Images were often made by relatively untrained painters. The earliest Christian art was a simplified interpretation of Greco-Roman figure painting. The emphasis was on storytelling through images of Christ and other biblical figures as well as through Christian symbols. In contrast to major changes in the size relationships between figures *(hierarchical scale)* in later Byzantine art, CHRIST TEACHING HIS DISCIPLES shows Christ only slightly larger than the faithful who surround him.

By the time Emperor Constantine acknowledged Christianity in 312, Roman attitudes had changed considerably. The grandeur of Rome was rapidly declining. As confidence in the material world fell, people turned inward to more spiritual values. The new orientation was reflected in art such as the colossal marble HEAD OF CONSTANTINE, once part of an immense figure. The superhuman head is an image of imperial majesty, yet the large eyes and immobile features express an inner spiritual life. The late Roman style of the facial features, particularly the eyes, is very different from the naturalism of earlier Roman portraits.

In 330, Constantine moved the capital of the Roman Empire east from Rome to the city of Byzantium, which he renamed Constantinople (present-day Istanbul). Although he could not have known it, the move would effectively split the empire in two. In 395, the Roman Empire was officially divided, with one emperor in Rome and another in Constantinople—the center of what became known as Byzantium or the Byzantine Empire. Over the course of the next century, the entire Empire was repeatedly attacked by nomadic Germanic tribes. They placed one of their own on the Imperial throne in 476.

Byzantium successfully repelled its invaders; Rome was not so fortunate. Under relentless attack from the Germanic tribes, and weakened from within by military rebellions and civil wars, the Western Roman Empire decayed and collapsed, ushering in the era in Europe known as the Middle Ages.

The eastern portion of the empire, however, did not collapse. Indeed, the Byzantine Empire survived well into the fifteenth century. Founded as a Christian continuation of the Roman Empire, Byzantium developed a rich and distinctive artistic style that continues today in the mosaics, paintings, and architecture of the Orthodox church of Eastern Europe.

Not only did Constantine grant Christianity official recognition, he also sponsored an extensive building program. Thus, in the late Roman and early Byzantine empires, we find the first great flowering of Christian art and architecture. For example, Christians adapted the Roman *basilica*, or assembly hall, for use in public worship. So begins the history of Christian church architecture. For the Romans, a basilica was a long hall flanked by columns with a semicircular *apse* at each end where government bodies and law courts met. One of the earliest Christian churches built was OLD ST. PETER'S BASILICA in Rome. Its long central aisle, now called the *nave*, ends in an apse, as in a Roman building. Here, Christians placed an altar.

Round or polygonal buildings crowned with domes had been used in earlier buildings such as Roman baths, and later in the PANTHEON. Beginning in the fourth century, such buildings were built for Christian services and took on Christian meaning. Domed, central-plan churches have dominated the architecture of Eastern Orthodox Christianity ever since.

In contrast to the external grandeur of Greek and Roman temples, early Christian churches were built with an inward focus. Their plain exteriors gave no hint of the light and beauty that lay inside.

The rapid construction of many large churches created a need for large paintings or other decorations to fill their walls. Mosaic technique (used by the Sumerians in the third millennium B.C.E. and later by the Greeks and Romans) was perfected and widely used in Early Christian churches. While

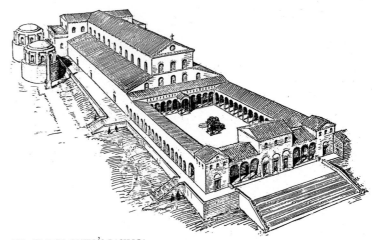

405 OLD ST. PETER'S BASILICA.
Rome. c. 320–335.

a. Reconstruction drawing.
Restoration study by Kenneth J. Conant.
Courtesy of the Francis Loeb Library, Graduate School of Design, Harvard University.

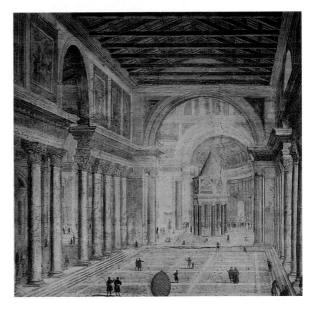

b. Interior view of basilica of Saint Peter's.
Fresco. S. Martino ai Monti, Rome, Italy
Photograph: Scala/Art Resource, NY.

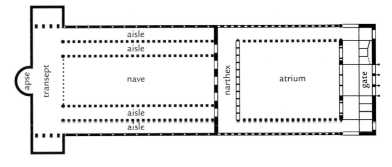

c. Plan.

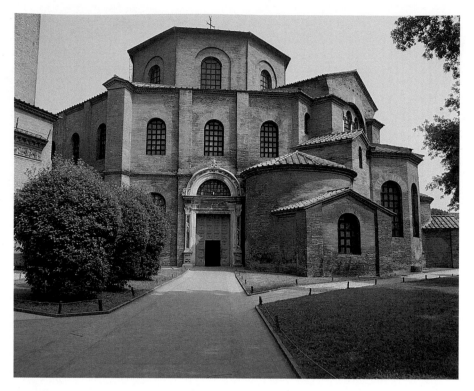

406 SAN VITALE. Ravenna, Italy. 526–547.

a. Exterior.
Photograph: Guglielmo Mairani/Garzla Nevi.

b. Plan.

other cultures knew of the art of attaching pieces of colored glass and marble (tesserae) to walls and floors, early Christians used smaller tesserae, with a greater proportion of glass, in a wider range of colors. Thus they achieved a new level of brilliance and opulence.

Ravenna, Italy, was briefly the capital of the Western Roman Empire (402–476), and was then recovered by Justinian for the Byzantine Empire (540–751). The many mosaics created in Ravenna in the fifth and sixth centuries show the transition from Early Christian to Byzantine style.

The most important sixth-century church is SAN VITALE in Ravenna. The glittering mosaic compositions that cover most of the interior surfaces depict the figures of Emperor Justinian and EMPRESS THEODORA in addition to religious figures and events. In a blending of religious and political authority, Justinian and Theodora are shown with halos, analogous to Christ and Mary, yet both are royally attired and bejeweled.

The elongated, abstracted figures provide symbolic rather than naturalistic depictions of the Christian and royal figures. Emphasis on the eyes is a Byzantine refinement of the stylized focus seen in the HEAD OF CONSTANTINE (page 274). Figures are depicted with heavy outline and stylized shading. The only suggestion of space has been made by overlap. Background and figures retain a flat, decorative richness typical of Byzantine art.

The arts of the Early Christian period were affected by an ongoing controversy between those who sought to follow the biblical prohibition against the making of images and those who wanted pictures to help tell the sacred stories. The Byzantine style developed as a way of inspiring the

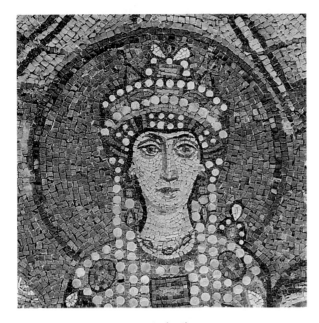

C. EMPRESS THEODORA. Mosaic detail.
Photographs: Scala/Art Resource, NY.

illiterate while keeping the biblical commandment that forbids the making of graven images. The Byzantine theory was that highly stylized (abstract) and decorative images could never be confused with a real person (as a naturalistic work might be). As a result, the naturalism and sense of depth found in Roman painting gradually gave way to Byzantine stylization.

By the tenth and eleventh centuries, Byzantine artists had created a distinct style that expressed Eastern Orthodox Christianity and also met the needs of a lavish court. The style had its roots in the Early Christian art of the late Roman Empire, as we have seen. But it also absorbed Eastern influences, particularly the flat patterns and nonrepresentational designs of Islam. Eastern influence continued with the hierarchical sizing and placement of subject matter in Byzantine church decoration.

After the ninth century, the inside of the dome of Hagia Sophia (see page 234) was adorned with a new kind of image, Christ as ruler of the universe—Christ as Pantocrator. This mosaic (now destroyed) became the inspiration for similar portrayals in smaller Byzantine churches such as

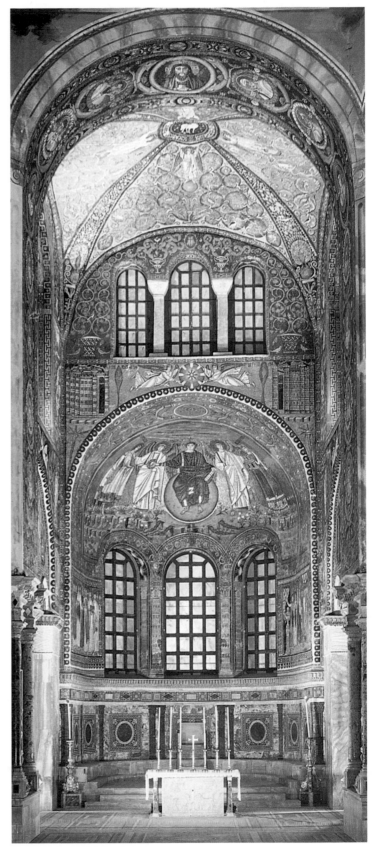

d. Interior.
Art Resource, NY.

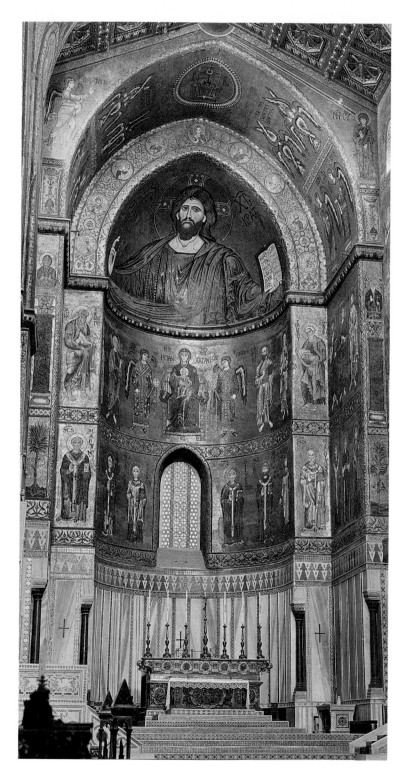

the Cathedral of Monreale, Sicily, where the mosaic of CHRIST AS PANTOCRATOR WITH MARY AND SAINTS shows typical Byzantine style employing hierarchic scale to express the greater magnitude of Christ relative to Mary, the saints, and angels portrayed in rows below him.

A row of windows circles the base of the dome, bringing light to the church interior. The effect of the mosaic surfaces depends on the direction of light from the windows and from artificial sources such as candlelight; each small tessera was placed on the adhesive surface and tilted to catch the light, producing a shimmering effect.

The Byzantine style is still followed by painters and others working within the tradition of the Eastern Orthodox church. Clergy closely supervise the iconography and permit little room for individual interpretation. Artists of the Eastern Orthodox faith seek to portray the symbolic or mystical aspects of religious figures rather than their physical qualities. The figures are painted in conformity to a precise formula. Small paintings, referred to as *icons* (from the Greek *eikon,* meaning image), are holy images that inspire devotion but are not worshiped in themselves. The making of portable icon paintings grew out of mosaic and fresco traditions.

Even within the relatively tight stylistic confines of the Orthodox style, occasionally an artist is able to make icons that not only have the required easy readability but also communicate powerful feeling. Such an artist was Andrei Rublev, one of the most highly regarded painters in Russian history. His OLD TESTAMENT TRINITY depicts a story in which Jewish patriarch Abraham entertained three strangers who later turned out to be angels: Christians have seen this story as foreshadowing their doctrine of the trinity. Rublev was able to give the scene a sweetness and tenderness through subtle facial expressions and elongation of bodies. The bright colors add intensity to the work, even in its present poor state.

407 CHRIST AS PANTOCRATOR WITH MARY AND SAINTS.
Apse mosaic. Cathedral of Monreale, Sicily.
Late 12th century.
Photograph: Scala/Art Resource, NY.

The design of the icon painting MADONNA AND CHILD ON A CURVED THRONE is based on circular shapes and linear patterns. Mary's head repeats the circular shape of her halo; circles of similar size enclose angels, echoing the larger circle of the throne. The lines and shapes used in the draped robes that cover the figures give scarcely a hint of the bodies beneath. Divine light is symbolized by the gold background that surrounds the throne in which the Virgin Mary sits. The large architectural throne symbolizes Mary's position as Queen of the City of Heaven. Christ appears as a wise little man, supported on the lap of a heavenly, supernatural mother.

In order that they be worthy of dedication to God, icons are usually made of precious materials. Gold leaf was used here for the background and costly lapis lazuli for the Virgin's robe.

THE MIDDLE AGES IN EUROPE

The one thousand years that followed the fall of the Western Roman Empire have been called the medieval period, or the Middle Ages, because they came between the time of ancient Greek and Roman civilizations and the rebirth, or renaissance, of Greco-Roman ideas in the fifteenth century.

Early Medieval Art

The art of the early Middle Ages took shape as Early Christian art absorbed a new influence: the art of the invaders. Many nomadic peoples traveled across the Eurasian grasslands called the Steppes, which extend from the Danube River in Europe to the borders of China. Their migrations occurred over a long period that began in the second millennium B.C.E. and lasted well into the Middle Ages.

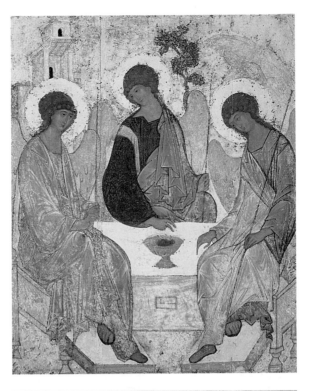

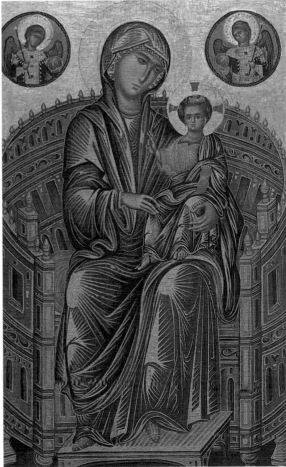

408 Andrei Rublev.
    OLD TESTAMENT TRINITY. c. 1410–1420.
    Tempera on panel. 55½" × 44½"
    Tretyakov Gallery, Moscow.
    Photograph: Scala/Art Resource, NY.

409 Byzantine School. MADONNA AND CHILD ON A
    CURVED THRONE. Byzantine, 13th century.
    Tempera on panel.
    32⅛" × 19⅜"; framed 35¾" × 22¹⁵⁄₁₆" × 3.
    Photograph © 2001 Board of Trustees, National Gallery of Art, Washington, D.C.
    Andrew W. Mellon Collection. 1937.1.1.(1)/PA.

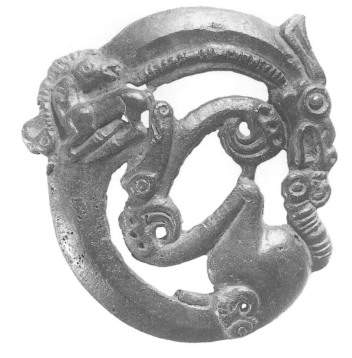

410 SCYTHIAN ANIMAL.
5th century B.C.E.
Bronze. Diameter 4".
The State Hermitage Museum, St. Petersburg, Russia.

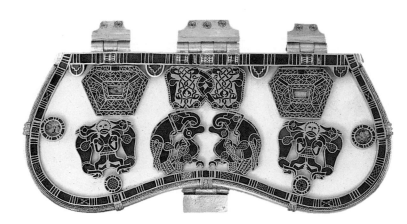

411 PURSE COVER.
From the Sutton Hoo Ship Burial, Suffolk, England.
Before 655.
Gold and enamel. Length 7½".
© British Museum, London.
Reproduced courtesy of the Trustees of the British Museum.

The Greeks called these nomads (and other non-Greeks) "barbarians." What little we know about them is derived from artifacts and records of literate cultures of the Mediterranean, Near East, and China, to whom the nomads were a menace. The Great Wall of China and Hadrian's Wall in Britain were built to keep out such invaders.

A long-lasting, varied, but interrelated art, known as the *animal style,* was developed by the Eurasian nomads. Because of their migrant way of life, their art consisted of small, easily portable objects such as items for personal adornment, weapons, and ornamental horse fittings for saddles, bridles, and harnesses. The style is characterized by active, intertwining shapes. The art of the animal style rarely depicts human beings; when it does, they play subordinate roles to animals.

Nomadic metalwork often exhibits exceptional skill. Because of frequent migrations and the durability and value of the art objects, the style was diffused over large geographic areas. Among the best-known works of nomadic art are small gold and bronze ornaments produced by the Scythians, whose culture flourished between the eighth and fourth centuries B.C.E. Their abstracted animal forms appear to have been adopted by groups in the British Isles, Scandinavia, and China. In the art of medieval Europe, similar animal forms appear later in woodcarving, stonecarving, and manuscript illumination, as well as in metal.

The gold and enamel PURSE COVER found in a grave at Sutton Hoo belonged to a seventh-century East Anglian king. The distinct variations of its motifs indicate that they are derived from several sources. The motif of a man standing between confronting animals appeared first in Sumerian art over three thousand years earlier (see page 262).

The meeting of decorative nomadic styles with Christianity can be seen most clearly in the illuminated holy books created in Ireland. The Irish had never been part of the Roman Empire, and in the fifth century they were Christianized without first becoming Romanized. During the chaotic centuries that followed the fall of Rome, Irish monasteries became the major centers of learning and the arts in Europe, and they produced numerous hand-lettered copies of religious manuscripts.

The initial letters in these manuscripts were embellished over time, moving first into the margin and then onto a separate page. This splendid initial page is the opening of St. Matthew's account of the Nativity in the BOOK OF KELLS, which contains the Latin Gospels. It is known as the CHI-RHO MONOGRAM because it is composed of the first two letters of Christ in Greek (XP) and is used to represent Christ or Christianity. Except for XP and two Latin words beginning the story of Christ's birth, most of the page is filled with a rich complexity of spirals and tiny interlacings. If we look closely at the knots and scrolls we see angels to the left of the X, a man's head in the P, and cats and mice at the base.

Romanesque

The stylistic term *Romanesque* was first used to designate European Christian architecture of the mid-eleventh to the mid-twelfth centuries, which revived Roman principles of stone construction, especially the round arch and the barrel vault. This term is now applied to all medieval art of western Europe during that period.

Byzantine art traditions continued in Southeastern Europe, while Romanesque art developed in a Western Europe dominated by feudalism and monasticism. Feudalism involved a complex system of obligations to provide services through personal agreements among local leaders of varying ranks. In addition to accommodating religious practices, monasteries provided shelter from a hostile world and served as the main sources of education.

Religious crusades and pilgrimages brought large groups of Christians to remote places, creating a need for larger churches. Romanesque builders increased the sizes of churches by doubling the length of the nave (the central space), doubling the side aisles, and building galleries above side aisles.

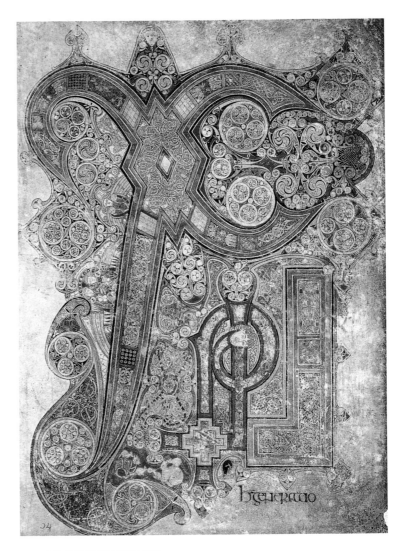

412 CHI-RHO MONOGRAM (XP).
Page from the BOOK OF KELLS.
Late 8th century.
The Board of Trinity College Library, Dublin, Ireland.
Reproduced courtesy of the Board of Trinity College Library.

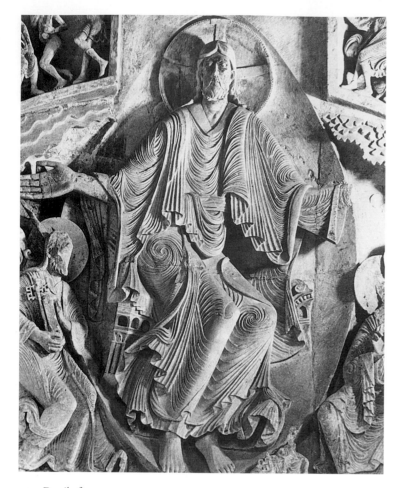

413 Detail of CHRIST OF THE PENTECOST.
Saint Madeleine Cathedral, Vézelay, France. 1125–1150.
Stone. Height of the tympanum 35½".

From *Art East and West* by Benjamin Rowland. Reproduced by
permission of the President and Fellows of Harvard University.

Churches continued to have wooden roofs, but stone vaults largely replaced fire-prone wooden ceilings, giving the new structures a close resemblance to Roman interiors. Consistent throughout the variety of regional styles was a common feeling of security provided by massive, fortresslike walls.

Romanesque churches feature imaginative stone carvings that are an integral part of the architecture. Subjects and models came from miniature paintings in illuminated texts, but sculptors gradually added a degree of naturalism not found in earlier medieval work. In addition to stylized and at times naive figures from biblical stories, relief carvings include strange beasts and decorative plant forms. The largest and most elaborate figures were placed over the central doorways of churches. Such figures were the first large sculpture since Roman times.

Deviation from standard human proportions enabled sculptors to give appropriately symbolic form to figures such as CHRIST OF THE PENTECOST. The mystical energy and compassion of Christ are expressed in this relief carving above the doorway of Saint Madeleine Cathedral at Vézelay, France. As worshippers enter the sanctuary, the image above them depicts Christ at the time he asked the Apostles and all Christians to take his message to the world. The image of Christ is larger in scale than the other figures, showing his relative importance. The sculptor achieved a monumental quality by making the head smaller than normal and by elongating the entire figure. Swirling folds of drapery are indicated with precise curves and spirals that show the continuing influence of the linear energy of the animal style and the CHI-RHO MONOGRAM. In abstract terms, the spiraling motion suggests Christ's cosmic power.

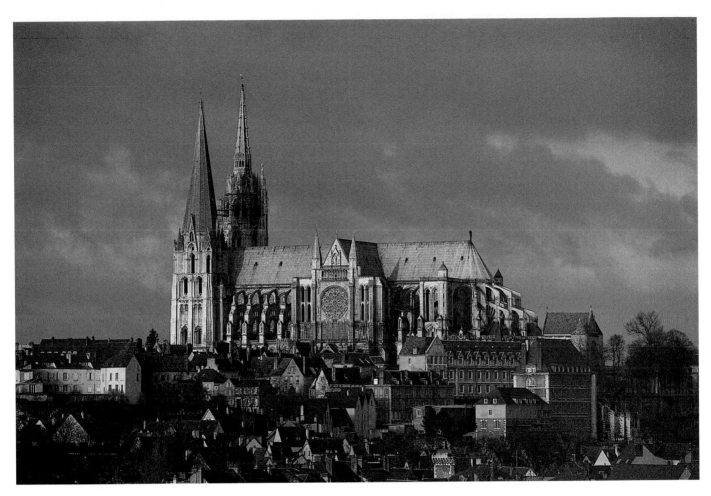

414 NOTRE DAME DE CHARTRES.
    Chartres, France. 1145–1513.
    Cathedral length 427'; facade height 157';
    south tower height 344'; north tower height 377'.
  a. View from the southeast.
    Photograph: © Adam Woolfitt, Sharpturn Productions.

Gothic

One of the major differences between the cultures of the East and the West is the restless energy of Europeans. This restless energy caused frequent changes in attitude that resulted in the changing styles of Western art. The Romanesque style had lasted barely a hundred years when the Gothic style began to replace it in about 1145. The shift is seen most clearly in architecture, as the Romanesque round arch was superseded by the pointed Gothic arch, developed in the mid-twelfth century (discussed on page 235).

Gothic cathedrals were expressions of a new age of faith that grew out of medieval Christian theology and mysticism. The light-filled, upward-reaching structures symbolize the triumph of the spirit over the bonds of earthly life, evoking a sense of joyous spiritual elation. Inside, the faithful must have felt they had actually arrived at the visionary Heavenly City.

Gothic cathedrals such as NOTRE DAME DE CHARTRES (Our Lady of Chartres) were the center of community life. In many cases, they were the only indoor space that could hold all the townspeople at once; thus, they were used for meetings, concerts, and religious plays. But most of all, they were places of worship. Above the town of Chartres, the cathedral rises, its spires visible for miles around.

The entire community cooperated in the building of NOTRE DAME DE CHARTRES, although those who began its construction never saw it in its final form. The cathedral continued to grow and change in major ways for over three hundred years. Although the basic plan is symmetrical and logically

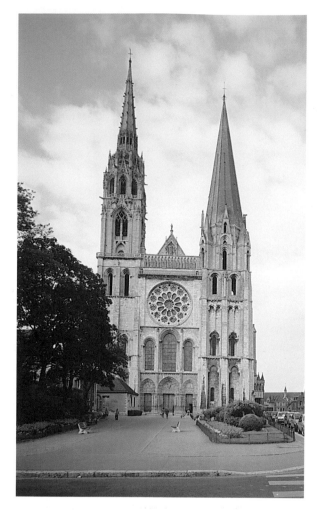

b. WEST FRONT.
Photograph: Duane Preble.

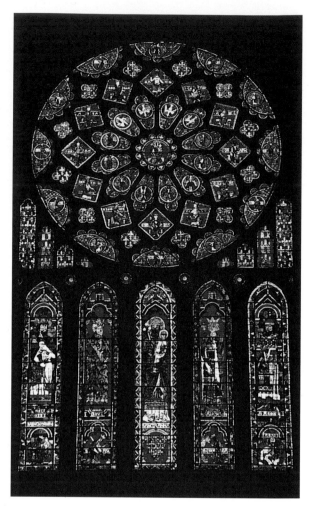

c. "ROSE DE FRANCE" WINDOW. c. 1233.
Photograph: Duane Preble.

organized, the architecture of CHARTRES has a rich, enigmatic complexity that is quite different from the easily grasped totality of the classical PARTHENON.

Chartres was partially destroyed by fire in 1194 and was rebuilt in the High Gothic style. One of the first cathedrals based on the full Gothic system, it helped set the standard for Gothic architecture in Europe. In its WEST FRONT, Chartres reveals the transition between the early and late phases of Gothic architecture. The massive lower walls and round arch portals were built in the mid-twelfth century. The north tower (on the left as one approaches the facade) was rebuilt with the intricate flamelike or *flamboyant* curves of the late Gothic style early in the sixteenth century, after the original tower collapsed in 1506.

Magnificent stained-glass windows of this period are so well integrated with the architecture that one is inconceivable without the other. The scriptures are told in imagery that transforms the sanctuary with showers of color, changing hour by hour. At Chartres, the brilliant north rose window, known as the ROSE DE FRANCE, is dedicated to the Virgin Mary, who sits in majesty, surrounded by doves, angels, and royal figures of the celestial hierarchy.

The statues of the OLD TESTAMENT PROPHET, KINGS, AND QUEEN to the right of the central doorway at the west entrance of CHARTRES are among the most impressive remaining examples of early Gothic sculpture. The kings and queen suggest Christ's royal heritage and also honor French monarchs of the time. The prophet on the left depicts Christ's mission as an apostle of God. In contrast to active, emotional Romanesque sculpture, the figures are passive and serene. Their elongated forms allow them to blend readily with the vertical emphasis of the architecture.

Although they are part of the total scheme, the figures stand out from the columns behind them. Their draped bodies, and especially their heads, reveal a developing interest in portraying human features. Such interest eventually led again to full portraiture and freestanding figures.

The temple relates to an idea expressed by Abbot Suger, the man credited with starting the Gothic era. At the Abbey church of St. Denis, where Suger began the Gothic style, he had an inscription placed on the entrance door stating his idea of the church's spiritual purpose:

*Whoever you may be, if you are minded to praise this
    door,*
*Wonder not at the gold, nor at the cost, but at the
    work.*
The work shines in its nobility; by shining nobly,
*May it illumine the spirit, so that, through its trusty
    lights,*
*The spirit may reach the true Light in which Christ
    is the Door.*
The golden door proclaims the nature of the Inward:
*Through sensible things, the heavy spirit is raised to
    the truth;*
From the depths, it rises to the light.[1]

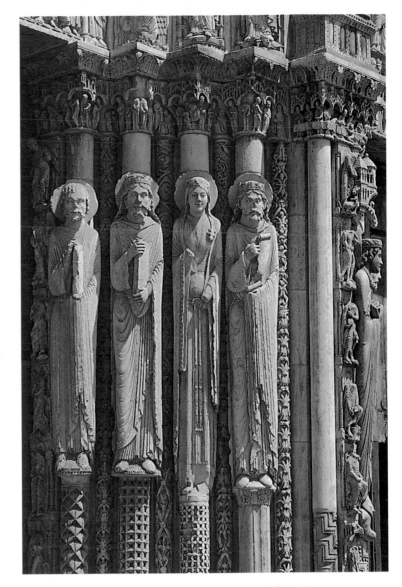

d. OLD TESTAMENT PROPHET, KINGS, AND QUEEN. c. 1145–1170.
Doorjamb statues from West (or Royal) Portal.
Photograph: Duane Preble.

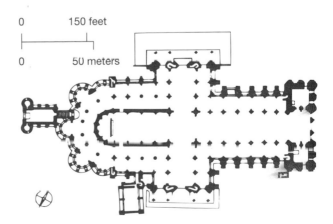

e. Plan based on Latin cross.

CHAPTER SEVENTEEN

RENAISSANCE AND BAROQUE EUROPE

A shift in attitude occurred in Europe as the religious fervor of the Middle Ages was increasingly challenged by logical thought and the new philosophical, literary, and artistic movement called *humanism*. Leading humanist scholars did not discard theological concerns, yet they supported the secular dimensions of life, pursued intellectual and scientific inquiry, and rediscovered the classical literature of Greece and Rome. The focus gradually shifted from God and the hereafter to humankind and the here and now.

THE RENAISSANCE

For many Europeans, the Renaissance was a period of achievement and worldwide exploration—a time of discovery and rediscovery of the world and of the seemingly limitless potential of individual human beings. The period began to take shape in the fourteenth century, reached its clear beginning in the early fifteenth century, and came to an end in the early seventeenth century. However, Renaissance thinking continues to influence our lives today, not only in Western countries but in all parts of the world where individualism, modern science, and technology influence the way people live. In art, new and more scientific approaches were brought to the quest for representational accuracy. The resulting naturalism dominated Western art for more than four hundred years.

The intellectuals of the time were the first in European history to give their own era an identifying name. They named their period the *Renaissance* — literally, Rebirth—an apt description for the period of revived interest in the art and ideas of classical Greece and Rome. Fifteenth-century Italians believed they were responsible for the rebirth of "the glory of ancient Greece," which they considered the high point of Western civilization. Yet Greco-Roman culture was not really reborn, because this "classical" heritage had never disappeared from the medieval West where Muslim scholars in Spain and Constantinople succeeded in keeping it alive. In essence, the Renaissance was a period of new and renewed understanding that transformed the medieval world, and laid the foundation for modern society.

In art, we can trace the beginnings of this new attitude to the fourteenth century. While Gothic and Byzantine painters continued to employ relatively flat symbolic styles, Gothic sculptors were moving from stylized abstraction toward greater naturalism and individuality in their figures.

The humanist enthusiasm for classical antiquity and a growing secularism led to revolutionary thinking in many areas. The first writer to reveal evidence of Renaissance thinking was the Italian poet Dante Alighieri, who lived during the thirteenth and fourteenth centuries and belonged primarily to the Middle Ages. The last major writer of the Renaissance was William Shakespeare, who lived three centuries later.

New values combined with technological advances brought forth an abundance of major artworks. Painting and sculpture were liberated from their medieval roles as supplements to architecture. Artists, who had been viewed as anonymous workers in the Middle Ages, came to be seen as individuals of creative genius.

The art of the Renaissance evolved in different ways in Northern and Southern Europe because the people of the two regions had different backgrounds, attitudes, and experiences. The Gothic style reached its high point in the north while Byzantine and Greco-Roman influences remained strong in the south. Italian Renaissance art grew from classical Mediterranean traditions that were human-centered and often emphasized monumentality and the ideal. In contrast, the art of the Northern Renaissance evolved out of pre-Christian, nature-centered religions that became God-centered through conversion to Christianity.

New directions in the course of human history are often begun by a small group or a single person of genius who seizes the opportunity that changing circumstances present. Such a person was Italian painter and architect Giotto di Bondone, known as Giotto. He departed from the abstract Byzantine style by portraying the feelings and physical nature of human beings. His innovative depictions of light, space, and mass gave a new sense of realism to painting. In LAMENTATION, Giotto depicted physical as well as spiritual reality. His figures are shown as individuals within a shallow, stagelike space, and their expressions portray personal feelings of grief not often seen in medieval art.

In retrospect, Giotto is considered not only a precursor of the Renaissance, but also the reinventor of naturalistic painting, which had not been seen in Europe since the decline of Rome a thousand years earlier. This "realism" is still an important current in Western painting.

The ancient Greeks had been concerned with idealized physical form; Roman artists had emphasized physical accuracy; and artists of the Middle Ages had focused on spiritual concerns rather than physical existence. In the Renaissance, as attention

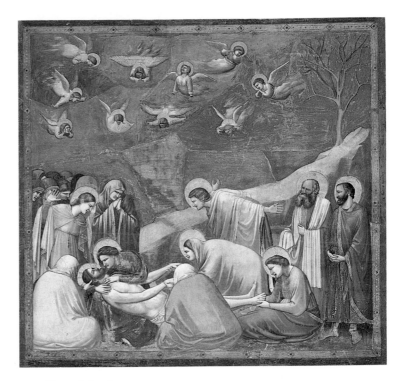

415　Giotto di Bondone. LAMENTATION.
Scrovegni Chapel, Padua, Italy. c. 1305.
Fresco. 72" × 78".
Photograph: Alinari/Art Resource, NY.

shifted from heaven to earth, artists portrayed Christian subjects in human terms. Italian leaders expressed a desire to equal or surpass the glory of ancient Greece and Rome and to imbue their achievements with the light of Christian understanding.

Italy was the principal homeland of the Renaissance. In time the movement spread northward, but it did not flourish everywhere in the West; it came late to Spain and Portugal, and it barely touched Scandinavia.

The Renaissance in Italy

Artistic and intellectual developments in the Italian city-states were aided by a flourishing economy set against a divided and chaotic political background. The great wealth of Italian merchants enabled them to compete with one another, and with church officials and nobility, for the recognition and power that came with art patronage.

Italian architects, sculptors, and painters sought to integrate Christian spiritual traditions with the rational ordering of physical life in earthly space.

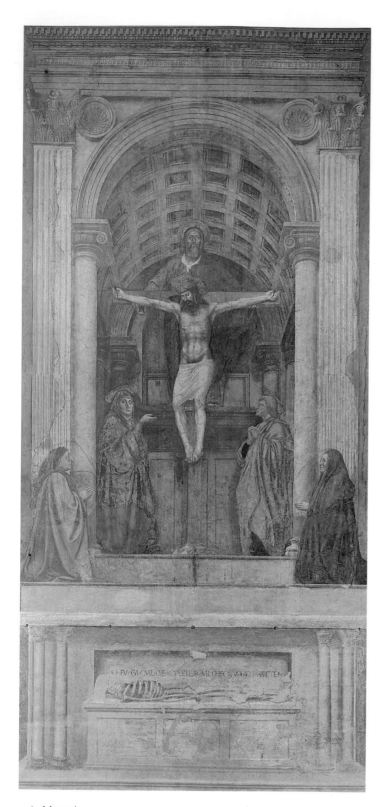

416 Masaccio.
THE HOLY TRINITY.
Santa Maria Novella, Florence. 1425.
Fresco. 21'10½" × 10'5".
Photograph: Scala/Art Resource, NY.

Artists began an intense study of anatomy and light, and they applied geometry to the logical construction of implied space through the use of linear perspective (see page 53). In turn, the careful observation of nature initiated by Renaissance artists aided the growth of science.

About one hundred years after Giotto, Masaccio became the first major painter of the Italian Renaissance. In his fresco THE HOLY TRINITY, the composition is centered on an open chapel in which is seen the Trinity: God the father, Christ the son, and between their heads a white dove symbolizing the Holy Spirit. Within the niche, Mary the mother of Jesus stands, gesturing to Christ; opposite her is St. John. Kneeling outside are the donors who paid for the painting, a husband and wife who headed a powerful banking family of that time. He is wearing the red robe that marks him as a member of the Florence city council. Below, a skeleton is lying on a sarcophagus beneath the inscription, "I was what you are, and what I am you shall become." If we view the painting from top to bottom, we move from spiritual reality to temporal reality.

THE HOLY TRINITY was the first painting based on the systematic use of linear perspective. Although perspective was known to the Romans in a limited way, it did not become a consistent science until architect Filippo Brunelleschi rediscovered and developed it in Florence early in the fifteenth century. Masaccio used perspective to construct an illusion of figures in three-dimensional space. The single vanishing point is below the base of the cross, about five feet above ground, at the viewer's eye level. Masaccio's perspective measurements were so precise that we can compute the dimensions of the interior of the illusionary chapel, which we see as a believable extension of the space occupied by the viewer. The setting also reveals Masaccio's knowledge of the new Renaissance architecture developed by Brunelleschi, which he based on Roman prototypes.

The figures in THE HOLY TRINITY have a physical presence that shows what Masaccio learned from the work of Giotto. In Giotto's work, however, body and drapery still appear as one; Masaccio's figures are clothed nudes, with garments draped like real fabric.

During the Italian Renaissance, the nude became a major subject for art, as it had been in Greece and Rome. Unclothed subjects are rare in medieval art (Adam and Eve, sinners in hell) and appear awkward, their bodies graceless. In contrast, sculpted and painted figures by Italian Renaissance artists appear as strong and natural as the Greek and Roman nudes that inspired them.

The great range and vitality of work by sculptor Donatello had a lasting influence on subsequent Renaissance sculpture and on European sculpture and painting for four centuries. Donatello brought the Greek ideal of what it means to be human into the Christian context. As a young adult he made two trips to Rome, where he studied medieval (Byzantine, Romanesque, and Gothic) as well as classical Greek and Roman art.

Donatello shows himself as a well-developed artist even in his early work. His bronze figure of DAVID was the first life-size, freestanding nude statue since Roman times. In it Donatello went beyond the classical ideal by including the dimension of personal expressiveness.

Although he was greatly attracted to the classical ideal in art, Donatello's sculpture was less idealized and more naturalistic than that of ancient Greece. He chose to portray the biblical shepherd, David—slayer of the giant Goliath and later to be king of the Jews—as an adolescent youth rather than as a robust young man. The sculptor celebrated the sensuality of the boy's body by clothing him only in hat and boots. It is not so much the face, but every shift in the figure's weight and angle that is expressive. The youth's position is derived from classical contrapposto. The few nudes that appeared in medieval art showed little sensual appeal and often portrayed shame and lust. Under the influence of humanist scholars who sought to surpass the Greeks and Romans in the nobility of form, the nude became a symbol of human worth and divine perfection, a representation of the "immortal soul."

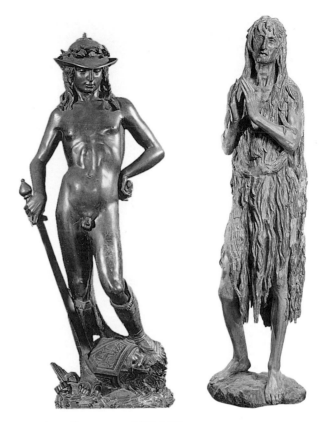

417 Donatello. DAVID. c. 1425–1430.
Bronze. Height 62¼".
Museo Nazionale del Bargello, Florence.
Photograph: Scala/Art Resource, NY.

418 Donatello. MARY MAGDALEN. c. 1455.
Wood, partially gilded. Height 74".
Museo dell'Opera del Duomo, Florence.
Photograph: Scala/Art Resource, NY.

During the Renaissance, artists received growing support from the new class of wealthy merchants and bankers, such as the Medici family, who, with great political skill, dominated the life of Florence and Tuscany. It is likely that Donatello created his bronze DAVID as a private commission for Cosimo de Medici, for the courtyard of the Medici palace.

A major influence on Donatello and other Renaissance artists was the renewal of Neoplatonist philosophy, embraced by the Medici family and their circle of philosophers, artists, historians, and humanists. These intellectuals believed that all sources of inspiration or revelation, whether from the Bible or classical mythology, are a means of ascending from earthly existence to mystical union with "the One." In this context, Donatello's DAVID was intended to be a symbol of divine beauty.

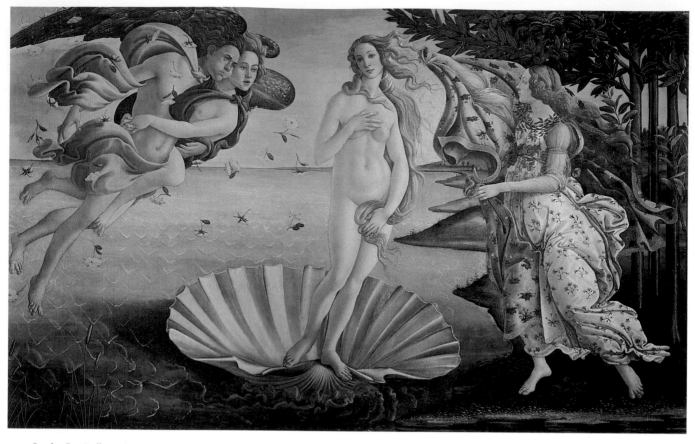

419 Sandro Botticelli. BIRTH OF VENUS. c. 1480.
Tempera on canvas. 5'8⅞" × 9'1⅞".
Uffizi Gallery, Florence.
Photograph: Scala/Art Resource, NY.

Donatello's work displayed a wide range of expression, from lyric joy to tragedy to extremes of religious passion. In contrast to the youthful and somewhat cocky DAVID, Donatello's MARY MAGDALEN (previous page) is haggard and withdrawn—a forcefully expressive figure of old age and repentance. For this late work, Donatello chose painted wood, the favorite medium of northern Gothic sculptors.

Another Medici commission is Sandro Botticelli's BIRTH OF VENUS, one of the first paintings of an almost life-size nude since antiquity. The large painting, completed about 1480, depicts the Roman goddess of love just after she was born from the sea. She is being blown to shore by a couple symbolizing the wind. As she arrives, Venus is greeted by a young woman who represents Spring. The lyric grace of Botticelli's lines shows Byzantine influence. The background is decorative and flat,

giving almost no illusion of deep space. The figures appear to be in relief, not fully three-dimensional.

The posture and gestures of modesty were probably inspired by a third-century B.C.E. Greco-Roman sculpture of Venus that Botticelli must have seen in the Medici family collection (see page 270). In her posture of introspection and repose, Botticelli's Venus combines the classical Greek idealized human figure with a Renaissance concern for thought and feeling.

It was revolutionary for an artist working within the context of a Christian society to place a nude "pagan" goddess at the center of a large painting, in a position previously reserved for the Virgin Mary. Botticelli's focus on classical mythology was—like Donatello's—based on Neoplatonist philosophy. Botticelli's ethereal Venus was intended to portray divine love—a celestial Venus.

The High Renaissance

Between about 1490 and 1530—the period known as the High Renaissance—Italian art reached a peak of accomplishment in the cities of Florence, Rome, and Venice. The three artists who epitomized the period were Leonardo, Michelangelo, and Raphael. They developed a style of art that was calm, balanced, and idealized, reconciling Christian theology with Greek philosophy and the science of the day.

Leonardo da Vinci was motivated by an insatiable curiosity and an optimistic belief in the human ability to understand the fascinating phenomena of the physical world. He believed that art and science are two means to the same end: knowledge.

Leonardo's investigative and creative mind is revealed in his journals, in which he documented his research in notes and drawings (see also pages 18 and 113). His notebooks are filled with studies of anatomy and ideas for mechanical devices, explorations that put him in the forefront of the scientific development of his time. His study of THE INFANT AND WOMB has a few errors, yet much of the drawing is so accurate that it could serve as an example in one of today's medical textbooks.

Leonardo was one of the first to give a clear description of the *camera obscura,* an optical device that captures light images in much the same way as the human eye. The concept of photography began with the Renaissance desire to create an equivalent to our visual perception of reality.

So frequently has Leonardo's world-famous portrait of MONA LISA been reproduced that it has become a cliché and the source of innumerable spoofs. Despite this overexposure, it is worthy of careful attention. It was one of Leonardo's favorite paintings. We can still be intrigued by the mysterious mood evoked by the faint smile and the strange, otherworldly landscape. The ambiguity is heightened by the hazy light quality that gives an amazing sense of atmosphere around the figure. This soft blurring of the edges—in Leonardo's words, "without lines or borders in the manner of smoke"—achieved through subtle value gradations, is called *sfumato* and was invented by Leonardo.[1] The effect,

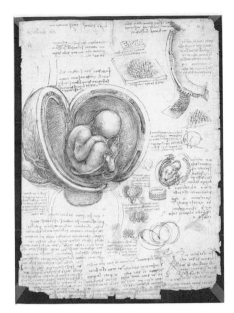

420 Leonardo da Vinci (1452–1519).
THE INFANT AND WOMB.
c. 1510.
Pen and ink. 11⅞" × 8⅜".
The Royal Collection
© 2002 Her Magesty Queen Elizabeth II

421 Leonardo da Vinci.
MONA LISA.
c. 1503–1506.
Oil on wood. 30¼" × 21".
Musée du Louvre, Paris.
Photograph: Scala/Art Resource, NY.

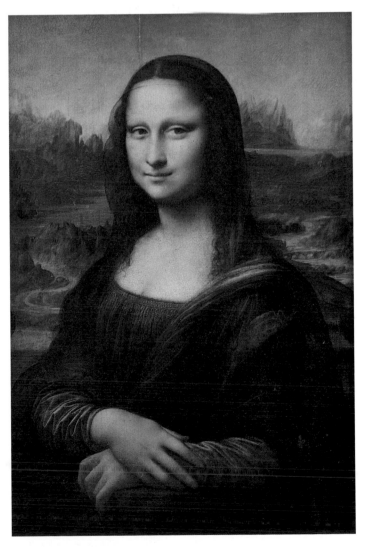

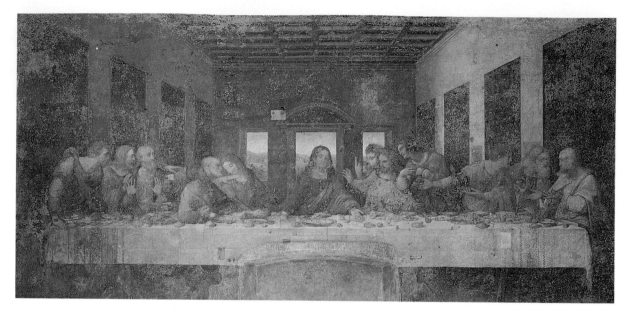

422 Leonardo da Vinci.
THE LAST SUPPER.
Santa Maria delle Grazie, Milan. c. 1495–1498.
Experimental paint on plaster. 14'5" × 28'¼".
Photograph: Scala/Art Resource, NY.

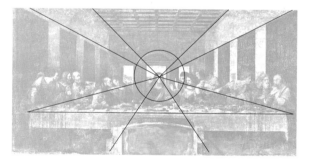

a. Perspective lines as both organizing
structure and symbol of content.

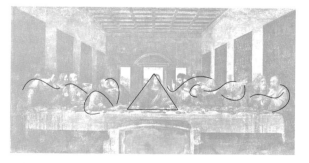

b. Christ's figure as stable triangle, contrasting with
active turmoil of the disciples.

heightened by chiaroscuro, amazed and impressed his contemporaries. MONA LISA's rich, luminous surface was achieved through the application of glazes (thin, translucent layers of paint).

The impact of Renaissance humanism becomes apparent when we compare THE LAST SUPPER by Leonardo with the Byzantine mosaic CHRIST AS PANTOCRATOR on page 278. In the Byzantine painting Christ is portrayed as a lofty being of infinite power. In Leonardo's painting, Jesus sits across the table from us—an accessible person who reveals his divinity in an earthly setting.

The naturalist style of the work contains a hidden geometry, which structures the design and strengthens the painting's symbolic content. The interior is based on a one-point linear perspective system, with a single vanishing point in the middle of the composition, behind the head of Christ. Leonardo placed Christ in the center, at the point of greatest implied depth, associating him with infinity. Over Christ's head an architectural pediment suggests a halo, further setting him off from the irregular shapes and movements of the surprised disciples on either side. In contrast to the anguished figures surrounding him, Christ is shown with his arms outstretched in a gesture of acceptance, his image a stable triangle.

Leonardo da Vinci—painter, sculptor, architect, town planner, writer, musician, scientist, engineer, and inventor—is the prototypical "Renaissance man," an extremely versatile individual with a record of high achievement in many fields.

Leonardo was the son of a young notary, Piero da Vinci, and a peasant girl of whom nothing is known. He grew up an only child in his father's household. In his mid-teens, he was apprenticed to Andrea del Verrochio, a leading artist in nearby Florence. Botticelli was one of his fellow apprentices.

Leonardo grew into a magnetic young man—tall, handsome, strong, graceful, charming, and enormously talented. He played the lute, sang beautifully, and made fascinating conversation. People loved to be near him, yet he remained essentially solitary. He formed few friendships over the course of his life, and he never married.

At age thirty he began seventeen years in the service of the Duke of Milan, primarily as a military engineer and secondarily as a court painter, sculptor, and architect. He also entertained the court as a musician and satirist and designed scenery and costumes for pageants. During this period he painted several important works, including THE LAST SUPPER.

It was also in Milan that he started to keep notebooks. Along with his few paintings, Leonardo's notebooks are his great legacy. They contain a lifetime of observations, inventions, and plans, all drawn in meticulous detail and annotated in secretive mirror writing. In his research drawings, he anticipated the development of such twentieth-century technology as the airplane, the parachute, and the armored tank. His range of subjects was enormous: Mathematics, anatomy, architecture, astronomy, optics, botany, geology, cartography, aeronautics, mechanics, civil engineering, urban planning, hydraulics, and weaponry all captured Leonardo's interest and benefited from his research.

Milan fell to French invaders in 1499 and Leonardo fled to Venice, where he was again employed as a military engineer. From there he went to Florence and worked on a portrait of an obscure merchant's third wife, the MONA LISA. The French called him back to Milan in 1506. He stayed until they were driven out six years later; then, hoping the Pope would have use for him, he journeyed to Rome.

Now in his sixties, Leonardo was increasingly haunted by a sense of futility. No building or invention of his had ever been built, no sculpture cast. Patrons had used his endless skills in frivolous or ignoble ways. Bored with what he could already do exquisitely well, he had left many paintings unfinished and ruined others with technical experiments. "Tell me if anything at all was done," he wrote over and over in his last notebooks. "Tell me if anything at all . . ."[2]

Yet what little he had finished was so spectacular that his fame was well established. In 1516, the new King of France, Francis I, offered Leonardo a house, a stipend, and the title of First Painter and Engineer and Architect to the King. The title was a formality; Francis expected nothing in return but the honor of the great man's presence and the pleasure of his conversation. Leonardo died in Cloux, near Aboise, France, in 1519.

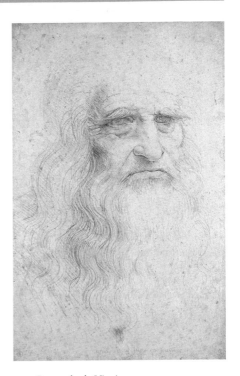

423   Leonardo da Vinci.
SELF-PORTRAIT. c. 1512.
Chalk on paper.
13" × 8¼".
Biblioteca Reale, Turin, Italy.
Photograph: Scala/Art Resource, NY.

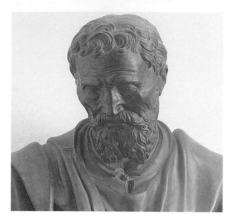

424   Daniele da Volterra.
MICHELANGELO BUONARROTI. 1565.
Detail of bronze bust.
Height of entire work 32".
Accademia, Florence.
Photograph: Alinari/Art Resource, NY.

Michelangelo Buonarroti was so greatly admired by his contemporaries that the poet Aristo referred to him as "Michael, more than human, Angel divine." Two biographies of Michelangelo were published in his lifetime. His noble, if irascible, character and his mistrust of human nature—including his own—make his life one of the most interesting known to us from the sixteenth century.

Michelangelo's father was a member of the minor nobility of Florence, a lazy, mean-spirited man who merely lived off the remains of the family fortune. Michelangelo's mother was unable to nurse him, so the infant was sent to stay with a wet nurse. The nurse's husband was a quarry worker in an area where stonecutting was a way of life. Michelangelo returned to his parents only for visits because his mother continued to suffer poor health. She died when Michelangelo was six years old. For four more years he continued to live as the son of the stonecutter and his wife, visiting his father only occasionally. He could neither read nor write, but he learned to use hammer and chisel.

When he was ten his father remarried, and Michelangelo returned home and was enrolled in school for the first time. In three years he learned to read and write in Italian but absorbed little else. Michelangelo drew whenever he could and neglected his other studies. He decided to leave school to become an artist, starting as an apprentice to the painter Ghirlandaio. His father and uncles looked down on artists and thought it a disgrace to have one in the house. Michelangelo's father never realized the importance of the arts, even when Michelangelo gained fame and fortune.

After a year, Michelangelo transferred to the school in the Medici gardens, where he was inspired by the beauty of the Medici collection of contemporary Italian, ancient Greek, and Roman art. He studied there for several years, in the company of the leading artists and scholars of the time. During the turmoil following the death of his patron, Lorenzo de Medici, Michelangelo left Florence for Rome. In Rome he completed the first of his major sculptures, including the PIETÀ, at the age of twenty-four (see page 86). His handling of the difficult subject and the beautiful finish of the work established his reputation and led to important commissions, including DAVID, when he returned to Florence. For the rest of his life, he went back and forth between Florence and Rome.

Although he considered himself primarily a sculptor, Michelangelo's painting on THE SISTINE CHAPEL ceiling is one of the world's most acclaimed works of art. The project was made enormous by Michelangelo himself; although the original plan called for twelve figures, Michelangelo included over three hundred.

No other artist has left such masterful accomplishments in four major art forms: sculpture, painting, architecture—and poetry. If he had not been a supreme architect, sculptor, and painter, Michelangelo might have been known to us as a writer. Perhaps the most revealing writings are his poems, which express his innermost feelings about his mind and soul as well as his art.

In his later years, in addition to architectural commissions—including the rebuilding of St. Peter's in Rome—Michelangelo worked as a city planner, completed some of his most important sculpture, and wrote many of his finest sonnets.

Michelangelo was very different from Leonardo, who was twenty-three years older. Michelangelo saw human beings as unique, almost godlike, while Leonardo saw them as one part of nature, which he viewed as a scientist as well as an artist. Michelangelo believed that in an artist's hands, "life" could be created through inspiration from God. For Michelangelo, sculpture and the process of its creation reflected people's struggle with their imperfect selves—souls in turmoil, bound in their bodies.

Michelangelo's life spanned nearly a century. From the time he was apprenticed at age thirteen until six days before his death at eighty-nine, he worked continuously. His last words were, "I regret that I have not done enough for the salvation of my soul and that I am dying just as I am beginning to learn the alphabet of my profession."[3]

In 1501, when he was twenty-six years old, Michelangelo obtained a commission from the city of Florence to carve a figure of David from an eighteen-foot block of marble that had been badly cut and then abandoned by another sculptor. The biblical hero David was an important symbol of freedom from tyranny for Florence, which had just become a republic. Other Renaissance artists such as Donatello had already given the city images of the young David, but it was Michelangelo's figure that gave the most powerful expression to the idea of David as hero, the defender of a just cause.

Michelangelo took DAVID's stance, with the weight of the body on one foot, from Greek sculpture. But the positions of the hands and tense frown indicate anxiety and readiness for conflict. Through changes in proportion and the depiction of inner feeling, Michelangelo humanized, then made monumental, the classical Greek athlete.

425 Michelangelo Buonarroti.
   a. DAVID. 1501–1504.
      Marble. Height of figure 14'3".
      Accademia, Florence
      Photograph: Duane Preble.
   b. DAVID. Close–up of head.
      Alinari/Art Resource,NY.

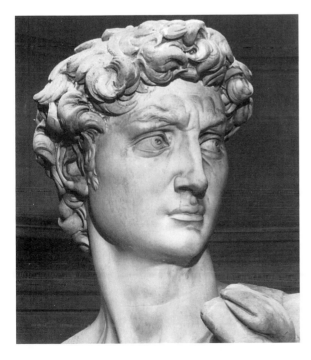

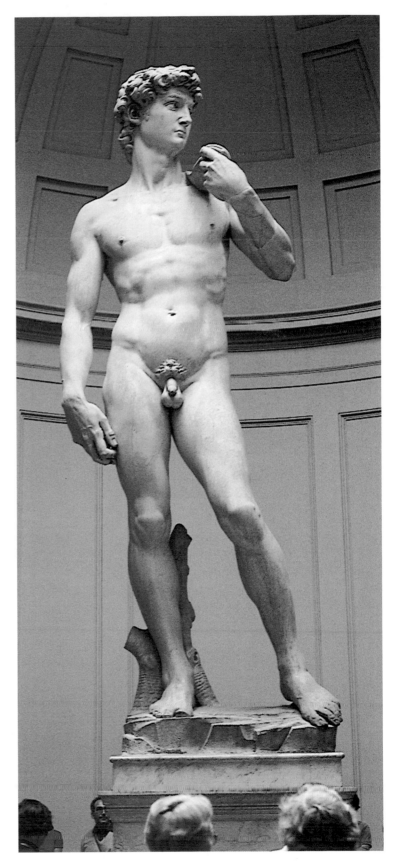

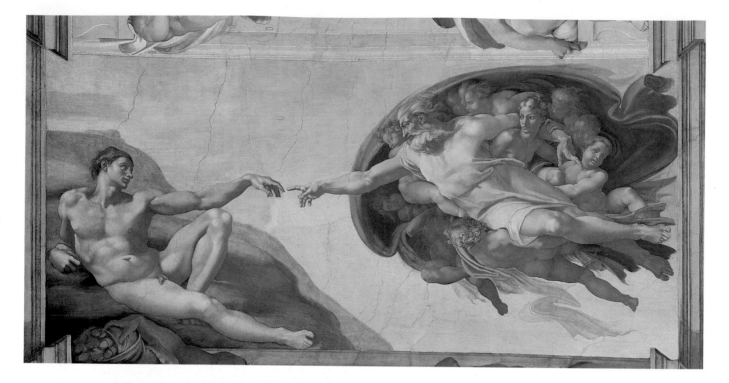

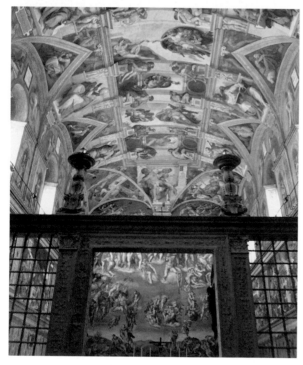

426 Michelangelo Buonarroti.
Frescoes on the ceiling and walls of THE SISTINE CHAPEL.
Vatican, Rome. 1508–1512.

a. THE CREATION OF ADAM, Fresco of the Sistine Chapel after
restoration. Vatican Museums, Rome, Italy.

b. THE SISTINE CHAPEL after restoration.
Vatican Museums, Rome, Italy. © Reuters NewMedia Inc./Corbis.

Michelangelo worked for three years on this sculpture. When it was finished and placed in the town square, the citizens of Florence were filled with admiration for the work and its creator. With this achievement, Michelangelo became known as the greatest sculptor since the Greeks.

Equally praised as a painter, Michelangelo had just begun work on what he thought would be his main sculptural commission, the tomb of Pope Julius II, when the Pope ordered him to accept a commission to paint THE SISTINE CHAPEL in the Vatican. Michelangelo began work on the ceiling in 1508 and finished it four years later. The surface is divided into three zones. In the highest are nine panels of scenes from Genesis, including THE CREATION OF ADAM. The next level contains prophets and sibyls (female prophets). The lowest level consists of groups of figures, some of which have been identified as Christ's biblical ancestors. *The Last Judgment*, painted later, fills the end wall above the altar.

The most-admired composition on the ceiling is the majestic portrayal of THE CREATION OF ADAM, in which God reaches out to give life to the first man. Eve, not yet mortal, stares at Adam from behind God's left arm.

The work powerfully expresses the Renaissance humanist concept of God: an idealized, rational man who actively tends every aspect of creation and has a special interest in humans. Michelangelo invented this powerful image, which does not exist in the Bible, to tell the story of the relationship between God and people from a Renaissance point of view.

Raphael Sanzio's warmth and gentleness were in sharp contrast to Leonardo's solitary, intellectual nature and Michelangelo's formidable moodiness. Of these three major creators of the High Renaissance, Raphael was the youngest and, in his life and art, the most expressive of the untroubled grace and radiance that marked the art of the period. His paintings present his awareness of the divine in human beings, the insight that was the driving enthusiasm of Italian Renaissance. For him life was an art form. It was as if he were saying, "Life is beautiful; human possibilities are limitless because we are one with God."

Among the most beloved of Raphael's many depictions of Mary and the infant Jesus are the superbly designed MADONNA OF THE CHAIR (page 83) and MADONNA OF THE MEADOWS altarpiece. Of much greater size and complexity is his mural painting THE SCHOOL OF ATHENS (page 53). Together, these paintings reveal Raphael's own harmonious resolution of the Renaissance desire to reconcile Christianity with the ideals of classical Greece and Rome.

Raphael was honored for centuries as Europe's greatest painter, yet he was also an accomplished archaeologist and architect. In addition to being principal artist for the Vatican, he was art director and city planner for Rome and made it his mission to restore the classic grandeur of the ancient capital city.

As the Early Renaissance was unfolding in Italy, a parallel new interest in realism arose in Northern Europe, where artists were even more concerned than the Italians with depicting life in the real world. Yet lingering medieval attitudes made the fifteenth-century art of the North as much a late phase of Gothic style as an early Renaissance style.

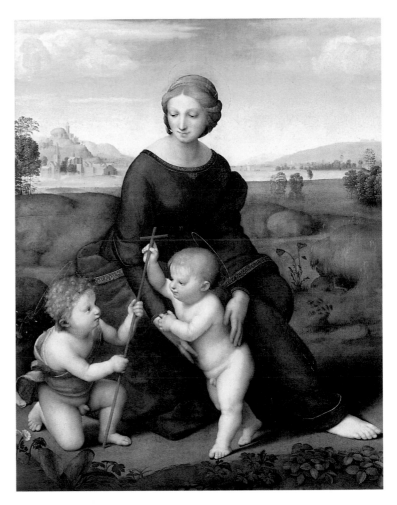

427 Raphael.
MADONNA OF THE MEADOWS. 1505.
Oil on panel. 3'8½" × 2'10¼".
Kunsthistorisches Museum, Vienna.

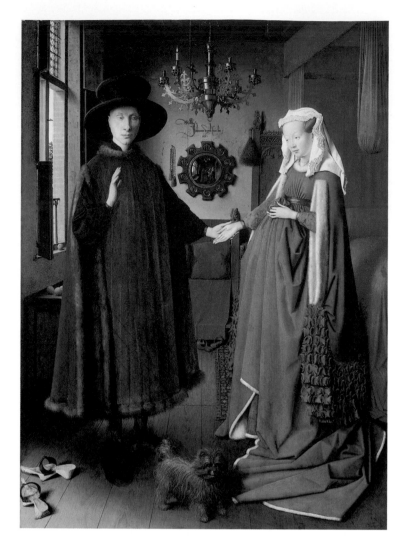

428 Jan van Eyck.
THE MARRIAGE OF GIOVANNI ARNOLFINI AND GIOVANNA
CENAMI. 1434.
Oil on oak panel. 33½" × 23½".
National Gallery, London, UK.
Photograph: Bridgeman Art Library/New York.

The Renaissance in Northern Europe

Jan van Eyck was a leading painter in Flanders, the region of present-day Belgium and adjacent parts of France and The Netherlands. He was one of the first to use linseed oil as a paint medium (see also pages 130–131). The fine consistency and flexibility of the new oil medium made it possible to achieve a brilliance and transparency of color that were previously unattainable. His oil paintings remain in almost perfect condition, attesting to his skill and knowledge of materials. Italian artists admired and were influenced by the innovations of van Eyck and other Flemish and Dutch artists.

On the same type of small wooden panels previously used for tempera painting, van Eyck painted in minute detail, achieving an illusion of depth, directional light, mass, rich implied textures, and the physical likenesses of particular people. Human figures and their interior settings took on a new, believable presence.

In spite of van Eyck's realistic detail, GIOVANNI ARNOLFINI AND HIS BRIDE has a Gothic quality in its traditional symbolism, formality, and vertical emphasis of the figures. At the time the portrait of the Arnolfini wedding was commissioned, the Church did not always require the presence of clergy for a valid marriage contract, and thus it was easy to deny that a marriage had taken place. Van Eyck's painting is thought to be a testament to the oath of marriage between Giovanni Arnolfini and Giovanna Cenami. As witness to the event, Jan van Eyck placed his signature and the date, 1434, directly above the mirror—and he himself appears to be reflected in the mirror (see detail on page 71).

Today the painting's Christian iconography, well understood in the fifteenth century, needs explanation. Many of the ordinary objects portrayed with great care have sacred significance. The single lighted candle in the chandelier symbolizes the presence of Christ; the amber beads and the sunlight shining through them are symbols of purity; the dog indicates marital fidelity. The bride's holding up her skirt suggestively in front of her stomach may indicate her willingness to bear children. Green, a symbol of fertility, was often worn at weddings.

In the early sixteenth century in Germany, Northern Renaissance master Albrecht Dürer further developed the practice of presenting instructive symbolism through detailed realism. His engraving THE KNIGHT, DEATH AND THE DEVIL (page 143) combines Christian symbols with familiar subjects in the Flemish tradition of van Eyck.

Pieter Bruegel was an independent thinker of far-reaching vision. As a young man he traveled extensively in France and Italy. Under the influence of Italian Renaissance painting, Bruegel developed a grand sense of composition and spatial depth. The focus of Bruegel's paintings was the lives and

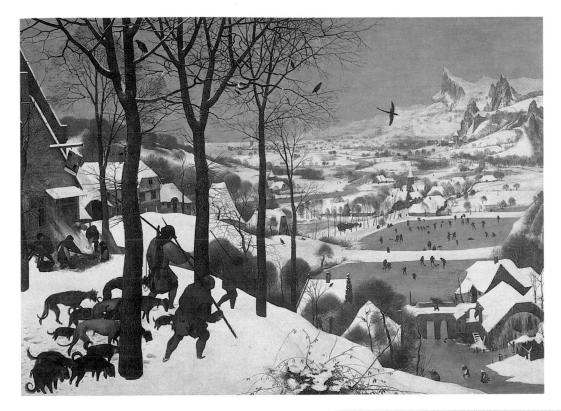

429 Pieter Bruegel.
THE RETURN OF THE
HUNTERS. 1565.
Oil on panel.
46½" × 63¾".
Kunsthistorisches Museum,
Vienna.

430 The Limbourg Brothers.
FEBRUARY, from
LES TRÈS RICHES HEURES
DU DUC DE BERRY.
1413–1416. 8⅞" × 5⅜".
Musée Condé, Chantilly, France.
Photograph: Giraudon/Art
Resource, NY.

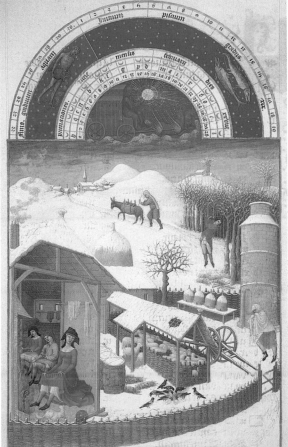

surroundings of common people, and toward the
end of his life he did a series of paintings representing the activities of the twelve months of the year.

One of the most beloved of the series is his
painting for January, THE RETURN OF THE HUNTERS.
Following the precedent set by manuscript painters
(illuminators) of medieval calendars, who depicted
each month according to the agricultural labor appropriate to it, Bruegel shows peasants augmenting
their winter diet by hunting. New here is the emphasis on nature's winter mood rather than on
human activity. The illusion of deep space, so important to this image, came from the innovations
of the Italians and was also inspired by Bruegel's
journey over the Alps. Views from high vantage
points are often seen in his work.

Compare Bruegel's painting with an illuminated
page for FEBRUARY from a late Gothic book of hours
painted by the Limbourg brothers in the early fifteenth century, before the Renaissance influence
reached the North. Notice how far landscape painting evolved in just one hundred fifty years. Although

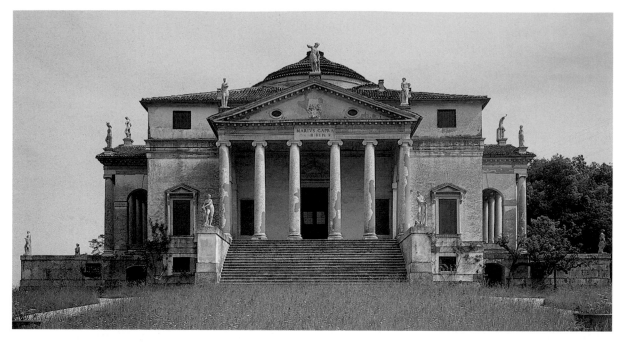

431　Andrea Palladio.
VILLA ROTONDA. Vicenza,
Italy. 1567–1570.
Photograph: Scala/Art Resource, NY.

there is a huge difference in the way space is depicted, in both paintings there is attention to nature and the details of everyday life. Bruegel achieved greater naturalism by portraying what he might see from one vantage point at a particular time; the Limbourg brothers implied various moments in time by creating an imaginary composite view.

Late Renaissance in Italy

The High Renaissance was followed by a period of turmoil, revolution, and new expectations. The early sixteenth century was a time of religious questioning and change that spawned the Protestant Reformation—the protest movement that sought to reform the Western Christian Church and resulted in the division into Protestant and Catholic churches. The tensions and exaggerations brought on by social change were apparent in major changes in art.

In the fifteenth century, Renaissance architects, sculptors, and painters had gone to great lengths to acquire knowledge of Greek and Roman ideas and to employ these ideas, along with contemporary concepts, in the creation of architecture they considered more beautiful than any done by their predecessors.

During the sixteenth century, architects made a deliberate effort to contradict classical rules even as they used classical forms. The most learned and influential architect was Andrea Palladio. His famous VILLA ROTONDA built near Vicenza, Italy, is intentionally unique, to the point of being capricious, yet reminiscent of the Roman Pantheon (see page 272). It has four identical sides, complete with porches resembling ancient temple façades, built around a central domed hall. The villa's design hardly satisfies the architectural goal of livability, but it was not intended for family living; it was designed for a retired monsignor as a kind of open summer house for social occasions. From its hilltop site, visitors standing in the central rotunda could enjoy four different views of the countryside.

Palladio's designs were published in books that were widely circulated throughout the Western world. For the next two centuries, architects and builders from Russia to London to Pennsylvania often used motifs that he developed, and his designs have even reappeared on Postmodern buildings in the last 25 years.

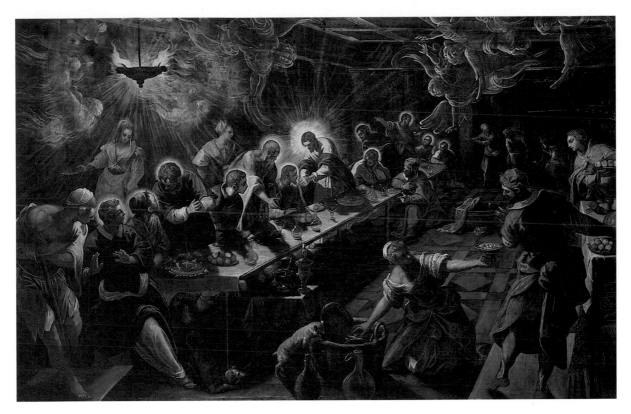

432 Jacopo Tintoretto.
THE LAST SUPPER. 1592–1594.
Oil on canvas. 12' × 18'8".
S. Giorgio Maggiore, Venice.
Photograph: Scala/Art Resource, NY.

By the mid-sixteenth century, it had become increasingly difficult for artists to surpass such forebears as Leonardo, Michelangelo, and Raphael. While the ideas of the Renaissance spread north, Mediterranean artists also faced change. Mannerism, the key trend in Southern Europe, dominated painting, sculpture, and architecture. Mannerist painters of the sixteenth century admired the drama and emotion found in the late work of Michelangelo and Raphael. The younger generation exaggerated these qualities, sometimes in contrived or mannered ways, to achieve their own unique expression. *Mannerism* is characterized by distortions of perspective, scale, and proportion; exaggerated color; and increased value contrast all aimed at provoking a sense of mystery and heightened emotion. The result was often ambiguous and disquieting, unlike the classical confidence inspired by High Renaissance art. Mannerism led from the High Renaissance of the early sixteenth century into Baroque art of the seventeenth century.

Paintings of Jacopo Tintoretto exhibit Mannerist qualities. His version of THE LAST SUPPER, completed when the artist was in his seventies, is a radical departure from Leonardo's calm, classical interpretation painted one hundred years earlier (page 292). After a lifetime working with the subject, Tintoretto transformed the earthly event into a supernatural vision. Christ seems farther away, distinguished only by a brilliant halo of light. The table, seen from a higher angle, is turned away from the picture plane in exaggerated perspective, creating a strong feeling of movement through diagonal forces. Angels appear overhead in the light and smoke of a blazing oil lamp. Disciples and attendants are caught at a moment of emotional intensity. Such vivid exaggerations of light, movement, spatial tension, and theatrical gesture became major storytelling devices for seventeenth-century artists.

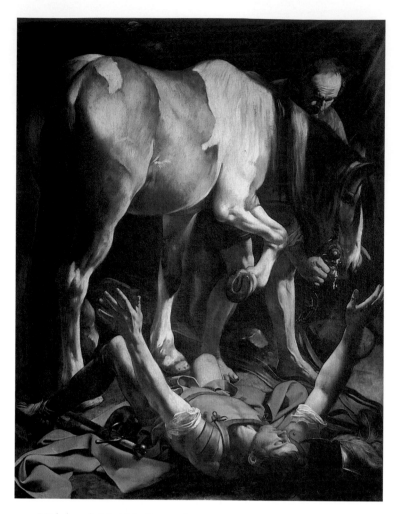

433 Michelangelo Merisi da Caravaggio.
THE CONVERSION OF SAINT PAUL. 1600–1601.
Oil on canvas. 100½" × 69".
Santa Maria del Popolo, Rome.
Photograph: Scala/Art Resource, NY.

BAROQUE

The era known as the Baroque period includes the seventeenth and most of the eighteenth centuries in Europe. Although Baroque generally refers to a period, the term is also used to describe the art that arose in Italy around 1600 and spread through much of Europe during the next two hundred years.

The Baroque period had far more varied styles than the Renaissance, yet much of the art shows great energy and feeling, and a dramatic use of light, scale, and balance. The goal of balanced harmony achieved by Renaissance artists such as Raphael in his SCHOOL OF ATHENS (page 53) and Michelangelo in his DAVID was set aside first by Mannerists and later by Baroque artists as they explored more inno-

vative uses of space and more intense ranges of light and shadow. Their art, with its frequent use of curves and countercurves, often appeals to the mind by way of the heart. Also, we can see a new degree of vivid realism in compositions employing sharp diagonals and extreme foreshortening.

The Counter Reformation developed in the late sixteenth and early seventeenth centuries as the Catholic Church's response to the Protestant Reformation and the growing impact of science. Many of the characteristics of the Baroque style were spawned and promoted by the Catholic Counter Reformation.

Michelangelo Merisi da Caravaggio's down-to-earth realism and dramatic use of light broke from Renaissance idealism and became the leading influences on other Baroque painters, north and south. Caravaggio created the most vivid and dramatic paintings of his time, using directed light and strong contrasts to guide the attention of the viewer and intensify the subject matter.

Emotional realism and theatrical use of chiaroscuro, especially in Caravaggio's night effects (called *tenebrism*), influenced later Baroque painters such as Rubens and Rembrandt. Displayed in a dark chapel, Caravaggio's paintings take on a vivid, lifelike quality intended to heighten the religious experience.

In THE CONVERSION OF SAINT PAUL, Caravaggio used light to imply a blinding flash, symbolizing the evangelist's conversion: "And suddenly there shined around him a light from heaven: and he fell to the earth" (Acts 9:3). The figure of Paul, in Roman dress, is foreshortened and pushed into the foreground, presenting such a close view that we feel we are right there. In keeping with the supernatural character of the spiritual events he portrayed, Caravaggio evoked a feeling for the mystical dimension within the ordinary world. He wanted his paintings to be accessible and self-explanatory, and for this purpose he brought the emotional intensity of his own rowdy life to the stories of the Bible. Some of the clergy for whom he painted rejected his style; his emotional realism was too strong for people accustomed to idealized aristocratic images that demonstrated little more than gestures of piety.

In post-Renaissance Rome, another artist who had as far-reaching an influence as Caravaggio was the sculptor and architect Gianlorenzo Bernini. Because Bernini's DAVID is life-size rather than monumental, viewers become engaged in the action. Rather than capture an introspective moment, as Michelangelo did (page 295), Bernini chose to depict David in a moment of tension, as he prepares to fling the stone at Goliath.

Bernini's elaborate orchestrations of the visual arts are the climax of Italian Baroque expression. The emotional intensity of his art is vividly apparent in his major work THE ECSTASY OF SAINT TERESA. It features a life-size marble figure of the saint and depicts one of her visions as she recorded it in her diary. In this vision, she saw an angel who seemed to pierce her heart with a flaming arrow of gold, giving her great pain as well as pleasure and leaving her "all on fire with a great love of God."⁴ Bernini made the visionary experience vivid by portraying the moment of greatest feeling, revealing spiritual passion through physical expression. Turbulent drapery heightens the emotional impact. His inventive departure from the naturalistic, classical norm soon influenced artists throughout Europe.

Flemish painter Peter Paul Rubens, a renowned diplomat and humanist, was the most influential Baroque artist in Northern Europe. He studied painting in Antwerp, then traveled to Italy in 1600. During a stay of several years he was greatly influenced by the work of Michelangelo, and to a lesser degree by the work of Raphael, Leonardo, and Caravaggio. When Rubens returned north, he won increasing acclaim and patronage; being a sophisticated businessman, he enjoyed an aristocratic lifestyle. His work came to be in such demand by the nobility and royalty of Europe that he established a large studio with many assistants. The exuberant sensuality of his compositions took Baroque painting to new heights. Although Rubens was noted for the voluptuous quality of

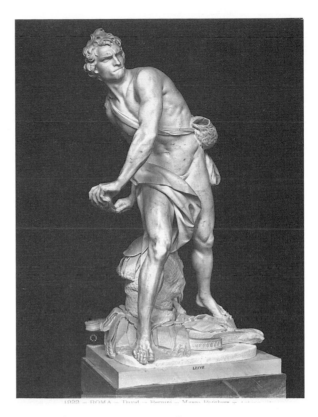

434 Gianlorenzo Bernini. DAVID. 1623.
Marble. Life-size.
Galleria Borghese, Rome.
Photograph: Alinari/Art Resource, NY.

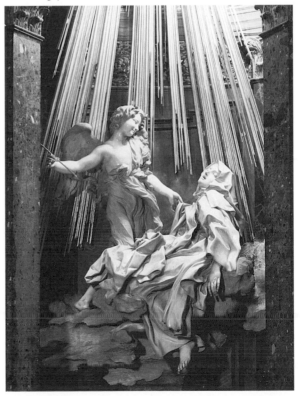

435 Gianlorenzo Bernini.
THE ECSTASY OF SAINT TERESA.
Detail of the altar, Cornaro Chapel, Santa Maria della Vittoria, Rome. 1645–1652. Marble. Life-size.
Photograph: Scala/Art Resource, NY.

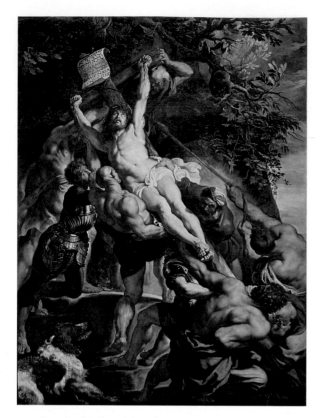

436 Peter Paul Rubens (Flemish, 1577–1640).
THE RAISING OF THE CROSS. 1610–1611.
Onze Lieve Vrouwkerk, Antwerp Cathedral, Belgium. Oil
on panel. 15'2" × 11' 2" (462 × 339 cm).
Photograph: Peter Willi/Bridgeman Art Library, London/NY.

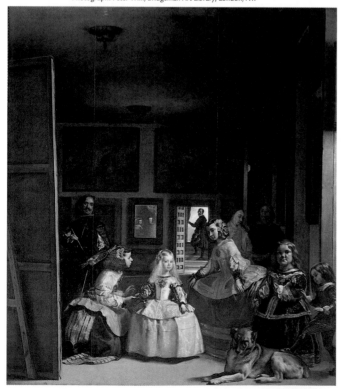

his nudes, there was a tendency for everything in his paintings to take on a similar sensuality. His free brushwork influenced many painters.

In RAISING THE CROSS, we see his interpretation of a religious subject, painted for an important cathedral in his homeland. The composition is arranged along a diagonal anchored at the bottom right by the well-muscled figure. This and other taut bodies in the work show the results of the artist's recent visit to Italy, where he saw works by Michelangelo and Caravaggio. At the same time, there is a high degree of realistic detail in the foliage and the dog at the bottom left that show Rubens's Flemish heritage from Jan van Eyck and others. The action and drama in the work make it seem to burst out of the frame, led by the upward glance of Christ. This visual dynamism, extending the action of the work into the viewer's space, marks the best Baroque painting.

While Rubens traveled Europe from England to Italy, Diego Velázquez was content to spend his entire career in the service of Philip IV, King of Spain. Philip was a broad-minded monarch who took delight in his chief painter's sometimes adventurous works. Such a painting is THE MAIDS OF HONOR, in which Velázquez plays an elaborate game. At first it is unclear who is the subject, since the artist himself is staring out from behind a canvas, brush in hand. The maids of honor encircle the king's daughter, who stares coquettishly at us, as if expecting something. She seems to be the center of the composition, as she stands in the brightest light. Another courtier stands in an illuminated doorway in the background. It is only when we see the mirror on the far wall, with the faces of the royal couple reflected in it, that we realize that this is a court portrait changed into a visual riddle. Velázquez painted a portrait of himself making a royal portrait! Like other Baroque works, this painting seems to reach out beyond its frame in a subtle dynamism of glance and image in which light and shadow play a major role.

437 Diego Velázquez.
THE MAIDS OF HONOR. 1656.
Oil on canvas. 10'5" × 9'.
Museo del Prado, Madrid.
Photograph: Erich Lessing/Art Resource, NY.

We have seen that Baroque characteristics are found in art that depicts both religious and nonreligious subjects. This was primarily because artists no longer relied wholly on the church for their support; many worked for nobles and aristocrats. In The Netherlands, the major patrons of art were middle-class merchants and bankers.

Jan Vermeer, Rembrandt van Rijn, and their peers painted views of the rich interiors of merchant homes and portraits of the middle class and the wealthy. Along with the new emphasis on scenes of daily life, religious art continued as a strong current in what is now The Netherlands; see, for example, Rembrandt's etching of CHRIST PREACHING (page 145).

As the result of recently won independence and booming international trade, Holland (part of The Netherlands) became a new type of society in the seventeenth century: predominantly middle class, wealthy, mercantile, materialistic, and Protestant. Among the middle and upper classes, there was widespread enjoyment of and investment in contemporary art. Many people collected, traded, and resold paintings at a profit. Favored subjects were the same ones enjoyed to this day: landscape, still life, genre scenes (depictions of everyday life), and portraits. Through Dutch painters, art became accessible and understandable in everyday terms.

Rembrandt remains one of the world's most revered artists. We can see why in his large work RETURN OF THE PRODIGAL SON. The story comes from the Bible: a disobedient son cuts himself off from his family, demands his inheritance early, wastes it in disorderly living, and ends up in dire poverty. When he reaches the end of his rope, he returns to his wealthy father and asks for a job feeding his hogs. The father is not scornful or judgmental, rather the opposite. He tenderly welcomes the haggard and forlorn young man. Rembrandt portrays this touching scene with great reserve and economy. We see the prodigal son's ragged clothing, and the father's gentle embrace. We also see standing at the right, hanging back guardedly, the father's other son.

Rembrandt's off-balance composition shows the influence of the Italian Baroque painters in its

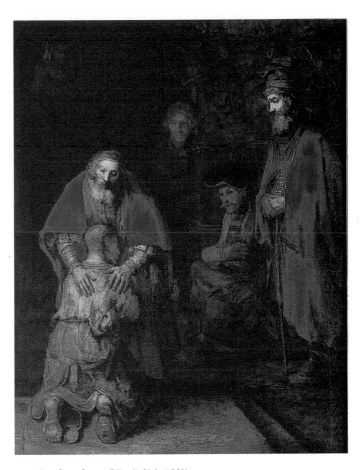

438 Rembrandt van Rijn (1606–1669).
RETURN OF THE PRODIGAL SON. c. 1668–1669.
Oil on canvas. 8'8" × 8'8" (265 × 205 cm).
Hermitage Museum, St. Petersburg. Scala/Art Resource, NY.

handling of light and dark. The story, however, is not of the miraculous vision of a saint, as in Caravaggio's CONVERSION OF ST. PAUL, but rather a miraculous restoration of affection between estranged people.

For Rembrandt meaning is conveyed through composition and paint application as well as subject matter. He delighted in the visual excitement that could be created with paint alone. The force of his brushwork is readily seen in his SELF-PORTRAITS on pages 9 and 132 and in his brush drawing on page 125.

Rembrandt's work has long influenced many painters—and, more recently, photographers—who have found his lighting techniques useful in directing the viewer's attention.

Rembrandt van Rijn was born in the elegant Dutch city of Leiden, the ninth of ten children of a prosperous miller. He began his art studies at fifteen, was apprenticed for three years to minor local artists, then traveled to Amsterdam to study briefly with a painter named Pieter Lastman, from whom he absorbed the influence of Caravaggio secondhand.

At nineteen, Rembrandt returned to Leiden and set up his own studio. Success came quickly, and in 1631 he moved to Amsterdam, a larger city offering more opportunities. There he married Saskia van Ulenborch, a beautiful, wealthy young woman from a good family. If we judge from his paintings of her over the years, it was a happy marriage.

By the end of the decade Rembrandt was the most celebrated painter in the city. He bought a large house in a fine neighborhood, lived lavishly, and collected paintings, costumes, and precious objects on a grand scale. Among his portraits are many of himself in assorted costumes and guises. He had so many pupils that he had to rent a warehouse for their work space.

Rembrandt's happiness was marred by the early deaths of their first three children. In 1641 his fourth child, Titus, was born. The next year Saskia died, and the challenging turmoil of his later life began.

Rembrandt's art grew more introspective. He turned increasingly to biblical subjects and landscapes. Fashionable portraits, his bread and butter, interested him less and less. His style, no longer so popular, brought fewer commissions. When Geertge Dircx, a nurse he had hired to help with Titus, became his common-law wife, his personal life raised eyebrows. A few years later he fell in love with another household servant, Hendrickje Stoffels. Geertge's subsequent departure was an extended ordeal, involving lawsuits, countersuits, and criminal charges. Hendrickje had two children with the painter and stayed with him until the end of her life. Because of a clause in Saskia's will, he was unable to marry Hendrickje, but his drawings and paintings of her are as affectionate as those of Saskia.

Rembrandt had always stretched his finances to the limit; and when the Dutch economy entered a shaky period in the 1650s, he was forced into bankruptcy. His house and all his possessions were sold in a series of auctions.

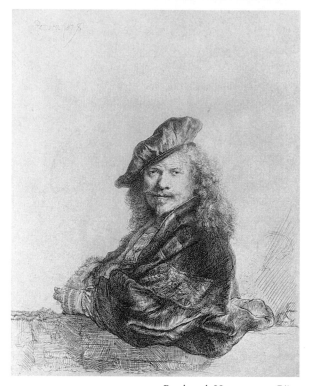

439   Rembrandt Harmensz van Rijn. SELF-PORTRAIT LEANING ON A LEDGE. 1639. Etching. 8⁵⁄₁₆" × 6⁵⁄₈".
The Metropolitan Museum of Art. Bequest of Mrs. H. O. Havemeyer, 1929. The H. O. Havemeyer Collection (29.107.25).

Ever loyal and supportive, Titus and Hendrickje formed a partnership to employ Rembrandt and to sell his work, thus shielding him legally from creditors. He moved with them to a smaller house in a far humbler part of town, where he lived in modest circumstances, continuing as a respected artist and receiving important commissions. Hendrickje died soon after, in 1663; Titus died in 1668. The next year, Rembrandt died.

Over one thousand drawings, etchings, and paintings survive, attesting to Rembrandt's vast output. To the very end, Rembrandt's art grew deeper and more insightful. In his last self-portraits, he had the look of a man whom nothing—no further drop of suffering—could touch, and yet there is not the slightest hint of self-pity. The same understanding and compassion radiates from his biblical scenes and portraits, making Rembrandt the most warmly human of the artists we consider great masters.

Jan Vermeer, another seventeenth-century Dutch painter, was also fascinated by light. His views of domestic life mark the high point of Dutch genre painting. Like Rembrandt, Vermeer was influenced by Caravaggio's use of light; unlike Caravaggio and Rembrandt, who used light for dramatic emphasis, Vermeer concentrated on the way light reveals each color, texture, and detail of the physical world. No one since Jan van Eyck had demonstrated such passion for seeing or such love for the visual qualities of the physical world.

Experimenting to learn to see more accurately, Vermeer evidently used a table-model camera obscura (see page 154). His intimate portrait THE GIRL WITH THE RED HAT was painted on a small wooden panel similar in size to the frosted glass on which the image would have appeared if a camera obscura of the period were used. Thus Vermeer may have taught himself to see with photographic accuracy by copying images from the ground glass. In THE GIRL WITH THE RED HAT, the focus has a narrow range. Only part of the girl's collar and the left edge of her cheek are in sharp focus; everything in front of and behind that narrow band becomes increasingly blurred. The carved lion's head on the arm of the chair in the foreground looks like shimmering beads of light, just as it would appear in an out-of-focus photograph.

Vermeer's understanding of the way light defines form enabled him to give his images a clear, luminous vitality. Much of the strength of the KITCHEN MAID comes from a limited use of color: yellow and blue accented by red-orange surrounded by neutral tones. Vermeer gave equal attention to the details and the way each detail relates to the whole composition. Notice, for example, the immense care given to the rendering of the subtle surface qualities of the wall with its nail holes and stains.

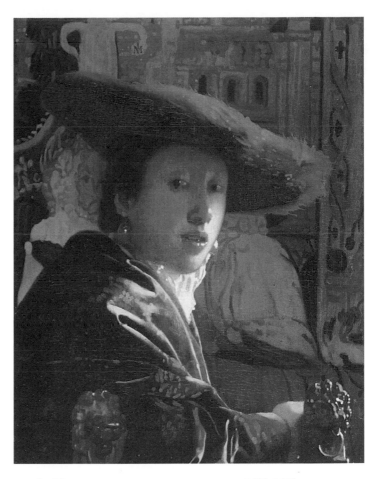

440 Jan Vermeer. THE GIRL WITH THE RED HAT. c. 1665–1666. Oil on panel, support: 9½" × 7⅛"; painted surface, 9" × 7¹⁄₁₆"; framed 15⅞" ×14"× 1¾".

441 Jan Vermeer.
THE KITCHEN MAID. c. 1658.
Oil on canvas. 18" × 16⅛".
Rijksmuseum, Amsterdam.

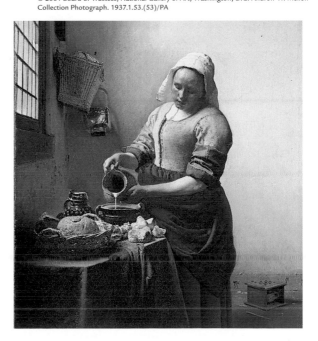

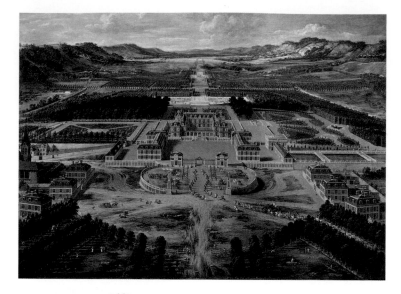

442 VERSAILLES. c. 1665.
Painting by Pierre Patel.
Musée du Louvre, Paris.
Photograph: Giraudon/Art Resource, NY.

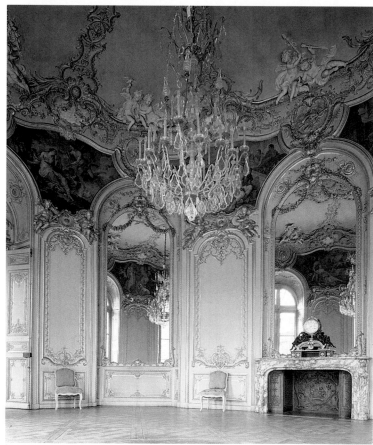

443 Germain Boffrand.
SALON DE LA PRINCESSE, HÔTEL DE SOUBISE.
Paris. Begun 1732.
Photograph: Hirmer Fotoarchiv, Munich, Germany.

During the Baroque period, French artists adopted Italian Renaissance ideas but made them their own; by the end of the seventeenth century, France had begun to take the lead in European art.

We can glimpse another view of seventeenth-century European life in the royal architecture and garden design of the French imperial villa of VERSAILLES, built for King Louis XIV. The main palace and its gardens exemplify French Baroque architecture and landscape architecture. Throughout the palace and gardens, cool classical restraint and symmetry balance the romance of Baroque opulence and grand scale.

VERSAILLES expressed the king's desire to surpass all others in the splendor of his palace. It is an example of royal extravagance, originally set in fifteen thousand acres of manicured gardens(!), twelve miles south of Paris. The vast formal gardens, with their miles of clipped hedges, proclaimed the king's desire to rule even over nature. This palace, which was also a governmental center, played an important role in the program of absolute monarchy that Louis XIV personified. Never more than here is the Baroque style allied with aristocracy.

Early in eighteenth-century France, the heavy, theatrical qualities of Italian Baroque art gradually gave way to the decorative *Rococo* style, a light, playful version of the Baroque. The curved shapes of shells were copied for elegantly paneled interiors and furniture, and they influenced the billowing shapes found in paintings. The arts moved out of the marble halls of palaces such as VERSAILLES and into fashionable town houses (called hotels) such as the HÔTEL DE SOUBISE.

The enthusiastic sensuality of the Rococo style was particularly suited to the extravagant and often frivolous life led by the French court and aristocracy. Some of the movement, light, and gesture of the Baroque remained, but now the effect was one of lighthearted abandon rather than dramatic action or quiet repose. Rococo paintings provided romantic visions of life free from hardships, in which courtship, music, and festive picnics filled the days.

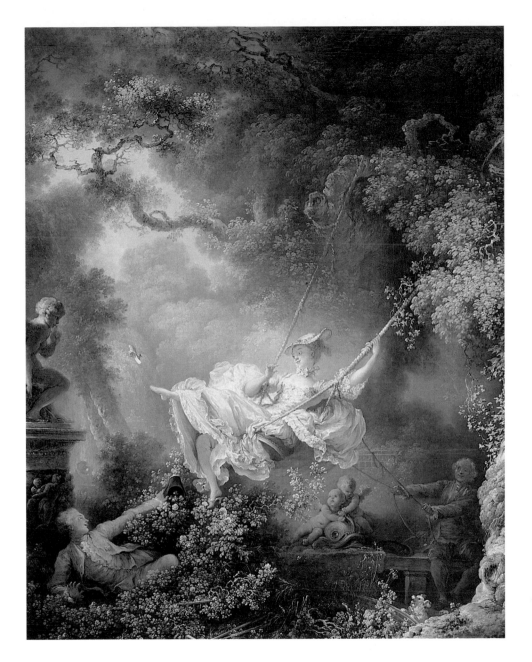

444 Jean Honoré Fragonard. THE SWING. 1767. Oil on canvas. 31⅞" × 25¼". Wallace Collection, London.

The aristocratic life of ease and dalliance is nowhere better depicted than in Jean-Honoré Fragonard's painting THE SWING. A well-dressed and idle young woman, attended by a dimly visible bishop, swings in a garden. At the lower left, a youth hides in the bushes and admires her. The story line of the work is provided by her flying shoe, which has come off and will soon land in the young man's lap. Fragonard learned the lessons of the Baroque well, as we can see in the off-balance composition arranged along the diagonal, and the contrasts of light and dark visible in the lush garden. But Baroque drama gives way here to sensuous abandon and light-as-air subject matter that typify the Rococo at its best.

Or worst. The next generation of French artists and intellectuals would rebel against the social irresponsibility portrayed in this type of art, which they saw as merely fluffy. The Enlightenment was already breaking out across Western Europe, and its new ideas of social equality and scientific inquiry would soon shake European art and culture to its core.

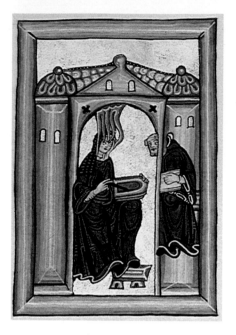

445 HILDEGARD'S VISION. From *Scivias* by Hildegard of Bingen. c. 1142–1152.
Facsimile of manuscript that belonged to the Wiesbaden Hessische Landesbibliotek.
Abeti St. Hildegard.

At the beginning of the feminist movement in the 1970s, many people began to notice that no women artists seemed to equal the achievements of male artists such as Michelangelo or Rembrandt. In fact, women artists were studied infrequently, and their work rarely appeared in textbooks. Art historian Linda Nochlin asked the question bluntly in a 1971 essay: "Why have there been no great women artists?"[5] An obvious answer might be that women's work has not reached the standard of quality set by great art. But, as Nochlin noted, the problem is much more complex than that.

The conditions for producing great art—or for excelling in any discipline—include family support, educational opportunity, community support, and patronage, as well as aptitude. Many artists now considered "great" benefited from most of these advantages. Yet the situation has been and still is discouraging, even hostile at times, for anyone who is not born white, moderately affluent, and male. Obstacles begin with the attitudes of parents, teachers, and others in power. What is amazing is that so many women have achieved so much against overwhelming odds.

From this perspective, there were few great women artists for the same reason that there were few great women scientists, ministers, or political leaders: They were kept out of most professions, including art.

Nevertheless, women have been creators since prehistoric times. Most of the ceramic pieces illustrated in this book were made by women. Most Persian carpets, Native-American baskets, and African textiles—including our cover—are also products of feminine hands. Western society classified this kind of work as crafts, not as art, and thus left it out of earlier accounts of art history. But to ignore these works is to ignore women's contributions over many cen-

turies. In addition, most of these works are unsigned or anonymous; they therefore get less attention than works attributed to known artists. This situation led one art historian to coin the phrase *Anonymous Was a Woman.*[6]

History provides well-documented accounts of injustices and discrimination against women artists. Works by women have often been incorrectly attributed to male teachers or to male relatives—on the assumption that no really good art could have been done by a woman. In 1723, Dutch painter Margareta Haverman, the second woman of her century to be elected to the French Royal Academy of Fine Arts, was expelled from the institution when its members, without apparent reason, decided that the work she submitted had been painted by her teacher. In 1859, sculptor Harriet Hosmer threatened a libel suit to force magazines to retract claims that men had done the work that bore her name. In 1875, American sculptor Anne Whitney lost a major commission when the jurors discovered that the work they had selected was by a woman. Racism has compounded the problem for women of color.

History can also tell us about women who overcame the odds. The twelfth-century nun Hildegard of Bingen, for example, was in charge of one of Germany's leading convents. Her musical compositions have only recently been rediscovered, but she contributed more than these. She corresponded with many of Europe's popes and one of these manuscripts, *Scivias*, was an autobiographical record of her prayer life.

HILDEGARD'S VISION is an illustration in *Scivias* made by nuns under her supervision. In the flattened-out style typical of medieval manuscripts, we see Hildegard receiving a vision of a brilliant light from heaven. It enters her eyes and head as she prepares to write it down in the presence of a monk. Hildegard characterized herself in her writings as an unassuming servant, a "feather on the breath of God," and the painting depicts her ready to transmit the divine will.

During the Renaissance in Italy, it became socially and politically correct for aristocrats to educate daughters as well as sons in the social arts. Although the idea was simply to produce women who could write poetry, dance, sing, paint, and excel in the art of conversation so that they would make good companions for aristocratic men, some women became highly accomplished artists. However, most were denied access to the training necessary for professional careers.

Sofonisba Anguissola was the first female artist of the Renaissance to achieve recognition throughout Europe. Anguissola studied with a portrait painter, and her well-publicized success led other male artists to accept female students. While still in her twenties, she became court painter to King Philip II of Spain. Her SELF-PORTRAIT of 1556 employs subtle Mannerist qualities that evoke a mystical mood.

European women artists were more numerous and better known during the Baroque period. Among the most remarkable was Artemisia Gentileschi, daughter of well-known artist Orazio Gentileschi. Although some of today's art historians consider Artemesia a better painter than her father, until recently her work received limited recognition because she was a woman.

While in her late teens, she was given drawing lessons by her father's friend and colleague Agostino Tassi.

The lessons were to have been held in the company of a female chaperone, but evidently the student-teacher relationship broke down. In 1612 Orazio Gentileschi accused Tassi of raping his daughter. Tassi pleaded innocent, but Artemesia did not waver in her testimony against him—despite being tortured with thumbscrews, ostensibly to elicit a confession of complicity or a denial of her claim. After a long trial, Tassi was acquitted of the charge.

Feminists and historians have made much of the relationship between her life—particularly the rape and its aftermath—and the violent subject matter of many of her paintings, including the series depicting the story of Judith from the Old Testament. To save her town from the advancing Assyrian army, Judith crossed enemy lines, seduced Holofernes, the Assyrian general, then beheaded him with his own sword. Although JUDITH AND THE MAIDSERVANT WITH THE HEAD OF HOLOFERNES does not show the gory decapitation (featured in her other paintings of the subject), the intensity of the moment is communicated clearly. The drama is intensified by bold use of theatrical light, sweeping curves, dramatic gestures, and warm colors.

Prior to the twentieth century, most of the women who achieved distinction in the visual arts had fathers or close male friends who were artists. A list of such women includes Rosa Bonheur (see chapter 21) and Marietta Robusti, both daughters of artists; Berthe Morisot (see page 144), who was closely associated with Edouard Manet; and Mary Cassatt (see page 146), who was a close friend of Edgar Degas.

Many other female artists whose works appear in this book have overcome major obstacles to become leading artists.

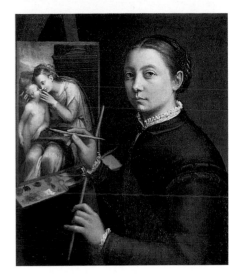

446 Sofonisba Anguissola
(Italian, 1527–1625).
SELF-PORTRAIT. 1556.
Oil on canvas.
66 × 57 cm.
Museum Zamek, Lancut Poland. © The Bridgeman
Art Library International Ltd.

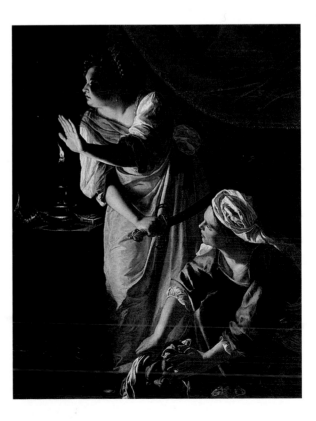

447 Artemisia Gentileschi.
JUDITH AND THE MAIDSERVANT WITH
THE HEAD OF HOLOFERNES. c. 1625.
Oil on canvas. 6'½" × 4'7¾".
Photograph ©1984 The Detroit Institute of Arts.
Gift of Mrs. Leslie H. Green.

Much of the art of the past that we enjoy today would have perished but for those people in each generation who cared for damaged works. Because art preserves tangible evidence of cultural hisory, preserving it is essential. But because art is subject to all the vicissitudes of nature and humanity, preserving it can also be very difficult.

A major work that has suffered grievously from both nature and humans is the beloved PARTHENON, a masterwork of world architecture (see p. 268 for a picture). After it served the Greeks as a temple of Athena, conquering Romans turned it into a brothel. Christians later used it as a church. The Turks of the Ottoman Empire refurbished it as a mosque for Muslim worship. When the Venetians attacked in 1687, the Turks converted it into an ammunition dump. In that year it was hit by Italian artillery and literally exploded.

In 1803, the British ambassador to the Ottoman court removed most of the marble sculpture from the building and took it to London, where it now remains. On the way, one of his ships ran aground and had to be salvaged. Overzealous cleaners in the British Museum in the 1930s scrubbed the surface of the sculptures with wire brushes, hopelessly damaging them. Meanwhile, what remains of the original building languishes under the impact of Athenian air pollution.

Every kind of art material presents its own particular set of challenges to restorers. The frescoes of the SISTINE CEILING, for example, were restored in a major campaign in the 1980s. Since fresco paint is very durable, restoring the works was mostly a matter of finding the proper cleaners to penetrate the layers of 400 years of air pollution, paint retouchings, varnish, mold, and candle smoke. When the work was completed, many were shocked to see for the first time the bright colors that Michelangelo used.

Most restorers of painting and sculpture today are trained in chemistry. They carefully analyze the surface and layers of works in their charge, often using a computer-aided process called mass spectrography. This preliminary chemical diagnosis informs them of the work's level of stability (or fragility), and suggests restorative methods.

Restorers must always decide how aggressively to treat a work's weaknesses; if the work is widely known, their decisions can be hotly debated. Restorers of the MONA LISA, for example, decided in the late 1990s not to remove the last layer of varnish from its surface, for fear of damaging Leonardo's paint underneath. This decision was hailed as respectful in some quarters and derided as too timid in others. In contrast, restorers of

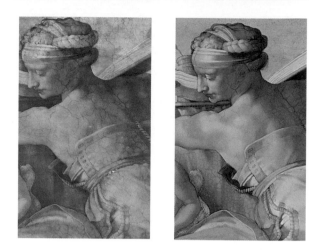

448 Michelangelo Buonarroti.
THE LIBYAN SIBYL; Detail of SISTINE CHAPEL ceiling frescoes, Vatican City.
a. before and
Photograph: Scala/Art Resource, NY.
b. after 1980s restoration. (See also page 296.)
Vatican Museums, Rome, Italy.

449 UCH MONUMENT COMPLEX.
Bahawalpur District, Punjab Province, Pakistan.
© Masood Khan/World Monuments Fund. Uch Monument Complex is on the World Monuments Watch *List of the 100 Most Endandered Sites*, a program of the World Monuments Fund.

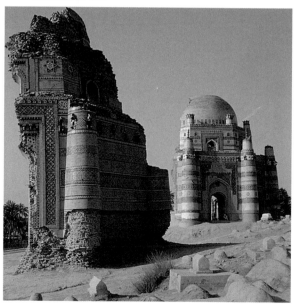

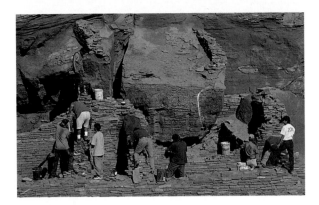

450 CORNERSTONES COMMUNITY PARTNERSHIP.
Hopi & Zuni youth working on restoring the Wapatki
National Monument. 1996.
Photograph: Ed Crocker/Cornerstone Community Partnerships.

Leonardo's LAST SUPPER recently added watercolor to the surface of the work, filling in gaps; this more assertive treatment was equally controversial for the opposite reasons.

One of the most celebrated recent cases of painting restoration involved intentional vandalism. In 1985, a Lithuanian independence activist entered the Hermitage Museum in St. Petersburg and threw acid on *Danae,* a large figural painting by Rembrandt. His attack left the work severely damaged, removing much paint and leaving descending trails of acid across most of its surface. The authorities who detained the man found explosives strapped to his legs under his clothing; apparently he had planned to commit suicide in the building, perhaps damaging other

works in the process. The Communist government urged the restorers to repaint *Danae* and make it appear that nothing had happened, but they resisted such an intrusive approach, biding their time by making chemical tests on the work until the government fell in 1989. They then restored it using more conservative means in a campaign that took seven years to complete. The work was placed back on display in 1997 together with photographs of the previously damaged surface. The museum published a book on the *Danae* story and it is widely circulated among painting restorers around the world.

However, for every high-profile work that is stabilized in a wealthy country,

hundreds of others slowly decay in poorer areas where resources are not as plentiful. These threatened works include important buildings in addition to paintings and sculpture.

The World Monuments Fund watches out for these, and publishes a list of the world's 100 most endangered sites every two years. Sites pictured in this book that have appeared on the list include the ancient city of Teotihuacan in Mexico; Machu Picchu in Peru; the Amenhotep Temple in Luxor, Egypt; the Roman city of Pompeii; Hagia Sophia in Istanbul; the Angkor Wat temple complex in Cambodia; and Borobudur in Indonesia. The Taj Mahal in India has been on the list twice, largely because air pollution from nearby oil refineries is damaging the marble surface of the building. The UCH MONUMENT COMPLEX in Pakistan was listed more recently; it has been a crossroads of cultures for many centuries. The site was probably founded by Alexander the Great. Its most ancient layers date back that far, suggesting that Uch was first used as a regional capital of his empire. It was later a Mongol administrative center during the eleventh and twelfth centuries, as that culture overran much of Asia and the Middle East. When Pakistan came back under Muslim control in the fifteenth century, Uch

then became an important nucleus for the Sufi sect, providing teachers and advisors to governors and princes throughout central Asia. The most impressive ruins at the site are the tombs and temples pictured here, where we see a mixture of architectural influences unique to that region. The site includes many priceless examples of brightly colored stonework in highly dramatic buildings. The fund's report says, "Today, Uch is stagnating, burdened by poverty, environmental degradation, and a breakdown of municipal management."

Restoration of such complexes is often a community affair. The CORNERSTONES COMMUNITY PARTNERSHIP for example, trains Native American youths in New Mexico to restore the ancient pueblos of their ancestors. Similar efforts have taken effect in Cambodia. Preservation of art works, always an uphill battle, engages creative minds and hands across the world.

CHAPTER EIGHTEEN

TRADITIONAL ARTS OF ASIA

Human beings have lived in Asia almost as long as they have in Africa. In Asia there occurred a similar development of ancient cultures, from hunting and gathering to agricultural village societies, to Bronze Age kingdoms, and so on. (For examples of ancient Asian art, see chapter 15.) Culturally as well as geographically, India is at the core of the continent. Many ideas that later permeated Asian societies originated in India and radiated outward. However, because each region of Asia also has its own local cultural forms, outright borrowing is rare. Rather, we can trace the passage of ideas and art styles across the continent as they were adapted and modified in various locations.

INDIA

In the 1930s, excavations at the sites of the ancient cities of Mohenjo-daro and Harappā revealed the remains of a well-organized society with advanced city planning and a high level of artistic production. The two cities served as focal points for a civilization that extended for one thousand miles along the fertile Indus Valley between three thousand and five thousand years ago. (Most of this valley, where Indian culture began, became part of Pakistan after Indian independence in 1947.)

Ancient Indus Valley sculpture already shows the particularly sensual naturalism that character-izes much of later Indian art. This quality enlivens the small, masterfully carved MALE TORSO from Harappā. The lifelike surface gives the torso an energized quality, as if it were animated by breath. The figure's protruding abdomen may reveal an early understanding of the importance of *prana*, or life-giving breath, a concept perpetuated by the ancient tradition of hatha yoga.

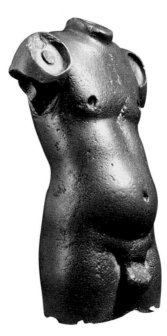

451 MALE TORSO.
Harappā, Indus Valley.
c. 2400–2000 B.C.E.
Limestone.
Height 3½".
National Museum of India.
New Delhi.
Photograph: Prithwish Neogy.

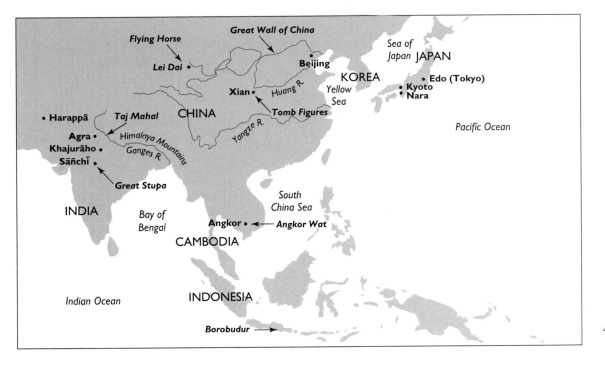

452 HISTORICAL
MAP OF ASIA.

Relatively few works of art have survived from the period between 1800 B.C.E., when the Indus Valley civilization declined, and 300 B.C.E., when the first Buddhist art appeared. Nevertheless, the years in that interval were important ones for the development of Indian thought and culture.

Starting around 1500 B.C.E., the Indian subcontinent was infiltrated and gradually taken over by nomadic Aryan tribes from the northwest. The Aryans' beliefs, gods, and social structure formed the foundation of the subsequent development of Indian civilization. Key Aryan beliefs that influenced later Indian thought include the idea that the universe evolves in repeated cycles of creation and destruction; that individuals are reincarnated after death; and that there is one supreme form of wisdom. These beliefs were spelled out in the main forms of Aryan literature, the Vedas (hymns) and Upanishads (philosophical works)—texts still regarded as sacred by many Indians.

The Aryans, being nomads, left behind very little of what we might call art. What came into being as Indian art is a synthesis of indigenous Indian art forms and the religious ideas of the nomadic Aryans.

Many Indian religions developed from the core beliefs of the Aryans. Their literature, for example, was accepted as scripture by Hindus. In the sixth century B.C.E., two highly influential spiritual leaders preached variations on Hindu beliefs. They were Siddhartha Gautama (563–483 B.C.E.), founder of Buddhism, and Mahavira, founder of Jainism. Although most Indians today are Hindus, Buddhism dominated the formative years of the development of Indian art, and it became a major cultural factor elsewhere in Asia.

Buddhist Art

The Buddhist religion began when Siddhartha Gautama achieved enlightenment. Seeking an answer to the question of human suffering, he arrived at what Buddhists call the Four Noble Truths: (1) Existence is full of suffering. (2) The cause of suffering is desire. (3) To eliminate suffering, one must eliminate desire. (4) To eliminate desire, one must follow the Eightfold Path of right views, right aspirations, right speech, right conduct, right livelihood, right effort, right mindfulness, and right contemplation. He also taught that if one achieves

TRADITIONAL ARTS OF ASIA   315

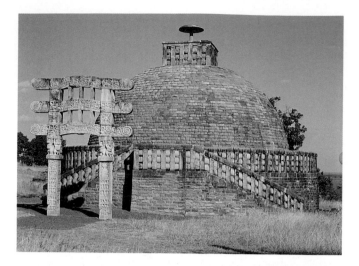

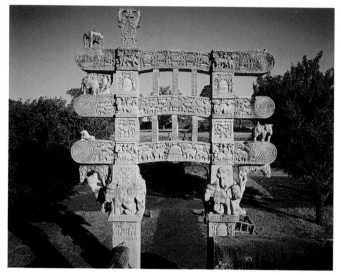

enlightenment, the endless cycle of death and rebirth will be broken, and the believer will experience a final rebirth in a pure spiritual realm. Siddhartha began to attract followers in the late sixth century B.C.E.; they called him the "Enlightened One" or the Buddha.

Early Buddhism did not include the production of images. Eventually, however, religious practice needed visual icons as support for contemplation, and images began to appear. The many styles of Buddhist art and architecture vary according to the cultures that produced them. As Buddhism spread from India to Southeast Asia and across central Asia to China, Korea, and Japan, it influenced (and was influenced by) native religious and aesthetic traditions.

An excellent example of early Indian Buddhist art is the domelike structure called the *stupa*, which evolved from earlier burial mounds. At THE GREAT STUPA at Sāñchī, four gates are oriented to the four cardinal directions. The devout walk around the stupa in a ritual path, symbolically taking the Path of Life around the World Mountain. Such stupas were erected at sacred locations, and relics (items belonging to a holy person) were usually buried in their core.

453a. STUPA I.
Sāñchī, India.
10 B.C.E.–15 C.E.
Scala/Art Resource/NY.

b. Eastern gate of
THE GREAT STUPA.
Photograph: Borromeo/Art Resource, NY.

454 EVOLUTION OF BUDDHIST ARCHITECTURE.
  a. Early Indian stupa. 3rd century to early 1st century B.C.E.
  b. Later Indian stupa. 2nd century C.E.
  c. Chinese pagoda. 5th to 7th centuries C.E.
  d. Japanese pagoda. 7th century C.E.

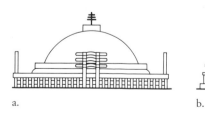

a.

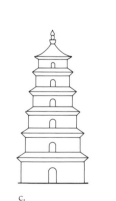

b.

c.

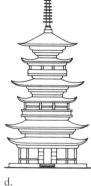

d.

The four gateways to THE GREAT STUPA include layers of sculpture in relief. These tell the story of the Buddha's life, but without depicting him directly. The characteristic sensuousness that we observed in the MALE TORSO from Harappā still enlivens these early monuments.

We can trace the EVOLUTION OF BUDDHIST ARCHITECTURE from its origin in India to its later manifestations in other parts of Asia. Buddhist pagodas developed from a merging of the Indian stupa and the traditional Chinese watchtower. The resulting broad-eaved tower structure was in turn adopted and changed by the Japanese.

Indian art was influenced by Western art when Alexander the Great conquered large parts of what is now Pakistan and Afghanistan in the fourth century B.C.E. This region, called Gandhara, continued its contacts with the Roman Empire during its peak years. Buddhist sculptors in the region developed a distinctive style of working that owes about equal amounts to East and West; the STANDING BODHISATTVA is an excellent example. Here the sculptor shows a knowledge of the realism of Roman portraiture, as well as the classical Greek method of showing a subject's body beneath the folds of the drapery in the legs. The subject, however, is Buddhist. A *bodhisattva* is a person who is on the point of achieving enlightenment, but delays it in order to remain on earth and teach others. Bodhisattva are usually depicted wearing rich garments and jewels.

The Indian Gupta dynasty (c. 320–540) is notable for major developments in politics, law, mathematics, and the arts. In the visual arts, the Gupta style combines native Indian ways of seeing with the naturalism of the Gandhara. Although slightly damaged, the carved stone STANDING BUDDHA is a fine example of Gupta sculpture. In its cool, idealized perfection, the refined Gupta style

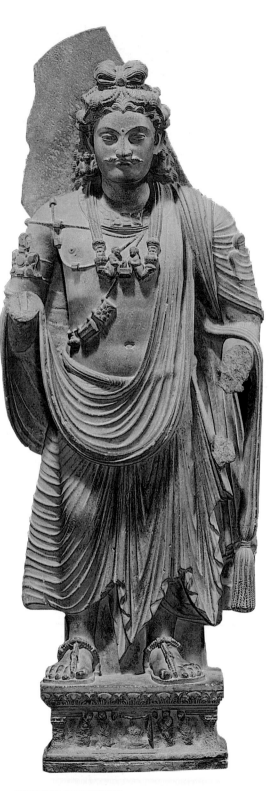

455 STANDING BODHISATTVA.
N.W. Pakistan, Gandhara region. Late 2nd century A.D. Kushana period. Gray schist, Height 43⅛".

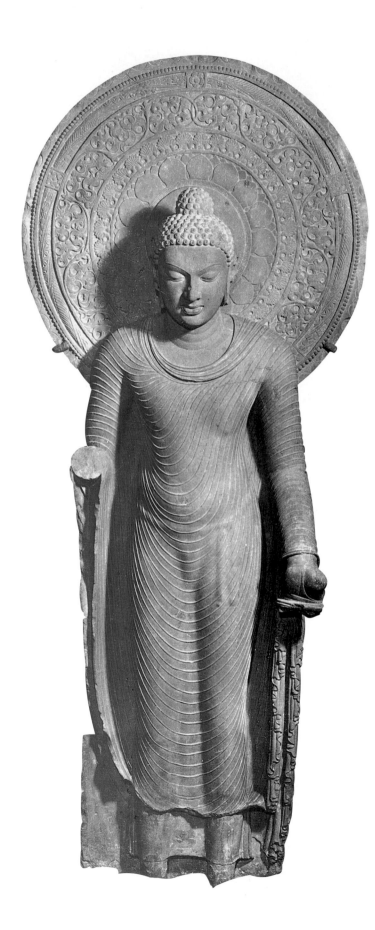

marks a period of high achievement in Indian art. Once again, the simplified mass of the figure seems to push out from within as though the body were inflated with breath. The rounded form is enhanced by curves repeated rhythmically down the figure. The drapery seems wet as it clings to and accentuates the softness of the body.

We can see similar Gupta elegance and linear refinement in the noble figure known as the "BEAUTIFUL BODHISATTVA" PADMAPANI, part of a series of elaborate paintings in the Ajanta Caves in Central India. The fine linear definition of the figure accents full, rounded shapes, exemplifying the Gupta ideal of relaxed opulence. The Gupta style was the principal one exported when Buddhism began to spread to China and Southeast Asia.

456 STANDING BUDDHA. 5th century.
Red sandstone. Height 5'3".
Indian Museum, Calcutta.

457 "BEAUTIFUL BODHISATTVA" PADMAPANI.
Detail of a fresco from Cave 1. Ajanta, India. c. 600–650
Duane Preble

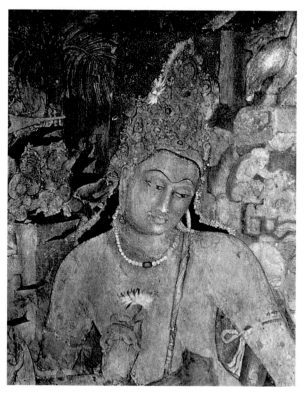

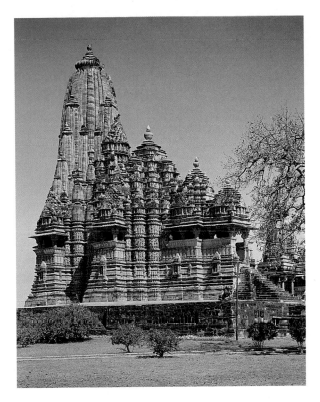

458 KANDARYA MAHADEVA TEMPLE.
Khajurāho, India. 10th–11th centuries.

a. Exterior
Photograph: Borromeo/Art Resource, NY.

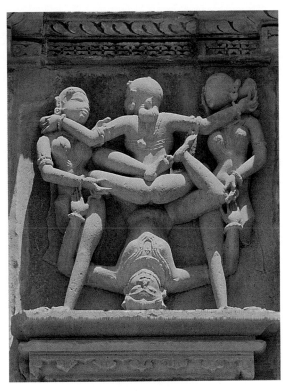

b. Scene from KANDARIYA MAHADEVA TEMPLE.
Erotic reliefs. Chandella dynasty, 1025–50 CE.
Khajuraho, Madhya Pradesh, India.
Photograph: Borromeo/Art Resource, NY.

Hindu Art

Hinduism recognizes three principal gods: Brahma, the creator of all things; Vishnu, the sustainer; and Shiva, the destroyer. These three gods intervene in human affairs at appropriate moments either to guarantee the continuing evolution of the cosmos, or to restore the proper balance of good and evil forces in the world. Most Hindu devotional practices are done individually (rather than in a group as is common in Christian worship), and Shiva is the god most often venerated in architecture and sculpture.

The Hindu temple is a major architectural form of India, and one of the world's most distinctive. It typically includes two parts: a porch, for the preparation and purification of the worshiper, and the Womb Chamber, called in Sanskrit the *garba griha*, the sacred room where an image of the god is kept.

The KANDARYA MAHADEVA TEMPLE at Khajurāho in north central India is one of the most spectacular and best preserved. A stairway leads to not one, but several porches, which allow access to the *garba griha*. The sacred chamber is marked on the outside by a tall tower that has replicas of itself on its sides. The rounded projecting forms, symbolizing both male and female sexuality, seem to celebrate the procreative energy existing in nature and within ourselves.

Shown here is one of six erotic scenes from the abundant sculpture on the outside of KANDARYA MAHADEVA TEMPLE. To the Hindu worshiper, union with God is filled with a joy analogous to the sensual pleasure of erotic love. The natural beauty and fullness of the human figures emphasize maleness and femaleness. Fullness seems to come from within the rounded forms, as we saw in the more ancient MALE TORSO from Harappā. The intertwining figures symbolize divine love in human form—an allegory of ultimate spiritual unity.

The complex corps of Hindu gods and goddesses depicted in Indian art represents all aspects

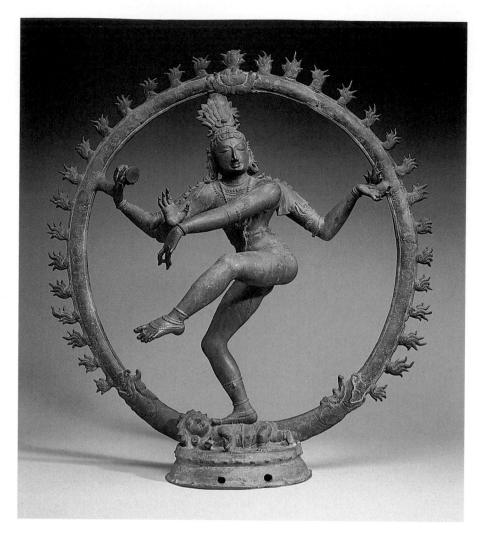

459   NĀTARĀJA: SHIVA AS KING SHIVA NĀTARĀJA, LORD OF THE DANCE.
South India, Chola Period, 11th century.
Bronze. Height 111.5 cm, (43⅛" × 40").
© 2001 The Cleveland Museum of Art.
Purchase from the J. H. Wade Fund (1930.331).

of human aspirations and experience. In later Hindu belief, Shiva encompasses in cyclic time the creation, preservation, dissolution, and re-creation of the universe. To show these roles, Shiva has been given various forms in Hindu sculpture. In an eleventh-century image from South India, SHIVA NĀTARĀJA, LORD OF THE DANCE, performs the cosmic dance within the orb of the sun. He tramples on the monster of ignorance as he holds sacred symbols in his hands. The encircling flame is the purifying fire of destruction and creation. He taps on a small drum to mark the cosmic rhythm of death and rebirth. As he moves, the universe is reflected as light from his limbs. The sculpture implies movement so thoroughly that motion seems contained in every aspect of the piece. Each part is alive with the rhythms of an ancient ritual dance. Multiple arms increase the sense of movement, while his face is composed and impassive, indicating that there is nothing to fear.

In the seventeenth and eighteenth centuries, northern Indian artists, influenced by the miniature painting traditions of Persia (see chapter 19), developed their own related, yet unique styles of painting. Figures in serene landscapes and religious legends were popular subjects. Hindu deities KRISHNA AND RADHA IN THE GROVE is charac-

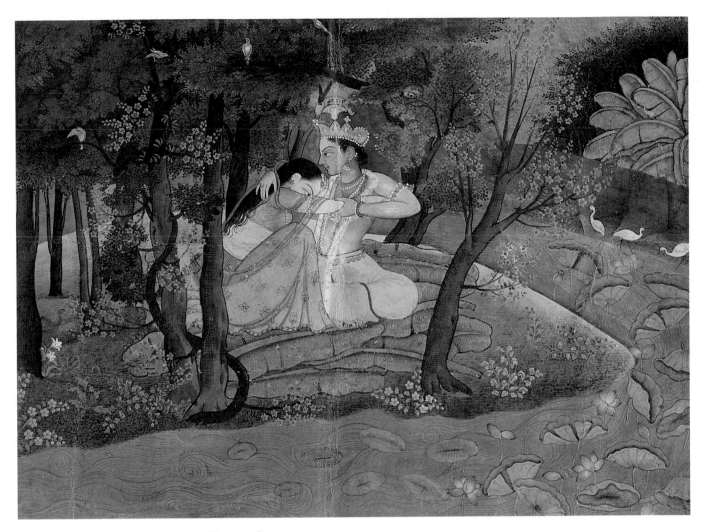

460 RADHA AND KRISHNA IN THE GROVE. Kangra style,
c. 1780. Gouache on paper. 4¾" × 6¾" (12.3 × 17.2 cm).
Victoria and Albert Museum, London/Art Resource, NY.

teristic of the romantic content and gracefully
flowing linear style of painters from the hill state
of Kangra. This painting echoes some of the
sumptuousness and sensuality of early Indian
sculpture. The legends of Krishna contain a wealth
of erotic references. As in Hindu temple sculpture
(see page 319), erotic themes in the painted legends of Krishna lead to deeper symbolic meanings.
Romantic love in the painting symbolizes the
soul's union with the divine.

Most of India was conquered by the Islamic
Mughal rulers in the early sixteenth century; that
part of Indian art will be a subject of chapter 19.

SOUTHEAST ASIA

The Bronze Age in Southeast Asia began when that
metal was first imported into the region about 800
B.C.E. Soon thereafter, the major cultural division of
the region appeared: The eastern coast, encompass-
ing most of what is now Vietnam, fell under Chinese
influence; most of the remainder willingly adopted
and transformed cultural influences from India.

Buddhism and Hinduism both spread south-
ward and eastward from India with traders and
merchants. Early Southeast Asian art is primarily
Buddhist; later monuments combine motifs, gods,
and figures from both religions. Each region of

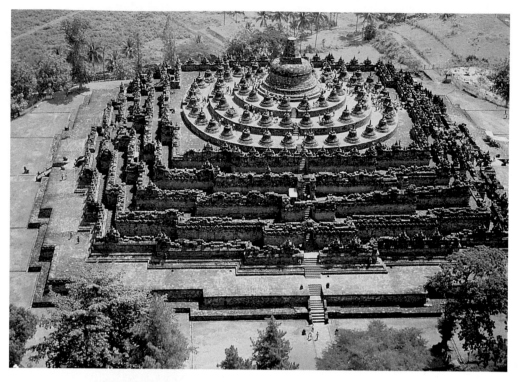

461 BOROBUDUR. Java. c. 800.
a. Aerial view.

Photograph: Robert Harding Picture Library.

b. CORRIDOR AT BOROBUDUR.
First Gallery.

Photograph: Werner Forman Archive.

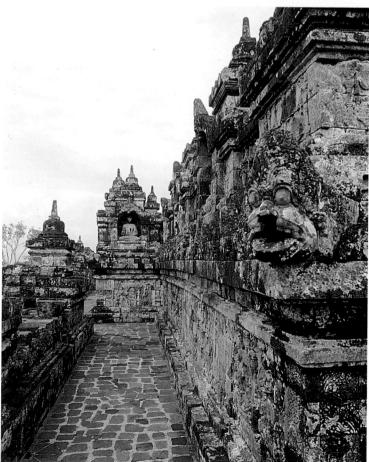

Southeast Asia developed its own interpretation of the major Indian styles.

By any standard, BOROBUDUR must rank among the major works of world art. Built about 800 C.E. on the island of Java (now part of Indonesia), it is an extremely elaborate version of an Indian stupa, or sacred mountain. Rising from a relatively flat plain, it stands above the local surroundings, measuring 105 feet high and 408 feet on a side. It is oriented to the four cardinal directions, with stairways at the four midpoints.

Pilgrims who come for spiritual refreshment may enter at any opening, and then walk around and climb the various terraces in a clockwise direction. More than ten miles of relief sculpture adorn the various CORRIDORS, telling stories that duplicate the journey to enlightenment. On the lower levels, the reliefs deal with the struggle of existence and the cycle of death and rebirth. Then come reliefs depicting the life of the Buddha. As pilgrims walk in these corridors, the high walls prevent them from seeing out, and the curves in the path limit the view ahead. Upper terrace reliefs depict the ideal world of paradise. However, there is still more to come.

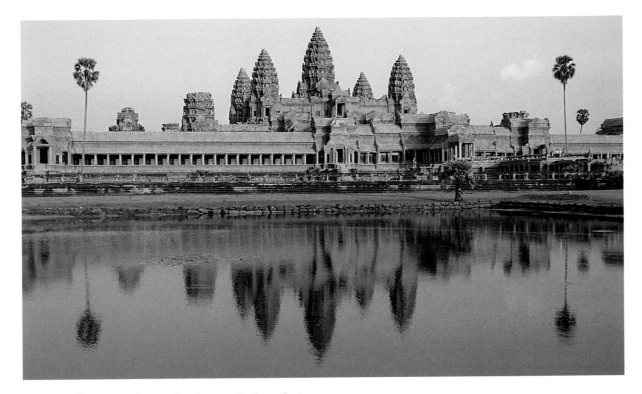

The final four circular levels permit the pilgrim to look out over the landscape and take in the broad view, suggesting enlightenment. Each of the seventy-two small hollow stupas contains a statue of a seated Buddha that is only dimly visible from the outside. At the very top is a sealed stupa whose contents the pilgrim can just guess at. Thus BOROBUDUR presents the Buddhist conception of the pathway through the cycles of birth and death, which culminates in enlightenment.

The sacred mountain of BOROBUDUR was a principal influence on the Cambodian temple of ANGKOR WAT, which was erected in the twelfth century near the capital of the Khmer empire. This was the most prosperous period in Cambodia's history, as the rulers mastered the science of irrigation and were able to make the jungles produce abundant crops. The people at that time seemed to accord their rulers near-divine status since the many stone carvings of Buddhas, Bodhisattvas, and Hindu gods appear also to be portraits of real people. The two religions were apparently considered compatible.

The temple, which faces due west, was originally surrounded by moats, as if to remind everyone

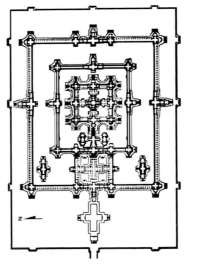

462 ANGKOR WAT.
c. 1120–1150.
a. West entrance.
Photograph: John Elk III/Bruce Coleman Inc.
b. Plan.

that management of water was the source of wealth. The many corridors have corbelled roofs, and inside they are decorated with low relief sculpture depicting primarily Hindu myths about the god Vishnu. (See one of the best of these, ARMY ON THE MARCH, on page 195.) The ruler of Cambodia thought of himself as a descendant of Vishnu, guarding the fertility of his domain. This emphasis on fertility in the design of ANGKOR WAT extends to the tops of the towers, which resemble sprouting buds.

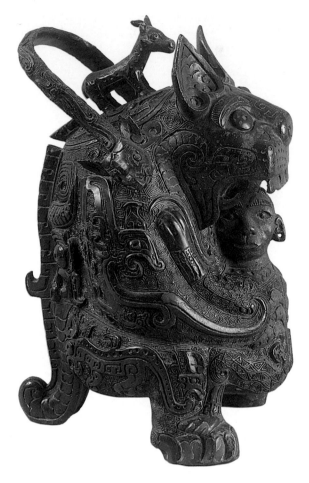

463 RITUAL VESSEL (LA TIGRESSE).
China. Shang dynasty. c. 1100–1000 B.C.E.
Cast bronze. Height 14".
Musée Cernushi, Paris. © MVP/negative: MC06155.

CHINA

Chinese civilization up to the modern period was characterized by the interaction of three traditions: Confucianism, Daoism, and Buddhism. The first two are Chinese creations, while Buddhism came from India. All three have interacted and influenced each other, imparting richness and variety to Chinese culture. Before these traditions developed, however, distinctive Chinese arts were already flourishing.

Some of the world's finest cast-bronze objects were produced in China during the Shang dynasty (sixteenth to eleventh centuries B.C.E.). In the RITUAL VESSEL, there is an overall compactness. As on other Shang containers, surfaces are covered with an intricate composite of animal forms: sometimes fragments of animals are combined, sometimes complete animals are depicted. In this piece, a deer acts as a handle for the lid; just behind the deer, an elephant's trunk comes out of a tiger's mouth, providing a third support. The man seems about to be devoured—his head is shown within the ferocious jaw of the tiger spirit—yet at the same time his hands are relaxed as he reaches to the animal for protection. An intriguing aspect of this vessel is the gentle expression on the man's face in relation to the aggressive, though protective power of the animal.

Most bronze vessels were used in rituals in honor of ancestors. The Chinese believed that one's ancestors live eternally in the spiritual realm, and from there they can influence worldly affairs—for better or worse. In the hope of improving their after-life, many persons were buried with most of their possessions. No one, however, was more vain in collecting objects for their burial than the emperor Qin Shihuangdi, who at the time of his death in 210 B.C.E. had unified China in something like its present form. (His dynastic name, Qin—pronounced chin—is the root of the word *China*.) So intent was he on guarding his afterlife that he ordered a massive army of life-size clay soldiers made for his protection. The TERRA COTTA WARRIORS number about six thousand in all, among them cavalrymen, archers, and foot soldiers. These lifelike figures in their huge tomb were not discovered until 1974, in one of the greatest archaeological finds in history.

The tombs from the Han dynasty (206 B.C.E.–221 C.E.) have yielded most of the surviving art work from that period in China, and from these remains we can learn a great deal about what interested and motivated at least the upper classes.

464 TERRA COTTA WARRIORS.
Pit No. 1, Museum of the First Emperor of Qin.
Shaanxi Province, China. Han Dynasty. c. 210 B.C.E.
Photograph: Hamilton Photography and Film Company.

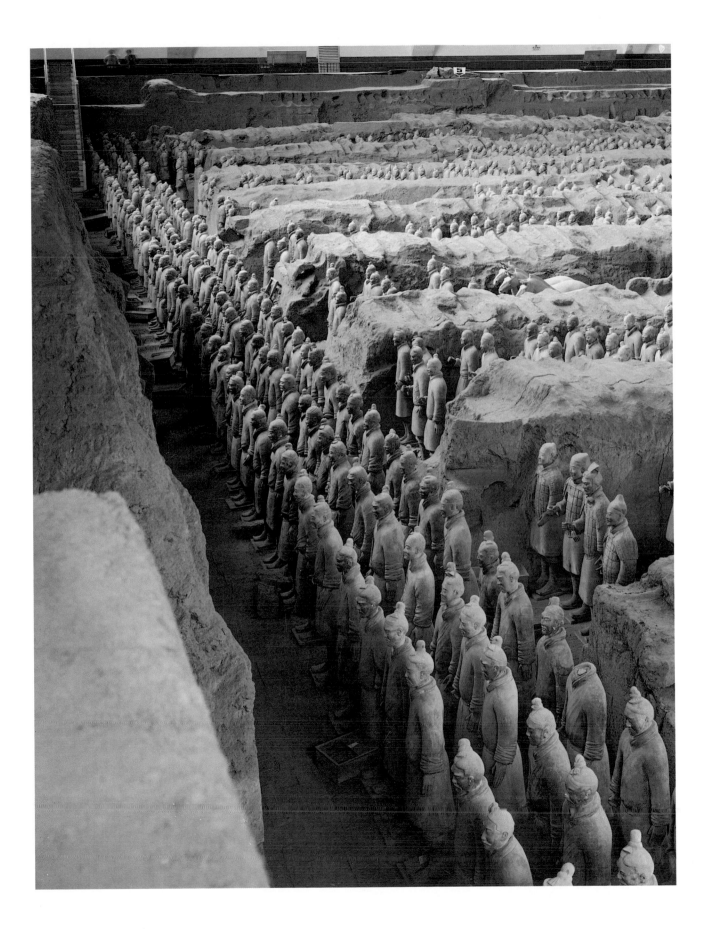

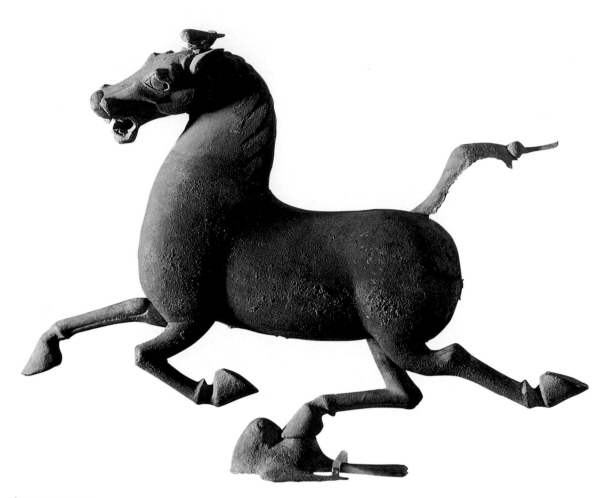

465 FLYING HORSE.
One leg resting on a swallow.
Eastern Han dynasty. 2nd century.
Bronze. 13½" × 17¾" (34.5 × 45 cm).
Excavated 1969 at Wu–Wai, Kansu.
National Museum, Beijing, China, Erich Lessing/Art
Resource, NY

Probably one of the best-known works from this period is the magnificent second-century FLY-ING HORSE found in Gansu Province. The sculptor gave a feeling of weightlessness to the horse by delicately balancing it on one hoof atop an abstract representation of a flying swallow. The curvaceous form and powerful energy of this elegant horse is vividly captured in a way that is typically Chinese.

Horses were prized possessions of royalty and aristocracy. Throughout Chinese history, they frequently appear in art as strong, noble animals. The horse is one of the twelve signs of the traditional Chinese zodiac, and persons born in the Year of

the Horse are said to possess strength, speed, and endurance.

Here the artist has understood the basic energy or life force of the animal, and rendered it faithfully. The quest to understand and depict this inner force, or *qi* in Chinese, animates a great deal of art production through the centuries in China.

Aside from tomb figures, there are few early Chinese representations of the human body in art. The most important tradition of sculpture based on the human figure began as Buddhism reached China from India some time during the first century C.E. Chinese artists then adopted the idealized, sacred images of Indian sculptors, with only minor changes. Some of the finest figures—those that express Buddhist compassion—are known as Avalokitesvara in India, Guan Yin in China, and Kwannon in Japan. The gentle smile and relaxed posture of the BODHISATTVA GUAN YIN symbolize kindness, patience, and wisdom. Guan Yin, also known as the Bodhisattva of Infinite Compassion, is a common figure for popular devotion in Buddhism, and here he is depicted in a typical Asian posture called "royal ease."

In painting, even more clearly than in sculpture, we see the Chinese reverence for nature. Traditionally, Chinese painters sought to manifest the spirit residing in every form. According to the beliefs of Daoism, an indigenous Chinese religion, a secret force called the Dao (or "the way" in English) animates all creation. A painter was taught to meditate before wielding a brush in order to achieve a balance between the impression received through the eyes and the perception of the heart and mind. After prolonged contemplation of nature, the artist painted from memory, working with ink and light color on silk or paper. Through painting, individuals nourished spiritual harmony within themselves and revealed divine energy to others. Daoism focuses on the relative nature of all things: There can be no death without life, no good without evil, and so forth. Behind the duality and illusion of the so-called real world is the unifying Dao. It is in this way that the universe functions, as one can see in the effortless flow of interacting forces of nature.

The Northern Song dynasty (960–1126) was a particularly important period for painting in China. During the eleventh century, a group of artist-intellectuals developed a new spirit in artistic expression. Many of these painters, who were poets, political leaders, and accomplished calligraphers, held that the artist's true character and emotions could be expressed through the abstract forms of calligraphic characters—and even through individual brush strokes. They were critical of those who painted for commercial rather than aesthetic reasons.

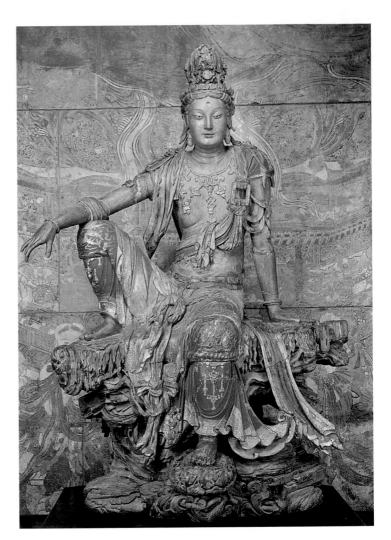

466 BODHISATTVA GUAN YIN,
THE WATER AND MOON GUANYIN BODHISATTVA.
11th–12th century. Northern Song (960–1127) or Liao Dynasty (916–1125). Chinese, Shanxi Province. Wood with paint. 95" × 65" (241.3 × 165.1 cm).

Nelson-Atkins Museum of Art, Kansas City, MO. Purchase: Nelson Trust. Photograph by Robert Newcombe. © 1993 The Nelson Gallery Foundation. All Rights Reserved.

467 Huai-su.
Detail of AUTOBIOGRAPHY.
Tang dynasty,
7th–10th centuries.
Ink on paper.
National Palace Museum,
Taipei, Taiwan, Republic of China.

Long valued in China, calligraphy is traditionally considered a more profound art than painting. Since ancient times, Chinese leaders of all kinds have been expected to express the strength of their character through elegant writing. By introducing calligraphic brush techniques for expressive purposes, painters sought to elevate painting to the levels that calligraphy and poetry had already attained. Huai-su, in AUTOBIOGRAPHY, and later masters drew inspiration from fourth-century Daoist poet, statesman, and master calligrapher Wang Xizhi. His style of writing, an improvement on earlier styles, has served as an inspirational model for generations of calligraphers to the present day. The stature of Wang Xizhi in China is comparable to that of Shakespeare and Rembrandt in the West and indicates the Chinese people's long-standing admiration for great calligraphy. Unfortunately, only a few original examples of his writing survive.

The flowering of calligraphy as an art form was due partly to the popularity of the new, looser style of writing that freed scholars from the angular formality of the characters that were used in official script. The fluid script enabled artists and poets to express themselves in a personal and spontaneous manner. With the spontaneous, gestural design of each brush stroke, the artist conveys the emotional as well as the intellectual content of the word or character being written. Poetry lies in the execution of the stroke as well as the phrase. In China, painting and writing are closely related, and Chinese artists often include poems within their paintings. The same brushes and ink are used for both, and in both each brush stroke is important in the total design. Artists "paint" their poems as much as they "write" their paintings.

Contemporaries of the court painter Fan Kuan regarded him as the greatest landscape painter of the Song dynasty. In his large hanging scroll TRAV-ELERS AMONG MOUNTAINS AND STREAMS, intricate brushwork captures the spirit of trees and rocks. Artists used many kinds of brush strokes, each identified by descriptive names such as "raveled rope," "raindrops," "ax cuts," "nailhead," and "wrinkles on a devil's face." Here "raindrop" and other types of brush strokes suggest the textures of the vertical face of the cliff. Men and donkeys, shown in minute scale, travel a horizontal path dwarfed by high cliffs rising sharply behind them. To highlight the stylized waterfall as the major accent in the design, Fan Kuan painted the crevice behind the waterfall in a dark wash and left the off-white silk unpainted to suggest the falling water. The vertical emphasis of the composition is offset by the almost horizontal shape of the light area behind the rocks in the lower foreground. The massive centrality of the composition is typical of the efforts of Northern Song artists to capture the more powerful aspects of nature.

When a vertical line intersects a horizontal line, the opposing forces generate a strong center of interest. Fan Kuan took advantage of this phenomenon by extending the implied vertical line of the falls to direct the viewer's attention to the travelers. Figures give human significance to the painting and, by their small scale, indicate the vastness of nature. Fan Kuan achieved his monumental landscape in part by grouping the fine details into a balanced design of light and dark areas.

The painting embodies ideas of Daoism and Neo-Confucianism, China's two major philosophical and spiritual traditions, in which nature is both emptiness and substance, interacting passive and active forces (yin and yang) that regulate the universe. One achieves harmony on Earth through a balance of these forces—female and male, void and solid, dark and light.

In both central and southern China, steep, mist-shrouded peaks have inspired Chinese painters for centuries. In the seventeenth century, Li Li-Weng wrote, "First we see the hills in the painting, then we see the painting in the hills." His words remind us that, although art depends on our

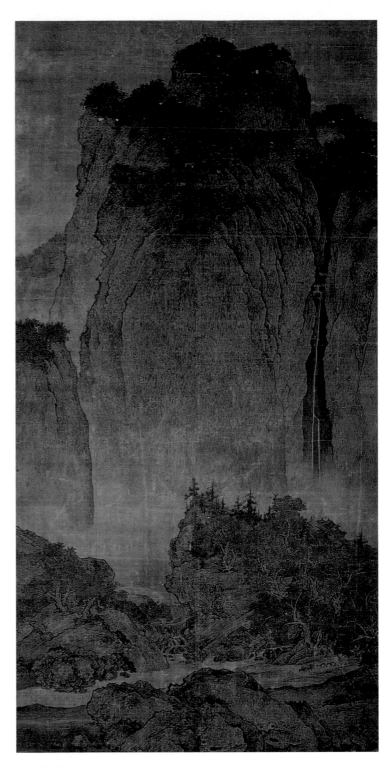

468 Fan Kuan.
TRAVELERS AMONG MOUNTAINS AND STREAMS.
Song dynasty. Early 11th century.
Hanging scroll, ink on silk. Height 81¼".
National Palace Museum, Taipei, Taiwan, Republic of China.

469 Wu Chen.
ALBUM LEAF from MANUAL OF INK BAMBOO. 1350.
Ink on paper. 16⅞" × 20½".
National Palace Museum, Taipei, Taiwan, Republic of China.

470 Yu-Jian.
MOUNTAIN VILLAGE IN A MIST. 13th century.
Ink on paper. Height 13".
Idemitsu Museum of Arts, Tokyo.

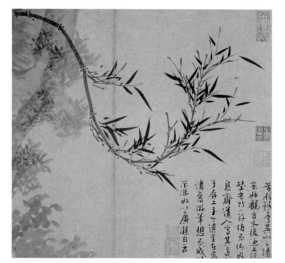

perception of nature, art also helps us to see nature with fresh eyes.

Northern Song painters helped prepare the way for another school of painting that flourished in Buddhist monasteries. Painters in the thirteenth century who espoused Chan (as Zen Buddhism is called in China) developed a bold style that used abbreviated, abstract references. Compared to the detailed representation in Fan Kuan's TRAVELERS AMONG MOUNTAINS AND STREAMS, priest Yu-Jian's painting of MOUNTAIN VILLAGE IN A MIST shows a simplified, loosely representational impression of a landscape. In this painting, the relationship of human beings to nature is again expressed by the figures and the barely suggested roof lines in an atmosphere of mist-obscured mountains. The white, unpainted surface is as visually strong as the brushwork. Whereas Fan Kuan's painting is detailed and formal, Yu-Jian's is suggestive and informal.

An unpainted surface standing for sky or clouds can also be a surface to write upon. Brush marks that indicate the landscape are expected to evoke a remembered experience rather than present what the eyes see. Here, the accompanying writing is a poem that also stimulates the memory image. The poem and the painting are parallel expressions. The practice of adding inscriptions to paintings be-

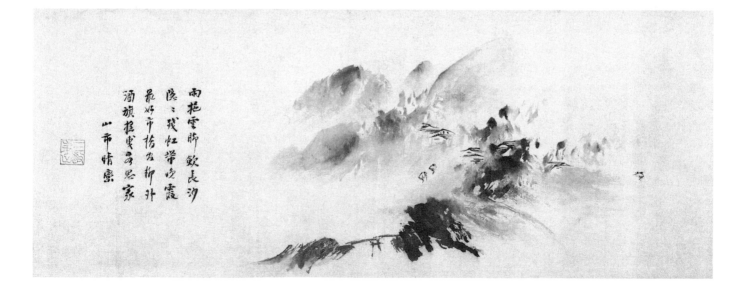

came common in the thirteenth and fourteenth centuries, and it has persisted through most of Chinese history.

Most of the important painters of the Song Dynasty were associated with offical art academies or monasteries; during the following Yuan Dynasty (1279-1368), the conquest of China by Mongols radically altered this scenario. The most creative artists refused to paint or teach for the foreign government; rather they lived outside official sponsorship. Devoting themselves to a life of art and poetry, they created a new style called *literati painting*.

The Yuan Dynasty literati painters made many innovations in brushwork and subject matter. They used the brush in new ways and saw old subjects with fresh eyes. An example is Huang Gongwang's DWELLING IN THE FUCHUN MOUNTAINS, pictured on p. 129. This long handscroll combines spontaneity and study in a powerful way.

The literati also pioneered the painting of bamboo. They did this because they saw symbolic meanings in its resistance to wind and storms. Just as bamboo bends without breaking, so must the creative artist in foreign-controlled China. A leading bamboo painter was Wu Chen, whose ALBUM LEAF is regarded as a masterpiece of the type.

In order to help assimilate their rich tradition, Chinese painters often copy (with personal variations) the works of earlier artists. Even fully mature painters will often produce a work in the style of an older master they particularly admire. This tendency reveals one of the basic precepts of Confucianism—respect for the past. The idea that a painter must fully comprehend tradition before expressing individuality was a hallmark of the artists who worked for the Imperial court in the sixteenth and seventeenth centuries, and they produced many works in which this homage is clear.

One of the most successful of these academic painters was Tang Yin, who worked in the early sixteenth century during the Ming Dynasty. His painting WHISPERING PINES ON A MOUNTAIN PATH owes a great deal to Fan Kuan's work TRAVELERS AMONG MOUNTAINS AND STREAMS. The manner of painting the rocks and the overall composition clearly show

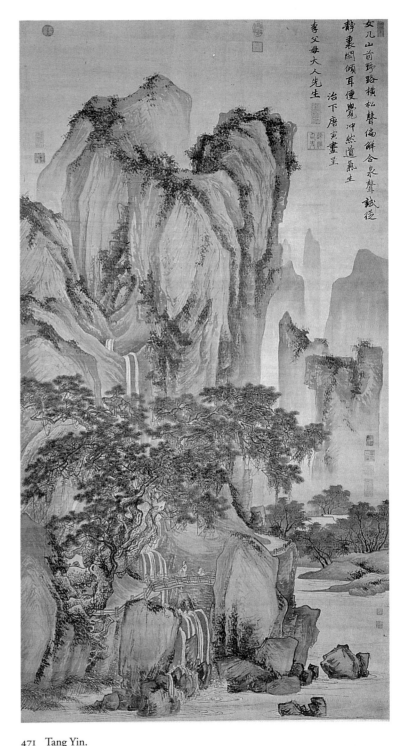

471 Tang Yin.
WHISPERING PINES ON A MOUNTAIN PATH.
Ming dynasty. c. 1516.
Hanging Scroll. 76" × 40".
National Palace Museum, Taipei, Taiwan, Republic of China.

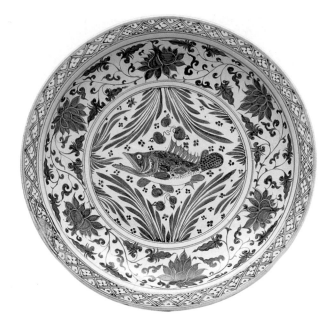

472 PORCELAIN PLATE. Mid-14th century.
Painted in underglaze blue. Diameter 18".
Metropolitan Museum of Art. Purchase, Mrs. Richard E. Linburn Gift.
Photograph: © 1989 Metropolitan Museum of Art. 1987.10.

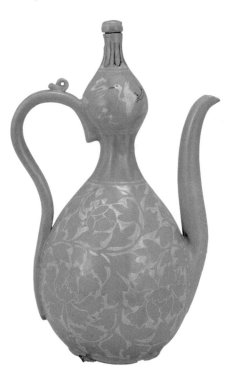

473 WINE PITCHER. Korea.
Koryo dynasty. Mid-12th century.
Stoneware with celadon glaze and inlaid
white and black slip. Height 13½".
National Museum of Korea, Seoul.
National Treasure No. 116.

that Tang was studying the work of Fan Kuan. In addition, Tang's inscribed poem shows his study of Daoism. The last three lines read:

The whispering pines dissolve in the rush of the
waterfall.
I listen with quiet absorption
And feel the spirit of Dao rising within me.[1]

The Chinese have traditionally held ceramic arts in high regard, and the history of pottery in China is primarily the story of Imperial sponsorship and nearly continuous technical advances. Probably the best-known type of Chinese ceramic is porcelain, made from a rare type of clay that when fired becomes pure white. Early porcelains, such as the PORCELAIN PLATE pictured here, were decorated with blue because that was the only color that could withstand the high temperatures necessary to fire porcelain correctly. The Chinese were the first to develop this type of pottery. After it was first imported into the Western world, European workshops tried for generations to duplicate its translucency and deep blue colors.

Throughout Asia, potters in different provinces and countries produced their own variations on Chinese ceramic styles. The WINE PITCHER shown here is an exquisite example of a Korean adaptation of the Chinese blue-green celadon glaze technique, with the addition of a new style of decoration. The potter etched out the background behind the flower decorations in the lower part of the vessel, and also etched the shapes of the flying cranes above. The potter then filled these lowered areas with white and black *slip* (liquid clay) before firing the vessel for the final time. This slip-inlay technique is a Korean invention, and here the smooth surface complements the graceful curves of the double-gourd shape and elegant handle of the pitcher. The shapes and decorations of this piece work so well together that the Korean government designated the WINE PITCHER a national treasure.

Bada Shanren (who also used the name Zhu Da) made paintings that combine technical mastery with a radically unconventional attitude toward art standards of his time. This combination led him to produce work that was, according to a critic who knew him, "strange and great."

Bada Shanren was born in the south central Chinese province of Jiangxi into the highest circles of Chinese society; he was a direct descendant of the founder of the Ming Dynasty, which ruled China from 1368 to 1644. As expected for members of this social class, his father, uncles, and grandfather were noted artists and poets.

Chinese rulers in those days assigned government positions based on one's performance in a series of examinations on literature and philosophy. At the age of nineteen, Bada passed the first round of these tests so successfully that he was named a National Scholar, a prime candidate for the final round of tests that would lead to a high post. It was then that unusual historical circumstances drastically changed his life.

Just as he was preparing for his future career, the Ming Dynasty was crumbling. The last Ming emperor hung himself in 1644, only months before Bada took the tests. Revolts and warfare ensued across China, and a foreign dynasty from Manchuria, called the Qing, established itself in

the capital, Beijing. It would be many years before its control was solidified.

Being of such high rank in the previous dynasty, Bada was in danger. All of his immediate family members were killed in the violence, and Bada fled the capital and took refuge in a Buddhist monastery under an assumed name. He became a monk and later rose to head the monastery, where he attracted hundreds of students.

As he was nearing fifty, he left the monastery and tried to live openly under his own name. But the tensions of the dynastic change had still not subsided; he was courted both by the Qing and old Ming loyalists. The first group wanted him to join the government; the other wanted him to lead a revolt.

Bada did neither, but rather began acting very strangely. Witnesses reported that he would wander the streets in rags, shouting. On the door of the abandoned building where he lived, he scrawled the word "dumb" (mute), and when visitors came he would laugh, drink, and paint with them, but would not talk. This behavior lasted for about five years, until he was taken in by a nephew.

Most historians believe that Bada was faking mental illness out of a desire to avoid taking sides in the political struggles of the day. In 1684, he gave up his feigned madness and lived in the provincial capital

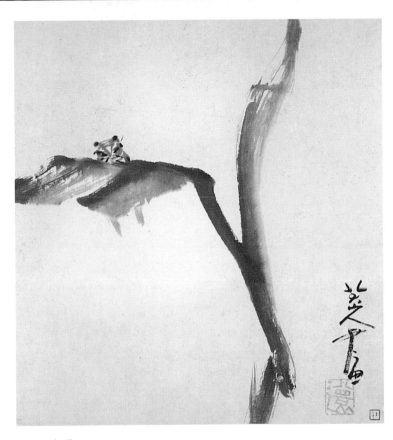

474 Bada Shanren.
CICADA ON A BANANA LEAF.
Qing dynasty. 1688–1689.
Leaf "f" from an album *Flowers and Birds*.
Ink on paper.
Freer Gallery of Art, Smithsonian Institution, Washington, D.C. F1955.21e.

of Nanchang as a recluse for the rest of his life, trading paintings for food.

And what paintings! His choice of subject matter was unusual, to say the least. In CICADA ON A BANANA LEAF the leaf, captured with a few slashing strokes of ink, holds up a melancholy cicada that stares intently back at us.

Beyond mere wildness, something deeper is going on here. The cicada is a symbol of immortality in China, as it seems to

rise up out of the ground alive when born. This cicada looks so broodingly unsure of itself that the work may reflect the insecurity of Bada's position as a descendant of a failed dynasty.

Bada's art was relatively unknown until the twentieth century. At last, when modern Chinese artists began looking for ways to update and question their own ancient traditions, they found in him a valued precursor.

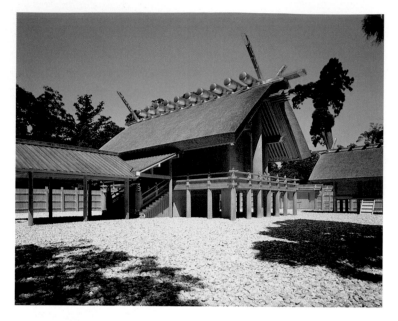

475 MAIN SHRINE.
Ise, Japan. c. 685. Rebuilt every twenty years.
Photograph: Kyoto News International, Inc.

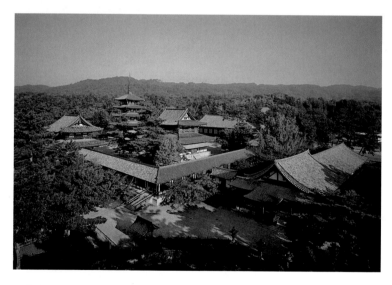

476 HORYUJI TEMPLE.
Nara, Japan. c. 670.
a. Aerial view.
Photograph: Asukaen Company, Ltd., Nara Japan.

JAPAN

Throughout its history, Japanese culture has been marked by alternating periods of nationalism, in which typically Japanese forms have prospered, and periods of open borrowing of foreign influences.

The indigenous religion of Japan is an ancient form of nature and ancestor worship called Shinto. In this religion, forests, fields, waterfalls, and huge stones are considered holy places where gods dwell. The Shinto shrines at Ise occupy a sacred site within a forest. The present MAIN SHRINE at Ise has been completely and exactly rebuilt every twenty years since the seventh century. Builders take wood for the shrine from the forest with gratitude and ceremonial care. As a tree is cut into boards, the boards are numbered so that the wood that was joined in the tree is reunited in the shrine. No nails are used; the wood is fitted and pegged. In keeping with the Shinto concept of purity, surfaces are left unpainted and the roof is natural thatch. The shrines at Ise combine simplicity with subtlety. Refined craftsmanship, sculptural proportions, and spatial harmonies express the ancient religious and aesthetic values of Shinto.

In the first wave of cultural borrowing that occurred more than a thousand years ago, the Japanese imported Buddhism, the Chinese writing system, and Chinese techniques of art and architecture. In fact, since much of ancient Chinese architecture has not survived, the best place to study it is in Japan on the Yamato plain near Kyoto, which served as the capital for many centuries.

The temple complex of HORYUJI exemplifies the Buddhist monastery as it existed in both China and Japan. In the center of the courtyard, we can see the many-storied pagoda, which has a symbolic function relating to its descent from Chinese watchtowers and Indian stupas (see page 316). Next to it is the KONDO, or Buddha hall, a meditation hall where statues are kept. In the center of one wall is a gate house; opposite it along the back wall is a larger lecture hall, where monks hear religious teaching. The oldest parts of HORYUJI date

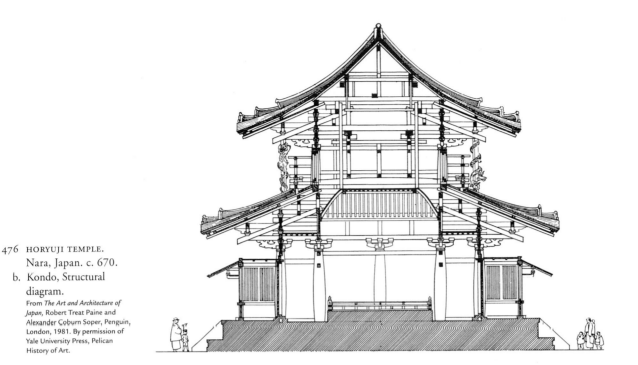

476 HORYUJI TEMPLE.
Nara, Japan. c. 670.

b. Kondo, Structural
diagram.

From *The Art and Architecture of Japan*, Robert Treat Paine and Alexander Coburn Soper, Penguin, London, 1981. By permission of Yale University Press, Pelican History of Art.

from the late seventh century, and are among the world's oldest surviving wooden buildings.

To hold up a two-story structure with a heavy tile roof, Japanese architects (influenced by Chinese predecessors) developed an elaborate bracketing system for the KONDO AT HORYUJI. The empty second story is merely an accent to show the importance of the building, but it also demonstrates the skill of the architect.

Japan has the oldest surviving royal family of any society. This longevity has been made possible by frequent military interventions in which the generals ruled on behalf of the emperors, as in the Kamakura period (1185–1333). The dominant taste of the leaders at that time favored a vigorous realism in art, and this is reflected in the wood portrait statue of MUCHAKU. Unkei, one of the greatest sculptors of Japan, created this life-size work depicting a legendary Buddhist priest from India holding an offering jar. The vividness of the facial expression and the delicacy of the hand gesture belie the wooden material from which it is carved.

Japanese painters of this period found the handscroll particularly effective for long narrative compositions that depict the passage of time.

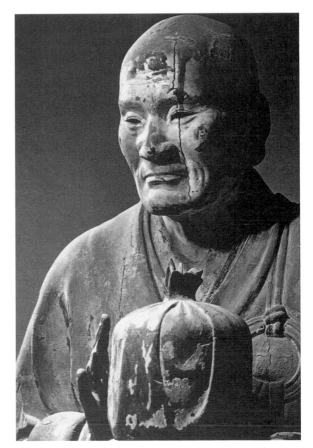

477 Unkei.
DETAIL OF MUCHAKU. c. 1208. Wood. Height 75".
Kofuku-ji Temple, Nara, Japan.

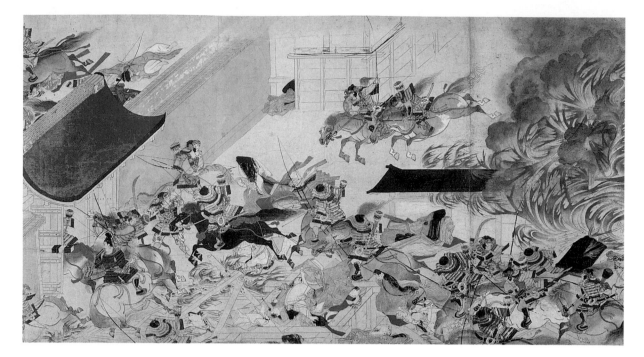

478 BURNING OF THE SANJO PALACE. SANJO-DEN YOUCHI NO EMAKI (Scroll with
depictions of the Night Attack on the Sanjo Palace). From the HEIJI
MONOGATARI EMAKI (illustrated Scrolls of the Events of the Heiji Era),
Japan. Second half of the 13th century. Kamakura period. Handscroll, ink
and colors on paper. Height 16" (41.3 × 699.7 cm).

BURNING OF THE SANJO PALACE is from the HEIJI
MONOGATARI, a scroll that describes the Heiji insur-
rection of 1159. As the scroll is unrolled from right
to left, the viewer follows a succession of events ex-
pertly designed to tell the story. Through effective
visual transitions, the horror and excitement of the
action are connected. The story builds from simple
to complex events, reaching a dramatic climax in
the scene of the burning palace, a highly effective
depiction of fire. The color of the flames emphasizes
the excitement of the historic struggle. Parallel diagonal lines and shapes, used to indicate the palace
walls, add to the sense of motion and provide a clear
geometric structure in the otherwise frantic activity
of this portion of the scroll. Today, such dramatic
events are presented through film or television.

Zen Buddhism, which spread to Japan from
China in the thirteenth century, provided a philosophical basis within which aesthetic activities were
given meaning beyond their physical form. Zen
teaches that enlightenment can be attained through
meditation and contemplation. The influence of

Zen on Japanese aesthetics can be seen in spontaneous and intuitive approaches to poetry, calligraphy, painting, gardens, and flower arrangements.

Zen Buddhist priest Sesshū is considered the
foremost Japanese master of ink painting. In 1467,
he traveled to China, where he studied the works of
Southern Song masters and saw the countryside
that inspired them. Chinese Chan (Zen) paintings,
such as Mu Qi's SIX PERSIMMONS (page 51) and
Yu-Jian's MOUNTAIN VILLAGE IN A MIST (page 330),
were greatly admired by the Japanese, and many
were brought to monasteries in Japan.

Sesshū adapted the Chinese style and set the
standard in ink painting for later Japanese artists.
He painted in two styles. The first was formal and
complex, while the second was a simplified, somewhat explosive style, later called *haboku,* meaning
"flung ink." HABOKU LANDSCAPE is abstract in its
simplification of forms and freedom of brushwork.
Sesshū suggested mountains and trees with single,
soft brush strokes. The sharp lines in the center
foreground indicating a fisherman, and the vertical

line above the rooftops representing the staff of a wine shop, are in contrast to the thin washes and darker accents of the suggested landscape.

In traditional Japan, folding screens provided privacy by separating areas within rooms. Artists have used the unique spatial properties of the screen format in highly original ways. In contrast to the European easel paintings that function like a window in the wall, a painted screen within the living space of a home becomes a major element in the interior.

Tawaraya Sōtatsu's large screen WAVES AT MATSUSHIMA consists of a pair of six-panel folding screens (on the following page). The screens are designed so that together or separately they form complete compositions. The subject is a pair of islands where there were very old Shinto shrines.

In keeping with well-established Japanese artistic practices, Sōtatsu created a composition charged with the churning action of waves, yet as solid and permanent in its design as the rocky crags around which the waters leap and churn. He translated his sensitive awareness of natural phenomena into a decorative, abstract design. Spatial ambiguity in the sky and water areas suggests an interaction that the viewer is to feel rather than to read as a literal transcription of nature. In addition to rhythmic patterns that fill much of the surface, boldly simplified shapes and lines are contrasted with highly refined details and eye-catching surprises. A flat, horizontal gold shape in the upper left, accentuated with a black line, signifies a cloud and reaffirms the picture plane. The strongly asymmetrical design, emphasis on repeated patterns, and relatively flat spatial quality are all typical of much Japanese painting from the sixteenth to the nineteenth centuries.

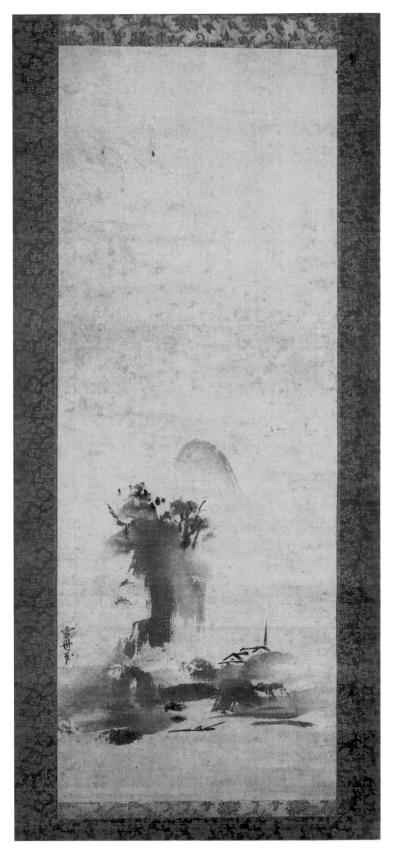

479 Sesshū, Japanese.
HABOKU LANDSCAPE. 1420–1506.
Muromachi Period. Hanging scroll,
ink on paper. 28¼" × 10½" (71.9 × 26.7 cm).
© The Cleveland Museum of Art. The Norweb Collection (CMA 55.43).

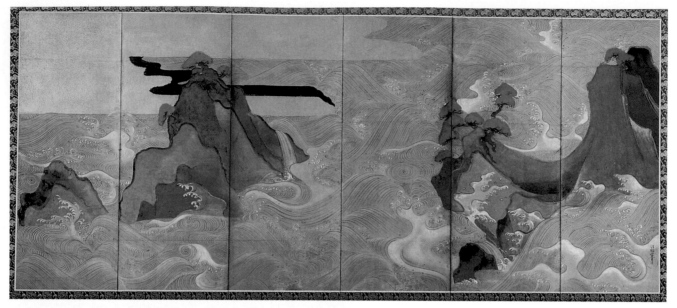

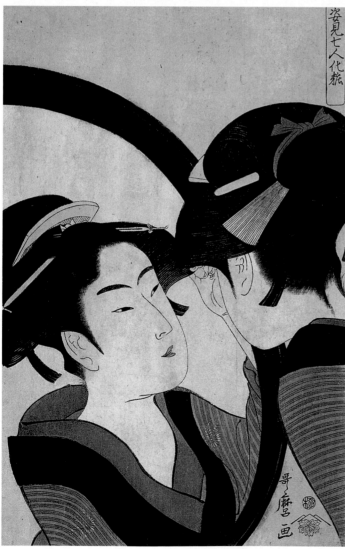

480 Tawaraya Sōtatsu (Japanese, active 1600–1630).
WAVES AT MATSUSHIMA.
17th century.
Folding screen, color and gold on paper. Image,
59⅞" × 141¼" (152 × 369.9 cm; overall, 166 × 369.9 cm).
Courtesy of the Freer Gallery of Art, Smithsonian Institution,
Washington, D.C. (F1906.231).

481 Utamaro Kitagawa (Japanese, 1754–1806).
REFLECTED BEAUTY, SEVEN BEAUTIES APPLYING MAKE-UP:
OKITA c. 1790. Woodblock print. 14¼" × 9½".
Honolulu Academy of Arts, Gift of James A. Michener, 1969 (15,490).

By the mid-seventeenth century, the art of woodcut printing had developed to meet the demand for pictures by the newly prosperous middle class. Japanese artists took the Chinese woodcut technique and turned it into a popular art form. For the next two hundred years, hundreds of thousands of these prints were produced. The prints are called *ukiyo-e*, meaning "pictures of the floating world," because they depict scenes of daily life, such as landscapes, popular entertainments, and portraits of theater actors.

Kitagawa Utamaro's woodcut REFLECTED BEAUTY transforms the then ordinary subject into a memorable image consisting of bold, curving outlines and clear, unmodeled shapes. As with most Japan-

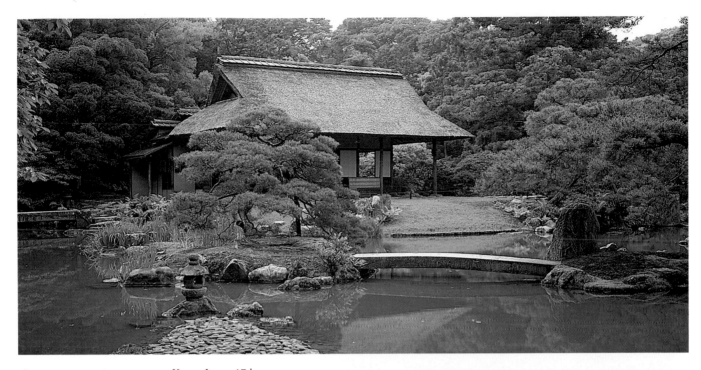

482 KATSURA DETACHED PALACE. Kyoto, Japan. 17th century.
  a. Gardens and tea house.
   Photograph courtesy of Kenzo Yamamoto.

ese paintings and prints, flat shapes are emphasized by the absence of shading. The center of interest is the reflected face of the woman, set off by the strong curve representing the mirror's edge. In contrast to Western composition with centered balance and subjects well within the frame, here the figure is thrust in from the right, and cut off abruptly by the edge of the picture plane, rather than being presented completely within the frame. This type of radically cropped composition was one of the elements of Japanese art that most intrigued European artists in the nineteenth century.

Japanese architects have also demonstrated the careful and subtle arrangement of clearly defined forms. KATSURA DETACHED PALACE, a seventeenth-century Japanese imperial villa, was built in Kyoto beside the Katsura River, whose waters were diverted into the garden to form ponds. All elements—land, water, rocks, and plants were integrated in a

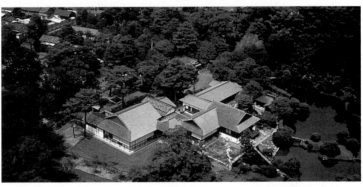

b. Aerial view of imperial gardens and villa.
   Photograph courtesy of Obayashi-Gumi, Construction Company.

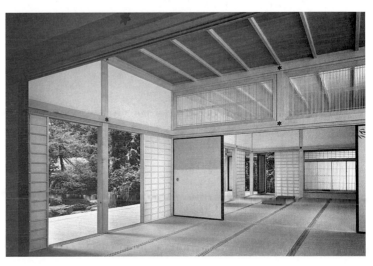

c. Interior of imperial villa.
   Photograph: Ezra Stoller © Esto.

garden design that blends human-made and natural elements. Because many of the palace walls are sliding screens, they can provide flexible interconnections between interior and exterior spaces.

For a royal palace, KATSURA is very humble. The complex was planned with no grand entrance either to the grounds or to the buildings. Instead, one approaches the palace along garden paths, watching unexpected views open up. Earth contours, stones, and waterways are combined to symbolize—on a small scale—mountains, rivers, fields, inlets, and beaches. The tea house, which imitates the traditional Japanese farmhouse, is constructed of common, natural materials. It provides the appropriate setting for the tea ceremony, which embodies the attitudes of simplicity, naturalness, and humility that permeate the entire palace grounds.

Domestic architecture has long been an important part of Japanese art. Modest houses, as well as palaces and Buddhist temples, have traditionally employed many of the structural and aesthetic principles of Shinto shrines. In the past, Japanese homes were related to the land and were often set in or built around a garden. Today small gardens provide intimacy with natural beauty, even in crowded city environments.

Traditional Japanese houses, such as those at KATSURA, are built of wood using post-and-beam construction. The result is essentially a roof on posts, allowing walls to be sliding screens rather than supports. The Japanese use of unpainted wood and the concept of spatial flow between indoors and outdoors have been major influences on modern architects in the West.

In the nineteenth century, European commerce and missionary work began to have a decisive impact across Asia. Various parts of Asia reacted differently to this new influence. India submitted, not always willingly, to colonial status under England. The Chinese tried to severely limit foreign influence on their culture, leading to conflicts which lasted into the twentieth century. The Japanese, in contrast, welcomed foreigners. A palace revolt in 1868 restored the Emperor to real power, and he began a vigorous program of cultural importation from the West which seems to be continuing even today.

The new policy of openness had immediate impact on the arts. The government gave stipends for Japanese artists to study in Europe, and invited Western artists and scholars to teach in Japanese universities. We see the results of this hybridization in paintings such as UPSTAIRS by Mitsutani Kunishiro. He studied in Paris near the turn of the century, and the work reflects his knowledge of painting in natural light gleaned from looking at Impressionist and Post-Impressionist paintings. At the same time, the subject matter is very Japanese.

Cultural trading between East and West continues into the present. We will consider some contemporary Asian artists in chapter 25.

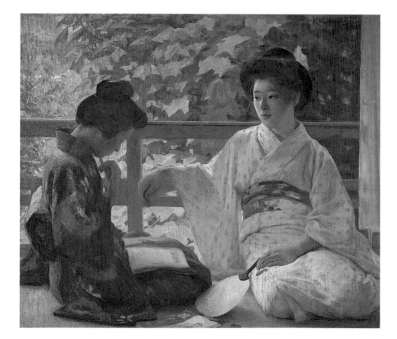

483   Mitsutani Kunishiro.
      UPSTAIRS. 1910.
      Oil on canvas. 105 × 120 cm.
      Collection of the Tokyo National Museum.

CHAPTER NINETEEN

THE ISLAMIC WORLD

Islam is one of the three major world religions built on the teachings of the religious seers of the Middle East. Although based on the revelations of prophet Mohammed, Islam shares fundamental beliefs and religious history with its predecessors Judaism and Christianity. An adherent of Islam is called a Muslim—Arabic for "one who submits to God."

Islamic history began in 622 C.E. with the Hegira, Mohammed's flight to what is now the city of Medina on the Arabian peninsula. The new religion spread quickly into much of what was once the Eastern Roman and Byzantine empires, then fanned out to include North Africa, Spain, and parts of Europe. Within one hundred years of the Prophet's death, Christian armies were repelling Muslim troops from Tours in central France. Islam is now the principal religion in the Middle East, North Africa, and some parts of Asia.

The Islamic invaders facilitated their conquests by allowing the peoples of conquered lands to retain their own religions and cultures, as the Romans had done. This strategy enabled the Muslim invaders, who had little art of their own in their early history, to borrow from earlier artistic traditions. At its height, from the ninth through the fourteenth centuries, Islamic culture developed into a synthesis of the religions, artistic and literary traditions, and scientific knowledge of the entire ancient world.

Unlike the medieval Christians, who rejected pre-Christian civilization and scholarship, Muslims adapted and built on the achievements of their predecessors. Muslim scholars translated the legacy of Greek, Syrian, and Hindu knowledge into Arabic, and Arabic became the language of scholarship from the ninth through the thirteenth centuries for Syrians, Jews, Persians, and Moors as well as Arabs. As medieval Europe languished from intolerance, isolationism, and feudalism, Islamic civilization flourished, producing outstanding achievements in the arts, sciences, administration, and commerce that were not attained in Europe until the height of the Renaissance, in the late fifteenth century.

Orthodox Islam prohibits the representation of human figures in art that will be used in a religious context. Mohammed taught that if an artist were to try to recreate the living forms of humans, he or she would be competing with Allah (God) who created everything. Mohammed also prohibited any pictures of himself while he was alive, claiming that he was not in any way exceptional—he was only a messenger. Thus figural arts are rare in Islam, and sculpture as Westerners know it is practically nonexistent. However, the art that evolved within this restriction is highly inventive, and reached its peak of success in the decorative arts and architecture.

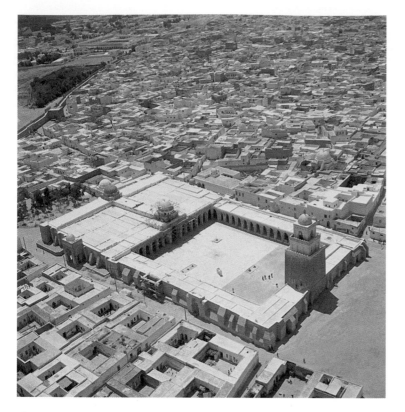

484 GREAT MOSQUE.
Kairouan, Tunisia. 836–875.
Photograph: Roger Wood/Corbis.

ARAB LANDS

When Islam first began to spread, local rulers took responsibility for building houses of worship in their territories. Early rulers usually adapted abandoned buildings, converting them into *mosques.* (The word is based on the Arabic *masjid,* which means "place of prostration.") The typical mosque must be big enough to accommodate all male worshipers for Friday prayers, during which they hear a sermon and bow down in the direction of Mecca, Islam's most holy city. (Women attend mosque worship only during the holy month of Ramadan.) The basic plan of a mosque is based on the design of the Prophet's house, which had an open courtyard bordered by porches held up with columns. Often, mosques include one or more *minarets* (towers), which mark the building's location and allow chanters to ascend and call the faithful to prayer.

An early mosque that still stands in something resembling its original condition is the GREAT MOSQUE in Kairouan, Tunisia. The open courtyard is surrounded by porches, with a minaret over the main entrance in the center of one short side. The deeper covered area opposite the minaret shelters the *mihrab,* the niche in the end wall that points the way to Mecca.

The ceramic arts are highly valued in Islam, and Arab potters in Iraq made a major advance when they perfected the luster technique, probably in the ninth century. This glaze effect, which imparts a metallic sheen to the surface of a vessel, is one of the most difficult to control in ceramics, and was equated in those days with alchemy, the effort to convert simple materials into gold. Most luster pottery was for the exclusive use of nobles and rulers. The PITCHER shown here has a very thin body, so that it was probably not used but only looked at. The Arabic script on the piece expresses praise and good wishes to the owner.

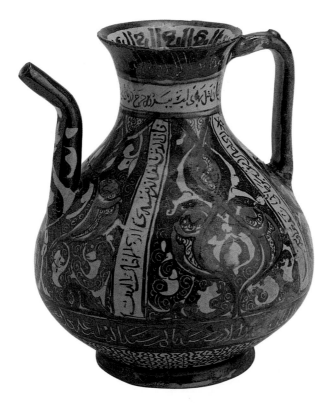

485 PITCHER (SPOUTED EWER).
Kashan. Early 13th century.
Luster over tin glaze. Height 6⅘".
Reproduced by permission of the Syndics of the
Fitzwilliam Museum, Cambridge, from the Ades Loan Collection.

SPAIN

Syrians first conquered Spain for Islam in the eighth century, but soon the region (together with bordering North Africa) became a distinct Muslim culture with important scientists, poets, philosophers, architects, and artists (see, for example, the Spanish LUSTER-PAINTED BOWL on page 82). Some of Europe's best libraries were in the Spanish Muslim cities of Córdoba and Granada, and respect for books and learning was higher here than in most other areas of the continent.

Calligraphy is a highly honored Islamic art because it is used to enhance the beauty of the word of Allah. The most respected practice for a calligrapher is the art of writing the words of the Koran, the sacred text of Islam, which Muslims believe was revealed in Arabic by Allah to Mohammed. In the Islamic world, the written TEXT OF THE KORAN is the divine word in visible form. According to Islamic tradition, God's first creation was the *qualam*, the slant-cut reed pen.

The decorative qualities of Arabic scripts combine well with both geometric and floral design motifs. We saw them combined in the PITCHER, but they work together with unforgettable effect in the COURT OF THE LIONS, which contains elaborate stucco arches resting on 124 white marble columns. Many of the walls seem to consist entirely of translucent webs of intricate decoration in marble, alabaster, glazed tile, and cast plaster. Light coming through the small openings in the decoration gives many of the rooms and courtyards a luminous splendor. Just above the columns is a horizontal band of calligraphy that expresses praise to Allah and blessings on visitors. (For another example of Spanish Muslim decoration, see the DECORATIVE PANEL FROM THE ALHAMBRA on page 14.)

The COURT OF THE LIONS is part of the much larger Alhambra, the royal palace and fort of the Muslim rulers in Granada. Occupying a commanding hill, the Alhambra was a self-contained city, with meeting rooms, royal residences, gardens, and housing for workers of various kinds. This was one of the last strongholds of Muslim rule in Spain, and when the last ruler abandoned it in 1492, the Spanish rulers kept it intact.

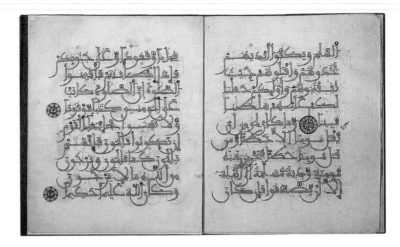

486 TEXT OF THE KORAN. North Africa or Spain. 11th century. Colors on paper.
MS no. 1544. Reproduced by kind permission of the Trustees of the Chester Beatty Library, Dublin.

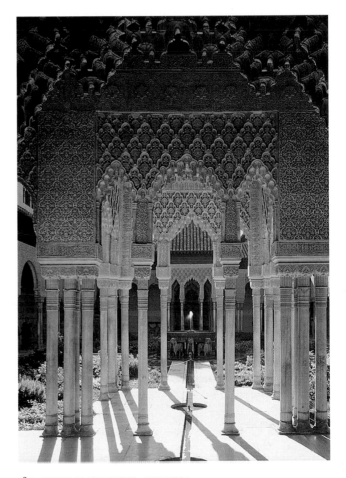

487 COURT OF THE LIONS, ALHAMBRA. Granada, Spain. 1309–1354.
Photograph: SuperStock, Inc.

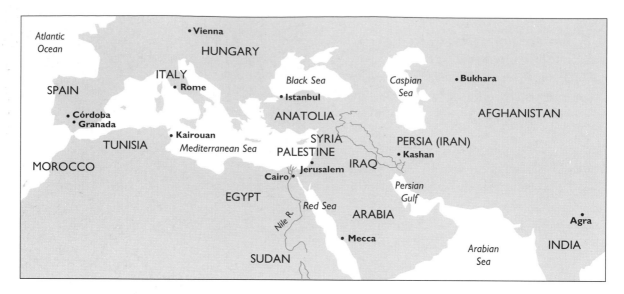

488 THE ISLAMIC WORLD.

PERSIA

Probably the best-known item of Persian art in the West is the carpet (see page 223 for the ARDABIL CARPET, one of the most impressive). Woven and knotted by women, men, and children, carpets were not only prized possessions; they were important to the history of Islamic arts as a means of spreading design ideas. Relatively portable, a carpet is a repository of motifs and compositions. Many decorative schemes on buildings or pottery were influenced by carpet design from distant regions.

Decorating architecture with tiles is an important offshoot of the ceramic arts, and this technique reached a peak of achievement in Persia. The MIHRAB shown here was taken from a mosque, where it pointed the way to Mecca for worshipers. The prohibition of images in the religious context means that the art cannot tell a story with human figures, as is common in the West. Islamic art makes up for this lack through extremely intricate designs that satisfy the sensuous urge for beauty while also engaging the mind's desire for order and pattern. Often, writing on a work implants ideas, as it does here in an outer band that quotes the Koran. In this way, a work such as this one can be absorbing to look at, spiritually uplifting, and aesthetically pleasing.

The MIHRAB has been separated from its original site, but it provides an example of the richness

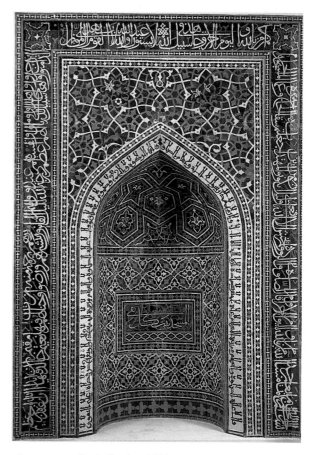

489 MIHRAB. Persia (Iran). c. 1354.
Glazed ceramic, cut and
assembled in mosaic. 11'3" × 7'6".
The Metropolitan Museum of Art.
Harris Brisbane Dick Fund, 1939. (39.20).
Photograph: © 1982 The Metropolitan Museum of Art.

of Persian decorative arts. Such techniques were often applied to entire buildings, as we see at the MIR-I-ARAB MADRASA in Uzbekistan. A *madrasa* is a Muslim theological school where the history of Islam and the interpretation of the Quran are taught. This one was named for its founder, a member of the philosophical Muslim sect known as Sufism.

The tasteful array of openings in two stories provide a counterpoint to the *iwan*, the large covered porch at the center. Behind are two domes, one marking the lecture hall and the other the founder's tomb. Most surfaces are dazzlingly covered with tiles in abstract patterns, showing how color is often integral to Islamic architecture.

Outside religious usage, the prohibition of images was relaxed, and Persian painters emerged as among the world's greatest illustrators as they made pictures to accompany handwritten copies of their major literary works. These illustrated books were prized possessions of the aristocracy. One of the best illustrations is SULTAN SANJAR AND THE OLD WOMAN, from the *Khamseh,* or "Five Poems," by Nizami (on the following page). The story is an allegory on vanity: The sultan was out riding with his courtiers one day when an old woman approached him, complaining that she had been robbed by one of his soldiers. Sanjar dismissed her, saying that her troubles were nothing compared to his with his military campaigns. The woman then confronted him, saying, "What good is conquering foreign armies when you can't make your own behave?"

The work is a careful composition with luxurious details in the fabrics, vegetation, and clouds. Subtle gestures help to tell the story, which takes place in the center. The method of rendering rocks in Persian painting owes a great deal to Chinese art, which the Persians knew (compare with TRAVELERS AMONG MOUNTAINS AND STREAMS on page 468). These paintings were most often produced in workshops, so that we do not generally know the artists' names; but in this case it seems fairly certain that the work is by Sultan-Muhammad, one of the two or three most highly regarded painters.

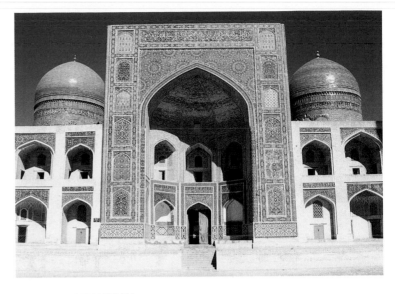

490 MIR-I-ARAB MADRASA.
Bukhara, Uzbekistan. 1535–1536. Facade.
Photograph: David Flack.

INDIA: THE MUGHAL EMPIRE

Descended from both Persians and Mongols, the Mughal rulers of India made a unique mix of cultures into a kingdom in the sixteenth and seventeenth centuries. Their subjects were Hindu, Jain, Zoroastrian, and even a few Christians. Only a minority (the upper classes) were Muslim. This meant that in the Mughal Empire, Islam evolved further from its Arab roots than anywhere up to that time.

Governing such a diverse people led the Mughal rulers to a level of tolerance unknown elsewhere in the world. Akbar, for example, who ruled from 1556 to 1605, ordered his ministers to learn about the various religions practiced in his realm, and he hired tutors to teach them. He also established a new religion that combined elements of all, and made himself the head of it, the better to resolve disputes. When Jesuit missionaries from Baroque Rome visited him, he entertained them lavishly, and bought Western religious prints from them for his art collection. He reversed the ancient rule against representation, saying that trying to copy Allah's handiwork by making pictures would, instead, lead artists to a deeper respect for divine creativity.

Under the influence of the empire's cultural mix, and the tolerant curiosity of most of its rulers, a Mughal painting style evolved that combined

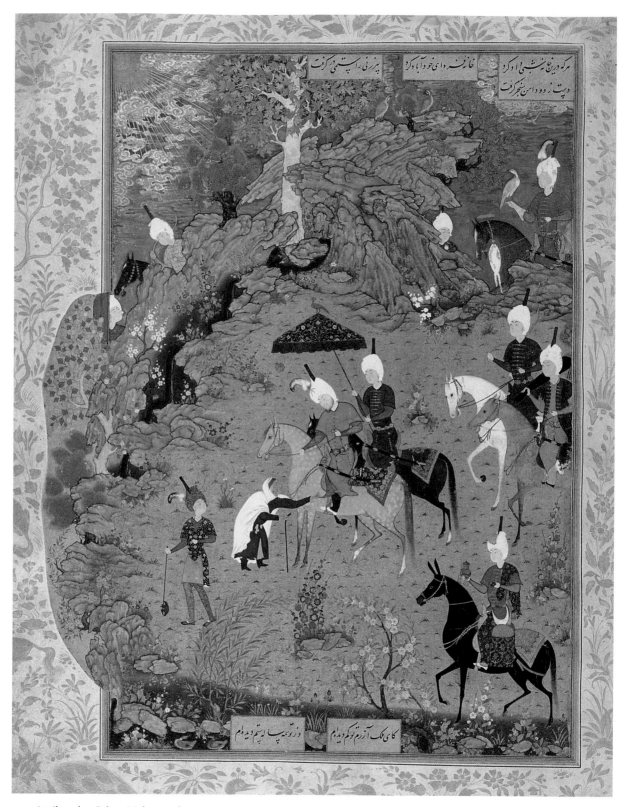

491 Attributed to Sultan-Muhammad.
SULTAN SANJAR AND THE OLD WOMAN, from the
KHAMSEH (FIVE POEMS) of Nizami, folio 181, 1539–1543.
Gouache on paper. 14½" × 10".
By permission British Library.

elements of European naturalism with Persian luxury and attention to detail. When a Portuguese trader brought to the court a turkey (which came not from Europe but the New World), the ruler Jahanghir ordered his favorite artist to make a picture of it. The result is TURKEY-COCK, one of the most vivid depictions of wildlife ever realized. The Arabic script tells the details of the gift. The boldness of its impact is equaled by the fineness of its details.

The last Mughal ruler to hold the realm together was Shah Jahan, who also created the most memorable piece of Mughal art, the TAJ MAHAL. Erected on the banks of a river between a guest house and a small mosque, the TAJ MAHAL (which means "Crown of the Palace") is a tomb for the ruler's favorite wife, who had died in childbirth. It sits before the four-part paradise garden that was traditional in Islam. The surface of the white marble exterior seems to change colors by catching sunlight at various angles. The proportions of the bulb-shaped dome make the building look light, as if it barely touches the ground. The walls seem paper-thin, with arch openings in a graceful rhythm. The paradise motif of the garden is continued in the long inscription over the central doorway arch, which is a quotation from the Koran. The total complex as it stands is incomplete, because Shah Jahan had envisioned an identical black marble tomb for himself just across the river, but this was never built. Even as it is, the TAJ MAHAL's combination of otherworldliness, beauty, and devotion has drawn visitors from across the world.

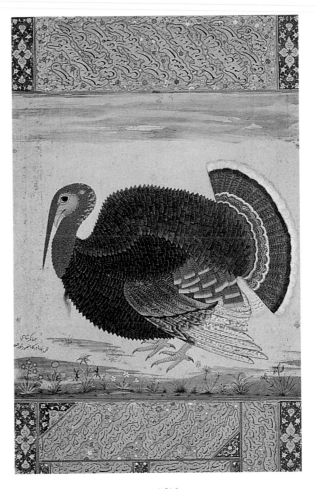

492 Mansur. TURKEY-COCK. c. 1612.
Gouache on paper, painted image. 5¼" × 5".
Victoria and Albert Museum, London.
Courtesy of the Trustees of the Victoria and Albert Museum, IM 135–1921.

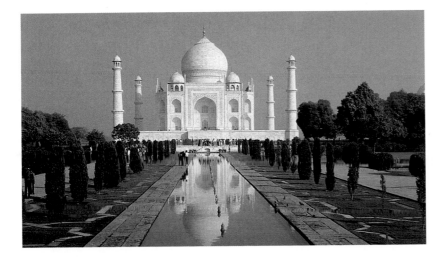

493 TAJ MAHAL.
Agra, India. 1632–1648.
Library, Getty Research Institute,
Photograph: Wim Swaan Collection (96.P.21).

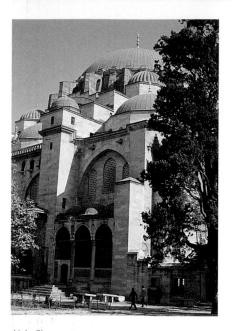

494 Sinan. SÜLEYMANIYE MOSQUE.
Istanbul, Turkey. 1550-1557.
Photograph: Index Ricerca Iconografica

The Ottoman Empire, the Muslim kingdom headquartered in Istanbul, reached its peak of prosperity under Sultan Süleyman in the sixteenth century, when Ottoman territories reached from Hungary to Saudi Arabia and from Cairo to Baghdad. Throughout those years the sultan's chief architect was Sinan, a man now recognized as one of the greatest architects in history. Over three hundred buildings, about a third of them mosques, are reliably attributed to him. His fame in the Muslim world is about equal in the Christian world to that of Michelangelo, whose near-contemporary he was.

Born into a Christian family, Sinan was trained under the Ottoman system of *devsirme*, under which the brightest and most talented young boys were selected for special service and given the best training. Converted to Islam, Sinan became a lifelong member of the Janissaries in 1521. They were the sultan's elite corps of generals and advisors, and in it Sinan traveled widely with the sultan on various military campaigns in the Middle East and Europe. These journeys afforded him the opportunity to visit many different types of buildings in the various regions that the sultan ruled. Imperial policy at that time dictated that buildings in the typical Ottoman style be erected throughout the realm, as a symbol of the sultan's power. Sinan began to distinguish himself as an architect by carrying out this task, designing buildings from Budapest in Hungary to Mecca in Saudi Arabia.

In 1538, the sultan named Sinan chief architect, a post that he held until his death. Most of his best surviving buildings are located in or near the Ottoman capital, where wealth and workers were most plentiful. Among these is the SÜLEYMANIYE MOSQUE in Istanbul. The account books from the project survive, and they show that Sinan supervised a total of 3523 workers, a testament to his organizing skills. The mosque resembles Hagia Sophia (see page 234), which the Ottomans regarded as the greatest building in history. But Sinan did not merely imitate the earlier building. The exterior of his mosque is far more visually interesting, as it shows domes and half-domes seemingly cascading down from the central mass.

The building that Sinan regarded as his best was the SELIMIYE MOSQUE, which he completed when he was near eighty years old and in the service of Süleyman's successor, Selim. Though this building is larger than the SÜLEYMANIYE MOSQUE, it looks lighter, because Sinan hid the buttresses that support the dome in the walls of the building. This structure allows the interior to flood with light, illuminating blue ceramic tiles and carefully selected marble and stone structural elements. Sinan boasted:

Those who consider themselves architects among the Christians say that in the realm of Islam no one can equal that of the Hagia Sophia; they claim that no Muslim architect would be able to build such a large dome. In this mosque, with the help of Allah and the support of Sultan Selim Khan, I erected a dome six cubits higher and four cubits wider than the dome of the Hagia Sophia.[1]

Indeed, the dome was higher, but it rode a little lower above the floor, so that the two buildings enclosed about equal interior space. Nevertheless, the mosque became an emblem of Ottoman prowess in architecture, a sign that Muslims could equal the great achievements of the past.

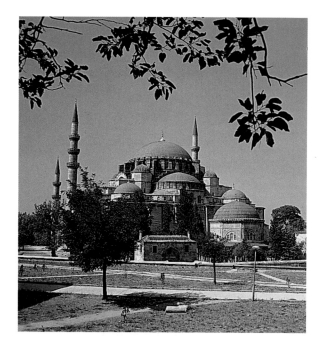

495 Sinan. SELIMIYE MOSQUE.
Edirne, Turkey. c. 1579.
Photograph: Tom Klobe.

CHAPTER TWENTY

AFRICA, OCEANIA, AND THE AMERICAS

When Westerners first encountered the peoples of Africa, Oceania, and the Americas, they regarded their cultures as "primitive"—that is, if left in isolation, they would develop as Western culture had, but perhaps at a slower rate. For centuries Westerners were blinded by this prejudiced and limited view.

Fortunately, most people in the West now realize that these cultures had very different patterns of development from those of Europe and Asia, and that the term "primitive" is not applicable to either their cultures or their arts. The many art forms of Africa, Oceania, and the Americas are based on long-lasting traditions, learned skills, and fine distinctions, just as Western art is. They are the product of cultural values and concerns. With the perspective of historical study, it has become obvious that Western art cannot be the "norm" for the world, just as no one culture is the norm for all peoples.

Each of these societies is composed of many different groups. It is not possible in a single chapter to present examples of art from all. We can consider here only a sampling of the works best known and understood by artists and art historians today.

AFRICA

The arts of the African continent are extremely varied, and the diversity of style reflects the variety of cultures on the continent. North of the Sahara, the art forms of Africa generally fall under the influence of Egyptian, Roman, or (most recently) Islamic traditions. These cultures were covered in previous chapters; here we will focus on sub-Saharan Africa.

Although most African styles from the past are highly abstract, some groups produced naturalistic works that astonished Europeans when they first encountered them. Among typical African art forms

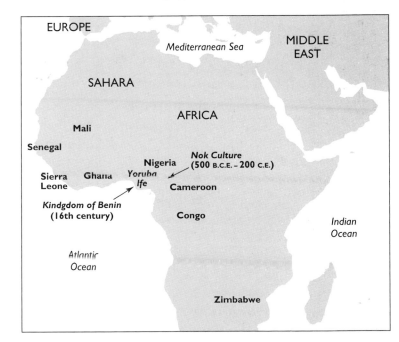

496 AFRICA.

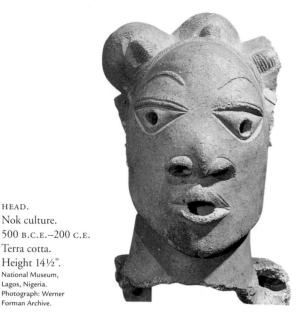

497 HEAD.
Nok culture.
500 B.C.E.–200 C.E.
Terra cotta.
Height 14½".
National Museum,
Lagos, Nigeria.
Photograph: Werner
Forman Archive.

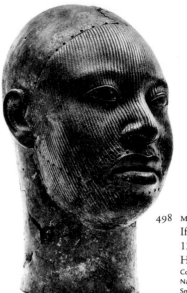

498 MALE PORTRAIT HEAD.
Ife, Nigeria.
12th century. Bronze.
Height 13½".
Collection of the Oni of Ife.
National Museum of African Art,
Smithsonian Institution.
Photograph: Eliot Elisofon Archives.

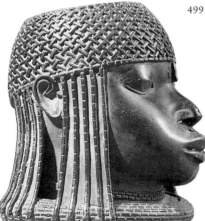

499 BENIN HEAD. Nigeria.
16th century.
Bronze. Height 9¼".
The Metropolitan Museum of Art, New York.
The Michael C. Rockefeller Memorial Collection. Bequest of Nelson A. Rockefeller, 1979
(79.206.86).

are masks and figures of terra cotta, bronze, stone, and wood. A great deal of traditional African sculpture is made for ritual use. In appreciating African art, knowledge of the cultural function of a work should go hand in hand with enjoyment of its form. Most museum displays of African art isolate the works in glass cases that make it difficult to understand their original function and context.

Tin miners digging in central Nigeria accidentally unearthed the oldest surviving examples of sub-Saharan art, such as the HEAD from the Nok culture. Archaeological evidence indicates that these works, of which hundreds have been found, date from the time of the Greeks and the Romans. Modeled in *terra cotta* (unglazed earthenware), they are nearly life-size. The heads, which are broken at the neck, were probably once attached to torsos. Their finely carved hair ornaments and facial features show that there had been sophisticated wood carving in that region. The vivid facial expression of the HEAD makes it seem like a portrait of an individual, but at the same time there is a degree of abstraction in the treatment of the eyes and nose. Little else has survived from the Nok culture. Although we know little about it, it seems to have heavily influenced other cultures of West Africa.

Concurrent with the Gothic era in twelfth-century Europe, a highly sophisticated art was being produced for the royal court of Ife, a sacred Yoruba city in southwestern Nigeria. In Ife, a naturalistic style of court portraiture developed that was stylistically and technically unlike anything to be found in Europe at the time. The MALE PORTRAIT HEAD, demonstrates its maker's great skill in the difficult craft of lost-wax bronze casting. Such thin-walled, hollow metal casting probably represents the culmination of many generations of cultural influences. Scarification lines emphasize facial contours; rows of small holes are believed to have held a beaded veil.

Anthropologists believe that in the fourteenth century, a master sculptor from Ife brought bronze casting to the neighboring kingdom of Benin. The BENIN HEAD exemplifies another court style, developed in Benin, that was somewhat abstract in comparison to the naturalism of Ife portrait sculpture.

When sixteenth-century Europeans first arrived in the kingdom of Benin, they were amazed to see cast bronze sculptures, palaces, and a highly organized city that compared favorably to their own capital cities. The ivory PORTRAIT OF A QUEEN MOTHER from Benin was carved in the sixteenth century, and modern versions are still worn on the oba's (king's) chest, or at his waist during important ceremonies. The crown worn by the Queen Mother consists of a row of alternating human heads and catfish. The heads were inspired by the "strange" dress, long, straight hair, and beard styles of Portuguese visitors.

The Bamana people of Mali are renowned for their carved wooden antelope figure headdresses, which young men attach to basketry caps and wear on top of their heads during agricultural ceremonies. When a new field is cleared, the most diligent male workers are selected to perform a dance of leaps in imitation of the mythical *tyi wara*, who taught human beings how to cultivate crops. The dance always includes both male and female TYI WARA DANCERS: the female is identified by a baby on her back, the male by a stylized mane. Abstracted antelope bodies become energized, almost linear forms. Rhythmic curves are accented by a few straight lines in designs that emphasize an interplay of solid mass and penetrating space.

The bold, uninhibited style of art of the grasslands region of Cameroon looks far removed from the aristocratic styles of Ife and Benin, even though it also was developed for royal courts. The separate areas of the LARGE DANCE HEADDRESS (see next page) are clearly defined by different patterns and textures. This heavy sculpture, worn by court officials, does not copy the human head but reinterprets it.

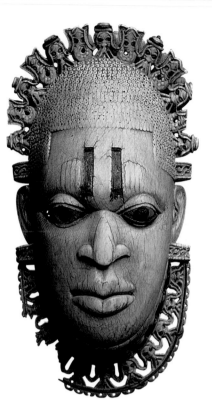

500 PENDANT MASK, COURT OF BENIN, PORTRAIT OF A QUEEN MOTHER. Nigeria, Africa. Early 16th century. Ivory, iron, copper. Height 9⅜".
The Metropolitan Museum of Art. The Michael C. Rockefeller Memorial Collection. Gift of Nelson A. Rockefeller, 1972 (1978.412.323). Photograph by Schecter Lee. © 1986 The Metropolitan Museum of Art.

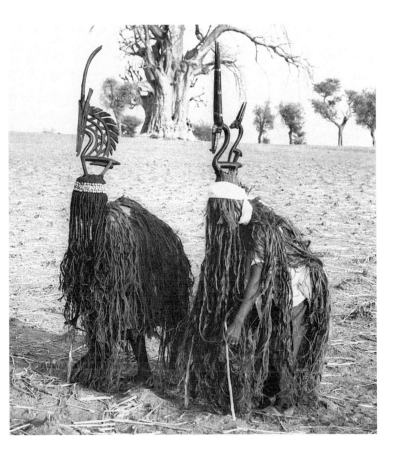

501 TYI WARA DANCERS. Mali.
Photograph: Dr. Pascal James Imperato.

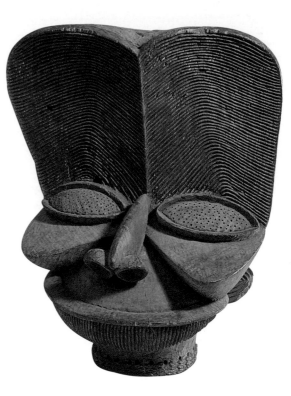

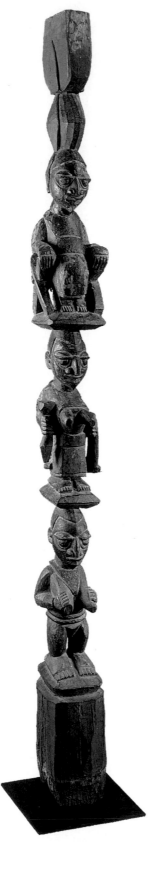

502 LARGE DANCE HEADDRESS.
Bamenda area, Cameroon, Africa.
19th century.
Wood. Height 26½".
Museum Rietberg, Zurich.
Edward von der Heydt Collection.
Photograph: Wettsin and Kauf.

503 Olembe Alaye.
HOUSE POST. Yoruba, Nigeria.
Mid-twentieth century.
Wood and paint. Height 83".
UCLA, Fowler Museum of Cultural History.

The Yoruba peoples of Nigeria have a long-established tradition of figural wood carving that makes use of diminutive proportions and almond-shaped parts. The HOUSE POST by Olembe Alaye is not only a literal support for a roof; it is also a meditation on the idea of support. Stacked in this composition are (from the top) an elder of the tribe seated in a folding chair, a woman holding a baby on her back, and a second woman holding her breasts in a traditional gesture of welcoming and respect. All three of these people are important to the maintenance of the society, as they represent wisdom, nurturing, and hospitality. All three personify characteristics that support the community.

The HOUSE POST takes on added meaning when we see it on location in a 1959 photograph of the TOMB OF FORMER CHIEF LISA. The chief was the "pillar of the community"; placing these posts at the front of his tomb added significance and honor to his memory. He is buried among other emblems of support that, all together, comprise tribal life.

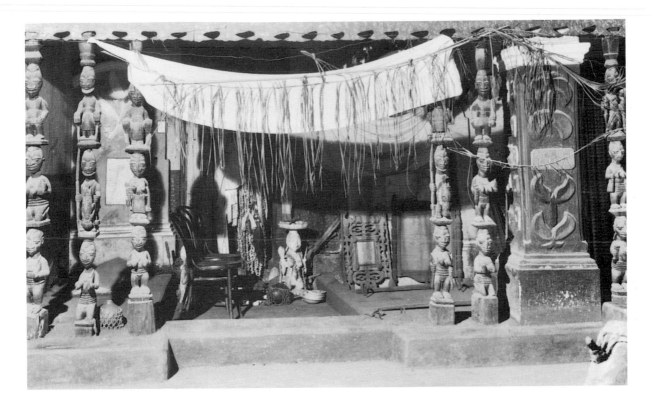

Not all African art has been made for royal or honorific uses. As with the antelope figures discussed earlier, much art is intended to influence future events for the better. One of the most distinctive examples is the POWER FIGURE from Congo. Someone who feels a need for spiritual power to solve a problem, answer a question, or promote a favorable outcome in a situation might make use of one of these figures. First, the person buys a plain wooden statue. In itself, it has no power, though it may be quite beautiful. Then a diviner or spirit counselor helps the purchaser add things to it. They may paint part of it, hang articles of clothing on it, attach charms to it, or drive nails into it. With each addition, the figure gains power, because each addition symbolizes an offered prayer, and each has a symbolic meaning. For example, anything made of iron is believed to have many powers, because it is used to make both weapons and plowing tools. A POWER FIGURE such as the one pictured may have so much force that it must be shielded from public view and handled with extreme care. However, after a time the power in the figure is spent, and it becomes practically worthless.

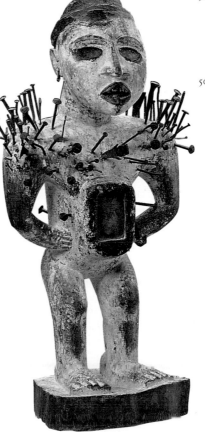

504 TOMB OF FORMER CHIEF LISA. Ondo, Nigeria. The HOUSE POST is third from left.
Photograph: W. Fagg, 1959. William B. Fagg Archive, UCLA Fowler Museum of Cultural History.

505 POWER FIGURE (NKONDE). Kongo people. Democratic Republic of Congo, 19th–20th century. Wood, pigment, metal, mirror, sacred material. Height 24" (61 cm).
©2000 Museum of Fine Arts, Boston. Gift of William E. and Bertha L. Teel, 1991. Courtesy, Museum of Fine Arts Boston, 1991.1064. Reproduced with permission. All Rights Reserved.

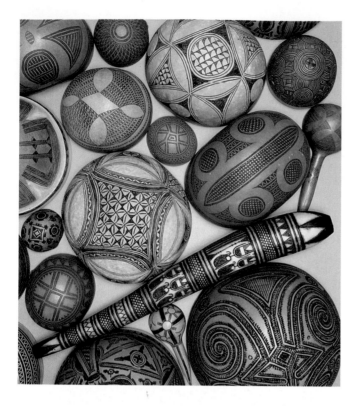

The art of pattern design is highly developed in many parts of Africa. In northern Nigeria, women embellish GOURDS with inventive incised patterns. The smooth surfaces lend themselves to carving and painting. Gourds have many uses in Africa, including storage and serving containers, musical instruments, and ritual objects.

In many African textile traditions, long, narrow strips of cloth are woven and then sewn together to make a piece of fabric large enough for a garment or blanket. For the TEXTILE from Sierra Leone, women wove strips with varied design motifs together so that the rhythmic patterns of the lengthwise pieces would line up to form crosswise stripes. Natural dye colors, rhythmic motifs, and subtle patterns were combined in elegant harmonies.

Nigerian women have found innovative ways to use the indigo dyes that tint their cotton cloth a rich, deep blue. Making ADIRE CLOTH such as the piece pictured here requires a stencil made from a sheet of tin. Women lay the stencils over the cloth, and press flour-and-water paste into the openings. When the stencil is lifted off, the patches of paste remain on the cloth and resist the action of the dye. The rest of the fabric takes on the typical deep blue color after repeated soakings, leaving the words and designs a lighter shade. The ADIRE CLOTH at the left contains repeated handprints, together with traditional Nigerian proverbs and sayings about the hand, such as "My hand is my closest friend."

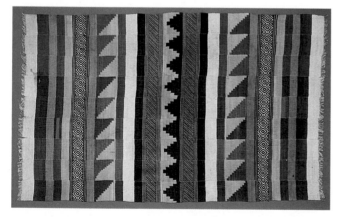

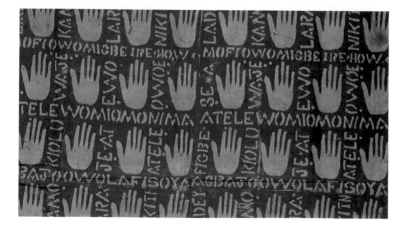

506 GOURDS.
Northern Nigeria. 20th century.
© UCLA Fowler Museum of Cultural History. Photograph: Richard Todd.

507 TEXTILE (KPOKPO).
Mende peoples, Sierra Leone and Libera.
Cotton, indigo dye, kola nut dye. 81½" × 49½".
National Museum of African Art and Natural Museum of Natural History.
Purchased with funds provided by the Smithsonian Collections Acquisition
Program, 1983–85, EJ10408. Photograph: Franko Khoury.

508 Detail of ADIRE CLOTH.
Yoruba, Lagos, Nigeria. 1984.
Dark and light blue cotton cloth, paste-resist and
stencils, natural indigo dye. Sewn in three pieces,
with two borders added. 76" × 62".
Collection of Flora *Edouwaye* Stewart Kaplan, New York.
Photograph: Sheldan Collins.

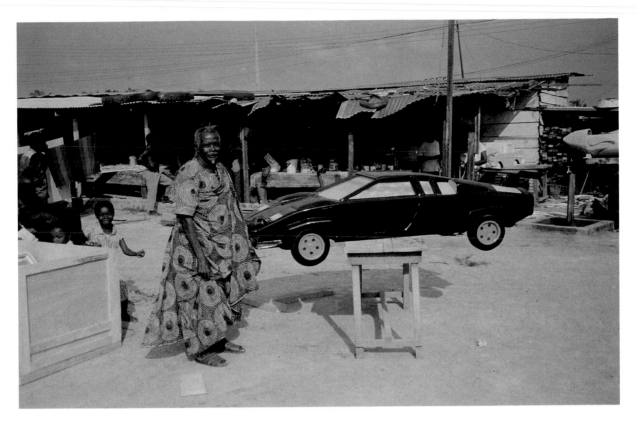

509 Kane Kwei with
LAMBORGHINI COFFIN. 1991.
Photograph: Ernie Wolfe III.
Courtesy Turkana Primitive/Ernie Wolfe Gallery, Los Angeles.

Looking only at the traditional arts of any society can be misleading. Within the indigenous societies of Africa, the pre-Columbian Americas, Oceania, and Australia, many traditional arts are no longer practiced and many of those that survive have lost their central roles in maintaining meaningful community life. Modern commerce, mass-produced material goods, and commercial mass media have transformed life around the world. Some societies with long-standing cultural traditions have been radically changed by these "modern" influences.

The impact of the amazing cross-cultural currents in today's global village is apparent in the work of Ghanaian artist Kane Kwei. His LAMBORGHINI COFFIN takes us beyond traditional African prototypes. In Ghana, as in many societies, the coffin is more than a container for the body: It is a vehicle to the next world. Traditionally, Ghanaian coffins reflect the profession, interests, or stature of the deceased. In 1970 Kwei, who had worked primarily as a

carpenter, was asked to make a coffin in the shape of a boat. It was greatly admired at the funeral and brought Kwei so many commissions that he started his own business: a fish for a fisherman, a cocoa pod for a planter, a Mercedes Benz for the owner of a taxi fleet. Kwei's coffins came to the attention of American gallery owner Ernie Wolfe, who encouraged him to make a variety of cars, which were exhibited in museums and galleries in the United States. From 1970 until his death in 1992, Kwei added a new dimension to his Ashanti tradition.

Not only has African art been influenced by modern Western society, it has also strongly influenced European art. When modern artists of the early twentieth century looked for ways to expand their visual vocabulary, many were drawn to African sculpture. They borrowed its forms, often without understanding its meanings and contexts. This borrowing was most important in the development of Cubism, as we shall see in chapter 22.

OCEANIA AND AUSTRALIA

Oceania is the collective name for the thousands of Pacific islands that comprise Melanesia, Micronesia, and Polynesia (including New Zealand). These islands were settled by migrants from Southeast Asia over a very long period, lasting from about 26,000 B.C.E., when New Guinea and Irian Jaya were populated, until about 800 C.E., when migrants reached New Zealand. Although it is difficult to generalize about Oceanic art, since the cultures, physical environments, and raw materials vary greatly over an enormous area, a few traditional beliefs seem to have been held in common across the Pacific, and these have influenced the creation of art.

First is the belief that the world as we know it was created by the union of the Earth Mother and the Sky Father. Their contact created life forms on the planet's surface. The Oceanic traditions view ancestors as intermediaries between people and the gods. Because ancestors who now live in the spirit world can intercede and influence future events, Oceanic artists have created many objects to honor or placate them. Another widely shared concept is *mana,* or spiritual power. *Mana* may reside in persons, places or things. Many art forms of Oceania were intended to possess this power, which can keep adversity at bay, promote community well-being, and enhance personal power and wisdom.

Oceanic peoples developed very little pottery because of a shortage of clay, and they were not acquainted with metal until traders introduced it in the eighteenth century. For tools, they used stone, bone, or shell; for houses, canoes, mats, and cloth, they used wood, bark, and small plants. Feathers, bone, and shells were employed not only for utensils and sculpture, but for personal adornment.

In the Solomon Islands and New Ireland (part of Melanesia), wood carvings and masks are designed to serve ritual purposes. In the art of many Melanesian societies, birds appear with human figures to act as guides or messengers between the physical world of the living and the spiritual world of deceased ancestors. The bird held by the CANOE PROW FIGURE from the Solomon Islands guides voyagers by acting as a protective spirit that watches out for shoals and reefs. Although the carving is only the size of a hand, it looks much larger because of the boldness of its form. The exaggerated nose and jaw help give the head its forward thrust. Against the blackened wood, inlaid mother-of-pearl provides strongly contrasting white eyes and rhythmically curving linear ZZZ bands.

In New Ireland, masks are made for funerary rites that commemorate tribal ancestors, both real and mythical. In this MASK, the elaborately carved, openwork panels are painted in strong patterns that accentuate—and at times oppose—the dynamic

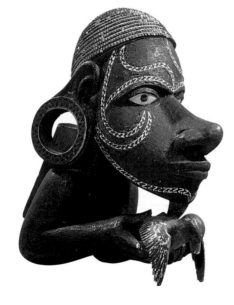

511 PROTECTIVE PROW FIGURE FROM A WAR CANOE.
New Georgia Island, Solomon Islands. 19th century. Wood with mother-of-pearl. Height 6½".
Museum fur Volkerkunde, Basle, Switzerland. Werner Forman/Art Resource, NY.

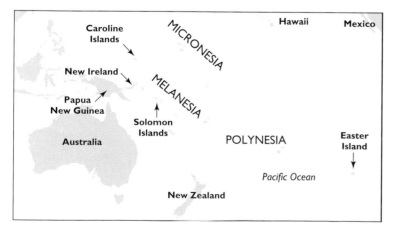

510 OCEANIA AND AUSTRALIA.

forms of the carving. Snail-shell eyes give the mask an intense expression. As in the Solomon Islands CANOE PROW FIGURE, a bird plays a prominent role. In the wings of this mask, chickens hold snakes in their mouths, a reference to the opposition of sky and earth. Anthropologists believe that this mask was used to remove bad influences from a ceremonial house. Once it had fulfilled its function, it was regarded as "used up," and was discarded.

Carvings made in Micronesia and in much of Polynesia are streamlined and highly finished. The Kapingamarangi COCONUT GRATER shows a fine integration of form and function. One sits on the "saddle" of the animal-like form and grates coconuts using the serrated blade at its head. The STANDING FIGURE from Nukuoro Atoll has a similar distinctive spare quality. Although Kapingamarangi and Nukuoro are in the southern part of Micronesia, their culture is Polynesian.

Polynesia covers a large, triangular section of the Pacific, from New Zealand to Hawaii to Easter Island. It is not surprising that the widely separated Polynesian islands and island groups developed

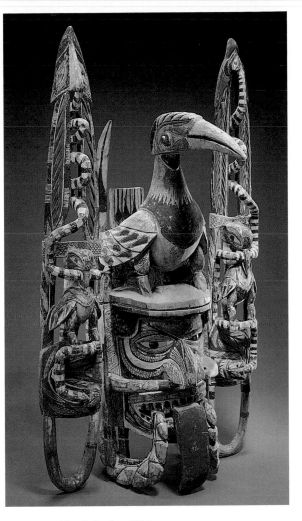

512 MASK. New Ireland. c. 1920.
Painted wood, vegetable fiber, shell. 37½" × 21⅓".
Photograph by Don Cole. © UCLA Fowler Museum of Cultural History.

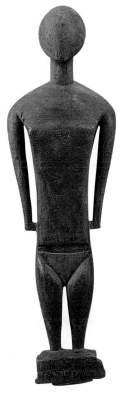

514 STANDING FEMALE
FIGURE.
Nukuoro Atoll,
Central Carolines.
Wood. Height 15⁹⁄₁₆".
19th century.
Honolulu Academy of Arts.
by Exchange 1943 (4752).

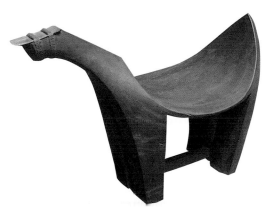

513 COCONUT GRATER.
Kapingamarangi, Caroline Islands. 1954.
Wood, shell blade attached with sennet. Height 19.5".
Courtesy of Keahonui Rosehill Newhouse.

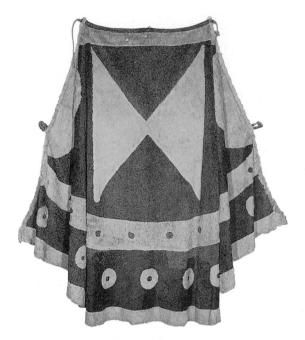

515 FEATHER CAPE. Hawaii. 18th century.
Network with feathers knotted into the mesh.
Height 4'1".
© Copyright The British Museum.

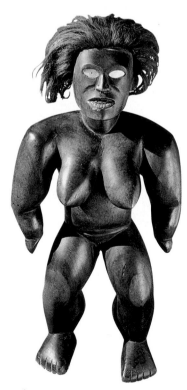

516 AUMAKUA
Wooden image from Forbes
Cave, Hawaii.
Koa wood. Height 29"
Seth Joel, Bishop Museum.

greatly varied arts that include both delicate and boldly patterned bark cloth, featherwork, shell-work, woodcarvings, and huge rock carvings.

The rich color and stunning designs of Hawaiian feather helmets and cloaks are among the world's most magnificent royal attire. Captain James Cook—the first European to officially visit the Hawaiian Islands—compared Hawaiian feather-works to "the thickest and richest velvet which they resemble both as to the feel and the glossy appearance."[1] In this FEATHER CAPE, the geometric figure and ground shapes are in pleasing relationship to one another as well as to the overall shape of the cape.

An outstanding example of semi-abstract Hawaiian sculpture is the forceful 'AUMAKUA (ancestral deity) found in the lava-tube burial cave of a chief or high priest. By eliminating extraneous details and carefully articulating the parts of the body, the sculptor increased the impact of the female figure's bold stance. Its power is enhanced by the attached reddish human hair, shell eyes, and open mouth with bone teeth. The arms-out, knees-bent, feet-apart position gives the figure a strong presence. Full upper arms taper to small forearms and even smaller hands. There is consistent use of full, rounded, almost inflated mass. The well-polished dark wood and inset material show a high degree of craftsmanship.

Many art forms come together in the MAORI MEETING HOUSE, which is a typical structure of traditional New Zealand. Such houses are used for extended family gatherings and rituals in honor of ancestors. The house pictured is named Ruatepupuke in honor of the ancient ancestor of a clan that still lives in the eastern corner of the north island.

Not only is the house named for the ancestor, it is meant to symbolize his presence. His face is at the top of the gable; the ridge represents his back; the rafters are his ribs; the outer upright posts symbolize his arms, as if he is on all fours, looking straight ahead. The front gable boards are painted in abstract patterns that derive from growing ferns. The faces of numerous other ancestors are carved in relief across the front of the house; most noticeable are the eyes of each, which are made from inlaid abalone shell. Through the doorway can be

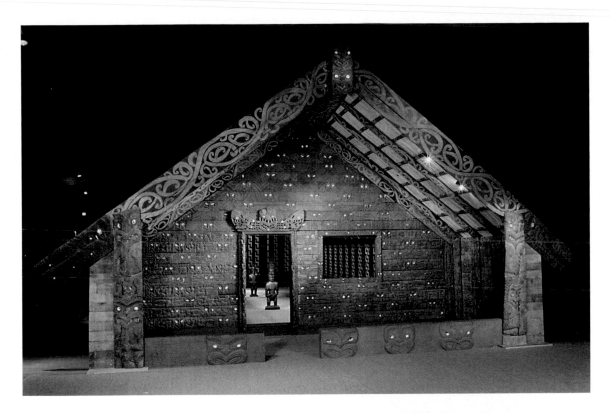

seen two center posts that hold up the ridge pole; these also represent ancestors. The inner walls alternate relief carvings with abstract patterns in matted flax called Tukutuku panels (see page 30).

The ridge pole above the porch is a relief carving of the Earth Mother and the Sky Father, who are the ancestors of all life forms. The degree of abstraction in these figures is typical of Maori carving, with swirling bands and spirals used in body decoration and derived from plant forms. This single board was carved in 1881; it cracked after drying unevenly. The slightly ferocious aspect of these figures indicates that they inhabit the spirit world, and this carving attempts to communicate some of their *mana*.

The human presence in Australia is very old. For tens of thousands of years before the invention of writing, Native Australians maintained an intimate bond with nature, as demonstrated by their art. While most other human groups gradually changed from wandering food foragers to settled farmers, manufacturers, and merchants, Native Australians continued to live as seminomadic hunter-gatherers without clothing or permanent shelters and with only a few simple but highly effective tools.

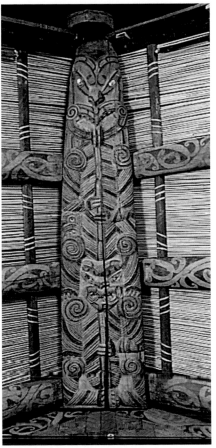

517 MAORI MEETING HOUSE.
Called "Ruatepupuke."
New Zealand. 1881.
Length 56'.
Height 13'10".
Neg.#A112508.3c.
Field Museum, Chicago. Photograph: Diane Alexander White, Linda Dorman.

a. Front view.
b. Ridge pole.

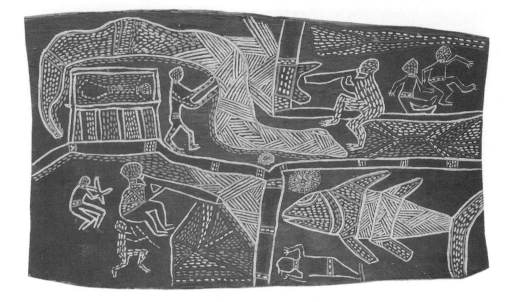

518 Bunia.
FUNERARY RITES AND SPIRIT'S
PATHWAY AFTER DEATH.
Australian bark painting.
Groote Eylantdt, Arnhem Land.
Northern Australia.
Axel Poignant Archive.

The recognition of their dependence on nature is evident in nearly all art done by Native Australians and other tribal peoples. Native Australians see the bond between themselves and nature as a close relationship established by creative beings in the mythical or Eternal Dreamtime. The many disciplines and practices related to spiritual life vary from tribe to tribe, but Dreamtime spirits are prominent in nearly all Native Australian groups.

In the bark painting entitled FUNERARY RITES AND SPIRIT'S PATHWAY AFTER DEATH, animal and human symbols tell a story, with time segments shown in four sections. In the upper left section, a dying man lies on a funeral platform; in the lower left, a *didjeridu* player and two dancers perform for him until he dies. In the upper right, the spirit of the dying man and his two wives also dance until he dies. After his death, the man's spirit leaves the platform and begins the journey to the spirit world; along the way he crosses over the great snake. In the lower right, he uses a stone to kill a large fish for food for the journey.

Native Australian myths have long been communicated through singing, chanting, dancing, and painting. In recent years, paintings (particularly those on bark) by Native Australians have attracted considerable attention from art collectors and galleries.

NATIVE NORTH AMERICA

Native peoples lived in North America for thousands of years before Europeans arrived on the continent. The oldest human-made artifacts—stone hearths and simple tools—may be twenty thousand to thirty thousand years old. Some carved bone tools and spear points are about ten thousand years old. However, surviving objects that most people would consider art are much more recent.

The Hopewell culture flourished from the second century B.C.E. to the sixth century C.E. Large Hopewell burial mounds, most of which were built in what is now Ohio, contained rich offerings placed in elaborate log tombs. The largest of these Hopewell structures is the GREAT SERPENT MOUND, now a park near the town of Peebles. The mound-builders first outlined the writhing design with rows of stones, then piled dirt between them. The serpent has a spiral tail, and its curving body ends with open jaws holding a large oval object. When it was first studied in the mid-nineteenth century, the snake's body was 4 feet 10 inches tall and 27 feet wide. If it were extended, it would be over 1200 feet long. This mysterious structure is one of hundreds of such earth works that early peoples built in the Midwest.

Hopewell artists included wood and stone carvers, potters, coppersmiths, and specialists who worked in shell and mica. The HAND, found in a

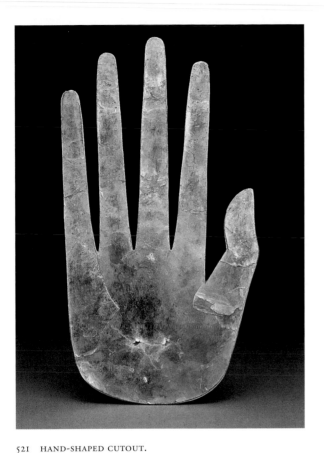

521 HAND-SHAPED CUTOUT.
Hopewell Mound, Ohio. c. 150.
Mica. 11⅓" × 6".
Ohio Historical Society, Columbus.
Photograph © 1985 The Detriot Institute of Arts.

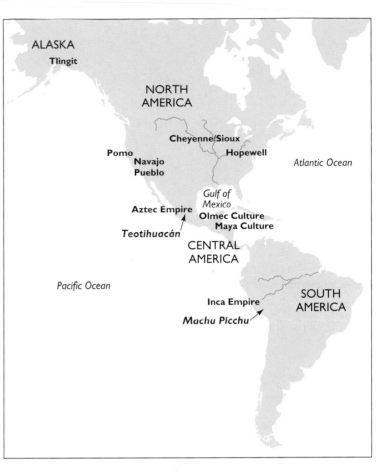

519 AMERICAS.

burial mound, has a striking, abstract quality; elongated fingers and a glowing surface strengthen its mysterious presence. Cut from a glistening, translucent sheet of mica, it seems to celebrate the coordination of eye and hand, mind and spirit, that is the source of all art.

Native Americans today produce an astonishing variety of art works, depending on their cultural tradition and the materials available in their region. In most cases, native art forms that are now practiced vigorously went through a period of disuse in the late nineteenth century when Indian reservations were first set up. Today many Native American artists are making traditional works, and many more are working in contemporary and even "cutting edge" styles. This section focuses on the traditional arts; contemporary work is a subject of chapter 25.

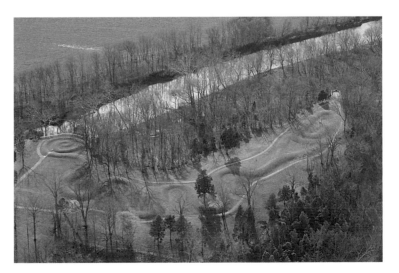

520 GREAT SERPENT MOUND.
Ohio. Adena culture.
100 B.C.E.–500 C.E. Uncoiled length 1254'.
Photograph: Mark C. Burnett/Photo Researchers Inc.

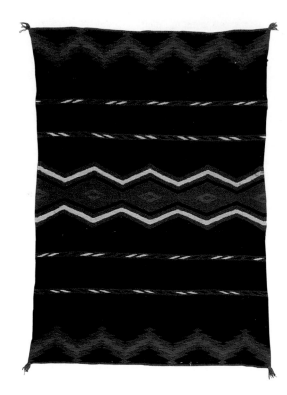

The Navajo of Arizona have been highly resourceful weavers for more than two centuries. The oldest surviving blankets are relatively simple designs, but interactions with other Native American groups, with white settlers, and with the international art market have transformed their art. While many men weave blankets today, the art form was traditionally a woman's province.

The nineteenth-century BLANKET shown here is made from hand-carded wool dyed with organic pigments. The chevron shapes indicate the influence of Mexican serapes, weavings that the Navajo saw during the period in the 1860s when they were uprooted by the U.S. Army and held in captivity in New Mexico. Despite their assimilation of various cultural influences, Navajo weavings seem to retain a high level of quality coupled with an effortless design sense. This accounts in part for their distinctive appearance.

The Pueblo peoples of the Southwest excel at many art forms, but they are best known for pottery, which is traditionally done by women. Maria Chino made the CEREMONIAL WATER JAR from earthenware

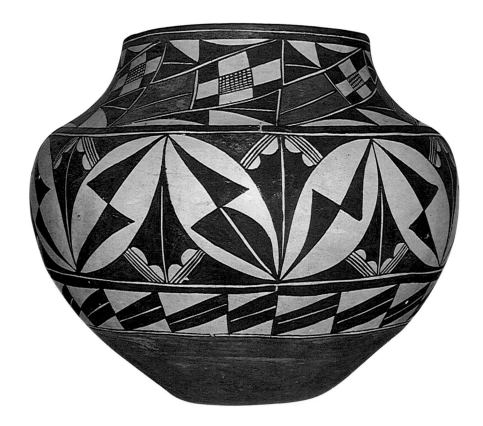

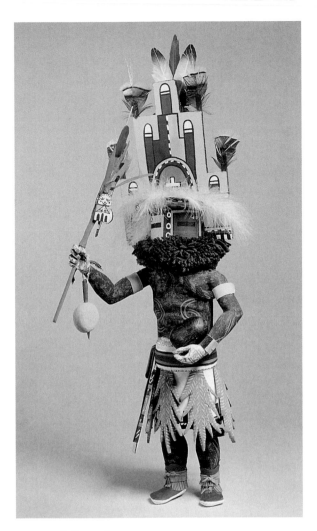

524 Marshall Lomakema.
HOPI KACHINA, HUMIS KATSINA FIGURE. 1971.
Shungopovi, AZ. Height: 34" (86.36 cm). Painted wood.
Courtesy of National Museum of the American Indian/Smithsonian Institution,
(24/7577). Photo by Carmelo Guadagno.

clay, and shaped it, according to traditional practice, without a potter's wheel. After firing it in an open fire on the ground, she painted it with natural pigments from the earth. The abstract symbols in Pueblo pots generally do not have a fixed meaning, but refer to the forces of nature or to community life. (Other examples are the San Ildefonso and Zuni Pots on page 96.) Pueblo pottery traditions are quite active now, but it was not always so. Near the beginning of the twentieth century, there was little being made until Nampeyo and others revived the ancient techniques (see essay on pages 215–216).

Most Pueblo peoples recognize the spirits of invisible life forces. These spirits, known in Zuni

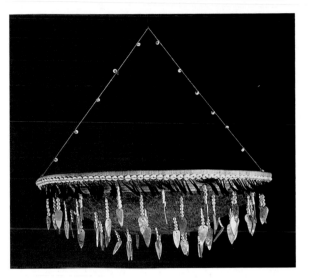

525 POMO FEATHER BASKET. California. 1937.
Feathers, beads and shells, 13½" × 3¼".
Courtesy of the Southwest Museum, Los Angeles. 811.6.1683/CT294.
Photograph by Larry Reynolds.

Pueblo and neighboring Hopi areas as *kachinas,* are impersonated by masked and costumed male members of the tribes, who visit the villages in a variety of forms, including birds, animals, clowns, and demons. During ceremonies they dance, present kachina figures to delighted children, provide humor, and occasionally give public scoldings. The carved and painted KACHINAS are made by Hopi and Zuni fathers and uncles as a means of teaching children their sacred traditions.

Native Americans of the Pacific Coast region produced some of the world's finest baskets. In northern California, Pomo artists made baskets of such incredible tightness that they can hold water. They vary greatly in size, shape, and decoration, from large containers up to four feet in diameter to tiny gift baskets less than a quarter of an inch across. Pomos wove strong geometric designs into many of their baskets and used ornaments such as feathers and shells to embellish others. Women were responsible for the highest artistic achievements in Pomo culture: the brightly colored FEATHER BASKETS. As with Pueblo pottery, the art of basketmaking was traditionally passed down in families from mother to daughter and aunt to niece. The instruction was frequently accompanied by training in other tribal traditions. Treasured pieces were made as gifts designed solely to delight the eye.

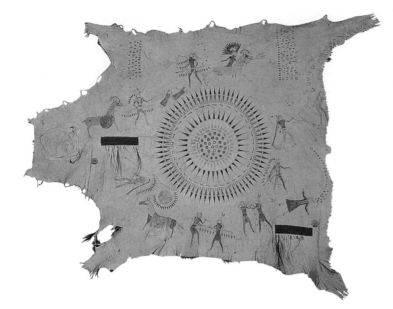

526 Mato Tope (Four Bears).
ROBE WITH MATO TOPE'S EXPLOITS. c. 1835.
Buffalo hide, red wool cloth, sinew, dyed porcupine quills, horsehair and
human hair; brown, yellow, and black pigment. 63" × 83¾".
Ethnographic Collection at the Bern Historical Museum. Photo: S. Rebsamen.

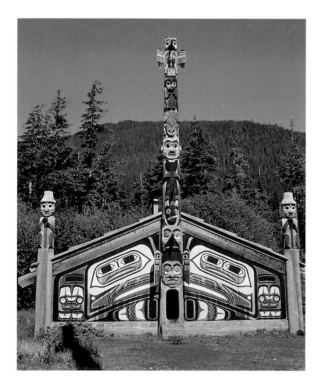

527 TLINGIT COMMUNITY HOUSE.
Ketchikan, Alaska.
Photograph: Steve McCutcheon.

Plains Indians practiced the traditional art of
painting on buffalo hides. Women generally made
abstract paintings on useful objects, such as the
BLACKFEET PARFLECHE on page 6. Men traditionally made representational paintings of their deeds
in battle, as we see in the ROBE WITH MATO TOPE'S
EXPLOITS. Mato Tope stretched this hide in the
sun to dry and then painted it with organic pigments in a water-based solution. Exploit paintings
are typically full of action, with the moving figures
seen in profile views with no horizon line. The best
examples date from before European contact, but
these are very rare. Our example was collected by a
fur trader and sent back to Switzerland. Later hides
depict more sophisticated battles with United
States Army troops. With the disappearance of the
buffalo and the creation of reservations, this art
form went through a fascinating evolution as artists
began to use watercolor and pencil on ledger books
supplied by trading posts. One of the best-known
of these warrior-artists was Howling Wolf, who is
the subject of the accompanying essay.

Northwest Coast tribes developed highly imaginative arts to depict their mythology. Elegant abstractions of animal subjects typify the painting and
sculpture of the Tlingit and other tribes that inhabit
the coastline from Seattle to Alaska. On house
walls, boxes, blankets, and even dishes, major features of a symbolic animal form are laid out in two-
dimensional abstract patterns. With its wide, gently
sloping roof, elaborately painted facade, and totem
poles, the TLINGIT COMMUNITY HOUSE is characteristic of the art and architecture of the region. A
totem is an object such as an animal or plant that
serves as an emblem of a family or clan; it often
symbolizes original, prehuman ancestors. The word
itself, from a Native American language of the
Upper Midwest, means "he is related to me."

The flat surfaces of the TLINGIT COMMUNITY
HOUSE show abstract shapes of beavers, bears,
whales, and ravens. The totem pole at the center
consists of such stacked symbols, which help a family clan to remember its history back to mythologi-
cal times. It is in fact like a family crest.

Plains Native American artist Howling Wolf's drawings reflect not only the artist's unique personal journey, but also larger currents of Native and white relations during a troubled time.

Born into the Southern Cheyenne tribe, Howling Wolf excelled from an early age at the arts of warfare. The young Howling Wolf counted his first act of bravery in 1867, when he was wounded while trying to capture the lead horse of a supply train sent to reinforce white settlers in Kansas. He soon rose in the ranks of the tribe to become a leader alongside his father.

With the arrival of large numbers of white people, however, the nature of Plains warfare evolved toward greater physical danger and the use of firearms. In this style of fighting, the U.S. Army was far more efficient than the Plains warriors, and Native peoples saw their lands steadily reduced.

In 1875, Howling Wolf was captured and subjected to an experiment that both changed his life and influenced the future course of U.S. government treatment of Native Americans. Both Howling Wolf and his father were among seventy-two captives that the Army regarded as particularly dangerous. In September 1875 they were sent to Fort Marion on the coast of Florida, under the command of Captain Richard Pratt,

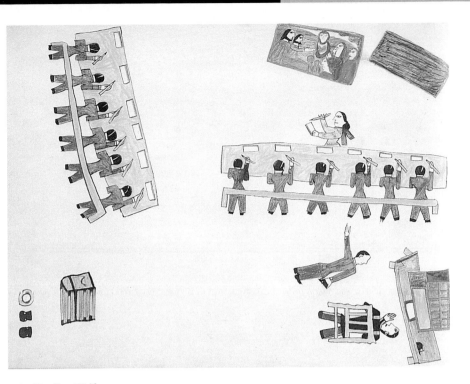

528   Howling Wolf.
CLASSROOM AT FORT MARION. 1876.
Colored pencil on paper. 8½" × 11".
New York State Library, Manuscript and Special Collections Section, Albany.

whose goal was to "civilize" them. The warriors would take Christian names, cut their hair, wear uniforms, and attend classes with teachers who would instill the skills of white society.

The experiment lasted three years, during which time Howling Wolf learned to read and write. He also made drawings that clearly show his inner struggle between his traditional values and the new ones he was being asked to adopt. In CLASSROOM AT FORT MARION, twelve former warriors are seated obediently at their desks as a teacher attempts to show them how to use a pen. Above the teacher's head is a chalkboard, and a larger rectangle shows a religious painting of the sort that commonly hung in classrooms of that time. In this picture within the picture, Howling Wolf experimented with Western perspective.

The rest of the work hovers guardedly between the flatness of traditional Plains painting and the demands of rendering three-dimensional blocks of space in the desks, the warriors, and the chest at the lower left. A confrontation seems to take place in the lower right corner, as a warrior re-

monstrates with an officer at his desk. In the uneasiness of the spacing, the rigidity of the poses, and the ambiguous multiple viewpoints in this work we can clearly see Howling Wolf's wary suspension between two cultures.

Howling Wolf was released from Fort Marion after three years. Resigned to giving up the struggle with white settlers, he returned to the Cheyenne reservation in Oklahoma, where he functioned more as a tribal leader than as an artist. Few works from his later life survive.

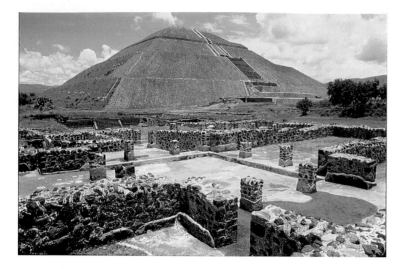

529　PYRAMID OF THE SUN.
Teotihuacan. 1st–7th century C.E.
700' wide, 200' high.
Photograph: John S. Flannery/Bruce Coleman Inc.

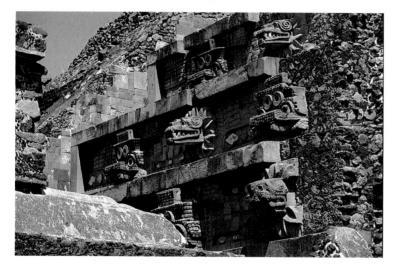

530　Detail of TEMPLE OF THE FEATHERED SERPENT.
Teotihuacan. 150–200 C.E.
Photograph: © Dr. E. R. Degginger/Color-Pic, Inc.

PRE-COLUMBIAN CENTRAL AND SOUTH AMERICA

A variety of highly sophisticated agricultural civilizations flourished in Mexico from about the time of Christ until the Spanish conquest of the 1520s. These cultures influenced one another through trade and conquest, and as a result they share many cultural forms, among them pyramids, calendars, and some important gods and myths. The earliest was the Olmec, who inhabited the Gulf Coast near what is now Veracruz (see the Olmec MASSIVE STONE HEAD on page 200). Probably more influential were the people who built the city of Teotihuacan, located in the central valley about forty miles north of where Mexico City is today.

The PYRAMID OF THE SUN in Teotihuacan is among the largest in the world, covering slightly more ground than the largest of the Great Pyramids of Giza. It rises only about half as high, probably in order to imitate the shape of the surrounding mountains. The pyramid lies over a cave that probably corresponds to the belief of many ancient Mexican cultures, that humanity first emerged from a hole in the ground. This thesis gets strong support from the fact that the pyramid is aligned to face the sunset on August 12, a date corresponding to the beginning of time in the Maya calendar. As we can see in the photograph, the pyramid of the sun was at the center of a large city, which archaeologists calculate was the world's sixth largest at its peak in 600 C.E.

At one end of the central avenue of Teotihuacan lies the TEMPLE OF THE FEATHERED SERPENT, which has sculptural decorations that influenced several other cultures. Alternating on the layers of the temple are relief heads of the Storm God, with its goggle eyes and scaly face, and the Feathered Serpent, its fanged head emerging from a plumed wreath. Teotihuacan itself was abandoned after burning in a mysterious fire in about the year 750 C.E. However, both of these gods were widely adopted by later cultures in ancient Mexico.

The Maya, whose descendants still live in what are now parts of Mexico, Guatemala, and Honduras, developed a written language, an elaborate calendar, advanced mathematics, and large temple complexes of stone.

The hundreds of stone temples at Tikal suggest that Maya priests had great power. TEMPLE 1, built during the classical Maya period, 300–900 C.E., rises over a great plaza in a Guatemalan rain forest. The two-hundred-foot-high pyramid has a temple at the top consisting of three rooms. Another Maya temple pyramid contained a burial chamber deep inside, similar to those found in Egyptian pyramids. Walls and roofs of Maya stone temples were richly carved and painted.

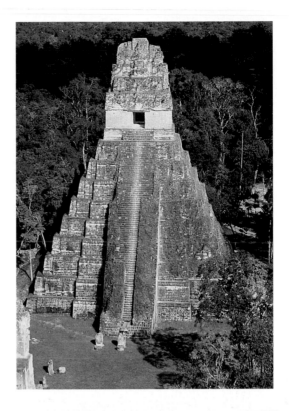

An excellent example of Maya sculpture from one such temple is LINTEL 24 from Yaxchilan, a site on the border between Mexico and Guatemala. This stone relief is best understood with the help of the written symbols along its edges, which have been recently decoded. Standing is the king, Lord Shield Jaguar, holding a flaming torch. The sculptor seems to have rendered effortlessly the casual fall of the feathers in his headdress. His wife Lady Xoc kneels before him performing a ritual. She draws blood from her pierced tongue, which she will blot with the pieces of paper in the basket in front of her. She wears richly patterned clothing that hints at highly developed textile arts of that time (none of which, unfortunately, survive). Her elaborate headdress is crowned with the goggle-eyed rain god, who looks almost directly upward from the back of Lady Xoc's head. Art historians regard highly the sculptor's evocation of the fleshiness of the figures, their subtle interaction, and the rich textures of their clothing. The writing on the work describes the action and even gives its date, 28 October 709.

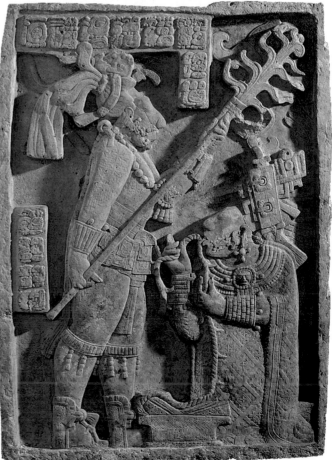

531   TEMPLE 1. Maya.
      Tikal, Guatemala. c. 300–900 C.E.
      Photograph: Hans Namuth/Photo Researchers, Inc.

532   LINTEL 24.
      Yaxchilan, Maya. 709 C.E.
      Limestone. Height: 43".
      © Copyright British Museum.

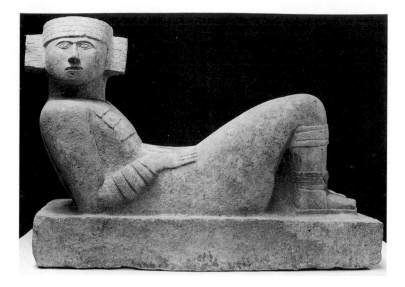

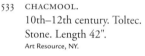

533 CHACMOOL.
10th–12th century. Toltec.
Stone. Length 42".
Art Resource, NY.

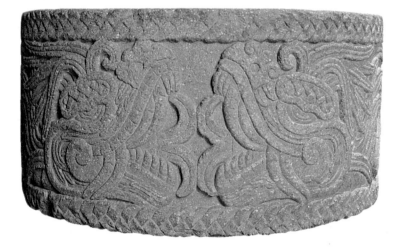

534 VESSEL OF THE FEATHERED SERPENT QUETZALCOATL.
Aztec. 1450–1521.
Stone. Height 19".
Museo Nacional de Antropología, Mexico City.

The Toltec civilization that developed in central Mexico between the ninth and thirteenth centuries forms a bridge between the decline of the Maya and the rise of the Aztecs. During a time of conflict and change, the Toltecs initiated a major new era in the highlands of central Mexico, distinguished by architectural innovations and massive carved figures. A Toltec form that also occurs in Aztec and Maya art is

the recumbent figure from Chichen Itza known by the Mayan name CHACMOOL. The bowl at the figure's waist held sacrificial offerings. Reclining figures such as this one were a strong influence on the modern sculpture of Henry Moore, whose RECUMBENT FIGURE is pictured on page 47.

The Aztecs were the most powerful kingdom in Mexico at the time of the Spanish Conquest; their art is in many respects a summation of preceding styles. The Aztecs (who called themselves the Mexica) settled in the early fourteenth century in the area where Mexico City now stands. Their principal temple was a dual pyramid in honor of the rain god and a war god, where they made human sacrifices of the prisoners they had taken in warfare with neighboring peoples. The Aztecs believed that such sacrifices were necessary in order to honor and recreate the self-sacrifice that the feathered serpent had performed in ancient times in order to ensure the continuation of the world. They believed that this original sacrifice had occurred at Teotihuacan, which they knew as an uninhabited ruin.

The feathered serpent is frequently depicted in Aztec sculpture, but rarely with more horrific effect than in the VESSEL OF THE FEATHERED SERPENT pictured here. Two snakes face each other, their fangs and split tongues forming a symmetrical design. The rather menacing aspect of this piece is typical of much Aztec stone sculpture, which reflects the militaristic and regimented nature of Aztec society. When the Spanish first visited the Aztec capital, they found the city cleaner and better-governed than most European cities. The Aztec also had highly developed arts of poetry and literature.

In the Andes of South America, Inca culture flourished for several centuries prior to the Spanish conquest of 1532. Spanish reports from the time tell of the magnificence of Inca art, but most of the culture's exquisite gold objects were melted down soon after the conquest, and all but a few of the refined fabrics have perished with age and neglect.

The Incas are perhaps best known for their supremely skillful shaping and fitting of stones. Their masonry is characterized by mortarless joints and the "soft" rounded faces of granite blocks.

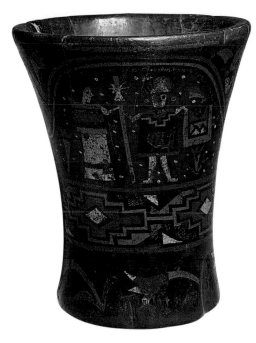

537 KERO CUP. Peru. Late 16th-17th century.
Wood with pigment inlay. 7⅜" × 6¹⁵⁄₁₆".
Brooklyn Museum of Art, Museum Expedition 1941,
Frank L. Babbott Fund. 41.1275.5

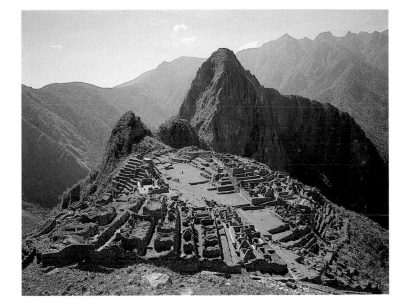

535 MACHU PICCHU. Inca. Peru.
Early 16th century.
Photograph: Ewing Krainen.

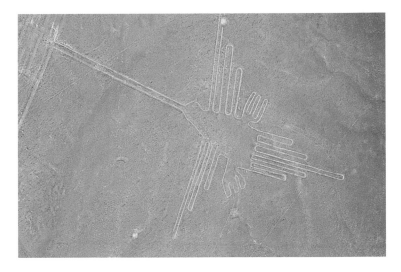

536 HUMMINGBIRD.
Nazca Valley, Peru.
Photograph: Georg Gerster/Photo Researchers, Inc.

MACHU PICCHU, an important ritual center, was built on a ridge in the eastern Andes, in what is now Peru, at an elevation of eight thousand feet. The city, which escaped Spanish detection, was planned and constructed in such a way that it seems to be part of the mountain. Respect for stones is an integral part of Inca culture. According to the Inca creation myth, two of their early ancestors who emerged from the earth immediately turned themselves into stones. Some stone shrines were regarded as living things requiring offerings and care.

On a desert plateau overlooking Nazca Valley, there is a crisscrossing of geometric lines and patterns in the dry yellow sand, presumably carved by the people of an ancient culture known as the Nazca. There are perfectly straight lines, some almost five miles long, and geometric patterns such as spirals, trapezoids, and triangles as well as abstracted images of various known and unknown birds and other animals, including the HUMMINGBIRD shown here. This gigantic sketch pad dwarfs the seemingly insignificant Pan American Highway that crosses one corner. Not until the age of airplanes were people able to see even one of these individual images in its entirety.

One of the few Inca art forms to survive the Spanish conquest intact was the KERO CUP carved from wood. These cups and many other objects are now held in museums far from the lands where they were made. The fate of traditional art objects in the modern world of international commerce is the subject of the following essay.

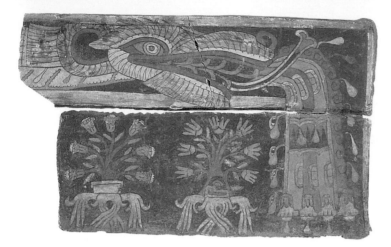

538　FEATHERED SERPENT AND FLOWERING TREES.
Probably Metepec, A.D. 650–750, Teotihuacan, Techinantitla, Mexico.
Height 24¼"

Fine Arts Museums of San Francisco, Bequest of Harald J. Wagner, 1985.104.1a–d (detail).

Most of us would like to think that museums acquire all of their goods through purchase at fair market price or through bequest of generous donors. Indeed, that is how museums most often add to their collections, but not always. Occasionally, items are presented to them that come from suspicious sources that the donors cannot document. Sometimes museums acquire objects from countries whose governments would not permit the export of the goods if they could prevent it. In a few celebrated cases, governments have requested the return of items they believe were taken illegally from their territories. This issue, which is called the return of cultural property, is currently very controversial throughout the museum world, and it has been the subject of much international negotiation. Here are two cases that have been in the news in recent years:

1. In 1897, English traders in Africa wanted to negotiate a business arrangement with the King of Benin. They sent a delegation to visit the royal court, but the king's representatives met this group several miles from the border and told the English that the king was performing a series of important rituals and could not discuss business. The English party came ahead anyway, but they were ambushed on the way and most of the traders were killed. The English then sent their army on a punitive expedition. They raided the Benin capital, taking many lives and seizing hundreds of bronzes (one of these is illustrated on page 350). Most of the art works entered the collection of the British Museum in London, and many others were given to other museums throughout England and Scotland. In January 1997, the King of Benin wrote to the director of the Glasgow Art Gallery and Museum requesting the return of the twenty-two bronzes and ivories for an upcoming series of royal ceremonies.

The director of the Glasgow Museum refused to return the Benin works, claiming that through their display to the Scottish public, the works "play an important role in introducing our visitors to the culture and religious beliefs of Benin . . . and, it has to be said, the history of British Imperialism."[2]

2. The de Young Museum in San Francisco received a telephone call in 1976 from the administrators of the estate of Harald J. Wagner, who had recently died. Wagner stated in his will that his art collection was to be donated to the de Young, and two curators visited the house that summer. There they found some seventy pieces of mural painting that had been taken off the walls of apartments in the ancient Mexican city of Teotihuacan. Among the fragments WAS FEATHERED SERPENT AND FLOWERING TREES. An examination revealed that the pieces had been pried off of the stucco walls with jack hammers or crowbars and loaded into trucks, and then somehow hauled out of Mexico. Wagner had sales receipts proving that he had bought them in Mexico in the 1960s, but removing these objects in the first place, and transporting them across the border, probably violated Mexican and American laws.

The de Young Museum invited Mexican experts to examine the mural paintings from Teotihuacan, and eventually returned more than half of them to the Mexican National Institute of Anthropology and History, the agency in charge of caring for historic sites. The Mexican government showed its gratitude to the de Young in 1993 by lending a large number of other works from Teotihuacan so that the museum could stage the largest exhibition ever held of works from that ancient city.

From these accounts, it is clear that the international trade in art is often a very delicate matter involving issues of national pride and public morality. Works of art are often hotly contested items, as much prized by their owners as coveted by those who would have them.

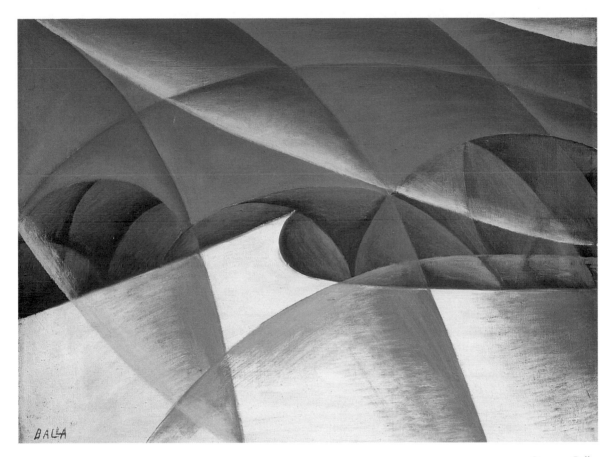

Giacomo Balla.
ABSTRACT SPEED THE CAR HAS PASSED. 1913.
Oil on canvas. 19¾" × 25¾".
Tate Gallery, London.

PART SIX
The Modern World

What generalizations could you make about twentieth-century art after glancing at the reproductions in this book's last five chapters?

The invention of photography freed painting from the need to be realistic. Why do artists continue to paint portraits instead of simply using a camera to capture someone's likeness?

Do the "stationary" visual arts such as painting and sculpture still have impact in a world dominated by film and television?

Is art today more or less difficult for the average person to understand than it was several hundred years ago? What changes might account for any difference?

Do artists build on the art of their predecessors in the way scientists build on the work of earlier scientists?

CHAPTER TWENTY-ONE

LATE EIGHTEENTH AND NINETEENTH CENTURIES

Three revolutions—the Industrial Revolution, which began in Britain about 1760; the American Revolution in 1775; and the French Revolution in 1789—launched the period of great social and technological change we call the modern age. The Industrial Revolution brought about the most significant shift in the way people lived since the Neolithic agricultural revolution ten thousand years earlier. Since the start of the Industrial Revolution, technological change has occurred at an ever increasing rate.

The Enlightenment, or Age of Reason, as the late eighteenth century has been called, was characterized by a shift to a more rational and scientific approach to religious, political, social, and economic issues. Belief in the importance of liberty, self-determination, and progress brought about an emphasis on democracy and secular concerns. Consistent belief systems that tended to unify the art of earlier societies became increasingly fragmented. Traditional values were challenged by the new atmosphere of independent investigation, by the radical changes brought about by technology, and by the increased mixing of peoples and cultures. Artists both expressed and abetted these changes.

In the Western world, a new self-consciousness regarding styles led to increasing uncertainty about the place of art and artists in society. In earlier periods, within each society, artists were more likely to adhere to one dominant style. Following the French Revolution and the subsequent break with traditional art patronage in France, a variety of styles developed simultaneously. Artists were freed from the artistic constraints imposed by their traditional patrons (royalty, aristocracy, wealthy merchants and bankers, and the church), but they were left to struggle financially until a new system of patronage emerged. Eventually, support came in the form of commercial galleries, private and corporate collectors, and museums.

NEOCLASSICISM

With the beginning of the French Revolution in 1789, the luxurious life that centered on the French court ended abruptly, and French society was disrupted and transformed. As the social structure and values changed, tastes changed.

One of the artists who led the way to revolutions in both art and politics was painter Jacques-Louis David. Believing that the arts should serve a political purpose in a time of social and governmental reform, he rejected what he saw as the frivolous immorality associated with the aristocratic Rococo style. When he painted OATH OF THE HORATII, David used an austere style called *Neoclassicism*. The term refers to the emulation of classical Greek and Roman art; much of the subject matter in Neoclassical art was Roman because Rome represented a republican, or nonmonarchical, government.

The subject of OATH OF THE HORATII is a story of virtue and the readiness to die for liberty, in which three brothers pledge to take the sword offered by their father to defend Rome. With such paintings, David gave revolutionary leaders an inspiring image of themselves rooted in history. "Take courage," was the painting's message, "your cause is a noble one and has been fought before."

David's Neoclassicism, seen in the rational, geometric structure of his composition, provides strong contrast to the lyrical softness of Rococo designs. The painting has the quality of classical (Greco-Roman) relief sculpture, with strong side light emphasizing the figures in the foreground. Even the folds in the garments are more like carved marble than soft cloth. The three arches of the columns give strength to the design and provide an historically appropriate setting for the Roman figures. The two center columns separate the three major parts of the subject. Vertical and horizontal lines parallel the edges of the picture plane, forming a stable composition that resembles a stage set.

The women at the right of THE OATH OF THE HORATII seem overcome by emotion, unable to participate in the serious decisions required of men who would defend their homeland. This painting reflects what was commonly believed at that time: that women are unfit for public life. Their exclusion from most professions was also followed in the art world, where women were banned from academy classes in which unclothed models were used. If a woman did succeed as an artist, it was because she either could afford private study or came from an artistic family.

In the works of the Neoclassicist Angelica Kauffmann, who overcame such obstacles, we see a different vision of woman's abilities. Born in Switzerland and trained by her father, Kauffmann spent six years in Italy before settling in London in 1768. She was elected a full member of the British Royal Academy two years later, the last woman to be so honored until the 1920s. Her work COR-NELIA, POINTING TO HER CHILDREN AS TREASURES was painted a year after David's OATH OF THE HOR-ATII. Cornelia is at the center of the work, talking to a friend seated at the right. The friend shows a string of jewels as if boasting about them, to which Cornelia replies that her children are her jewels.

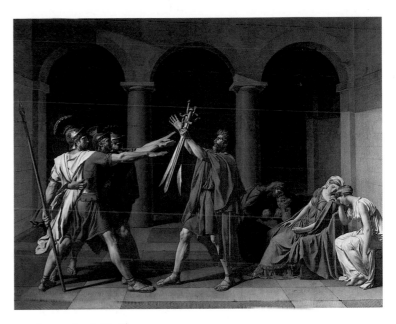

539 Jacques-Louis David.
OATH OF THE HORATII. 1784.
Oil on canvas. 10'10" × 14'.
Musée du Louvre, Paris.
Photograph: Scala/Art Resource, NY.

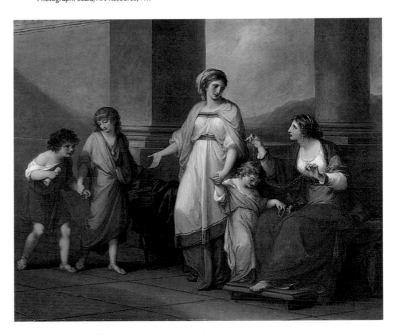

540 Angelica Kauffmann (born Swiss, 1741–1807).
CORNELIA, POINTING TO HER CHILDREN AS HER TREASURES.
c. 1785. Oil on canvas. 40" × 50". Signed on base of column at right: Angelica Kauffmann pinxt.
Virginia Museum of Fine Arts, Richmond. The Adolf D. and Wilkins C. Williams Fund.
Photograph: Ann Hutchison. © Virginia Museum of Fine Arts. 75.22/50669.2

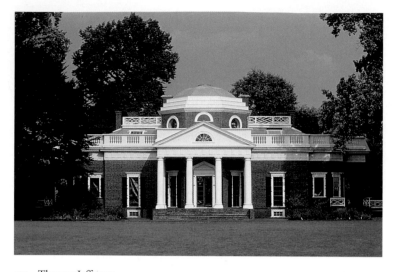

541 Thomas Jefferson.
MONTICELLO. Charlottesville, Virginia. 1793–1806.
Courtesy of the Thomas Jefferson Memorial Foundation.

Indeed, to a student of Roman history, this was true: Cornelia's children adopted her well-known democratic beliefs and went on to become important figures in the development of the Roman political system.

The new classical (that is, Neoclassical) spirit was also felt in architecture. American architecture achieved international stature for the first time with the work of statesman-architect Thomas Jefferson. His original design for his home, MONTICELLO, was derived from Palladio's Renaissance reinterpretation of Roman country-style houses (see page 300). Then, during his years in Europe as Minister to France (1784–1789), Jefferson was strongly influenced by French, Italian, and Roman architecture. Thus, when he rebuilt his home between 1793 and 1806, he had the second story removed from the center of the building and replaced by a dome on an octagonal drum. He added a large Greco-Roman portico (a porchlike roof supported by columns), making the entire design reminiscent of the PANTHEON (see page 272) by way of contemporary French Neoclassical architecture. In comparison with the first MONTICELLO, the second version has a monumental quality that reflects Jefferson's increasingly classical conception of architecture.

Both MONTICELLO and Jefferson's designs for the University of Virginia show the Roman phase of Neoclassical American architecture, often called the Federal or Jeffersonian Style. Jefferson aimed for an architecture capable of expressing the values of the new American republic. In its fusion of classical Greek, Roman, Renaissance (Palladian), and eighteenth-century forms, his architecture shows an originality that sets it apart. Jefferson's Neoclassical style is reflected in much of American architecture before the Civil War. Neoclassical architecture can be found in practically every city in the United States, and it continues to dominate Washington, D.C.

ROMANTICISM

The Enlightenment celebrated the power of reason; however, an opposite reaction, Romanticism, soon followed. This new wave of emotional expression motivated the most creative artists in Europe from about 1825 to 1850. The word Romanticism comes from *romances,* popular medieval tales of adventure written in romance languages.

Whereas Neoclassicism refers to a specific style, *Romanticism* refers to an attitude that inspired a number of styles. Romantic artists, musicians, and writers held the views that imagination and emotion are more valuable than reason, that nature is less corrupt than civilization, and that human beings are essentially good. Romantics championed the struggle for human liberty and celebrated nature, rural life, common people, and exotic subjects in art and literature. They wanted to assert the validity of subjective experience and to escape Neoclassicism's fixation on classical forms.

Spanish artist Francisco Goya was a Romantic painter and printmaker. A contemporary of David, he was aware of the French Revolution and he personally experienced some of the worst aspects of the ensuing Napoleonic era, when French armies invaded Spain and much of the rest of Europe. Goya at first welcomed Napoleon's invading army because his sympathies were with the French Revolution and he had lost confidence in the king of Spain. But he soon discovered that the occupying

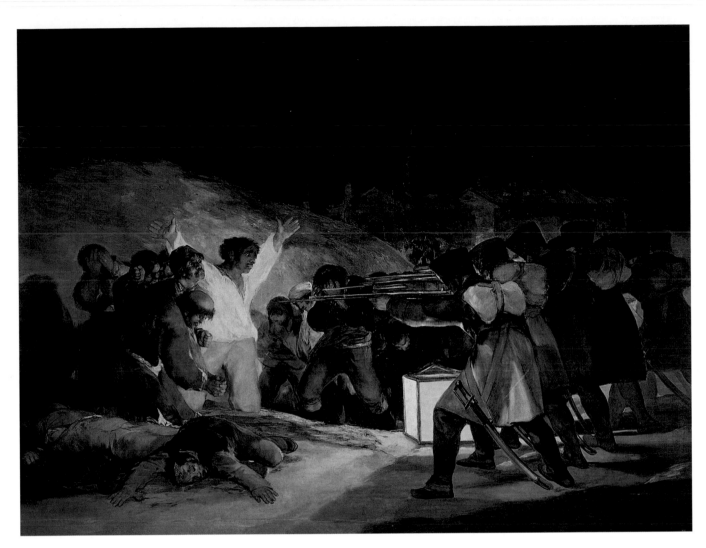

542 Francisco de Goya y Lucientes (1746–1828).
THE THIRD OF MAY. 1814. Oil on canvas. 8'9" × 13'4".
Museo del Prado, Madrid, Spain. Erich Lessing/Art Resource, NY.

army was destroying rather than defending the ideals he had associated with the Revolution. Madrid was occupied by Napoleon's troops in 1808. On May 2, a riot broke out against the French in the central square. Officers fired from a nearby hill, and the cavalry was ordered to cut down the crowds. The following night, firing squads were set up to shoot anyone who appeared in the streets. Later, Goya vividly and bitterly depicted these brutalities in his powerful indictment of organized murder, THE THIRD OF MAY, 1808, painted in February 1814.

The painting is enormous, yet so well conceived in every detail that it delivers its message in-stantly. A structured pattern of light and dark areas organizes the scene, giving it impact and under-scoring its meaning. Goya focuses attention on the soldiers by means of value shifts that define a wedge shape formed by the hill and the brightly lighted area on the ground. Mechanical uniformity marks the faceless firing squad, in contrast to the ragged group that is the target. From the soldiers' dark shapes, we are led by the light and the lines of the rifles to the man in white. The focal point is this man, raising his arms in a gesture of defiance. THE THIRD OF MAY, 1808 is not a mere reconstruc-tion of history; it is a universal protest against the brutality of tyrannical governments.

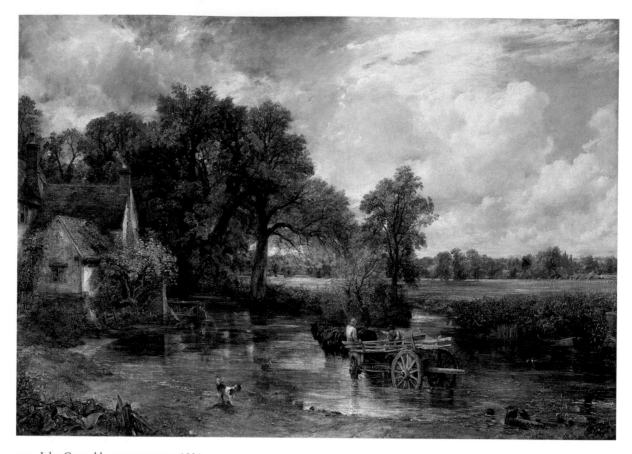

543 John Constable. THE HAY WAIN. 1821.
Oil on canvas. 50½" × 73".
Reproduced by courtesy of the Trustees, The National Gallery Company, Ltd. London.
© National Gallery, London.

During the early nineteenth century, English painting was dominated by an interest in landscape—a response to the increasingly sooty air and sprawling factories of the Industrial Revolution.

The son of a wealthy miller, Romantic painter John Constable grew up in the English countryside and developed a love of nature that was to stay with him all his life. Although he developed his detailed paintings in his studio in the traditional way, he preceded them with numerous oil sketches he completed outdoors. Constable was not the first to paint such studies on location, but he was unique in the attention he gave to the intangible qualities of light and weather. He decried what he saw as the decline of art caused by "the imitation of preceding styles, with little reference to nature."[1] He said that he wished to paint nature as if he were seeing it for the first time.

When Constable's painting THE HAY WAIN was exhibited in the annual Paris exhibition of 1824, French artists were amazed by the English painter's vision of landscape. Constable broke away from conventional formulas of color and technique. His innovative use of individual strokes of varied color and his use of flecks of white to suggest shimmering sunlight brought him ridicule from contemporary critics and, two generations later, praise from the French Impressionists.

In the United States, the work of Romantic painter Thomas Cole helped to stimulate enthusiasm for the grandeur and beauty of the vast American wilderness. Cole is recognized as the founder of the Hudson River School, an important group of American landscape painters. Like Constable, Cole began with on-site oil and pencil sketches, then made his large paintings in his studio. The broad,

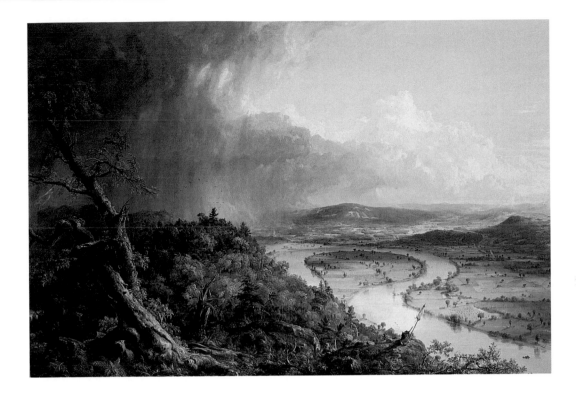

544 Thomas Cole.
THE OXBOW. 1836.
Oil on canvas.
51½" × 76".
The Metropolitan Museum of Art,
New York. Gift of Mrs. Russell Sage,
1908. (08.228)
Photograph: © 1995 The
Metropolitan Museum of Art.

panoramic view, carefully rendered details, and light-filled atmosphere of paintings such as THE OXBOW became the inspiration for American landscape painting for several generations; see also Asher Durand's KINDRED SPIRITS on page 54.

In nineteenth-century America it was difficult to obtain the education necessary to become a professional artist; for an African American it was almost impossible. Nevertheless, with the help of antislavery sponsors, a few succeeded.

Robert S. Duncanson was one of the first African-American artists to earn an international reputation. As the son of a Scots-Canadian father and an African-American mother, he may have had an easier time gaining recognition as an artist than those who did not straddle the color line. Prior to settling in Cincinnati, he studied in Italy, France, and England, and he was heavily influenced by European Romanticism. With BLUE HOLE, LITTLE MIAMI RIVER, Duncanson reached artistic maturity. He modified the precise realism of the Hudson River School with an original, poetic softening. He orchestrated light, color, and detail to create an intimate and engaging reverie of a person in nature.

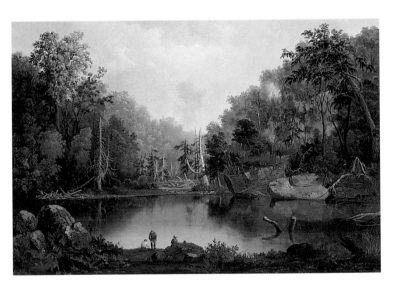

545 Robert S. Duncanson.
BLUE HOLE, LITTLE MIAMI RIVER. 1851.
Oil on canvas. 29¼" × 42¼".
Cincinnati Art Museum.
Gift of Norbert Heermann and Arthur Helbig. 1926.18.

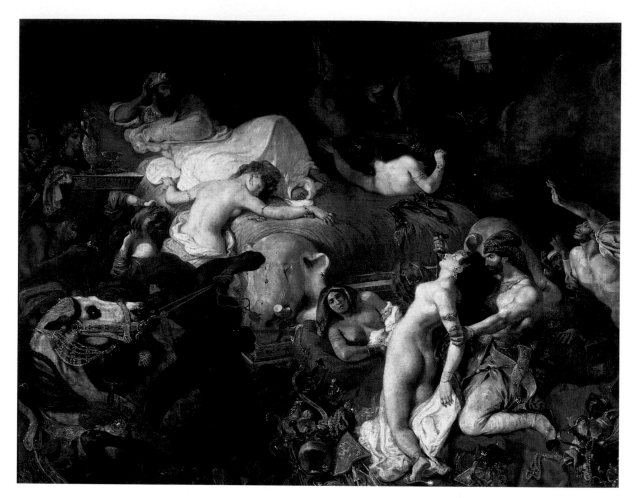

546 Eugène Delacroix. THE DEATH OF SARDANAPALUS. 1827.
Oil on canvas. 12'1½" × 16'2⅞".
Musée du Louvre, Paris.
Photograph: Kavaler/Art Resource, NY.

In France, the leading Romantic painter was Eugène Delacroix. Delacroix's painting THE DEATH OF SARDANAPALUS exhibits the many qualities that distinguish Romanticism from the Neoclassicism of David and his followers. The story is based on an imaginative piece of literature by Lord Byron: Sardanapalus is an Assyrian king in a hopeless military situation. Rather than surrender, he takes poison and orders all of his favorite possessions brought before him and destroyed in an orgy of violence. Delacroix composed this writhing work along a diagonal, and lit it using strong chiaroscuro in a way that recalls certain Baroque paintings (see page 304). His brushwork is loose and open, or *painterly,* not at all like the cool precision of Neoclassicism.

Delacroix used all of these devices in order to enhance the viewer's emotional response to a horrifying, if imagined, event. The Romantic painters in general stressed strong viewer involvement, use of color equal in importance to drawing, and dramatic movement, in contrast to the detached rationality and clear idealism of the Neoclassicists.

PHOTOGRAPHY

The camera, perfected by the painter Daguerre (see page 155), was initially seen by landscape and portrait painters as a threat to their livelihood. In fact, it freed painters from the roles of narrator and illustrator, allowing them to explore dimensions of inner experience that had been largely neglected in

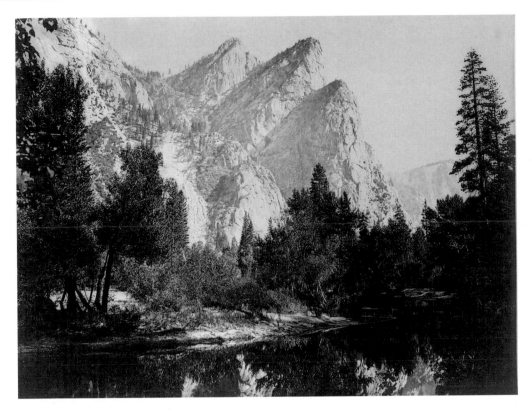

547   Carleton E. Watkins.
THE THREE BROTHERS—4480 FEET—YOSEMITE.
1861. Photograph.
Library of Congress.

Western art since the Renaissance. Photography offered new opportunities to fuse images of objective reality with personal visions.

In its first two generations, the new medium was put to many uses. The perfection of glass-plate negatives in the 1850s made possible reproductions of photographs, though the technology was still quite cumbersome to use. Photographers had to smear glass plates with just the right amount of toxic chemicals, expose the plate for the correct number of seconds, and develop the negative almost immediately.

Carleton Watkins in 1861 journeyed into the Sierra Nevada to photograph the THREE BROTHERS in Yosemite valley. This image is part of a portfolio of landscape photographs that he made for sale, signing each one as if it were a painting. These photographs were widely circulated, and they influenced the U.S. Congress to set aside Yosemite as a National Park.

Delacroix was one of the first to recognize the difference between camera vision and human vision. He believed that photography was potentially of great benefit to art and artists. In an essay for students, Delacroix wrote:

A daguerreotype is a mirror of the object; certain details almost always overlooked in drawing from nature take on in it characteristic importance, and thus introduce the artist to complete knowledge of construction as light and shade are found in their true character.[2]

Félix Tournachon, called Nadar, was—like many other photographers—an artist who came to prefer photography to drawing and printmaking. He gained fame as a balloonist, and from a hot air balloon he made the first aerial photographs. He even took the first underground photographs in the sewers and catacombs of Paris, using artificial lighting techniques and long exposures.

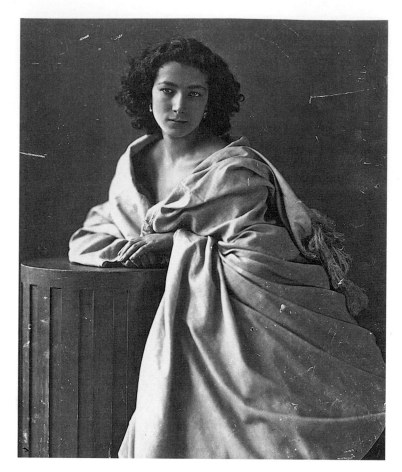

548 Nadar (Félix Tournachon).
SARAH BERNHARDT. 1855.
Photograph printed from a collodion negative.
International Museum of Photography at
George Eastman House, Rochester, New York.

Nadar recognized that photography was merely a mechanical process and that the photographer had to be intelligent and creative in order to make significant works of art with a camera. The most notable artists, writers, and intellectuals of Paris went to him to have their portraits made. His photograph of French actress SARAH BERNHARDT is an evolutionary link between the Romantic painted portraits of nineteenth-century women and the glamour photography of today. Another pioneer

portrait photographer was Julia Cameron, who began photographing at age forty-eight and created an impassioned body of work (see page 156).

As both a tool and a way of seeing, photography influenced the next major stylistic development: Realism.

Both Neoclassicism and Romanticism had their beginnings in rebellion. But by mid-century each had become institutionalized, functioning as a conservative force in French artistic life. At the state-sponsored École des Beaux Arts, or School of Fine Arts, students were taught by members of the Academy of Fine Arts (an organization of government-approved artists) that "great painting" demanded "classical" technique and "elevated" subject matter found in history, mythology, literature, or exotic locations.

Delacroix accused Academy members of teaching beauty as though it were algebra. Today, we still use the term *academic art* for generally unimaginative works that follow stale formulas laid down by an academy or school, especially the French Academy of the nineteenth century.

French Academy members played a major role in selecting artists for a huge annual exhibition known as the Salon. Participating in the Salon was virtually the only way an artist might become known to the public. The art history of the rest of the nineteenth century is largely one of rebellion against such institutions and authority figures. Vast changes in art and the artist's role in society were about to topple the dominance of the French Academy.

REALISM

Realism describes a style of art and literature that depicts ordinary existence without idealism, exoticism, or nostalgia. We have seen it before the nineteenth century, notably in Roman sculpture and Flemish and Dutch painting. By mid-century, a growing number of artists were dissatisfied with both the Neoclassicists' and the Romantics' attachment to mythical, exotic, and historical subjects. They believed that art should deal with human ex-

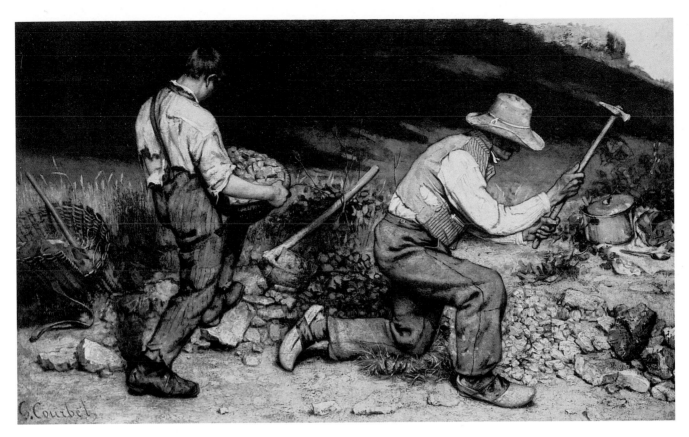

549 Gustave Courbet (1819–1877).
THE STONE BREAKERS. 1849 (destroyed in 1945).
Oil on canvas. 5'5" × 7'10".
The Bridgeman Art Library International Ltd.

perience and observation. They knew that people in the nineteenth century were living a new kind of life, and wanted art to show it.

In the 1850s, French painter Gustave Courbet revived Realism with new vigor by employing a direct, painterly technique for the portrayal of the dignity of ordinary things and common life. In doing so, he laid the foundation for a rediscovery of the extraordinary visual qualities of everyday experience.

THE STONE BREAKERS shows Courbet's rejection of Romantic and Neoclassical formulas. His subject is neither historical nor allegorical, religious nor heroic. The men breaking stones are ordinary road workers, presented almost life-size. Courbet

did not idealize the work of breaking stones or dramatize the struggle for existence; he simply said, Look at this.

Courbet's detractors were sure that he was causing artistic and moral decline by painting what they considered unpleasant and trivial subjects on a grand scale. They accused him of raising "a cult of ugliness" against cherished concepts of Beauty and the Ideal. Realism was perceived as nothing less than the enemy of art, and many believed that photography was the source and the sponsor of this disaster. When THE STONE BREAKERS was exhibited in Paris in the Salon of 1850, it was attacked as unartistic, crude, and socialistic. From then on, Courbet set up his own exhibits—the beginning of

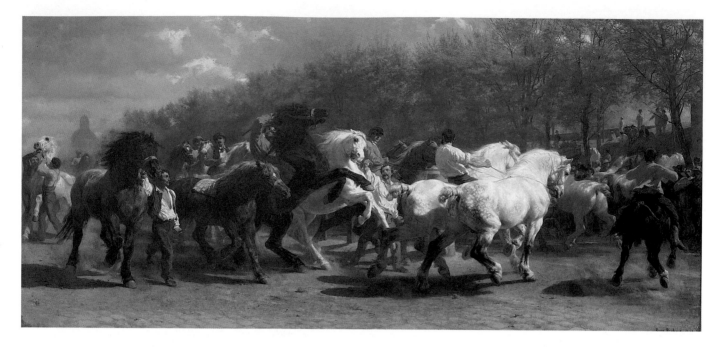

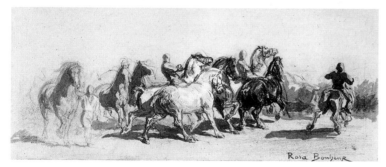

550 Rosa Bonheur. THE HORSE FAIR. 1853–1855.
Oil on canvas. 8' × 16'7½".
The Metropolitan Museum of Art, NY.
Gift of Cornelius Vanderbilt, 1887.
Photograph: © 1997 The Metropolitan Museum of Art, NY.

551 Rosa Bonheur. STUDY FOR THE HORSE FAIR. c. 1853.
Black chalk, gray wash heightened with white, on beige paper.
5⅜" × 13¼".
The Metropolitan Museum of Art, NY.
Bequest of Edith H. Proskauer, 1975. (1975.319.2)

the continuing practice of independent shows organized by artists themselves.

Courbet was one of the first to finish his paintings outdoors, working directly from nature. Previously, most landscape painting had been done in the artist's studio from memory, sketches, and reference materials such as rocks and plants brought in from outside. When portable tubes of oil paint became available in 1841, artists were able to paint outdoors without preliminary drawings or preconceived plans. By working directly from subjects outdoors, painters were able to capture first impressions. This shift in practice opened up whole new ways of seeing and painting.

Of his own work, Courbet said,

To know in order to create, that was my idea. To be able to represent the customs, the ideas, the appearance of my own era . . . to create living art; that is my aim.[3]

Realism of a more popular sort was practiced by Rosa Bonheur, who specialized in painting rural scenes with animals. In THE HORSE FAIR, she captured the surging energy of a group of horses offered for sale, some of them untamed. Many scholars believe that the figure on horseback in the blue-green coat near the center of the picture is a portrait of the artist wearing men's clothing. If so, it was one of several unconventional personal characteristics that she adopted in order to help her career (see accompanying essay).

The Realist paintings of American artist Thomas Eakins are remarkable for their humanity and insight into the everyday world. A comparison

The list of awards that Rosa Bonheur earned in her lifetime was impressive by any standard: First Medal at the Paris Salon; Grand Cross of the French Legion of Honor; Commander of the Order of Isabella the Catholic; Member of the Order of King Leopold of Belgium. She was the first woman ever to receive most of these honors. She was also a friend to Queen Victoria of England and the French Emperor Napoleon III. Yet Rosa Bonheur also led an unusual personal life that showed clearly the difficulties that a woman of her day had to face if she wanted a career.

Her most important early influence was her father, Raymond, a drawing teacher. He was a Saint-Simonian Socialist—that is, he believed all wealth should be shared because everybody was equal; girls were as worthy as boys and should be raised the same way. These beliefs are somewhat radical even today, but he took them even further. He believed that a new savior would come to the human race, as Christ had done in ancient times, and that this new Messiah would be a woman. Hence he took special pains to educate his daughters, an unusual step for that period.

Rosa Bonheur decided as a teenager to become an artist, and benefitted from her father's teaching; in fact, she soon surpassed him. Since the Academy forbade women from studying the nude model, she decided to specialize in painting country scenes with animals. There was a ready market for such works, partly because France was industrializing and people from the country were moving to the city in great numbers. People wanted to remember country life, and Bonheur became their painter. A few Parisian artists had already specialized in this subject, but she soon surpassed them too.

The main problem inherent in her career choice was that she would have to do things that women just did not do: spend a lot of time on farms and ranches, become an expert rider, and sketch animal anatomy in slaughterhouses. All of these she did, apparently with pleasure.

She found that she could do her work with more ease and comfort if she cut her hair short and wore trousers. Cutting the hair was not a problem, but for a woman to wear trousers in public was illegal. Well, not exactly: She had to get a permit from the local police and renew it every six months. The stack of papers was found among her possessions after she died.

She was not the first woman to adopt a male appearance as a career move. The novelist Amandine Dupin, eighteen years older than Bonheur, had scandalized Paris by wearing men's clothing and using the pen name George Sand; Bonheur admired her.

How else might a woman forward her career in a male-dominated society? Bonheur always insisted that her only goals were convenience and career advancement: "If, however, you see me dressed as I am, it is not in the least in order to make me into an original, but simply in order to facilitate my work. Consider that, at a certain period in my life, I spent whole days at the slaughterhouse."[4]

She never married, regarding it as a hindrance. Rather, she lived most of her life with her friend Natalie Micas in a home filled with pets. The two of them were active in the Society for the Prevention of Cruelty to Animals. Her favorite males, she said, were the bulls that she painted.

Meanwhile, her work kept selling and gaining honors. She bought a country estate next to the Emperor's family home. When Empress Eugenie arrived at her door to present her with the Legion of Honor, the artist kept Her Majesty waiting while she threw a robe on over her pants.

To the end of her life, Bonheur lived the dichotomy of the successful and honored career

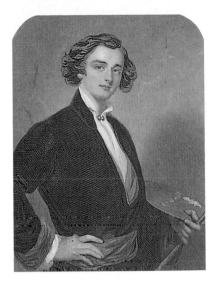

552   W. H. Mote.
ROSA BONHEUR. 1856.
Engraving after R. Buckner.
Picture Collection, The New York Public Library, Astor, Lenox and Tilden Foundations.

woman forced into an unconventional personal life. Accused of seeming unfeminine, she defended herself in a way that rings as a call for women's equality:

Why wouldn't I be proud of being a woman? My father, that enthusiastic apostle of humanity, repeated to me many times that woman's mission was to uplift the human race, that she was the Messiah of future centuries. I owe to his doctrines the great and proud ambition that I conceived for the sex to which I take glory in belonging, and whose independence I will uphold until my last day. Moreover, I am persuaded that the future belongs to us.[5]

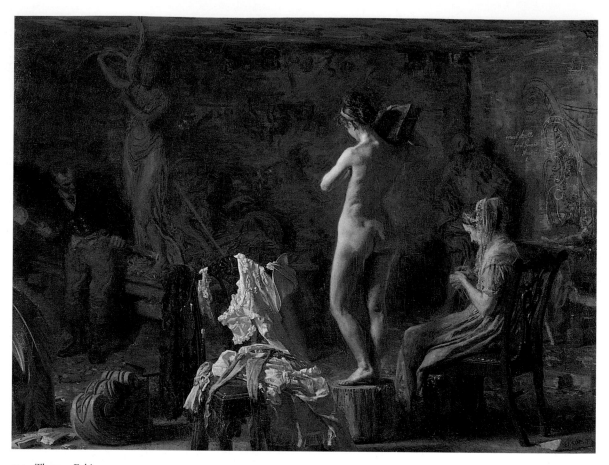

554 Thomas Eakins.
WILLIAM RUSH CARVING HIS ALLEGORICAL FIGURE OF THE SCHUYLKILL RIVER. 1876–77.
Oil on canvas on Masonite. 20⅛" × 26⅛".
Philadelphia Museum of Art. Gift of Mrs. Thomas Eakins and Miss Mary A. Williams. 1929-184-27.
Photo by Graydon Wood, 2000.

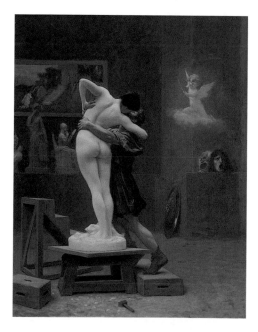

of the paintings of Eakins and those of his teacher, Jean Léon Gérôme, shows the contrast between Realism and officially sanctioned academic art. The attitude Eakins presented is one of great respect for the beauty of the ordinary human being. Gérôme may have been equally interested in ordinary beauty, yet he created a painting based on classical and academic ideals. Eakins's insistence on painting people the way they actually look led him to escape the bondage of stylization imposed by the rules of the academy; it also led to shock and rejection by the public and much of the art world.

553 Jean Léon Gérôme.
PYGMALION AND GALATEA. c. 1860.
Oil on canvas. 35" × 27".
The Metropolitan Museum of Art, New York.
Gift of Louis C. Raegner, 1927.
Photograph: © 1989 The Metropolitan Museum of Art, 27.200.

In the academic painting PYGMALION AND GALATEA, Gérôme placed the woman, Galatea, on a pedestal, both literally and figuratively. The Greek myth of Pygmalion tells of a sculptor who carved a statue of a woman so beautiful that he fell in love with his sculpture. Pygmalion prayed to Aphrodite, goddess of love, who responded by making the figure come to life. The sentimental approach (note the cupid), smooth finish, and mild eroticism are typical of academic art. In his painting WILLIAM RUSH SCULPTING HIS ALLEGORICAL FIGURE, Eakins presented a Realist view of the sculptor's trade: A model poses as the artist chisels away at the left; nineteenth-century decorum demanded that a chaperone be present. Eakins selected this subject because William Rush was the first American artist to use nude models, bringing controversy on himself in the 1820s.

We can see Eakins's influence in the work of his student and friend Henry Ossawa Tanner, who was the best known African-American painter before the twentieth century. At the age of thirteen, Tanner watched a landscape painter at work and decided to become a painter. While studying with Eakins at the Academy of Fine Arts in Philadelphia, Tanner changed his subject matter from landscapes to scenes of daily life. In 1891, after an exhibition of his work was largely ignored, Tanner moved to France, where he remained for most of the rest of his life. He found less racial prejudice in Paris than in the United States. His paper "The American Negro in Art," presented at the 1893 World's Congress on Africa in Chicago, voiced the need for dignified portrayals of blacks, and he offered his painting THE BANJO LESSON as a model.

The lively realism of THE BANJO LESSON reveals Tanner's considerable insight into the feelings of his subjects, yet he avoids the sentimentality that was common in many late nineteenth-century American paintings. This painting shows the influence of Eakins in its detail and the influence of the Impressionists in Tanner's use of light and color.

The most important predecessor of Impressionism in French art is without a doubt Edouard Manet, who was the most controversial artist in

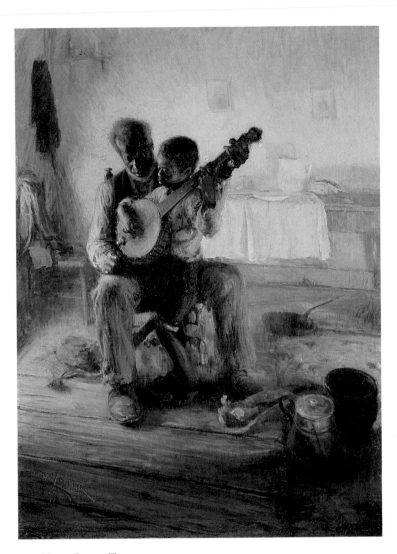

555   Henry Ossawa Tanner.
THE BANJO LESSON. 1893.
Oil on canvas. 49" × 35½".
Hampton University Museum, Hampton, Virginia.

Paris in the 1860s. He studied with an academic master, but soon broke away from traditional teaching in an effort to update the art of the Old Masters (Tintoretto, Velázquez, and Rembrandt, for example) by infusing painting with a dose of realism inherited from Gustave Courbet. In addition, Manet often flattened out the figures in his paintings under the influence of the Japanese prints that he knew and admired. His loose, open brushwork and sometimes commonplace subjects were

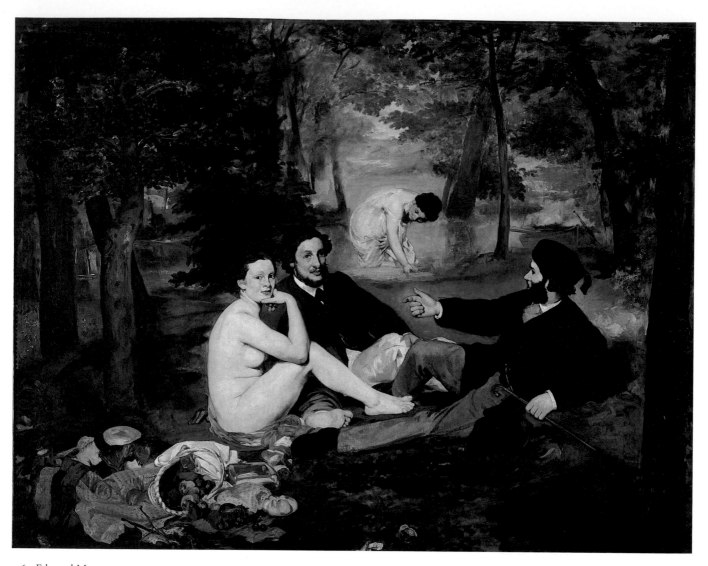

556 Edouard Manet.
LUNCHEON ON THE GRASS (LE DÉJEUNER SUR L'HERBE). 1863.
Oil on canvas. 84" × 106".
Photograph: Herve Lewandowski, Musée d' Orsay, Paris.
© Reunion des Musées Nationaux/Art Resource, NY.

an inspiration to younger painters who led the Impressionist movement. Manet's painting LUNCHEON ON THE GRASS scandalized French critics and the public—because of the way it was painted as well as the subject matter. Manet painted the female figure without shading, employed flat patches of color throughout the painting, and left bare canvas in some places. He concentrated on the interplay among the elements of form that make up the composition: light shapes against dark, cool colors accented by warm colors, directional forces, and active balance. Manet's concern with visual issues over content or storytelling was revolutionary.

Renaissance illusion of depth is greatly diminished here. Manet's emphasis on the interaction of dark and light shapes and his deemphasis of both chiaroscuro and perspective cause us to look at the surface of the painting rather than simply through it as an illusionary window onto nature.

The juxtaposition of a female nude with males dressed in clothing of the time shocked viewers, but such a combination was not new. Nude and clothed figures in landscape derives from a tradition going back to Renaissance and even Roman compositions that depicted ancient myths or stories from the Bible. However, in Manet's painting,

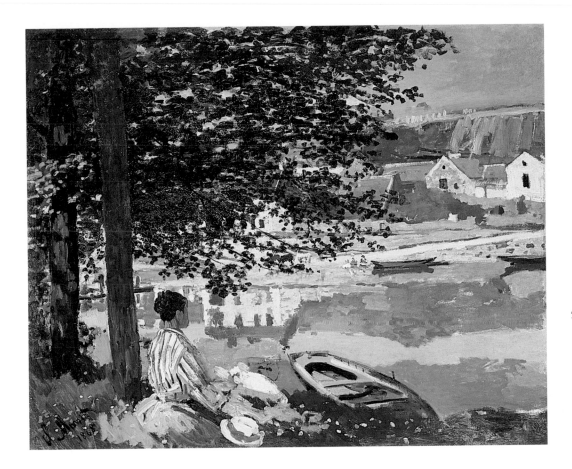

there is no allegory, no history, no mythology, and not even a significant title to suggest morally redeeming values. Manet based his composition (but not his meaning) on the figures in an engraving of a Renaissance drawing by Raphael, who in turn had been influenced by Roman relief sculpture.

It is ironic that Manet, who had such reverence for the art of the past, would be attacked by the public and the critics for his radical innovations. Simultaneously, he was championed by other artists as a leader of the avant-garde. Manet became the reluctant leader of an enthusiastic group of young painters who later formed the group known as the Impressionists.

Under Manet's influence, Claude Monet abandoned the use of heavy earth colors and broad stroke painting techniques. Monet's paintings ON THE SEINE and BATHING AT LA GRENOUILLÈRE (see page 97) both pay homage to and progress from Manet's LUNCHEON ON THE GRASS. Monet had adopted Manet's color-patch technique and ap-

plied it to painting vivid colors generated by sunlight. Monet's idyllic glimpses of contemporary life, painted with an emphasis on qualities of light and color, are the beginnings of *Impressionism.*

IMPRESSIONISM

In 1874, a group of young painters who had been denied the right to show in the Salon of 1873 organized an independent exhibition of their work. These artists, opposing academic doctrines and Romantic ideals, turned instead to the portrayal of contemporary life. They sought to paint "impressions" of what the eye actually sees rather than what the mind knows. This is no simple goal; we usually generalize what we think we see from the most obvious fragments. A river may become a uniform blue-green in our minds, whereas direct, unconditioned seeing shows a rich diversity of colors.

Landscape and ordinary scenes painted outdoors in varied atmospheric conditions, seasons, and times of day were among the main subjects of

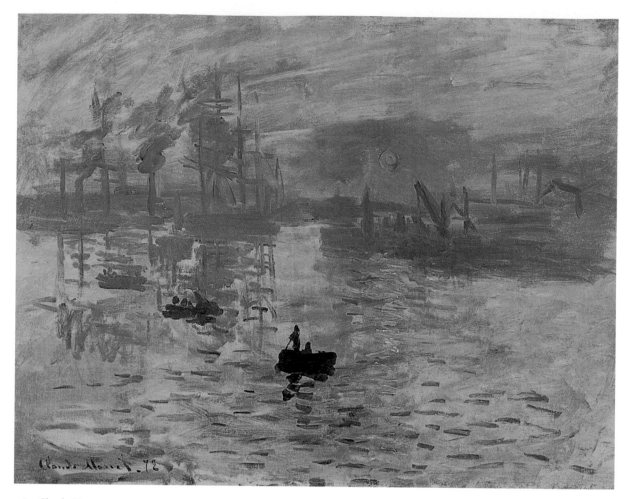

558 Claude Monet. IMPRESSION: SUNRISE. 1872.
Oil on canvas. 19½" × 25½".
Musée Marmottan, Paris.

these artists. They were dubbed Impressionists by a critic who objected to the sketchy quality of their paintings. The term was suggested by one of Monet's versions of IMPRESSION: SUNRISE. Although the critic's label was intended to be derogatory, the artists adopted the term as a fitting description of their work.

From direct observation and from studies in physics, the Impressionists learned that we see light as a complex of reflections received by the eye and reassembled by the mind during the process of perception. Therefore they used small dabs of color that appear merely as separate strokes of paint when seen close up, yet become lively depictions of subjects when seen at a distance. Monet often applied strokes of pure color placed next to each

other, rather than colors premixed or blended on the canvas. The viewer perceives a vibrancy that cannot be achieved with mixed color alone. The effect was startling to eyes accustomed to the muted, continuous tones of academic painting.

The Impressionists enthusiastically affirmed modern life. They saw the beauty of the world as a gift and the forces of nature as aids to human progress. Although misunderstood by their public, the Impressionists made visible a widely held optimism about the promise of the new technology.

Impressionism was strongest between 1870 and 1880. After 1880, it was Claude Monet who continued for more than forty years to advance Impressionism's original premise. Instead of painting from sketches, he and most of the others in the

Claude Monet grew up in Le Havre, a bustling port town on the north coast of France. In high school, he developed a reputation for drawing caricatures. A local picture framer exhibited them in his shop, and there they caught the eye of a painter named Eugène Boudin.

Monet's senior by sixteen years, Boudin was a pioneer in the new practice of painting outdoors, working directly from nature. He encouraged Monet to pursue art seriously and invited him along on a painting excursion. The experience started Monet on the path he would follow all his life. "Boudin set up his easel and began to paint," Monet later recalled. "I looked on with some apprehension, then more attentively, and then suddenly it was as if a veil was torn from my eyes; I had understood. I had grasped what painting could be."[6]

Monet continued his studies in Paris, where he immersed himself in the lively artistic debates of the day. He met and admired the controversial painters Courbet and Manet. He met other art students, Renoir among them, who shared his passion for painting nature and modern life. In time, they would become famous as leading Impressionists.

Fame was long in coming, however; Monet was over forty before his paintings sold well enough to guarantee a living for himself and his family. In the meantime, life was difficult. From dawn to dusk he painted; in the evening, by lamplight, he wrote letters—letters asking for money, letters stalling creditors, letters trying to arrange for his work to be seen and sold.

As Monet's artistic vision deepened, he realized that every shift in light and atmosphere created a new subject. He would arrive at a site with as many as a dozen canvases, working on each one in turn as the light changed. His painting grew increasingly subjective as he strove to express not only light but his feelings about the changing qualities of light. Relentlessly self-critical, he was often driven to despair by his work, and he destroyed dozens of canvases he considered failures.

In back of his house at Giverny, the small town outside Paris where he finally settled, Monet created a water lily pond that became the favorite subject of his final years. In old age, he embarked on one of his most ambitious projects: a series of huge paintings of the water surface, its shimmering reflections of sky and clouds punctuated with floating flowers. Shown end to end, they form dazzling panoramas over six feet tall and twenty-eight feet long. Monet intended them as a gift to the French government, and one of his last acts before he died was to send a letter declaring them finished.

As you read in the next chapter about the radical movements that followed World War I, remember that the last and purest of the Impressionists was still painting from dawn to dusk every day, creating masterpieces of Impressionism long after the course of "art history" had moved on.

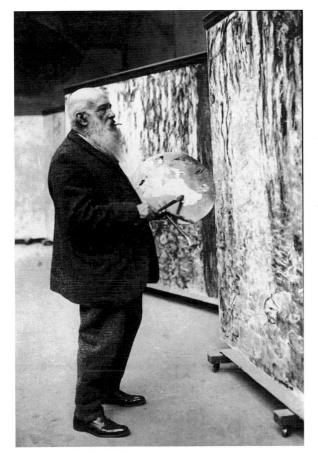

559   CLAUDE MONET on his eightieth birthday. 1920.
Collection Roger-Viollet.
Photograph: Liaison Agency.

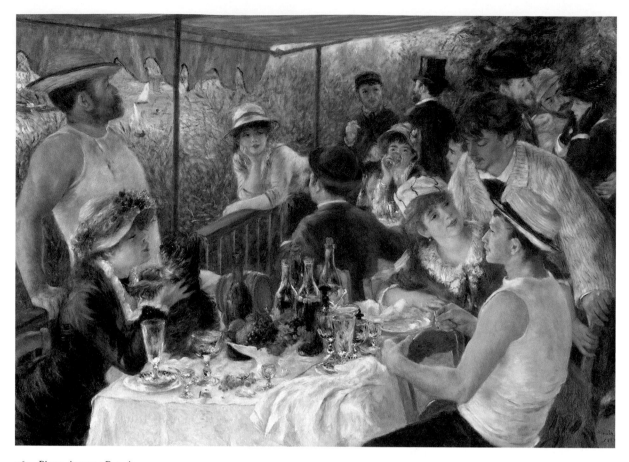

560 Pierre-Auguste Renoir.
THE LUNCHEON OF THE BOATING PARTY. 1881.
Oil on canvas. 51" × 68".
The Phillips Collection, Washington, D.C.

group painted outdoors. Monet returned to the same subjects again and again in order to record the moods and qualities of light at different times of day and at different seasons.

Monet's BATHING AT LA GRENOUILLÈRE (page 97) and Renoir's THE LUNCHEON OF THE BOATING PARTY both depict a popular Impressionist theme: middle-class people enjoying leisure activities along the Seine, the river that flows through Paris. These paintings also reveal similarities and differences between the styles of the two painters.

Monet's concern with the visual phenomena of light and color contrasts with the later work by Renoir, who by then was more concerned with composition. In THE LUNCHEON OF THE BOATING PARTY, as in Monet's paintings, rich colors, highlights, and shadows create a lively surface. But by 1881, Renoir had begun to move away from the

lighter, more diffuse Impressionist imagery of the 1870s toward more solid forms and more structured design; we see this if we compare this painting to his 1872 work on page 98. Renoir's disregard for true linear perspective, as seen in the lines of the railing and table top, reflects the declining interest in naturalistic illusions of depth. More obvious is his interest in portraying the solidity of the figures in a memorable composition.

The young men and women depicted are conversing, sipping wine, and generally enjoying the moment. The Industrial Revolution had created an urban middle class with leisure, a love of the new technology, and a taste for fashion—and the Impressionists chronicled their lives.

Edgar Degas exhibited with the Impressionists, although his approach differed from theirs. He shared with the Impressionists a directness of ex-

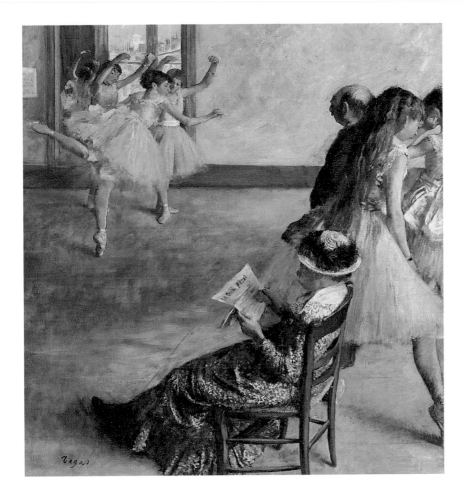

561 Edgar Degas.
THE BALLET CLASS.
c. 1879–1880.
Oil on canvas. 32⅜" × 30¼".
Philadelphia Museum of Art.
Purchased with the W. P. Wilstach Fund.
W1937-2-1.

pression and an interest in portraying contemporary life, but he combined the immediacy of Impressionism with a highly inventive structured approach to design not found in the work of those painters. Degas, along with the Impressionists, was influenced by the new ways of seeing and composing that he saw in Japanese prints and unposed street-scene photography.

Conventional European compositions placed subjects within a central zone. Degas, however, used surprising, lifelike compositions and effects that often cut figures at the edge. The tipped-up ground planes and bold asymmetry found in Japanese prints inspired Degas to create paintings filled with intriguing visual tensions, such as those in THE BALLET CLASS, in which two diagonal groups of figures appear on opposite sides of an empty center.

Degas depicted ballet classes in ways that showed their unglamorous character. Often, as here, he was able to turn his great ability to the task of defining human character and mood in a given situation. The painting builds from the quiet, disinterested woman in the foreground, up to the right, then across to the cluster of dancing girls, following the implied sightline of the ballet master. The stability of the group on the right contrasts with the smaller, irregular shape of the girls before the mirror. Degas managed to balance spatial tensions between near and far and to create interesting contrasts between stable and unstable, large and small. He emphasized the line in the floor, which he brought together with the top of the woman's newspaper to guide the viewer's eye. The angle of the seated woman's foot brings us around to begin again.

American painter Mary Cassatt went to Paris in the late 1860s to further her artistic development. She was strongly influenced by the work of Manet and Degas. Following an invitation by Degas, she joined and exhibited with the Impressionists. Later, she was among the many European

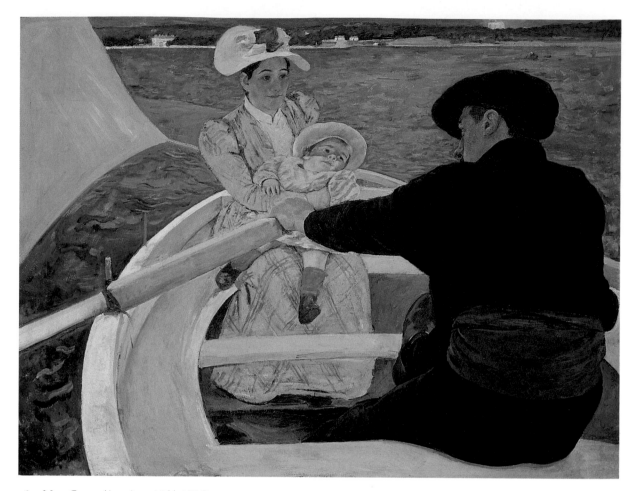

562 Mary Cassatt (American, 1844–1926).
THE BOATING PARTY. 1893–1894.
Oil on canvas. 35⁷⁄₁₆" × 46⅛"; framed 44⅛" × 54¼".

and American artists who were influenced by Japanese prints and casual compositions of late nineteenth-century do-it-yourself photography. A resemblance to Japanese prints is readily apparent in the simplicity and bold design of THE BOATING PARTY. Cassatt refined her subject in sweeping curves and almost flat shapes.

There is, in addition, subtle feminist content in this work. The difference in clothing styles between the woman and the man shows that she has hired him to take her and the child out for a boat ride. This was an unusually assertive thing for a woman to do for herself in those days, and the glances between all three persons in the painting show some of the social tension that would have accompanied this event. The work is typical of Cassatt in its focus on the world of women and their concerns.

Painters such as Manet, Monet, Renoir, Degas, and Cassatt rejected the artificial poses and limited color prescribed by the Academy. Because they rebelled against accepted styles, they made few sales in their early years. Many who were considered outsiders, set apart from the conventional art of their time, we now consider masters of nineteenth-century art and precursors of twentieth-century art.

The Impressionist group disbanded after its exhibition in 1886, but its influence was immeasurable—in spite of the fact that Impressionist paintings were looked upon with indifference, even hostility, by most of the public and the critics until the 1920s. From the perspective of our time, Impressionism was the most important artistic movement of the nineteenth century.

French artist Auguste Rodin was at least as important to sculpture as his contemporaries, the Impressionist and Post-Impressionist painters, were to painting. Rodin became the first sculptor since Bernini (see page 303) to return sculpture to the status of a major art form, renewed with emotional and spiritual depth.

In 1875, after training as a sculptor's helper, Rodin traveled to Italy where he was impressed by the work of the Renaissance masters Donatello and Michelangelo. Rodin was the first to use Michelangelo's unfinished pieces (see page 200) as an inspiration for making unfinishedness an expressive quality. In contrast to Michelangelo, however, Rodin was primarily a modeler rather than a carver.

In 1880, he was commissioned to make a bronze door, *The Gates of Hell*, for a proposed museum of decorative arts. The large project was unfinished at Rodin's death, but many of the figures that are part of the door, including THE THINKER, modeled in clay and cast in bronze, and THE KISS, carved in marble (page 31), were enlarged as independent pieces. Of THE THINKER, Rodin wrote that his first inspiration had been Dante, but he rejected the idea of a thin, ascetic figure.

Guided by my first inspiration I conceived another thinker, a naked man, seated upon a rock, his feet drawn under him, he dreams. The fertile thought slowly elaborates itself within his brain. He is no longer dreamer, he is creator.[7]

In the place of Christ in judgment, often seen over the doorways of medieval churches, Rodin projects the universal artist/poet as creator, judge, and witness, brooding over the human condition. Rodin combined a superb knowledge of anatomy with modeling skill to create the fluid, tactile quality of hand-shaped clay. He restored sculpture as a vehicle for personal expression after it had lapsed into mere decoration and heroic monuments.

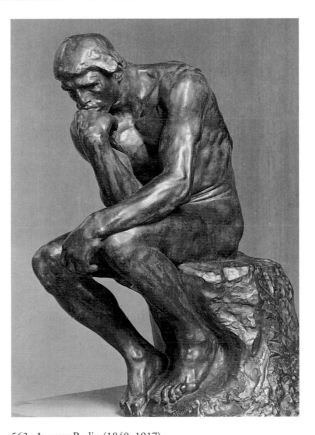

563 Auguste Rodin (1840–1917).
THE THINKER (LE PENSEUR). c. 1910
Bronze. Life-size.
The Metropolitan Museum of Art, NY. Gift of Thomas F. Ryan, 1910 (11.173.9)

THE POST-IMPRESSIONIST PERIOD

Post-Impressionism refers to trends in painting starting in about 1885 that followed Impressionism. The Post-Impressionist painters did not share a single style; rather, they built on or reacted to Impressionism in highly individual ways. Some felt that Impressionism had sacrificed solidity of form and composition for the sake of momentary impressions. Others felt that Impressionism's emphasis on the direct observation of nature and everyday life did not leave enough room for personal expression or spiritual content. Among those whose works best exemplify Post-Impressionist attitudes were Dutch artist Vincent van Gogh and French artists Paul Gauguin, Georges Seurat, and Paul Cézanne.

Gauguin and van Gogh brought to their work expressive, emotional intensity and a desire to make their thoughts and feelings visible. They

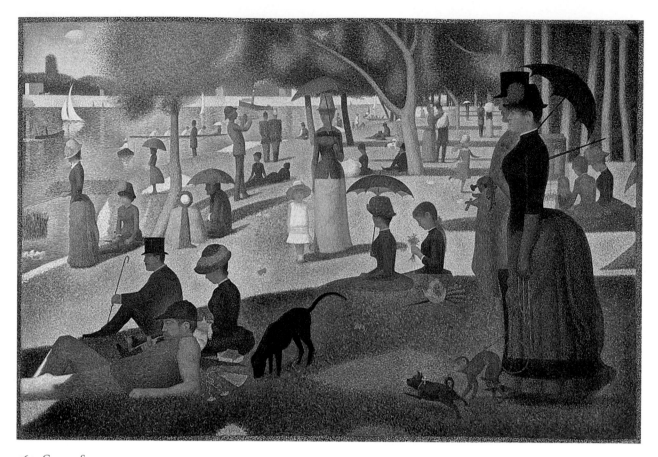

564 Georges Seurat.

A SUNDAY ON LA GRANDE JATTE. 1884–1886.
Oil on canvas. 81" × 120⅜".
Helen Birch Bartlett Memorial Collection. 1926.224.

often used strong color contrasts, shapes with clear contours, bold brushwork, and, in van Gogh's case, vigorous paint textures. Their art greatly influenced twentieth-century expressionist styles.

Seurat and Cézanne were interested in developing formal structure in their paintings. Each in his own way organized visual form to achieve structured clarity of design. Their paintings influenced twentieth-century formalist styles.

Cézanne and Seurat based their work on the observation of nature, and both used visibly separate strokes of color to build rich surfaces. Seurat's large painting A SUNDAY ON LA GRANDE JATTE has the subject matter, light, and color qualities of Impressionism, but this is not a painting of a fleeting moment. It is a carefully constructed composition of lasting impact. Seurat set out to systematize the optical color mixing of Impressionism and to create a more solid, formal organization with simplified shapes. He called his method *divisionism,* but it is more popularly known as *pointillism.* With it, Seurat tried to develop and apply a "scientific" technique. He arrived at his method by studying the principles of color optics that were being formulated at the time. Through the application of tiny dots of color, Seurat achieved a vibrant surface based on optical mixture (see page 66 for a detail).

Seurat preceded A SUNDAY ON LA GRANDE JATTE with more than fifty drawn and painted preliminary studies in which he explored the horizontal and vertical relationships, the character of each shape, and the patterns of light, shade, and color. The final painting shows the total control that Seurat sought through the application of his method.

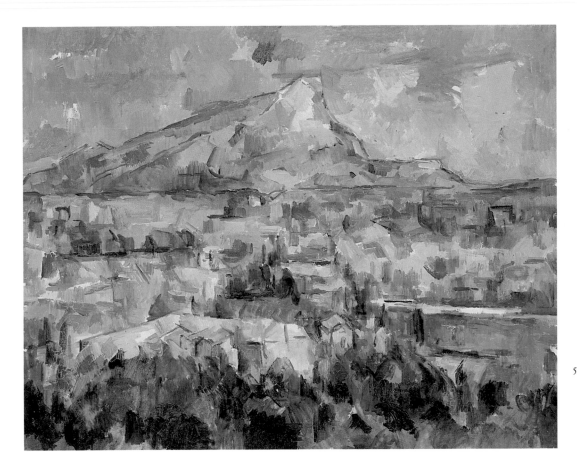

565 Paul Cézanne.
MONT SAINTE-VICTOIRE.
1902–1904.
Oil on canvas.
27½" × 35¼".
Philadelphia Museum of Art: The
George W. Elkins Collection.
E1936-1-1

The frozen formality of the figures seems surprising, considering the casual nature of the subject matter; yet it is precisely this calm, formal grandeur that gives the painting its strength and enduring appeal.

Like Seurat, Cézanne sought to achieve strength in the formal structure of his paintings. "My aim," he said, "was to make Impressionism into something solid and enduring like the art of the museums."[8]

Cézanne saw the planar surfaces of his subjects in terms of color modulation. Instead of using light and shadow in a conventional way, he relied on carefully developed relationships between adjoining strokes of color to show solidity of form and receding space. He questioned, then abandoned, linear and atmospheric perspective and went beyond the appearance of nature, to reconstruct it according to his own interpretation.

Landscape was one of Cézanne's main interests. In MONT SAINTE-VICTOIRE, we can see how he flattened space yet gave an impression of air and depth with some atmospheric perspective and the use of warm advancing and cool receding colors. The dark edge lines around the distant mountain help counter the illusion of depth. There is an important interplay between the illusion of depth and the fact of strokes of color on a flat surface. Cézanne simplified the houses and trees into patches of color that suggest almost geometric planes and masses. His open (not blended) brush strokes and his concept of a geometric substructure in nature and art offered a range of possibilities to those who studied his later paintings. Of the many important painters working in France around the turn of the century, Cézanne had the most lasting effect on the course of painting in the twentieth century. His art both built on, and departed from, Impressionism.

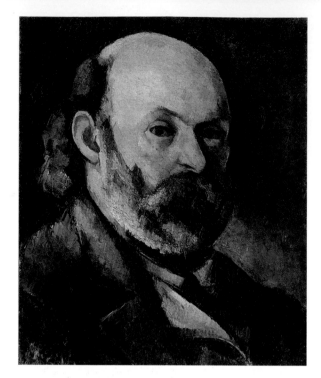

566 Paul Cézanne.
SELF-PORTRAIT.
Oil on canvas.
Hermitage Museum, St. Petersberg.
Photograph: Scala/Art Resource, NY.

Paul Cézanne was born in Aix-en-Provence, a quiet provincial town in the south of France. As a schoolboy his passion was poetry, and his friends, including the future novelist Emile Zola, thought of him as a budding literary genius. Bowing to the wishes of his father, a wealthy banker, Cézanne enrolled in a local college to study law. But Zola, who had gone to Paris to be in the center of things, goaded Cézanne into declaring himself an artist and moving to the capital.

In Paris, Cézanne studied at the Académie Suisse, where his fellow students included many future Impressionists. In his early career, he painted from his imagination, not from nature; his subjects were often violent or erotic, the drawing seems barely competent, and he laid the paint on thickly, clumsily, passionately. The journey from these awkward beginnings to the mastery of his final years is one of the most impressive and moving self-transformations in the history of art.

Around 1870, Cézanne began to paint directly from nature and to discipline himself in this approach. Cézanne exhibited twice with the Impressionists, but the critics attacked him so viciously that he refused to show his work again. He returned to Aix, where for almost twenty years he worked in a self-imposed exile from the art world.

His personal life changed during those years as well: he married his mistress of seventeen years, when their son Paul was already twelve. Cézanne had kept their existence from his parents, afraid of angering his father and losing the meager allowance he provided. Later that year his father died, making Cézanne a wealthy man who was free to pursue his art without money worries.

In 1895, the young art dealer Ambrose Vollard offered the reclusive painter a show in Paris. Cézanne sent one hundred fifty canvases, the finest of twenty years of work, wrapped in bundles of newsprint. The exhibit came as a revelation even to his old Impressionist friends. "It is great painting," wrote Pissarro. "My enthusiasm pales against Renoir's. Even Degas is seduced . . . Monet, all of us."[9]

Cézanne was never popular with critics or the public during his lifetime, but he became a hero to the next generation of painters, many of whom made the pilgrimage to Aix to meet him. Still he worked all day every day, trying to realize more fully his sensations in response to nature.

In one of his last letters, he wrote his son, "Here on the bank of this river, the motifs multiply, the same subject seen from different angles gives a subject for study of the most powerful interest and so varied that I think I could occupy myself for months without changing position, simply bending a little more to the right or left."[10] This is as clear a description of a painter's state of grace as we are ever likely to have.

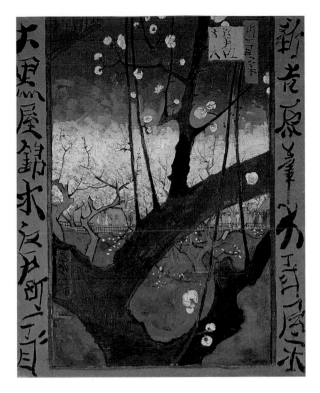

567   Vincent van Gogh, after Hiroshige.
    JAPONAISERIE: FLOWERING PLUM TREE. 1887.
    Oil on canvas. 21½" × 18".
    Vincent van Gogh Foundation/Van Gogh Museum, Amsterdam.

568   Vincent van Gogh.
    THE SOWER. 1888.
    Oil on canvas. 17⅜" × 22⅛".
    Vincent van Gogh Foundation/Van Gogh Museum, Amsterdam.

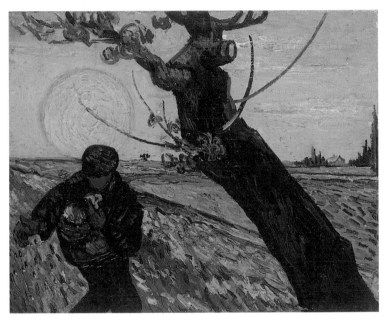

With Vincent van Gogh, late nineteenth-century painting moved from an outer impression of what the eye sees to an inner expression of what the heart feels and the mind knows.

From Impressionism, van Gogh learned the expressive potential of open brushwork and relatively pure color; but the style did not provide enough freedom to satisfy his desire to express his feelings. Van Gogh intensified the surfaces of his paintings with textural brushwork that recorded each gesture of his hand and gave an overall rhythmic movement to his paintings. He began to use strong color in an effort to express his emotions more clearly. In letters to his brother Theo, he wrote,

. . . instead of trying to reproduce exactly what I have before my eyes, I use color more arbitrarily so as to express myself forcibly. . . .

I am always in hope of making a discovery there to express the love of two lovers by a marriage of two complementary colors, their mingling and their opposition, the mysterious vibrations of kindred tones. To express the thought of a brow by the radiance of a light tone against somber background.[11]

As did other artists of the period, van Gogh developed a new sense of design from studying and even copying Japanese prints, as in FLOWERING PLUM TREE. In THE SOWER, the Japanese influence on van Gogh's sense of design is clearly seen in the bold, simplified shapes and flat color areas. The wide band of a tree trunk cuts diagonally across the composition; its strength balances the sun and its energy coming toward us with the movement of the sower.

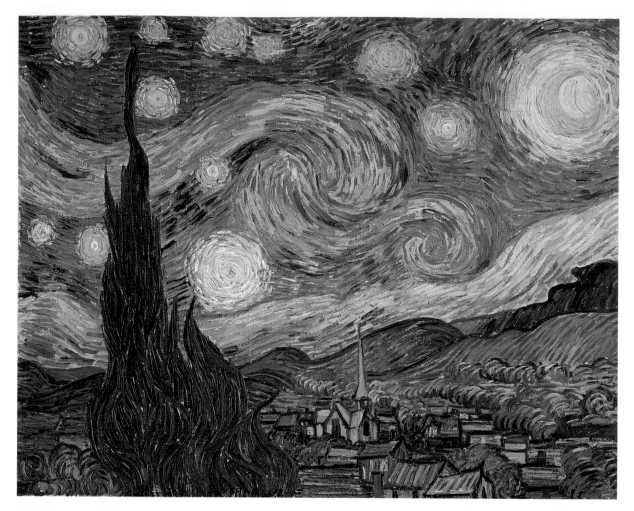

569   Vincent van Gogh.
THE STARRY NIGHT. 1889.
Oil on canvas. 29" × 36¼" (73.7 x 92.1 cm).
The Museum of Modern Art, New York. Acquired through the Lillie P. Bliss Bequest.
Photograph: © 2002 The Museum of Modern Art, New York.

A strong desire to share personal feelings and insights motivated van Gogh. In THE STARRY NIGHT, his observation of a town at night became the point of departure for a powerful symbolic image. Hills seem to undulate, echoing tremendous cosmic forces in the sky. The small town nestled into the dark forms of the ground plane suggests the scale of human life. The church's spire reaches toward the heavens, echoed by the larger, more dynamic upward thrust of the cypress trees in the left foreground. (The evergreen cypress is traditionally planted beside graveyards in Europe as a symbol of eternal life.) All these elements are united by the surging rhythm of lines that express van Gogh's passionate spirit and mystical vision. Many know of van Gogh's bouts of mental illness, but few realize that he did his paintings between seizures, in moments of great clarity.

French artist Paul Gauguin, like van Gogh, was highly critical of the materialism of industrial society. This attitude led Gauguin to admire the honest life of the Brittany peasants of western France. In 1888, he completed THE VISION AFTER THE SERMON, the first major work in his revolutionary new style. The large, carefully designed painting shows Jacob and the angel as they appear to a group of

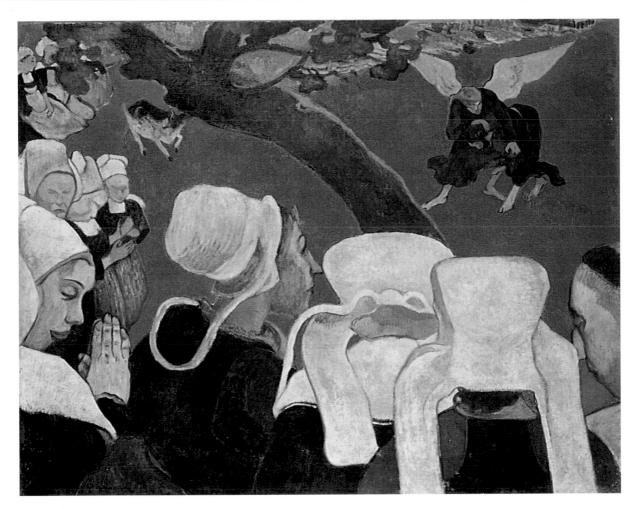

570 Paul Gauguin.
THE VISION AFTER THE SERMON (JACOB WRESTLING WITH THE ANGEL). 1888.
Oil on canvas. 28¾" × 36½".
National Gallery of Scotland, Edinburgh.

Brittany peasants in a vision inspired by the sermon in their village church.

The symbolic representation of unquestioning faith is an image that originated in Gauguin's mind rather than in his eye. With it, Gauguin took a major step beyond Impressionism. In order to avoid what he considered the distraction of implied deep space, he tipped up the simplified background plane and painted it an intense, "unnatural" vermilion. The entire composition is divided diagonally by the trunk of the apple tree, in the manner of Japanese prints. Shapes have been reduced to flat curvilinear areas outlined in black, with shadows minimized or eliminated.

Both van Gogh's and Gauguin's uses of color were important influences on twentieth-century painting. Their views on color were prophetic. The subject, Gauguin wrote, was only a pretext for symphonies of line and color.

In painting, one must search rather for suggestion than for description, as is done in music. . . . Think of the highly important musical role which colour will play henceforth in modern painting.[12]

Gauguin retained memories of his childhood in Peru that persuaded him that the art of ancient and non-Western cultures had a spiritual strength

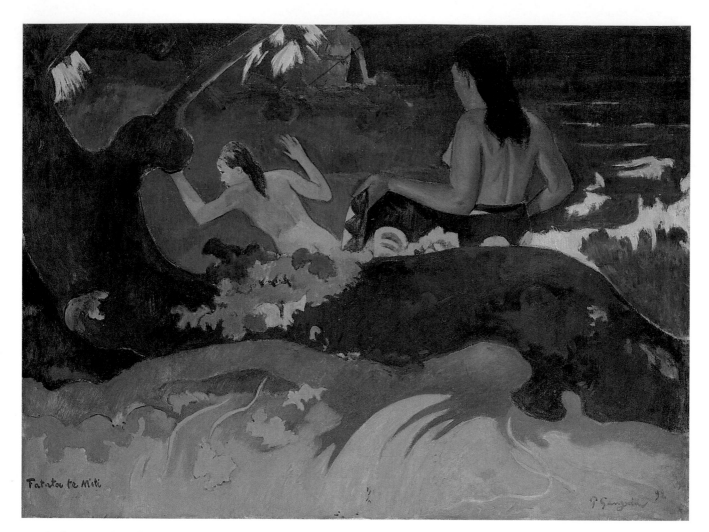

571   Paul Gauguin. (French, 1848-1903).
FATATA TE MITI (BY THE SEA). 1892.
Oil on canvas, 67.9 x 91.5 cm (26¾" × 36").
Chester Dale Collection. Photograph ©2002 Board of Trustees, National Gallery of Art, Washington, D.C.
1963. 10.149. (1813)/PA

that was lacking in the European art of his time. He wrote:

Keep the Persians, the Cambodians, and a bit of the Egyptians always in mind. The great error is the Greek, however beautiful it may be.[13]

A great thought system is written in gold in Far Eastern art.[14]

Gauguin's desire to rejuvenate European art and civilization with insights from non-Western traditions would be shared in the early twentieth century by Matisse, Picasso, and the German Expressionists. They adopted Gauguin's vision of the artist as a spiritual leader who could select from the past, and from various world cultures, anything capable of releasing the power of self-knowledge and inner life.

At the end of his life, Gauguin tried to break completely with European civilization by going to Tahiti. In FATATA TE MITI, he combined flat, curvilinear shapes with tropical and fanciful colors.

For Gauguin, art had become above all a means of communicating through symbols, a "synthesis," he called it, of visual form carrying memory, feelings, and ideas. These beliefs link him to

"I want to establish the right to dare everything," Gauguin wrote on the eve of his death.[15] Battered by bronchitis, neuralgia, syphilis, and a series of strokes, alone, impoverished, and halfway around the world from France, Gauguin had indeed dared everything—not only in his art, but in his life.

Paul Gauguin was twenty-three when a family friend introduced him to the world of art and artists. Immersing himself in the new art of his day, he collected works by Cézanne, Degas, and others, and he began to paint in his spare time. By 1879, he was exhibiting with the Impressionist artists he so admired. His job as a stockbroker had become an unbearable distraction, and when he lost it in the aftermath of a financial crash a few years later, he decided not to look for another: He would be an artist. He was then thirty-five, with a pregnant wife and four children. It quickly became clear that he could not support his family as an artist, and after two years of arguments and compromises, his wife moved back to her family, taking the children with her.

Gauguin sought a place to paint that would nourish his vision of an art in touch with the primal mysteries of life. He moved first to Brittany, drawn to the primitive lives of the Breton peasants. In 1887, he painted on the Caribbean island of Martinique, but he fell ill, ran out of money, and had to return to France. The following year he joined van Gogh in the south of France, but their idealistic plans for an artists' commune disintegrated into disastrous quarrels.

Convinced that he had to escape the "disease of civilization," Gauguin voyaged to Tahiti in 1891. He left its Westernized capital, Papeete, for a grass hut in a remote village, where he took a teenage bride, fathered a child, and steeped himself in the island's myths and legends. Despite the pressure of constant poverty, Gauguin transformed the raw material of Tahiti into a dream of earthly paradise, where a sensual people lived in harmony with their gods.

In 1893, Gauguin returned to France, confident that his Tahitian work would bring him success. It did not come. Lonely and disillusioned, he returned to Tahiti in 1895 and found it more Westernized than before. Frustrated and angry, he fought with the colonial authorities and railed against the missionaries. His health was failing rapidly, he was desperate for money, and he grew so despondent he attempted

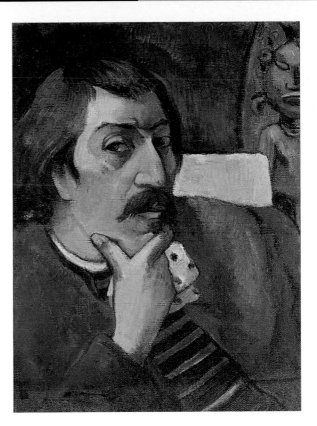

suicide. Again he set off in search of a simpler life, sailing in 1901 to the Marquesas Islands, where he died two years later.

"It is true that I know very little," Gauguin wrote to a friend. "But who can say if even this little, worked on by others, will not become something great?"[16] In Paris, in 1906, a large retrospective of Gauguin's work made the extent of his achievement clear for the first time. His achievement was considerable, and, built on by Picasso, Matisse, and many others, his "little" did indeed become something great.

572 Paul Gauguin.
PORTRAIT OF THE ARTIST WITH THE IDOL. c. 1893.
Oil on canvas. 17¼" × 12⅞".
Collection of the McNay Art Museum, Bequest of Marion Koogler McNay.

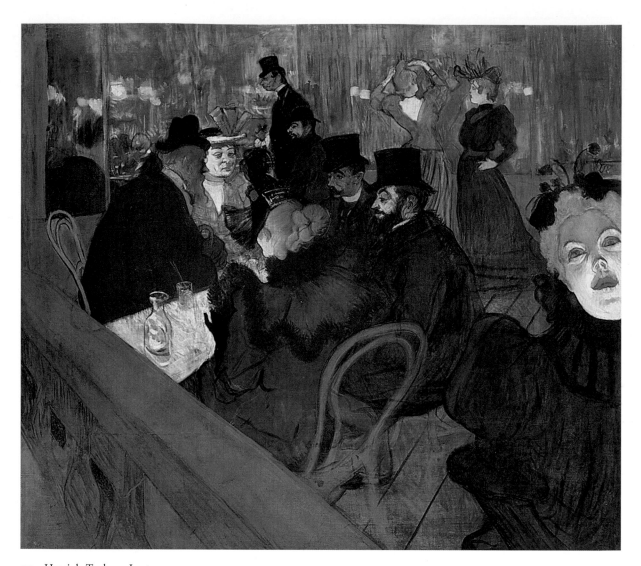

573   Henri de Toulouse-Lautrec.
AT THE MOULIN ROUGE. 1892–1895.
Oil on canvas. 48⅜" × 55¼".

Symbolism, a movement in literature and the visual arts that developed around 1885.

Reacting against both Realism and Impressionism, Symbolist poets and painters sought to lift the mind from the mundane and the practical. They employed decorative forms and symbols that were intentionally vague or open-ended in order to create imaginative suggestions. The poets held that the sounds and rhythms of words were part of their poems' deeper meaning; the painters recognized that line, color, and other visual elements were ex-

pressive in themselves. Symbolism, a trend rather than a specific style, provided the ideological background for twentieth-century abstraction; it has been seen as an outgrowth of Romanticism and a forerunner of Surrealism.

Henri de Toulouse-Lautrec, another Post-Impressionist, painted the gaslit interiors of Parisian nightclubs and brothels. His quick, long strokes of color define a world of sordid gaiety. Toulouse-Lautrec was influenced by Degas (see page 391), whose work he greatly admired. In AT THE MOULIN

ROUGE, Toulouse-Lautrec used unusual angles, cropped images, such as the face on the right, and expressive, unnatural color to heighten feelings about the people and the world he painted. His paintings, drawings, and prints of Parisian nightlife influenced twentieth-century's expressionist painters and his posters influenced graphic designers (see page 149).

Norwegian painter Edvard Munch traveled to Paris to study the works of his contemporaries, especially Gauguin, van Gogh, and Toulouse-Lautrec. What he learned from them, particularly from Gauguin's works, enabled him to carry Symbolism to a new level of expressive intensity. Munch's powerful paintings and prints explore depths of emotion—grief, loneliness, fear, love, sexual passion, jealousy, and death.

In THE SHRIEK Munch takes the viewer far from the pleasures of Impressionism and extends considerably van Gogh's expressive vision. In this powerful image of anxiety, the dominant figure is caught in isolation, fear, and loneliness. Despair reverberates in continuous linear rhythms. Munch's image has been called the soul-cry of our age.

The nineteenth-century invention of photography, along with the discovery of non-Western art and the rediscovery of pre-Renaissance art, strongly affected the direction of Western art. As the century progressed, artists sought a deeper reality by breaking away from the artificial idealism of officially recognized academic art.

This fresh beginning was full of self-assurance, as seen in the optimistic mood of Impressionism. Yet the process of seeing the visual world anew brought with it added levels of awareness, as the appearance of things came to be less important than the relationship between viewer and reality. Once again, it became the artist's task to probe and reveal hidden worlds, to make the invisible visible. Artists gave increasing importance to the elements of form and to the formal structure of seen and invented imagery. Nature was internalized and transformed in order to portray a greater reality as the stage was set for even bigger changes in the twentieth century.

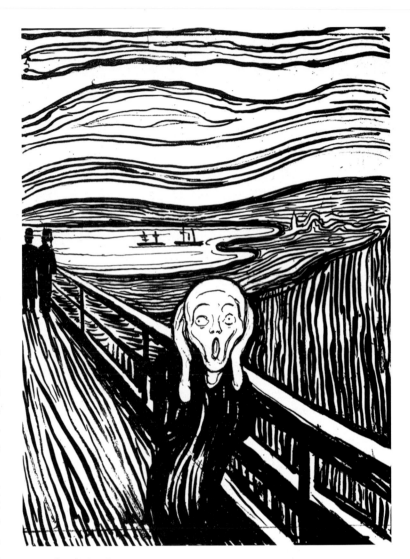

574 Edvard Munch.
THE SHRIEK. 1896.
Lithograph, printed in black, composition, 13¹⁵⁄₁₆" × 10" (35.4 x 25.4 cm).
The Museum of Modern Art, New York. Matthew T. Mellon Fund.
Photograph: © 2002 The Museum of Modern Art, New York.
© 2002 The Munch Museum/The Munch-Ellingsen Group/Artists Rights Society (ARS), New York.

CHAPTER TWENTY-TWO

EARLY TWENTIETH CENTURY

During the first decade of this century, Western views of reality changed radically. In 1900, Sigmund Freud published *The Interpretation of Dreams,* a vast work that explored the structure and power of the subconscious mind. In 1903, the Wright brothers flew the first power-driven aircraft. In 1905, Albert Einstein changed our concepts of time, space, and substance with his theory of relativity. Matter could no longer be considered solid; it was recognized as a field of energy. Simultaneously, great changes occurred in art, and some of them were inspired by scientific discoveries. In 1913, Russian artist Wassily Kandinsky described how deeply he was affected by the discovery of subatomic particles:

A scientific event cleared my way of one of the greatest impediments. This was the further division of the atom. The crumbling of the atom was to my soul like the crumbling of the whole world.[1]

The art of the twentieth century is the result of a series of revolutions in thinking and seeing. Its characteristics are those of the century itself: rapid change, diversity, individualism, and exploration—followed by abundant discoveries. Twentieth-century artists, as well as scientists, have challenged preconceptions of the nature of reality, and they have made visible new levels of consciousness.

The explosion of new styles of art at the beginning of this century grew from Impressionist and Post-Impressionist innovations. Yet in their search for forms to express the new age, European artists looked to ancient and non-Western cultures for inspiration and renewal. In so doing, they overturned the authority of the Renaissance, which had dominated Western artistic thought for five hundred years.

TOWARD ABSTRACTION

Early twentieth-century art continued the general shift from naturalistic to abstract art begun in the late nineteenth century. The comparison in chapter 2 of two works of sculpture, both titled THE KISS (page 31), illustrates the transition from nineteenth- to twentieth-century thinking. Rodin, the leading sculptor of the nineteenth century, created a naturalistic work. Brancusi, the leading sculptor of the early twentieth century, produced an abstract interpretation.

Sculptor Constantin Brancusi changed the way we think about forms in space. Before Brancusi, sculptors in the Western world made statues. Since Brancusi, sculptors have made many other kinds of three-dimensional forms as well as statues—works collectively called sculpture. It was Brancusi's development of abstract and nonrepresentational sculpture that led to the shift.

A sequence of Brancusi's early work shows his radical break with the past. His SLEEP of 1908 has an appearance similar to Rodin's romantic naturalism. In his SLEEPING MUSE of 1911, Brancusi simplified the subject as he moved from naturalism to abstraction. THE NEWBORN of 1915 is stripped to essentials. Brancusi said, "Simplicity is not an end in art, but one arrives at simplicity in spite of oneself, in approaching the real sense of things."[2]

Comparisons can be made between Brancusi's work and Cycladic sculpture over four thousand years old. Ancient sculpture from the Cyclades (islands of the Aegean Sea) has a distinctive, highly abstract elegance similar to Brancusi's. It is known that Brancusi spent time in the Louvre studying the collection that included ancient sculpture, such as the CYCLADIC HEAD.

Brancusi shared with other leading Parisian artists an interest in African and other non-Western arts, but the main influence on his sculpture was the folk art of his native Romania and his childhood in a peasant community with a strong wood-carving tradition.

When he was thirteen years old, Brancusi left his family. After supporting himself at menial jobs for several years, he attended art school where he

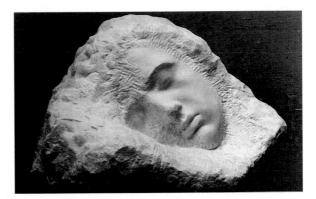

575 Constantin Brancusi.
SLEEP. 1908.
Marble. 6½" × 12".
National Museum, Bucharest, Romania. Photograph courtesy Musée National d'Art Moderne, Paris. © 2002 Artists Rights Society (ARS), New York/ADAGP, Paris.

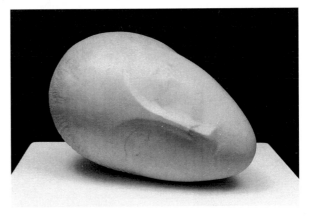

576 Constantin Brancusi.
SLEEPING MUSE. 1909–1911.
Marble. 7" × 10⅝" × 8".
Hirschhorn Museum and Sculpture Garden, Smithsonian Institution, Gift of Joseph H. Hirschhorn (1966). © 2002 Artists Rights Society (ARS), New York/ADAGP, Paris.

578 CYCLADIC II.
Female statuette.
2700–2300 B.C.E.
Syros group. Marble.
Height 10½".
Photograph: Herve Lewandowski.
Louvre Museum, Paris, France.
© Reunion des Musées Nationaux/
Art Resource, NY.

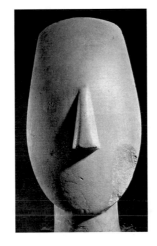

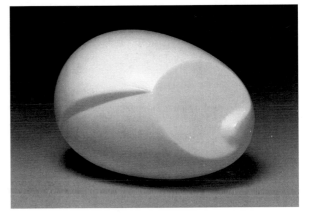

577 Constantin Brancusi.
THE NEWBORN. 1915.
Marble. 6" × 8½".
Philadelphia Museum of Art. The Louise and Walter Arensberg Collection.
© 2002 Artists Rights Society (ARS), New York/ADAGP, Paris.

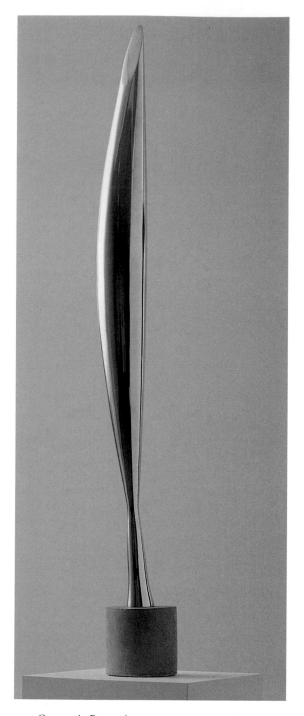

579 Constantin Brancusi.
BIRD IN SPACE. 1928.
Bronze (unique cast). Height 54"× 8 ½" × 6 ½"
(137.2 × 21.6 × 16.5 cm).
The Museum of Modern Art, New York. Given anonymously.
Photograph: © 2002 The Museum of Modern Art New York.
© 2002 Artists Rights Society (ARS), NY/ADAGP, Paris.

studied sculpture. The rigorous and traditional program was based on the close study of anatomy.

In 1904 Brancusi went to Paris where he attended the École des Beaux Arts (the French School of Fine Arts). Later he worked briefly in Rodin's studio. When he was invited by Rodin to become his assistant, Brancusi is said to have turned him down with the reply, "Nothing can grow under big trees."

Brancusi's early work shows the influence of Rodin, but Brancusi went on to develop his own vision as an artist. He abandoned modeling in favor of carving. Brancusi was a superb craftsman who possessed great sensitivity to the character of his materials—primarily metal, stone, and wood. "We must try not to make materials speak our language. We must go with them to a point where others will understand their language." [3]

Brancusi sought to go beyond the surface embellishments that had dominated European sculpture since the Gothic period and to make viewers conscious of form. He brought about a revival of carving. Brancusi's expressive strength was achieved by carefully reducing forms to their essence. As a result his sculptures are endowed with an almost sacred aura; they invite contemplation.

In BIRD IN SPACE, Brancusi transformed inert mass into an elegant, uplifting form. The implied soaring motion of the "bird" embodies the idea of flight. The highly reflective polish given to the bronze surface adds considerably to the form's weightless quality. Brancusi started working on this visual concept about a decade after the Wright brothers initiated the age of human flight, but long before the world was filled with streamlined aircraft, cars, pens, and telephones. Brancusi said, "All my life I have sought the essence of flight. Don't look for mysteries. I give you pure joy." [4]

Modern art, because it was so new and so radical, presented many problems relating to the definition of the term "art." Suddenly it was much more difficult to tell if a given object was art or not, let alone to judge its quality. In a unique court case of 1928, a Federal District Court judge was forced to decide if Constantin Brancusi's sculpture BIRD IN SPACE was in fact a work of art. This is what took place:

The American photographer Edward Steichen was returning from Europe with the piece in his possession. He told the customs inspectors that it was a work of art and was thus exempt from import duty (as works of art have been in America since 1913). The inspectors did not believe him. They classified BIRD IN SPACE as a "domestic utensil or surgical instrument" and charged him $240.

Steichen paid the duty, but—believing he was wronged by the decision, he complained to his friend, the well-known art patron Gertrude Vanderbilt Whitney. Whitney, the founder of the Whitney Museum of American Art, mounted a lawsuit against the government so that Steichen could recover his money.

The case was *Brancusi* vs. *The United States*, and lawyers for both sides called witnesses. Testifying for the government, the customs inspectors described their bafflement at seeing the piece. Traditional art historians took the stand and expressed doubt, both about BIRD IN SPACE and about modern art in general. The principal witness for Steichen and Brancusi was the artist Jacob Epstein, a friend of the Whitney family who had also known Brancusi for fifteen years. The government's lawyer questioned Epstein closely about his qualifications as an artist, and then proceeded to the point[5]:

Lawyer: Do you make painting your profession?

Epstein: No, sculpture is my profession.

Lawyer: Do you have anything to do with making sculpture similar to the exhibit one (BIRD IN SPACE)?

Epstein: Well, all sculptures are different.

Lawyer: I asked you if you made anything like exhibit one.

Epstein: I may not have the desire to make it.

Lawyer: I did not ask you that.

Judge: Answer the question. Did you make anything like that exhibit?

Epstein: No.

Lawyer: In all your thirty years?

Epstein: No, I have not made anything like that.

Lawyer: Do you consider from the training that you have had and based on your experience you had in these different schools and galleries—do you consider that a work of art?

Epstein: I certainly do.

Lawyer: When you say you consider that a work of art will you kindly tell me why?

Epstein: Well, it pleases my sense of beauty, gives me a feeling of pleasure. Made by a sculptor, it has to me a great many elements, but consists in itself as a beautiful object. To me it is a work of art.

Epstein then described Brancusi's reputation among modern artists, and said that the type of abstraction that Brancusi realized in BIRD IN SPACE was similar to the simplifications often found in Egyptian sculpture. He offered as evidence a small statue of a hawk. Government lawyers tried to get him to say that Brancusi's work did not resemble a bird, but Epstein held his ground. There the cross-examination ended, and both sides rested.

The judge decided that BIRD IN SPACE was indeed art. The decision read in part:

"There has been developing a so-called new school of art, whose exponents attempt to portray abstract ideas rather than to imitate natural objects. Whether or not we are in sympathy with these newer ideas and the schools which represent them, we think the facts of their existence and their influence upon the art world as recognized by the courts must be considered.

"The object now under consideration is shown to be for purely ornamental purposes, its use being the same as that of any piece of sculpture of the old masters. It is beautiful and symmetrical in outline, and while some difficulty might be encountered in associating it with a bird, it is nevertheless pleasing to look at and highly ornamental, and as we hold under the evidence that it is the original production of a professional sculptor, and is in fact a piece of sculpture and a work of art according to the authorities above referred to, we sustain the protest. . . ."

And Steichen got his money back.

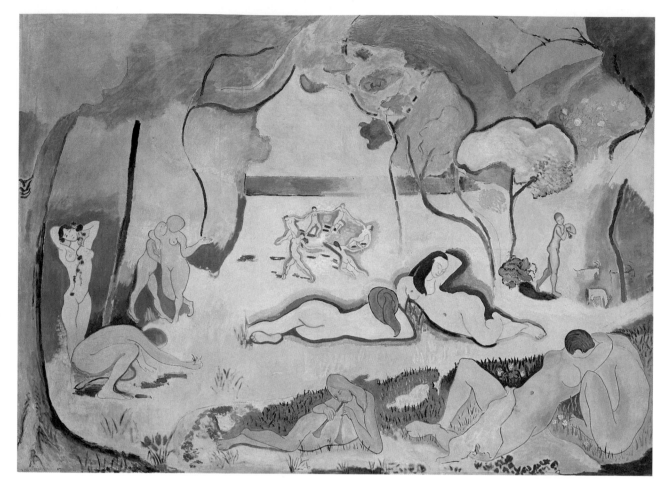

580 Henri Matisse. LE BONHEUR DE VIVRE. 1905–1906.
Oil on canvas. 69⅛" × 94 ⅞"(175 × 241 cm). BF#719.

THE FAUVES AND EXPRESSIONISM

By the turn of the century, many young painters in France had been attracted to Seurat's divisionist method. Its formalist, rational approach seemed perfectly suited to a progressive, scientific era. For some young painters just starting out, divisionism offered a systematic way to escape the weight of the past and to counter the oppressive influences of their academic teachers and the outdated Impressionists.

Soon, however, some of these artists felt imprisoned rather than liberated by divisionism. They wanted to express themselves more directly, more spontaneously. Led by Henri Matisse, a group of painters that included André Derain drew inspira-

tion from the expressive color of Gauguin and van Gogh. They studied Cézanne's pictorial constructions in colored planes. Their own use of color grew increasingly intense and subjective.

In 1905, their first group exhibit shocked the public. A critic of that show derisively called them *les fauves* (the wild beasts). According to Matisse, the epithet was never accepted by the group; it was merely a tag found useful by critics.

Matisse's painting JOY OF LIFE is a major early work in a long career and a masterpiece of what came to be known as *Fauvism*. Pure hues vibrate across the surface; lines, largely freed from descriptive roles, align with simplified shapes to provide a lively rhythm in the composition. The seemingly

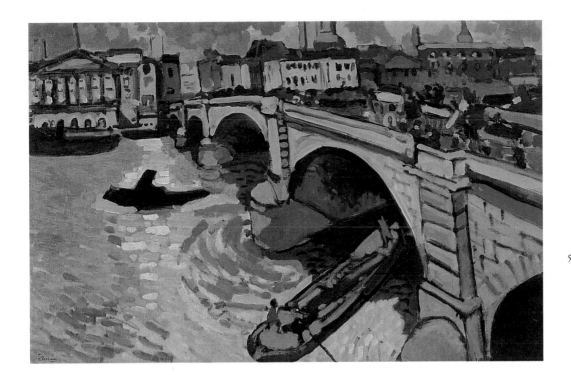

581 André Derain.
LONDON BRIDGE. 1906.
Oil on canvas. 26" × 39"
(66 × 99.1 cm).
The Museum of Modern Art, New York.
Gift of Mr. and Mrs. Charles Zadok.
Photograph © 2002 The Museum of
Modern Art, New York. © 2002 Artists
Rights Society (ARS), New York,
ADAGP, Paris.

careless depiction of the figures is based on Matisse's knowledge of human anatomy and drawing. The intentionally direct, childlike quality of the form serves to heighten the joyful content.

In Derain's LONDON BRIDGE, brilliant, invented color is balanced by some use of traditional composition and perspective. Derain spoke of intentionally using discordant color. It is an indication of today's acceptance of strong color that Derain's painting does not appear disharmonious.

The Fauve movement lasted little more than two years, from 1905 to 1907, yet it was one of the most influential developments in early twentieth-century painting. The Fauves took an even more decisive step in freeing color from its traditional role of describing the natural appearance of an object. In this way, their work led to an increasing use of color as an independent expressive element.

We can categorize Fauvism as an expressive style. *Expressionism* is a general term for art that emphasizes inner feelings and emotions over objective depiction. In Europe, romantic or expressive tendencies can be traced from seventeenth-century Baroque art to the early nineteenth-century painting of Delacroix, who in turn influenced the expressive side of Post-Impressionism (particularly van Gogh).

A few German artists at the beginning of the century shared the expressionist goals of the Fauves. Their desire to express attitudes and emotions was so pronounced and sustained that we call their art *German Expressionism.* They developed imagery characterized by vivid, often angular simplifications of their subjects, dramatic color contrasts, with bold, at times crude finish used to heighten their emotional and psychological meanings. Like their Fauve counterparts, the German Expressionists built on the achievements of Gauguin and van Gogh and the soul-searching paintings of Munch. They felt compelled to use the power of expressionism to address the human condition, often exploring such themes as natural life, sorrow, passion, spirituality, and mysticism. As their art developed, it absorbed formal influences from medieval German art, Fauvism, Slavic folk art, African and Oceanic art, and Cubism.

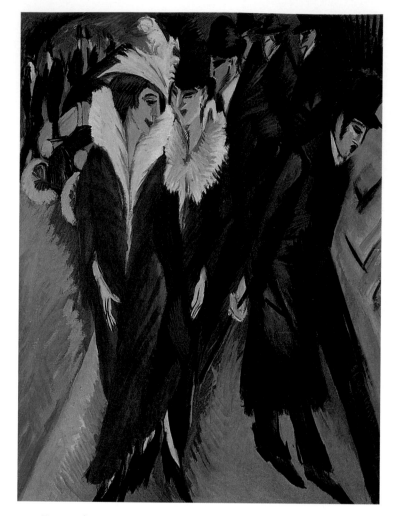

582 Ernst Ludwig Kirchner.
STREET, BERLIN. 1913.
Oil on canvas. 47½" × 35⅞" (120.6 × 91.1 cm).
The Museum of Modern Art, New York. Purchase. Photograph
©2002 The Museum of Modern Art, New York.

and establish a new, vigorous aesthetic that would form a bridge between the Germanic past and modern experience. They first exhibited as a group in 1905, the year of the first Fauve exhibition.

Kirchner's concern for expressing human emotion gave his work a quality similar to that which he admired in Munch's work. Kirchner's early paintings employed the flat color areas of Fauvism; by 1913, he had developed a style that incorporated the angularities of Cubism (discussed presently), African sculpture, and German Gothic art. In STREET, BERLIN, elongated figures are crowded together with the use of repeated diagonal lines to create an urban atmosphere charged with energy. Dissonant colors, chopped out shapes, and rough, almost crude, brushwork heighten the emotional impact.

The Blue Rider group was led by Russian painter Wassily Kandinsky, who lived in Munich between 1908 and 1914 and who shared with his German associates a concern for developing an art that would turn people away from false values, toward spiritual rejuvenation. He believed that a painting should be "an exact replica of some inner emotion"; in BLUE MOUNTAIN, painted in 1908, he created a "choir of colors" influenced by the vivid, freely expressive color of the Fauves.[6]

Kandinsky's paintings evolved toward an absence of representational subject matter. In BLUE MOUNTAIN, subject matter had already become secondary to the powerful effect of the visual elements released from merely descriptive roles.

By 1910, Kandinsky had made the shift to totally nonrepresentational imagery in order to concentrate on the expressive potential of pure form freed from associations with recognizable subjects. He sought a language of visual form comparable to the independent aural language we experience in music. The rhythms, melodies, and harmonies of music please or displease us because of the way they affect us. By titling his painting WITH THE BLACK ARCH NO. 154, Kandinsky referred to the dominant visual element in the painting, which is similar to a composer's naming a composition

The range of German Expressionist feeling is evident in the compassionate depictions of the poor and helpless by Käthe Kollwitz (pages 99 to 101), and the graphic clarity of prints by Emil Nolde (page 141).

Two groups typified the German Expressionist movement of the early twentieth century: the Bridge (*die Brücke*) and the Blue Rider (*der blaue Reiter*). Ernst Ludwig Kirchner, architecture student turned painter, was the founder of the Bridge. The group included several of his fellow architectural students, Emil Nolde, and others. They appealed to artists to revolt against academic painting

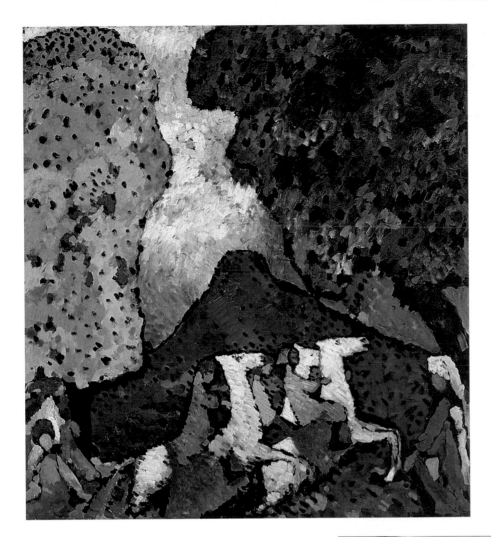

583 Vasily Kandinsky.
BLUE MOUNTAIN (DER BLAUE BERG).
1908–1909. Oil on canvas.
41¾" × 38"(106 × 96.6 cm).
The Solomon R. Guggenheim Museum, N Y. Gift,
Solomon R. Guggenheim, 1941. 41.505. Photograph by
David Heald. © The Solomon R.Guggenheim Founda-
tion, NY. © 2002 Artists Rights Society (ARS),
NY/ADAGP, Paris.

584 Wassily Kandinsky.
WITH THE BLACK ARCH NO. 154.
1912.
Oil on canvas. 74" × 77⅛".
Cliche phototheque des Collections du Centre Georges
Pompidou/Musee national d'art moderne, Paris.
Photo: Phillippe Migeat © Centre G.Pompidou © 2002
Artists Rights Society (ARS), New York/ ADAGP, Paris.

"Symphony No. 2 in D Major." Weightless curves float across large free shapes in a painted world of interactive energies.

Kandinsky said that the content of his paintings was "what the spectator *lives* or *feels* while under the effect of the *form and color combinations* of the picture."[7] He was an outstanding innovator in the history of art, and his revolutionary nonfigurative works played a key role in the development of subsequent nonrepresentational styles. His purpose was not simply aesthetic: he saw his paintings as leading a way through an impending period of catastrophe to a great new era of spirituality. Kandinsky felt art could provide a spiritual nourishment for the modern world—a level of fulfillment no longer offered by religion.

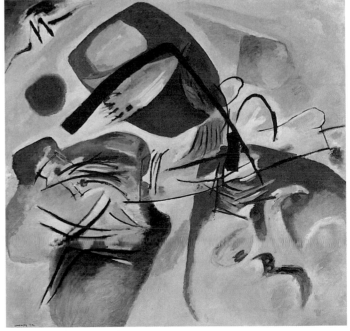

CUBISM

While living in Paris, Spanish artist Pablo Picasso shared ideas and influences with French artist Georges Braque. Together they pursued investigations that led to Cubism, the most influential movement of the early twentieth century. Cubism heavily influenced the spatial design (basic visual structure) of many of the notable paintings and sculptures of the century. During the same period, the bold use of bright, invented color initiated by Fauvism was another strong current of influence. In terms of design, color contributes to but is secondary to structure. Through its indirect influence on architecture and the applied arts, Cubism has become part of our daily lives.

It is interesting to trace Picasso's artistic development in relation to the emergence of Cubism. In 1906, the year Matisse completed JOY OF LIFE, Picasso painted SELF-PORTRAIT WITH PALETTE, which has a unique, abstract flatness not present in his earlier work. The boldly simplified surfaces and shapes were influenced by the abstract, pre-Roman Iberian sculpture of Spain such as the IBERIAN STONE RELIEF.

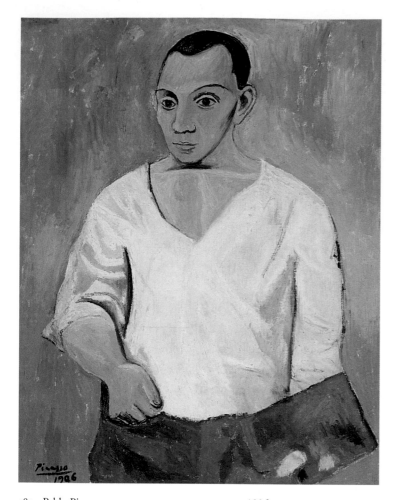

585 Pablo Picasso. SELF-PORTRAIT WITH PALETTE. 1906.
Oil on canvas. 36¼" × 28¾".
Philadelphia Museum of Art. A.E. Gallatin Collection. 1950-1-1.
Photo by Graydon Wood, 1990.
© 2002 Estate of Pablo Picasso/Artists Rights Society (ARS), NY.

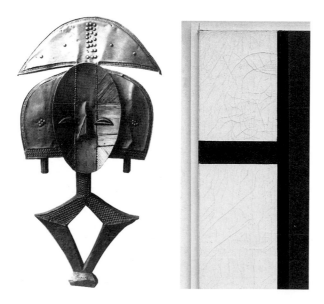

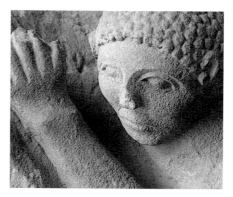

586 IBERIAN STONE RELIEF.
Museo Arqueológico Nacional, Madrid.

587 BAKOTA FUNERARY FIGURE.
French Equatorial Africa, probably 20th century.
Brass sheeting over wood. Length 27½".
Catalog #323686, Department of Anthropology, Smithsonian Institution.

588 ETOUMBI MASK.
French Congo. Wood. Height 14".
Musée Barbier-Mueller, Geneva.
Photograph: P. A. Ferrazzini.

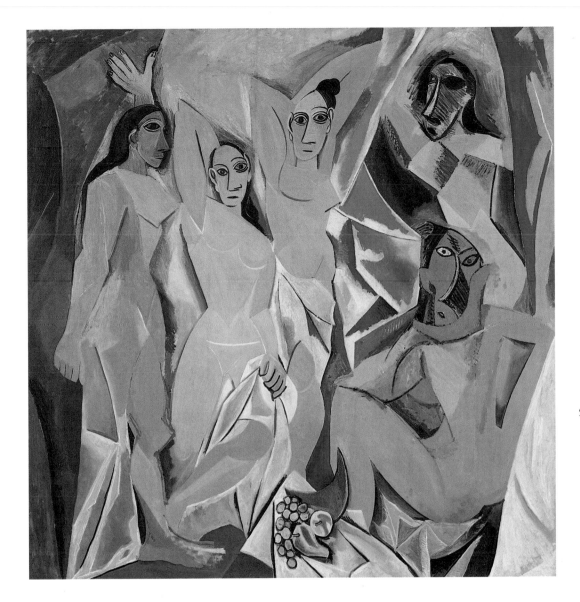

Picasso absorbed influences quickly, keeping only what he needed to achieve his objectives. His breakthrough painting, LES DEMOISELLES D'AVIGNON, shows a radical departure from tradition. Rejecting the accepted European notion of ideal beauty, Picasso created an entirely personal vocabulary of form influenced by Cézanne's faceted reconstructions of nature and by the inventive abstraction, vitality, and power he admired in African sculpture such as the BAKOTA FUNERARY FIGURE and the ETOUMBI MASK.

Picasso's new approach astonished even his closest friends. Georges Braque, who did as much as Picasso to develop Cubism, was appalled when he first saw LES DEMOISELLES in 1907. "You may give

all the explanations you like," he said, "but your painting makes one feel as if you were trying to make us eat cotton waste and wash it down with kerosene."[8] In LES DEMOISELLES D'AVIGNON, the fractured, angular figures intermingle with the sharp triangular shapes of the ground, activating the entire picture surface. This reconstruction of image and ground, with its fractured triangulation of forms and its merging of figure and ground was the turning point. With this painting, Picasso exploded the lingering Renaissance approach to the human figure in art and the legacy of Renaissance perspective. In short, he overturned many of the traditions of Western art. LES DEMOISELLES thus set the stage and provided the impetus for the development of

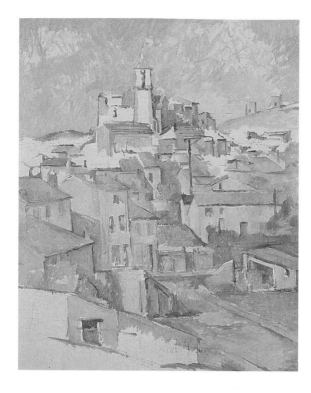

Cubism. Though some art historians have come to decry the work's negative depiction of women, viewers are challenged by the painting's hacked-out shapes and overall intensity.

A comparison of two paintings—Cézanne's GARDANNE, completed in 1886, and Braque's HOUSES AT L'ESTAQUE, completed in 1908, shows the beginning of the progression from Cézanne's Post-Impressionist style to the Cubist approach developed by Braque and Picasso.

Picasso made the first breakthrough, but Braque did the most to develop the refined vocabulary of Cubism. Braque admired Cézanne's continuous probing, his doubt, and his dogged determination to get at the truth of his subjects. In a series of landscapes painted in the south of France (where Cézanne had worked), Braque took Cézanne's faceted planar constructions a step further. Picasso's development of figure and ground interactions was also a springboard for paintings such as Braque's HOUSES AT L'ESTAQUE.

Instead of the sequential progression into depth that had been common in European painting since the Renaissance, Braque's shapes define a rush of forms that pile up rhythmically in shallow, ambiguous space. Buildings and trees seem interlocked in an active spatial system that pushes and pulls across the picture surface.

HOUSES AT L'ESTAQUE, one of the first Cubist paintings, provided the impetus for the movement's name: When Matisse saw this painting, he declared it to be a bunch of little cubes. Although this observation does not accurately describe Cubist form, Cubism became the name by which the movement was identified. From 1908 to 1914, Braque and Picasso were equally responsible for bringing Cubism to maturity. They worked for a

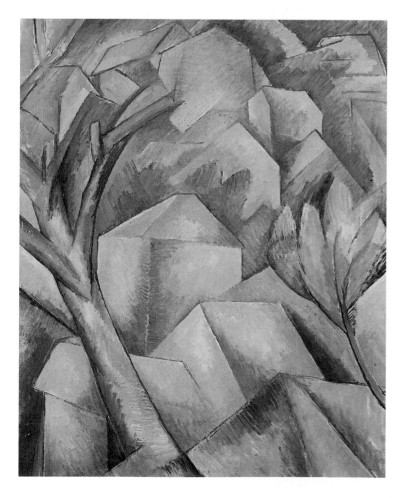

590   Paul Cézanne.
      GARDANNE. 1885–1886.
      Oil on canvas. 31½" × 25¼", (80 × 64.2 cm).
      The Metropolitan Museum of Art.
      Gift of Dr. and Mrs. Franz H. Hirschland, 1957. (57.181).
      Photograph: © 1991 The Metropolitan Museum of Art.

591   Georges Braque. (1882-1963)
      HOUSES AT L'ESTAQUE. 1908.
      Oil on canvas. 28½" × 23".
      Fundation RUPF, Bern, Switzerland. Giraudon/Art Resource, NY.
      © 2002 Artists Rights Society (ARS), NY/ADAGP, Paris.

time in increasingly neutral tones, in an effort to achieve formal structure devoid of the emotional distractions of color.

By 1910, Cubism had become a fully developed style. During the *analytical* phase of Cubism (1910 to 1911), Picasso, Braque, and others analyzed their subjects from various angles, then painted abstract, geometric references to these views. Because mental concepts of familiar objects are based on experiences of seeing many sides, they aimed to show objects as the mind, rather than the eye, perceives them. Georges Braque's THE POR-TUGUESE is a portrait of a man sitting at a café table strumming a guitar. The subject is broken down into facets and recombined with the background. Figure and ground thus collapse into a shallow and jagged pictorial space.

Cubism, although radical in appearance, was actually a new phase of the classical approach to visual form. It was a rational, formalist counterpart to the subjective emphasis of the Fauves and other expressionists. Above all, it was a reinvention of pictorial space. The Cubists realized that the two-dimensional space of the picture plane was unique—a form of space quite different from the three-dimensional space we occupy. Natural objects were points of departure for abstract images, demonstrating the essential unity of forms within the spaces that surround and penetrate them. Cubism is a reconstruction of objects, based on geometric abstraction. By looking first at Cézanne's GARDANNE, then at Braque's HOUSES AT L'ESTAQUE, and finally at THE PORTUGUESE, we see a progression in which forms seem to build, then spread across the surface in interwoven planes.

A new kind of construction of planes in actual space came about when Picasso assembled his sheet-metal GUITAR (see next page) and thereby extended the Cubist revolution to sculpture. Many consider GUITAR one of this century's most significant sculptures, since it began what has become a dominant trend toward sculptural construction. Before GUITAR, most sculpture was carved or modeled. Since GUITAR, much of contemporary sculpture has been constructed.

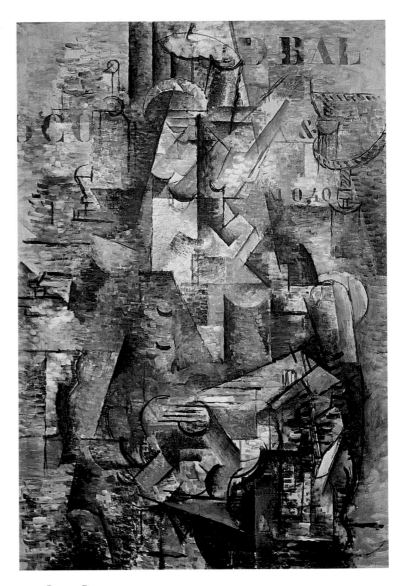

592 Georges Braque.
THE PORTUGUESE. 1911.
Oil on canvas. 46" × 32".
Kunstmuseum, Basel, Switzeland. Giraudon/Art Resource, NY.
©2002 Artists Rights Society (ARS), New York/ADAGP, Paris.

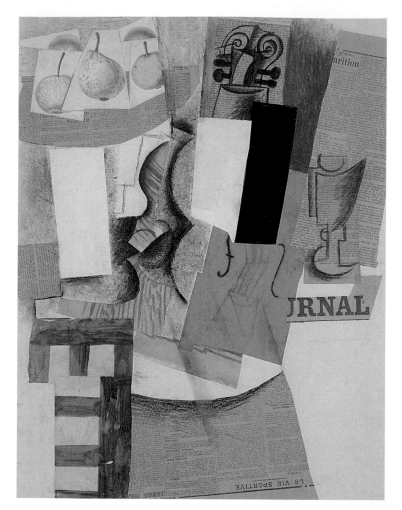

In 1912, Picasso and Braque modified Analytical Cubism with color, textured and patterned surfaces, and the use of cutout shapes. The resulting style came to be called Synthetic Cubism. Artists used pieces of newspaper, sheet music, wallpaper, and similar items, not re-presented but actually *presented* in a new way. The newspaper in THE VIOLIN is part of a real Paris newspaper. The shapes, which in earlier naturalistic, representational paintings would have been "background," have been made equal in importance to foreground shapes. The whole image reads as relatively flat. Picasso chose traditional still-life objects; but rather than paint the fruit, he cut out and pasted printed images of fruit. Such compositions, called *papier colle* in French, or pasted paper, became known as *collage* in English. Analytical Cubism involved taking apart, or breaking down, the subject into its various aspects; Synthetic Cubism was a process of building up or combining bits and pieces of material.

593   Pablo Picasso (Spanish, 1881-1973)
VIOLIN AND FRUIT. 1913.
Charcoal colored papers, gouache, painted paper collage.
25¼" × 19½".
Philadelphia Museum of Art: A.E. Gallatin Collection, 1952-61-106.
© 2002 Estate of Pablo Picasso/Artists Rights Society (ARS), New York.

594   Pablo Picasso.
GUITAR. Paris, winter 1912–13.
Construction of sheet metal and wire.
30½" × 13¾" × 7⅝" (77.5 × 35 × 19.3 cm)
The Museum of Modern Art, New York. Gift of the artist.
Photograph © 2002 The Museum of Modern of Modern Art, New York.
© 2002 Estate of Pablo Picasso/Artists Rights Society (ARS), NY.

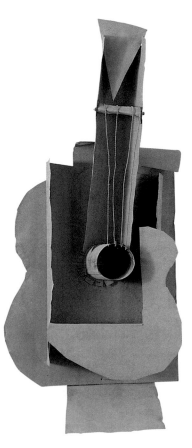

Even before he could talk, Pablo Picasso showed skill in drawing. Years later, he could remember the colors of things he saw in early childhood.

Born in the southern Spanish town of Málaga to artistic parents, Picasso first studied art with his father, a drawing teacher. At the age of ten he moved with his family to La Coruña on the Atlantic coast, then to Barcelona four years later, when the future Cubist was fourteen. Such was his skill at drawing, that upon arrival he passed the entrance examinations for the School of Fine Arts. He won his first gold medal at an exhibition in his home town in 1897.

At the age of sixteen he entered the Royal Academy in Madrid, but attended only briefly because he regarded the teaching methods as oppressive. Returning to Barcelona in 1899, he began to frequent the advanced art circles where Modern art was practiced and hotly debated. His own work evolved rapidly through Symbolism and Post-Impressionism to expressive portraits of social outcasts and poor people.

At twenty-five, Picasso became fascinated with the expressive force of art from outside Western traditions. He became particularly interested in the African and Oceanic sculpture that Gauguin and later the Fauves had "discovered."

From 1904 to 1945 he lived in Paris. His early work shows his ability to assimilate varied influences and his interest in exploring new modes of expression. There are conflicting accounts regarding when and where Picasso first saw African sculpture. He claimed that his first encounter with African sculpture and masks was in an exhibition late in 1907, after he had finished LES DEMOISELLES. Other artists and writers, including Matisse and Gertrude Stein, told of showing Picasso African sculpture in 1906. His paintings and sculpture of the period certainly show a familiarity with sculpture and masks of the Ivory Coast and the metal-covered figures of the Gabon. By 1909 Picasso had become a serious collector of African art.

In their development of Cubism, Picasso and Braque drew inspiration from the inventive abstractions of African sculpture and the structural translation of nature seen in paintings by Cézanne.

Picasso exhibited in the first Surrealist exhibition in Paris in 1925, but he did not sign the group's manifesto. Like the Surrealists, he became increasingly involved with the political unrest in Europe during the 1930s. After a short period of rest and retreat, Picasso produced a long series of drawings and paintings that expressed his anguish over the growing political violence that led to World War II (see GUERNICA, page 119).

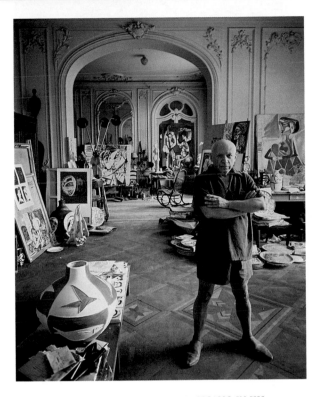

595 PICASSO IN HIS STUDIO AT CANNES. c. 1965.
© Arnold Newman/Getty Images.

Any written biography of Picasso is only a footnote to the autobiographical content of much of his art. In his many variations on the themes of the artist at work and the artist with his model, we recognize that Picasso is commenting on his own experience. Within and beyond his images of the life of an artist there is the ebb and the flow, the inspiration and the crises of Picasso's turbulent love life. Five very different women, who shared his life, appear again and again in his art.

His later work included ceramics and huge numbers of prints and drawings in addition to many paintings. Hardworking and prolific until the end of his life, he was a key figure who gave visual expression to the essential character of his time. In its diversity,

Picasso's art relates to most of the twentieth century's art movements. With his prodigious imagination and many innovative changes in style and media, Picasso inspired generations of younger artists who often made whole careers sparked by just one phase of his creative evolution.

Picasso's stature in the twentieth century is comparable to Michelangelo's during the Renaissance: both artists lived nearly a century, both became famous early in life, both lived during periods of incredible change, and both were at the forefront of the artistic developments of their times.

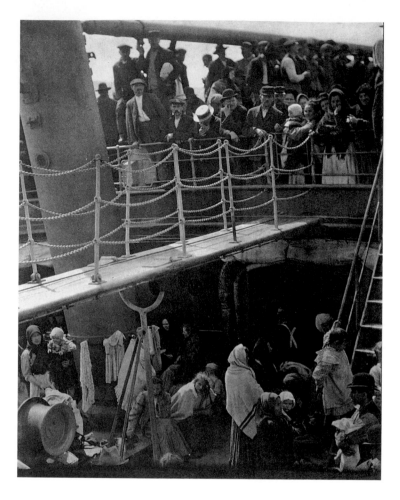

THE MODERN SPIRIT IN AMERICA

As Picasso and Braque took the steps that led to Cubism, American photographer Alfred Stieglitz was also reconsidering the geometry of design on the picture plane. When Picasso saw Stieglitz's photograph THE STEERAGE, he said, "This photographer is working in the same spirit as I am."[9]

THE STEERAGE looked "chopped up" to many people. Some of the artist's friends felt that it should have been two photographs rather than one. Stieglitz, however, saw the complex scene as a pattern of interacting forces of light, shade, shape, and direction. Aboard a ship headed for Europe, he saw the composition of this photograph as "a round straw hat, the funnel leaning left, the stairway leaning right, the white drawbridge with its railings made of circular chains, white suspenders crossing on the back of a man on the steerage below, round shapes of iron machinery, a mast cutting into the sky, making a triangular shape. . . . I saw a picture of shapes and underlying that the feeling I had about life."[10] He rushed to his cabin to get his camera, hoping the relationships would not change. Nothing had shifted, and he made the photograph he considered his best.

Stieglitz made major contributions toward establishing photography as an art of comparable importance to traditional media (see p. 159 for another work). He also played a key role in introducing the new European painting and sculpture to Americans. In 1907, he opened a gallery in New York and began showing the work of the most progressive European artists, including photographers. He was the first in America to show works by Cézanne, Matisse, Brancusi, Picasso, and Braque. Following the exhibition of art by these European pioneers, Stieglitz began to show work by those who

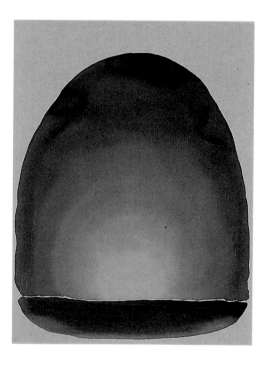

596 Alfred Stieglitz. THE STEERAGE. 1907. From CAMERA WORK, NEW YORK, NO. 34, October 1911.
Photogravure, 7¾" × 6½" (19.7 × 16.5 cm).
The Museum of Modern Art, New York. Gift of Alfred Stieglitz. Copy Print © 1999 The Museum of Modern Art, New York.

597 Georgia O'Keeffe.
LIGHT COMING ON THE PLAINS NO II. 1917.
Watercolor on newsprint. 11⅞" × 8⅞".
Amon Carter Museum, Fort Worth, Texas 1966.32.
© 2002 The Georgia O'Keeffe Foundation/Artists Rights Society (ARS), New York.

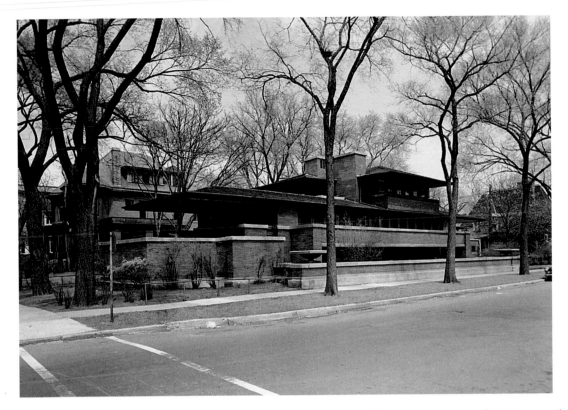

598 Frank Lloyd Wright.
ROBIE HOUSE.
Chicago, Illinois. 1909.

would become leading American artists, including Georgia O'Keeffe (see also pages 33 to 34).

O'Keeffe's work from the time of World War I was innovative, consisting mostly of abstractions based on nature. LIGHT COMING ON THE PLAINS, for example, uses fine gradations of tone to suggest the moments of anticipation before sunrise. She based this work on experiences living in the Texas panhandle where she taught school, but the painting also refers to what she later recalled as her earliest memory: a warm, enfolding, mystical light.

Between 1905 and 1910, traditional concepts of form in space were being challenged in architecture as well as in sculpture, painting, and photography. While Cubism was developing in painting, leading American architect Frank Lloyd Wright was designing "prairie houses," in which he often omitted or minimized walls between living and dining rooms and between interior and exterior spaces. Wright's concept of open plans has changed the way people design living spaces. In many contemporary homes, kitchen, dining room, and living room now join in one continuous space, and indoors often intermingles with outdoors.

In his ROBIE HOUSE of 1909, a striking canti-levered roof reaches out and unifies a fluid design of asymmetrically interconnected spaces. Through Wright's influence, the open flow of spaces became a major feature of contemporary architecture. To get a feeling of how far ahead of his time Wright was, imagine the incongruity of a new 1909 automobile that could have been parked in front of the ROBIE HOUSE the year it was completed. (For more on Frank Lloyd Wright and his architecture, see pages 248 to 249.)

The American public had its first extensive look at leading developments in European art during the Armory Show held in New York in 1913. This show of over sixteen hundred works became the best known and the most influential art exhibition ever held in the United States. Americans, especially young American artists, were able to see key works by Impressionists, Post-Impressionists, and Fauves—particularly Matisse, who was much maligned by critics. Also shown were paintings by Picasso, Braque, Léger, Duchamp, and sculpture by Brancusi. As a result, Cubism and other forms of abstract art spread to America.

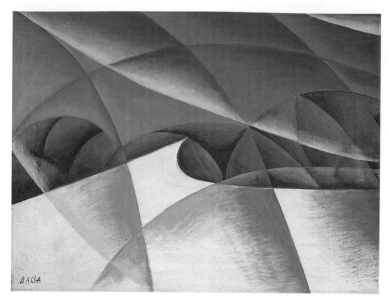

599 Giacomo Balla (1871-1958).
ABSTRACT SPEED-THE CAR HAS PASSED. 1913.
Oil on canvas. 19¾" × 25¾".
Tate Gallery, London/Art Resource, NY.
©2002 Artists Rights Society (ARS), New York/SIAE, Rome.

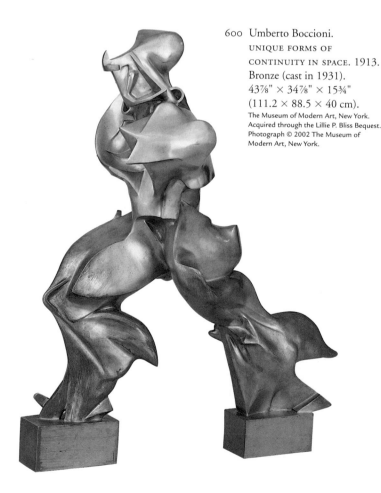

600 Umberto Boccioni.
UNIQUE FORMS OF
CONTINUITY IN SPACE. 1913.
Bronze (cast in 1931).
43⅞" × 34⅞" × 15¾"
(111.2 × 88.5 × 40 cm).
The Museum of Modern Art, New York.
Acquired through the Lillie P. Bliss Bequest.
Photograph © 2002 The Museum of
Modern Art, New York.

FUTURISM AND THE CELEBRATION OF MOTION

The Italian Futurists were among the many artists who gained their initial inspiration from Cubism. To the shifting planes and multiple vantage points of Cubism, Futurists such as Giacomo Balla and Umberto Boccioni added a sense of speed and motion and a celebration of the machine.

By multiplying the image of a moving object, Futurists expanded the Cubist concepts of simultaneity of vision and metamorphosis. In 1909, the poet Filippo Tommaso Marinetti proclaimed in the *Initial Manifesto of Futurism:* "the world's splendor has been enriched by a new beauty; the beauty of speed . . . a roaring motorcar . . . is more beautiful than the Victory of Samothrace."[11]

The Futurists translated the speed of modern life into works that captured the dynamic energy of the new century. Giacomo Balla intended his work AB-STRACT SPEED THE CAR HAS PASSED to depict the rushing air and dynamic feeling of a vehicle passing. This "roaring motorcar" is passing at about 35 miles an hour, but at that time this was the pinnacle of speed.

An abstract sculpture of a striding figure climaxed a series of Umberto Boccioni's drawings, paintings, and sculpture. Boccioni insisted that sculpture should be released from its usual confining outer surfaces in order to open up and fuse the work with the space surrounding it. In UNIQUE FORMS OF CONTINUITY IN SPACE, muscular forms seem to leap outward in flamelike bursts of energy. During this period, the human experience of motion, time, and space was transformed by the development of the automobile, the airplane, and the movies. Futurist imagery reflects this exciting period of change.

French artist Marcel Duchamp, working independently of the Futurists, brought the dimension of motion to Cubism. His NUDE DESCENDING A STAIRCASE, NO. 2 was influenced by stroboscopic photography, in which sequential camera images show movement by freezing successive instants (see p. 58 for an example).

Through sequential, diagonally placed, abstract references to the figure, the painting presents the movement of a body through space, seen all at once, in a single rhythmic progression. Our sense of gravity intensifies the overall feeling of motion. When the painting was displayed at the Armory Show in New York in 1913, it caused cries of dismay and was seen as the ultimate Cubist madness. The painting, once described as "an explosion in a shingle factory," has remained an inspiration to artists who use repetition and rhythm to express motion.

Sonia Delaunay expressed motion in her paintings through color contrasts. Her large work BAL BULLIER is an interpretation of couples moving about on the floor of one of Paris's leading night clubs of the time. We see Cubist influence in the work, as it is composed of flat shapes that overlap in shallow space. But the added push and pull of contrasting color contributes both depth and motion to the composition. It was difficult to stretch a canvas twelve feet across, so the artist used mattress ticking.

Delaunay was an early crusader for the integration of Modern art into everyday things. Even as she painted, she made bookbindings, embroideries, textiles, and fashions that included ideas from the latest Modern art movements. She started her own clothing design studio in 1922, where she specialized in what she called Simultaneous Dresses. Not for many years would such ideas take hold in the mass market.

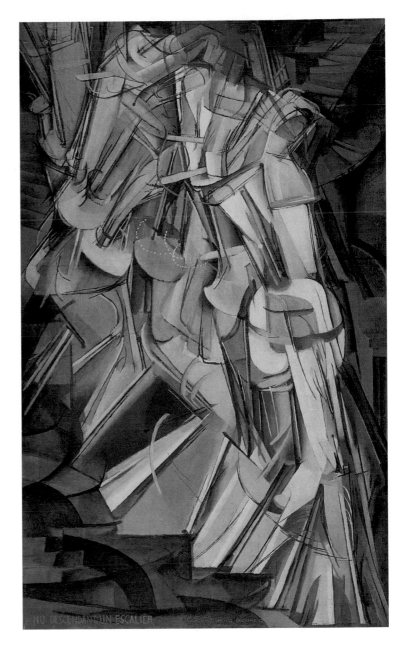

601 Marcel Duchamp
     (American, b. France 1887–1968).
     NUDE DESCENDING A STAIRCASE,
     NO. 2, 1912. Oil on canvas. 58" × 35".
     Philadelphia Museum of Art. The Louise and Walter Arensberg
     Collection, 1950-134-59. Photo by Graydon Wood, 1994.
     © 2002 Artists Rights Society (ARS), New York/ADAGP,
     Paris/Estate of Marcel Duchamp.

602 Sonia Delaunay.
     BAL BULLIER. 1913.
     Oil on mattress ticking, 0.97 × 3.9 m.
     Collections du Centre Georges Pompidou/Musée nationale d'art
     moderne, Paris. Photo J.F. Tomasian © Centre G. Pompidou.

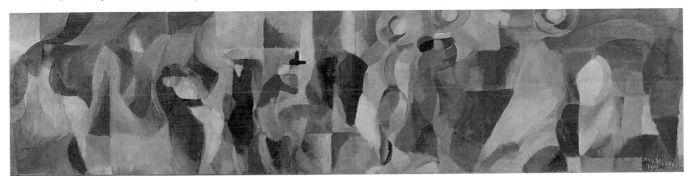

CHAPTER TWENTY-THREE

BETWEEN WORLD WARS

In 1914, enthusiasm for grand patriotic solutions to international tensions led citizens of many countries into World War I, a murderous and protracted conflict involving many European countries and eventually the United States. History has revealed that the war was far more devastating than the people of the time were led to believe. Over ten million were killed and twice that number wounded by machinery devised, but no longer controlled, by human reason. The promise of a whole new generation was lost in the world's first experience with mechanized mass killing.

As a result of the war, the political and cultural landscape was changed forever. The war set the stage for the Russian Revolution and paved the way for the Nazis of Germany and the Fascists of Italy. Governments assumed new powers to mobilize people and material, to dictate economic life, to censor public expression, and, by controlling information, to manipulate the way people thought. Dissent was denounced as unpatriotic.

Writers, photographers, and artists were prevented by governments and the self-censoring press from communicating the horror of the war. Many writers and artists produced propaganda, remained silent, or fought in the war. A great many were killed.

It was not until after the war had ended that those artists and writers who survived were able to express their perceptions of the catastrophe that shaped the world. Many sensitive people either were stifled by cynicism or sought relief in idealistic schemes for reform.

During the postwar era there was a gap between the older generation who had "bought" the propaganda and the young who had been in the trenches, between the official party line and the reality understood by the informed public. In the arts, movements emerged to protest the insanity and to mend the gulf between idealism and actuality.

DADA

Dada began in protest against the horrors of World War I. It became an aggressive assault on corrupt values by an international group of young writers and artists. Those who began the movement in Zurich chose the intentionally ambiguous word *Dada* as their rallying cry. One member of the group assumed that it referred to *da, da,* Slavic for "yes, yes." The two-syllable word was well suited for expressing the essence of what was an attitude, not a style. In the eyes of the Dadaists, the destructive absurdity of war was caused by traditional, narrow-minded values, which they set out to overturn. According to artist Marcel Janco,

Dada was not a school of artists, but an alarm signal against declining values, routine and speculation, a desperate appeal on behalf of all forms of art, for a creative basis on which to build a new and universal consciousness of art.[1]

French artist and poet Jean Arp said,

While the thunder of guns rolled in the distance, we sang, painted, glued, and composed for all our worth. We are seeking an art that would heal mankind from the madness of the age.[2]

Dadaists maintained that humankind had demonstrated that it was without reason. In order to make a new beginning, the Dadaists rejected all accepted moral, social, political, and aesthetic values. They felt it was pointless to try to find order and meaning in a world in which so-called rational behavior had produced only chaos and destruction. They sought to shock the middle class into seeing the absurdity of the Western world's social and political situation.

The Dadaists celebrated play and spontaneity. Their literature, art, and staged events were often based on chance rather than premeditation. Poets selected words at random; artists joined elements in startling, irrational combinations.

For Marcel Duchamp, mechanically produced things were a reservoir of un-self-conscious art objects. In his view, a reproduction of the MONA LISA was a ready-made object, in the same class as bicycle wheels, kitchen stools, and snow shovels. L.H.O.O.Q. is an "assisted readymade" by Duchamp, expressing his view that art had become simply a precious commodity. He poked fun with his "corrections," a penciled moustache and goatee and a new title. The unusual title is a vulgar pun in French, comprehensible to those who can hear the sentence in the sound of the letters pronounced in French. Translated into English, it reads, "She has a hot tail." Duchamp's outrageous irreverence toward one of the world's most revered paintings was an attempt to shake people out of a pattern of unthinking acceptance of cultural values.

Man Ray, an American, was a friend of Duchamp. His Dada works include paintings, photographs, and assembled objects. In 1921, in Paris, Man Ray saw an iron displayed in front of a shop selling housewares. He purchased the iron, a box of tacks, and a tube of glue. After gluing a row

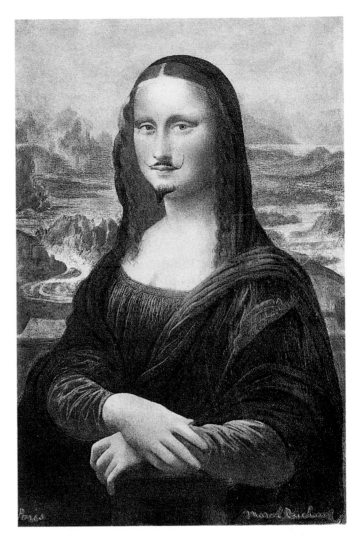

603 Marcel Duchamp.
L.H.O.O.Q. 1919.
From BOITE—EN—VALSIE." Pencil on reproduction of Leonardo's MONA LISA. 7¾" × 4¾".
Philadelphia Museum of Art: Louise and Walter Arensburg Collection.
© 2000 Artists Rights Society (ARS) NY/ADAGP, Paris/Estate of Marcel Duchamp.

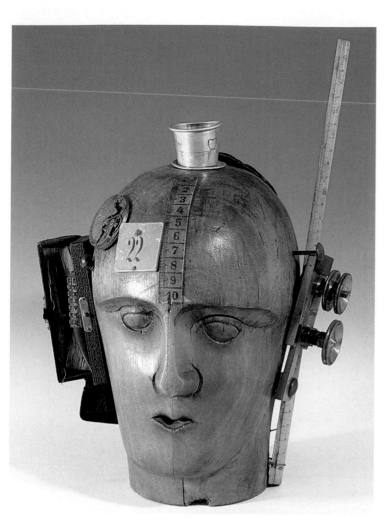

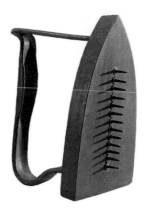

of tacks to the smooth surface of the iron, he titled his assemblage THE GIFT—thus creating an ironic contradiction.

One memorable Dada sculpture, Raoul Hausmann's THE SPIRIT OF OUR TIME, continues to express a truth about the twentieth century. We would like to know ourselves, yet we succumb to the playthings of our technology and ignore the sound of silence. Have the artifacts of our mass production turned us into hollow-headed robots who simply receive and transmit information and are unable to think for ourselves? Hausmann seems to have anticipated the world of artificial intelligence and the ubiquitous head-set radios, tape, and CD players.

Dadaists expanded on the Cubist idea of collage with *photomontage*, in which parts of photographs are combined in thought-provoking ways. In THE MULTI-MILLIONAIRE, by Dadaist Hannah Höch, man, the artifact-making industrialist, stands as a fractured giant among the things he has produced.

Some Dadaists maintained that "Art is dead." They often intended to be antiaesthetic. Ironically, they created a new aesthetic that has had lasting influence on the twentieth century.

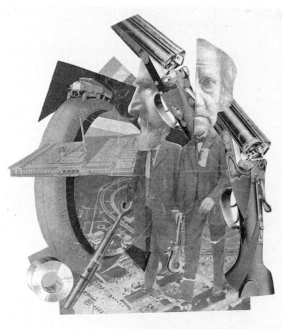

605 Raoul Hausmann.
THE SPIRIT OF OUR TIME. 1919.
Combine. Height 12¾".
Musee National d'Art Modern, Georges Pompidou Centre, Paris.
© Artists Rights Society (ARS), NY/ADAGP, Paris.

606 Hannah Höch.
THE MULTI-MILLIONAIRE. 1923.
Photomontage. 14" × 12".
Galerie Berinson, Berlin.
© 2002 Artists Rights Society (ARS), NY/VG Bild-Kunst, Bonn.

FANTASY AND METAPHYSICS

The highly personal and inventive art of Paul Klee provided inspiration for both Dadaists and their heirs, the Surrealists. Although Klee belonged to neither group, his work paralleled these movements and he exhibited with both groups.

As Klee developed his art, he tried to free himself from the accumulation of history in an effort to begin all over again. He discovered ways to tap the resources of his own unconscious, enabling him to create fantastic images. Klee spoke of his receptivity to such inspiration:

. . . everything vanishes around me and good works rise from me of their own accord. My hand is entirely the implement of a distant sphere. It is not my head that functions but something else, something higher, something more remote. I must have great friends there, dark as well as bright. . . . They are all very kind to me.[3]

Both whimsy and mystery pervade Klee's fantastic TWITTERING MACHINE. A major part of the intrigue comes from the title and its relationship to the "machine." We participate in the fun as we imagine the twittering sounds that will come forth when the crank is turned. As a machine it is absurd—a kind of useless Dada object. (See p. 40 for another of his works.)

Earlier in the century, when Cubism was maturing, Marc Chagall assimilated the influence of the Cubists by blending their use of geometric abstraction with his own imaginative use of subject matter. His fantasy-filled paintings such as the BIRTHDAY and I AND THE VILLAGE (page 44) incorporate symbolism drawn from Eastern European Jewish Hasidism, folklore, and childhood memories of Russian life.

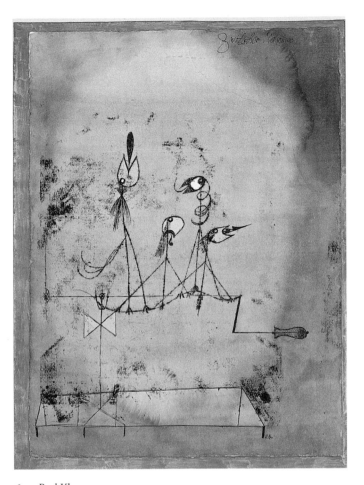

607 Paul Klee.
TWITTERING MACHINE (ZWITSCHER–MASCHINE). 1922.
Watercolor, and pen and ink on oil transfer drawing on paper, mounted on cardboard.
25¼" × 19" (63.8 × 48.1 cm).
The Museum of Modern Art, New York. Purchase.
Photograph: © 2002 The Museum of Modern Art, NY.
© 2002 Artists Rights Society (ARS), NY/VG Bild-Kunst, Bonn.

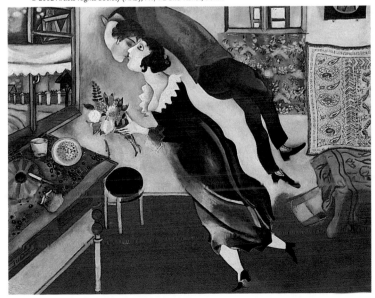

608 Marc Chagall.
THE BIRTHDAY (l'ANNIVERSAIRE). 1915.
Oil on cardboard. 31¾" × 39¼".
The Museum of Modern Art, New York.
Acquired through the Lillie P. Bliss Bequest.
Photograph © 2002 The Museum of Modern Art, NY.
© 2002 Artists Rights Society (ARS), NY/ADAGP, Paris.

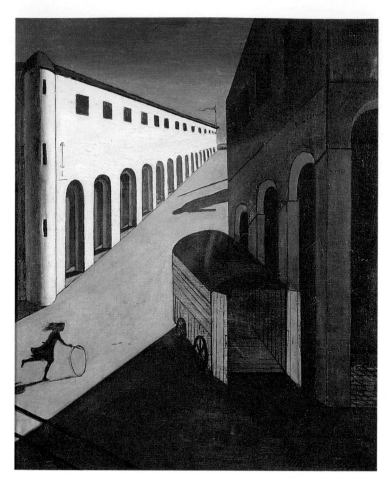

609 Giorgio De Chirico.
THE MYSTERY AND MELANCHOLY OF A STREET. 1914.
Oil on canvas. 34¼" × 28⅛".
Private collection. Photograph © Allan Mitchell
© 2002 Artists Rights Society (ARS)/SIAE, Rome.

Many of Chagall's paintings show people "flying" or with their feet off the ground, as a metaphor for love. Chagall's immense outpouring of work included prints and stained glass as well as paintings. His images arc filled with delightful combinations of gestures, objects, environments, and figures from his life and imagination.

Italian painter Giorgio De Chirico had a more direct role as a precursor of Surrealism than Klee or Chagall. In THE MYSTERY AND MELANCHOLY OF A STREET, De Chirico used distorted linear perspective, with conflicting vanishing points, to create an eerie space peopled by faceless shadows. The painting speaks the symbolic language of dreams and mystery. According to the artist,

everything has two aspects: the current aspect, which we see nearly always and which ordinary men see, and the ghostly and metaphysical aspect, which only rare individuals may see in moments of clairvoyance and metaphysical abstraction.[5]

De Chirico sought to create an alternative reality that could communicate with the unconscious by removing objects from the real world and presenting them in incongruous relationships.

SURREALISM

In the 1920s a group of writers and painters gathered to proclaim the omnipotence of the unconscious mind, thought to be a higher reality than the conscious mind. Their goal was to make visible the imagery of the unconscious. They were indebted to the shocking irrationality of Dadaism, the fantastic creations of Chagall and Klee, and especially the dream images of De Chirico. They also drew heavily on the new psychology of Sigmund Freud.

The new movement, *Surrealism*, was officially launched in Paris in 1924 with the publication of its first manifesto, written by poet-painter André Breton. In it he defined the movement's purpose as

the future resolution of these two states, dream and reality, which are seemingly so contradictory, into a kind of absolute reality, a surreality, if one may so speak.[6]

Shortly before Chagall's marriage, his bride-to-be, Bella, brought him flowers on his birthday. In Bella's autobiography, she wrote of their rapture:

Soon I forget the flowers. You work with your brushes . . . You pour on color . . . Suddenly you jump in the air . . . You float among the rafters. You turn your head and you twist mine too . . . and both together we rise over the clean little room.

"How do you like my picture?" you ask . . . You wait and are afraid of what I may tell you. "It's very good . . . you float away so beautifully. We'll call it the Birthday."[4]

Among the members of the Surrealist group were Spanish painters Salvador Dali and Joan Miró.

Dali's THE PERSISTENCE OF MEMORY evokes the eerie quality of some dreams. Mechanical time wilts in a deserted landscape of infinite space. The warped, headlike image in the foreground may be the last remnant of a vanished humanity. It may also be a self-portrait, complete with protruding tongue.

Dali and Miró represent two opposite tendencies operating in Surrealism. Dali's illusionary deep space and representational techniques create near-photographic dream images that make the impossible seem believable. The startling juxtaposition of unrelated objects creates a nightmarish sense of a superreality beyond the everyday world. This approach has been called Representational Surrealism. In contrast, Miró's Abstract Surrealism provides suggestive elements that give the widest possible play to the viewer's imagination and emphasize color and design rather than storytelling content.

To probe deep into the unconscious, Miró and others used automatic processes, sometimes called *automatism,* in which chance was a key factor. With the adoption of spontaneous and "automatic" methods, the Surrealists sought to expand consciousness by transcending limits of rational thought.

Miró's evocative paintings often depict imaginary creatures. He made them by scribbling on the canvas and then examining the results to see what the shapes suggested. The bold, organic shapes in WOMAN HAUNTED BY THE PASSAGE OF THE DRAGON-FLY, BIRD OF BAD OMEN are typical of his mature work.

The wild, tormented quality, however, is unusual for Miró and reflects his reaction to the times. Miró pointed out that this painting was done at the time of the Munich crisis that helped precipitate World War II. Even though there is a sense of terror here, Miró's underlying playful optimism is apparent.

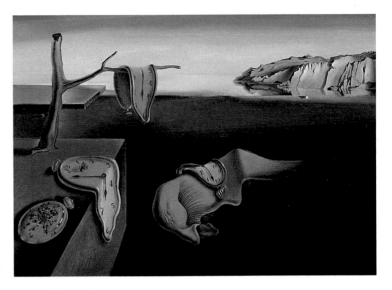

610 Salvador Dali.
THE PERSISTENCE OF MEMORY (PERSISTANCE DE LA MEMOIRE). 1931.
Oil on canvas. 9½" × 13" (24.1 × 33 cm).
The Museum of Modern Art, New York. Anonymous gift.
Photograph © 2002 The Museum of Modern Art, New York.
© 2002 Kindom of Spain, Gala-Salvador Dali Foundation/Artists Rights Society, (ARS), NY.

611 Joan Miró (Spanish 1893–1983).
WOMAN HAUNTED BY THE PASSAGE OF THE BIRD-DRAGONFLY OMEN OF BAD NEWS. 1938.
Oil on canvas. 31½" × 124" (80 × 315 cm).
The Toledo Museum of Art, Toledo, Ohio.
Purchased with funds from the Libbey Endowment.
Gift of Edward Drummond Libbey. 1986.25
© 2002 Artists Rights Society (ARS), NY/ADAGP, Paris.

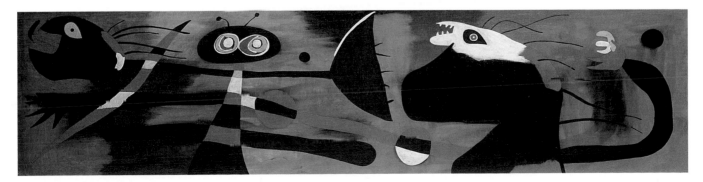

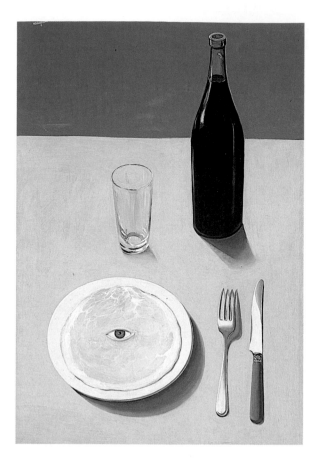

Belgian Surrealist René Magritte used an illogical form of realism, similar to Dali's in surface appearance but quite different in content. Magritte's paintings engage the viewer in mind-teasing mystery and playful humor. Everything depicted in PORTRAIT is ordinary; the impact comes from the unsettling placement of an eye looking back at us from a plate of ham.

Mexican painter Frida Kahlo was one of many artists who, though not a part of the Surrealist group in Europe, knew these artists and chose to build on their discoveries. Her painting THE TWO FRIDAS shows herself as a split personality, divided between her European and Mexican heritage. As each stares back at us, we see their hearts plainly visible, joined by blood vessels. This is an allusion both to ancient Aztec human sacrifice and to the artist's own surgical traumas. Her many self-portraits provide insight to an exceptional person who lived life with passionate intensity in spite of incredible physical problems. (See "Compelling Autobiographer.")

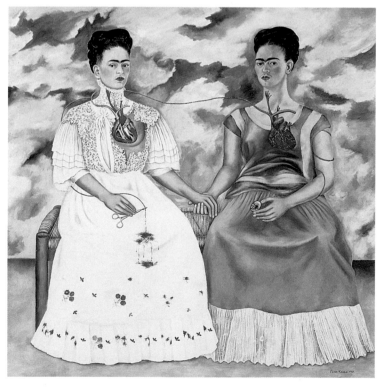

612   René Magritte.
      PORTRAIT. 1935.
      Oil on canvas. 28⅞" × 19⅞" (73.3 × 50.2 cm).
      The Museum of Modern Art, New York.
      Gift of Mrs. Kay Sage Tanguy.
      Photograph: © 2002 The Museum of Modern Art, NY.
      © 2002 C. Herscovici, Brussels/Artists Rights Society (ARS), NY.

613   Frida Kahlo (1907–1954).
      THE TWO FRIDAS. 1939.
      Oil on canvas. 5'8½" square.
      Schalkwijk/Art Resource, NY. © 2002 Banco de Mexico Diego Rivera & Frida Kahlo
      Museums Trust. Av. Cinco de Mayo No. 2, Col. Centro, Del. Cuauhtemoc 06059,
      Mexico, D.F. Reproduction authorized by the Instituto Nacional de Bellas Artes and
      Literature.

Frida Kahlo was a strong-willed, determined woman in a society that taught women to be passive.

Born in a suburb of Mexico City, she was the child of a photographer of German descent and a part-Spanish, part-Indian mother. When she was six years old she was stricken with polio. The painful disease caused her to be isolated for nine months and left her with one leg shorter and thinner than the other. At age eighteen she was in a trolley car accident that was followed by ineffective orthopedic treatments and thirty-two operations over the course of her life.

Chronic physical suffering caused by her illness and the accident led to a preoccupation with her severely damaged body—often the central subject in her paintings. In spite of her pain, her art reveals her feelings of connection with nature and with the creative energy that flows through all life. In her paintings, details of nature are integrated with elements of dreams and fantasies.

When her work was shown in Paris in 1938, it received favorable attention from leading Surrealists. However, Kahlo's unique style is probably more indebted to

Mexican narrative folk painting than to European Surrealism. Her paintings contain a mixture of folk art motifs, Surrealist elements, and autobiographical variations on the theme of mythical woman.

Her life was as unconventional as her art: she had two stormy marriages to the artist Diego Rivera, numerous affairs, and friendships with leading international leftist and Surrealist leaders.

In her complex self-portrait, THE LOVE EMBRACE OF THE UNIVERSE . . . , Kahlo celebrated the ultimate resolution of her relationship to her husband, the painter Diego Rivera, shown cradled in her arms like an infant. The painting's layered symbols suggest the underlying unity behind the light/dark, love/pain dualities of human experience. Kahlo's image is echoed on expanding levels of sustaining strength, from personal power, to mother Earth, to cosmic embrace.

Kahlo nurtures Rivera as the baby she could never have. Through his size, position, and pale skin she indicates his vulnerability, while simultaneously portraying *Dieguitto's* (little Diego's) spiritual insight by painting an enlarged third eye on his forehead. Kahlo is calm, yet sheds a tear. The world she created is the world that she felt created her.

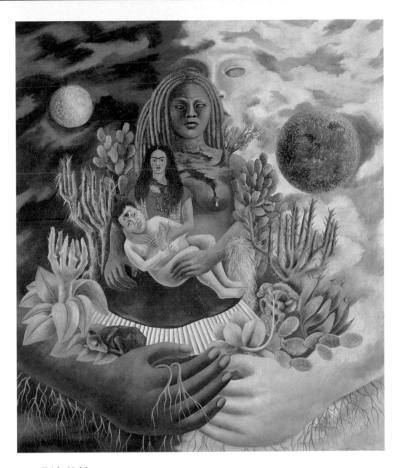

614 Frida Kahlo.
THE LOVE EMBRACE OF THE UNIVERSE, THE EARTH (MEXICO), DIEGO, ME, AND SEÑOR XOLOTL. 1949. Oil on masonite. 27½" × 23⅞" (70.1 × 60.5 cm).
Courtesy of Centro Cultural Arte Contemporaneo, Mexico City, Jacques and Natasha Gelman Collection.
© 2000 Banco de Mexico Diego Rivera and Frida Kahlo Museums Trust.
Av. Cinco de Mayo No. 2, Col. Centro, Del. Cuauhtemoc 06059, Mexico, D.F. Schalkwijk.

Kahlo's dramatic, bohemian personality enriched her distinctive painting style. Since her death in 1954, her international reputation has greatly increased. In the 1980s her psychologically loaded self-portraits found an appreciative new audience. Kahlo has become the heroine of the Mexican avant-garde and the subject of several books and a feature-length movie.

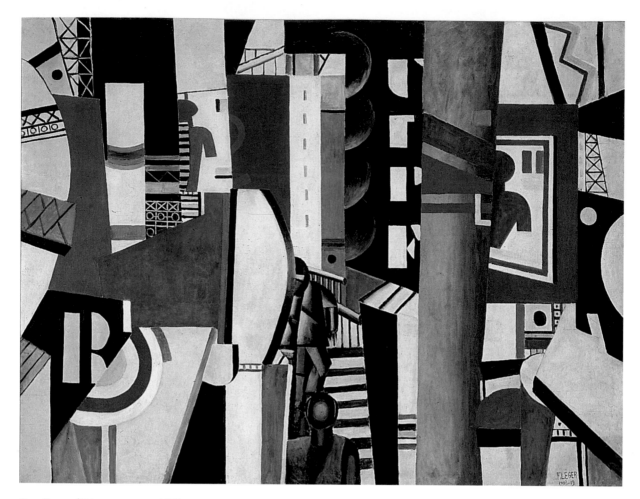

615 Fernand Léger. THE CITY. 1919.
Oil on canvas. 91" × 177½".
Philadelphia Museum of Art. A. E. Gallatin Collection, 1952-61-58.
© 2002 Artists Rights Society (ARS), NY/ADAGP, Paris.

THE INFLUENCE OF CUBISM

Of all Modern art movements, Cubism has been probably the most influential. Beginning in Paris, it spread to many parts of the world. This style makes possible many ambiguities between presence and absence, representation and abstraction, figure and ground. It suggests meanings that are relative and contingent. Far from presenting the world as stable and predictable, Cubism suggests constant change and evolution. An art historian wrote, "By devaluing subject matter, or by monumentalizing simple, personal themes, and by allowing mass and void to elide, the Cubists gave effect to the flux and paradox of modern life and the relativity of its values."[7]

Thus Cubism makes visible some important characteristics of modern life.

In his large painting THE CITY, Fernand Léger crushed jagged shapes together, collapsing space in a composition reminiscent of a Cubist portrait or still life. The forms in his paintings look machine-made, rounded and tubular; this is in keeping with the urban bustle that is the work's subject.

Russian artists took Cubism in the direction of complete abstraction. A leader there was Kazimir Malevich, who branded his style Suprematism. His painting SUPREMATIST COMPOSITION: AIRPLANE FLYING shows in its title that the artist was familiar with Futurism: its subject is a speeding modern airplane. Yet Malevich so simplified the Cubist pictorial language that we are left with a succession of flat irregular rectangles against a pure background.

Malevich believed that shapes and colors in a painting always communicate, no matter what the subject of the work. Ideally, he thought, art should not need subject matter. This is why he named his movement Suprematism, because he wanted to focus on the supremacy of shape and color in art over external stimuli. He shared some points of view with his fellow Russian Wassily Kandinsky, whom he knew (see p. 3 for a work). But while Kandinsky (who worked in Germany) painted brash, expressive works, Malevich's constant urge to simplify makes him the more radical painter.

One of Fernand Léger's students, Tarsila do Amaral, took Léger's brand of Cubism back to her home in Brazil in 1924, where she participated in a Modern art movement called Anthropophagism. The nearly unpronounceable word means cannibalism, because that is what she thought Brazilian artists should do: cannibalize European styles and let them nourish Brazilian artists, so they could create something new.

Her painting titled ABAPORU shows the influence of Léger's tubular figures as they overlap in an ill-defined flat space. The work's title is a word from an indigenous Brazilian language. It means "The One Who Eats," suggesting both the alleged cannibalism of Brazil's ancient peoples, and also the artist's modern version. The idea that artists could cannibalize the European styles had great influence on other Latin American artists as they explored Modernism elsewhere on that continent.

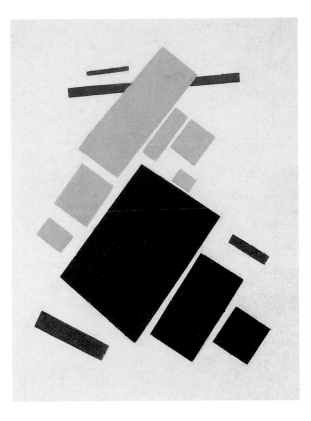

616 Kasimir Malevich.
SUPREMATIST COMPOSITION: AIRPLANE FLYING. 1915. (dated 1914). Oil on canvas, 22⅞" × 19" (58.1 × 48.3 cm).
The Museum of Modern Art New York. Acquisition confirmed in 1999 by agreement with the Estate of Kazimir Malevich and made possible with funds from the Mrs. John Hay Whitney Bequest (by exchange). Photograph © 2002 The Museum of Modern Art.

617 Tarsila do Amaral.
ABAPORU. 1928.
Oil on canvas, 34" × 29".
Museo de Arte Latinoamericano, Buenos Aires.

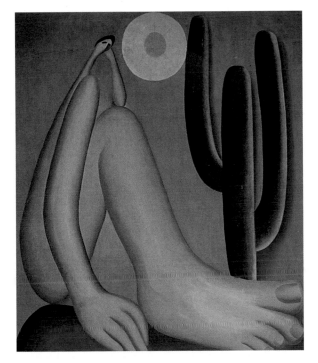

BUILDING A NEW SOCIETY

Several art movements emerged in the years after World War I. Pioneer abstractionists felt that the nonrepresentational language of form they were creating would provide an ideal basis for the utopian society they sought. Constructivism, in Russia, focused on developing a new visual language for a new industrial age. De Stijl, in Holland, advocated the use of basic forms, particularly rectangles, horizontals, and verticals. Both movements spread throughout Europe and were adapted by the Bauhaus in Germany.

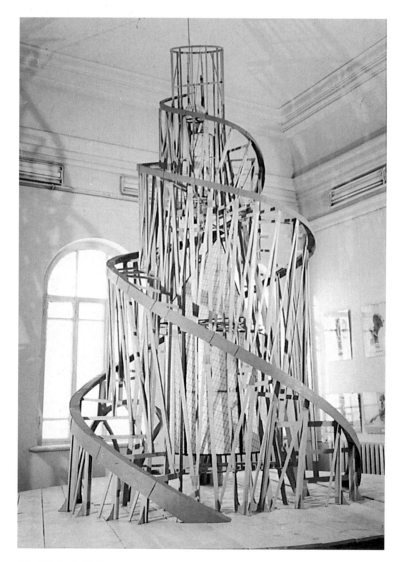

618 Vladimir Tatlin.
MODEL FOR MONUMENT TO THE
THIRD INTERNATIONAL. 1919–1920.
Photograph: Sovfoto/Eastfoto
© Estate of Vladimir Tatlin/Licensed by VAGA, NY

Constructivism

Constructivism was a revolutionary sculptural movement that began in Russia, inspired in part by abstraction of Malevich and others. Seeking to create art that was relevant to modern life in form, materials and content, Constructivists began making the first nonrepresentational constructions out of such modern materials as plastic and electroplated metal.

The Constructivists were in concert with the Cubists in rejecting the traditional view of sculpture as a static volume defined by mass and created by modeling and carving. The name of the movement came from their preference for constructing planar and linear forms that suggested a dynamic quality and, whenever possible, contained moving elements. Mass had previously been the main element in sculpture; with the Constructivists, space became primary.

Vladimir Tatlin's MODEL FOR MONUMENT TO THE THIRD INTERNATIONAL embodies many Constructivist ideas. Indebted about equally to Cubist sculpture and to the Eiffel Tower, this daring structure was intended to be 1,300 feet high. Built primarily of steel and glass, with its structure on the outside, it was to house inside it three office buildings that would rotate at varying speeds: once an hour, a day, and a month. The double spiral ramps symbolized the ascent of humanity to a new stage of evolution, which Tatlin thought was the new Communist state then being established in Russia. The monument would reflect the dynamism and progress of that social experiment. Tatlin's model was widely exhibited in Europe, but the project was too revolutionary to be realized.

Supported by the majority of artists, the Russian government of the middle 1920s decided to tolerate only art that the public could easily understand. A number of Modern artists then realized that they must work elsewhere to develop and promote their ideas. By leaving Russia, they were able to make a contribution to international sculpture, design, and painting.

De Stijl

Another of the many movements inspired by the formal qualities of Cubism was *De Stijl* (The Style). In 1917, a small group of Dutch artists, led by painter Piet Mondrian, began to employ nonrepresentational geometric elements in a group style that involved both two- and three-dimensional art forms. (See p. 97 for a discussion of the concept of a group style.) Their goal was the creation of a world of universal harmony. Armed with the newly independent vocabulary of "pure" visual form, they created an inventive body of work in painting, architecture, furniture, and graphic design.

Mondrian's evolution as an artist represents the origin and essence of De Stijl. Working to free painting completely from both the depiction of nameable objects and the expression of personal feelings, he developed an austere style based on the expressive potential of fundamental visual elements and their relationships. He sought to create a new aesthetic that would provide a poetic vitality capable of setting standards of harmony for the new technological age.

From 1917 until his death in 1944, Mondrian was the leading spokesperson for an art reflecting universal order. For Mondrian, the universal elements were straight lines, the three primary colors, and rectangular shapes. He reduced painting to four elements: line, shape, color, and space. COMPOSITION WITH RED, YELLOW, AND BLUE, completed in 1930, exemplifies his totally nonrepresentational later work.

In 1940, Mondrian left Europe for New York, where he spent the last four years of his life. New York was a joy to him because it seemed to be a celebration of human achievement. He was fascinated by the geometric, technological world, its neon lights, and especially the staccato rhythms of American jazz. His enthusiasm for music, dancing, and his new environment gave his final paintings, such as BROADWAY BOOGIE-WOOGIE, a pulsing, rhythmic energy.

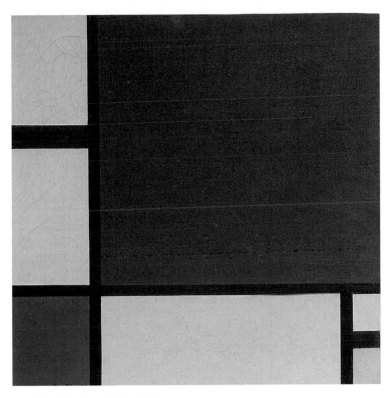

619   Piet Mondrian (1872–1944).
COMPOSITION WITH RED, YELLOW, AND BLUE. 1930.
Oil on canvas. 19" × 19".
Private collection, Zurich. Switzerland. Giraudon/Art Resource, NY.
© 2002 Artists Rights Society (ARS), NY/Beeldrecht, Amesterdam.

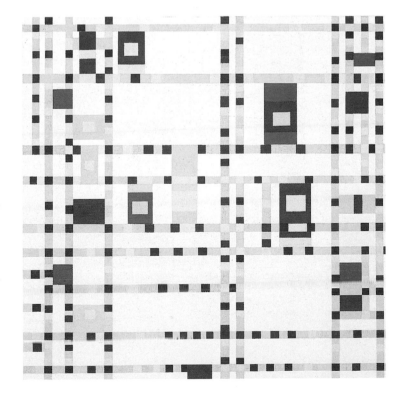

620   Piet Mondrian.
BROADWAY BOOGIE-WOOGIE. 1942–1943.
Oil on canvas. 50" × 50" (127 × 127 cm).
The Museum of Modern Art, New York. Given anonymously.
Photograph © 2002 The Museum of Modern Art, NY. © 2002
Artists Rights Society (ARS), NY/Beeldrecht, Amsterdam.

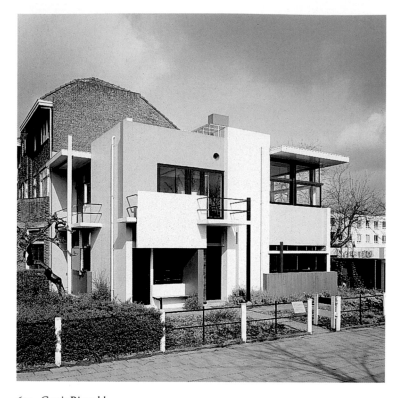

621 Gerrit Rietveld.
SCHRÖDER HOUSE, UTRECHT. 1924.
Centraal Museum Utrecht, The Netherlands.
© 2002 Artists Rights Society (ARS), NY/Beeldrecht, Amsterdam.

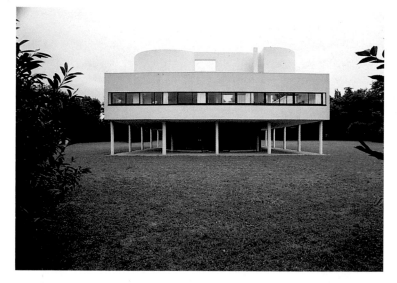

622 Le Corbusier.
VILLA SAVOYE. Poissy, France. 1928–1930.
© 2002 Artists Rights Society (ARS), NY/ADAGP, Paris/FLC.
Photograph: Prithwish Neogy.

International Style Architecture

The search for a new visual language engaged architects as well as painters. Ideas about form developed by the Constructivists, the De Stijl artists, and previously by American architect Frank Lloyd Wright, were carried further by architects stimulated by the structural possibilities of modern materials including steel, plate glass, and reinforced concrete.

About 1918, a new style of architecture emerged simultaneously in Germany, France, and the Netherlands and came to be called the *International Style.* Steel-frame curtain-wall construction methods made it possible to build structures characterized by undecorated rectilinear planes. Extensive use of glass in non-load-bearing exterior walls brought abundant light and flexible space to interiors. In many International Style buildings, asymmetrical designs created dynamic balances of voids and solids. Unlike Frank Lloyd Wright, who blended houses with their natural surroundings, architects working in the International Style deliberately created a visual contrast between natural and manufactured forms.

Dutch architect Gerrit Rietveld was associated with Mondrian and De Stijl. His SCHRÖDER HOUSE in Utrecht, built for a woman, was an early classic of the International Style. Its design of interacting planes, spaces, and primary colors are closely related to Mondrian's paintings.

In France, the principles of the International Style of architecture were basic to the early work of leading architect, city planner, and painter Charles-Édouard Jeanneret, known by the pseudonym Le Corbusier. His drawing on page 240 represents his philosophy that a basic structural frame allows complete freedom in terms of the placement of interior and exterior walls. His most significant early work is the VILLA SAVOYE. The second-floor living area seems to float on slender reinforced-concrete columns above a smaller, deeply recessed entrance and service area on the ground. A private interior terrace opens to the sky on the upper level, joined to the living room by floor-to-ceiling panels of plate glass. Le Corbusier called his houses "machines for living."

The International Style buildings designed by Walter Gropius for the Bauhaus (see page 240) clearly reflect the concepts of both De Stijl and Constructivism. Today, the spare style that Mondrian and the Bauhaus helped to initiate can be seen in the design not only of buildings, but of books, interiors, clothing, furnishings, and many other articles of daily life.

Architect and designer Ludwig Mies van der Rohe was one of the most influential figures associated with the Bauhaus and the International Style. In 1938, he emigrated to the United States. There, his ideas and works strongly influenced the post–World War II development of the rectilinear, metal-and-glass-sheathed, steel-frame skyscraper.

623 Max Beckmann.
 DEPARTURE. 1932–1933.
 Oil on canvas; triptych, center panel 7'¾" × 45⅜"; side panels each 7'¾" × 39¼".
 The Museum of Modern Art, New York. Given anonymously (by exchange).
 Photograph: © 2002 The Museum of Modern Art, NY.
 © 2002 Artists Rights Society (ARS), NY/VG Bild-Kunst, Bonn.

POLITICAL PROTEST

Expressionism continued as the dominant trend in German art despite the fact that the Bridge and Blue Rider groups were largely dispersed by the devastation of World War I. Reactions to the war and the social and political situation of the 1920s and 1930s led to some of Expressionism's major works. Two exponents of German Expressionism and its values were Käthe Kollwitz and Max Beckmann.

Beckmann's experience working in a field hospital during World War I led him to shift from his early Impressionist-influenced mode to an expressive style in which he could speak forcefully of the misery he saw.

After years of public acceptance and professional success, Beckmann was classified as a degenerate artist by the Nazis. Fifteen German museums were forced to remove his paintings. He painted his great triptych (three-panel painting) DEPARTURE in secret during the early years of the Nazi regime. Suggestions of Christian symbolism include the altarpiece-related triptych format and a Christlike fisherman-king. Beckmann's moral

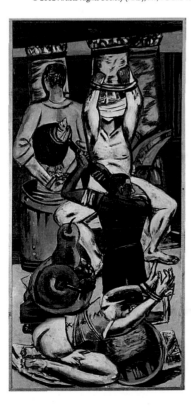
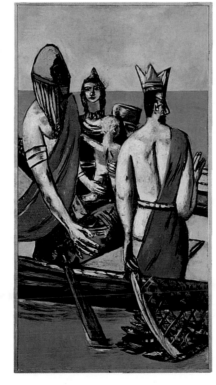
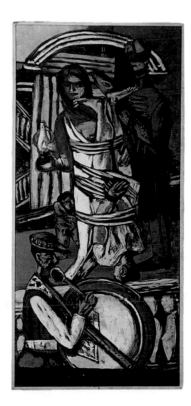

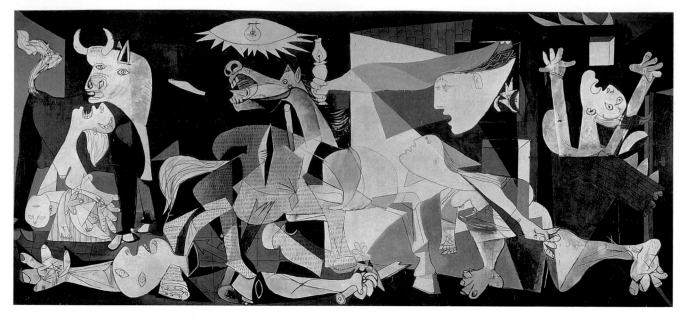

624   Pablo Picasso. GUERNICA. 1937.
Oil on canvas. 11'5½" × 25'5¼".
Museo Nacional Centro de Arte Reina Sofía. Giraudon/At Resource, NY.
© 2002 Estate of Pablo Picasso/Artists Rights Society (ARS), NY.

content and symbolism are presented with the direct vigor of a circus sideshow. When the triptych was shipped out of Germany in 1937, Beckmann fooled Hitler's inspectors by labeling it "Scenes from Shakespeare's *Tempest*." Beckmann, forced to go into hiding, fled first to Holland, then to the United States. In retrospect, we see DEPARTURE as an allegory of good and evil as well as a portrayal of Beckmann's personal experience and desire to escape a society gone mad.

Hitler's rise to power in the 1920s and 1930s all but destroyed the German Expressionist movement, although many of its leading artists had already left Germany by then. The Bauhaus, the most influential art school of the early twentieth century, was closed by the Nazis in 1933. In 1938, about five thousand paintings and sculptures and twelve thousand prints and drawings by German Expressionist artists were confiscated.

Between 1936 and 1939, while Hitler held power in Germany, Spain underwent a bloody civil war. With military support from Germany and Italy, General Francisco Franco emerged as dictator.

Throughout the 1920s and into the 1930s, Spanish-born Pablo Picasso continued to produce innovative drawings, paintings, prints, posters, and sculptures. Many of these works were filled with strange distortions and dislocations related to Surrealism. In 1937, while the Spanish Civil War was in progress, Picasso was commissioned by the doomed Spanish democratic government to paint a mural for the Paris Exposition. For several months he was unable to begin work. Suddenly, on April 26, 1937, he was shocked into action by the "experimental" mass bombing of the defenseless Basque town of Guernica. To aid his bid for power, General Franco had allowed Hitler to use his war machinery on the town as a demonstration of military power. The bombing, which leveled the fifteen-square-block city center, was the first incidence of saturation bombing in the history of warfare. Hundreds died, and more were strafed with machine gun fire from German aircraft as they fled the city into neighboring fields.

Picasso, appalled by this brutality against the people of his native country, called upon all his powers to create the mural-size painting GUERNICA. Although Picasso's GUERNICA stems from a specific incident, it is a statement of protest against the senseless brutality of all war.

GUERNICA covers a huge canvas more than 25 feet long. It is painted in somber black, blue-blacks, whites, and grays. A large triangle embedded under the smaller shapes holds the whole scene of chaotic destruction together as a unified composition. GUERNICA combines Cubism's intellectual restructuring of form with the emotional intensity of earlier forms of Expressionism and Abstract Surrealism. Details show some of the personal symbolism Picasso used to portray ideas and feelings beyond the protest of a single incident. In dream symbolism, a horse often represents a dreamer's creativity. Here the horse is speared and is dying in anguish. Beneath the horse's feet a soldier lies in pieces; near his broken sword a faint flower suggests hope. Above, a woman reaches out from an open window, an oil lamp in hand. Near the old-fashioned lamp and above the horse's head is an eyelike shape with an electric light bulb at the center. Jagged rays of light radiate out from the bottom edge. The sun? An eye? Sometimes an eye representing the eye of God was painted on the ceiling of medieval churches. The juxtaposition between old and new sources of illumination could be a metaphor relating to enlightenment. God's eye, in this context, may symbolize the creative energy of God subverted by human beings for destructive rather than creative ends.

During the 1940s, while German forces occupied France, Picasso was allowed to paint in his studio in Paris even though his art was considered degenerate by the Nazis. One day German soldiers came to his door with a small reproduction of GUERNICA. They asked, "Did you do this?" Picasso replied, "No, you did."[8] On another occasion during the war, Picasso remarked that "painting is not done to decorate apartments. It is an instrument of war for attack and defense against the enemy."[9]

Unfortunately, the type of aerial bombardment that he decried in GUERNICA soon became a common strategy, used by all sides in the war.

Between the world wars, a socially and politically committed form of art called *social realism* became common in many countries. This style took many forms, but they all include a retreat from the

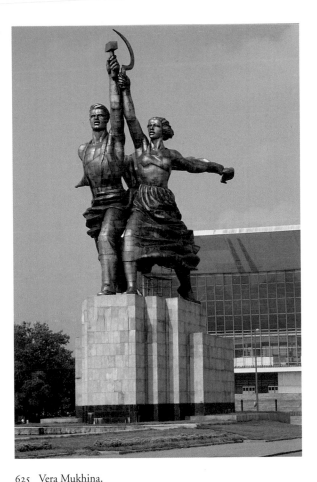

625 Vera Mukhina.
MONUMENT TO THE PROLETARIAT
AND AGRICULTURE. 1937.
Stainless steel. 78' high.
All-Russia Exposition Gounds, Moscow.
Photograph: Sovfoto/Eastfoto, TASS.

radical innovations of Modern art and a desire to communicate more readily with the public about social causes and issues. In Nazi Germany and in Communist Russia and China this style became an officially sponsored "norm" for art, which artists could ignore only if they did not care to have a successful career. A good example of Russian Social Realism is Vera Mukhina's MONUMENT OF THE PROLETARIAT AND AGRICULTURE. Her huge statue, which depicts a male factory worker and a female farm worker in stainless steel 78 feet high, was first exhibited at the Paris World's fair of 1937. Later set up in Moscow, it expresses the hopes and ideals of the workers' state, which came crashing down in 1991 with the fall of the Communist regime.

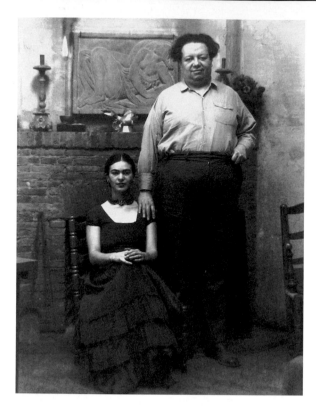

626 DIEGO RIVERA AND
FRIDA KAHLO. c. 1930.
Peter A. Juley & Son Collection.
Smithsonian American Art
Museum, Washington, DC.

"The earliest memory I have," Diego Rivera wrote, "is that I was drawing."[10] He drew all the time on anything he could find. His astonished parents found that the only way to contain him was literally: they gave him a room with walls covered in blackboard and an endless supply of crayons, chalks, and pencils. The magical hours he spent there must have made a deep impression on the budding artist, for he became, in time, the most celebrated muralist of our century.

Rivera grew up in Mexico City. From age twelve he attended a prestigious art school. At twenty he won a scholarship to Europe. He settled in Paris, where he quickly caught up with the latest developments in art and became known as a leading Cubist painter.

In 1918, Rivera entered a difficult period of searching and growth. He abandoned Cubism and looked increasingly back over art history. In medieval cathedrals and Renaissance frescoes art had a task—an important story to tell to an entire society. Was this no longer possible? Did art now have to appeal only to the few? Did modern society have no great tasks for its artists?

An answer came in 1920 from Mexico. The revolution begun in 1911 had triumphed at last, and the new government planned an ambitious public works program. It called on its artists to beautify public buildings with murals that would celebrate the country's rich cultural heritage and teach a largely illiterate people the history of their own political struggle.

Rivera returned to Mexico the next year. He later recalled,

My homecoming produced an aesthetic exhilaration which it is impossible to describe. . . . In everything I saw a potential masterpiece—the crowds, the markets, the festivals, the marching battalions, the working men in the shops and in the fields.[11]

Rivera believed that the New World should declare its artistic independence from Europe. He looked to the living tradition of folk art and to the ancient works of the Aztec, Maya, and other American civilizations to provide healthy roots for new artistic growth. His finest frescoes are vast compositions that orchestrate hundreds of figures and incidents with narrative clarity. Invited to work in the United States, Rivera was fascinated by the genius of bridges, skyscrapers, industrial buildings, and machine-design. "Your engineers are your great artists," he told a (North) American friend.[12]

Rivera had three wives over the course of his life, including the painter Frida Kahlo (see page 429), whom he married in 1929. They made a striking couple—he was enormous, she was slight. Her parents said it was "like a marriage between an elephant and a dove."[13] Yet in temperament she was every inch his equal. Although their relationship was often stormy, hers was the only opinion he sought—and listened to—about his work in progress.

Rivera provided lasting statements on the social issues of his day. He is remembered as a champion of the overworked and underpaid.

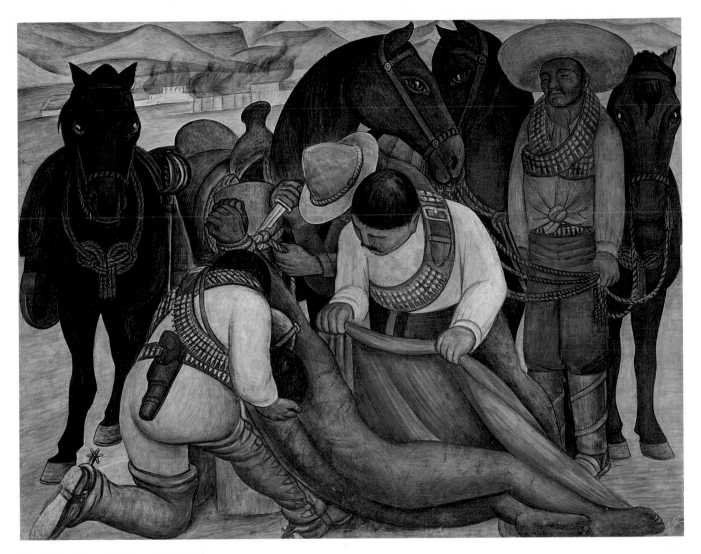

627 Diego Rivera (Mexican, 1886–1959).
THE LIBERATION OF THE PEON. 1931. Fresco. 73" × 94¼".
Philadelphia Museum of Art. Given by Mr. and Mrs. Herbert Cameron.1943–46–1. Photo by Graydon Wood, 1994.
© 2002 Banco de Mexico Diego Rivera & Frida Kahlo Museums Trust. Av. Cinco de Mayo No. 2, Col. Centro, Del.
Cuauhtemoc 06059, Mexico, D.F. Reproduction authorized by the Instituto National de Bellas Artes and Literature.

Mexican social realism took the form of mural paintings that embodied the ideals of the revolution of 1910–1917, when a popular uprising overthrew a long-entrenched dictatorship. The Mexican government in 1921 embarked on a program to pay artists an hourly wage to decorate public buildings with murals that spoke to the people about the recent revolution and about their long history. Inspired by the murals of the Italian Renaissance and by pre-Columbian wall paintings of ancient Mexican cultures, the muralists envisioned a national art that would glorify the traditional Mexican heritage and promote the new post-revolutionary government. Diego Rivera's fresco THE LIBERATION OF THE PEON is a good example that deals with a common event of the revolution: the landlord's house burns in the background, while revolutionary soldiers untie the peon from a stake and cover his naked body, which is scarred by repeated lashings. This work is a variation of a large painting on a wall of the Ministry of Education in Mexico City. Both Diego Rivera and fellow muralist José Clemente Orozco visited the United States, where they influenced American mural painting (a work by Orozco is pictured on page 84).

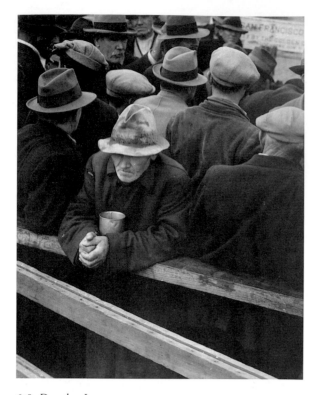

628 Dorothea Lange.
WHITE ANGEL BREAD LINE, SAN FRANCISCO. 1933.
Photograph.
The Oakland Museum of California, City of Oakland.
Copyright The Dorothea Lange Collection. Gift of Paul S. Taylor.
A67.137.33001.1

During the Depression years of the 1930s, the United States government maintained an active program of subsidy for the arts. The Works Progress Administration (WPA) commissioned painters to paint murals in public buildings, and the Farm Security Administration (FSA) hired photographers and filmmakers to record the eroding dustbowl and its workworn inhabitants. With government support, the art of documentary filmmaking reached a peak of achievement.

Photographer Dorothea Lange documented the helplessness and hopelessness of the urban unemployed. Her sensitive study, A DEPRESSION BREADLINE, SAN FRANCISCO, is a powerful image of a difficult period.

AMERICAN PAINTING

In the 1930s, the spread of the Depression, along with political upheaval, helped motivate artists in America to search for both national and personal identity. American artists were caught between a largely indifferent public at home and a feeling, both at home and abroad, that American art was merely provincial. In this atmosphere of cultural inferiority, an American regionalism developed, based on the idea that artists in the United States could find their identity by focusing attention on the subject matter that was uniquely American.

629 Edward Hopper
(American, 1882–1973).
NIGHTHAWKS. 1942.
Oil on canvas.
30" × 60"
(84.1 × 152.4 cm).
The Art Institute of Chicago,
Friends of American Art Collection.
1942.51. Photograph
© 1998 The Art Institute of
Chicago. All rights reserved.

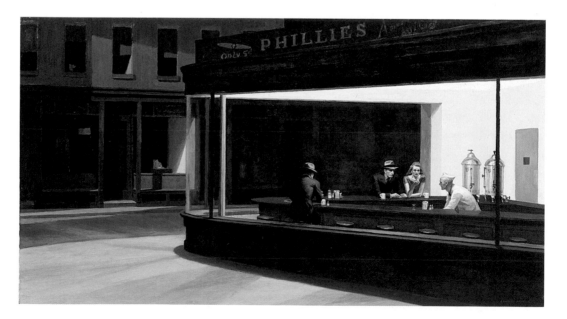

Edward Hopper made several trips to Europe between 1906 and 1910, but he remained apart from European avant-garde movements as he portrayed the loneliness that permeated much of American life. NIGHTHAWKS shows Hopper's fascination with the mood of people in a particular place and time. The haunting effect of his paintings comes largely from his carefully organized compositions and his emphasis on controlled use of light and shadow areas. Both Hopper and the Impressionists were interested in light, but for different purposes: Hopper employed it to clarify and organize structure, whereas the Impressionists used light in ways that seemed to dissolve structure.

Regional painter Grant Wood studied art in Paris in the early 1920s. Although he never worked with Cubist or Expressionist ideas, he did identify with modern trends and began making freely brushed paintings derived from Impressionism. After years of little success, Wood returned to his birthplace in rural midwestern America and dedicated himself to memorializing the unique character of the land, the people, and their way of life. Childhood experience as an Iowa farm boy and the perception of his artistic maturity combined to make Grant Wood an astute observer of rural America.

Wood's personal style of crisp realism was inspired by the paintings of the Northern Renaissance masters such as van Eyck, Dürer, and Holbein. He also drew on American folk painting and the characteristically stiff, long-exposure portraits taken by late nineteenth-century photographers. Wood, like van Eyck, calculated every aspect of design and all details of the subject matter to enhance the content of his paintings.

The idea for the famous painting AMERICAN GOTHIC came to Wood when he saw a modest farmhouse built in Carpenter Gothic style. The restrained color, simplification of round masses such as trees and people, and use of detail are typical of Wood's paintings. The two figures are echoed in the pointed-arch window shapes. Vertical lines and paired elements dominate. For example, the lines of the pitchfork are repeated in the man's overalls and shirt front. The upright tines of the fork seem

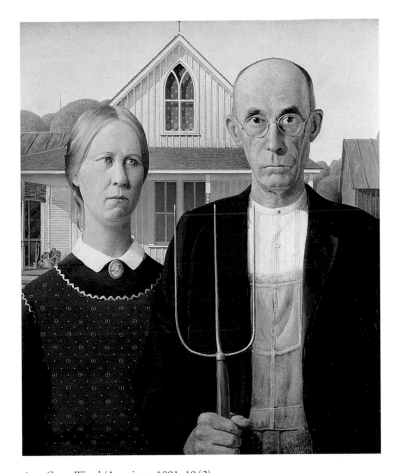

630 Grant Wood (American, 1891–1942).
AMERICAN GOTHIC. 1930.
Oil on beaverboard. 29⅞" × 24⅞"
(74.3 × 62.4 cm).

to symbolize the pair's firm, traditional stance and hard-won virtue. Wood's AMERICAN GOTHIC has become a national icon that speaks clearly to many. It continues to spark a wealth of responses.

The most forceful spokesperson for an original American art was Thomas Hart Benton. In 1908, Benton went to Paris to study European art. He and Rivera both painted in modern styles early in their careers, but Benton's conservative midwestern background and traditional art training led him to be more impressed with the work of Italian Renaissance masters than with the French moderns.

After 1918, Benton worked to create an art that was American in both form and content—a

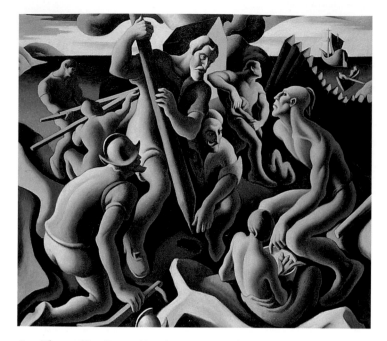

631 Thomas Hart Benton (American, 1889–1975).
PALISADES, from the series AMERICAN HISTORICAL EPIC. c. 1919–1924.
Oil on cotton duck on aluminum honeycomb panel. 66⅛" × 72".
Photograph Jamison Miller © 1996 The Nelson Gallery Foundation. The Nelson-Atkins Museum of Art, Kansas City, Missouri. Bequest of the artist. © T. H. Benton and R. P. Benton Testamentary Trusts/Licensed by VAGA, NY.

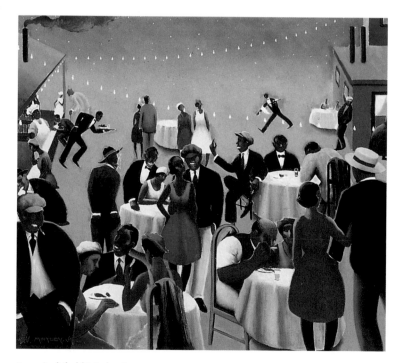

632 Archibald Motley, Jr.
BARBECUE. 1934.
Oil on canvas. 36¼" × 40⅛".
Howard University Gallery of Art, Washington, D.C.

realistic style that would be easily understood by all, based on the depiction of American themes. Some of the strength for both figures and composition came from the influence of Michelangelo. Benton transformed Renaissance and modern influences in a highly personal style in which all forms are conditioned by strong curvilinear rhythms. The push and pull of shapes in shallow space, emphasized by contrasting light and dark edges, shows what Benton learned from Cubism.

PALISADES was part of a series of paintings, titled AMERICAN HISTORICAL EPIC, which Benton never completed. In contrast to conventional histories that feature great men, Benton wanted to create a people's history, one that depicted the actions of ordinary people on the land. Here, the European colonizers are staking out and dividing up the land, while the Indians, in contrast, are sharing their knowledge of growing corn, which the newcomers will need for survival.

There was also a strong social realist movement among African Americans during this period, a part of the cultural resurgence of the Harlem Renaissance, which included music and literature as well as the visual arts. One of the principal painters was Archibald Motley, Jr., who created BARBECUE in 1934. The work is ebullient and full of motion, and also shows an interest in how figures look under artificial light. Motley specialized in depicting all aspects of the urban black experience, including on occasion gamblers and drinkers during Prohibition. Such subject matter did not endear him to pretentious art patrons, but Motley replied, "I have tried to paint the Negro as I have seen him and as I feel him, in myself without adding or detracting, just being frankly honest."[13]

The emigration of large numbers of people to the United States just before and after World War II brought about a reexamination of the role of art in modern life. Expatriated European artists brought new ideas and purposes to America. As a result, the regional, narrative styles of painters such as Thomas Hart Benton lost favor, and New York became the new center for the exchange of creative energies among artists from many nations.

CHAPTER TWENTY-FOUR

ACCELERATED CHANGE: MODERN ART AFTER 1945

At the end of World War II, Europe lay in ruins—financially, emotionally, and physically. Many prominent European artists had fled from Nazi oppression to the United States, which emerged from the war economically strong and optimistic. This influx from Europe coincided with America's newfound confidence. As artists flocked to New York in the way they once had to Paris, the city became, for the first time, a center of artistic innovation.

Among the artists who settled in New York were Mondrian, Léger, Duchamp, Dali, and Hans Hofmann. They worked, taught, exhibited, and generally stirred things up, opening new possibilities for American artists. Modernism was no longer a distant, European phenomenon; its leading practitioners were in the United States.

War had altered the consciousness of the developed world in subtle but profound ways. The Nazi genocide machine had taken human cruelty to a new low, and the atomic bomb gave humankind terrifying new powers: People were now living in a world they had the technology to destroy. These conditions formed the background for art and life in Europe and the United States for most of the postwar period.

ABSTRACT EXPRESSIONISM AND RELATED ART

The horrors of World War II, in which millions of people lost their lives in battle or in concentration camps, led artists to rethink the relationship between art and life. Again, dislocations caused by war led artists to explore visual realms other than the representational and narrative. The result was *Abstract Expressionism*, a culmination of the expressive tendencies in painting from van Gogh and Gauguin through Fauvism and German Expressionism. Immediate inspiration came from the motives and spontaneous methods of Surrealism—in particular, the abstract Surrealism of Miró.

German artist Hans Hofmann was one of the most influential of the European immigrants. Both a painter and a well-loved teacher, he made a major contribution to new American art from the 1930s through the 1950s. Hofmann stressed a balance between spontaneity and formal structure, and this approach became a model for generations of American painters. By 1940, he had begun using poured paint and bold color. IDOLATRESS I (see next page) is an excellent example of his style from the war years. The bright colors of the work reflect the artist's early studies with Henri Matisse, and the flat organic shapes recall Picasso's cubism of the GUERNICA period of the 1930s. IDOLATRESS I appears to have been painted in a headlong rush of energy, yet it also shows careful composition in the precarious balance of suggestive shapes.

Hofmann and other European émigrés influenced many American painters, leading them to move away from the dominant realist styles of the 1930s and experiment with more expressive and

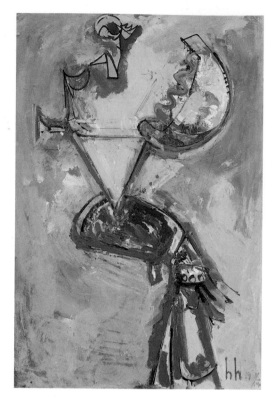

633 Hans Hofmann. IDOLATRESS I. 1944.
Oil and aqueous media on Upsom board.
60⅛" × 40⅛".
University of California, Berkeley Art Museum; gift of the artist. Photo:
by Benjamin Blackwell. (©) Regents of the University of California.

inventive ways of creating art. The unparalleled crisis of the World War also led them to move away from public issues of history and social comment that Depression-era painting emphasized. As a result, they began to paint in styles that were both stylistically innovative and personal.

Jackson Pollock, the leading innovator of Abstract Expressionism, studied with Thomas Hart Benton in the 1930s. The rhythmic structure of Benton's style and Hofmann's early drip-and-pour techniques were influences on Pollock's poured paintings of the late 1940s and early 1950s. Searching for ways to express primal human nature, Pollock also studied Navajo sand painting and psychologist Carl Jung's theories of the unconscious.

The act of painting itself became a major part of the content of Pollock's paintings. Pollock created AUTUMN RHYTHM by dripping thin paint onto the canvas rather than brushing it on. By working on huge canvases placed on the floor, Pollock was able to enter the space of the painting physically and

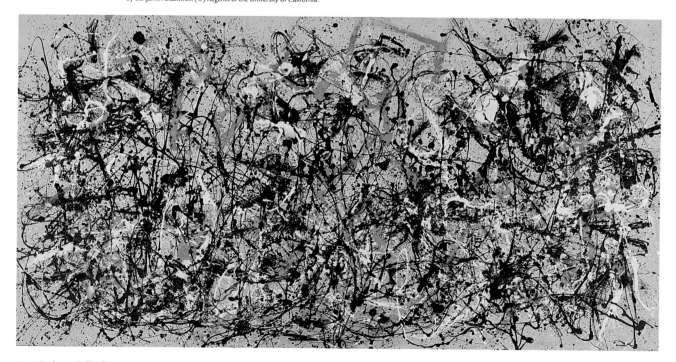

634 Jackson Pollock. AUTUMN RHYTHM. (NUMBER 30), 1950.
Oil on canvas. 105" × 207" (266.7 × 525.8 cm).
Signed and dated (lower right): Jackson Pollock 50.
The Metropolitan Museum of Art, George A. Hearn Fund, 1957. (57.92).
Photograph © 1985 The Metropolitan Museum of Art. (c) 2002 The Pollock-
Krasner Foundation/Artists Rights Society (ARS), New York.

psychologically. The huge format allowed ample room for his sweeping gestural lines. Pollock dripped, poured, and flung his paint, yet he exercised control and selection by the rhythmical, dancing movements of his body. A similar approach in the work of many of his colleagues led to the term *action painting*.

A different, but related, painting style that evolved at about the same time was *color field,* a term for painting that consists of large areas of color, with no obvious structure, central focus, or dynamic balance. The canvases of color field painters are dominated by unified images, images so huge that they engulf the viewer. They are not about environments; they are environments in themselves.

Mark Rothko is now best known as a pioneer of color field painting, although his early works of the 1930s were urban scenes. By the 1940s, influenced by Surrealism, he began producing paintings inspired by myths and rituals. In the late 1940s, he gave up the figure and began to work primarily through color. In works such as BLUE, ORANGE, RED Rothko was able to use color to evoke moods ranging from joy and serenity to melancholy and death. By superimposing thin layers of paint, he achieved a variety of qualities from dense or heavy to atmospheric and luminous. Rothko's paintings have a highly sensuous appeal and—due to their size—a monumental presence.

Helen Frankenthaler's work also evolved during the height of Abstract Expressionism. In 1952, she pioneered staining techniques as an extension of Jackson Pollock's poured paint and Mark Rothko's fields of color. Brush strokes and paint texture were eliminated as she spread liquid colors across horizontal, unprimed canvas. As the thin pigment soaked into the raw fabric, she coaxed it into fluid, organic shapes. Pale, subtle, and spontaneous, MOUNTAINS AND SEA marked the beginning of a series of paintings that emphasize softness and openness and the expressive power of color. The twenty-four-year-old Frankenthaler painted it in one day, after a trip to Nova Scotia. This large, influential painting is a pivotal work in the history of mid-twentieth-century art.

635　Mark Rothko.
BLUE, ORANGE, RED. 1961.
Oil on canvas. 90¼"× 81¼".
Hirschhorn Museum and Sculpture Garden, Smithsonian Institution, Washington, D.C. Gift of Joseph H. Hirschhorn Foundation (1966). Photograph: Lee Stalsworth. © 2002 Kate Rothko Prizel and Christopher Rothko/Artists Rights Society (ARS), NY. HMSG 66.4420.

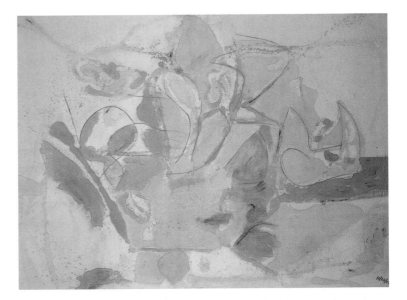

636　Helen Frankenthaler.
MOUNTAINS AND SEA. 1952.
Oil on canvas. 7'2⅝" × 9'9¼".
Collection of the artist, on loan to The National Gallery of Art, Washington, D.C.
© Helen Frankenthaler 1999.

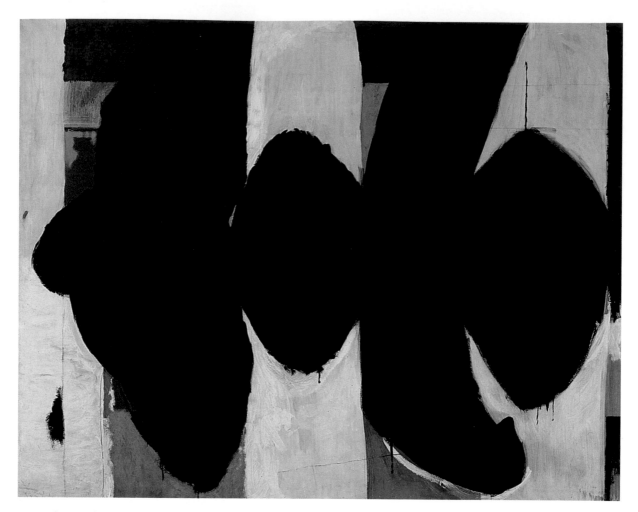

637　Robert Motherwell. ELEGY TO THE SPANISH REPUBLIC NO. 34, 1953–1954.
Oil on canvas. 80" × 100".
Albright-Knox Art Gallery, Buffalo, NY. Gift of Seymour H. Knox, Jr. (1957).
© Dedalus Foundation, Inc./Licensed by VAGA, NY, NY.

Robert Motherwell's series of paintings titled ELEGY TO THE SPANISH REPUBLIC is permeated with a tragic sense of history. Unlike many Abstract Expressionists, Motherwell began with a specific subject as his starting point. His elegies brood over the destruction of the young Spanish democracy by General Franco in the bloody Spanish Civil War of the 1930s. Heavy black shapes crush and obliterate the lighter passages behind them.

The influence of Expressionist and Surrealist attitudes on Willem de Kooning's work is evident in his spontaneous, emotionally charged brushwork and provocative use of shapes. Throughout his career, De Kooning emphasized abstract imagery, yet he felt no compulsion to ban recogniz-

able subject matter. After several years of working without subjects, he began a series of large paintings in which ferocious female figures appear. These canvases, painted with slashing attacks of the brush, have an overwhelming presence. In WOMAN AND BICYCLE, the toothy smile is repeated in a savage necklace that caps tremendous breasts. While it explodes with the energies of Abstract Expressionism, this work is controversial among feminists for the horrendous image of women that it presents.

Norman Lewis was an African-American artist who participated in Abstract Expressionism from its inception. Like most of the Abstract Expressionists, during the 1930s Lewis painted in a social realist style, depicting urban poverty that he observed

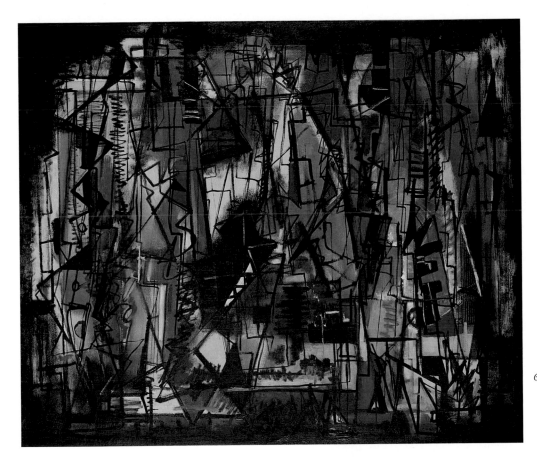

639 Norman Lewis. (1909-1979).
UNTITLED. c. 1947.
Oil on canvas. 30" × 36" signed.
Private Collection, NY.
Courtesy Michael Rosenfeld Gallery, NY
and Landor Fine Arts.

in his neighborhood of Harlem. During and after World War II, he was increasingly influenced by Modern art. His UNTITLED work from 1947 documents his shift toward a more spontaneous and improvisational style. Lewis's art differs from other Abstact Expressionists in that it seems more poetic and reserved. In addition, his painting at times shows traces of nature or, as we see in this work, city life.

In the ten years following the end of the war, European art differed from American art in two principal ways: First, many Europeans ventured less into abstraction, often retaining some trace of the human figure in their art. A prime example of this is the sculptor Alberto Giacometti, whose MAN

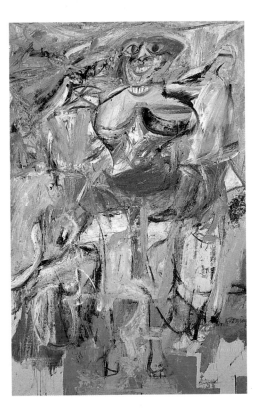

638 Willem de Kooning. WOMAN AND BICYCLE. 1952–1953.
Oil on canvas. 76½" × 49" (194.3 × 124.5 cm).
Collection of Whitney Museum of Art, New York. Purchase, 55.35.
Photgraph © 2000: Whitney Museum of American Art, NY. (c) 2002 Willem
de Koonig Revocable Trust/Artists Rights Society (ARS), NY.

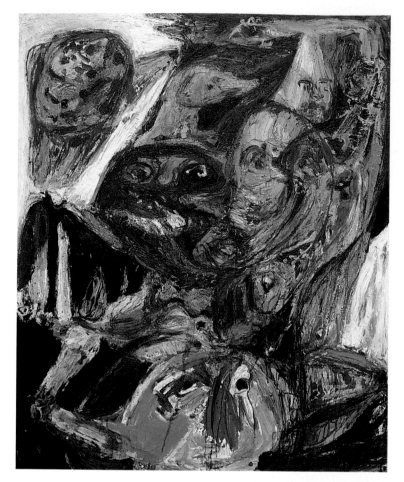

POINTING is illustrated on page 46. In painting, Danish artist Asger Jorn made explosive figural works that often combined heavily worked paint surfaces with ironic titles. In his painting THE GREAT VICTORY, instead of a scene of triumph we see a group of leering, monstrous heads emerging from murky depths. With their art, Giacometti and Jorn often commented on the basic aloneness of individuals, and the disappointments of an exhausted and devastated postwar European society.

Second, some Europeans were more innovative than Americans in their use of materials. Alberto Burri, for example, used burlap sacks in a series of works in the early 1950s. His SACK WITH RED includes tattered pieces of fabric crudely stitched to the surface of the canvas. During the war, the artist served in the Italian army as a doctor; his use of bright red is meant to symbolize blood, and the burlap represents a temporary bandage. Burlap had a further symbolic significance in that it held grain that the United States sent to Italy as postwar foreign aid. These burlap works are Burri's effort to symbolically bind up Europe's wounds after the havoc of the war.

640 Asger Jorn.
THE GREAT VICTORY. 1955–1956.
Oil on canvas. 127 × 104.5 cm.
Photograph: Lars Bay.
© Silkeborg Kunstmuseum, Silkeborg, Denmark.

641 Alberto Burri. (b. 1915).
SACKING AND RED, 1954.
Various media on canvas. 86.4 × 100.3 cm.
Tate Gallery, London/Art Resource, NY.

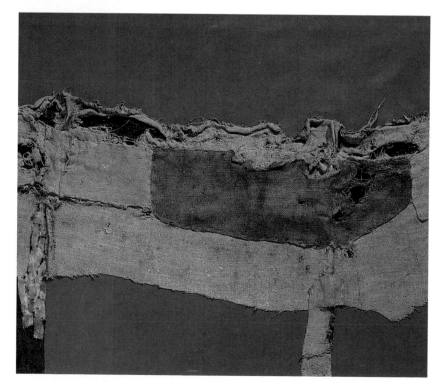

David Smith, for many critics the most important American sculptor of the postwar period, took the formal ideas of Cubism and gave them an American vigor. His assembled metal sculpture balanced formal qualities with the elemental energy of Abstract Expressionist painting. His use of factory methods and materials provided new options for the next generation of sculptors. Smith's late work included the stainless steel CUBI series, based on cubic masses and planes balanced dynamically above the viewer's eye level. The scoured surfaces of the steel reflect light in ways that seem to dissolve their solidity. Smith intended the sculpture to be viewed outdoors in strong light, set off by green landscape.

PHOTOGRAPHY AND ARCHITECTURE AT MID-CENTURY

In the late 1940s, at the dawn of the age of television, camera imagery began to proliferate into what has become today's mass-media environment. During this period some "art" photographers made their own contributions to the way we see. Both straight and manipulated approaches to image making were employed as photographers explored new frontiers of experience. There was an active exchange of visual ideas among photographers and painters, another phase in the dialog between these artists that started when photography was invented.

Harry Callahan, one of the most original and influential photographers of this time, continually renewed his vision and awakened viewers' awareness in the process. Working from an impersonal exploratory base, he achieved images expressing "my feelings and visual relationships to life within me and about me."[1] His MULTIPLE TREES is a dance of moving energy related to, yet different from, the dynamic action communicated in the paintings of Abstract Expressionists.

Social documentary photography took a leap forward in the postwar years in the hands of Swiss-born Robert Frank. He crisscrossed the United

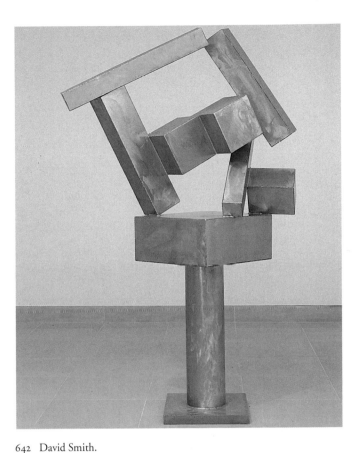

642 David Smith.
CUBI XVII. 1963.
Polished stainless steel. 107¾" × 64⅜" × 38⅛".
Dallas Museum of Art.
The Eugene and Margaret McDermott Fund.
© Estate of David Smith/Licensed by VAGA, NY.

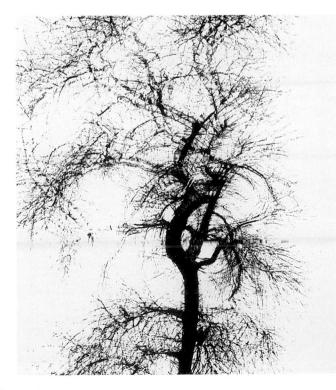

643 Harry Callahan. (American, b. 1912).
MULTIPLE TREES. 1949.
Gelatin silver multiple exposure
photograph. 9½" × 9 7/16" (24.1 × 24 cm)

The Museum of Fine Arts, Houston. Museum purchase with funds provided by the Museum Collectors. ACC: 87.168.
© The Estate of Harry Callahan, courtesy of Pace/McGill, Gallery, NY.

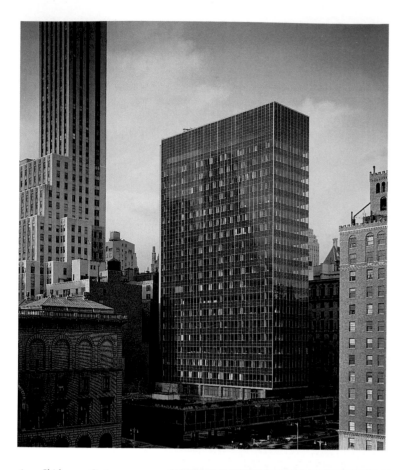

States in the middle 1950s, photographing telling images of loneliness and obsolescence in his prosperous adopted country. TROLLEY, NEW ORLEANS is an interesting composition of rectangles and reflections that resonate against the shape of the image as a whole. Only after looking for awhile at this finely crafted print do we notice that the passengers are segregated by race. Frank published his pictures in a 1958 portfolio called *The Americans* which also set a new standard of quality for the printing of photography books.

Most architects at mid-century were still involved with the International Style (introduced on page 240), but in a more reserved and austere way. LEVER HOUSE in New York City pointed the way for future office buildings for the next twenty-five years: It is a steel-and-glass box that looks slick and convenient and modern. Most American cities have such buildings; another is pictured on page 241. Later architects would revolt against it, but for a generation this ultra-clean look represented the image of the American corporation.

645 Skidmore, Owings, and Merrill.
LEVER HOUSE. 1952.
New York City.

Ezra Stoller © Esto. All rights Reserved.

644 Robert Louis Frank (American, b. 1924).
TROLLEY, NEW ORLEANS.
From THE AMERICANS.
Silver gelatin print.

Restricted gift of Photography Gallery, 1961.943. Photograph ©2000 The Art Institute of Chicago.

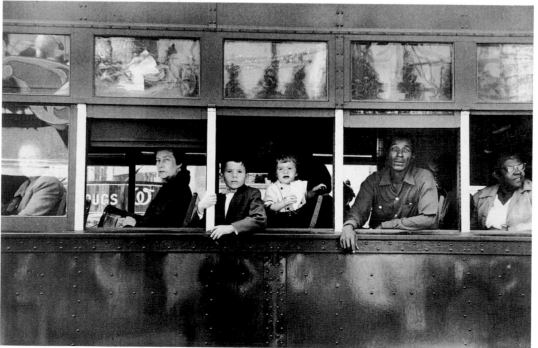

NEO-DADA

Most leading artists of the 1940s and 1950s chose not to deal with recognizable subject matter. They avoided any reference to the appearance of the environment in which they lived. In the mid-1950s, a few young artists began to acknowledge, confront, and even celebrate the visual diversity of the urban scene; they wanted to move beyond the exclusive, personal nature of Abstract Expressionism.

Under the influence of avant-garde composer John Cage, who urged artists to pay attention to the lives they were living, Robert Rauschenberg began combining ordinary objects and collage materials with abstract expressionistic brushwork in what he called "combine-paintings." The essence of creative thinking involves combining elements of the expected world in order to make an unexpected, previously unthinkable new thing. Such is the startling presence of Rauschenberg's MONOGRAM. What is a stuffed, long-haired angora goat doing standing in the middle of a collage-painting with a tire around its middle? The artist is acting as a prankster, in the spirit of the Surrealist artists such as Magritte (see page 428).

Rauschenberg's CANYON recalls the work of Dada artists; the strange assemblage offers glimpses of seemingly unrelated objects and events and acts as a symbol for the wild juxtapositions of modern life. Instead of blocking out the chaotic messages of city streets, TV, and magazines, Rauschenberg incorporates the trash of urban civilization in his art, renewing our sense of mystery.

In the early 1960s, with the aid of the new technique of photographic screen printing, Rauschenberg brought together images from art history and documentary photographs. In TRACER (see next page) he combined expressionist painting with modified parts of art reproductions and news photographs so that art history, the Vietnam War, and street life interact with one another. Just as we can move from sports to dinner to televised wars and sitcoms, Rauschenberg's work assembles the unrelated bits and pieces of everyday experience.

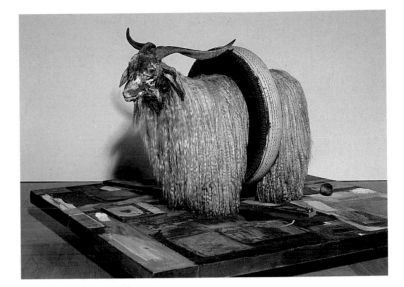

646 Robert Rauschenberg.
MONOGRAM. 1955–1959.
Freestanding combine. 42" × 64" × 64½".
Moderna Museet, Stockholm.
© Robert Rauschenberg/Licensed by VAGA, NY.

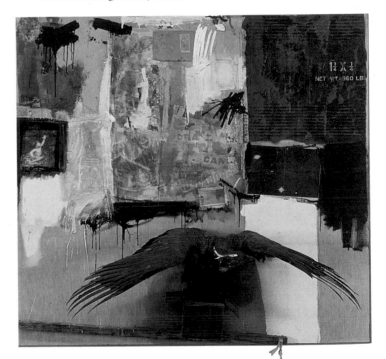

647 Robert Rauschenberg.
CANYON. 1959.
"Combine painting" of oil on canvas, wood, printed matter, stuffed eagle, pillow tied with cord, etc.
81¾" × 70" × 24".
Photograph courtesy of Leo Castelli Gallery, New York.
© Robert Rauschenberg/Licensed by VAGA, NY.

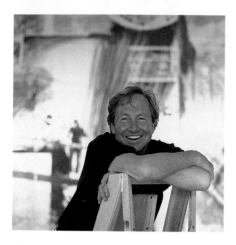

649   ROBERT RAUSCHENBERG.
Photograph: © Ed Chappell.

If it weren't for the Navy, Robert Rauschenberg might never have discovered art at all.

One-quarter Cherokee, Rauschenberg was born in Port Arthur, Texas. He had little exposure to art before he was seventeen, and originally he intended to become a pharmacist. Growing up, he enjoyed drawing, but "art" was something for other people.

He spent three years in the Navy during World War II, working in a naval hospital. One day, while on leave in California, he wandered into his first museum. Among the paintings he saw were two he recognized from reproductions on playing cards. "That was the first time I realized you could actually be an artist," he recalled.[2]

But how to become one? Again chance stepped in: a girlfriend in Los Angeles was returning home to Kansas City; if she could get him into the Kansas City Art Institute, would he come with her? Rauschenberg studied at the Institute for about a year. Next he went briefly to Paris (he thought all artists were supposed to). Then he spent time at the experimental Black Mountain College in North Carolina, where he met and began working with composer John Cage. Eventually, he settled in New York, where he supplemented his income by designing window displays for fashionable Fifth Avenue stores. He continued to work with Cage, and he met Jasper Johns. Rauschenberg and Johns became the inspiration for a new avant-garde, a new synthesis of art and ordinary life.

New York now has hundreds of galleries for new art, but in the 1950s there were only five. The community of artists was small, intense, and poor, yet there was high energy and optimism. Rauschenberg experimented endlessly. When he ran out of canvas, he painted on whatever came to hand—most notoriously, his old bed quilt. Soon he was using ordinary objects almost exclusively, connecting art to daily life in a direct, exhilarating way. Anything that looked interesting could find itself in a Rauschenberg.

In 1964, he received international acclaim when he won the grand prize for painting at the Venice Biennale.

In the 1980s he began to devote most of his energy (and income) to a project called ROCI (pronounced "rocky"), the Rauschenberg Overseas Cultural Interchange. ROCI grew out of the artist's experiences in the 1970s, when he collaborated with traditional craftsworkers and artists in China, India, and Tibet. He was struck by how little the peoples of the world know about each other and how making art together improved communication.

His first project in the new millennium was *Synapsis Shuffle.* This huge work consists of 52 panels of collaged imagery gathered over the artist's long career. At the first exhibition of the work in mid-2000, he invited twelve celebrities to arrange the panels in any order they wished.

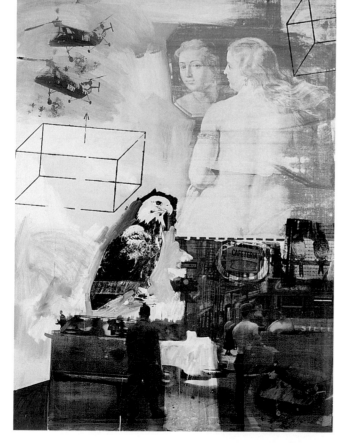

648   Robert Rauschenberg (American, born 1925). TRACER. 1963. Oil and silkscreen on canvas, 84⅛" × 60".

Photograph: Jamison Miller © 2002 The Nelson Gallery Foundation. The Nelson-Atkins Museum of Art, Kansas City, Missouri. (Purchase) F84-70. © Robert Rauschenberg/Licensed by VAGA, New York, N.Y.

Rauschenberg often discussed art-making with Jasper Johns during their formative years in the 1950s. Whereas Rauschenberg's work is filled with visual complexity, Johns' work is deceptively simple. His large early paintings were based on common graphic forms such as targets, maps, flags, and numbers. He was interested in the difference between signs (emblems that carry meaning) and art. In Johns' work, common signs play a dual role: they have the power of Abstract Expressionist forms in their size, bold design, and painterly surface qualities, yet they represent familiar objects and thus bring art back to everyday life. In his TARGET WITH FOUR FACES, a sign (target) becomes a painting, while the faces (sculpture) are perceived as a sign.

As with Man Ray's THE GIFT (page 424), Johns' common subjects are now objects of contemplation. His irony relates back to Dada and forward to Conceptual Art. The Neo-Dada works of Johns and Rauschenberg provided a bridge between Abstract Expressionism and later Pop Art. In fact, Johns and Rauschenberg are not Pop artists, but champions of art in an environment saturated with media-promoted icons of popular culture.

The Neo-Dada spirit also broke out in Europe, where in 1958 Yves Klein greeted visitors at an empty gallery, in a show he called "The Void." Italian artist Piero Manzoni turned people into "works of art" by signing their bodies and clothing. Niki de Saint Phalle made paintings and collages, and then symbolically killed them by piercing them with nails, darts or even gunshots. ST. SEBASTIAN OR THE PORTRAIT OF MY LOVE contains one of her husband's shirts and neckties below a dart board. The artist drove dozens of nails into the shirt, and then threw darts at the board. These works by Saint Phalle and others continue the irreverent aspects of the spirit of Dada.

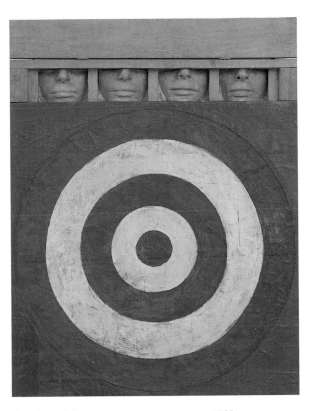

650 Jasper Johns, TARGET WITH FOUR FACES. 1955.
Assemblage: encaustic on newspaper and collage on canvas with objects, 26" × 26", surmounted by four tinted plaster faces in wood box with hinged front. Box, closed, 3¾" × 26" × 3½". Overall dimensions with box open, 33⅝" × 26" × 3".
The Museum of Modern Art, NY. Gift of Mr. and Mrs. Robert C. Scull. Photograph: © 2002 The Museum of Modern Art, NY. © Jasper Johns/Licensed by VAGA, NY.

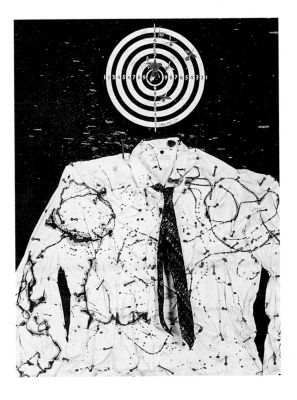

651 Niki de Saint Phalle.
ST. SEBASTIEN, OR THE PORTRAIT OF MY LOVE. 1960.
Oil, fabric, darts, and nails on wood and dart board.
28½" × 21¾" × 2¾".
Collection of the artist.
© 2000 Artists Rights Society (ARS), NY/ADAGP, Paris.

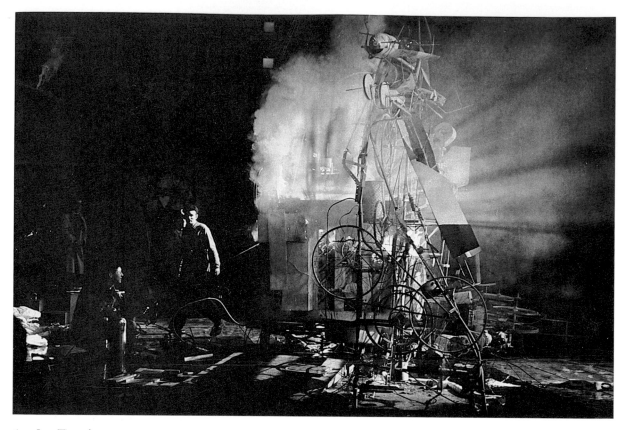

652   Jean Tinguely.
HOMAGE TO NEW YORK: A SELF-CONSTRUCTING,
SELF-DESTRUCTING WORK OF ART. 1960.
Photograph: David Gahr.
© 2002 Artists Rights Society (ARS), NY/ADAGP, Paris.

EVENTS AND HAPPENINGS

Artists have continued to extend the boundaries of the visual arts until they can no longer simply be defined as aesthetic objects. In addition to easel paintings, there are now room-size installation pieces; in addition to traditional sculpture, there are earthworks. And, in addition to stationary art objects, there are living, moving art events.

For Swiss sculptor Jean Tinguely, life was play, movement, and perpetual change. Tinguely made machines that do just about everything except work in the manner we expect. Although much kinetic art has celebrated science and technology, Tinguely enjoyed a mocking yet sympathetic relationship to machines and machine fallibility. "I try to distill the frenzy I see in the world, the mechanical frenzy of our joyful, industrial confusion."[3]

In 1960, Tinguely built a large piece of mechanized sculpture that he put together from materials gathered from junkyards and stores in and around New York City. The result was a giant assemblage designed to destroy itself at the turn of a switch—which it did in the courtyard of the Museum of Modern Art in New York City on March 17, 1960. The environmental sculpture was appropriately called HOMAGE TO NEW YORK: A SELF-CONSTRUCTING, SELF-DESTRUCTING WORK OF ART. Tinguely's HOMAGE TO NEW YORK was an event, similar in its effect to a Happening.

Happenings are cooperative events in which viewers become active participants in partly planned, partly spontaneous performances that combine loose scenarios and considerable improvisation. Strictly speaking, Happenings are drama with "structure but no plot, words but no dialogue, actors but no characters, and above all, nothing logical or continuous."[4] Unlike Dada and Surrealist events, the first Happenings were frequently nihilistic, without a relieving sense of humor. No help was given the viewer, who was expected to find his or her own answers. Happenings led to more controlled, more focused types of art events.

The term Happening was first used by Allan Kaprow in the late 1950s. There were no spectators at Kaprow's Happening, HOUSEHOLD. At a preliminary meeting, participants were given parts. The action took place at an isolated rural dump, amid smoldering piles of refuse. The men built a wooden tower on a trash pile while the women constructed a nest on another mound. During the course of a series of interrelated events, the men destroyed the nest and the women retaliated by pulling down the men's tower. In the process, participants gained a new perspective on the theater of life in our time.

POP ART

Inspired by Neo-Dada, Pop Art emerged as human contact with the natural world was rapidly being cut off by a flood of manufactured objects, advertising signs, and urban sprawl. Poet Ogden Nash summed up the situation: "I think that I shall never see / A billboard lovely as a tree. / Perhaps unless the billboards fall, / I'll never see a tree at all."[5]

The term Pop is short for "popular," for art that deals with the images of commercially-driven "mass culture." Like the Dadaists and Neo-Dadaists before them, Pop artists wanted to challenge cultural assumptions.

Whereas Abstract Expressionism had celebrated each artist's individual feelings and personal touch, Pop artists created cool, mechanical images that hid all evidence of their hands at work. Commercial art, long denigrated by fine artists, became a source of inspiration. Pop painters used photographic screenprinting and airbrush techniques to achieve the surface characteristics of such anonymous mass-produced imagery as advertising, food labels, and comic books.

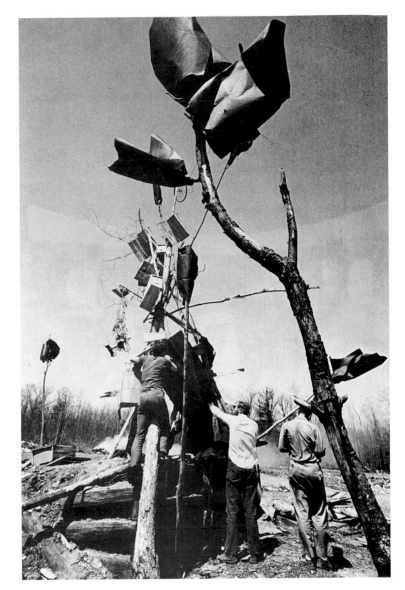

653 Allan Kaprow.
HOUSEHOLD. Happening commissioned by Cornell University, performed May 1964.
Photograph: Solomon A. Goldberg.

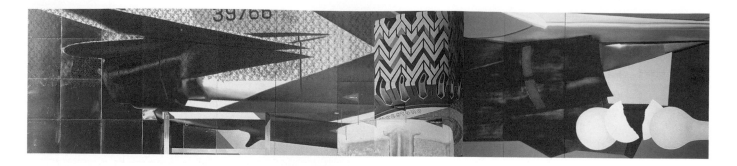

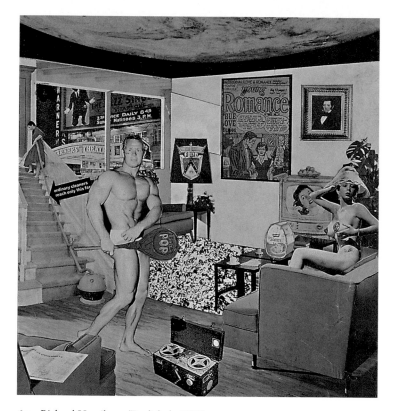

654 Richard Hamilton, (English, b. 1922).
JUST WHAT IS IT THAT MAKES TODAY'S HOMES SO
DIFFERENT, SO APPEALING? 1959.
Collage. 10¼" × 9¾".
Kunsthalle, Tübingen, Germany.
© 2002 Artists Rights Society (ARS), NY/DACS, London.

Pop Art appeared almost simultaneously in London and New York. In London, a group of young artists made collages with images cut from popular, mostly American, magazines. Decades earlier, Dada artists such as Hannah Höch (see page 424) had produced photomontages with similar raw material. But for the Londoners, the purposes were different. In 1957, English artist Richard Hamilton published a somewhat tongue-in-cheek list of characteristics of Pop Art for the London artists who were beginning to work in this vein. The list includes qualities of contemporary mass culture these artists chose to address. Hamilton wrote that Pop Art should be:

> *Popular (designed for a mass audience)*
> *Transient (short-term solution)*
> *Expendable (easily forgotten)*
> *Low-cost*
> *Mass-produced*
> *Young (aimed at youth)*
> *Witty*
> *Sexy*
> *Gimmicky*
> *Glamorous*
> *Big business*[6]

Pop Art's media sources include the comic strip, the advertising blowup, the famous-name-brand package, and the visual clichés of billboard, newspaper, movie theater, and television. Elements from all these mass media are included in Hamilton's collage JUST WHAT IS IT THAT MAKES TODAY'S HOMES SO DIFFERENT, so appealing? Hamilton's work is a hilarious parody of the superficiality and materialism of modern popular culture. In it, we

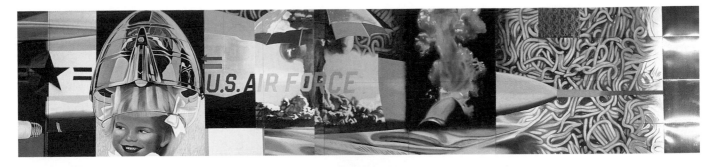

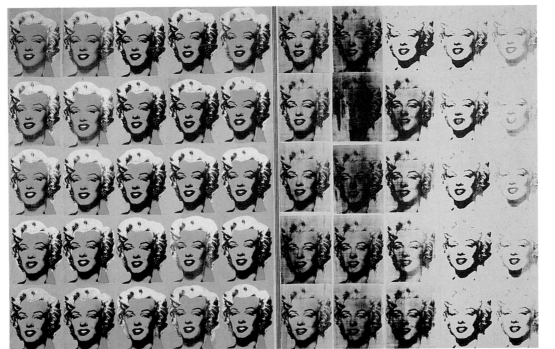

655 James Rosenquist.
F-III. 1965.
Oil on canvas with
aluminum, four parts.
10' × 86'.
Private collection.
© James Rosenquist/Licensed
by VAGA, NY.

656 Andy Warhol.
MARILYN DIPTYCH. 1962.
Tate Gallery, London/Art Resource,
NY. © 2002 Andy Warhol
Foundation for the Visual
Arts/Artists Rights Society (ARS), NY.

see the word Pop along with the origins and images of the Pop style.

American artist James Rosenquist worked as a billboard painter after attending art school and college. Later, he incorporated his experiences in a mature style that presents impersonally rendered montages of contemporary American popular culture. He drew on the techniques and imagery of his sign painting experience, painting huge close-up details of faces, natural forms, and industrial objects with a mechanical airbrush.

Rosenquist's huge mural F-III filled all four walls of the Leo Castelli Gallery in New York City when it was first presented in 1965. The image of an F-111 jet—an enormously expensive experimental fighter—sweeps across his wall-to-wall environment of 1960s Americana. Rosenquist mixed symbols of affluence and destruction in his billboard-sized painting, which includes—in addition to a jet fighter plane—a hair dryer, a child of ambitious parents, a tire, light bulbs, a beach umbrella, and a mushroom cloud from a nuclear bomb.

No American artist in the 1960s sparked more public indignation than Andy Warhol. He didn't invent Pop Art, but he was its most visible and controversial exponent. Like Rosenquist, Warhol began his career as a commercial artist. When he moved into the fine-art sphere in the early 1960s, Warhol came as an inventive subversive. MARILYN MONROE DIPTYCH is his meditation on celebrity

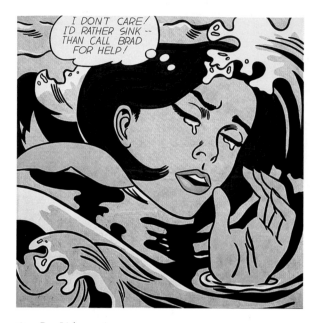

657 Roy Lichtenstein.
DROWNING GIRL. 1963.
Oil and synthetic polymer paint on canvas.
67⅝" × 66¾" (171.6 × 169.5 cm).
The Museum of Modern Art, New York. Philip Johnson Fund
and gift of Mr. and Mrs. Bagley Wright.
Photograph: © 2002 The Museum of Modern Art, NY.

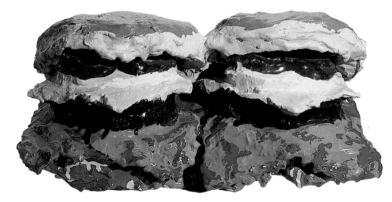

658 Claes Oldenburg.
TWO CHEESEBURGERS WITH EVERYTHING
(DUAL HAMBURGERS). 1962.
Burlap soaked in plaster, painted with enamel.
7" × 14¾" × 8⅝" (17.8 × 37.5 × 21.8 cm).
The Museum of Modern Art, New York. Philip Johnson Fund.
Photograph: © 2002 The Museum of Modern Art, NY.

status. The work gives us the actress's face 50 times over, in smudged black-and-white and garish color. The work seems to be telling us that a celebrity is a packaged commodity. This was news in the 1960s; today most people seem to realize it. Warhol's work called attention to the pervasive and uniformly insistent character of our commercial environment. The repetition of mass imagery has become our cultural landscape and our mythology; the "canned" popular image is a giant filter and equalizer of everything from processed foods to presidential candidates.

In DROWNING GIRL and other paintings, Roy Lichtenstein used comic book images with their bright primary colors, impersonal surfaces, and characteristic printing dots. His work is a commentary on a world obsessed with consumer goods, sex, and violence. He saw Pop Art as "involvement with what I think to be the most brazen and threatening characteristics of our culture, things we hate, but which are also powerful in their impingement on us."[7]

For several decades, Claes Oldenburg has been finding inspiration in the common, mass-produced artifacts of American society. His lumpy, gloopy TWO CHEESEBURGERS WITH EVERYTHING (known as DUAL HAMBURGERS) needs no explanation. There it is! Oldenburg enjoys taking mundane objects and remaking them into icons; see another project on page 39. Rather than turn away from the funk of neo-America, Oldenburg embraces it:

I am for Kool-Art, 7-UP art, Pepsi-art, Sunshine art, 39 cents art . . . Menthol art . . . Rx art . . . Now art . . . I am for U.S. Government Inspected Art, Grade A art, Regular Price art, Yellow Ripe art, Extra Fancy art, Ready-to-eat art.[8]

Since prehistoric times, art has helped people to describe, to understand, and to gain a sense of positive interaction with their surroundings. Cave dwellers—our ice-age ancestors—painted the animals that were a major feature of their environment; modern city dwellers draw inspiration from an urban environment, making art of the signs and symbols of popular culture.

MINIMAL AND HARD-EDGE

Pop Art was just one reaction against the self-absorbed quality of Abstract Expressionism. In the late 1950s and early 1960s, a number of artists who began as painters rejected painting because they felt it lacked the concreteness and presence of three-dimensional forms. However, their minimalist sculpture frequently has more in common with architecture and painting than it does with traditional sculpture. Instead of being emotionally charged, the works are nonsensual, impersonal, geometric structures.

Among those who went from painting to sculpture was Donald Judd. He worked with industrial materials such as sheet metal, aluminum, and molded plastics, which had not previously been used for art; his UNTITLED combines stainless steel and plexiglass. Judd was a leading artist and the major spokesman for the Minimalist movement. In his essay "Specific Objects," he wrote about the aims of his art:

It isn't necessary for a work to have a lot of things to look at, to compare, to analyze one by one, to contemplate. The thing as a whole, its quality as a whole, is what is interesting. . . . In the new work the shape, image, color, and surface are single, and not partial and scattered.[9]

Other painters and sculptors took different approaches. Some painters shared an interest in what they saw as the essence of painting: a flat, colored surface. Quick-drying acrylic paints, which were developed at this time, lend themselves to uniform application and to the use of tape to obtain shapes with precise edges—a style called *hard-edge.* This somewhat misleading term refers to works concerned not only with linear definition but with the relationship of color to form.

The most complete application of Minimalism occurs in sculpture, yet painters were also involved. As paintings became objects rather than reflections of objects, they began to function as environments in themselves instead of as representations of environments.

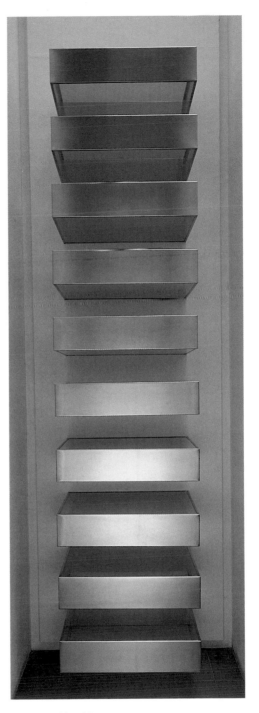

659   Donald Judd.
UNTITLED. 1967.
Stainless steel and plexiglass, ten units, 9⅛ × 40 × 31".
Height 14'3".
Collection of the Modern Art Museum of Fort Worth. Museum Purchase,
The Benjamin J. Tillar Memorial Trust.
© Donald Judd Foundation/Licensed by VAGA, New York, NY.

660 Ellsworth Kelly.
BLUE, GREEN, YELLOW, ORANGE, RED. 1966.
Oil on canvas 5 panels, Overall: 60" × 240 "
(152 × 609.6 cm).

Solomon R. Guggenheim Museum, NY. Photograph by Ellen Labenski
© The Solomon R. Guggenheim Foundation, New York. (FN 67.1833)

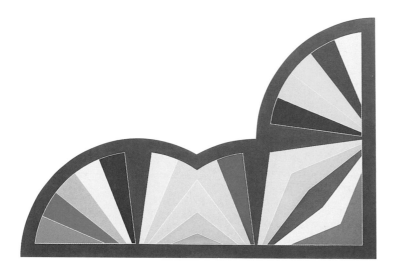

661 Frank Stella. (American, b. 1936).
AGBATANA III. 1968.
Fluorescent acrylic on canvas.
120" × 180 " (305 × 457 mm).
© Allen Memorial Art Museum, Oberlin College, Ohio. Ruth C.
Roush Fund for Contemporary Art and National Foundation for
the Arts and Humanities Grant, 1968. © 2002 Frank Stella/Artists
Rights Society (ARS), New York.

Ellsworth Kelly's bold paintings are richly hued studies of color and form. BLUE, GREEN, YELLOW, ORANGE, RED is self-explanatory in at least a superficial sense. At a deeper level, Minimalism is a quest to see if art can do without representation, storytelling, or personal feeling. If the work had curved lines, modeled color, or paint strokes, it would not be as pure. Rather, the subject seems to be color itself: how we respond to it, and how different colors interact with each other in our field of view. It is an optical experiment that throws away a great many of the traditional rules. Such quests for the essence of art motivated many in those years.

Frank Stella's rigorous hard-edge paintings of the 1960s emphasize the flatness of the picture plane and its boundaries. He treated his paintings like constructed objects rather than pictures. In AGBATANA III, Stella replaced the traditional rectangular format with a distinctive outer profile to further extend the concept of the surface as an object in its own right rather than as a field for illusions. External boundaries of the overall shape are arrived at internally. There is no figure-ground relationship; within the painting, everything is figure. Interwoven bands of both muted and intense colors pull together in a tight spatial weave.

Stella's intellectual conception of the painting-as-object brought him close to the realm of sculpture and aligned him with Minimalism. Minimalists admired the unified, all-at-once, nonrelational character of works by such artists as Pollock and Rothko. Minimalism depends on such a total impression. Formal properties are reduced to essentials.

CONCEPTUAL ART

During the last decades of the twentieth century, artists have reacted ever more quickly to each successive aesthetic movement. Pushing back the limits, the next reductive step after Minimalist art became no art at all—that is, an art of ideas rather than objects. Conceptual Art, in which an idea takes the place of the art object, was an outgrowth of Minimalism and a reaction to Pop. The Conceptual movement was heavily indebted to Marcel Duchamp, the first champion of an art of ideas.

Joseph Kosuth, the most rigorous early Conceptualist, was angered at the materialism of the art market and Pop Art's embrace of commercialism. In 1965, he produced ONE AND THREE CHAIRS, which consisted of a wooden chair, a photograph of the same chair, and a photographic enlargement of a dictionary definition of the word "chair."

Another notable Conceptual work was *Ice,* by Rafael Ferrer. In 1969, Ferrer put together an assemblage of ice blocks and autumn leaves on the Whitney Museum's entry ramp. When collectors complained about the ephemeral nature of his creation, Ferrer suggested that the iceman's bill might be collected as a kind of "drawing." In the true spirit of Conceptualism, this work is not illustrated here.

SITE WORKS AND EARTHWORKS

In the late 1960s, a number of artists working under the influence of Minimalism and Conceptual Art went beyond the prevailing idea of sculpture as a portable precious object. They began creating works that are inseparable from the sites for which they were designed. In *site-specific* works, the artist's sensitivity to the location determines the composition, scale, medium, and even the content of each piece.

When Bulgarian artist Christo was a student, he was alienated by the narrowness of his country's officially prescribed social realist art. His enthusiasm was aroused, however, by government-sponsored trips to the countryside, during which he and other art students advised farmers on how to improve the appearance of the landscape for foreigners traveling on the *Orient Express.*

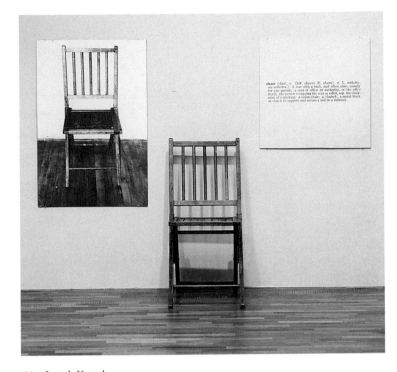

662 Joseph Kosuth.
ONE AND THREE CHAIRS. 1965.
Wooden folding chair, photographic copy of a chair, and photographic enlargement of dictionary definition of chair.
Chair, 32⅜" × 14⅞" × 20⅞" (82 × 37.8 × 53 cm).
Photo panel, 36" × 24⅛" (91.5 × 61.1 cm).
Text panel, 24" × 24⅛" (61 × 61.3 cm).
The Museum of Modern Art, New York. Larry Aldrich Foundation Fund.
Photograph: © 2002 The Museum of Modern Art, NY. ©2002 Joseph Kosuth/ Artists Rights Society (ARS) , New York.

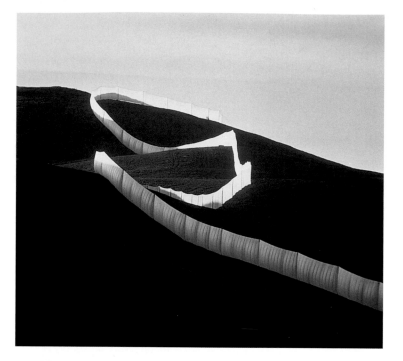

Christo first made his living as a portrait painter. Later, he joined a group of artists in Paris who were presenting objects as art rather than making painted or sculpted representations of objects. In collaboration with his wife he began wrapping in fabric objects ranging in size from a motorcycle to a mile of sea cliffs in Australia.

One of Christo and Jeanne-Claude's most ambitious projects was RUNNING FENCE, a temporary environmental artwork that was as much a process and an event as it was sculpture. The eighteen-foot-high white nylon fence ran from the ocean at Bodega Bay in Sonoma County, California, through 24.5 miles of agricultural and dairy land. RUNNING FENCE was a unique event, ultimately involving thousands of people. The project required political action, the agreement of landowners, and the help of hundreds of workers. They raised the necessary funds for this and other projects by selling drawings and collages of their works.

663 Christo and Jeanne–Claude. RUNNING FENCE.
Sonoma and Marin Counties, California. 1972–1976.
5.48 meters (18 ft.) × 39.4 kilometers (24½ miles)
Nylon fabric and steel poles.
© 1976 Christo.
Photograph: Wolfgang Volz.

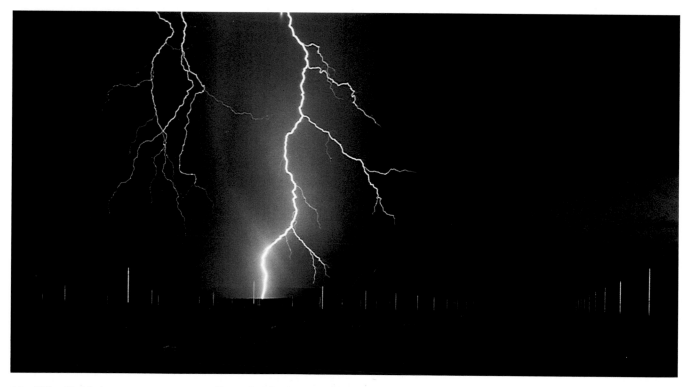

664 Walter De Maria. THE LIGHTNING FIELD. Quemado, New Mexico. 1977.
400 stainless-steel poles, average height 20'7"; land area 1 mile × 1 kilometer.
Photograph: John Cliett. © Dia Center for the Arts, New York.

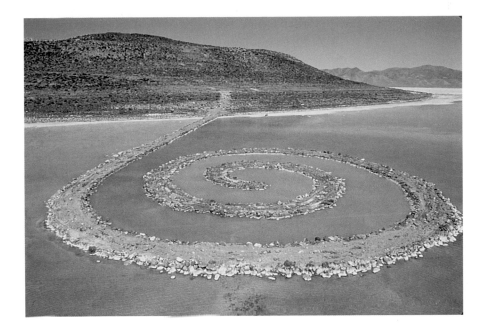

665 Robert Smithson.
SPIRAL JETTY.
Great Salt Lake, Utah. 1970.
Earthwork, Length 1500', width 15'.
© Gianfranco Gorgoni Art. © Estate of Robert Smithson/Licensed by VAGA, New York, NY.

The seemingly endless ribbon of white cloth made the wind visible and caught the changing light as it stretched across the gently rolling hills, appearing and disappearing on the horizon. The simplicity of RUNNING FENCE relates it to Minimalist art, but the fence itself was not presented as an art object. It was the focal point for a work that included the interweaving of people, process, object, and place.

Walter De Maria's THE LIGHTNING FIELD is a site sculpture designed to be viewed over a period of time. The work consists of four hundred stainless steel poles arranged in a rectangular grid over an area measuring one mile by one kilometer (0.6 mile) in west central New Mexico. The sharpened tips of the poles form a level plane, a kind of monumental bed of nails. Each of the poles can act as a lightning conductor during the electrical storms that occur frequently over the desert. Actual strikes are rare, however. Early and late in the day the poles reflect the sun, creating accents of technological precision in sharp contrast to the otherwise natural landscape. Purposely isolated from the art-viewing public, THE LIGHTNING FIELD combines aspects of both Conceptual and Minimalist art.

Viewers must arrange their visits through the Dia Foundation, which commissioned the piece. Once there, they are left to study the work and make their own interpretations.

Site works are environmental constructions, frequently made of sculptural materials, designed to interact with, but not permanently alter, the environment. *Earthworks* are sculptural forms made of materials such as earth, rocks, and sometimes plants. They are often very large, and they may be executed in remote locations. Earthworks are usually designed to merge with or complement the landscape. Many site works and earthworks show their creators' interest in ecology and in the earthworks of ancient America.

Robert Smithson was one of the founders of the earthworks movement. His SPIRAL JETTY, completed at Great Salt Lake, Utah, in 1970, has since gone in and out of view several times with changes in the water level. Its natural surroundings emphasize its form as willful human design. Although our society has no supportive, agreed-upon symbolism or iconography, we instinctively respond to universal signs like the spiral, which are found in nature and in ancient art.

The earthworks and site works movements have helped redirect relationships among architecture, sculpture, and the environment.

Although site-specific works can be commissioned, they are almost never resold unless someone buys the land of which they are a part. Artists who create conceptual art, earthworks, site works, and performance art share a common desire to subvert the gallery-museum-collector syndrome, to present art as an experience rather than as a commodity.

INSTALLATIONS AND ENVIRONMENTS

While some artists were creating outdoor earthworks and site works, others were moving beyond the traditional concepts of indoor painting and sculpture. Since the mid-1960s, artists from diverse backgrounds and points of view have fabricated interior installations and environments rather than portable works of art. Some installations alter the entire spaces they occupy; others are experienced as large sculpture; most of them assume the viewer to be a part of the piece.

James Turrell's installations challenge assumptions about the truth of what we see. By manipulating light and space, Turrell creates environments that cause shifts in viewers' perceptions. His work goes beyond the lean physical structures of Mini-

malism, and beyond Conceptualism's reliance on words and ideas, to dwell on the mysterious and at times awe-inspiring interaction of light, space, and time. Light becomes a tangible physical presence in works such as AMBA, where viewers are coaxed into paying attention to their own perceptions.

The work is about your seeing. It is responsive to the viewer. As you move within the space or as you decide to see it, one way or another, its reality can change.[10]

What really interests me is having the viewer make discoveries the same way the artist does . . . instead of having the viewer participate vicariously, through someone else. . . . You determine the reality of what you see. The work is the product of my vision, but it's about your seeing. The poles of the realm in which I operate are the physical limitations of human vision and the learned limits of perception, or what I call "prejudiced perception." Encountering these prejudices can be an amazing experience, and if someone can come to these discoveries directly, the way the artist does, the impact is greater and so is the joy.[11]

Turrell has also created what he calls Skyspaces by removing sections of ceilings to expose the sky. (One is illustrated on page 210.)

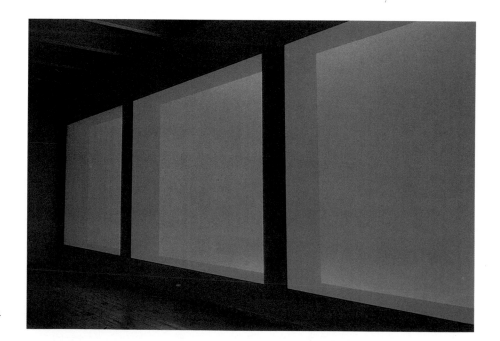

666 James Turrell.
AMBA. 1982.
Light installation.
Photograph courtesy of the artist.

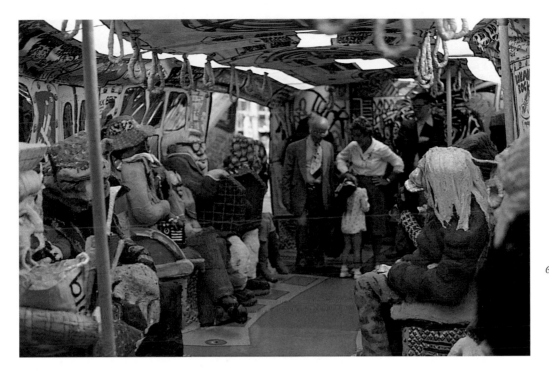

667 Red Grooms and the Ruckus
Construction Company.
RUCKUS MANHATTAN. 1976.
Mixed media installation.
Photographed at the Marlborough Gallery,
NY. © 2002 Red Grooms/Artists Rights
Society (ARS), NY.
Photograph: Duane Preble.

A far cry from Turrell's cool perceptual magic are the narrative, whimsical installations of Red Grooms. RUCKUS MANHATTAN, a refreshing, wildly humorous installation, was created by Grooms and a group called the Ruckus Construction Company. Grooms defines *ruckus* as "a beautiful southern word meaning a disorderly commotion."[12] The elaborate sculptural extravaganza featured caricatures of many famous New York City landmarks, including a 30-foot-tall World Trade Center, a subway train, the Woolworth Building, a Times Square porno shop, a Staten Island ferry one could "ride" on, and the Statue of Liberty in red platform shoes, holding a cigar in her raised right hand. The installation was a marvelous cartoon mix of theater, circus, carnival, parade, and amusement park. Realistic details were everywhere, including steam puffing out of manholes.

Viewers became a part of the work as they mingled with papier-mâché and cutout figures in a complex of walk-in buildings, shops, subway cars, and bridges that was installed first in Manhattan's Marlborough Gallery in the summer of 1976. As living people and papier-mâché people blended in the chaos of the minicity, it seemed as though all Manhattan and all the world were a giant cartoon.

EARLY FEMINISM

In the late 1960s, many women artists began to realize that they faced discrimination in their careers. It was rare for women to be taken seriously in artists' groups; galleries were more willing to exhibit the work of men than of women; and museums collected the work of men far more often than that of women. Moreover, it seemed to the early feminists that making art about their experience as women might doom them to obscurity in a male-dominated art world. In the early 1970s in New York and California, they began to take action.

Lucy Lippard, an influential art critic and a strong supporter of women artists, argues, "The overwhelming fact remains that a woman's experience in this society —social and biological—is simply not like that of a man. If art comes from the inside, as it must, then the art of men and women must be different, too."[13] The work of some women artists definitely is influenced by their gender and their interest in feminist issues.

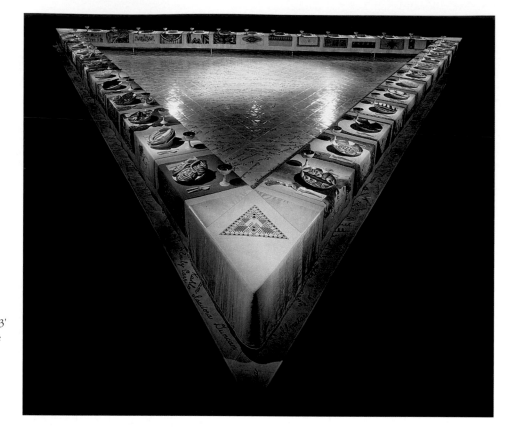

668 Judy Chicago. THE DINNER PARTY.
1979. Mixed Media, 48' × 48' × 42' × 3'
installed. Triangular table on white tile
floor.
Collection: The Dinner Party Trust.
Photograph: © Donald Woodman. © 2002 Judy
Chicago/Artists Rights Society (ARS), New York.

California feminists tended to work collaboratively, and to make use of media that have been traditionally associated with "craft work" and with women: ceramics and textiles. THE DINNER PARTY was a collaboration of many women (and a few men), organized and directed by Judy Chicago over a period of five years. This cooperative venture was in itself a political statement about the supportive nature of female experience, as opposed to the frequently competitive nature of the male.

A large triangular table contains place settings for thirty-nine women who made important contributions to world history. These run a wide gamut, from Egyptian Queen Hatshepsut to Georgia O'Keeffe. The names of 999 additional notable women of achievement are inscribed on ceramic tiles below the table. Each place setting includes a hand-embroidered fabric runner and a porcelain plate designed in honor of that woman. Some of the plates are painted with flat designs; others have modeled and painted relief motifs; many are explicitly sexual, embellished with flowerlike female genitalia.

The project proved to be as controversial as it was historically informative. Exhibited widely and to great acclaim after it was created, THE DINNER PARTY has never found a permanent home. When not on display, it sits crated in a warehouse.

East Coast feminists were more pointed in their protests. Some of them formed the group Women Artists in Revolution (WAR), which picketed museums. In response to private dealers who were reluctant to show work by women, they formed their own collaborative gallery, Artists in Residence (AIR). Nancy Spero, a leader in East Coast feminist circles, participated in both groups. Her work from the late 1960s and early 1970s used uncommon media such as paper scrolls, stencils, and printing to document subjects such as the torture and abuse of women. Her later scrolls, such as REBIRTH OF VENUS, attempt to present images of women different from those commonly seen in art.

In the segment illustrated here, an ancient statue of the love goddess Venus is split open to reveal a woman sprinter who runs directly toward the viewer. The contrast between the two images is difficult to miss. Woman as love object gives way to woman as achiever. (Compare this work to Botticelli's Renaissance BIRTH OF VENUS on p. 290.)

Feminists from both coasts combined their efforts with art historians in an effort to research, document, and celebrate the accomplishments of women artists of the past who had been neglected. One of the first woman artists "rediscovered" was still very much alive: sculptor Louise Bourgeois, whose work had been dealing with feminist issues for the preceding forty years.

Bourgeois depicts femaleness from within instead of looking at it from the outside, as male artists have done for centuries. Her sculpture describes the experience of being female in terms of organic shapes placed in tenuous relationships. It explores helplessness, fear, nurturing, and sexuality—as well as aggression, rage, and protest.

According to Bourgeois, the underlying motivations for her art stem from unresolved psychological conflicts of her childhood. In one of her most powerful works, THE DESTRUCTION OF THE FATHER, she alludes to the Greek myth of Cronos devouring his children. In this sculpture, Bourgeois turned to an ancient myth to exorcise her fear of her domineering father. "It is a very murderous piece," Bourgeois pointed out in her retrospective catalogue. Its inspiration lay in the "impulse that comes when one is under too much stress and one turns against those one loves the most."[14] Bourgeois's monumental rubber and mixed-media sculpture is profoundly threatening; it describes a deep division between genders and generations.

Researchers and art historians continue to uncover and publicize work by women throughout history, and each edition of this book has benefited from the effort by including more of them. Because Feminism has influenced most contemporary art movements since the 1970s, it makes little sense to separate feminist artists in discussions of the styles of the last quarter-century.

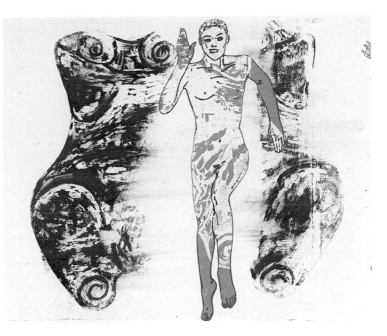

669 Nancy Spero.
REBIRTH OF VENUS. Detail. 1984.
Handprinting on paper. 12" × 62'.
Courtesy Jack Tilton Gallery and P.P.O.W., New York.
Photograph: David Reynolds

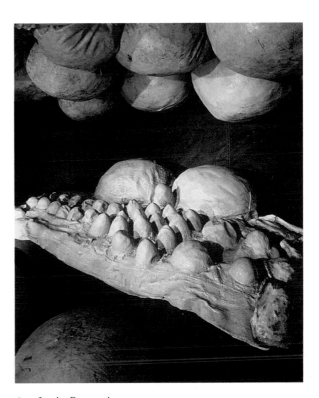

670 Louise Bourgeois.
THE DESTRUCTION OF THE FATHER. 1974.
Latex, plaster, wood and fabric. 93⅝" × 142⅝" × 97⅞".
Courtesy Cheim & Read, NY. Photograph: Estate of Peter Moore/Licensed by VAGA, NY.

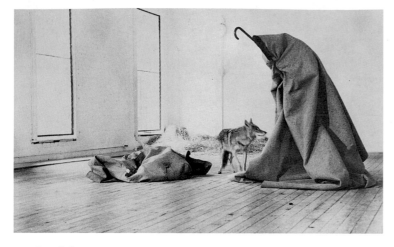

671 Joseph Beuys.
I LIKE AMERICA AND AMERICA LIKES ME. 1974.
Performance at Rene Block Gallery.
Courtesy: Ronald Feldman Fine Arts, New York.
Photograph: © Caroline Tisdall. © 2002 Artists Rights Society (ARS), NY/VG Bild-Kunst, Bonn.

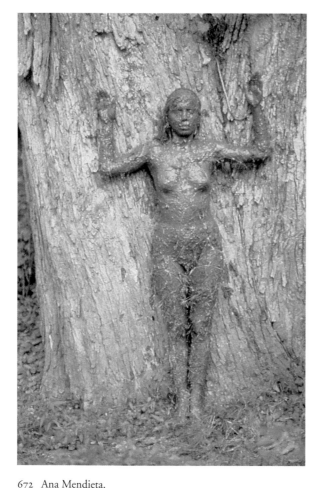

672 Ana Mendieta.
TREE OF LIFE SERIES. 1977.
Performance at Old Man's Creek, Iowa City, Iowa.
Photograph: Collection Ignacio C. Mendieta.
Courtesy of the estate of Ana Mendieta and Galerie Lelong, NY.
© Estate of Ana Mendieta.

PERFORMANCE ART

In performance art, artists do not use traditional media at all. Rather, they perform actions before an audience or in nature. Thus this art form contains both visual art and drama, and has historical antecedents in Futurist and Dada performances of the early twentieth century as well as to Expressionist painting. An Abstract Expressionist painting is the frozen record of an event (the act of making a painting). The next step was easy: eliminate the record and concentrate on the event itself. The record was in the remembered experience of the participants and in a few photographs. Forms of art such as Conceptual art, which emphasize idea and process over art-as-object, are related to current modes of performance art.

One of the most influential performance artists of the 1960s and 1970s was German-born Joseph Beuys. He carried out actions that resonated with deep symbolic significance, as if he were a healer or shaman. For one 1965 piece, he swathed his head in honey and gold leaf, and carried a dead rabbit around an art gallery explaining to it the paintings on view, touching the rabbit's lifeless paw to each. Some people, he later said, were as insensitive in their daily lives as the rabbit was in the art gallery. Arriving in New York for the first time in 1974, he immediately plunged into a work called COYOTE: I LIKE AMERICA AND AMERICA LIKES ME. Met at the airport by an ambulance, he was wrapped in felt and taken to a gallery, where he lived for a week with a coyote. The animal symbolized the wild West; copies of the *Wall Street Journal* were delivered daily to represent contemporary, business-oriented culture. He meant to heal the breach between the two.

Cuban émigré Ana Mendieta used her own body in several works as a symbol of the earth and natural cycles. In the TREE OF LIFE SERIES, she coated her body with mud and grasses and stood against ancient tree trunks. She intended in these pieces to show the essential equivalence between femaleness and natural processes such as birth and growth. For her, as for many early feminists, biology accounted for most of the differences between

MIERLE UKELES

Like Conceptual art and Minimalism, Performance can take art to its very edges. Mierle Ukeles's 1974 work A.I.R. WASH was one such occasion. For three hours, this artist kept a stretch of New York City sidewalk spotless. She scrubbed until her rags tore. She wiped the street behind passers-by. Each hour she announced in a loud voice in all four directions that what she was doing was art. This work, which indeed involved "work," was documented in photographs. Was it art? Her answer to the question, which involves core American democratic ideas, can be found on the CD-ROM that accompanies this book.

673 Mierle Laderman Ukeles.
A.I.R. WASH. 1973.
Performance.

women and men. Through the natural cycles of their bodies, she seems to be saying, women are closer to the rhythms of the earth.

PHOTOREALIST PAINTING AND SUPERREALIST SCULPTURE

The deadpan quality of Pop Art led some painters and sculptors in the late 1960s and 1970s to make finely crafted works with a similar message. Whereas Pop often looks mass-produced, these later realist styles insist on the laborious, handmade finish. Despite the movements that rejected realism in favor of nonrepresentational form, it was inevitable that some artists would continue to paint realistically while others would return to some aspect of art's role as a recorder of appearances. The principal difference between the paintings of Photorealists and most earlier realist painting is that the Photorealists are not telling stories; most of them, including Richard Estes, choose subjects with no narrative significance. The cool objectivity of Photorealism shows the influence of Pop Art, but Photorealism does not use Pop's mass-media subjects.

In preparation for each of his paintings, Estes takes many photographs. He then paints complex composite images of common cityscapes, often devoid of people but full of the character of urban life. Estes painted HORN AND HARDART AUTOMAT (next page) with a traditional brush, giving the surface an active and personal paint quality when viewed at close range. His sensitive application of abstract values in each composition makes Estes one of the most consistently rewarding of the artists who work with photographically inspired realism.

A sculptural counterpart to Photorealism can be seen in the work of Duane Hanson. His superrealist figures, cast in polyester and fiberglass and then painted in minute detail, are unsettling when experienced face-to-face. Viewers marvel at the incredible technique, but for Hanson, technique is a means, not an end. Hanson not only imitates reality, he sometimes presents ideas about reality that are unpleasant. He takes a documentary approach to realist sculpture. His figures are ordinary people, with no trace of idealism. Carefully selected clothing and other props are important parts of each of Hanson's pieces, and he gives considerable

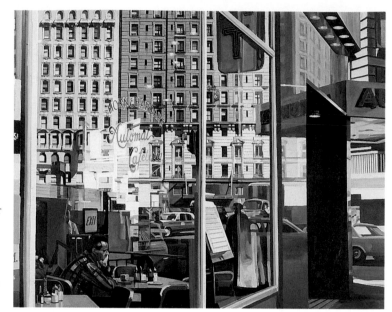

674 Richard Estes.
HORN AND HARDART
AUTOMAT. 1967.
Oil on masonite.
48" × 60".
Collection of Mr. and Mrs.
Stephen D. Paine, Boston.
© Richard Estes/Licensed by
VAGA, NY/Marlborough
Gallery, NY.

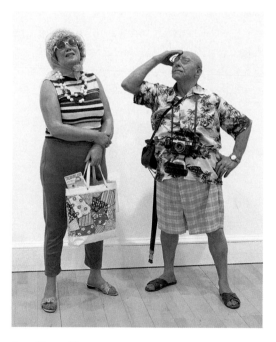

675 Duane Hanson.
TOURISTS. 1970.
Fiberglass and polychromed polyester.
64" × 65" × 67".
National Gallery of Scotland. © Estate of Duane Hanson/License by
VAGA, New York, NY.

thought to relationships among figure, clothing, and articles.

Hanson's figures are so intensely realistic, having lifelike hair, clothing, and skin, that people who come upon them often begin to interact with them before realizing that they are not alive.

TOURISTS is a pointed social comment on Americans in general and American tourists in particular. The overweight figures, encumbered with possessions, look like people we know or have seen many times. The content of this piece suggests a love-hate relationship with middle-class America.

Simply defined, censorship is the alteration or removal of works of art from public view. It is probably as old as art itself, and it has been done for reasons that are many and varied. Consider the following historical cases, many of which involve works that are illustrated in this book:

In 726 the Byzantine Emperor Leo III ordered the total destruction of Christian icons in the realm (a few are pictured on page 279). He believed that prayer in the presence of images encouraged idolatry, and under his orders thousands of paintings of Christ, Mary, and the Saints were destroyed. The policy lasted for most of the rest of that century.

Michelangelo depicted a great many nude people in his paintings in the Sistine Chapel in the Vatican (see page 296). Many of these figures have since had loincloths painted over them on orders from popes who believed them too revealing. When the works were restored in the 1990s, only about half of these later additions were removed, so that visitors today do not see the works exactly as they were when the artist finished them.

Japanese prints were subject to many censorship laws in the eighteenth and nineteenth centuries. These laws (which were not always enforced with equal zeal), required prints to display the artist's signature and a seal of approval from a censor. The print pictured on this page, IWAI HANSHIRO IV, has both in the lower right and left. One of the most famous print artists, Utamaro, once broke the laws by making a print of the emperor. He was ordered held in chains for thirty days, and he died shortly thereafter. One of his works is pictured on page 338.

Hollywood movies were not granted First Amendment free-speech protection until 1952. Prior to that, most studios abided by a variety of state laws and an industry Production Code that forbade depictions of nudity, childbirth, members of ethnic minorities in starring roles, drug use, suggestive dancing, or ridicule of religion.

Chinese artist Xu Bing created A BOOK FROM THE SKY in 1985, and exhibited it shortly thereafter to great acclaim at the National Museum of Fine Arts in Beijing. The work consists of 400 handmade books spread on the floor to resemble Chinese outdoor newspapers; all of the printed characters are the artist's own invention, fictitious and meaningless. After the Chinese government cracked down on democracy activists in 1989, official opinion changed about this work. The Ministry of Culture accused the artist of encoding subversive intent in the work, and he was placed under surveillance. He migrated to the United States in 1990.

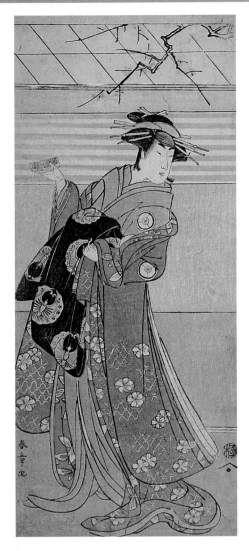

676 Katsukawa Shunsho. IWAI HANSHIRO IV AS MISTRESS OF SOGA-NO-JURO. 1792. Color woodcut.
Wallach collection, Miriam and Ira D. Wallach. Division of Art, Prints and Photographs, New York Public Library, Astor, Lenox, and Tilden Foundations.

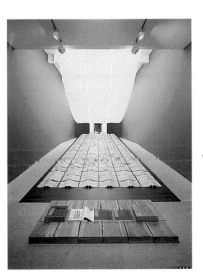

677 Xu Bing. A BOOK FROM THE SKY. 1987–1991. Museo Nacional Centro de Arte Reina Sofia, Madrid, Spain.
Courtesy Xu Bing.

We can see from these cases that censorship may be carried out for religious, moral, or political reasons, when civil authorities decide that the artist's freedom matters less than other important values.

Today, artists in the United States seem to enjoy very wide lattitude to create as they please. This right was best codified in a 1973 court case, *Miller v. California,* which held that a work may be censored only if it is demonstrably obscene; that is, if the "average person, applying contemporary community standards," finds it so, and if "the work taken as a whole lacks serious literary, artistic, political, or scientific value." Thus our modern society, which places high value on individual achievement and personal self-expression, seems to tip the balance in favor of freedom for artists.

Yet controversies continue; even in our day there are still efforts to restrict artistic expression. Where artists see attempted censorship, others see efforts to protect values. Here are some recent cases of attempts to alter or suppress expression:

The television network MTV reviews all videos submitted to it for broadcast. About one-third of videos that are eventually played on the network are re-edited by their makers in response to requests from the network before airing.

In 1996 a museum curator in Utah received a traveling exhibition of sculptures by Auguste Rodin that he had ordered (see an example of Rodin's work on page 31). He did not put all of the works on view, however, because some of them contained a degree of nudity that he thought was incompatible with Mormon teachings. Therefore the Utah public did not get to see a representative sample of sculpture by this artist.

Since the middle 1980s, controversy has swirled around the issue of public funds for controversial art. Many Americans are comfortable with the idea that artists should be able to create as they please, but many also assert a government right to censor works that are aided by tax dollars. Here are two such cases:

In 1996 four performance artists received grants from the National Endowment for the Arts, and proceeded to create works that many found controversial. The director of the Endowment withdrew their grants in response to clamor from some members of Congress, and the artists in turn sued in court, alleging that they were censored. The Supreme Court sided with the government. Shortly thereafter, the National Endowment abolished grant programs aiding individual artists, and it is not likely to reinstate them.

New York Mayor Rudolph Giuliani tried to close the Brooklyn Museum in the fall of 1999 over the painting HOLY VIRGIN MARY by Chris Ofili. Giuliani found the work offensive to Roman Catholicism because it portrayed Mary as a black woman with exaggerated features, and because the work had pieces of elephant dung attached to it. Since the museum operates in a city-owned building, the mayor went to court to try to evict it and cut off its maintenance funds if the directors did not remove the work from view. The artist responded that he was himself Catholic, and that it is common to use elephant dung in some forms of art in Africa, where he was born. The court sided with the artist and the museum. Far from suppressing Ofili's work, the mayor's lawsuit brought record-breaking crowds.

These cases demonstrate that artistic creation is often contested territory in which wider struggles over values, culture, and politics resonate. They also show that history is full of attempts by civic leaders to harness the power of art to shape the public mind.

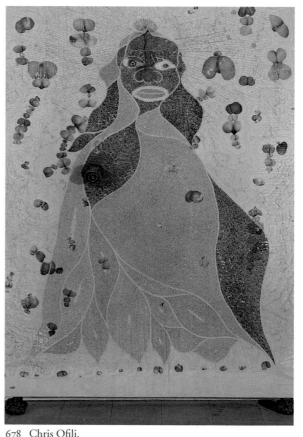

678   Chris Ofili.
THE HOLY VIRGIN MARY. 1996.
Mixed media on canvas. 8' × 6' (243.8 × 182.8 cm).
Victoria Miro Gallery.

CHAPTER TWENTY-FIVE

RECENT DIVERSITY

Most art critics and historians agree that sometime in the late 1970s or early 1980s, Modern art came to an end. That is, the impulses and drives that caused Modern art had practically spent themselves. Just as the Italian Renaissance, the Gupta Dynasty in India, and the Nok Culture of West Africa all were eventually supplanted by new styles, new cultural values, or new sources of support, so was Modern art.

A closer look will help clarify the change. Modern art was based on rejecting tradition and breaking rules. Each new movement found some rule to break: use of representational color, regular perspective, and recognizable subject matter are only a few of the rules that modern artists cast aside.

The impulse to depart from the norm lost its impact when it *became* the norm in most Western societies. In Western societies, we now look intently forward: to the next year, to the next presidential term, or to the next line of computers; not backward to the wisdom of our elders, ancient rituals, or eternal principles. Departing from the norm is widely seen as healthy. In fact, this was the slogan of a chain of fast food restaurants in the early 1990s: "Sometimes you just gotta break the rules."

A related fact is that the public now accepts, or at least tolerates, most Modern art. Exhibitions of work by such former rule-breaking radicals as Henri Matisse, Paul Gauguin, Paul Cézanne, and Claude Monet fill museums with visitors. All of the ten most expensive paintings ever sold at auction are modern works (five by Picasso; three by van Gogh; one each, by Cézanne and Renoir). The modern-style Vietnam Veterans Memorial has become a national shrine. Most Modern art is no longer controversial.

At this time in the development of art, it seems that there are no rules left to break. One can do something new for only so long before repetition occurs. While it is still possible to employ themes that offend people today, it is very difficult to make a style as new as (say) Cubism, Expressionism, Constructivism, or Minimalism. Most artists have given up trying.

The impact of this change is not yet clear. Art of our own time is always the most difficult to evaluate. In general, it seems that most artists of the present generation are not keenly interested in perfecting form, creating beauty, or fine-tuning their sense of sight. They mostly want to comment on life in all of its aspects. They want to create work that illuminates the relationships between what we see and how we think. Rather than being objects of timeless beauty, most art since the 1980s consists of objects laden with information about the period we live in. This chapter will present some movements of the present generation; many of the artists discussed in this chapter could be placed in more than one category, but most would prefer not to be categorized at all.

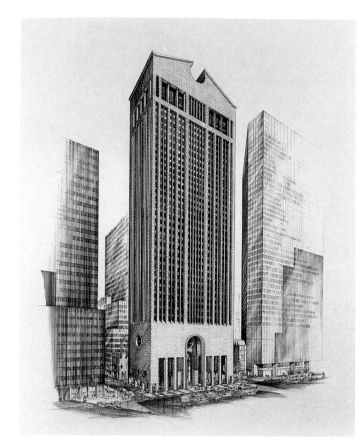

679 Johnson and Burgee.
A.T. & T. BUILDING.
New York City. 1978–1984.
Photo by Gil Amiaga, NYC.

POSTMODERN ARCHITECTURE

The history of architecture has been characterized by refinements followed by overturnings, with the young and the imaginative always finding some degree of inadequacy in the work of their immediate predecessors. A growing discontent with the sterile anonymity of the mid-century International Style (see the LEVER HOUSE on page 450) led many architects to rebel and to look once again at meaning, history, tradition, and context. Their departure from architectural modernism was dubbed Postmodern in the late 1970s.

Postmodernists feel that the unadorned functional purity of the International Style makes all buildings look the same, offers no identity relative to purpose, no symbolism, no meaning, no mystery, no excitement. Postmodern architects enjoy the very qualities of modern life that the proponents of machine aesthetics sought to escape: complexity, ambiguity, contradiction, nostalgia, romance, and the rich vulgarity of popular taste. One of the important Postmodern architects, Robert Venturi, wrote a book in 1972 that brought the entire profession to attention with its self-explanatory title: *Learning from Las Vegas.*

Postmodern architects embrace an eclectic mix of historical influences, decorative tendencies, and the popular styles of architecture and applied arts that the general public can relate to. The Postmodernists divorce themselves and their work from the accepted meanings of "traditional" and "modern" and do not value one more than the other. The attitudes associated with Postmodernism are a part of all the arts, including literature. In the visual arts, the Postmodern style is perhaps best known and most easily seen in architecture.

Architect Philip Johnson's career has spanned both the Modern and Postmodern movements. He has been known since mid-century as an advocate of Modernism and, with Mies van der Rohe, designed the SEAGRAM BUILDING (page 241), a landmark of the International Style. But the pure glass-enclosed box, repeated a thousand times in cities throughout the world, became too severe, too limited for Johnson and his younger colleagues. In high-rise buildings such as the A.T. & T. BUILDING in New York City,, he reversed himself. Here Johnson and John Burgee brought back warmth and delight with a decorative upper story that brings together elements from several historical styles.

The architecture of Michael Graves reflects a personal blend of traditional classicism and inventive irony. His PUBLIC SERVICES BUILDING is both formal and playful. Its exterior makes reference to a pair of fluted classical columns sharing a single capital. These off-color vertical elements are set in a pool of reflecting mirror windows, which detaches them from any function in the building's structure. The remainder of the façade consists of anonymous rows of square openings, an ironic reference to the bureaucrats inside.

When Japanese architect Arata Isozaki made his first trip to Europe in 1960, he became fascinated by the classical architectural spaces of ancient Rome, by medieval towns, and by the villas of Andrea Palladio (see page 300). Isozaki, who calls himself a "guerrilla architect," seeks to create buildings with mystery, excitement, and surprise rather than quiet beauty. His TEAM DISNEY BUILDING shows a playful departure from the cool rationality of Modernism.

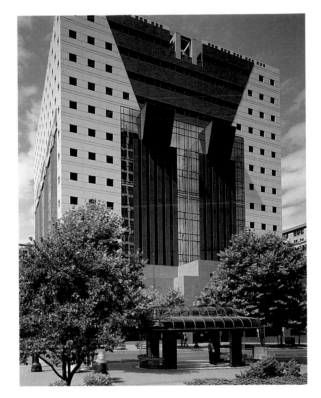

680   Michael Graves.
PUBLIC SERVICES BUILDING.
Portland, Oregon. 1980–1982.

681   Arata Isozaki.
TEAM DISNEY BUILDING.
Orlando, Florida. 1990.
Photograph: © Charles Jencks.

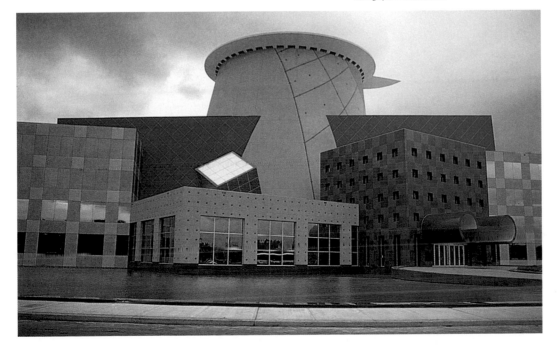

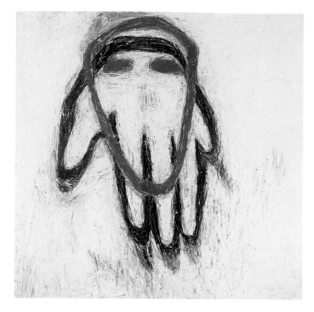

682 Susan Rothenberg (American, 1945–).
BLUE HEAD. 1980–1981.
Acrylic on canvas. 114" × 114". Signed on reverse, center
Susan Rothenberg 1980–18 Head (Blue).
Virginia Museum of Fine Arts, Richmond.
Gift of The Sydney & Frances Lewis Foundation. © Virginia Museum of Fine Arts.
© 2002 Susan Rothenberg/Artists Rights Society (ARS), NY.

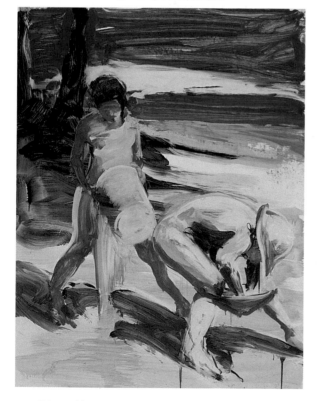

683 Eric Fischl.
UNTITLED. 1986.
Oil on paper. 46" × 35".
Private collection. Courtesy Mary Boone Gallery, New York.

PAINTING

As Modernism came to an end, many painters in America and Europe began to revive expressive, personal styles in a movement known as Neo-Expressionism. This was partly in response to the impersonality and generally aesthetic orientation of movements such as Conceptual Art and Minimalism, and to the ironic, tongue-in-cheek quality of Pop Art and related trends.

One of the first Neo-Expressionists was Susan Rothenberg, who in the 1970s began making symbolic, heavily brushed works in which subject matter teeters on the brink of recognizability. After the cleansing blankness of Minimalism, Rothenberg could return to figurative images with original vision; what emerges is almost ethereal.

She works in a narrow range of tones, using a muted palette of white, beige, silvery or dark gray, with a bit of blue. Her BLUE HEAD, which outlines a horse's head in front of a human hand, is a haunting image that remains outside persistent attempts at explanation. It is a primal sign operating in the interval between the known material world and the mystery beyond.

Eric Fischl is another master of painterly brushwork. Like Rothenberg, he moved from abstract art to representation. His UNTITLED view of children washing sand from their bathing suits shows a love of gesture and color. Fischl paints with direct fluidity, drawing the viewer into the magical process of creating pictures out of paint. His seductive paint application is often overshadowed by subject matter that sometimes shocks viewers with its psychological and sexual implications.

The German painter Anselm Kiefer combines the aggressive paint application of Abstract Expressionism with nineteenth-century feelings for history and mythology. Kiefer gives equal attention to moral and aesthetic issues. His paintings, loaded with symbolism, mythology, and religion, probe the German national conscience and reveal the grim confusion felt by many postwar Germans. Kiefer sees art as having the power to provide a spiritual catharsis; yet his disturbing work presents more questions than answers.

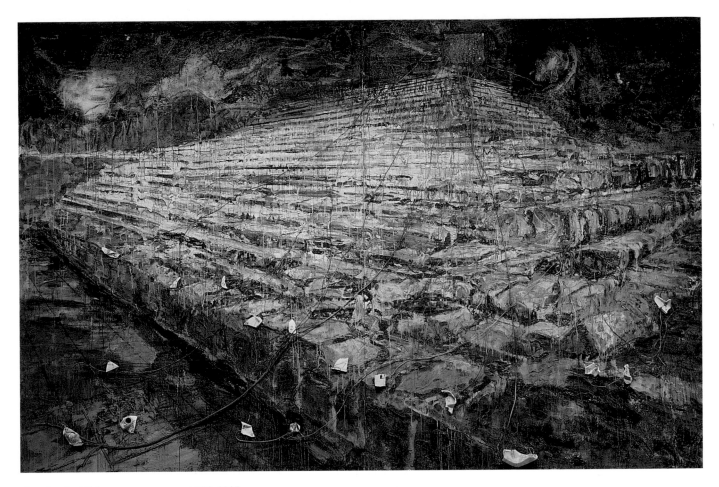

684 Anselm Kiefer. OSIRIS AND ISIS. 1985–1987.
Oil, acrylic, emulsion, clay, porcelain. lead copper wire, and circuit
board on canvas. 150" × 229½" × 6½" (381 × 560.7 × 16.5 cm).
San Francisco Museum of Modern Art. Purchased through a gift of Jean Stein, by exchange,
the Mrs. Paul L. Wattis Fund, and the Doris and Donald Fisher Fund. Photograph by Ben Blackwell.

OSIRIS AND ISIS recalls the ancient Egyptian myth of the cycle of death and rebirth. Osiris symbolized the indestructible creative forces of nature; according to legend, the god was slain and cut into pieces by his evil brother. Isis, sister and wife of Osiris, found and buried the pieces, making each burial place sacred. In another version of the story, Isis collected the pieces and brought Osiris back to life. In Kiefer's huge painting, the goddess Isis (in the form of a TV circuit board) sits on top of a pyramid, sending out a network of wires attached to fragments of the dismembered Osiris. The heavily textured surface, consisting of paint, mud, earth, rock, tar, and bits of ceramic and metal, intensifies the image's disturbing power.

Some see Kiefer's anguish-filled, end-of-the-world paintings as dreary and depressing; others feel Kiefer is calling on his fellow Germans to move beyond guilt to an era of renewed hope.

The Neo-Expressionists tend to favor painting because a seemingly infinite variety of surface textures and colors are possible. Every creative decision can leave a trace on the finished work, registering like a barometer every twitch in sensibility. Other artists use the various media of painting because they are good for storytelling. The artist can construct a two-dimensional world with the utmost freedom. This interest in narration is a dominant tendency in contemporary painting.

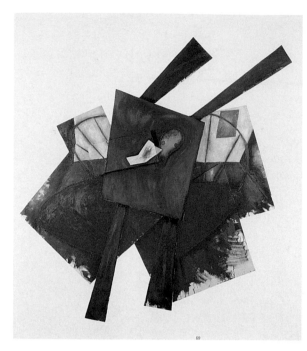

685   Elizabeth Murray.
MORE THAN YOU KNOW. 1983.
Oil on nine canvases. 108" × 111" × 8".
Photography courtesy of Pace Wildenstein.
Collection of The Edward R. Broida Trust, Florida.
© 1983 Elizabeth Murray.

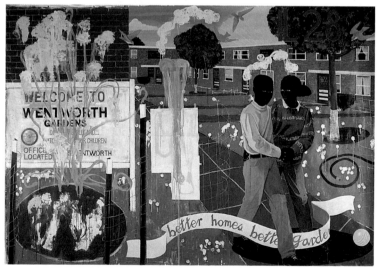

686   Kerry James Marshall.
BETTER HOMES BETTER GARDENS. 1994.
Acrylic and collage on canvas. 8'4" × 12'.
Collection of Denver Art Museum.
Photograph courtesy Jack Shainman Gallery, New York City.

Elizabeth Murray combines personal meanings with explosively innovative form in works such as MORE THAN YOU KNOW. The painting dates from the time between the birth of her two children; however, beyond the general outlines of a room with two red chairs, there is little here to suggest the experience of motherhood. Her personal information is only the launching pad for a fascinatingly jagged array of canvas fragments that do not fit together, but still seem to cohere. Murray's vibrant and exuberant paintings leave a great deal of the story for the viewer to make up from the suggestive shapes.

Kerry James Marshall grew up in housing projects in Alabama and Los Angeles, and he wants to correct a popular vision of those places as crime-ridden. His 1994 work BETTER HOMES BETTER GARDENS is part of a series of paintings that he made on Chicago housing projects which contain the word "garden" in their names. This one is obviously set in Wentworth Gardens, and it depicts a couple walking down a flowered pathway in a low-rise setting. At the left is a fenced area enclosing a communal flower garden. Three of the artist's trademark bluebirds fly across the upper portion of the scene, and all seems peaceful. Whatever else happens in housing projects, they are places of community and neighborhood feeling, he seems to be telling us.

Yet for all its optimism, there are ironic touches in this work. The perfectly spiraled garden hose, the white blotches over the heads of the couple, and the flowered entry with the "Welcome" sign add a note of complexity to the mood, casting a flickering shadow over its sweetness. The inscription "IL 2-8" in the upper right reminds us that this is both an illustration, and a painter's painting that is in fact rigorously composed. It is based on a solid grid of horizontals, verticals, and a few diagonals. Though the work is optimistic, Marshall is not merely painting an idealistic scene.

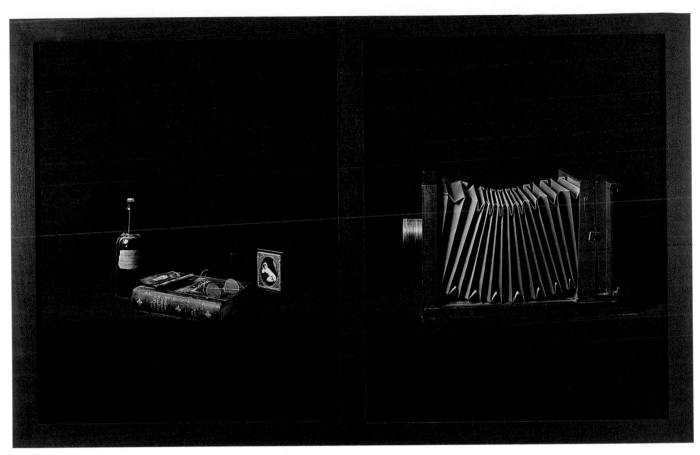

687 Sarah Charlesworth.
STILL LIFE WITH CAMERA. 1995.
Cibachrome photographs in wood frame. 50" × 80" overall.
Photo courtesy Gorney Bravin & Lee, New York.

PHOTOGRAPHY

The Postmodern movement has been a primary influence on recent photography. The principal new insight that Postmodernists brought to the medium was the perhaps unsurprising notion that a photograph is not merely a "straight" record of fact. There are ways of composing, taking, developing, and printing pictures that serve to encode information and influence viewers. Photographers influenced by Postmodernism show through their pictures that they know their medium is not an objective one. Even the most straightforward scenes can have hidden meanings. Postmodernists want to show us that the camera can influence us in ways we may not suspect, and the camera itself has a certain way of seeing.

Sarah Charlesworth was an early leader in the Postmodern photography movement. A longtime associate of Conceptual artist Joseph Kosuth (see his ONE AND THREE CHAIRS on page 461), Charlesworth takes thought-provoking pictures of pictures. Her 1995 work STILL LIFE WITH CAMERA consists of two images in overlapping frames. On the left is a still life similar to those of traditional painting (see A SMOKE BACKSTAGE on page 27); on the right, an antique camera. Both panels are photographs printed with relatively new Cibachrome technology, a favorite of Postmodern photographers because of its high resolution.

As we look at this work, we see a camera taking in a scene, except that the scene is not natural, but arranged according to old traditions. The implication is that photographers and painters never take reality as they find it, but rather always interpret. We are implicated in the situation because we are

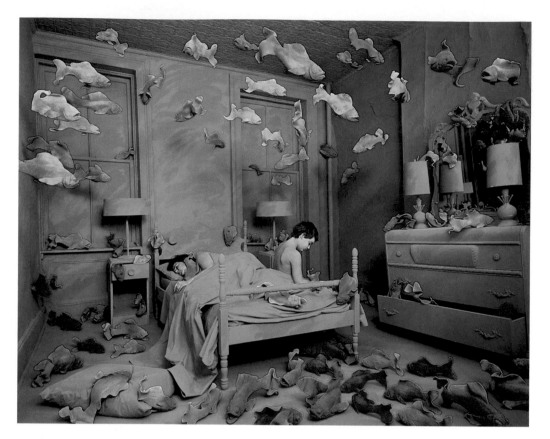

688　Sandy Skoglund.
REVENGE OF THE GOLDFISH.
1981. Cibachrome print.
30" × 40".
Courtesy of the artist.

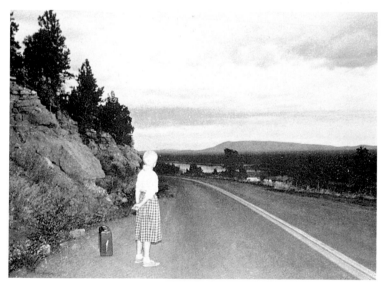

689　Cindy Sherman.
UNTITLED FILM STILL. 1979.
Black and white photograph.
Courtesy Cindy Sherman and Metro Pictures.

looking not at real objects but constructed versions of them. Thus our seeing is never pure, but always conditioned by culture and training. The camera, even as it records reality, also assists us in classifying it.

Sandy Skoglund goes farther down this path. She invents impossible scenes, and then photographs them. REVENGE OF THE GOLDFISH is a hilarious nightmare in which a suburban bedroom is taken over by the once-confined goldfish. Her photographs purposely have very little to do with what we call reality, and we are not likely to take her pictures as "the truth."

Cindy Sherman's photographs of the late 1970s were among the first to be called Postmodern. She took black-and-white photos of herself, posing with props in scenes that corresponded to stereotyped female characters from popular culture. IN UNTITLED FILM STILL #48, for example, she stands on a deserted road at dusk, her back to us, hastily packed suitcase at her side. As in many "teen movies" of the 1950s and 1960s, she is the misunderstood daughter running away from home. Other photos from the series depict the girl next door, daddy's little girl, the anxious young career woman, the oppressed housewife. Without referring to specific movies, Sherman's photos are imagined stills from popular film types that have helped to form stereotypical images of women. She seems to be saying that our popular culture of movies and television programs typecasts women in certain roles, and thus keeps women from realizing themselves.

Sherman's work is influenced about equally by Pop Art, Performance Art, and Feminism. She differs from the early feminists, though, in presenting women as a product of the culture and not of biology. In her eyes, culture has a much larger role in forming women than does nature.

SCULPTURE

The range of options available to sculptors has rarely been wider. Partly in reaction to the simplicity of Minimal and Conceptual art, sculptors today draw on a range of techniques and materials. One task that seems to have motivated many of the best of them in recent years is exploring the symbolic value of shapes. How can a shape "mean something"? What range of memories and feelings are viewers likely to attach to a given figure? At what point does a form "take shape" so that a viewer can recognize it? Are they likely to see what the creator had in mind? These are some of the questions that sculptors have been posing with their pieces in recent years.

Martin Puryear, an African American, thoughtfully probes such questions. Combining elegant craftsmanship, organic creativity, and humor, Puryear's deceptively simple sculptures include references to shelters, canoes, trestle bridges, coffins, and basketry. Puryear's work has a distinctly American eloquence that arises from a pioneering tradition of self-reliance and disciplined craftsmanship. His OLD MOLE recalls the delicate skeleton of an animal, the whimsical humor of a folk tale, and the austere sophistication of Minimalist sculpture.

Indian-born English sculptor Anish Kapoor takes these explorations in a more ritualistic direction

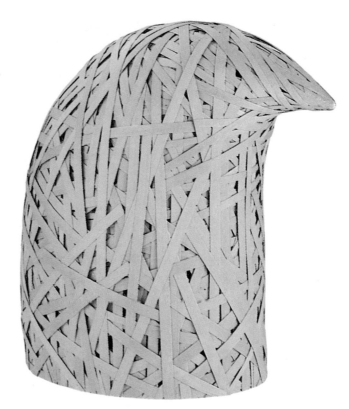

690 Martin Puryear.
OLD MOLE. 1985.
Red cedar. 61" × 61" × 32".
Philadelphia Museum of Art. Purchased with gifts (by exchange) of Samuel S. White 3rd and Vera White, and Mr. and Mrs. C.G. Chaplin and with funds contributed by Marion Boulton Stroud, and Mr. and Mrs. Dennis Alter and Mrs. H. Gates Lloyd. 1986-70-1.

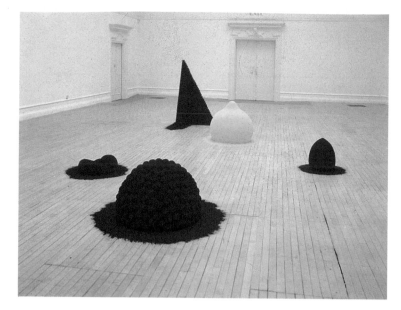

691 Anish Kapoor.
TO REFLECT AN INTIMATE PART OF THE RED. 1981.
Pigment and mixed media.
Installation: 78" × 314" × 314".

Photo: Andrew Penketh, London. Courtesy Barbara Gladstone.

692 Kiki Smith.
ICE MAN. 1995.
Silicon bronze.
80" × 29¼" × 12"
(203.2 × 74.3 × 30.5 cm).
© 1995 Kiki Smith.
Photograph: Ellen Page Wilson.
Courtesy of Pace Wildenstein.

in his work TO REFLECT AN INTIMATE PART OF THE RED. He deployed across a gallery floor several shapes that allude to ancient religious structures such as Maya pyramids, Indian stupas, and onion-shaped domes. Kapoor sprinkles his sculpture with powder, an action that also seems ritualistic. The translation of these shapes into an art gallery context raises questions about how their spiritual meanings come about, and how much of that meaning is kept in the new context.

Probably the most potent symbol in sculpture is the human body, and many artists today allude to it in order to illuminate the ways in which our culture gives it meaning. Most recent sculptors who depict the body see it not as a vehicle for idealism or beauty, but rather for commenting on the ways in which culture shapes our bodies and how we think about them.

Kiki Smith is a hero to many feminists because of the way she has modeled, in resin, wax, and papier mâché, full-body depictions of wounded women. These pieces drew attention to the silent suffering of many victims of domestic violence, but in recent years she has broadened her focus. She is as likely now to concentrate attention on the inside of the body and its functions, some of which are infrequently dealt with in art. Like many artists today, she is also influenced by current events. In 1995, when the body of a frozen Stone Age man with skin intact was found in the Alps, she fashioned ICE MAN as a commentary. The piece, showing the unclothed man in the frozen position in which he was found, is modeled life-size in silicon bronze. The material gives the surface a dark color similar to that of the dead man's skin. Smith simplified the facial features, leaving the work's title the only sure clue to the source of the piece. She hung the work on the wall of the gallery, slightly above eye level, attached by its back. Thus it became for viewers an object of curiosity, a specimen, just as the frozen Stone Age man was for the anthropologists who studied it at great length.

PUBLIC ART

We have seen that cultural diversity and rapid change have led to variety in styles of art and personal responses to works of art. Because there is no longer general agreement on what constitutes "good" art, selection of a work of art for a public place can be an emotional and often a political issue. Although most people will readily accept the decisions of experts in other areas, many believe they have the right to view or not view art and to decide for themselves what art they want to see. The placement of an artwork in a public space makes it accessible, but this may lead to a feeling that some so-called art experts have decided what the public should learn to like. In the case of government art commissions, people who dislike the "art" may be further distressed when they realize that their tax dollars helped pay for it.

The idea of public art goes back to ancient times. Government and religious leaders have commissioned many of history's best-known artists to execute works for the public. However, it is only in recent decades that we have seen a steady stream of commissions for public art given to large numbers of American artists.

During the 1960s, government leaders began to spend money in new areas. Since the arts are considered beneficial for individuals and communities, it seemed appropriate that city, state, and national governments become involved in bringing the arts to the public. A high percentage of today's public art is now commissioned by government agencies.

Among the largest sponsors of public art is the federal government's General Services Administration (GSA) Art-in-Architecture program, begun in 1962. The program requires that one-half of one percent of the cost of each new government building be spent for art to be located in or around the new building. States, cities, and counties subsequently implemented similar programs, with varying percentages designated for the purchase or commissioning of works of art.

The federal government's National Endowment for the Arts (NEA) was created in 1965.

Among the NEA's many programs is the Art in Public Places Program, from which communities can request matching funds for commissions of large outdoor artworks. Public art pictured in this book includes works by Ginzel and Jones (page 57), Louise Nevelson (page 102), Claes Oldenburg (page 39), and Beverly Pepper (page 80). As the new millennium begins, government agencies have less money for such projects than they had in the past.

The VIETNAM VETERANS MEMORIAL (see next page), located on the Mall in Washington, D.C., has become America's best-known public art. The 250-foot-long, V-shaped black granite wall bears the names of the nearly sixty thousand American servicemen and women who died or are missing in Southeast Asia. The nonprofit Vietnam Veterans Memorial Fund, Inc. (VVMF) was formed in 1979 by a group of Vietnam veterans who believed that a symbol of recognition of the human cost of the war would help speed the process of national reconciliation. Controversy over American involvement in the war had caused returning veterans to receive less than a hero's welcome.

In 1980, Congress authorized the site, and the VVMF announced a national design competition. The VVMF set design criteria specifying that the memorial be reflective and contemplative in character, harmonize with its surroundings, contain the names of all those who died or remain missing, and make no political statement about the war. After examining 1,421 entries, the jury of internationally recognized artists and designers unanimously selected the design of twenty-one-year-old Maya Ying Lin of Athens, Ohio, then a student at Yale University. Lin had visited the site and created a design that would work with the land rather than dominate it. "I had an impulse to cut open the earth . . . an initial violence that in time would heal. The grass would grow back, but the cut would remain, a pure, flat surface, like a geode when you cut it open and polish the edge. . . . I chose black granite to make the surface reflective and peaceful."[1]

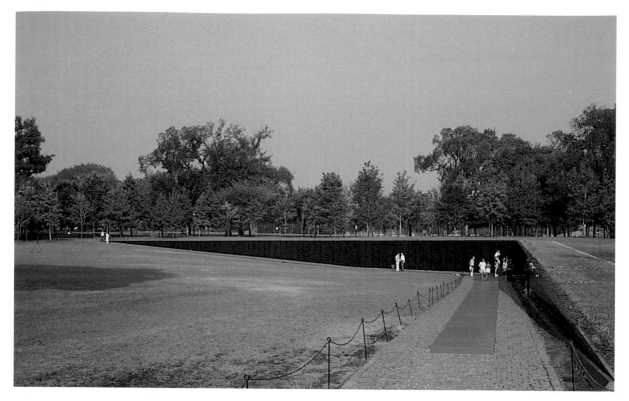

693 Maya Lin. VIETNAM VETERANS MEMORIAL.
The Mall, Washington, D.C. 1980–1982.
Black granite. Each wall 10'1" × 246'9".
Photograph: Duane Preble.

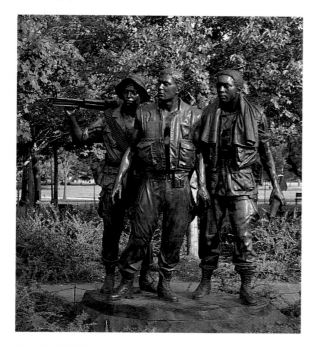

694 Frederick Hart.
VIETNAM MEMORIAL SCULPTURE.
The Mall, Washington, D.C. 1984.
Bronze. Life-size.
Photograph: Duane Preble.

Initial reaction by the press was favorable, and in Spring 1981 the Commission of Fine Arts and other government agencies approved the design. But several months later, a Vietnam veteran appeared before the commission and called the proposed design a "black gash of shame." He hit a nerve, and subsequent accusations in the press called the design "unheroic," "defeatist," and "death-oriented." Veterans were divided on the issue. It was, indeed, a hard design to explain. In January 1982, the Secretary of the Interior put the project on hold.

A compromise was reached several months later when it was decided that a figurative sculpture and a flag would be added to the site. Frederick Hart was chosen to create a naturalistic bronze statue to be located in a cluster of small trees near the wall. In time, the compromise seemed to please all sides. The wall was dedicated on Veterans Day 1982, and the Hart statue in 1984. Most of the modernists who were dismayed at the idea of

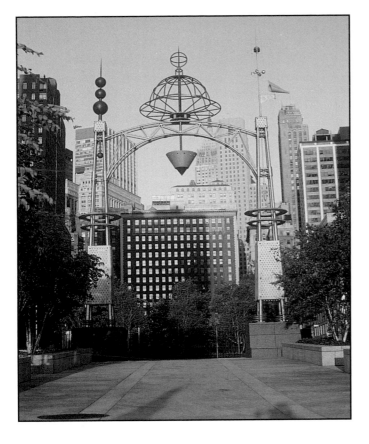

R. M. FISCHER

Battery Park City in New York is an effort to combine the expertise of specialists with input from citizens to integrate public art into a mixed commercial and residential area. This new neighborhood, which took shape in the early 1980s, was planned as a redevelopment project in a run-down area of Manhattan. Apartments, hotels, schools, and shops now occupy the 982-acre site.

R. M. Fischer's RECTOR GATE marks a strategic location between an apartment complex and a riverside park. Visitors and residents walking from one to the other pass under this fanciful structure, which is laden with symbolic motifs from science fiction movies, heroic engineering projects, and more practical TV towers or antennae.

695   R. M. Fischer.
RECTOR GATE. 1988.
Stainless steel, bronze, granite, lighting.
50' × 28'.
Courtesy the artist.

cluttering up the site with yet another bronze commemorative statue were pleasantly surprised by the quality of the figurative VIETNAM MEMORIAL SCULPTURE and the fact that it complements the wall from a distance rather than competes with it. Despite public clamor for a traditional monument, a majority of the thousands of tourists who flock to the memorial each day never see the Hart sculpture; they are drawn to the wall.

Lin's bold, eloquently simple design creates a memorial park within a larger park. The polished black surface reflects the surrounding trees and lawn, and the tapering segments point to the Washington Monument in one direction and the Lincoln Memorial in the other. Names are inscribed in chronological order by date of death, each name given a place in history. As visitors walk toward the center, the wall becomes higher and the names pile up inexorably. The monument, visited by thousands each day, has—for many—the power to console and heal.

The fragmented nature of contemporary American culture presents a dilemma for both artists and those who sponsor public art. Should the freedom of the creative individual be unquestioned, with the hope that the public will follow, or at least accept, the art that results? Or should the public, or some part of the public, have a voice in setting guidelines for selection or actually select the art that becomes part of the public environment—particularly when the art is paid for by tax dollars? Just how democratic should the process be? On the one hand, we could rely entirely on experts, whose tastes are often different from those of the public; at the other extreme, with a lot of public input, we might yield to the lowest common denominator of popular taste.

ISSUE-ORIENTED ART

Many artists in the last twenty years have sought to link their art directly to important or controversial questions. Issue-oriented artists believe that if they limit their art to aesthetic matters,

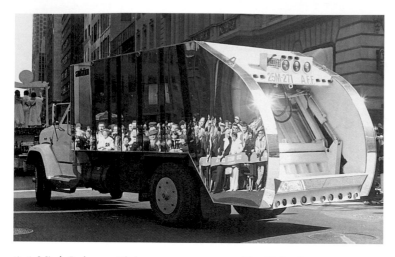

696 Mierle Laderman Ukeles. THE SOCIAL MIRROR. New York. 1983.
20-cubic yard garbage collection truck fitted with hand-tempered glass
mirror with additional strips of mirrored acrylic.

Courtesy The New York City Department of Sanitation. Photograph: D. James Dee.

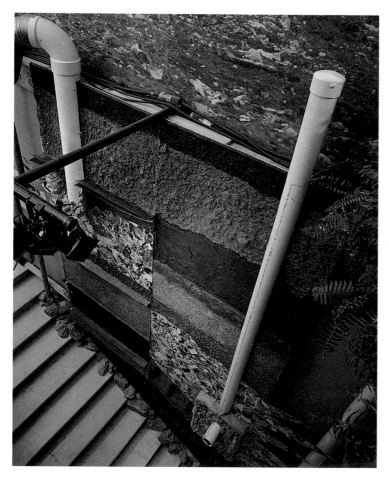

697 Mierle Laderman Ukeles with New York City Department of Sanitation.
LANDFILL CROSS SECTION. 1990.
Layers of clays, soils, geosynthetic materials, methane venting system.
Courtesy Ronald Feldman Fine Arts, New York.
Photograph: D. James Lee.

then their work will be only a distraction from
pressing problems. Furthermore, they recognize
that what we see has a powerful influence on how
we think, and they do not want to miss an opportunity to influence both.

Mierle Laderman Ukeles, spurred by New
York's ongoing garbage crisis and her own experiences as a mother, began to consider the importance
to society of "maintenance work," the repetitive
tasks such as garbage collection that are necessary
for social functioning. (See also her work on page
469 and the discussion on the CD-ROM.) Since
1978, Ukeles has been an unsalaried artist-in-
residence for the New York City Department of
Sanitation, where she makes pieces that are based
on the apparent everydayness of Conceptual Art. In
1979 and 1980 she joined the daily rounds of sanitation workers and their supervisors; then for eleven
months she completed an eight-hour-a-day performance piece in which she shook the hands of the
more than 8,500 workers taking care of New York's
mountains of garbage. With each handshake she
said, "Thank you for keeping New York City alive."

For a parade, Ukeles covered the sides of a
garbage truck with mirrors, creating THE SOCIAL
MIRROR. The piece enabled people to see themselves
as the starting point of the process, the source of the
garbage. In the 1990 piece LANDFILL CROSS SECTION,
she installed layers of a landfill, including its
methane gas vents, beside a stairway so that viewers
could see what happened to some of the waste that
they generated. The result was not only educational,
but a surprisingly interesting visual composition.

Photographer Richard Misrach is similarly motivated by concern for the environment. His photograph SUBMERGED LAMPPOST, SALTON SEA captures
the silent yet ironic beauty of a small town in California that was flooded by a misguided irrigation
system. In other works he has documented in chill-
ing detail the bloated carcasses of animals killed on
military proving grounds in Nevada. His brand of
nature photography is in opposition to the common calendars that include soothing views of pris-
tine landscapes. He wants us to know that such
scenes are fast disappearing.

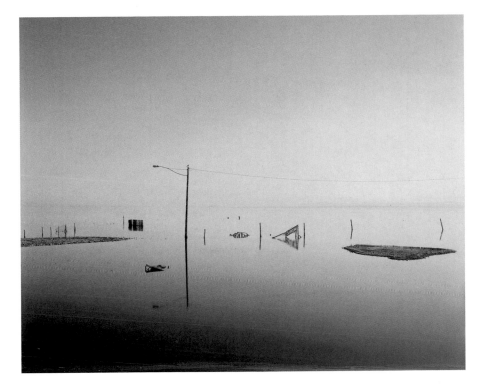

698 Richard Misrach.
SUBMERGED LAMPPOST, SALTON SEA. 1985.
Photograph (chromogenic color print).
Courtesy Robert Mann Gallery. © Richard Misrach.

699 Barbara Kruger.
UNTITLED (I SHOP THEREFORE I AM). 1987.
Photographic silkscreen/vinyl. 111" × 113".
Courtesy Mary Boone Gallery, New York.

Barbara Kruger was trained as a magazine designer, and this profession shows in her piece UNTITLED (I SHOP THEREFORE I AM). She invented the slogan, which sounds as though it came from advertising. The position of the hand, too, looks like it came from an ad for aspirin or sleeping medication. Our products define us, don't they? We are what we shop for, and often we buy a product because of what it will say about us and not for the thing itself. These are some of the messages present in this simple yet fascinating work. Perhaps its ultimate irony is that the artist had it silkscreened onto a shopping bag.

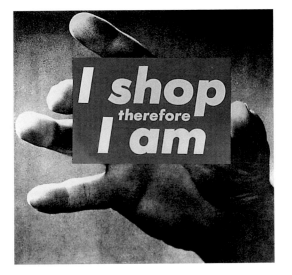

Artists who create works about racism and class bias have often attempted to show how common practices of museum display may unwittingly contribute to such problems. In 1992, the Maryland Historical Society invited African-American artist Fred Wilson to rearrange the exhibits on one floor to create an installation called MINING THE MUSEUM. (See next page.) He spent a year preparing for the show, rummaging through the Society's basement and documentary records; the results were surprising. He found no portraits, for example, of noted African-American Marylanders Benjamin Banneker (who laid out the boundaries of the District of Columbia), Frederick Douglass (noted abolitionist and journalist), or Harriet Tubman (founder of the Underground Railroad). He found instead busts of Henry Clay, Andrew Jackson, and Napoleon Bonaparte, none of whom ever lived in Maryland. He exhibited those three busts next to three empty pedestals to symbolize the missing African Americans. He set out a display of

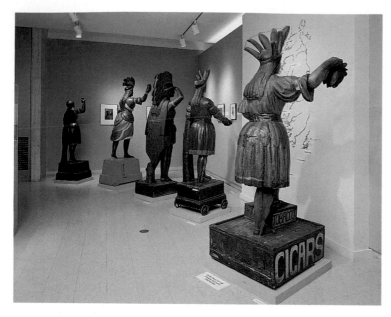

700 Fred Wilson.
MINING THE MUSEUM. 1992.
Installation. Cigar Store Indians facing photographs
of Native American Marylanders.
Maryland Historical Society.
Photograph: Jeff D. Goldman.

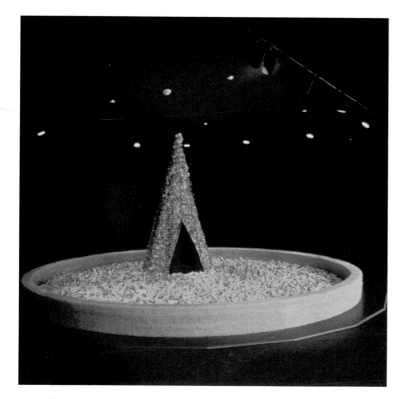

701 Cildo Meireles.
OLVIDO (OBLIVION). 1987–89.
Native American tent, banknotes, bones, candles, soundtrack. 157½" × 315".
Courtesy of the Artist and Galerie Lelong, New York.

Colonial Maryland silverware and tea utensils, but included a pair of slave shackles. This lesser-known form of metalwork was perhaps equally vital to the functioning of nineteenth-century Maryland. He dusted off the Society's collection of wooden cigar-store Indians and stood them, backs to viewers, facing photographs of real Native Americans who lived in Maryland. In an accompanying exhibition brochure he wrote that a museum should be a place that can make you think. When MINING THE MUSEUM was on display, attendance records soared.

Brazilian artist Cildo Meireles communicates his concerns about environmental destruction through the impact of large-scale installations such as OLVIDO (OBLIVION). A conical form shingled with paper money stands on a deep layer of bones—symbols of death. Candles, important to Catholic religious practice, form an encircling wall. The leaflike money on the central cone is currency from the nations of North, Central, and South America, which previously had indigenous populations; it represents the greed and exploitation that have doomed generations of Native Americans. The installation includes a soft sound track that evokes sounds of chanting priests or perhaps distant traffic—but is actually the sound of chain saws rapidly destroying rain forests. Meireles comes from a family long known for its advocacy of Native rights, and this installation denounces the destruction of indigenous cultures and the environment in which they once thrived.

William Kentridge's animated films trace the emergence of a new South Africa as it comes to grips with its history of apartheid. HISTORY OF THE MAIN COMPLAINT tells a story of a real estate speculator who is rendered semi-conscious in an auto accident. As he slowly comes to himself in the hospital, his gradually clarifying memory tells him in flashbacks that others died in the crash, and also that he was the cause of it. The protagonist's story is an allegory of South Africa itself as it slowly awakens from the grim reality of racism. The artist made this film laboriously, in the fashion of an old cartoon, drawing hundreds of the story's moments in charcoal on paper and then photographing them in sequence.

THE GLOBAL PRESENT

Communication and travel technologies are making the world seem smaller and smaller. The Internet, air travel, fax machines, cable television, and international migration are bringing us all into ever closer proximity. Since the fall of communism, the world is no longer as divided by ideology as it was for the preceding half-century, thus contributing to a more fluid world culture. Many businesses, for example, are not confined by national boundaries anymore; they may raise money in one country, buy raw materials in another, set up manufacturing facilities in a third, and sell the final product around the world.

The trend toward globalization has had some interesting consequences: Mexican soap operas are extremely popular in the Philippines. Residents of Papua New Guinea can watch reruns of the 1980s television show *Dallas* in local bars. Latin American novels influenced Chinese filmmakers of the 1980s and 1990s. During the Persian Gulf War, Iraqi dictator Saddam Hussein followed the conflict on CNN. At this writing, the world's tallest building is located in Kuala Lumpur, Malaysia; soon a planned bank in Shanghai will overtake it. Ethnic "minorities" already make up the majority of students in many American public school systems. By the year 2015, according to the United Nations, only one of the world's fifteen largest urban areas will be located in the United States (New York City, tied for eighth place with Tianjin, China). None of the top fifteen will be European. To function successfully and to live peacefully, it is becoming increasingly necessary that we understand cultures beyond our own.

The globalization of culture has also had a profound impact on art. Contemporary art forms such as conceptual, installation, and performance art have spread around the world. Innovative work is emerging in unexpected places, as artists in many countries employ increasingly international modes of expression to interpret the contemporary world in the light of their own traditions. This union of the cosmopolitan and the local is a major source of the new creative effort that has always fertilized art. A few examples from Americans and from disparate

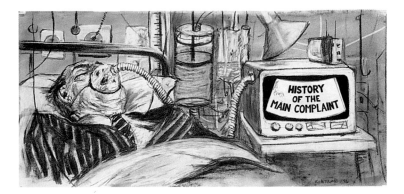

702 William Kentridge.
Drawing from HISTORY OF THE MAIN COMPLAINT. (Title Page). 1996.
Charcoal and pastel on paper. 60 × 122 cm.
Courtesy of the Goodman Gallery, South Africa.

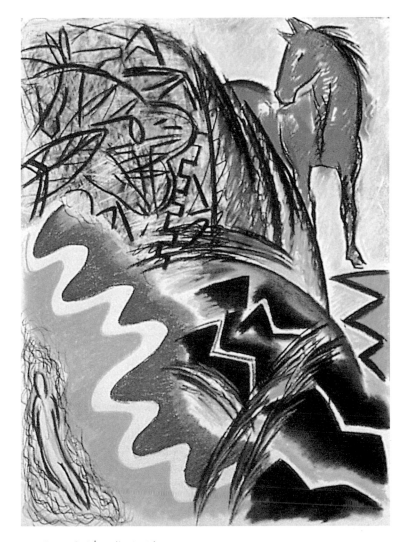

703 Jaune Quick-to-See Smith.
PETROGLYPH PARK. 1986.
Pastel on paper. 30" × 22".
Private collection. Courtesy Steinbaum Krauss Gallery, New York.

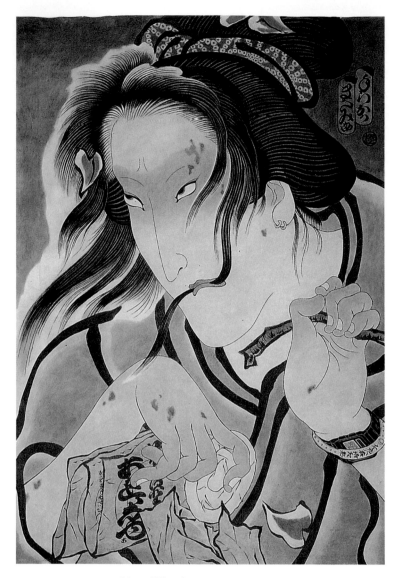

704 Masami Teraoka. GEISHA AND AIDS NIGHTMARE
from the AIDS SERIES. 1989–1990.
Watercolor on canvas. 106½" × 74".
Courtesy of the artist and Pamela Auchincloss Gallery/Arts Management.
Photograph: Lynda Hess.

continents will have to suffice to indicate the directions that art is taking.

Jaune Quick-to-See Smith uses a linear Abstract Expressionist style that links the symbols and markings of her French, Cree, Shoshone, and Flathead Native American heritage with the influences of Neo-Expressionist painters. In PETROGLYPH PARK (previous page), Smith used colors and ancient motifs of the Southwest landscape and the horse, a symbolically important animal to many Native American cultures.

We can see some of the complexity of today's multicultural world in the meticulous paintings of Masami Teraoka. He explores contemporary issues in a style based on the traditional woodblock prints popular in Japan from the seventeenth through the nineteenth centuries (see page 146). Both Japanese prints and Teraoka's paintings refer to worldly pleasures, but Teraoka's works, with references to hamburgers, ice cream cones, cameras, and condoms, are clearly of the late twentieth century.

With great wit and skillful design, Teraoka combines clichés of Eastern tradition and Western subject matter in highly inventive images that play on some of the ironies of contemporary East-West relations or focus on social and environmental hazards. In his GEISHA AND AIDS NIGHTMARE, the despairing courtesan realizes that it is already too late for the protection she clutches. In a 1970s series he confronted issues such as McDonald's Hamburgers invading Japan. His recent paintings involve the media blitz, virtual reality, and the e-mail jungle.

Issues now causing soul searching for many people in this ideologically shrinking world are the interlocking questions of personal and ethnic identity. Does an artist from one part of the world need to stick with the traditional styles still associated with that part of the world? Is it appropriate for an American artist to paint in a traditional Chinese style or visa versa?

Senegalese artist Fodé Camara feels strongly that Africans—and by implication everybody else—have the right to make any art they choose. Their work does not have to be recognizable as African. When asked if he saw himself as African, Camara replied, "Yes, I am very African because Africa is above all amalgamation and recycling."[2] In PARCOURS–TRICOLORE II, Camara presents a large colorful, boldly designed painting depicting an abstract standing figure, his own silhouette, with imprints of his hands, and suggestions of Goré, the former slave depot island off Dakar. By painting in sections, on three horizontal panels and then dividing his image in four vertical bands, Camara has provided a visual structure for his strong color and active brushwork. His use of symbols is personal and thought provoking.

Arpita Singh of New Delhi makes vivid works that chronicle women's concerns in India. Her 1993 painting DURGA is a reinterpretation of a well-known Hindu myth. In ancient times the world was besieged by the Buffalo Demon, and the gods could not subdue him. Finally the gods had the idea of combining all of their strength into the form of one woman, Durga, who grew multiple arms and took on unprecedented powers in order

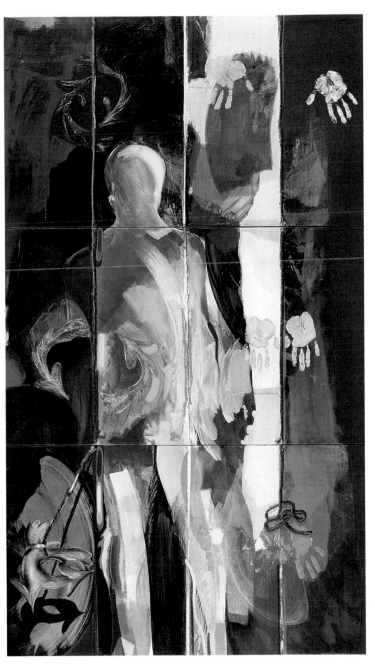

705 Fodé Camara.
PARCOURS–TRICOLORE II. 1988.
Oil on canvas. 82" × 47".
Collection Abdourahim Agne.
Courtesy of the artist and The Museum
for African Art, NY.
Photograph: Jerry L. Thompson.

706 Arpita Singh.
DURGA. 1993.
Oil on canvas. 29⅞" × 24".
Private collection.
Photo: Center of International
Modern Art, Calcutta.

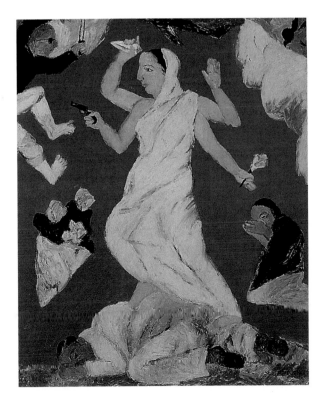

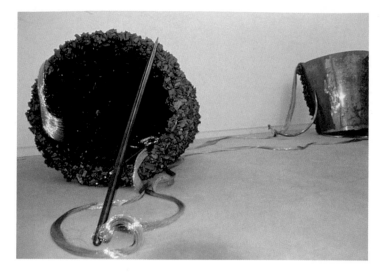

707 Tunga.
PALINDROMO INCESTO. 1994.
Installation view.
Courtesy of the artist and Luhring Augustine.

to stop the monster. This subject appears frequently in ancient Hindu temple sculpture, but Singh put the story in modern form. Here Durga wears a veil and holds a pistol along with the traditional blessing symbols of the shell and flower. Stepping over one foe, she confronts another who brandishes a knife. As in the myth, Durga is calm and collected as she does her duty to rid the world of a scourge. Admiring women kneel nearby. The artist used a heavily brushed and painterly style, coupled with unclear perspective depth and angular figures, to suggest vivid action. At the center is the heroine, who combines surging energy with poise and calm.

The installations of Brazilian artist Tunga combine an element of fantasy with a strong physical presence. PALINDROMO INCESTO, for example, has been re-created several times in slightly different forms. Three large metal buckets are magnetized and have varying amounts of metal fragments clinging to their surfaces. These are echoed by three metal rings suspended above the floor. Long braided strands of copper wire hold the rings and snake across the floor, joining the other elements. The work is puzzling at first glance, but the artist does not intend it to make logical sense. Drawing inspiration from the Surrealists' subversion of ratio-

nality, this work alludes to exploitative copper mining, womens' sewing (the buckets resemble thimbles, the copper wire thread), and home decoration for the holiday season. The title, with its reference to taboos and verbal play, defies explanation. The work's large size and rich combination of textures make it both memorable and somewhat eerie.

Contemporary concerns mix eloquently with Chinese traditions in the art of Cai Guo Qiang. For a 1997 museum exhibition in New York, Cai created CULTURAL MELTING BATH. The work's title refers to the "melting pot," or meeting ground of ethnicities, that characterizes New York City (and many other cities in the world these days). He lifted twelve huge stones from the bottom of a Chinese lake and arranged them in the museum under a large gauze tent according to the principles of *feng-shui,* the ancient Chinese art of domestic interior design. At the center, he placed a Western hot tub that bubbled and steamed reassuringly (visitors were allowed to bathe in it periodically). A mixture of herbs floated in the water, tinting it yellow and perfuming the space. Above, hanging from the ceiling, Cai installed a gnarled banyan tree root, and suspended from it a small cage containing a pair of white finches. The installation, which is based on traditional Chinese beliefs about the makeup of the universe, combined four of the five basic elements: water, earth, wood, and metal. By carefully arranging them, the artist hoped to give reassurance, and help soothe the frayed nerves of the modern city-dwellers who inhabit an increasingly multicultural world. One art critic who viewed the piece called it "calming and visually stunning."

Our final work in this book embodies a look ahead at the future of art. When the Cincinnati Contemporary Art Center outgrew its spaces in 1999, the directors had to consider what sorts of exhibits they would be likely to display in a new building: performances, videos, installations, and even paintings. They decided that they could not easily predict what the future course of art might be, and hence they wanted a building that incorporated uncertainty and unpredictablility into its very design.

They hired London-based Zaha Hadid to design the building, because they believed her to be most able to create a multi-story structure that would express the constant flux of contemporary art (see the biography of Hadid on page 245). The new CINCINNATI CONTEMPORARY ART CENTER has a translucent skin on the outside, so that passersby will see some of the art displayed within. The entry lobby is planned to be an inviting space, with galleries visible above as if suspended from the ceiling. A ramp with switchbacks gives access to the exhibition spaces while providing periodic glimpses of the lobby and the city outside. Each of these galleries is radically different in shape and structure, so that viewers cannot predict what sort of space lies ahead. This seems an excellent metaphor for the future of art, as we viewers proceed along a ramp toward yet-unseen works whose very unpredictability can be exciting, interesting, and stimulating.

This book has attempted to present a small portion of the seemingly boundless variety of art that has characterized human artistic expression. We have seen that art comes from basic feelings that all of us share. Through their work, most artists attempt to understand and interact with life, to find purpose and meaning in it. Art and human life vary considerably across time and space, but the primary purpose of art endures. Creative expression is a response to being alive.

Appreciation for the artistic dimension within each of us is as important as the recognition of the roles of art and artists in society at large. In the process of strengthening our understanding and appreciation for the art produced by recognized masters, we must not neglect the art within ourselves. To prevent such a dead end, it is necessary to give equal care and attention to the development of the artist within.

Art offers us a way to go beyond mere physical existence. The ideas, values, and approaches that constitute the basis of the visual arts can continue to enrich our lives and surroundings. We form art. Art forms us.

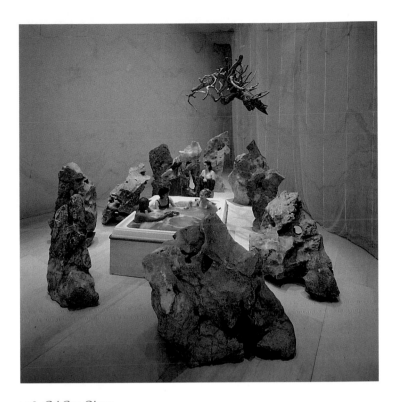

708   Cai Guo Qiang.
CULTURAL MELTING BATH:
PROJECTS FOR THE TWENTIETH CENTURY. 1997.
Installation in the Queens Museum of Art.
12 stones, hot tub, banyan tree root, pair of finches, herbs, netting. Dimensions variable.
Photograph: Hiro Ihara.

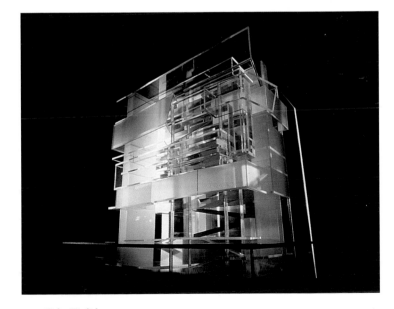

709   Zaha Hadid.
CINCINNATI CONTEMPORARY ART CENTER.
Presentation Model, 1998.
Photo courtesy Cincinnati Contemporary Art Center.

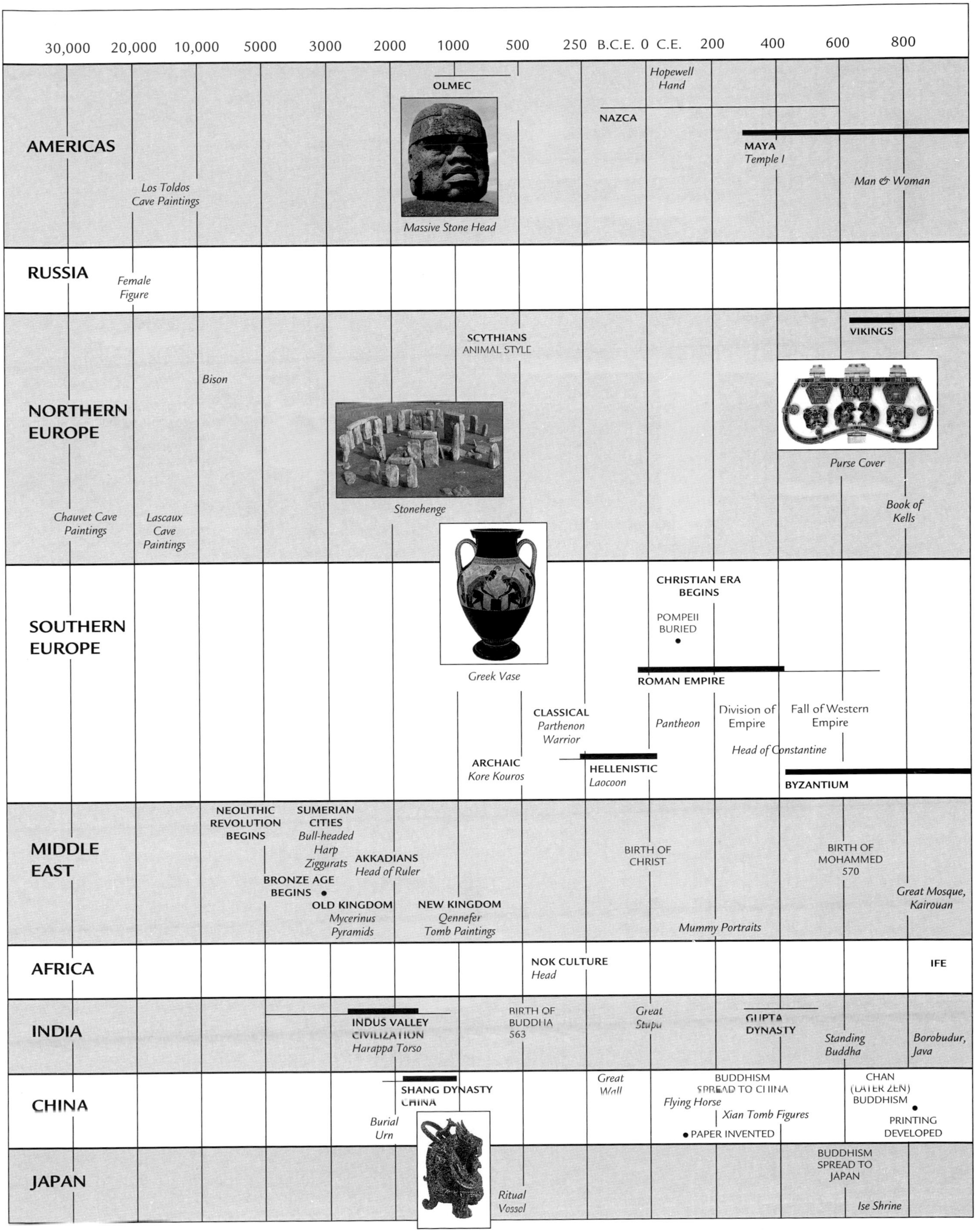

Timeline scale: 30,000 20,000 10,000 5000 3000 2000 1000 500 250 B.C.E. 0 C.E. 200 400 600 800

AMERICAS
- Los Toldos Cave Paintings
- OLMEC
- *Massive Stone Head*
- NAZCA
- Hopewell Hand
- MAYA — *Temple I*
- Man & Woman

RUSSIA
- *Female Figure*

NORTHERN EUROPE
- Bison
- Chauvet Cave Paintings
- Lascaux Cave Paintings
- Stonehenge
- SCYTHIANS ANIMAL STYLE
- VIKINGS
- *Purse Cover*
- Book of Kells

SOUTHERN EUROPE
- Greek Vase
- ARCHAIC — *Kore Kouros*
- CLASSICAL — *Parthenon Warrior*
- HELLENISTIC — *Laocoon*
- CHRISTIAN ERA BEGINS
- POMPEII BURIED
- ROMAN EMPIRE
- *Pantheon*
- Division of Empire
- Fall of Western Empire
- *Head of Constantine*
- BYZANTIUM

MIDDLE EAST
- NEOLITHIC REVOLUTION BEGINS
- SUMERIAN CITIES — *Bull-headed Harp* — Ziggurats
- BRONZE AGE BEGINS
- AKKADIANS — *Head of Ruler*
- OLD KINGDOM — *Mycerinus* — Pyramids
- NEW KINGDOM — *Qennefer Tomb Paintings*
- BIRTH OF CHRIST
- *Mummy Portraits*
- BIRTH OF MOHAMMED 570
- Great Mosque, Kairouan

AFRICA
- NOK CULTURE — *Head*
- IFE

INDIA
- INDUS VALLEY CIVILIZATION — *Harappa Torso*
- BIRTH OF BUDDHA 563
- *Great Stupa*
- GUPTA DYNASTY
- *Standing Buddha*
- Borobudur, Java

CHINA
- SHANG DYNASTY CHINA
- *Burial Urn*
- *Ritual Vessel*
- Great Wall
- BUDDHISM SPREAD TO CHINA
- *Flying Horse*
- PAPER INVENTED
- *Xian Tomb Figures*
- CHAN (LATER ZEN) BUDDHISM
- PRINTING DEVELOPED

JAPAN
- BUDDHISM SPREAD TO JAPAN
- Ise Shrine

| 1000 | 1100 | 1200 | 1300 | 1400 | 1450 | 1500 | 1550 | 1600 | 1650 | 1700 | 1750 | 1800 | 1850 |

Machu Picchu

HUDSON RIVER SCHOOL

Durand
Cole

INCA   *Inca Shirt*

DECLARATION
OF INDEPENDENCE

CIVIL
WAR

AZTEC

Vessel of the Feathered Serpent Quetzcoatl

Hildegard
of Bingen

Crystal Palace

NEO-CLASSICISM
David
Kauffmann

GOTHIC
Chartres Cathedral

REFORMATION

ROMANTICISM
Delacroix
Constable
Turner

Holbein

The Kitchen Maid
Vermeer

FRENCH
REVOLUTION   Courbet

ROMANESQUE

van Eyck

Dürer

Rembrandt

ROCOCO
Fragonard

INVENTION OF
PHOTOGRAPHY

Daguierre
Nadar

Tree of Jesse

RENAISSANCE   Botticelli
Lippi   Leonardo

Giotto

Raphael   Palladio

BAROQUE

Michelangelo
David

Caravaggio
El Greco

Bernini

Goya

Carriera

COUNTER REFORMATION

BYZANTIUM

Alhambra

Süleymaniye Mosque

Ardabil Carpet

D'Arenberg Basin

IFE   *Male Portrait Head*

Benin Head

Kandarya Temple

MUSLIM INVASION
OF INDIA

Fan Kuan
Travelers

GUNPOWDER
INVENTED

Mansur
Turkey Cock

Tang Yin
Whispering Pines on a Mountain Path

Bada
Shanren

Ryoan-ji Garden

Katsura

UKIYO-E

Sengai   Utamaro

Hokusai

Burning of the Sanjo Palace

Sotatsu
Waves at Matsushima

Hiroshige

Timeline years: 1870 1880 1890 1900 1910 1920 1930 1940 1950 1960 1970 1980 1990 2000

AMERICAS

WORLD WAR I

HARLEM RENAISSANCE
Lawrence
Motley

● FIRST TALKING FILM

WORLD WAR II

ABSTRACT EXPRESSIONISM
Pollock
de Kooning
Hofmann
Frankenthaler

Rauschenberg

● FIRST MOON LANDING

CONCEPTUAL

POP
Rosenquist
Warhol

PHOTOREALISM
Estes

Meireles

REGIONALISM
Wood
Benton

MINIMAL
T. Smith
Held

Rothenberg

POST-MODERNISM

F.L. Wright

Eisenstein

Nampeyo
Seed Jar

Cassatt
The Letter

O'Keeffe
Oriental Poppies

Kabakov

RUSSIA

CONSTRUCTIVISM
Tatlin

NORTHERN EUROPE

Manet

IMPRESSIONISM
Monet
Renoir
Degas
Rodin

POST-IMPRESSIONISM
Cézanne
Gauguin
van Gogh

CUBISM
Braque
Picasso

INTERNATIONAL STYLE

NEO-EXPRESSIONISM
Kiefer

Jorn

BAUHAUS

DE STIJL
Mondrian
Rietveld

FAUVISM
Matisse

Brancusi

DADA
Duchamp
Höch

PERFORMANCE
Beuys

GERMAN EXPRESSIONISM
Kirchner
Nolde
Kollwitz

SURREALISM
Miró   Magritte
Dali

Cézanne
The Turn in the Road

FUTURISM
Balla
Boccioni

Burri

SOUTHERN EUROPE

Balla
Dynamism of a Dog on a Leash

Aulenti
Italian Pavilion

MIDDLE EAST

Congo Power Figure

Fodé   **AFRICA**

Singh   **INDIA**

Rawanchaikul

Bakota Funerary Figure

NOTE: In presenting the Artforms Time Line, it has been necessary to use several different scales to indicate both long and short spans of years on a few pages. If a ten-year scale were used to cover the entire 32,000-year period presented, the time line would be more than a hundred feet long.

CHINESE REVOLUTION

CHINA

Cai
Projects for Extraterrestrials

JAPAN

Tange   Takaezu   Ando

GLOSSARY

The following terms are defined according to their usage in the visual arts. Words in *italics* are also defined in the glossary.

abstract art Art that departs significantly from natural appearances. Forms are modified or changed to varying degrees in order to emphasize certain qualities or content. Recognizable references to original appearances may be very slight. The term is also used to describe art that is *nonrepresentational*.

Abstract Expressionism An art movement, primarily in painting, that originated in the United States in the 1940s and remained strong through the 1950s. Artists working in many different styles emphasized spontaneous personal expression in large paintings that are *abstract* or *nonrepresentational*. One type of Abstract Expressionism is called *action painting*. See also *Expressionism*.

abstract Surrealism See *Surrealism*.

academic art Art governed by rules, especially works sanctioned by an official institution, academy, or school. Originally applied to art that conformed to standards established by the French Academy regarding composition, drawing, and color usage. The term has come to mean conservative and traditional art.

academy An institution of artists and scholars, originally formed during the Renaissance to free artists from control by guilds and to elevate them from artisan to professional status. In an academy, art is taught as a humanist discipline along with other disciplines of the liberal arts.

achromatic Having no color (or *hue*); without identifiable hue. Most blacks, whites, grays, and browns are achromatic.

acrylic (acrylic resin) A clear plastic used as a *binder* in paint and as a casting material in sculpture.

action painting A style of *nonrepresentational* painting that relies on the physical movement of the artist by using such gestural techniques as vigorous brushwork, dripping, and pouring. Dynamism is often created through the interlaced directions of the paint's impact. A subcategory of *Abstract Expressionism*.

additive color mixture The mixture of colored light. When light colors are combined (as with overlapping spot lights), the mixture becomes successively lighter. Light primaries, when combined, create white light. See also *subtractive color mixture*.

additive sculpture Sculptural form produced by adding, combining, or building up material from a core or *armature*. Modeling in clay and welding steel are additive processes.

aerial perspective See *perspective*.

aesthetic Pertaining to the sense of the beautiful and to heightened sensory perception in general.

aesthetics The study and philosophy of the quality and nature of sensory responses related to, but not limited by, the concept of beauty. Within the art context: The philosophy of art focusing on questions regarding what art is, how it is evaluated, the concept of beauty, and the relationship between the idea of beauty and the concept of art.

afterimage The visual image that remains after an initial stimulus is removed. Staring at a single intense *hue* may cause the cones, or color receptors, of the eye to become fatigued and perceive only the complement of the original hue after it has been removed.

airbrush A small-scale paint sprayer that allows the artist to control a fine mist of paint.

analogous colors or **analogous hues** Closely related *hues*, especially those in which a common hue can be seen; hues that are neighbors on the color wheel, such as blue, blue-green, and green.

analytical Cubism See *Cubism*.

aperture In photography, the *camera* lens opening and its relative diameter. Measured in f-stops, such as f/8, f/11, etc. As the number increases, the size of the aperture decreases, thereby reducing the amount of light passing through the *lens* and striking the film.

apse A semicircular end to an aisle in a *basilica* or a Christian church. In Christian churches an apse is usually placed at the eastern end of the central aisle.

aquatint An *intaglio* printmaking process in which *value* areas rather than lines are etched on the printing plate. Powdered resin is sprinkled on the plate, which is then immersed in an acid bath. The acid bites around the resin particles, creating a rough surface that holds ink. Also, a *print* made using this process.

arcade A series of *arches* supported by columns or piers. Also, a covered passageway between two series of arches or between a series of arches and a wall.

arch A curved structure designed to span an opening, usually made of stone or other masonry. Roman arches are semicircular; Islamic and Gothic arches come to a point at the top.

armature A rigid framework serving as a supporting inner core for clay or other soft sculpting material.

art criticism The process of using formal analysis, description, and interpretation to evaluate or explain the quality and meanings of art.

Art Nouveau A style that originated in the late 1880s based on the sinuous curves of plant forms. It was used primarily in architectural detailing and the applied arts.

artist's proof A trial print, usually made as an artist works on a plate or block, to check the progress of a work.

assemblage Sculpture using preexisting, sometimes "found" objects that may or may not contribute their original identities to the total content of the work.

asymmetrical Without *symmetry*.

atmospheric perspective See *perspective*.

automatism The condition of being automatic; action without conscious control. Employed by *Surrealist* writers and artists to allow unconscious ideas and feelings to be expressed.

balance An arrangement of parts achieving a state of equilibrium between opposing forces or influences. Major types are symmetrical and asymmetrical. See *symmetry*.

Baroque The seventeenth-century period in Europe characterized in the visual arts by dramatic light and shade, turbulent composition, and exaggerated emotional expression.

barrel vault See *vault*.

bas relief See *relief sculpture*.

Basilica A roman town hall, with three aisles and an *apse* at one or both ends. Christians appropriated this form for their churches.

Bauhaus German art school in existence from 1919 to 1933, best known for its influence on design, leadership in art education, and its radically innovative philosophy of applying design principles to machine technology and mass production.

beam The horizontal stone or timber placed across an architectural space to take the weight of the roof or wall above; also called a *lintel.*

binder The material used in paint that causes *pigment* particles to adhere to one another and to the *support;* for example, linseed oil or acrylic polymer.

bodhisattva A type of Buddhist holy person who is about to achieve enlightenment, but postpones it to remain on earth to teach others. Frequently depicted in the arts of China and Japan.

buttress A *support,* usually exterior, for a wall, *arch,* or *vault* that opposes the lateral forces of these structures. A flying buttress consists of a strut or segment of an arch carrying the thrust of a vault to a vertical pier positioned away from the main portion of the building. An important element in *Gothic* cathedrals.

Byzantine art Styles of painting, design, and architecture developed from the fifth century C.E. in the Byzantine Empire of ancient eastern Europe. Characterized in architecture by round *arches,* large *domes,* and extensive use of *mosaic;* characterized in painting by formal design, *frontal* and *stylized* figures, and rich use of color, especially gold, in generally religious subject matter.

calligraphy The art of beautiful writing. Broadly, a flowing use of line, often varying from thick to thin.

camera A mechanical or digital device for taking photographs. It generally consists of a light-proof enclosure with an *aperture,* which allows a controlled light image to pass through a shuttered *lens* and be focused on a photosensitive material.

camera obscura A dark room (or box) with a small hole in one side, through which an inverted image of the view outside is projected onto the opposite wall, screen, or mirror. The image is then traced. This forerunner of the modern camera was a tool for recording an optically accurate image.

cantilever A beam or slab projecting a substantial distance beyond its supporting post or wall; a projection supported only at one end.

capital In architecture, the top part, cap stone, or head of a column or pillar.

cartoon 1. A humorous or satirical drawing. 2. A drawing completed as a full-scale work-ing drawing, usually for a *fresco* painting, *mural,* or tapestry.

carving A *subtractive* process in which a sculpture is formed by removing material from a block or mass of wood, stone, or other material, with the use of sharpened tools.

casting A substitution or replacement process that involves pouring liquid material such as molten metal, clay, wax, or plaster into a mold. When the liquid hardens, the mold is removed, and a form in the shape of the mold is left.

catacombs Underground burial places in Ancient Rome. Christians and Jews often decorated the walls and ceilings with paintings.

ceramics Clay hardened into a relatively permanent material by firing. A practitioner of the ceramic arts is a ceramist.

chiaroscuro Italian word meaning "light-dark." The gradations of light and dark *values* in *two-dimensional* imagery; especially the illusion of rounded, three-dimensional form created through gradations of light and shade rather than line. Highly developed by *Renaissance* painters.

chroma See *intensity.*

cinematography The art and technique of making motion pictures, especially the work done by motion picture camera operators.

classical 1. The art of ancient Greece and Rome. In particular, the style of Greek art that flourished during the fifth century B.C.E. 2. Any art based on a clear, rational, and regular structure, emphasizing horizontal and vertical directions, and organizing its parts with special emphasis on balance and proportion. The term classic is also used to indicate recognized excellence.

closed form A self-contained or explicitly limited form; having a resolved balance of tensions, a sense of calm completeness implying a totality within itself.

coffer In architecture, a decorative sunken panel on the underside of a ceiling.

collage From the French *coller,* to glue. A work made by gluing various materials, such as paper scraps, photographs, and cloth, on a flat surface.

colonnade A row of columns usually spanned or connected by *beams* (lintels).

color field painting A movement that grew out of *Abstract Expressionism,* in which large stained or painted areas or "fields" of color evoke aesthetic and emotional responses.

color wheel A circular arrangement of contiguous spectral <u>hues</u> used in some color systems. Also called a color circle.

complementary colors Two *hues* directly opposite one another on a *color wheel* which, when mixed together in proper proportions, produce a neutral gray. The true complement of a color can be seen in its *afterimage.*

composition The combining of parts or elements to form a whole; the structure, organization, or total form of a work of art. See also *design.*

Conceptual art An art form in which the originating idea and the process by which it is presented take precedence over a tangible product. Conceptual works are sometimes produced in visible form, but they often exist only as descriptions of mental concepts or ideas. This trend developed in the late 1960s, partially as a way to avoid the commercialization of art.

content Meaning or message contained and communicated by a work of art, including its emotional, intellectual, symbolic, thematic, and narrative connotations.

contrapposto Italian for "counterpose." The counterpositioning of parts of the human figure about a central vertical axis, as when the weight is placed on one foot causing the hip and shoulder lines to counterbalance each other—often in a graceful S-curve.

cool colors Colors whose relative visual temperatures make them seem cool. Cool colors generally include green, blue-green, blue, blue-violet, and violet. Warmness or coolness is relative to adjacent hues. See also *warm colors.*

crosshatching See *hatching.*

Cubism The most influential style of the twentieth century, developed in Paris by Picasso and Braque, beginning in 1907. The early mature phase of the style, called analytical Cubism, lasted from 1909 through 1911. Cubism is based on the simultaneous presentation of multiple views, disintegration, and geometric reconstruction of subjects in flattened, ambiguous pictorial space; figure and ground merge into one interwoven surface of shifting planes. Color is limited to *neutrals.* By 1912, the more decorative phase called synthetic or collage Cubism began to appear; it was characterized by fewer, more solid forms, conceptual rather than observed subject matter, and richer color and texture.

curtain wall A non-load-bearing wall.

curvilinear Formed or characterized by curving lines or edges.

cutting ratio The ratio of film actually used in a movie after editing to the amount that was shot during production.

Dada A movement in art and literature, founded in Switzerland in the early twentieth century, which ridiculed contemporary culture and conventional art. The Dadaists shared an antimilitaristic and anti-aesthetic attitude, generated in part by the horrors of World War I and in part by a rejection of accepted canons of morality and taste. The anarchic spirit of Dada can be seen in the works of Duchamp, Man Ray, Hoch, Miro, and Picasso. Many Dadaists later explored *Surrealism.*

daguerreotype An early photographic process developed by Louis Daguerre in the 1830s which required a treated metal plate. This plate was exposed to light, and the chemical reactions on the plate created the first satisfactory photographs.

depth of field The area of sharpness of focus in front of and behind the subject in a photograph. Depth of field becomes greater as the aperture is decreased and the f-stop number is increased.

De Stijl A Dutch purist art movement begun during World War I by Mondrian and others. It involved painters, sculptors, designers, and architects whose works and ideas were expressed in *De Stijl* magazine. De Stijl, Dutch for "the style," was aimed at creating a universal language of *form* that would be independent of individual emotion. Visual form was pared down to primary colors plus black and white, and rectangular shapes. The movement was influential primarily in architecture.

direct painting Executing a painting in one sitting, applying wet over wet colors.

divisionism See *Pointillism.*

dome A generally hemispherical roof or *vault.* Theoretically, an *arch* rotated 360 degrees on its vertical axis.

dressed stone Stone used for building that is cut to fit into a masonry wall.

drypoint An *intaglio* printmaking process in which lines are scratched directly into a metal plate with a steel needle. Also, the resulting *print.*

earthenware A type of clay used for ceramics. It fires at between 1100–1150° C., and is porous after firing.

earthworks Sculptural forms made from earth, rocks, or sometimes plants, often on a vast scale and in remote locations. Some are deliberately impermanent.

eclecticism The practice of selecting or borrowing from earlier styles and combining the borrowed elements.

edition In printmaking, the total number of *prints* made and approved by the artist, usually numbered consecutively. Also, a limited number of multiple originals of a single design in any medium.

elevation In architecture, a scale drawing of any vertical side of a given structure.

encaustic A painting medium in which *pigment* is suspended in a *binder* of hot wax.

engraving An *intaglio* printmaking process in which grooves are cut into a metal or wood surface with a sharp cutting tool called a burin or graver. Also, the resulting *print.*

entasis In *classical* architecture, the slight swelling or bulge in the center of a column, which corrects the illusion of concave tapering produced by parallel straight lines.

etching An *intaglio* printmaking process in which a metal plate is first coated with acid-resistant wax, then scratched to expose the metal to the bite of nitric acid where lines are desired. Also, the resulting *print.*

Expressionism The broad term that describes emotional art, most often boldly executed and making free use of distortion and symbolic or invented color. More specifically, Expressionism refers to individual and group styles originating in Europe in the late nineteenth and early twentieth centuries. See also *Abstract Expressionism.*

Fauvism A style of painting introduced in Paris in the early twentieth century, characterized by areas of bright, contrasting color and simplified shapes. The name *les fauves* is French for "the wild beasts."

feminism In art, a movement among artists, critics, and art historians that began in an organized fashion in the 1970s. Feminists seek to validate and promote art forms that express the unique experience of women, and to redress oppression by men.

feng shui An ancient Chinese method of interior design that seeks to align spiritual forces within the space to be arranged.

figure Separate shape(s) distinguishable from a background or *ground.*

flying buttress See *buttress.*

folk art Art of people who have had no formal, academic training, but whose works are part of an established tradition of style and craftsmanship.

font The name given to a style of type. The text of *Artforms* is printed in the Adobe Garamond font.

foreshortening The representation of *forms* on a *two-dimensional* surface by shortening the length in such a way that the long axis appears to project toward or recede away from the viewer.

form In the broadest sense, the total physical characteristics of an object, event, or situation.

format The shape or proportions of a *picture plane.*

fresco A painting technique in which *pigments* suspended in water are applied to a damp lime-plaster surface. The pigments dry to become part of the plaster wall or surface. Sometimes called *true fresco* or *buon fresco* to distinguish is from painting over dry plaster.

frieze A narrow band of *relief sculpture* that usually occupies the space above the columns of a classical building.

frontal An adjective describing an object that faces the viewer directly, rather than being set at an angle or *foreshortened.*

Futurism A group movement that originated in Italy in 1909. One of several movements to grow out of *Cubism.* Futurists added implied motion to the shifting planes and multiple observation points of the Cubists; they celebrated natural as well as mechanical motion and speed. Their glorification of danger, war, and the machine age was in keeping with the martial spirit developing in Italy at the time.

gesso A mixture of glue and either chalk or plaster of Paris applied as a *ground* or coating to surfaces in order to give them the correct properties to receive paint. Gesso can also be built up or molded into *relief* designs, or carved.

glaze In *ceramics,* a vitreous or glassy coating applied to seal and decorate surfaces. Glaze may be colored, transparent, or opaque. In oil painting, a thin transparent or translucent layer brushed over another layer of paint, allowing the first layer to show through but altering its color slightly.

Gothic Primarily an architectural style that prevailed in western Europe from the twelfth through the fifteenth centuries, characterized by pointed *arches,* ribbed *vaults,* and flying *buttresses,* that made it possible to create stone buildings that reached great heights.

gouache An opaque, water-soluble paint. *Watercolor* to which opaque white has been added.

ground The background in two-dimensional works—the area around and between *figure(s)*. Also, the surface onto which paint is applied.

Happening An event conceived by artists and performed by artists and others, usually unrehearsed and without a specific script or stage.

hard-edge A term first used in the 1950s to distinguish styles of paintings in which shapes are precisely defined by sharp edges, in contrast to the usually blurred or soft edges in *Abstract Expressionist* paintings.

hatching A technique used in drawing and linear forms of printmaking, in which lines are placed in parallel series to darken the value of an area. Crosshatching is drawing one set of hatchings over another in a different direction so that the lines cross.

Hellenistic Style of the later phase of ancient Greek art (300–100 B.C.E.), characterized by emotion, drama, and interaction of sculptural forms with the surrounding space.

hierarchic proportion Use of unnatural *proportions* or *scale* to show the relative importance of figures.

high key Exclusive use of pale or light *values* within a given area or surface.

horizon line In linear *perspective,* the implied or actual line or edge placed on a *two-dimensional* surface to represent the place in nature where the sky meets the horizontal land or water plane. The horizon line matches the eye level on a two-dimensional surface. Lines or edges parallel to the ground plane and moving away from the viewer appear to converge at *vanishing points* on the horizon line.

hue That property of a color identifying a specific, named wavelength of light such as green, red, violet, and so on. Often used synonymously with *color.*

humanism A cultural and intellectual movement during the *Renaissance,* following the rediscovery of the art and literature of ancient Greece and Rome. A philosophy or attitude concerned with the interests, achievements, and capabilities of human beings rather than with the abstract concepts and problems of theology or science.

icon An image or symbolic representation (often with sacred significance).

iconography The symbolic meanings of subjects and signs used to convey ideas important to particular cultures or religions, and the conventions governing the use of such forms.

impasto In painting, thick paint applied to a surface in a heavy manner, having the appearance and consistency of buttery paste.

implied line A line in a composition that is not actually drawn. It may be a sight line of a figure in a composition, or a line along which two *shapes* align with each other.

Impressionism A style of painting that originated in France about 1870. (The first Impressionist exhibit was held in 1874.) Paintings of casual subjects were executed outdoors using divided brush strokes to capture the light and mood of a particular moment and the transitory effects of natural light and color.

installation A type of art medium in which the artist arranges objects or art works in a room, thinking of the entire space as the medium to be manipulated. Also called *environments.*

intaglio Any printmaking technique in which lines and areas to be inked and transferred to paper are recessed below the surface of the printing plate. *Etching, engraving, drypoint,* and *aquatint* are all intaglio processes. See also *print.*

intensity The relative purity or saturation of a *hue* (color), on a scale from bright (pure) to dull (mixed with another hue or a *neutral*).

intermediate color A *hue* between a primary and a secondary on the color wheel, such as yellow-green, a mixture of yellow and green.

International Style An architectural style that emerged in several European countries between 1910 and 1920. Related to purism and *De Stijl* in painting, it joined structure and exterior design into a noneclectic form based on rectangular geometry and growing out of the basic function and structure of the building.

Isometic perspective See *perspective.*

iwan A high, vaulted porch frequently used in Islamic architecture to mark an important building or entrance.

kachina One of many deified ancestral spirits honored by Hopi and other Pueblo Indians. These spiritual beings are usually depicted in doll-like forms.

kiln An oven in which pottery or *ceramic* ware is fired.

kinetic art Art that incorporates actual movement as part of the design.

kore Greek for "maiden." An archaic Greek statue of a standing clothed young woman.

kouros Greek for "youth." An archaic Greek statue of a standing nude young male.

lens The part of a *camera* that concentrates light and focuses the image.

linear perspective See *perspective.*

linoleum cut A *relief* process in printmaking, in which an artist cuts away negative spaces from a block of linoleum, leaving raised areas to take ink for printing.

lintel See *beam.*

literati painting In Asian art, paintings produced by cultivated amateurs who are generally wealthy and devoted to the arts, including calligraphy, painting, and poetry. Most commonly used to describe work of painters not attached to the royal courts of the Yuan, Ming, and Qing Dynasties (fourteenth to eighteenth centuries) in China.

lithography A planographic printmaking technique based on the antipathy of oil and water. The image is drawn with a grease crayon or painted with *tusche* on a stone or grained aluminum plate. The surface is then chemically treated and dampened so that it will accept ink only where the crayon or tusche has been used.

local color The actual color as distinguished from the apparent color of objects and surfaces; true color, without shadows or reflections. Sometimes called *object color.*

logo Short for "logotype." Sign, name, or trademark of an institution, a firm, or a publication, consisting of letter forms, borne on one printing plate or piece of type.

loom A device for producing cloth by interweaving fibers at right angles.

lost wax A *casting* method. First a model is made from wax and encased in clay or casting plaster. When the clay is fired to make a mold, the wax melts away, leaving a void that can be filled with molten metal or other self-hardening liquid to produce a cast.

madrasa In Islamic tradition, a building that combines a school, prayer hall, and lodging for students.

Mannerism A style that developed in the sixteenth century as a reaction to the classical rationality and balanced harmony of the High *Renaissance;* characterized by dramatic use of space and light, exaggerated color, elongation of figures, and distortions of *perspective, scale,* and *proportion.*

mass Three-dimensional form having physical bulk. Also, the illusion of such a form on a *two-dimensional* surface.

mat Border of cardboard or similar material placed around a picture as a neutral area between the frame and the picture.

matte A dull finish or surface, especially in painting, photography, and *ceramics.*

medium (pl. media or mediums) 1. A particular material along with its accompanying technique; a specific type of artistic technique or means of expression determined by the use of particular materials. 2. In paint, the fluid in which *pigment* is suspended, allowing it to spread and adhere to the surface.

mihrab A niche in the end wall of a *mosque* that points the way to the Muslim holy city of Mecca.

minaret A tower outside a *mosque* where chanters stand to call the faithful to prayer.

Minimalism A *nonrepresentational* style of sculpture and painting, usually severely restricted in the use of visual elements and often consisting of simple geometric shapes or masses. The style came to prominence in the late 1960s.

mixed media Works of art made with more than one *medium.*

mobile A type of sculpture in which parts move, often activated by air currents. See also *kinetic art.*

modeling 1. Working pliable material such as clay or wax into *three-dimensional* forms. 2. In drawing or painting, the effect of light falling on a three-dimensional object so that the illusion of its *mass* is created and defined by *value* gradations.

monochromatic A color scheme limited to variations of one *hue;* a hue with its *tints* and/or *shades.*

montage 1. A composition made up of pictures or parts of pictures previously drawn, painted, or photographed. 2. In motion pictures, the combining of separate bits of film to portray the character of a single event through multiple views.

mosaic An art medium in which small pieces of colored glass, stone, or ceramic tile called *tessera* are embedded in a background material such as plaster or mortar. Also, works made using this technique.

mosque House of public prayer in the Muslim religion. From the Arabic *masjid,* "place of prostration."

mural A large wall painting, often executed in *fresco.*

narrative editing A filmmaking process in which a film editor makes a version of a scene by combining many shots from various camera angles.

nave The tall central space of a church or cathedral, usually flanked by side aisles.

negative shape A background or *ground* shape seen in relation to foreground or *figure* shape(s).

Neoclassicism New classicism. A revival of classical Greek and Roman forms in art, music, and literature, particularly during the eighteenth and nineteenth centuries in Europe and America. It was part of a reaction against the excesses of *Baroque* and *Rococo* art.

Neolithic art A period of ancient art after the introduction of agriculture but before the invention of bronze. *Neolithic* means "new stone age" to distinguish it from *Paleolithic,* or "old stone age."

neutrals Not associated with any single *hue.* Blacks, whites, grays, and dull gray-browns. A neutral can be made by mixing complementary hues.

nonobjective See *nonrepresentational art.*

nonrepresentational Art without reference to anything outside itself—without representation. Also called "nonobjective"—without recognizable objects.

object color See *local color.*

offset lithography Planographic printing by indirect image-transfer from photomechanical plates. The plate transfers ink to a rubber-covered cylinder, which "offsets" the ink to the paper. Also called photo-offset and offset lithography.

oil paint Paint in which the *pigment* is held together with a *binder* of oil, usually linseed oil.

opaque Impenetrable by light; not transparent or translucent.

open form A form whose contour is irregular or broken, having a sense of growth, change, or unresolved tension; form in a state of becoming.

optical color mixture Apparent rather than actual color mixture, produced by interspersing brush strokes or dots of color instead of physically mixing them. The implied mixing occurs in the eye of the viewer and produces a lively color sensation.

organic shape An irregular, non-geometric shape. A shape that resembles any living matter. Most organic shapes are not drawn with a ruler or a compass.

original print A print done by an artist or under his or her direct supervision. Not a reproduction.

painterly Painting characterized by openness of form, in which shapes are defined by loose brushwork in light and dark color areas rather than by outline or contour.

Paleolithic art A very ancient period of art coincident with the Old Stone Age, before the discovery of agriculture and animal herding.

pastels 1. Sticks of powdered pigment held together with a gum binding agent. 2. Pale colors or *tints.*

performance art Dramatic presentation by visual artists (as distinguished from theater artists such as actors and dancers) in front of an audience, usually apart from a formal theatrical setting.

persistence of vision An optical illusion that makes cinema possible. The eye and mind tend to hold seen images for a fraction of a second after they disappear from view. Quick projection of slightly differing images creates the illusion of movement.

perspective A system for creating an illusion of depth or *three-dimensional* space on a *two-dimensional* surface. Usually used to refer to linear perspective, which is based on the fact that parallel lines or edges appear to converge and objects appear smaller as the distance between them and the viewer increases. Atmospheric perspective (aerial perspective) creates the illusion of distance by reducing color saturation, value contrast, and detail in order to imply the hazy effect of atmosphere between the viewer and distant objects. *Isometric perspective* is not a visual or optical interpretation, but a mechanical means to show space and volume in rectangular forms. Parallel lines remain parallel; there is no convergence. A work executed in *one-point perspective* has a single *vanishing point.* A work in *two-point perspective* has two of them.

photomontage The process of combining parts of various photographs in one photograph.

photorealism A style of painting that became prominent in the 1970s, based on the cool objectivity of photographs as records of subjects.

photo screen A variation of *silkscreen* in which the stencil is prepared photographically.

picture plane The *two-dimensional* picture surface.

pigment Any coloring agent, made from natural or synthetic substances, used in paints or drawing materials.

plate mark An impression made on a piece of paper by pressing a printing plate onto it. A plate mark is usually a sign of an *original print*.

Pointillism A system of painting using tiny dots or "points" of color, developed by French artist Georges Seurat in the 1880s. Seurat systematized the divided brushwork and *optical color mixture* of the *Impressionists* and called his technique "Divisionism."

Pop Art A style of painting and sculpture that developed in the late 1950s and early 1960s, in Britain and the United States; based on the visual cliches, subject matter, and impersonal style of popular mass-media imagery.

porcelain A type of clay for ceramics. It is white or grayish and fires at between 1350–1500° C. After firing, it is translucent and rings when struck.

positive shape A *figure* or foreground shape, as opposed to a *negative* ground or background shape.

post-and-beam system (post and lintel) In architecture, a structural system that uses two or more uprights or posts to support a horizontal beam (or lintel) which spans the space between them.

Post-Impressionism A general term applied to various personal styles of painting by French artists (or artists living in France) that developed from about 1885 to 1900 in reaction to what these artists saw as the somewhat formless and aloof quality *Impressionist* painting. Post-Impressionist painters were concerned with the significance of form, symbols, expressiveness, and psychological intensity. They can be broadly separated into two groups—expressionists, such as Gauguin and van Gogh, and formalists, such as Cezanne and Seurat.

Post-Modern An attitude or trend of the 1970s, 1980s, and 1990s. In architecture, the movement away from or beyond what had become boring adaptations of the *International Style,* in favor of an imaginative, eclectic approach. In the other visual arts, Post-Modern is characterized by influence from all periods and styles, including modernism, and a willingness to combine elements of all styles and periods. Although modernism makes distinctions between high art and popular taste, Post-Modernism makes no such value judgments.

primary colors Those *hues* that cannot be produced by mixing other hues. *Pigment* primaries are red, yellow, and blue; light primaries are red, green, and blue. Theoretically, pigment primaries can be mixed

together to form all the other hues in the spectrum.

prime In painting, a primary layer of paint or sizing applied to a surface that is to be painted.

print (artist's print) A multiple original impression made from a plate, stone, wood block, or screen by an artist or made under the artist's supervision. Prints are usually made in *editions,* with each print numbered and signed by the artist.

proportion The size relationship of parts to a whole and to one another.

realism 1. A type of *representational art* in which the artist depicts as closely as possible what the eye sees. 2. Realism. The mid-nineteenth-century style of Courbet and others, based on the idea that ordinary people and everyday activities are worthy subjects for art.

registration In color printmaking or machine printing, the process of aligning the impressions of blocks or plates on the same sheet of paper.

reinforced concrete (ferroconcrete) Concrete with steel mesh or bars embedded in it to increase its tensile strength.

relief printing A printing technique in which the parts of the printing surface that carry ink are left raised, while the remaining areas are cut away. Woodcuts and linoleum prints (linocuts) are relief prints.

relief sculpture Sculpture in which *three-dimensional* forms project from the flat background of which they are a part. The degree of projection can vary and is described by the terms high relief and low relief.

Renaissance Period in Europe from the late fourteenth through the sixteenth centuries, which was characterized by a renewed interest in human-centered *classical* art, literature, and learning. See also *humanism.*

representational art Art in which it is the artist's intention to present again or represent a particular subject; especially pertaining to realistic portrayal of subject matter.

reproduction A mechanically produced copy of an original work of art; not to be confused with an original *print* or art print or artist's print.

rhythm The regular or ordered repetition of dominant and subordinate elements or units within a design.

ribbed vault See *vault.*

Rococo From the French "rocaille" meaning "rock work." This late *Baroque* (c. 1715–

1775) style used in interior decoration and painting was characteristically playful, pretty, romantic, and visually loose or soft; it used small *scale* and ornate decoration, *pastel* colors, and asymmetrical arrangement of curves. Rococo was popular in France and southern Germany in the eighteenth century.

Romanesque A style of European architecture prevalent from the ninth to the twelfth centuries with round *arches* and barrel *vaults* influenced by Roman architecture and characterized by heavy stone construction.

Romanticism 1. A literary and artistic movement of late eighteenth- and nineteenth-century Europe, aimed at asserting the validity of subjective experience as a countermovement to the often cold formulas of *Neoclassicism;* characterized by intense emotional excitement, and depictions of powerful forces in nature, exotic lifestyles, danger, suffering, and nostalgia. 2. Art of any period based on spontaneity, intuition, and emotion rather than carefully organized rational approaches to form.

Salon An official art exhibition in France, juried by members of the offical French *Academy.*

santero Literally "saint-maker." A person in Hispanic traditions who carves or paints religious figures.

saturation See *intensity.*

scale The size or apparent size of an object seen in relation to other objects, people, or its environment or *format.* Also used to refer to the quality or monumentality found in some objects regardless of their size. In architectural drawings, the ratio of the measurements in the drawing to the measurements in the building.

screenprinting (serigraphy) A printmaking technique in which stencils are applied to fabric stretched across a frame. Paint or ink is forced with a squeegee through the unblocked portions of the screen onto paper or other surface beneath.

secondary colors Pigment secondaries are the *hues* orange, violet, and green, which may be produced in slightly dulled form by mixing two *primaries.*

serif Any short lines that end the upper and lower strokes of a letter.

serigraphy See *screenprinting.*

setback The legal distance that a building must be from property lines. Early setback requirements often increased with the height of a building, resulting in step-like recessions in the rise of tall buildings.

shade A *hue* with black added.

shape A *two-dimensional* or implied two-dimensional area defined by line or changes in value and/or color.

shutter In photography, the part of the *camera* that controls the length of time the light is allowed to strike the photosensitive film.

silk screen See *screenprinting.*

simulataneous contrast An optical effect caused by the tendency of contrasting forms and colors to emphasize their difference when they are placed together.

site-specific art Any work made for a certain place, which cannot be separated or exhibited apart from its intended environment.

size Any of several substances made from glue, wax, or clay, used as a filler for porous material such as paper, canvas, or other cloth, or wall surfaces. Used to protect the surface from the deteriorating effects of paint, particularly oil paint.

slip Clay that is thinned to the consistency of cream, and used as paint on *earthenware* or *stoneware* ceramics.

stoneware A type of clay for ceramics. Stoneware is fired at between 1200–1300°C. and is nonporous when fired.

storyboard A series of drawings or paintings arranged in a sequence, used by directors and editors to help visualize the narrative flow of a film or video.

stupa The earliest form of Buddhist architecture, a dome-like structure probably derived from Indian funeral mounds.

style A characteristic handling of *media* and elements of form, which give a work its identity as the product of a particular person, group, art movement, period, or culture.

stylized Simplified or exaggerated visual *form* which emphasizes particular or contrived design qualities.

subtractive color mixture Mixture of colored *pigments* in the form of paints, inks, pastels, and so on. Called subtractive because reflected light is reduced as pigment colors are combined. See *additive color mixture.*

subtractive sculpture Sculpture made by removing material from a larger block or form.

support The physical material that provides the base for and sustains a *two-dimensional* work of art. Paper is the usual support for drawings and prints; canvas or panels are supports in painting.

Surrealism A movement in literature and visual arts that developed in the mid-1920s

and remained strong until the mid-1940s; grew out of *Dada* and *automatism.* Based upon revealing the unconscious mind in dream images, the irrational, and the fantastic, Surrealism took two directions: *representational* and *abstract.* Dali's and Magritte's paintings, with their uses of impossible combinations of objects depicted in realistic detail, typify representational Surrealism. Miro's paintings, with his use of abstract and fantastic shapes and vaguely defined creatures, are typical of abstract Surrealism.

symbol A form or image implying or representing something beyond its obvious and immediate meaning.

symmetry A design (or composition) with identical or nearly identical form on opposite sides of a dividing line or central axis; formal *balance.*

Synthetic Cubism See *Cubism.*

tempera A water-based paint that uses egg, egg yolk, glue, or casein as a *binder.* Many commercially made paints identified as tempera are actually *gouache.*

tessera Bit of colored glass, ceramic tile, or stone used in a *mosaic.*

texture The tactile quality of a surface or the representation or invention of the appearance of such a surface quality.

three-dimensional Having height, width, and depth.

throwing The process of forming clay objects on a potter's wheel.

tint A *hue* with white added.

trompe l'oeil French for "fool the eye." A *two-dimensional* representation that is so naturalistic that it looks actual or real (or *three-dimensional*).

true fresco See *fresco.*

truss In architecture, a structural framework of wood or metal based on a triangular system, used to span, reinforce, or support walls, ceilings, piers, or beams.

tunnel vault (barrel vault) See *vault.*

tusche In *lithography,* a waxy substance used to draw or paint images on a lithographic stone or plate.

two-dimensional Having the dimensions of height and width only.

typography The art and technique of composing printed materials from type.

unity The appearance of similarity, consistency, or oneness. Interrelational factors that cause various elements to appear as part of a single complete form.

value The lightness or darkness of tones or colors. White is the lightest value; black is the darkest. The value halfway between these extremes is called middle gray. Sometimes called *"tone."*

vanishing point In linear *perspective,* the point on the *horizon line* at which lines or edges that are parallel appear to converge.

vantage point The position from which the viewer looks at an object or visual field; also called "observation point" or "viewpoint."

vault A masonry roof or ceiling constructed on the principle of the *arch.* A tunnel or barrel vault is a semicircular arch extended in depth; a continuous series of arches, one behind the other. A groin vault is formed when two barrel vaults intersect. A ribbed vault is a vault reinforced by masonry ribs.

vehicle Liquid emulsion used as a carrier or spreading agent in paints.

vertical placement A method for suggesting the third dimension of depth in a two-dimensional work by placing an object above another in the composition. The object above seems farther away than the one below.

video art An art form first developed in the 1970s, in which artists use video equipment to stage and film performances or capture spontaneous events.

volume 1. Space enclosed or filled by a three-dimensional object or figure. 2. The implied space filled by a painted or drawn object or figure. Synonym: *mass.*

warm colors Colors whose relative visual temperature makes them seem warm. Warm colors or *hues* include red-violet, red, red-orange, orange, yellow-orange, and yellow. See also *cool colors.*

warp In weaving, the threads that run lengthwise in a fabric, crossed at right angles by the *weft.* Also, the process of arranging yarn or thread on a *loom* so as to form a warp.

wash A thin, transparent layer of paint or ink.

watercolor Paint that uses water-soluble gum as the *binder* and water as the *vehicle.* Characterized by transparency. Also, the resulting painting.

weft In weaving, the horizontal threads interlaced through the *warp.* Also called woof.

woodcut A type of *relief print* made from an image that is left raised on a block of wood.

Magdalena Abakanowicz (mahg-dah-*lay*-nuh ah-bah-kah-*no*-vich)

Ácoma (*ah*-koh-mah)

Alhambra (al-*am*-bra)

Tarsila do Amaral (tar-*see*-lah doo ah-mah-*rahl*)

Angkor Wat (*ang*-kohr waht)

Sofonisba Anguissola (so-fah-*niss*-bah ahn-*gwees*-so-la)

José Raphael Aragón (ho-*say* rah-fah-*el* ah-rah-*gohn*)

Ardabil (ar-*dah*-bil)

Gae Aulenti (gay ow-*len* tee)

'Aumakua (ahow-mah-*koo*-ah)

avant garde (ah-vahn *gard*)

Judy Baca (*bah*-kah)

Giacomo Balla (*jah*-koh-moh *bahl*-la)

Jean-Michel Basquait (jawn mee-*shell* bos-kee-ah)

Bauhaus (*bow*-house)

Benin (ben-een)

Gianlorenzo Bernini (jahn-low-*ren*-tsoh ber-*nee*-nee)

Joseph Bueys (*yo*-sef boyce)

Umberto Boccioni (oom-*bair*-toh boh-*choh*-nee)

Bodhisattva (boh-dee-*saht*-vah)

Germaine Boffrand (zher-*main*-bof-*frohn*)

Rosa Bonheur (buhn-*er*)

Borobudur (boh-roh-boo-*duhr*)

Sandro Botticelli (bought-tee-*chel*-lee)

Louise Bourgeois (boorzh-*wah*)

Constantin Brancusi (*kahn*-stuhn-teen brahn-*koo*-see)

Georges Braque (zhorzh brahk)

Pieter Bruegel (*pee*-ter *broy*-guhl)

Michelangelo Buonarroti, see *Michelangelo*

Alberto Burri (ahl-*bair*-toe boo-ree)

Cai Guo Quang (tseye gwoh *chyang*)

Callicrates (kah-*lik*-rah-teez)

Fodé Camara (foe-day cah-*mah*-rah)

Annibale Carraci (ahn-*nee*-bahl-lay cah-*rah*-chee)

Michelangelo da Caravaggio (mee-kel-*an*-jay-loe da car-ah-*vah*-jyoh)

Rosalba Carriera (roh-*sal*-bah car-*yair*-ah)

Henri Cartier-Bresson (on-*ree* car-tee-*ay* bruh-*sohn*)

Mary Cassatt (cah-*sat*)

Paul Cézanne (say-*zahn*)

Marc Chagall (shah-gahl)

Chartres (*shahr*-truh)

Chauvet (show-*vay*)

Dale Chihuly (chi-*hoo*-lee)

Chilkat (*chill*-kaht)

Maria Chino (*chee*-noh)

Giorgio de Chirico (*johr*-jyo de *key*-ree-co)

chola (*choh*-lah)

Christo (*kree*-stoh)

Constantine (*kahn*-stuhn-teen)

conté (kahn-tay)

contrapposto (kohn-trah-*poh*-stoh)

Gustave Courbet (*goos*-tahv koor-*bay*)

Cycladic (sik-*lad*-ik)

Louis Jacques Mandé Daguerre (loo-*ee* zhahk mon-*day* dah-*gair*)

Honoré Daumier (awn-ohr-*ay* doh-mee-ay)

Jacques-Louis David (zhahk loo-*ee* dah-*veed*)

John DeAndrea (dee-*ann*-dray-ah)

Edgar Degas (ed-gahr duh-*gah*)

Willem de Kooning (*vill*-em duh *koe*-ning)

Eugène Delacroix (oo-*zhen* duh-lah-*kwah*)

André Derain (on-*dray* duh-*ran*)

de Stijl (duh steel)

Richard Diebenkorn (*dee*-ben-korn)

Donatello (dohn-ah-tell-loh)

Henry Dreyfuss (*dray*-fuhs)

Marcel Duchamp (mahr-*sell* doo-*shahm*)

Albrecht Dürer (*ahl*-brekht *duh*-ruhr)

Thomas Eakins (*ay*-kins)

Sergei Eisenstein (sair-gay *eye*-zen-schtine)

M. C. Escher (*esh*-uhr)

Fan Kuan (fahn kwahn)

feng shui (fung shway)

Eric Fischl (*fish*-il)

Jean-Honoré Fragonard (zhon oh-no-*ray* fra-go-*nahr*)

Helen Frankenthaler (frank-en-*thahl*-er)

fresco (*fres*-coh)

Ganges (*gan*-jeez)

Paul Gauguin (go-*gan*)

Frank Gehry (*ger*-ree)

Artemisia Gentileschi (ahr-tuh-*mee*-zhyuh jen-till-*ess*-kee)

Jean Léon Gérôme (zhon *lay*-on zhay-*roam*)

Lorenzo Ghiberti (low-*rent*-soh ghee-*bair*-tee)

Alberto Giacometti (ahl-*bair*-toh jah-ko-*met*-tee)

Giotto di Bondone (*joht*-toe dee bone-*doe*-nay)

Francisco Goya (fran-*sis*-coe go-*yah*)

Walter Gropius (*val*-tuhr *grow*-pee-us)

Guan Yin (*gwan* yeen)

Guernica (*gwar*-nih-kah)

Zaha Hadid (*zah*-hah hah-*deed*)

Hagia Sophia (hah-zhah so-*fee*-ah)

Suzuki Harunobu (soo-*zoo*-key hah-roo-*noh*-boo)

Hatshepsut (hah-*shep*-soot)

Heiji Monogatari (hay-jee mo-no-gah-*tah*-ree)

Hannah Höch (*hahn*-nuh hohk)

Hans Hofmann (*hahns* hohf-mahn)

Hokusai (hohk-*sy*)

Pieter de Hooch (*pee*-tuhr duh *hohk*)

Victor Horta (*veek*-tohr *ore*-tah)

Horyuji (hohr-*yoo*-jee)

Huang Gongwang (hwang gung-*wang*)

Huangshan (hwanhng-shahn)

Hung-Chih (hung jeh)

Ictinus (ick-*tee*-nuhs)

Inca (*eenk*-ah)

Ise (*ee*-say)

Arata Isozaki (ahr-ah-tah ee-so-*zah*-kee)

Asger Jorn (*az*-ger yorn)

Ilya Kabakov (*ill*-ya *kob*-ah-kohv)

kachina (kah-*chee*-nah)

Frida Kahlo (*free*-dah *kah*-loh)

Kandarya Mahadeva (gan-dahr-reeah mah-hah-*day*-vuh)

Vasily Kandinsky (vass-see-lee can-*din*-skee)

Anish Kapoor (ah-*neesh*-kah-*puhr*)

Katsura (kah-*tsoo*-rah)

Gyorgy Kepes (gee-*yohr*-gee kep-esh)

Khamerernebty (kahm-er-er-*neb*-tee)

Anselm Kiefer (*ahn*-sehlm kee-fuhr)

Ernst Ludwig Kirchner (*airnst loot*-vik *keerkh*-ner)

Paul Klee (clay)

Käthe Kollwitz (*kay*-teh *kahl*-wits)

Torii Kiyonobu (tor-ee-ee kee-oh-*noh*-boo)

Torii Kiyotada (tor-ee-ee kee-oh-*tah*-dah)

Krishna (*krish*-nuh)

Mistutani Kunishiro (meet-soo-*tah*-nee koo-nee-*shee*-roh)

Laocoön (lay-*ah*-koh-ahn)

Lascaux (lass-coe)

Le Corbusier (luh core-boo-zee-ay)

Fernand Léger (fair-*non* lay-*zhay*)

Roy Lichtenstein (*lick*-ten-steen)

Maya Lin (*my*-uh *lin*)

Fra Filippo Lippi (frah fill-*leep*-poh *leep*-pee)

Marshall Lomokema (loh-moh-kem-ah)

Machu Picchu (*mah*-choo *peek*-choo)

Ma Fen (mah fen)

René Magritte (ruh-*nay* muh-*greet*)

mandala (mahn-dah-lah)

Edouard Manet (ay-*dwahr* mah-*nay*)

Etienne-Jules Marey (ay-tee-*en* zhyool mah-*ray*)

Mansur (mahn-soor)

Maori (mow-ree)

Marisol (mah-ree-*sohl*)

Masaccio (mah-*sach*-chyo)

Henri Matisse (on-*ree* mah-*tees*)

Mato Tope (*mah*-toh *toh*-pay)

Maya (*my*-uh)

de Medici (deh *meh*-dee-chee)

Cildo Meireles (*seel*-doe may-*ray*-les)

Ana Mendieta (ah-nah men-*dyet*-ah)

Michelangelo Buonarroti (mee-kel-*an*-jay-loe bwoh-nah-*roe*-tee)

Ludwig Mies van der Rohe (*loot*-vik *mees* vahn dair *roh*-eh)

Mihrab (*mee*-rahb)

Richard Misrach (*miz*-rahk)

Igor Mitoraj (*ee*-gor *mee*-tohr-eye)

Paula Modersohn-Becker (*moh*-dur-zohn *bek*-ur)

Piet Mondrian (*peet* mohn-dree-ahn)

Claude Monet (*klohd* muh-*nay*)

Berthe Morisot (*bairt* moh-ree-*zoh*)

mosque (mahsk)

Alphonse Mucha (*ahl*-fohns *moo*-chah)

Vera Mukhina (*vir*-ah moo-*kee*-nah)

Edvard Munch (*ed*-vard *moonk*)

Mu Qi (moo-chee)

Eadweard Muybridge (*ed*-wurd *my*-brij)

Mycerinus (miss-uh-*ree*-nuhs)

Nadar (Felix Tournachon) (nah-*dar* *fay*-leeks toor-nah-*shohn*)

Nampeyo (nam-pay-oh)

Emil Nolde (*ay*-meal *nohl*-duh)

Notre Dame de Chartres (*noh*-truh dahm duh *shahr*-truh)

Claes Oldenburg (klahs ol-den-burg)

Olmec (*ohl*-mek)

José Clemente Orozco (ho-*say* cleh-*men*-tay oh-*rohs*-coh)

Nam June Paik (nahm joon pahk)

Andrea Palladio (ahn-*dray*-uh pahl-*lah*-dyo)

Giovanni Paolo Pannini (jyo-*vahn*-nee *pah-oh*-lo pah-*nee*-nee)

parfleche (par-*flesh*)

Parvati (par-*vah*-tee)

Pablo Picasso (pab-lo pee-*cah*-so)

Jackson Pollock (*pah*-lock)

Polyclitus (pol-ee-*cly*-tus)

Pompeii (pahm-*pay*)

Pont du Gard (pohn duh *gahr*)

Nicholas Poussin (nee-coh-*law* poo-*san*)

pietá (pee-ay-*tah*)

Pierre-Paul Prud'hon (proo-*dohn*)

Qennifer (*ken*-eh-fer)

Quetzalcoatl (kets-ahl-*kwah*-til)

Radha (*rad*-dah)

Robert Rauschenberg (*roh*-shen-buhrg)

Gerrit Reitveld (*gair*-it *ryt*-velt)

Rembrandt van Rijn (*rem*-brant van *ryne*)

Pierre August Renoir (pee-*err* oh-*goost* ren-*wahr*)

Gerhardt Richter (*gair*-hart *rick*-ter)

Leni Riefenstahl (len-ee *ree*-fen-shtahl)

Diego Rivera (dee-*ay*-goh ree-*vay*-rah)

Sabatino Rodia (roh-*dee*-uh)

Francois August Rodin (frahn-*swah* oh-*goost* roh-*dan*)

Henri Rousseau (on-*ree* roo-*soh*)

Andre Rublev (*ahn*-dray *ru*-blof)

Niki de Saint Phalle (*nee*-kee duh san *fall*)

Sāñchī (*sahn*-chee)

Raphael Sanzio (ra-fay-el *sahn*-zee-oh)

Hideo Sasaki (hid-*ay*-oh sah-sah-*kee*)

Sassetta (suh-*set*-tuh)

scythian (*sith*-ee-ahn)

George Segal (*see*-guhl)

Sesshū (seh-shoo)

Georges Seurat (zhorzh sir-*ah*)

Bada Shanren (*bah*-dah *shan*-ren)

Shiva Nātarāja (*shih*-vuh nah-tah-*rah*-jah)

Katsukawa Shunsho (kaht-soo-*kah*-wah *shun*-so)

Sinan (*see*-nahn)

Tawaraya Sōtatsu (tah-wa-*rah*-ya *soh*-taht soo)

Alfred Stieglitz (*steeg*-lits)

stupa (*stoo*-pah)

Toshiko Takaezu (tosh-ko tah-kah-*ay*-zoo)

Tang Yin (tahng yin)

Kenzo Tange (ken-zo tahn-gay)

Vladimir Tatlin (vlah-*dee*-meer taht-lin)

Teotihuacan (tay-oh-tee-wah-*cahn*)

Masami Teraoka (ma-sah-mee tair-ah-oh-ka)

Jean Tinguely (zhon tan-*glee*)

Jacobo Tintoretto (*ha*-coh-boh teen-toh-*ray*-toh)

Tlingit (*kling*-git)

Félix Gonzáles Torres (*feh*-leeks gohn-*sa*-les *tohr*-res)

Henri de Toulouse-Lautrec (on-*ree* duh too-*looz* low-*trek*)

tuku-tuku (*too*-koo-*too*-koo)

James Turrell (tuh-*rell*)

Tutankhamen (too-tahn-*kahm*-uhn)

Jerry Uelsmann (*uhlz*-man)

Unkei (ung-kay)

Mierle Laderman Ukeles (merl lay-duhr-man *yoo*-kuh-lees)

Ur (er)

Kitagawa Utamaro (kit-ah-*gah*-wah ut-ah-*mah*-roh)

Henry van de Velde (vahn duh-*vel*-deh)

Theo van Doesburg (*tay*-oh van dohz-*buhrg*)

Jan van Eyck (*yahn* van *ike*)

Vincent van Gogh (*vin*-sent van goe; also, van *gawk*)

Diego Velázquez (dee-*aye*-goh bay-*ahht*-kehth; also, vay-*las*-kes)

Robert Venturi (ven-*tuhr*-ee)

Jan Vermeer (*yahn* ver-*mair*)

Versailles (vair-*sy*)

Leonardo da Vinci (lay-oh-*nahr*-doh dah *veen*-chi)

Peter Voulkos (*vool*-kohs)

Andy Warhol (*wohr*-hohl)

Willendorf (*vill*-en-dohrf)

Xu Bing (shoo bing)

Yu-Jian (yu-jee-en)

ziggurat (*zig*-uh-raht)

NOTES

CHAPTER 1

1. Kenneth C. Lindsay and Peter Vergo, eds., *Kandinsky, Complete Writings on Art* (Boston: G.K. Hall, 1982), 383.

2. Wasily Kandinsky, "Concerning the Spiritual in Art," translated K. C. Lindsay and P. Vergo, *Art in Theory 1900–1990*, edited by Charles Harrison and Paul Wood (London: Blackwell, 1992), 94.

3. C. L. Barnhart and Jess Stein, eds., *The American College Dictionary* (New York: Random House, 1963), 70.

4. Georgia O'Keeffe, *Georgia O'Keeffe* (New York: Viking, 1976), opposite plate 13.

5. Charles Glueck, "A Brueghel from Harlem," *The New York Times* (February 22, 1970): sec. 2, 29.

6. Quoted in "Romare Bearden," *Current Biography* (1972), p. 30.

7. Julia Marcus, "Romare Bearden," *Smithsonian* (March 1981): 74.

8. Ibid., 72.

9. Félix González-Torres, interview with Tim Rollins, in *Félix González-Torres* (New York: Artpress, 1993), 23.

10. Clive Bell, "The Aesthetic Hypothesis," *Art in Theory 1900–1990: An Anthology of Changing Ideas,* edited by Charles Harrison and Paul Wood (Cambridge, MA: Blackwell, 1992), 115.

CHAPTER 2

1. Don Fabun, *The Dynamics of Change* (Englewood Cliffs, NJ: Prentice Hall, 1968), 9.

2. Lawrence Weschler, *Seeing Is Forgetting the Name of the Thing One Sees: A Life of Contemporary Artist Robert Irwin* (Berkeley: University of California Press, 1982).

3. Edward Weston, *The Daybooks of Edward Weston,* edited by Nancy Newhall (Millerton, NY: Aperture, 1973), vol. 2, 181.

4. Henri Matisse, "The Nature of Creative Activity," *Education and Art,* edited by Edwin Ziegfeld (New York: UNESCO, 1953), 21.

5. Douglas Davis, "New Architecture: Building for Man," *Newsweek* (April 19, 1971): 80.

6. Betty Burroughs, ed., *Vasari's Lives of the Artists* (New York: Simon & Schuster, 1946), 191.

7. Leo Tolstoy, *What Is Art?* (London: Walter Scott, 1899), 50.

8. Bergen Evans, *Dictionary of Quotations* (New York: Delacorte Press, 1968), 340.

9. Erich Fromm, "The Creative Attitude," *Creativity and Its Cultivation,* edited by Harold H. Anderson (New York: Harper-Collins, 1959), 44.

10. Andrew Derain, *ArtNews* (April 1995): 118.

11. John Holt, *How Children Fail* (New York: Pitman, 1964), 167.

12. Oswald Sirén, *The Chinese on the Art of Painting* (New York: Schocken Books, 1963), 56.

13. Gyorgy Kepes, *The Language of Vision* (Chicago: Paul Theobald, 1944), 9.

14. "Notes d'un peintre sur son dessin," *Le Point IV* (1939): 14.

15. Jean Schuster, "Marcel Duchamp, vite," *le surréalisme* (Spring 1957): 143.

16. Georgia O'Keeffe, *Georgia O'Keeffe* (New York: Viking, 1976), opposite plate 23.

CHAPTER 3

1. Maurice Denis, *Theories 1870–1910* (Paris: Hermann, 1964), 13.

2. Henry Moore, *Henry Moore* (London: Edbury Press, 1986), 125.

3. Quoted in "National Airport: A New Terminal Takes Flight," *Washington Post,* (July 16, 1997). Accessed at http://www.washingtonpost.com/wp-srv/local/longterm/library/airport/architect.htm, May 14, 2000.

4. Ray Bethers, *Composition in Pictures* (New York: Pitman, 1949), 163; originally in *Manifesto of the Futurist Painters* (Italy, 1910).

5. Faber Birren, *Color Psychology and Color Theory* (New Hyde Park, NY: University Books, 1961), 20.

CHAPTER 4

1. R. G. Swenson, "What is Pop Art?" *Art News* (November 1963): 62.

2. Elizabeth McCausland, "Jacob Lawrence," *Magazine of Art* (November 1945): 254.

3. Jack D. Flam, *Matisse on Art* (New York: Dutton, 1978), 36; originally in "Notes d'un peintre," *La Grande Revue* (Paris, 1908).

4. Ibid.

5. Henri Matisse, "Notes of a Painter," translated by Alfred H. Barr, Jr., *Problems of Aesthetics,* edited by Eliseo Vivas and Murray Krieger (New York: Holt, 1953), 259–260; originally in "Notes d'un peintre," *La Grande Revue* (Paris, 1908).

6. Ibid., 260.

CHAPTER 5

1. *The Diaries and Letters of Kaethe Kollwitz,* translated by Richard and Clara Winston (Chicago: Henry Regnery, 1955), 52.

2. *Louise Nevelson: Atmospheres and Environments* (New York: Whitney Museum, 1980), 55.

3. Diana MacKown, *Dawns and Dusk* (New York: Scribner, 1976), 14.

4. "Louise Nevelson: A Conversation with Barbara Diamonstein," *Nevelson: Maquettes for Monumental Sculpture* (New York: Pace Gallery, 1980), 2.

5. Ibid., 7.

CHAPTER 6

1. Barbara Rose, ed., *Readings in American Art Since 1900* (New York, 1975), 28.

2. Martin Filler, "The Shock of the Hughes," *Vanity Fair* (November 1990): 226.

3. *Time* (April 29, 1991): 29.

4. *Time* (September 23, 1991): 75.

5. "Robert Hughes," *Esquire* (June 1988): 223.

6. Filler, "The Shock of the Hughes," 226.

7. Rick Steves, *Mona Winks: Self-guided Tours of Europe's Top Museums* (London: John Muir; New York: Norton, 1988).

CHAPTER 7

1. Frederick Franck, *The Zen of Seeing: Seeing/Drawing as Meditation* (New York: Vintage, 1973), 6.

2. David Hockney, *David Hockney* (New York: Abrams, 1977), 271.

3. Robert Wallace. *The World of Van Gogh* (New York: Time-Life, 1969), 90.

4. Anthony Blunt, *Picasso's Guernica* (New York: Oxford University Press, 1969), 28.

5. Ichitaro Kondo and Elsie Grilli, *Katsushika Hokusai* (Rutland, VT: Tuttle, 1955), 13.

CHAPTER 8

1. Quoted in Erika Doss, *Spirit Poles and Flying Pigs: Public Art and Cultural Democracy in American Communities* (Washington, D.C.: Smithsonian Institution Press, 1995), p, 176.

2. Ibid., p. 179.

3. Ibid., p. 180.

CHAPTER 10

1. Minor White, Foreward to *Ansel Adams,* edited by Liliane De Cock (New York Graphic Society, 1972).

2. "Edwin Land," *Time* (June 26, 1972): 84.

3. Henri Cartier-Bresson, *The Decisive Moment* (New York: Simon & Schuster, 1952), 14.

4. Margaret Bourke-White, *Portrait of Myself* (New York: Simon & Schuster, 1963), 13.

5. Ibid., 64.

6. Ibid.

7. Ibid., 142.

8. Ibid., 308.

9. James L. Enyeart, *Jerry N. Uelsmann, Twenty-Five Years: A Retrospective* (Boston: Little, Brown, 1982), 37.

CHAPTER 11

1. Quoted in Brad Weiners, "Color Him a Provocateur," *Wired Magazine* (December 1996): http://www.wired.com/wired/archive/4.12/kalman.htm

CHAPTER 12

1. Henry Hopkins, *Fifty West Coast Artists* (San Francisco: Chronicle Books, 1981), 25.

2. Ruth Butler, *Western Sculpture: Definitions of Man* (New York: HarperCollins, 1975), 249; from an unpublished manuscript in the possession of Roberta Gonzáles, translated and included in the appendices of a Ph.D dissertation by Josephine Whithers, *The Sculpture of Julio Gonzáles: 1926–1942* (New York: Columbia University, 1971).

3. Brassaï, *Conversations with Picasso* (Paris: Gallimard, 1964), 67.

4. Brassaï, Gyula Hala´sz. *Picasso and Company.* (New York, Doubleday, 1966), 52.

5. *Alexander Calder* (New York: Abrams, 1979), 13.

6. Ibid., 15.

7. Quoted in Lucy Lippard, *Mixed Blessings: New Art in a Multicultural America* (New York: Pantheon 1990), p. 86.

8. Brandon Taylor, *Avant-Garde and After: Rethinking Art Now* (New York: Prentice Hall, 1995), 157.

CHAPTER 13

1. Quoted in Thalia Gouma-Peterson, *Miriam Schapiro: Shaping the Fragments of Art and Life* (New York: Abrams, 1999), p. 29.

2. Ruth Bunzel, *The Pueblo Potter* (New York: Columbia University Press, 1929), 56.

3. Quoted in Rose Slivka and Karen Tsujimoto, *The Art of Peter Voulkos,* (Tokyo: Kodansha, 1995), p. 50.

4. John Coyne, "Handcrafts," *Today's Education,* November–December 1976: 75.

5. Grace Glueck, "In Glass, and Kissed by Light," *The New York Times,* Aug. 29, 1997, Bl.

6. Quoted in *Expressions in Wood: Masterworks from the Wornick Collection* (Oakland: Oakland Museum of California, 1996), p. 64.

7. Kathleen McCann, "Diane Itter: Paying Tribute to the Artist," *Fiberarts.* September–October 1992: 46. Reprinted by permission of the Publisher, Altamont Press, Inc., Asheville, NC.

8. *Abakanowicz* (New York: Abbeville, 1982), 127.

9. Faith Ringgold, *We Flew Over the Bridge: The Memoirs of Faith Ringgold* (Boston: Little, Brown, 1995).

10. Ibid.

11. Ibid.

CHAPTER 14

1. Louis Sullivan, "The Tall Office Building Artistically Considered," *Lippincott Monthly Magazine,* March 1896: 408.

2. Zaha Hadid: Complete Buildings and Projects (New York: Rizzoli, 1998), p. 28.

3. Ibid., p. 43.

4. Frank Lloyd Wright, *The Future of Architecture* (New York: Horizon Press, 1953), 227.

5. Michael Demarest, "He Digs Downtown," *Time,* (August 24, 1981): 46.

6. Will Durant, *The Story of Philosophy,* 2nd ed. (New York: Simon & Schuster, 1933), 141.

7. Humphry Osmond, "Some Psychiatric Aspects of Design," in *Who Designs America,* Laurence B. Holland, ed., (Garden City, New York: Anchor Books, 1966), 316.

CHAPTER 15

1. "Picasso Speaks," *The Arts,* (May 1923): 319.

CHAPTER 16

1. Titus Burckhardt, *Chartres and the Birth of the Cathedral* (Bloomington, IN: World Wisdom Books, 1996), 47.

CHAPTER 17

1. David Piper, *The Illustrated History of Art* (New York: Crescent Books, 1991), 130.

2. Jacob Bronowski, "Leonardo da Vinci," *Renaissance Profiles,* edited by J. H. Plumb (New York: HarperCollins, 1976), 84.

3. *The World of Michelangelo* (New York: Time-Life, 1966), 192.

4. Saint Teresa of Jesus, *The Life of Saint Teresa of Jesus,* translated by David Lewis, edited by Benedict Zimmerman (Westminster, MD: Newman, 1947), 266.

5. Linda Nochlin, "Why Have There Been No Great Women Artists?" *Art News,* January 1971, 22–39 ff.

6. Mira Bank, *Anonymous Was a Woman* (New York: St. Martins, 1979).

CHAPTER 18

1. Wen C. Fong, "The Literati Artists of the Ming Dynasty," Wen C. Fong and James C. Y. Wyatt, *Possessing the Past: Treasures from the National Palace Museum, Taipei* (New York: Metropolitan Museum of Art, 1996), 387.

CHAPTER 19

1. From Sinan's autobiography, quoted in Sheila Blair and Jonathan Bloom, *Art and Architecture of Islam, 1250–1800* (New Haven: Yale University Press, 1994), 226.

CHAPTER 20

1. James Cook, *A Voyage to the Pacific Ocean* (Dublin: H. Chambelayne 1784) vol. 2, 206.

2. Julian Spalding, letter to the King of Benin, January 10, 1997. Published in *Art Newspaper,* April 1997.

CHAPTER 21

1. C. R. Leslie, *Memoirs of the Life of John Constable* (London: J. M. Dent, 1913), 274.

2. Beaumont Newhall, "Delacroix and Photography," *Magazine of Art* (November 1952), 300.

3. Margaretta Salinger: Gustave Courbet, 1819–1877, *Miniature Album XH* (New York: Metropolitan Museum of Art, 1955), 24.

4. From *Reminiscences of Rosa Bonheur,* published in 1910 and quoted in Wendy Slatkin, ed., *The Voices of Women Artists* (Englewood Cliffs, NJ: Prentice Hall, 1993), 132.

5. Ibid., 132.

6. William Seitz, *Claude Monet* (New York: Abrams, 1982), 13.

7. Albert E. Elsen, *Rodin* (New York: Museum of Modern Art, 1963), 53; from a letter to critic Marcel Adam, published in an article in *Gil Blas* (Paris: July 7, 1904).

8. John Rewald, *Cézanne: A Biography* (New York: Abrams, 1986), 208.

9. Michael Howard, *Cézanne* (London: Bison Group, 1990), 6.

10. *Cézanne and the Post-Impressionists,* McCall's Collection of Modern Art (New York: McCall Books, 1970), 5.

11. Vincent van Gogh, *Further Letters of Vincent van Gogh to His Brother, 1886–1889* (London: Constable, 1929), 139, 166.

12. Ronald Alley, *Gauguin* (Middlesex, England: Hamlyn, 1968), 8.

13. Paul Gaugin, *Lettres de Paul Gauguin à Georges-Daniel de Monfried* (Paris: Georges Cres, 1918), 89.

14. John Russell, *The Meanings of Modern Art* (New York: HarperCollins, 1974), 35.

15. Jean Leymerie, "Paul Gauguin," *Encyclopedia of World Art* (London: McGraw-Hill, 1971), vol. 6, 42.

16. Yann Le Pichon, *Gauguin: Life, Art, Inspiration* (New York: Abrams, 1987), 240.

CHAPTER 22

1. Wassily Kandinsky, "Reminiscences," *Modern Artists on Art,* edited by Robert L. Herbert (Englewood Cliffs, NJ: Prentice Hall, 1964), 27.

2. Alfred H. Barr, Jr., ed., *Masters of Modern Art,* 1955 (New York: Museum of Modern Art, 1955), 124.

3. Dorothy Dudley, "Brancusi," *Dial,* February 1927: 124.

4. H. H. Arnason, *History of Modern Art,* rev. ed. (New York: Abrams, 1977), 146.

5. Quotes from the trial and the decision come from "Bird in Space in the Dock," *The Art Newspaper,* 63 (October 1996): 28–29.

6. William Fleming, *Art, Music and Ideas* (New York: Holt, 1970), 342.

7. Ibid., 342.

8. Roland Renrose, *Picasso: His Life and Work* (New York: Schocken, 1966), 125.

9. Nathan Lyons, ed., *Photographers on Photography* (Englewood Cliffs, NJ: Prentice Hall, 1966), 133.

10. Beaumont Newhall, *The History of Photography* (New York: Museum of Modern Art, 1964), 111.

11. Joshua C. Taylor, *Futurism* (New York: Museum of Modern Art, 1961), 124.

CHAPTER 23

1. Hans Richter, *Dada 1916–1966* (Munich: Goethe Institut, 1966), 22.

2. Paride Accetti, Raffaele De Grada, and Arturo Schwarz, *Cinquant'annia Dada—Dada in Italia 1916–1966* (Milan: Galleria Schwarz, 1966), 39.

3. Alfred H. Barr, Jr., ed., *Masters of Modern Art* (New York: Museum of Modern Art, 1955), 131.

4. Ibid., 133.

5. William Fleming, *Art, Music and Ideas* (New York: Holt, 1970), 346.

6. André Breton, *Manifestos of Surrealism,* translated by Richard Seaver and Helen R. Lane (Ann Arbor: University of Michigan Press, 1972), 14.

7. Sam Hunter and John Jacobus, *Modern Art.* (New York: Harry N. Abrams, 1985), p. 148.

8. Lael Wertenbaker, *The World of Picasso* (New York: Time-Life, 1967), 130.

9. Herbert Read, *A Concise History of Modern Painting* (New York: Praeger, 1959), 160.

10. Betram Wolfe, *The Fabulous Life of Diego Rivera* (New York: Stein and Day, 1963), 18.

11. *Diego Rivera: A Retrospective* (New York: Norton, 1986), 19.

12. Wolfe, *The Fabulous Life of Diego Rivera,* 277.

13. *The Concise Oxford Dictionary of Art and Artists* (Oxford: Oxford University Press, 1990), 398.

14. Romare Bearden and Harry Henderson, *A History of African American Artists* from 1792 to the Present (New York, 1993), 152.

CHAPTER 24

1. Sherman Paul, *Harry Callahan* (New York: The Museum of Modern Art, 1967), 6.

2. Barbara Rose, *An Interview with Robert Rauschenberg* (New York, Vintage, 1987), 9.

3. Edward Lucie-Smith, *Sculpture Since 1945* (London: Phaidon, 1987), 77.

4. Calvin Tomkins, *The World of Marcel Duchamp* (New York: Time-Life, 1966), 162.

5. Ogden Nash, "Song of the Open Road" (after "Trees," by Joyce Kilmer), © 1932. Originally published in the *New Yorker.* Reprinted by permission.

6. *Richard Hamilton: Catalogue of an Exhibition at the Tate Gallery,* March 12–April 19, 1970 (London: Tate Gallery, 1970), 31.

7. R. G. Swenson, "What Is Pop Art?" *Art News* (November 1963): 25.

8. Claes Oldenberg, "I am for an art . . ." from *Store Days, Documents from the Store (1961) and Ray Gun Theater (1962),* selected by Claes Oldenberg and Emmett Williams (New York: Something Else Press, 1967).

9. Donald Judd, "Specific Objects," *Arts Yearbook* 8 (1965): 78.

10. Julia Brown, *Occluded Front: James Turrell* (Los Angeles: Fellows of Contemporary Art, Lapis Press, 1985), 15.

11. Patricia Failing, "James Turrell's New Light on the Universe," *Art News* (April, 1985): 71. Copyright 1985 Patricia Failing.

12. Grace Glueck, "Odd Man Out: Red Grooms, the Ruckus Kid," *Art News* (December 1973): 27.

13. Lucy R. Lippard, *From the Center: Feminist Essays on Women's Art.* (New York: Dutton, 1976), 48.

14. *Louise Bourgeois* (New York: Museum of Modern Art, 1982), 95.

CHAPTER 25

1. Joel L. Swerdlow, "To Heal a Nation," *National Geographic,* May 1985: 557.

2. Susan Vogel, *Africa Explores, 20th Century African Art* (New York: Prestel), 184.

SUGGESTED READING

General Reference

Barnet, Sylvan. *A Short Guide to Writing About Art,* 5th ed. New York: Longman, 1997.

Dictionary of Art, The. 34 vols. New York. Grove's Dictionaries, 1996.

Dissanayake, Ellen. *Homo Aestheticus: Where Art Comes From and Why.* New York: Free Press, 1992.

Dissanayake, Ellen. *What Is Art For?* Seattle: University of Washington Press, 1988.

Gablik, Suzi. *Conversations Before the End of Time.* New York: Thames and Hudson, 1995.

Goldwater, Robert, and Marco Treves, eds. *Artists on Art.* New York: Pantheon, 1958.

Lucie Smith, Edward, ed. *The Thames and Hudson Dictionary of Art Terms.* New York: Thames and Hudson, 1984.

Read, Herbert, and Nikos Stangos, eds. *The Thames and Hudson Dictionary of Art and Artists.* London: Thames and Hudson, 1985.

PART 1
WHAT IS ART FOR?

Canaday, John. *What is Art? An Introduction to Painting, Sculpture & Architecture.* New York: Knopf, 1980.

Edwards, Betty. *Drawing on the Artist Within: A Guide to Innovation, Invention and Creativity.* New York: Simon & Schuster, 1986.

Johnson, Jay. *American Folk Art of the Twentieth Century.* New York: Rizzoli, 1983.

London, Peter. *No More Secondhand Art: Awakening the Artist Within.* Boston: Shambhala, 1989.

Lowenfeld, Viktor. *Creative and Mental Growth,* 8th ed. New York: Macmillan, 1987.

May, Rollo. *The Courage to Create.* New York: W. W. Norton, 1975.

McKim, Robert. *Experiences in Visual Thinking,* 2nd ed. Monterey, California: Brooks/Cole, 1980.

Samuels, Mike, M.D., and Nancy Samuels. *Seeing with the Mind's Eye: The History, Techniques and Uses of Visualization.* New York: Random House, 1975.

PART 2
THE LANGUAGE OF VISUAL EXPERIENCE

Anderson, Donald M. *The Art of Written Forms.* New York: Holt, Rinehart & Winston, 1969.

Arnheim, Rudolf. *Art and Visual Perception,* rev. ed. Berkeley: University of California Press, 1974.

Baudrillard, Jean. *The Ecstasy of Communication,* tr. Bernard and Caroline Schutze. Brooklyn, NY: Semiotext(e), 1988.

Dosczi, Gyorgy. *The Power of Limits: Proportional Harmonies in Nature, Art and Architecture.* Boulder: Shambhala, 1981.

Kepes, Gyorgy. *Language of Vision.* Chicago: Paul Theobald, 1949.

Nelson, George. *How to See.* Boston: Little, Brown, 1977.

Shahn, Ben. *The Shape of Content.* New York: Random House, 1957.

Varley, Helen, ed. *Colour.* London: Mitchell Beazley, 1980.

PART 3
TWO-DIMENSIONAL MEDIA

Burgoyne, Patrick. *The New Internet Design Project: The Best of Graphic Art on the Web.* New York: Rizzoli, 1999.

Cartier-Bresson, Henri. *The Decisive Moment.* New York: Simon & Schuster, 1952.

Castleman, Riva. *Prints of the Twentieth Century,* rev. ed. New York: Thames and Hudson, 1988.

Cooper Union for the Advancement of Science and Art, *Techo-Seduction,* New York: Cooper Union, 1997.

Edwards, Betty. *Drawing on the Right Side of the Brain,* rev. ed. Los Angeles: Tarcher, 1989.

Franck, Frederick. *The Zen of Seeing: Drawing as Meditation.* New York: Random House, 1973.

Goldstein, Nathan. *The Art of Responsive Drawing,* 4th ed. Englewood Cliffs, N.J.: Prentice Hall, 1992.

Goodman, Cynthia. *Digital Visions: Computers and Art.* New York: Abrams, 1987.

Ivins, William M. *Prints and Visual Communication.* New York: Plenum, 1969.

London, Barbara, with John Upton. *Photography,* 5th ed. New York: Longman, 1994.

Lupton, Ellen. *Mixing Messages: Graphic Design in Contemporary Culture.* New York: Cooper-Hewitt National Design Museum, 1996.

Mast, Gerald. *A Short History of the Movies.* New York: Macmillan, 1986.

Mayer, A. Hyatt. *Prints and People: A Social History of Printed Pictures.* Princeton: Princeton University Press, 1980.

Mayer, Ralph. *Artists Handbook of Materials and Techniques,* 5th ed. New York: Viking, 1991.

Newhall, Beaumont. *The History of Photography,* rev. ed. New York, Museum of Modern Art, 1982.

Nicolaides, Kimon. *The Natural Way to Draw.* Boston: Houghton Mifflin, 1975.

Piper, David. *Looking at Art: An Introduction to Enjoying Great Paintings of the World.* New York: Random House, 1984.

Sachs, Paul J. *Modern Prints and Drawings: A Guide to a Better Understanding of Modern Draughtsmanship.* New York: Knopf, 1954.

Smith, Stan, and Friso Ten Holt, eds. *The Artist's Manual: Equipment, Materials, Techniques.* New York: Mayflower Books, 1980.

Wilson, Marjorie. *Teaching Children to Draw: a Guide for Teachers & Parents.* Englewood Cliffs, N.J.: Prentice Hall, 1982.

Wye, Deborah. *Thinking Print: From Books to Billboards, 1980–95.* New York: Abrams and Museum of Modern Art, 1996.

PART 4
THREE-DIMENSIONAL MEDIA

Bacon, Edmund N. *The Design of Cities,* rev. ed. New York: Penguin, 1976.

Camusso, Lorenzo, and Sandro Bortone, *Ceramics of the World: From 4000 B.C to the Present.* New York: Abrams, 1991.

Gardiner, Stephen. *Introduction to Architecture.* Oxford: Equinox, 1983.

Le Normand-Romain, Antoinette, et al. *Sculpture: The Adventure of Modern Sculpture in the Nineteenth and Twentieth Centuries.* New York: Rizzoli, 1986.

Lucie-Smith, Edward. *The Story of Craft: The Craftsman's Role in Society.* Ithaca, New York: Cornell University Press, 1981.

Macaulay, David. *Cathedral: The Story of Its Construction.* Boston: Houghton Mifflin, 1973.

Mayer, Barbara. *Contemporary American Craft Art.* Salt Lake City: Gibbs M. Smith, 1988.

Meggs, Philip B. *A History of Graphic Design.* New York: Van Nostrand Reinhold, 1992.

Rubinstein, Charlotte Streifer. *American Women Sculptors: A History of Women Working in Three Dimensions.* Boston: G. K. Hall, 1990.

Salvadori, Mario. *Why Buildings Stand Up.* New York: W. W. Norton, 1980.

Scully, Vincent, Jr. *Modern Architecture: The Architecture of Democracy.* New York: Braziller, 1977.

Speight, Charlotte and John Toki. *Hands in Clay: An Introduction to Ceramics,* 3rd ed. Mountain View, Calif.: Mayfield, 1994.

Thomas, Michel, Cristine Mainguy, and Sophie Pommier. *Textile Art.* New York: Rizzoli, 1985.

Watkin, David A. *A History of Western Architecture.* London: Barrie & Jenkins, 1986.

Wines, James. *De-Architecture.* New York: Rizzoli, 1987.

PART 5
ART AS CULTURAL HERITAGE

Bahn, Paul G. *Journey Through the Ice Age.* Berkeley: University of California, 1997.

Blair, Sheila, and Jonathan M. Bloom. *The Art and Architecture of Islam, 1250–1800.* New Haven: Yale University Press, 1994.

Blier, Suzanne Preston. *The Royal Arts of Africa: The Majesty of Form.* New York: Abrams, 1998.

Chadwick, Whitney. *Women, Art, and Society,* 2nd rev. ed. London: Thames and Hudson, 1996.

Coe, Ralph T. *Lost and Found Traditions: Native American Art 1965-1985.* New York: American Federation of the Arts, 1986.

Cole, Herbert M. *Icons: Ideals and Power in the Art of Africa.* Washington: Smithsonian, 1989.

Dreamings: The Art of Aboriginal Australia. New York: Braziller and the Asia Society Galleries, 1988.

Dwyer, Jane P., and Edward B. Dwyer. *Traditional Arts of Africa, Oceania and the Americas.* San Francisco: The Fine Arts Museums of San Francisco, 1973.

Ettinghausen, Richard. *The Art and Architecture of Islam, 650–1250.* New York: Penguin, 1987.

Feest, Christian. *Native Arts of North America.* New York: Thames and Hudson, 1992.

Fine, Elsa H. *Women and Art: A History of Women Painters and Sculptors from the Renaissance to the 20th Century.* Montclair, N.J.: Allanheld & Schram, 1978.

Fleming, William. *Art, Music, and Ideas,* 8th ed. New York: Holt, Rinehart & Winston, 1991.

Gombrich, E.H. *The Story of Art,* 15th ed. Englewood Cliffs, N.J.: Prentice Hall, 1989.

Guerrilla Girls, *The Guerrilla Girls' Bedside Companion to the History of Western Art.* New York: Penguin, 1998.

Heller, Nancy G. *Women Artists: An Illustrated History.* New York: Abbeville, 1987.

Janson, H. W. *History of Art,* 5th ed., revised by Anthony Janson. New York: Abrams, 1997.

Kennedy, Jean. *New Currents, Ancient Rivers: Contemporary African Artists in a Generation of Change.* Washington, D. C.: Smithsonian, 1992.

Lee, Sherman. *A History of Far Eastern Art,* 5th rev. ed. Englewood Cliffs, New Jersey: Prentice-Hall, 1997; New York: Abrams, 1997.

Mead, S. M. *Exploring the Visual Arts of Oceania.* Honolulu: University Press of Hawaii, 1979.

Metropolitan Museum of Art, *Mexico: Splendors of Thirty Centuries.* New York: Metropolitan Museum, 1990.

Pfeiffer, John E. *The Creative Explosion: An Inquiry into the Origins of Art and Religion.* New York: Harper & Row, 1982.

Reti, Ladislao, ed. *The Unknown Leonardo.* New York: McGraw-Hill, 1974.

Ruspoli, Mario. *The Cave of Lascaux: The Final Photographic Record.* London: Thames & Hudson, 1987.

Stanley-Baker, Joan. *Japanese Art.* New York: Thames & Hudson, 1984.

Stokstad, Marilyn. *Art History.* New York: Abrams, 1995.

Sullivan, Michael. *The Arts of China,* 3d ed. Berkeley: University of California, 1984.

Wood, Michael. *Art of the Western World.* New York: Simon and Schuster, 1989.

PART 6
THE MODERN WORLD

Arnason, H. H. *History of Modern Art: Painting, Sculpture, Architecture, Photography,* 4th ed. New York: Abrams, 1986.

Asia Society Galleries. *Contemporary Art in Asia: Traditions/Tensions.* New York: Asia Society, 1996.

Beardsley, John. *Earthworks and Beyond.* New York: Abbeville, 1984.

Beckett, Wendy. *Contemporary Women Artists.* New York: Universe, 1988.

Bearden, Romare, and Harry Henderson. *A History of African-American Artists from 1792 to the Present,* New York: Pantheon, 1993.

Broude, Norma, and Mary D. Garrard, eds. *The Expanding Discourse: Feminism and Art History.* New York: HarperCollins, 1992.

Canaday, John. *Mainstreams of Modern Art,* 2nd ed. New York: Henry Holt, 1981.

Cockcroft, Eva, John Weber, and James C. Cockcroft. *Toward a People's Art: A Contemporary Mural Movement.* New York: Dutton, 1977.

Fleming, Ronald Lee, and Renata von Tscharner. *Place Makers: Creating Public Art That Tells You Where You Are.* New York: Harcourt, Brace, Jovanovich, 1986.

Foster, Hal, ed. *The Anti-Aesthetic: Essays on Postmodern Culture.* Seattle: Bay Press, 1983.

Friedman, Mildred. *De Stijl: 1917-1931.* New York: Abbeville, 1992.

Goldberg, Vicki. *The Power of Photography: How Photographs Changed Our Lives.* New York: Abbeville, 1991.

Henri, Adrian. *Total Art: Environment, Happenings, and Performance.* New York: Praeger, 1974.

Hughes, Robert. *American Visions: The Epic Story of Art in America.,* New York: Knopf, 1997.

Jencks, Cahrles. *The Language of Post-Modern.* New York: Rizzoli, 1991.

Lancaster, Clay. *The Japanese Influence in America.* New York: Abbeville, 1985.

Lippard, Lucy. *Mixed Blessings: New Art in a Multicultural America.* New York: Pantheon 1990.

Lovejoy, Margot. *Postmodern Currents: Art and Artists in the Age of Electronic Media.* Englewood Cliffs, N.J.: Prentice Hall, 1992.

Neff, Terry Ann R. *In the Mind's Eye: Dada and Surrealism.* New York: Abbeville, 1985.

Pelfrey, Robert H., with Mary Hall-Pelfrey. *Art and Mass Media.* New York: Harper & Row, 1985.

Quirarte, Jacinto. *Mexican American Artists.* Austin: University of Texas Press, 1973.

Richter, Hans. *Dada: Art and Anti-Art.* New York: Abrams, 1970.

Rickey, George. *Constructivism: Origins and Evolution.* New York: Braziller, 1967.

Rosenblum, Naomi. *A History of Women Photographers.* New York: Abbeville, 1994.

_____. *A History of Photography,* 3d ed. New York: Abbeville, 1997.

Sandler, Irving. *American Art of the 1960s.* New York: Harper & Row, 1988.

———. *Art of the Postmodern Era.* New York: Icon, 1996.

Selz, Peter. *Art in Our Times: A Pictorial History, 1890-1980.* New York: Abrams, 1981.

Sonfist, Alan, ed. *Art in the Land: A Critical Anthology of Environmental Art.* New York: Dutton, 1983.

Spelman College. *Bearing Witness: Contemporary Works by African American Women Artists.* New York: Rizzoli, 1996.

Stern, Robert A. M. *American Architecture: Innovation and Tradition.* New York: Rizzoli, 1985.

Stiles, Kristine, and Peter Selz. *Theories and Documents of Contemporary Art: A Sourcebook of Artists' Writings.* Berkeley: University of California Press, 1996.

Sullivan, Edward J., ed. *Latin American Art in the Twentieth Century.* London: Phaidon, 1996.

Tuchman, Maurice, *The Spiritual in Art: Abstract Painting 1890-1985.* New York: Abbeville, 1986.

Wheeler, Daniel. *Art Since Mid-Century.* New York: Vendome, 1991.

SUGGESTED WEBSITES

Direct links to these and many other websites are located at the *Artforms* website at http://prenhall.com/artforms

General Reference

The Web Museum
http://sunsite.unc.edu/wm/
An on-line source for hundreds of images of art works from many periods and cultures.

Words of Art
http://www.arts.ouc.bc.ca/fiar/glossary/gloshome.html
An on-line glossary of theory and critical terms, searchable like a dictionary.

Researching Your Art Object
http://www.i/pi.com/artsource/wcidman.html
Links to bibliographies, magazines, dictionaries of art terms, and artists' biographies. All are readable in Adobe Acrobat portable document file format.

Mark Harden's Artchive
http://www.artchive.com
A source for images of art works from many historical periods. Searchable by artist's name or by movement.

The Artcyclopedia
http://www.artcyclopedia.com
This site provides links to art images on the web, with links to educational sites and articles.

Major Museum Websites

These are among the best museum sites. They offer informative tours of parts of their permanent collections, with images that can be viewed at full screen and supporting text.

Detroit Institute of Art
http://www.dia.org

The Louve Museum, Paris
http://www.louvre.fr

The Prado Museum, Madrid
http://museoprado.mcu.es/prado/html

Hermitage Museum, St. Petersburg
http://www.hermitagemuseum.org

Art Institute of Chicago
http://www.artic.edu/aic/index.html

PART 1
ART IS . . .

Kandinsky's Abstractions
http://www.glyphs.com/art/kandinsky/
A very informative site that documents all of Kandinsky's works in the series *Compositions*. All surviving works are available in full-screen reproductions. Because of the number of images, it takes extra time to load.

Museum of International Folk Art
http://www.state.nm.us/moifa/MOIFAhome/MOIFAhome.html
Changing on-line exhibits, guide to the permanent collection, and teaching guides to temporary exhibitions.

PART 2
THE LANGUAGE OF VISUAL EXPERIENCE

Color Matters
http://www.colormatters.com/culturematters.html
A directory of information about the cultural significance of colors, taking Jan Van Eyck's painting *Giovanni Arnolfini and His Bride* as an example.

The Web Museum: Impressionism
http://sunsite.unc.edu/wm/paint/glo/impressionism/
Several screens of information on the rise and development of the movement, with many works.

Claes Oldenburg: An Anthology
http://www.artnetweb.com/oldenburg/contents.html
A website devoted to a recent nationally traveling exhibition of work by this Pop artist, who often employed extreme distortions of scale in his works.

Museum of Bad Art
http://www.glyphs.com/moba
The official website of the not entirely serious Museum of Bad Art, located outside Boston. Images of many works from the collection, which they describe as "art too bad to be ignored." Includes the painting illustrated in Chapter 6.

PART 3
TWO-DIMENSIONAL ARTS

TypoGRAPHIC
http://www.typographic.rsub.com/
A timeline of the history of Western Typography, with important typeface inventors and links to their creations.

Liquitex Paint Company
http://www.liquitex.com/aboutus/made/home.cfm
This corporate site explains how artists' oil paints are made, with pictures of each step.

George Eastman House
http://www.eastman.org/
A very informative site on the history of photography, with on-line collections galleries and a timeline of the evolution of photography.

Walker Art Center Gallery 9
http://www.walkerart.org/gallery9
A site devoted to display of digital works created for the World Wide Web. Rotating schedule of on-line works, with information and commentary.

Spencer Museum Graphic Arts Page

http://www.ukans.edu/~sma/prints.html

An informative site with close-up reproductions of prints in various media, and links to educational sites about printmaking processes.

PART 4
THREE-DIMENSIONAL ARTS

The Henry Moore Foundation

http://www.henry-moore-fdn.co.uk/hmf/

A starting point for finding information about this important modern sculptor. Chronology, biography, images of works, and links to other sites.

Christo and Jeanne-Claude Home Page

http://www.christojeanneclaude.net/

Photos, information, and history of the outdoor projects of Christo and Jeanne-Claude.

Women in Architecture

http://www.bluffton.edu/~sullivanm/women/contents.html

Biographical information on some prominent twentieth-century women architects, with links to related sites.

Nineteenth-Century Sculpture

http://www.bc.edu/bc_org/avp/cas/fnart/art/19th_sculp.html

A searchable directory of works and artists, covering all European nineteenth-century movements.

Textiles Through Time

http://www.interlog.com/~gwhite/ttt/tttintro.html

The starting point for further information about textile arts. Contains links to many other museums, galleries, and informational sites.

PART 5
ART AS CULTURAL HERITAGE

The Chauvet Cave

http://www.culture.fr/culture/arcnat/chauvet/en/gvpda-d.htm

A French Government site on the newest discovery of cave art. Contains information about the discovery and many views of the cave paintings.

Universes in Universe

http://www.universes-in-universe.de/e_map.htm

A large directory of information on the arts of Africa, Oceania, and the Americas. Searchable by country or region, with information on art history, museums, and cultural events.

Virtual Sistine Chapel

http://oar.rm.astro.it/amendola/sistinab.html

Information about the commissioning of the chapel, the artists who worked on its decorations, and thumbnails of its major art works, which can be viewed at full screen.

Islamic and Arab Arts and Architecture

http://islamicart.com/

A rich and attractively designed site, with information and pictures of Architecture, Calligraphy, and Textiles. Includes a glossary of terms and names of important artists and architects.

Kyoto Museum of Art

http://www.kyohaku.go.jp/

Nicely designed site that features masterpieces of Japanese art in several media.

National Palace Museum, Taiwan

http://202.39.81.6/

The North American mirror site of this museum, which houses what may be the world's best collection of traditional Chinese art in all media.

PART 6
THE MODERN WORLD

The Age of Enlightenment

http://mistral.culture.fr/files/imaginary_exhibition.html

A French government site on the NeoClasssical period, with background information, index of artists, and links to works in French museums.

The On-Line Picasso Project

http://www.tamu.edu/mocl/picasso/

An encyclopedic site on Picasso's life and art, containing articles from encyclopedias, remembrances of persons who knew him, images, and other information divided into fourteen categories.

The Andy Warhol Museum

http://www.warhol.org

This site offers reproductions of works by the master of Pop Art and information on the movement.

A.I.R. Gallery

http://www.airnyc.org/history.cfm

A history of one of the first feminist art galleries devoted to promoting the work of women artists.

Artnet Magazine

http://www.artnet.com/magazine/frontpage.asp

An on-line magazine about contemporary art, with exhibtion news and reviews. Linked to a full-service art site with art world news and information.

The International Dada Archive

http://www.lib.uiowa.edu/dada

A compendium of information and links to sites about the Dada movement and its major artists.

Smithsonian American Art Museum

http://nmaa-ryder.si.edu/collections/index.html

Besides displaying works, this site contains several educational modules about various periods of art in the United States.

INDEX

ABOUT THE AUTHOR

Revising author Patrick Frank is Assistant Professor of Art History at the University of Kansas, where he specializes in modern Latin American art. After receiving M.A. and Ph.D. degrees from George Washington University, he taught Art History in several higher education environments, from rural community colleges to private universities. Before coming to Kansas, his previous faculty appointment was at the University of Colorado at Boulder, where he refocused the introductory Art History courses from Western art to World art. His recent scholarly work has dealt with the printmaker José Guadalupe Posada. He authored the book *Posada's Broadsheets: Mexican Popular Imagery 1890-1910* (University of New Mexico Press). He also curated an exhibition, *Bandits and Bullfighters: Heroes and Anti-Heroes in Prints by Posada*, which opened in 1998 at the Colorado Springs Fine Arts Center before beginning a national tour. His essays and reviews have appeared in *The New Art Examiner*, *Goya: Revista de Arte*, *Third Text,* and the alternative publications *Drunken Boat* and *Anarchy: A Journal of Desire Armed.* His involvement with *Artforms* began when he first taught from it in 1991.